Better Homes and Gardens®

ANNUAL•
Recipes
1997

Better Homes and Gardens® Books
Des Moines, Iowa

Nectarine-Pistachio
Tart (page 189)

*A*nniversaries, birthdays—these milestones that mark our lives—are always good times to look back at where we've been. They're also a good time to remind ourselves that we play an important role in the making of our own heritage, the legacy we'll leave to those we love.

This year, the entire family of Better Homes and Gardens® editors and designers has spent a good deal of time steeped in our own 75-year history—not only to assess what's gone by but also to make sure we keep alive our tradition of helping Americans live better lives.

It's been an especially exciting year for our food editors. They've been handed the perfect excuse to review and renew not only the recipes but also the cooking traditions that have warmed the souls of Americans for 75 years. Looking through January, you'll find recipes that you, our readers, claim as some of your forever-favorites. July offers our all-time hottest grilled recipes, and November and December host holiday memories—old and new.

So dig in and enjoy. This year you're truly getting the best of the best when it comes to America's most trusted source for family food and fun.

Jean LemMon, Editor in Chief

the editors

*T*here are foods to suit any occasion, from a Saturday brunch with friends to, say, a magazine's 75th anniversary. It's our pleasure to help you find just the right taste for your events, large and small. Our food editors—from left, Jeanne Ambrose, David Feder, Nancy Byal, and Richard Swearinger—share your passion for good food and making it better. Their recipes are tested thoroughly in the home-style kitchens at Better Homes and Gardens. *Taste and appearance are important, but each recipe also gets tested for its ease and speed of preparation. The editors spend time in our kitchens so you can save time in yours. That's more than the magazine's promise—that's a personal commitment from Nancy, David, Jeanne, and Richard. In this book, you'll find a year of their work in the recipes they've tested and tasted and now recommend to you.*

Better Homes and Gardens® Books

An imprint of Meredith® Books

Better Homes and Gardens® Annual Recipes 1997

Project Editor: *Jennifer Darling*
Contributing Editor: *Shelli McConnell*
Associate Art Director: *Lynda Haupert*
Copy Chief: *Angela K. Renkoski*
Editorial and Design Assistants: *Judy Bailey, Jennifer Norris, Karen Schirm*
Test Kitchen Director: *Sharon Stilwell*
Illustrator: *Thomas Rosborough*
Cover Photographer: *Scott Little*
Electronic Production Coordinator: *Paula Forest*
Production Director: *Douglas M. Johnston*
Production Manager: *Pam Kvitne*
Assistant Prepress Manager: *Marjorie J. Schenkelberg*

Meredith® Books

Editor in Chief: *James D. Blume*
Design Director: *Matt Strelecki*
Managing Editor: *Gregory H. Kayko*
Executive Food Editor: *Lisa Holderness*

Vice President, General Manager: *Jamie L. Martin*

Better Homes and Gardens® Magazine

Editor in Chief: *Jean LemMon*
Executive Food Editor: *Nancy Byal*
Associate Editors: *David Feder, R.D.; Jeanne Ambrose; Richard Swearinger*

Meredith Publishing Group

President, Publishing Group: *Christopher M. Little*
Vice President and Publishing Director: *John P. Loughlin*

Meredith Corporation

Chairman of the Board: *Jack D. Rehm*
President and Chief Executive Officer: *William T. Kerr*

Chairman of the Executive Committee: *E. T. Meredith III*

Our seal assures you that every recipe in
Better Homes and Gardens® Annual Recipes 1997 has been
tested in the Better Homes and Gardens® Test Kitchen.
This means that each recipe is practical and
reliable, and meets our high standards of taste appeal.
We guarantee your satisfaction with this book for
as long as you own it.

Cover photograph: *Buttermilk-Pecan Brownies with
Sour Cream Frosting, Cheesecake Swirl Brownies,
and Fudgy Brownies (pages 140–141)*
Page 1: *Fresh Fruit with Minted Yogurt (page 189)*

*Some of the images in this book are used by permission
of Zedcor, Inc., Tucson, AZ, from the 100,000 image and the
30,000 image DeskGallery® collections. 1-800-482-4567.*

All of us at Better Homes and Gardens® Books are
dedicated to providing you with the information and ideas you need
to create tasty foods. We welcome your comments
and suggestions. Write to us at: Better Homes and Gardens Books,
Cookbook Editorial Department, 1716 Locust Street, RW-240,
Des Moines, IA 50309–3023.

*If you would like to order additional copies
of this book, call 1-800-439-4119.*

CONTENTS

When this symbol appears with a recipe, rest assured that you can prepare the dish—start to finish—in 30 minutes or less.

Any recipe that bears this low-fat symbol has met our guideline of having no more than 10 grams of fat per serving (see page 8).

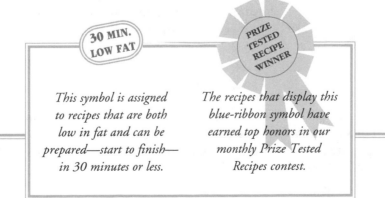

30 MIN. LOW FAT

*This symbol is assigned
to recipes that are both
low in fat and can be
prepared—start to finish—
in 30 minutes or less.*

PRIZE TESTED RECIPE WINNER

*The recipes that display this
blue-ribbon symbol have
earned top honors in our
monthly Prize Tested
Recipes contest.*

NUTRITION INFORMATION

With each recipe, we give you useful nutrition information you easily can apply to your own needs. First read "What You Need" (below) to determine your dietary requirements. Then refer to the Nutrition Facts listed with each recipe. You'll find the calorie count and the amount of fat, saturated fat, cholesterol, sodium, carbohydrates, fiber, and protein for each serving. In most cases, along with the Nutrition Facts per serving, you'll find the amount of vitamin A, vitamin C, calcium, and iron noted as a percentage of the Daily Values. The Daily Values are dietary standards set by the Food and Drug Administration. To stay in line with the nutrition breakdown of each recipe, follow the suggested number of servings.

HOW WE ANALYZE

The Better Homes and Gardens® Test Kitchen computer analyzes each recipe for the nutritional value of a single serving.

◆ The analysis does not include optional ingredients.

◆ We use the first serving size listed when a range is given. For example: If we say a recipe "Makes 4 to 6 servings," the Nutrition Facts are based on 4 servings.

◆ When ingredient choices (such as margarine or butter) appear in a recipe, we use the first one mentioned for analysis. The ingredient order does not mean we prefer one ingredient over another.

◆ When milk is a recipe ingredient, the analysis is calculated using 2-percent milk.

WHAT YOU NEED

The dietary guidelines below suggest nutrient levels that moderately active adults should strive to eat each day. As your calorie levels change, adjust your fat intake, too. Try to keep the percentage of calories from fat to no more than 30 percent. There's no harm in occasionally going over or under these guidelines, but the key to good health is maintaining a balanced diet *most of the time.*

Calories:	About 2,000
Total fat:	Less than 65 grams
Saturated fat:	Less than 20 grams
Cholesterol:	Less than 300 milligrams
Carbohydrates:	About 300 grams
Sodium:	Less than 2,400 milligrams
Dietary fiber:	20 to 30 grams

LOW-FAT RECIPES

For recipes that meet our low-fat criteria, a main-dish serving must contain 10 or fewer grams of fat. For side dishes or desserts, the serving must contain 5 or fewer grams of fat. These recipes are flagged with a low-fat symbol.

JANUARY
Resolutions Come True

30-minute recipes indicated in RED.
Low-fat and no-fat recipes indicated
with a ♥.
Photographs indicated in italics.

After the holiday goodies are gone comes the season of recovery. No wonder so many New Year's resolutions involve food: less fat, healthier meals, more creative menus. You can do even better. Want healthy and interesting from the same meal? Look for low-fat surprises, such as Gourmet Pizza or Pork Chop Barbecue, which taste like summer in the hammock.

For something to lift your spirits, how about a taste of the international? Sure, travel might be nice, but a stay-at-home budget is well served by homemade tastes from other lands: Greek Croustade, Thai Turkey, Sicilian Meat Roll, or Caribbean Callaloo.

RICOTTA PUFFS

Prep: 30 min. ◆ Bake: 20 min.

*This recipe earned Lisa D. Gillett
of Aurora, Colorado, $100
in the magazine's monthly contest.*

1   17¼-oz. pkg. frozen puff
    pastry (2 sheets), thawed

◆◆◆

½   cup ricotta cheese
½   cup chopped roasted red
    sweet pepper
3   Tbsp. grated Romano cheese
1   Tbsp. snipped fresh parsley
1   tsp. dried oregano, crushed
½   tsp. pepper

◆◆◆

Milk
Grated Romano cheese

1 Unfold the pastry on a lightly floured surface. Using a sharp knife, cut each puff pastry sheet into nine 3-inch squares; set aside.

2 For filling, in a medium mixing bowl stir together the ricotta cheese, roasted red sweet pepper, the 3 tablespoons Romano cheese, parsley, oregano, and pepper.

3 Moisten the edges of each pastry square with milk. Spoon about 2 teaspoons filling onto 1 side of each pastry square. Fold the other side of the pastry over the filling. Seal, using the tines of a fork. With a sharp knife, cut slits in the top of each pastry bundle. Brush with milk and sprinkle with additional Romano cheese.

4 Arrange pastry bundles on a baking sheet. Bake in a 400° oven about 20 minutes or till golden. Remove from baking sheet and cool on wire rack for 5 minutes before serving. Makes 18 pastries.

Nutrition facts per pastry: 137 cal., 10 g total fat (1 g sat. fat), 3 mg chol., 137 mg sodium, 10 g carbo., 0 g fiber, 3 g pro. *Daily values:* 3% vit. A, 19% vit. C, 3% calcium.

GREEK CROUSTADE

Prep: 40 min. ◆ Bake: 30 min.

The spinach, feta cheese, and phyllo dough make it Greek; the edible pastry shell holding the thick vegetable mixture makes it a croustade (pronounced kroo-STAHD).
(See the photograph on page 40.)

1   10-oz. pkg. frozen chopped
    spinach
¼   cup chopped onion
3   Tbsp. butter or margarine
3   Tbsp. all-purpose flour
¼   tsp. dried tarragon or fennel
    seed, crushed
¼   tsp. pepper
¾   cup milk
2   beaten eggs
1   cup cream-style cottage
    cheese
⅔   cup crumbled feta cheese

◆◆◆

10 sheets frozen phyllo dough
    (17×12-inch rectangles),
    thawed
½   cup butter or margarine,
    melted

1 Cook the spinach according to the package directions; drain well, pressing out excess liquid. In a medium saucepan cook the onion in the 3 tablespoons butter or margarine till tender. Stir in the flour, tarragon or fennel seed, and pepper. Add milk all at once. Cook and stir till mixture is thickened and bubbly. Stir about half of the hot mixture into eggs; return all to saucepan. Stir in the cottage cheese, feta cheese, and spinach; set aside.

2 Unroll the phyllo dough; remove 1 sheet of phyllo dough at a time. (As you work, cover the remaining phyllo dough with plastic wrap to prevent it from drying out.) Lightly brush the first sheet with some of the ½ cup melted butter or margarine. Fold phyllo in thirds lengthwise; brush the top with butter or margarine.

3 Place an end of the folded sheet in the center of a 12- or 14-inch pizza pan, extending it over side of pan. Repeat with the remaining phyllo dough and butter or margarine; arrange strips spoke-fashion evenly around pan. (The ends of each sheet will overlap in the center and be about 3 inches apart at outer ends.)

4 Spread the spinach mixture in an 8-inch circle in the center of the pastry. Starting with the last phyllo strip placed in the pan, lift the end of the strip up and bring it toward the center of the filling. Holding the end with both hands, twist end several times; coil and tuck end under to form a rosette. Lay rosette over filling, leaving a 3-inch opening in center (filling should be visible).

5 Repeat with the remaining phyllo strips in the reverse order in which they were placed in the pan. Drizzle any remaining butter or margarine over all. Bake in a 375° oven for 30 to 35 minutes or till golden. Cut croustade into wedges and serve warm. Makes 10 appetizer servings.

Nutrition facts per serving: 272 cal., 20 g total fat (12 g sat. fat), 96 mg chol., 532 mg sodium, 15 g carbo., 0 g fiber, 9 g pro. *Daily values:* 32% vit. A, 4% vit. C, 13% calcium, 8% iron.

DRIED TOMATO-PESTO SPREAD

Prep: 40 min. ◆ Chill: 4 to 24 hr.
See the photograph on page 38.

1 8-oz. pkg. cream cheese, softened
½ cup crumbled feta cheese (2 oz.)
2 cloves garlic, minced
1 Tbsp. milk
1 cup firmly packed fresh basil leaves
1 cup firmly packed fresh parsley sprigs
½ cup grated Parmesan cheese
¼ cup pine nuts, walnuts, or almonds
2 cloves garlic, minced
3 Tbsp. olive oil or cooking oil
2 Tbsp. pine nuts, walnuts, or almonds, toasted
½ cup oil-packed dried tomatoes, drained and finely chopped
Crackers or toasted French bread slices

1 In a food processor bowl or mixing bowl, combine the cream cheese, feta cheese, 2 cloves garlic, and milk. Cover and process or beat with an electric mixer on medium speed till almost smooth.

2 For pesto, in a clean food processor bowl or blender container, combine the basil, parsley,

Parmesan cheese, ¼ cup nuts, 2 cloves garlic, and olive oil. Cover and process or blend with several on-off turns till almost smooth, stopping machine several times and scraping sides; set aside.

3 Line a 3½- to 4-cup mold with plastic wrap. Sprinkle the 2 tablespoons toasted nuts over bottom of mold. Spoon one-fourth cheese mixture atop nuts, spreading evenly. Carefully spread with half the pesto. Add another one-fourth of cheese mixture.

4 Sprinkle tomatoes atop cheese in mold. Add another one-fourth cheese mixture and the remaining pesto. Spread remaining cheese mixture atop. Cover; chill at least 4 hours or overnight. To serve, unmold cheese onto a platter. Serve with crackers or French bread. Serves 16.

Nutrition facts per tablespoon: 162 cal., 13 g total fat (6 g sat. fat), 25 mg chol., 230 mg sodium, 7 g carbo., 0 g fiber, 6 g pro. *Daily values:* 9% vit. A, 10% vit. C, 8% calcium, 7% iron.

GARLIC-FETA CHEESE SPREAD

Prep: 15 min. ◆ Chill: 1 to 24 hr.

This recipe earned Joanne Spencer of Brookfield, Connecticut, $200 in the magazine's monthly contest.

1 cup crumbled feta cheese (4 oz.)
½ of an 8-oz. pkg. cream cheese or reduced-fat cream cheese (Neufchâtel), softened

THE CLEVER COOK

A MASTER CHOPPER

A pastry blender is a great tool for chopping soft foods. For instance, when making guacamole or egg salad, I use my pastry blender to chop the avocado or hard-cooked eggs, mixing in the other ingredients at the same time.

Maxye Spens Henry
Thousand Oaks, California

⅓ cup mayonnaise or reduced-calorie mayonnaise
1 clove garlic, minced
¼ tsp. dried basil, crushed
¼ tsp. dried oregano, crushed
⅛ tsp. dried dillweed
⅛ tsp. dried thyme, crushed
Fresh thyme (optional)
Assorted vegetables and unsalted crackers (optional)

1 In a food processor bowl or mixing bowl, combine the feta cheese, cream cheese, mayonnaise, garlic, basil, oregano, dillweed, and dried thyme. Cover and process or beat with electric mixer on medium speed till combined. Transfer to a serving bowl. Cover and chill till serving time. If desired, garnish with fresh thyme and serve with vegetables and crackers. Makes 1½ cups.

Nutrition facts per tablespoon: 51 cal., 5 g total fat (2 g sat. fat), 11 mg chol., 84 mg sodium, 0 g carbo., 0 g fiber, 1 g pro. *Daily values:* 2% vit. A, 2% calcium.

PEPPERED CHUTNEY ROAST

Prep: 20 min. ◆ Marinate: 4 to 8 hr.
Roast: 35 min.

When the occasion calls for a splurge, beef tenderloin is a top choice. This simple preparation does the rich meat delicious justice. (See the photograph on page 38.)

¾ cup unsweetened pineapple juice
½ cup steak sauce
⅓ cup port wine
⅓ cup Worcestershire sauce
¼ cup lemon juice
1 tsp. seasoned salt
1 tsp. lemon-pepper seasoning
1 tsp. dry mustard
◆◆◆
1 2½- to 3-lb. beef tenderloin
1 tsp. cracked black pepper
3 slices bacon, cooked and drained
½ cup chutney, snipped

1 For marinade, in a medium bowl mix pineapple juice, steak sauce, port wine, Worcestershire sauce, lemon juice, seasoned salt, lemon-pepper, dry mustard, and 1 teaspoon *pepper;* set aside.

2 Score meat by making shallow cuts at 1-inch intervals diagonally across tenderloin in a diamond pattern. Repeat on second side. Place meat in a large plastic bag; set in a large bowl. Pour marinade over meat; close bag. Refrigerate for 4 to 8 hours *(but no longer),* turning meat occasionally to distribute marinade. Drain, reserving marinade.

3 Rub beef tenderloin with the cracked pepper. Place meat on a rack in a shallow roasting pan.

Insert meat thermometer. Roast, uncovered, in a 425° oven 30 to 45 minutes or till meat thermometer registers 135°. Baste the tenderloin twice during roasting with the reserved marinade. Remove roast from the oven and arrange bacon strips along the top. Spoon the chutney evenly over tenderloin. Return the roast to the oven for 5 to 10 minutes more or till the meat reaches 140° (center will be medium-rare; for a medium to medium-well roast, cook till meat thermometer inserted near center registers 150°). The meat's temperature will rise 5° upon standing. Transfer meat to a serving platter. Let stand, covered, about 15 minutes before slicing. Serves 12.

Nutrition facts per serving: 172 cal., 7 g total fat (3 g sat. fat), 55 mg chol., 141 mg sodium, 8 g carbo., 0 g fiber, 19 g pro. *Daily values:* 6% vit. C, 16% iron.

SICILIAN MEAT ROLL

Prep: 20 min. ◆ Bake: 1¼ hr.

Your favorite Italian flavors are wrapped into this meat loaf. Serve the meat loaf with hot pasta, tossed with butter and herbs, and a spinach salad. (See the photograph on page 38.)

2 slightly beaten eggs
¾ cup soft bread crumbs (1 slice)
½ cup tomato juice
2 Tbsp. snipped fresh parsley
½ tsp. dried oregano, crushed
¼ tsp. salt
¼ tsp. pepper
1 small clove garlic, minced
2 lb. lean ground beef
◆◆◆
6 1-oz. thin slices cooked ham
1¾ cups shredded mozzarella cheese (7 oz.)

1 In a large mixing bowl combine the eggs, bread crumbs, tomato juice, parsley, oregano, salt, pepper, and garlic. Stir in the ground beef, mixing well.

2 On foil, pat meat mixture into a 12×10-inch rectangle. Arrange the ham slices atop meat, leaving a ¾-inch border around all edges. Sprinkle *1½ cups* of the shredded mozzarella cheese over the ham. Starting from a short end, carefully roll up meat, using foil to lift; seal edges and ends. Place roll, seam side down, in a 13×9×2-inch baking pan.

3 Bake in a 350° oven about 1¼ hours or till temperature registers 170° and juices run clear. (Center of meat roll will be pink due to ham.) Sprinkle the remaining shredded mozzarella over top of roll. Return to oven about 5 minutes or till cheese melts. Makes 8 to 10 servings.

Nutrition facts per serving: 323 cal., 19 g total fat (8 g sat. fat), 152 mg chol., 604 mg sodium, 4 g carbo., 0 g fiber, 33 g pro. *Daily values:* 8% vit. A, 14% vit. C, 16% calcium, 18% iron.

OLD-TIME BEEF STEW

Prep: 35 min. ◆ Cook: 2¾ hr.

Here's how our editors described this popular recipe back in 1962: "It's the browning—long and lazy— that gives a stew the rich color and flavor. Gentle cooking is what makes the meat tender."

1½ lb. boneless beef stew meat, cut into 1-inch cubes
2 Tbsp. cooking oil
4 cups water
1 large onion, sliced

2 cloves garlic, minced
2 Tbsp. Worcestershire sauce
1 Tbsp. lemon juice
1 tsp. sugar
½ tsp. salt
½ tsp. paprika
¼ tsp. pepper
1 bay leaf
⅛ tsp. ground allspice

◆◆◆

6 medium carrots, peeled and
   bias-sliced into ¾-inch
   chunks
4 medium potatoes, cut into
   1-inch chunks
1 lb. small white onions,
   peeled and halved

◆◆◆

½ cup cold water
¼ cup all-purpose flour
   Salt
   Pepper
   Snipped fresh parsley
   (optional)

1 In a large pot cook all of the stew meat at once in hot oil over medium-high heat for 15 to 20 minutes or till brown, stirring occasionally. Drain off excess fat. Add the 4 cups water, sliced onion, garlic, Worcestershire sauce, lemon juice, sugar, salt, paprika, pepper, bay leaf, and allspice to pot. Bring just to boiling; reduce heat. Simmer, covered, for 2 hours, stirring occasionally.

2 Stir in the carrots, potatoes, and halved onions. Return to boiling; reduce heat. Simmer, covered, about 30 minutes more or till meat and vegetables are tender. Discard bay leaf.

3 In a screw-top jar shake together the ½ cup cold water and flour till combined. Stir into stew.

Menu

Old-Time Beef Stew
(see page 12)

◆◆◆

Light Bread
(see page 22)

◆◆◆

Salad of mixed greens topped with pear slices and purchased poppy seed salad dressing

◆◆◆

Gingersnap cookies with vanilla ice cream

Cook and stir till thickened and bubbly; cook 1 minute more. Season stew to taste with salt and pepper. To serve, spoon stew into bowls. If desired, sprinkle each serving with snipped parsley. Makes 6 main-dish servings.

Nutrition facts per serving: 389 cal., 13 g total fat (4 g sat. fat), 82 mg chol., 338 mg sodium, 37 g carbo., 5 g fiber, 31 g pro. *Daily values:* 171% vit. A, 37% vit. C, 5% calcium, 30% iron.

PORK CHOP BARBECUE

Prep: 30 min. ◆ Bake: 25 min.

Remember this satisfying dinner—served with home fries and green beans—for a soothing supper on a wintry night. Be careful not to overbake the chops so they stay moist and tender.
(See the photograph on page 40.)

½ cup water
3 Tbsp. vinegar
2 Tbsp. sugar
1 Tbsp. prepared mustard

¼ tsp. salt
¼ to ½ tsp. black pepper
⅛ tsp. ground red pepper
1 medium onion, cut into thin
   wedges
1 lemon slice
½ cup catsup
2 Tbsp. Worcestershire sauce
1 tsp. liquid smoke

◆◆◆

6 rib pork chops, cut ¾ inch
   thick
1 to 2 Tbsp. cooking oil

1 In a small saucepan combine the water, vinegar, sugar, mustard, salt, black pepper, and red pepper. Add the onion and lemon slice. Bring mixture to boiling; reduce heat. Simmer, uncovered, for 20 minutes. Add the catsup, Worcestershire sauce, and liquid smoke. Bring to boiling. Remove from heat. Remove the lemon slice and discard.

2 In a large skillet brown pork chops, half at a time, in hot oil over medium-high heat. Place chops in a 3-quart rectangular baking dish. Pour sauce evenly over chops.

3 Bake, uncovered, in a 350° oven for 25 to 30 minutes or till pork chops are slightly pink in center and juices run clear, turning chops once. To serve, transfer pork chops to a warm serving platter. Pour sauce over all. Makes 6 servings.

Nutrition facts per serving: 190 cal., 10 g total fat (3 g sat. fat), 44 mg chol., 475 mg sodium, 13 g carbo., 1 g fiber, 14 g pro. *Daily values:* 2% vit. A, 24% vit. C, 1% calcium, 6% iron.

COQ AU VIN ROSETTES

Prep: 45 min. ◆ Bake: 35 min.

The classic coq au vin (kohk-oh-VAHN) is a French stew of chicken, mushrooms, onion, and herbs cooked with wine. This recipe wraps all of those flavors into an elegant, creamy pasta dish.

1½ lb. skinless, boneless chicken breast halves
3 cups sliced fresh mushrooms (8 oz.)
½ cup chopped onion
2 Tbsp. margarine or butter
¾ cup dry white wine
½ tsp. dried tarragon, crushed
½ tsp. white pepper
⅛ tsp. salt

◆◆◆

8 lasagna noodles, cooked and drained
1 8-oz. pkg. cream cheese, cut up
½ cup dairy sour cream
2 Tbsp. all-purpose flour
½ cup half-and-half, light cream, or milk
1 cup shredded Gruyère cheese (4 oz.)
1 cup shredded Muenster cheese (4 oz.)
1 whole almond (optional)*
3 Tbsp. slivered almonds, toasted (optional)
Snipped fresh parsley or tarragon (optional)

1 Cut chicken into 1-inch pieces. In a large skillet cook the mushrooms and onion in margarine over medium-high heat 4 to 5 minutes or till tender, stirring occasionally. Add chicken, wine, dried tarragon, pepper, and salt. Bring just to boiling; reduce heat. Simmer, covered, for 5 minutes, stirring once. Remove from heat.

Savory Turkey-Sauced Pasta (see right)

◆◆◆

Salad of mixed greens, tossed with purchased Italian salad dressing and sprinkled with chopped toasted nuts

◆◆◆

Breadsticks

◆◆◆

Chocolate Cream Cheese Cake (see page 24)

2 Meanwhile, halve lasagna noodles lengthwise. Curl each into a 2½-inch diameter ring and place, cut side down, in a 3-quart rectangular baking dish. Using a slotted spoon, spoon chicken mixture into center of lasagna rings, reserving liquid in skillet. Add the cream cheese to reserved liquid; heat and stir just till melted. Stir together the sour cream and flour; blend in half-and-half, light cream, or milk. Add sour cream mixture and cheeses to skillet. Cook and stir over medium heat till thickened and bubbly. Spoon sauce over lasagna rings. If desired, insert a whole almond in 1 of the rings and sprinkle slivered almonds atop all.

3 Bake, covered, in a 325° oven about 35 minutes or till heated through. Spoon sauce over lasagna rings when served. If desired, garnish with snipped parsley or tarragon. Makes 8 servings.

*Note: According to folklore, the lucky diner who finds the whole almond is blessed with good luck.

Nutrition facts per serving: 517 cal., 30 g total fat (16 g sat. fat), 132 mg chol., 358 mg sodium, 21 g carbo., 1 g fiber, 36 g pro.*Daily values:* 31% vit. A, 3% vit. C, 26% calcium, 17% iron.

SAVORY TURKEY-SAUCED PASTA

Start to finish: 35 min.

2 cups sliced fresh mushrooms
⅓ cup sliced green onions
2 cloves garlic, minced
1 Tbsp. olive oil or cooking oil
1 14½-oz. can stewed tomatoes
1½ cups cubed cooked turkey or chicken
1¼ cups chicken broth
1 cup frozen peas
1 Tbsp. snipped fresh thyme or ½ teaspoon dried thyme, crushed
¼ tsp. salt
¼ tsp. pepper
1 8-oz. carton light dairy sour cream
2 Tbsp. cornstarch

◆◆◆

8 oz. gemelli, rotini, or other pasta

1 In a large saucepan cook mushrooms, green onions, and garlic in hot oil till mushrooms are tender. Carefully add the stewed tomatoes, turkey, chicken broth, peas, thyme, salt, and pepper. Bring to boiling; reduce heat. Simmer, covered, 5 minutes. Stir together the sour cream and cornstarch; add to skillet. Cook and stir till thickened and bubbly; cook and stir 2 minutes more.

2 Meanwhile cook the pasta according to package directions; drain. To serve, toss the hot pasta with the turkey mixture. Makes 6 servings.

Nutrition facts per serving: 353 cal., 10 g total fat (3 g sat. fat), 41 mg chol., 513 mg sodium, 46 g carbo., 2 g fiber, 21 g pro. *Daily values:* 12% vit. A, 22% vit. C, 7% calcium, 24% iron.

SWIRLED VEGETABLE TURKEY LOAF

Prep: 30 min. ◆ Bake: 1 hr.

What appears to be ordinary meat loaf turns into colorful pinwheels when sliced.

1 beaten egg
2 Tbsp. catsup
¼ cup seasoned fine dry bread crumbs
1 tsp. dry mustard
¾ tsp. salt
½ tsp. lemon-pepper seasoning
1½ lb. ground raw turkey

◆◆◆

    Nonstick spray coating
1 cup sliced fresh mushrooms
½ cup finely shredded carrot
2 cups torn fresh spinach
2 Tbsp. apple jelly, melted

1 In a large mixing bowl combine egg, catsup, bread crumbs, mustard, salt, and lemon-pepper seasoning. Add ground turkey; mix well. On waxed paper pat the mixture to a 10×8-inch rectangle.

2 Spray a large nonstick skillet with nonstick spray coating. Add mushrooms and carrots. Cook over medium heat till tender and

any liquid is evaporated. Add spinach; cook and stir till wilted. Remove from heat; spread atop turkey rectangle to within 1 inch of edges. Starting from a short end, carefully roll up meat, using waxed paper to lift; seal edges and ends. Place loaf, seam side down, in a shallow baking pan.

3 Bake loaf, uncovered, in a 350° oven 1 to 1¼ hours or till juices are no longer pink in center of loaf. To serve, brush with apple jelly. Makes 8 servings.

Nutrition facts per serving: 155 cal., 7 g total fat (2 g sat. fat), 58 mg chol., 472 mg sodium, 8 g carbo., 1 g fiber, 13 g pro. *Daily values:* 30% vit. A, 9% vit. C, 3% calcium, 11% iron.

PRIZE TESTED RECIPE WINNER

THAI TURKEY

Start to finish: 25 min.

This recipe earned Kelli Whiting of Indianapolis, Indiana, $100 in the magazine's monthly contest.

⅔ cup water
2 Tbsp. soy sauce
1 Tbsp. honey
2 tsp. toasted sesame oil
2 tsp. curry powder
1 tsp. cornstarch
⅛ to ¼ tsp. crushed red pepper

◆◆◆

    Nonstick spray coating
1 small onion, cut into thin wedges
1 red sweet pepper, cut into thin strips
12 oz. cooked turkey, cut into bite-size strips (about 3 cups)
1 clove garlic, minced

    Hot cooked rice
    Sliced serrano peppers (optional)

1 For sauce, in a small mixing bowl stir together the water, soy sauce, honey, sesame oil, curry powder, cornstarch, and crushed red pepper; set aside.

2 Spray a large skillet or wok with nonstick spray coating. Cook and stir the onion wedges and red pepper strips over medium heat till tender. Stir in the turkey strips and garlic. Stir in sauce. Cook and stir till thickened and bubbly. Cook and stir for 1 minute more. Serve over hot cooked rice. If desired, garnish with serrano peppers. Serves 4.

Nutrition facts per serving with rice: 335 cal., 11 g total fat (3 g sat. fat), 81 mg chol., 576 mg sodium, 31 g carbo., 1 g fiber, 27 g pro. *Daily values:* 20% vit. A, 53% vit. C, 3% calcium, 21% iron.

ROASTED POTATO AND TURKEY SALAD

Prep: 30 min. ♦ Bake: 45 min.

This recipe earned Amy Loucks of Cambridge, Massachusetts, $200 in the magazine's monthly contest.

12 whole tiny new potatoes (about 1 lb.)
2 Tbsp. olive oil
½ tsp. salt
½ tsp. pepper

♦♦♦

⅓ cup olive oil
2 Tbsp. Dijon-style mustard
4 cloves garlic, minced
½ tsp. pepper

♦♦♦

1 lb. cooked turkey, cut into bite-size strips (3 cups)
4 slices bacon or turkey bacon, crisp-cooked, drained, and crumbled
1 small red onion, sliced and separated into rings
¼ cup snipped fresh Italian parsley
6 cups torn mixed greens, such as romaine, spinach, and leaf lettuce

1 Scrub potatoes; prick 2 or 3 times with a fork. Place potatoes in a shallow baking pan and drizzle with the 2 tablespoons olive oil. Sprinkle with salt and ½ teaspoon pepper. Bake in a 400° oven about 45 minutes or till potatoes are tender, stirring twice. Cool completely. Cut cooled potatoes into quarters.

2 For dressing, in a small bowl whisk together the ⅓ cup olive oil, Dijon-style mustard, garlic, and ½ teaspoon pepper.

3 In a large bowl combine the potatoes, turkey, bacon, onion, and parsley. Add the dressing, tossing gently to coat. To serve, arrange the mixed greens on salad plates; spoon turkey mixture atop. Makes 6 main-dish servings.

Nutrition facts per serving: 359 cal., 20 g total fat (3 g sat. fat), 63 mg chol., 422 mg sodium, 20 g carbo., 2 g fiber, 26 g pro. *Daily values:* 10% vit. A, 39% vit. C, 4% calcium, 20% iron.

LOW FAT

TURKEY ENCHILADAS

Prep: 40 min. ♦ Bake: 44 min.

Hooray for today's new ingredients that help us enjoy great-tasting, healthful meals. By using lower-fat dairy products in this Tex-Mex casserole, you save 5 grams of fat per enchilada.

½ cup chopped onion
½ of 8-oz. pkg. reduced-fat cream cheese (Neufchâtel), softened
1 Tbsp. water
1 tsp. ground cumin
¼ tsp. pepper
⅛ tsp. salt
4 cups chopped cooked turkey or chicken breast
¼ cup chopped pecans, toasted
12 7- to 8-inch flour tortillas Nonstick spray coating

♦♦♦

1 10¾-oz. can reduced-sodium condensed cream of chicken soup
1 8-oz. carton light dairy sour cream
1 cup skim milk

2 to 4 Tbsp. finely chopped pickled jalapeño peppers

♦♦♦

½ cup shredded reduced-fat sharp cheddar cheese (2 oz.)
Snipped fresh cilantro or parsley (optional)
Chopped tomato and sweet pepper (optional)

1 In a small saucepan cook the onion, covered, in a small amount of *water* over medium heat till tender; drain. In a medium mixing bowl stir together the cream cheese, the 1 tablespoon water, cumin, pepper, and salt. Stir in the cooked onion, turkey, and toasted pecans.

2 Wrap the tortillas in foil. Heat in a 350° oven for 10 to 15 minutes or till softened. (Or, if using a microwave, wrap the tortillas in a microwave-safe paper towel and cook on high for 30 to 60 seconds or till softened.) Meanwhile, spray a 3-quart rectangular baking dish with nonstick coating. For each enchilada, spoon about ¼ cup of the turkey mixture onto a tortilla; roll up. Place tortilla, seam side down, in the baking dish. Repeat with remaining filling and tortillas.

3 For sauce, in a medium mixing bowl stir together the cream of chicken soup, sour cream, milk, and jalapeño peppers. Pour the mixture over the enchiladas. Bake, covered, in a 350° oven about 40 minutes or till heated through.

4 Sprinkle the enchiladas with the shredded cheddar cheese. Bake enchiladas, uncovered, for

4 to 5 minutes more or till the cheese is melted. If desired, top with the snipped cilantro or parsley, tomatoes, and sweet pepper. Makes 12 enchiladas.

Nutrition facts per enchilada: 272 cal., 10 g total fat (3 g sat. fat), 57 mg chol., 398 mg sodium, 22 g carbo., 1 g fiber, 22 g pro. *Daily values:* 10% vit. A, 1% vit. C, 11% calcium, 13% iron.

GOURMET PIZZA

Prep: 20 min. ◆ Bake: 22 min.

Create your own gourmet-style pizza by mixing and matching the suggested toppings in the tip at right. Or, use your imagination and top it with your own favorites.

1 recipe **Italian Pizza Sauce** or **Pimiento Sauce** (see right)
1 16-oz. loaf frozen whole wheat bread dough, thawed
  Yellow cornmeal
1 teaspoon dried Italian seasoning or oregano, crushed, or ½ teaspoon dried rosemary, crushed

2 cups assorted **meat** and/or **vegetables** (see tip, right)
  Cheese (see tip, right)

1 Prepare either the Italian Pizza Sauce or the Pimiento Sauce. For crust, lightly grease a 15×10×1-inch baking pan and sprinkle pan with cornmeal. On a lightly floured surface, roll the dough to a 16×11-inch rectangle. Transfer dough to the prepared pan. Build up edges slightly. *Do not let rise.* Bake in a 425° oven about 12 minutes or till brown. Spread prepared sauce over hot crust. Layer with seasonings and your choice of meat, vegetables, and cheese. Bake for 10 to 15 minutes more or till bubbly and hot. Makes 9 main-dish servings.

Italian Pizza Sauce: In a food processor bowl or blender container, place one 14½-ounce can *Italian-style stewed tomatoes.* Cover and process or blend till smooth. Add one 6-ounce can *low-sodium tomato paste;* process or blend till combined.

Pimiento Sauce: In a bowl combine one 15-ounce can *low-sodium tomato sauce;* two 4-ounce jars *sliced pimiento,* drained; 2 teaspoons *balsamic vinegar or red wine vinegar;* ¼ teaspoon *garlic powder;* ¼ teaspoon *salt;* and ½ teaspoon *pepper.*

Nutrition facts per serving using Italian Pizza Sauce, ham, spinach, squash, red onion, mozzarella cheese, and Parmesan cheese: 262 cal., 7 g total fat (3 g sat. fat), 27 mg chol., 932 mg sodium, 34 g carbo., 3 g fiber, 19 g pro. *Daily values:* 28% vit. A, 37% vit. C, 14% calcium, 11% iron.

DESIGNER PIZZA TOPPINGS

Some like pizza plain; others like it loaded. Use the following list of meat, vegetables, and cheese to create a gourmet-style pizza of your own.

MEAT

2 cups sliced cooked ham; chopped cooked chicken; or canned shrimp, rinsed and well drained

VEGETABLES

◆ Frozen chopped spinach, thawed and well drained
◆ Sliced zucchini and/or yellow summer squash
◆ Chopped red or green sweet pepper or roasted red sweet pepper
◆ Sliced fresh mushrooms
◆ Chopped red onion
◆ Chopped plum tomatoes
◆ Thinly sliced green onion
◆ Cooked* and thinly sliced fennel bulb and/or cooked* and chopped eggplant
  *Cook the fennel bulb or eggplant, covered, in a small amount of boiling, salted water for 3 to 5 minutes or till tender.

CHEESE

1½ cups shredded part-skim mozzarella cheese or reduced-fat Monterey Jack cheese (about 6 ounces), plus ½ cup grated Parmesan cheese, grated Romano cheese, shredded reduced-fat cheddar cheese, or crumbled feta cheese

Vegetarian Chili
(see below)

◆◆◆

Mixed grain bread or
crusty hard rolls

◆◆◆

Salad of fresh spinach,
apple wedges, and
feta cheese

CALLALOO

Prep: 30 min. ◆ Cook: 1¼ hr.

In the Caribbean, callaloo (kal-uh-LOO), a Creole-style soup made from callaloo leaves, is as commonplace as sandy beaches and reggae music. Look for the leaves in specialty food shops.

1 lb. fresh or frozen fish fillets
1 cup chopped onion
2 cloves garlic, minced
2 Tbsp. margarine or butter
1 lb. fresh greens with stems,
    such as callaloo leaves,
    mustard greens, spinach,
    or Swiss chard
5 cups chicken broth
½ cup coconut milk (optional)
4 oz. salt pork
1 fresh chili pepper, seeded
    and chopped*
½ tsp. dried thyme, crushed
2 cups sliced okra or one
    10-oz. pkg. frozen cut
    okra
1 6-oz. pkg. frozen crabmeat,
    thawed
3 cups hot cooked rice

1 Partially thaw fish, if frozen. Cut fish into 1-inch pieces. Cover and chill till ready to use.

2 In a large pot cook onion and garlic in hot margarine or butter till tender. Meanwhile, tear greens into bite-size pieces, discarding stems. Stir greens into onion mixture. Add broth, coconut milk (if using), salt pork, chili pepper, and thyme. Bring to boiling; reduce heat. Simmer, covered, till greens are very tender. For callaloo or mustard greens, allow 1 hour; for spinach or Swiss chard, allow 20 to 30 minutes.

3 Remove and discard salt pork. Stir in okra. Return to boiling; reduce heat. Simmer, covered, 5 minutes. Stir in fish and crabmeat. Return to boiling; reduce heat. Simmer, uncovered, 5 to 7 minutes or till fish flakes. Serve soup over rice in bowls. Makes 6 main-dish servings.

*****Note:** Because chili peppers contain volatile oils that can burn skin and eyes, wear plastic or rubber gloves or work under cold running water. If your bare hands touch the chili peppers, wash hands and nails well with soap and water.

Nutrition facts per serving: 439 cal., 22 g total fat (7 g sat. fat), 66 mg chol., 1285 mg sodium, 32 g carbo., 3 g fiber, 28 g pro. Daily values: 31% vit. A, 63% vit. C, 11% calcium, 18% iron.

VEGETARIAN CHILI

Prep: 25 min. ◆ Cook: 2 hr.

2 Tbsp. olive oil or cooking oil
1½ cups chopped celery
1½ cups chopped green sweet
    pepper
1 cup chopped onion
3 cloves garlic, minced

◆◆◆

2 28-oz. cans tomatoes, cut up
3 15- to 16-oz. cans beans
    (kidney, black, garbanzo,
    great northern, and/or
    pinto), rinsed and drained
½ cup raisins
¼ cup red wine vinegar
3 to 4 tsp. chili powder
1 Tbsp. snipped fresh parsley
1 tsp. sugar
1½ tsp. dried basil, crushed
1½ tsp. dried oregano, crushed
1½ tsp. ground cumin
1 tsp. ground allspice
½ tsp. salt
¼ tsp. bottled hot pepper sauce
1 bay leaf
1 12-oz. can beer
¾ cup cashews
1 cup shredded Swiss,
    mozzarella, or cheddar
    cheese (4 oz.)(optional)

1 In a 4- to 6-quart pot heat oil. Add celery, green sweet pepper, onion, and garlic. Cover and cook over medium heat about 10 minutes or till vegetables are tender, stirring occasionally.

2 Stir in *undrained* tomatoes, drained beans, raisins, vinegar, chili powder, parsley, sugar, basil, oregano, cumin, allspice, salt, hot pepper sauce, bay leaf, and ¼ teaspoon *pepper*. Bring to boiling; reduce heat. Simmer, covered, 1½ hours. Stir in beer. Return to boiling. Simmer, uncovered, for 30 minutes or to desired consistency. Remove bay leaf. Stir in cashews. If desired, sprinkle cheese atop each serving. Makes 12 cups (8 main-dish servings).

Nutrition facts per serving: 333 cal., 11 g total fat (2 g sat. fat), 0 mg chol., 960 mg sodium, 52 g carbo., 12 g fiber, 16 g pro. Daily values: 17% vit. A, 80% vit. C, 12% calcium, 31% iron.

HOMEMADE WONTON SOUP

Start to finish: 1¼ hr.

20 **Shrimp and Pork Wontons**
   (see below)
 4 **cups chicken broth**
 ½ **cup thinly bias-sliced carrot**
 5 **to 6 green onions, slivered**
   (½ cup)
 1 **1-inch piece gingerroot**
   Several dashes toasted
   sesame oil
   Fresh cilantro (optional)

1 In a 3-quart saucepan bring 6 cups *water* to boiling. With a spoon place wontons, 1 at a time, into boiling water; reduce heat. Simmer, uncovered, for 5 minutes. (If using frozen wontons, do not thaw; after adding, return water to boiling before simmering.) Drain; rinse with cool water.

2 Meanwhile, in a 2-quart saucepan combine chicken broth, carrot, green onions, and gingerroot. Bring to boiling; reduce heat. Simmer, covered, for 2 to 4 minutes or till vegetables are crisp-tender. Remove gingerroot and discard. Stir in sesame oil. Divide wontons among bowls; ladle broth mixture atop. If desired, sprinkle with cilantro. Makes 4½ cups (4 to 6 servings).

Shrimp and Pork Wontons: For filling, thaw one 6-ounce package *frozen, peeled, cooked shrimp*. Finely chop shrimp; combine with ½ cup finely chopped *cooked pork*, ½ cup finely chopped *mushrooms,* ½ cup sliced *green*

HOW TO WRAP A WONTON

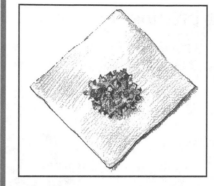

Step 1: Use 1 recipe Shrimp and Pork Wontons (see below) and 40 wonton skins. Top center of each skin with 1 teaspoon filling.

Step 2: Fold the lower corner of the wonton over the filling and bring its point up; tuck under the wonton's filling.

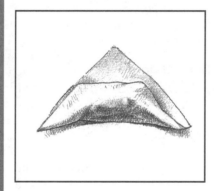

Step 3: Roll the wonton up slightly to cover the filling, leaving about 1 inch of skin unrolled at the top corner.

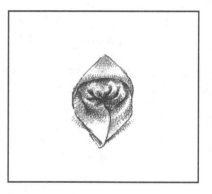

Step 4: Moisten a side corner. Grasp corners; overlap them over the filling, attaching moistened corner to other corner.

onions, 2 tablespoons finely chopped *pimiento,* 2 tablespoons snipped *fresh cilantro,* 2 tablespoons *soy sauce,* and ⅛ teaspoon *ground red pepper.*

Using the directions in the tip above, fill one 1-pound package *wonton wrappers* (40) with filling. Use half the wontons for soup (see left). Freeze remaining wontons for a second batch of soup. To

freeze, place wontons on a baking sheet in a single layer. Freeze till solid. Place frozen wontons in a freezer bag or container and freeze for up to 3 months.

Nutrition facts per serving: 215 cal., 4 g total fat (1 g sat. fat), 57 mg chol., 1,330 mg sodium, 27 g carbo., 1 g fiber, 17 g pro. *Daily values:* 49% vit. A, 12% vit. C, 4% calcium, 20% iron.

Nutrition Hits and Myths

With each new year or even the change of seasons, come new goals and resolutions, many of which revolve around our diets. Before you resolve to change your diet, consider this: We're fed various nutrition dogma all our lives, but a lot of what we accept as nutrition gospel is closer to nutrition myth. These myths, when more closely examined, can raise a host of valid questions.

While there are no hard answers in the study of nutrition, here are some answers to a few of the most commonly asked nutrition questions.

◆ Is poultry healthier than beef? Not necessarily. An ounce of beef has more B-12, zinc, and iron than an ounce of poultry. If fat is the issue, there are cuts of beef every bit as lean as poultry. Take note of these comparisons for 3.5-ounce, uncooked portions of the following meats:

Meat	Total Fat g	Saturated Fat g	Cholesterol mg
Sirloin steak, choice	7.2	2.8	89
Chicken, skin on, light and dark meat	13.6	3.8	88
Turkey, packaged ground	12.8	4.5	90

Source: Bowes and Church's Food Values of Portions Commonly Used, 16th Edition, 1994

◆ Do carbohydrates make you fat? Any food can make you fat, not just those foods high in carbohydrates. Carbohydrates, like protein, provide 4 calories per gram; fat provides 9 calories per gram. Complex carbohydrates (starches such as bread, pasta, rice, and potatoes), especially those derived from whole grains, are the body's best source of energy nourishment when they replace saturated fats and excess protein in the diet. Eating more calories than you work off and leading a sedentary life are what add the poundage.

◆ Are eggs really bad for you? Eggs are an excellent source of high-quality, inexpensive protein. Eggs are also lower in cholesterol than once believed—an average egg has about 210 mg cholesterol. The American Heart Association, noting recent research that indicates eggs don't by themselves significantly raise blood cholesterol levels, now says it is possible for healthy persons who have normal blood cholesterol levels to enjoy 1 or 2 eggs a day.

◆ If I eat too much salt, will I get high blood pressure? Salt does not cause an otherwise healthy person to develop hypertension. Unless you already have hypertension problems or are diagnosed as salt-sensitive, you don't need to limit your salt intake. This doesn't mean you can eat your weight in salt every day. What it does mean is you can relax and enjoy those salted pretzels, from time to time.

◆ Is honey better for you than table sugar? There really isn't a whole lot of difference between honey and table sugar (sucrose). Honey is composed of mostly fructose (fruit sugar) with some sucrose and glucose as well. Simple sugars, such as table sugar, honey, maple sugar, date sugar, and brown sugar, are all processed by the body in the same manner. Like table sugar, they all provide 4 calories per gram. *A word of caution:* Do not feed

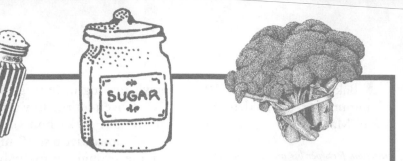

honey to infants under one year of age. Honey can contain trace amounts of botulism spores which a mature digestive system can handle but could mean a fatal case of botulism for babies.

◆ If I eat too much sugar, will I get diabetes? For someone with a blood sugar disorder, sugar can aggravate the condition if intake isn't regulated. But, like salt, the substance itself does not cause the disease. There is a caveat: Too much food, especially sugars and fats, leads to obesity. Obesity can lead to insulin resistance and possibly to diabetes. A balanced diet plus moderate exercise—about half an hour's worth each day—can help prevent that from happening.

◆ Is all fat bad? The human body needs fat—as a source of energy, as a transporter and storer of nutrients, for nerve function, and for cell structure. Unfortunately, the "eat less fat" message promoted by health professional groups such as the American Dietetic Association and the American Heart Association often is misinterpreted as a blanket condemnation of fat. Here's the true message from the pros: Healthy persons with blood cholesterol levels around 200 mg or less usually need not worry about fat intake as long as they enjoy a wide variety of foods in moderation and get some exercise.

◆ Will I lose weight if I go on a vegetarian diet? That depends on how you eat overall. A vegetarian diet is not automatically a low-fat diet. Deep-fried vegetables have more fat than a grilled, skinless chicken breast. Vegetarians who fill up on nuts, cheese, and full-fat dairy products as their main sources of protein (versus, say, beans and peas) could find themselves on a diet higher in fat than the person whose daily menu includes lean meats and plenty of fresh fruits and steamed vegetables.

Once Upon a Time

In the 1920s, people were encouraged to eat pickles "for health." The scientific basis for pickle-popping was nebulous, to be sure. Nutrition myths will be with us forever. For the most part these myths are harmless—a plethora of pickles never hurt anyone—but they are a reminder that there are no magic foods no matter how much we want to believe in them.

NO FAT
WINTER FRUIT BOWL
Prep: 25 min. ◆ Cool and chill: 2 hr.

This sweet-tart combo adds a colorful accent to any meal.

3 medium grapefruit
◆◆◆
½ cup sugar
½ cup orange marmalade
2 cups fresh cranberries (8 oz.)
◆◆◆
3 medium bananas
Fresh mint sprig (optional)

1 To section grapefruit, cut off the ends of a grapefruit, then use a long, thin-bladed knife to cut out the core. Resting an end of the grapefruit on a cutting board, cut off the peel in strips. Peel the grapefruit apart and simply lift or pull each segment off the membrane, working over a bowl to catch the juice.

2 Set grapefruit sections aside (should have about 3 cups). Add enough *water* to reserved grapefruit juice to measure 1 cup. In a medium saucepan combine the 1 cup grapefruit juice, sugar, and marmalade. Bring to boiling, stirring to dissolve sugar; reduce heat. Add cranberries; cook and stir for 5 to 8 minutes or till skins pop. Remove from heat; cool. Add grapefruit. Cover and chill.

3 Just before serving, slice the bananas and stir into chilled grapefruit mixture. If desired, garnish with fresh mint. Makes about 6½ cups (10 servings).

Nutrition facts per serving: 148 cal., 0 g total fat, 0 mg chol., 3 mg sodium, 39 g carbo., 3 g fiber, 1 g pro.
Daily values: 2% vit. A, 55% vit. C, 1% calcium, 2% iron.

UP-AND-DOWN BISCUITS

Prep: 20 min. ◆ Bake: 10 min.

To eat these fun biscuits, peel away one of the up-and-down layers, which are generously spiced with cinnamon. (See the photograph on page 41.)

2 cups all-purpose flour
3 Tbsp. sugar
4 tsp. baking powder
½ tsp. cream of tartar
½ cup shortening
⅔ cup milk
◆◆◆
¼ cup margarine or butter, melted
¼ cup sugar
2 to 3 tsp. ground cinnamon

1 Grease twelve 2½-inch muffin cups; set aside. In a medium bowl mix flour, the 3 tablespoons sugar, baking powder, cream of tartar, and ½ teaspoon *salt.* Using a pastry blender, cut in shortening till mixture resembles coarse crumbs. Make a well in the center; add milk all at once. Stir just till dough clings together.

2 On a lightly floured surface, knead dough gently 10 to 12 strokes. Divide dough in half. Roll out half of the dough to a 12×10-inch rectangle. Brush with half of the melted margarine or butter. Combine the ¼ cup sugar and cinnamon; sprinkle half over dough. Cut rectangle into five 12×2-inch strips. Stack the 5 strips on top of one another. Cut into six 2-inch squares. Place squares, cut side down, in prepared muffin cups. Repeat with remaining dough, margarine or butter, and sugar mixture.

3 Bake in a 450° oven 10 to 12 minutes or till golden. Serve warm. Makes 12.

Nutrition facts per biscuit: 216 cal., 13 g total fat (3 g sat. fat), 1 mg chol., 262 mg sodium, 23 g carbo., 1 g fiber, 2 g pro. *Daily values:* 5% vit. A, 11% calcium, 8% iron.

LIGHT BREAD

Prep: 30 min. ◆ Rise: 2 hr.
Bake: 25 min.

This bread dough is so easy, all you'll need to mix it is a sturdy spoon. Toasted and spread with jam for breakfast, this bread is a family pleaser.

½ cup sugar
½ cup shortening
2 tsp. salt
1 cup warm milk (110° to 115°)
2 beaten eggs
◆◆◆
1 cup warm water (110° to 115°)
2 pkg. active dry yeast
6¼ to 6¾ cups all-purpose flour

1 In a large mixing bowl combine sugar, shortening, and salt. Add warm milk and stir to soften shortening; cool. Using a wooden spoon, beat in eggs.

2 In a bowl stir together warm water and yeast; let stand 5 minutes. Stir yeast mixture into shortening mixture. Add *4 cups* of the flour; beat with a wooden spoon till smooth. Add enough remaining flour to make a soft dough. Turn dough out onto floured surface; knead in enough remaining flour to make a moderately stiff dough that is smooth and elastic (6 to 8 minutes). Place in greased

bowl, turning once to grease surface. Cover; let rise in warm place till double (1¼ hours). Punch dough down; let rest 10 minutes. Divide dough into halves or thirds. Shape into loaves. Place in 2 greased 9×5×3-inch loaf pans or 3 greased 8×4×2-inch loaf pans. Let dough rise till double (45 to 60 minutes).

3 Bake in 375° oven about 25 minutes or till golden. Cover with foil the last 5 to 10 minutes, if necessary, to prevent over-browning. Remove loaves from pans and cool on a wire rack. If desired, wrap bread in moisture- and vapor-proof wrap and freeze for up to 3 months. Makes 2 or 3 loaves (36 servings).

Nutrition facts per serving: 117 cal., 3 g total fat (1 g sat. fat), 12 mg chol., 126 mg sodium, 19 g carbo., 1 g fiber, 3 g pro. *Daily values:* 1% calcium, 6% iron.

Light Pan Rolls: Prepare bread as directed, except after first rising, divide dough into 36 pieces. Gently pull each dough piece into a ball, tucking edges beneath. Place rolls in 2 greased 13×9×2-inch baking pans. Let rise till double (45 to 60 minutes). Bake in a 375° oven 15 to 20 minutes or till golden. Cool. Makes 36.

EASY PEACH CRISP

Prep: 12 min. ◆ Bake: 12 min.
See the photograph on page 44.

1 12-inch Italian bread shell (Boboli)
1 21-oz. can peach or apple pie filling

⅓ cup quick-cooking rolled
  oats
¼ cup packed brown sugar
3 Tbsp. all-purpose flour
3 Tbsp. butter or margarine,
  melted

1 Place the Italian bread shell on a pizza pan or large baking sheet. Top with the peach or apple pie filling, spreading evenly. In a small mixing bowl stir together rolled oats, brown sugar and flour. Stir in the melted butter or margarine till well combined. Sprinkle atop pie filling. Bake in a 400° oven for 12 to 15 minutes or till heated through. Serves 8.

Nutrition facts per serving: 334 cal., 8 g total fat (1 g sat. fat), 8 mg chol., 389 mg sodium, 61 g carbo., 1 g fiber, 8 g pro. *Daily values:* 13% vit. A, 13% vit. C, 6% calcium, 12% iron.

PRIZE TESTED RECIPE WINNER

BRANDIED CRANBERRY-APRICOT BARS

Prep: 1 hr. ◆ Bake: 40 min.

If Sharon Davidson of Reno, Nevada, had her way, she'd start every meal with dessert. "I have a sweet tooth and so does the rest of my family," she says. Her love of baking helped her create these bars, which won the September 1996 Prize Tested Recipes contest in the Best-Ever Bar Cookies category and earned our first annual Grand Prize.

⅓ **cup golden raisins**
⅓ **cup dark raisins**
⅓ **cup dried cranberries**
⅓ **cup snipped dried apricots**
⅓ **cup brandy or water**

◆◆◆

1 **cup all-purpose flour**
⅓ **cup packed brown sugar**
⅓ **cup margarine or butter,**
  softened

◆◆◆

2 **eggs**
1 **cup packed brown sugar**
⅓ **cup all-purpose flour**
1 **tsp. vanilla**
⅓ **cup chopped pecans**
  Powdered sugar

1 In a saucepan combine the golden raisins, dark raisins, dried cranberries, apricots, and brandy or water. Bring to boiling. Remove from heat. Let stand for 20 minutes; drain.

2 In a medium mixing bowl stir together the 1 cup flour and ⅓ cup brown sugar. Using a pastry blender, cut in the softened margarine or butter till mixture resembles coarse crumbs. Press into an ungreased 8×8×2-inch baking pan. Bake in a 350° oven about 20 minutes or till golden.

3 Meanwhile, in a medium mixing bowl beat the eggs with an electric mixer on low speed for 4 minutes. Stir in 1 cup brown sugar, ⅓ cup flour, and the vanilla till combined. Stir in the drained fruit and pecans. Pour fruit mixture over crust; spread evenly.

4 Bake about 40 minutes more or till a wooden toothpick inserted near the center comes out clean, covering with foil the last 10 minutes to prevent overbrowning. Cool in pan on a wire rack. Sift powdered sugar over top. To serve, cut into bars. Makes 16.

Nutrition facts per serving: 221 cal., 8 g total fat (4 g sat. fat), 42 mg chol., 72 mg sodium, 32 g carbo., 1 g fiber, 2 g pro.

BREAD SPREADS

Add a tasty zip to your breads by serving them with one of these yummy spreads. You can stir a spread together in about 5 minutes, but let it chill at least 1 hour before serving to allow its flavors to blend.

NUT BUTTER

Mix ½ cup finely chopped almonds or walnuts; ¼ cup butter or margarine, softened; and ¼ cup apricot or peach preserves. Makes 1 cup.

CITRUS BUTTER

Mix ½ cup butter or margarine, softened; 1 tablespoon powdered sugar; and 1 teaspoon finely shredded orange or lemon peel. Makes ½ cup.

ONION-PARMESAN BUTTER

Mix ½ cup butter or margarine, softened; 2 tablespoons grated Parmesan cheese; and 2 teaspoons sliced green onion. Makes ½ cup.

HERB BUTTER

Mix ½ cup butter or margarine, softened; and ½ teaspoon each dried thyme and marjoram, crushed, or 1 teaspoon dried basil, crushed. Makes ½ cup.

PIMIENTO BUTTER

In a food processor bowl or blender container, combine one 4-ounce jar sliced pimientos, drained; 1 tablespoon anchovy paste; and 1 clove garlic, minced. Cover and process or blend till pimientos are pureed and mixture is smooth. Stir pimiento mixture into ½ cup butter or margarine, softened. Makes about 1 cup.

CHOCOLATE CREAM CHEESE CAKE

Prep: 50 min. ◆ Bake: 25 min.

One of our recipe collectors wrote, "If you could see the original recipe, you'd note the yellowed tape and multiple spills that set this recipe apart from others. I serve it anytime I need a perfect, never-fail, delicious dessert."

The original dark chocolate cake appeared in our magazine in 1975; now, 22 years later, we're introducing a white chocolate variation.

(See the photographs on page 43.)

2½ cups all-purpose flour
1½ tsp. baking powder
½ tsp. baking soda
¼ tsp. salt
◆◆◆
1 8-oz. pkg. cream cheese, softened
⅔ cup butter or margarine, softened
1 tsp. vanilla
5 oz. unsweetened chocolate, melted and cooled
8 cups sifted powdered sugar*
⅓ cup milk
1 to 2 cups sifted powdered sugar*
◆◆◆
3 large eggs
1 cup milk
◆◆◆
½ cup seedless red raspberry preserves
White Chocolate Stars (optional) (see above right)
Fresh red raspberries (optional)

1 Grease and flour three 8×1½- or 9×1½-inch cake pans; set aside. In a large mixing bowl stir together flour, baking powder, baking soda, and salt; set aside.

2 In a large mixing bowl beat together cream cheese, butter or margarine, and vanilla with an electric mixer on medium speed till fluffy. Add melted chocolate; beat till well blended. Alternately beat in the 8 cups powdered sugar and the ⅓ cup milk. Transfer 3½ cups of the mixture to another large mixing bowl to use for the cake batter; set aside. You should have about 2 cups of the mixture remaining, which will be used for the frosting. To this frosting mixture, beat in enough of the additional 1 to 2 cups sifted powdered sugar to make it of spreading consistency. Cover frosting and refrigerate till needed.

3 Add the eggs to the 3½ cups cream cheese mixture; beat on medium speed 1 minute. Add flour mixture and the 1 cup milk alternately to the egg mixture, beating on low speed after each addition just till combined. Pour batter into prepared pans. (If you don't have 3 cake pans of the same size, chill a portion of cake batter for up to 1 hour before baking.)

4 Bake in a 350° oven 25 to 30 minutes for 8-inch pans and 22 to 25 minutes for 9-inch pans or till a wooden toothpick inserted near center comes out clean. Cool in pans 10 minutes. Remove from pans and cool on wire racks.

5 Remove frosting from refrigerator about 30 minutes before frosting the cake. Place a cake layer on a serving plate; spread with half of the raspberry preserves. Top with a second layer; spread with remaining jam. Top with third cake layer. Spread top and sides with frosting. Cut in wedges to serve. If desired, garnish each serving with a White Chocolate Star and fresh raspberries. Makes 16 servings.

*Note: It's important to sift the powdered sugar before measuring. To sift, place powdered sugar in a sieve over a bowl. Use a spoon to stir the powdered sugar while pressing it through the sieve.

White Chocolate Stars: In a small saucepan heat and stir 2 ounces *white chocolate baking squares* and 1 teaspoon *shortening* over low heat till melted and smooth. Cool slightly. Transfer mixture to a heavy, self-sealing plastic bag; seal. Cut a tiny hole in a corner of bag. Use hole to pipe chocolate into star shapes on a piece of waxed paper. Let dry.

Nutrition facts per serving: 495 cal., 19 g total fat (10 g sat. fat), 78 mg chol., 251 mg sodium, 81 g carbo., 1 g fiber, 6 g pro. *Daily values:* 16% vit. A, 7% calcium, 13% iron.

White Chocolate Cream Cheese Cake: Prepare the cake as directed, except use 5 ounces *Nestlé's white chocolate baking squares* for the unsweetened chocolate. (Do not substitute.) Garnish cake with the *fresh red raspberries, White Chocolate Curls* (see below), and additional *powdered sugar.*

White Chocolate Curls: Carefully draw a sharp vegetable peeler across the broad surface of two or three 2-ounce *white baking bars* at warm room temperature. Use curls immediately or carefully place on paper towels in a single layer in a covered storage container. Chill till needed.

PUMPKIN-PECAN PIE

Prep: 25 min. ◆ Bake: 50 min.

When you can't decide between pumpkin or pecan for your holiday pie, let this delicious recipe come to your rescue. (See the photograph on page 41.)

1 recipe Pastry for Single-
  Crust Pie (see right)

◆◆◆

3 slightly beaten eggs
1 15-oz. can pumpkin
¾ cup sugar
½ cup dark corn syrup
1 tsp. vanilla
¾ tsp. ground cinnamon
1 cup chopped pecans

◆◆◆

  Whipped cream (optional)
  Ground cinnamon (optional)

1 Prepare Pastry for Single-Crust Pie. On a lightly floured surface use your hands to slightly flatten dough. Roll dough from center to edges into a circle about 12 inches in diameter. To transfer pastry, wrap it around the rolling pin. Unroll pastry into a 9-inch pie plate. Ease pastry into plate, being careful not to stretch it. Trim pastry to ½ inch beyond edge of pie plate. Fold under extra pastry. Crimp the edge.

2 For filling, in a medium mixing bowl combine the eggs, pumpkin, sugar, corn syrup, vanilla, and the ¾ teaspoon cinnamon; mix well. Place the pastry-lined pie plate on the oven rack. Carefully pour filling into pastry shell. Sprinkle with pecans.

3 Bake in a 350° oven 50 to 55 minutes or till knife inserted near the center of pie comes out clean. Cool on a rack. If desired, serve with whipped cream sprinkled with cinnamon. Serves 8.

Pastry for Single-Crust Pie: In a medium mixing bowl stir together 1¼ cups *all-purpose flour* and ¼ teaspoon *salt*. Using a pastry blender cut in ⅓ cup *shortening* till pieces are pea-size. Using 4 to 5 tablespoons *cold water* total, sprinkle water, 1 tablespoon at a time, over flour and toss with a fork till all the dough is moistened. Shape dough into a ball.

Nutrition facts per serving: 412 cal., 20 g total fat (4 g sat. fat), 80 mg chol., 109 mg sodium, 55 g carbo., 3 g fiber, 6 g pro. *Daily values:* 120% vit. A, 4% vit. C, 3% calcium, 20% iron.

APPLE-WALNUT COBBLER

Prep: 20 min. ◆ Bake: 50 min.

A cross between a coffee cake and a pudding, this dessert cuts nicely into squares. Or, spoon portions into dessert cups and pass the cream. (See the photograph on page 41.)

5 cups thinly sliced, peeled
  tart apples (such as
  Cortland, Granny Smith,
  Jonathan, or Rome
  Beauty)
¾ cup chopped walnuts
¼ cup sugar
½ tsp. ground cinnamon
1 cup all-purpose flour
½ cup sugar
1 tsp. baking powder
1 beaten egg
½ cup evaporated milk
⅓ cup margarine or butter,
  melted
  Half-and-half or light cream
  (optional)

1 Lightly grease a 2-quart square baking dish. Spread the apples in the dish. Sprinkle with ½ cup of the walnuts, the ¼ cup sugar, and the cinnamon. In a medium mixing bowl stir together the flour, the ½ cup sugar, and baking powder.

2 In a small bowl combine the egg, evaporated milk, and melted margarine or butter. Stir the egg mixture into dry ingredients till smooth. Pour evenly over apples; sprinkle with remaining walnuts.

3 Bake in a 325° oven for 50 to 55 minutes or till a wooden toothpick inserted in the center comes out clean. Cut into squares and serve cobbler warm. If desired, serve with half-and-half or light cream. Makes 9 servings.

Nutrition facts per serving: 304 cal., 15 g total fat (3 g sat. fat), 28 mg chol., 143 mg sodium, 41 g carbo., 2 g fiber, 5 g pro. *Daily values:* 10% vit. A, 5% vit. C, 7% calcium, 7% iron.

FROSTED BUTTERSCOTCH COOKIES

Prep: 30 min. ◆ Bake: 10 min.

2½ cups all-purpose flour
1   tsp. baking soda
½   tsp. baking powder
½   tsp. salt
1½ cups packed brown sugar
½   cup shortening
2   slightly beaten eggs
1   tsp. vanilla
1   8-oz. carton dairy sour cream
⅔   cup chopped walnuts
1   recipe Browned Butter Frosting (see below)
    Walnut halves (optional)

1 In a bowl combine flour, soda, baking powder, and salt; set aside. In a mixing bowl beat brown sugar and shortening with an electric mixer on medium to high speed till combined. Add eggs and vanilla; beat till combined. Alternately add flour mixture and sour cream, beating after each addition. Stir in walnuts.

2 Drop dough by rounded teaspoons 2 inches apart onto greased cookie sheet. Bake in a 375° oven for 10 to 12 minutes or till edges are lightly browned. Cool cookies on a wire rack. Spread cooled cookies with Browned Butter Frosting. If desired, top each cookie with a walnut half. Makes 60 cookies.

Browned Butter Frosting: In a medium saucepan heat and stir ½ cup *butter* over medium-low heat till golden brown *(do not scorch)*. Remove from heat. Stir in 3½ cups *sifted powdered sugar,* 1½ teaspoons *vanilla,* and 5 to 6 teaspoons *hot water.* Beat till frosting is easy to spread. Use immediately. If frosting begins to set up as you work, stir in a few drops hot water; beat smooth again. Makes about 1⅓ cups frosting.

Nutrition facts per frosted cookie: 105 cal., 5 g total fat (2 g sat. fat), 13 mg chol., 63 mg sodium, 14 g carbo., 0 g fiber, 1 g pro. *Daily values:* 2% vit. A, 1% calcium, 2% iron.

CHOCOLATE-COVERED CHERRY COOKIES

Prep: 30 min. ◆ Bake: 10 min.

For these fudgy treats, you spread the frosting on the cookies before baking. Just be sure to use real chocolate (not imitation) so the cookies will bake properly.
(See the photograph on page 42.)

1½ cups all-purpose flour
½   cup unsweetened cocoa powder
½   cup butter or margarine
1   cup sugar
¼   tsp. baking soda
¼   tsp. baking powder
¼   tsp. salt
1   egg
1½ tsp. vanilla

◆◆◆

48 undrained maraschino cherries (about one 10-oz. jar)
1   6-oz. pkg. semisweet chocolate pieces
½   cup sweetened condensed milk

1 Combine flour and cocoa powder; set aside. In a mixing bowl beat butter with an electric mixer till softened. Add sugar, soda, baking powder, and salt. Beat till combined. Add egg and vanilla; beat. Gradually beat in flour mixture.

2 Shape dough into 1-inch balls; place on an ungreased cookie sheet. Press down center of each ball with thumb. Drain maraschino cherries, reserving juice. Place a cherry in the center of each cookie. In a small saucepan combine chocolate pieces and sweetened condensed milk; heat till chocolate is melted. Stir in *4 teaspoons* reserved cherry juice.

3 Spoon about 1 teaspoon frosting over each cherry, spreading to cover cherry. If necessary, thin frosting with additional cherry juice. Bake in a 350° oven about 10 minutes or till done. Remove to wire rack; cool. Makes 48 cookies.

Nutrition facts per cookie: 81 cal., 3 g total fat (1 g sat. fat), 11 mg chol., 45 mg sodium, 12 g carbo., 0 g fiber, 1 g pro. *Daily values:* 2% vit. A, 1% calcium, 2% iron.

THE CLEVER COOK

PRETZELS FOR NUTS

When baking chocolate chip, raisin, or oatmeal drop cookies, I substitute coarsely crushed pretzels for any chopped nuts called for in the recipe. You get the taste and texture of nuts with almost none of the fat.

T. Stephens
Ohio

FEBRUARY
Fuel for the Fire

30-minute recipes indicated in RED
Low-fat and no-fat recipes indicated
with a ♥.
Photographs indicated in italics.

Winter's worst calls for a cook's best—hearty foods to take on the season. Fight back the chill with the zesty flair of Savory Mexican Pork Roast or Pasta with Ratatouille. For a taste of all-American warmth, savor an award-winning Southwestern Meat Loaf or quick-and-easy Beef Steak with Red Onion Relish.

Brighten those long shadows of February with Raspberry-Almond Rolls, Apple Butter Coffee Cake, or an Apricot-Almond Tart.

Is cooking ever more satisfying than when winter whistles 'round a window steamed by the stove? Put another log on the fire and another hearty meal on your plates.

**Beef Steak with Red
Onion Relish
(see below right)**

◆◆◆

**Roasted Garlic Mashed
Potatoes
(see page 46)**

◆◆◆

**Salad of mixed greens,
orange sections, and
toasted walnuts**

◆◆◆

Whole wheat rolls

SAVORY MEXICAN PORK ROAST

Prep: 25 min. ◆ Cook : 1½ hr.

1 2½- to 3-lb. boneless
    pork shoulder roast
    (rolled and tied)
2 Tbsp. cooking oil
1 14½-oz. can tomatoes,
    undrained and cut up
1 cup reduced-sodium chicken
    broth
½ cup picante sauce
1 medium onion, chopped
1 medium green sweet pepper,
    chopped
1 Tbsp. chili powder
½ tsp. ground cumin
⅛ tsp. ground pepper
4 medium carrots, thinly sliced
4 stalks celery, thinly sliced

◆◆◆

1 Tbsp. cornstarch
    Hot cooked mashed potatoes

1 Trim fat from meat. In a
Dutch oven brown roast on all
sides in hot oil. Drain off fat. Add
the undrained tomatoes, chicken
broth, picante sauce, onion, green

sweet pepper, chili powder, cumin
and ground pepper to Dutch
oven. Bring to boiling; reduce
heat. Simmer, covered, for 1 hour.
Add carrots and celery. Simmer,
covered, for 30 to 40 minutes
more or till meat is tender.
Remove meat to a platter, reserving vegetables and juices in Dutch
oven. Keep meat warm.

2 For sauce, combine the
cornstarch and ¼ cup *cold water*.
Stir into vegetable mixture. Cook
and stir till thickened and bubbly.
Cook and stir for 2 minutes more.
Serve the sauce with the meat and
and mashed potatoes. Serves 8.

Nutrition facts per serving: 384 cal., 18 g
total fat (6 g sat. fat), 95 mg chol., 730 mg
sodium, 30 g carbo., 3 g fiber, 28 g pro.
Daily values: 94% vit. A, 50% vit. C, 6%
calcium, 19% iron.

BEEF STEAK WITH RED ONION RELISH

Start to finish: 25 min.

*A good steak can easily be part of a
healthful diet. Choose a lean cut, such
as sirloin, and trim off any excess fat.*

1 lb. boneless beef sirloin
    steak, cut ¾ inch thick
¼ to 1 tsp. coarsely ground
    pepper
2 tsp. cooking oil

◆◆◆

1 large red onion, thinly sliced
    and separated into rings
¼ cup dry red wine
½ tsp. dried sage, crushed
¼ tsp. salt

1 Cut the steak into 4 equal
portions and rub both sides with
the ground pepper. In a large

nonstick skillet heat oil over
medium-high heat. Add the
steaks and cook about 4 minutes
on each side or till medium doneness. Remove the steaks from the
skillet, reserving drippings. Keep
steaks warm.

2 In the skillet cook onion in
drippings over medium heat for 5
to 7 minutes or till crisp-tender.
Carefully add wine, sage, and salt.
Cook 1 to 2 minutes or till most
of the liquid is evaporated. Serve
onion mixture with steaks. Makes
4 servings.

Nutrition facts per serving: 246 cal., 12 g
total fat (4 g sat. fat), 76 mg chol., 200 mg
sodium, 3 g carbo., 1 g fiber, 26 g pro.
Daily values: 2% vit. C, 1% calcium,
20% iron.

GREEK MEAT LOAF

Prep: 20 min. ◆ Bake: 50 min.

*Cool cucumber sauce tops each serving
of this Greek-inspired meat loaf.*

⅓ cup dairy sour cream
½ cup peeled, seeded, and
    chopped cucumber
2 Tbsp. chopped red onion
1 clove garlic, minced
¼ tsp. dried mint or
    basil, crushed

◆◆◆

1 beaten egg
½ cup sliced pitted ripe olives
¼ cup fine dry bread crumbs
¼ cup crumbled feta cheese
    (1 oz.)
¼ cup milk
½ tsp. dried mint or
    basil, crushed
8 oz. lean ground beef
8 oz. lean ground lamb
½ cup chopped tomato

1 For sauce, stir together the sour cream, cucumber, onion, garlic, ¼ teaspoon mint or basil, ⅛ teaspoon *pepper,* and dash *salt.* Cover and chill.

2 For meat loaf, in a large mixing bowl combine the egg, olives, bread crumbs, feta cheese, milk, ½ teaspoon mint or basil, ¼ teaspoon *salt,* and ¼ teaspoon *pepper.* Add the ground beef and lamb; mix well. In a shallow baking pan pat mixture into a 7×3×2-inch loaf. Bake in 350° oven about 50 minutes or till no pink remains.

3 To serve, cut meat loaf into slices. Spoon some of the sauce over each serving and sprinkle with tomato. Makes 4 servings.

Nutrition facts per serving: 367 cal., 25 g total fat (11 g sat. fat), 151 mg chol., 557 mg sodium, 10 g carbo., 1 g fiber, 26 g pro. *Daily values:* 12% vit. A, 11% vit. C, 13% calcium, 17% iron.

SOUTHWESTERN MEAT LOAF

Prep: 15 min. ◆ Bake: 65 min.

This recipe earned Bernard Merino of San Francisco $100 in the magazine's monthly contest.

- 1 slightly beaten egg
- ¾ cup soft bread crumbs (1 slice bread)
- ¾ cup salsa
- ⅓ cup raisins
- ¼ cup finely chopped almonds, toasted
- ¼ cup finely chopped onion
- ½ tsp. sugar

- ½ tsp. salt
- ¼ tsp. ground cinnamon
- ⅛ tsp. ground cloves
- 1½ lb. ground beef

◆◆◆

- ¼ cup salsa
  Salsa (optional)

1 In a large mixing bowl stir together egg, bread crumbs, the ¾ cup salsa, raisins, almonds, onion, sugar, salt, cinnamon, and cloves. Add ground beef and mix well. In a shallow baking pan pat meat mixture into an 8×4×2-inch oval loaf. (Or, pat meat mixture into an 8×4×2-inch loaf pan.) Bake in 350° oven for 1 hour.

2 Drain off fat. Insert a meat thermometer into center of loaf. Spoon the ¼ cup salsa over meat loaf. Bake 5 to 10 minutes more or till thermometer reaches 160°. Transfer to a serving platter. Let stand 10 minutes before serving.

3 To serve, cut the meat loaf into slices. If desired, serve meat loaf with additional salsa. Makes 6 servings.

Nutrition facts per serving: 312 cal., 18 g total fat (6 g sat. fat), 107 mg chol., 426 mg sodium, 14 g carbo., 1 g fiber, 25 g pro. *Daily values:* 6% vit. A, 21% vit. C, 3% calcium, 20% iron.

POT ROAST MADRAS

Prep: 35 min. ◆ Cook: 2 hr.

The combination of ginger, curry, and turmeric takes this spicy roast beyond the ordinary.

- 1 2- to 2½-lb. boneless beef chuck pot roast
- 1 tsp. ground ginger
- 1 tsp. curry powder
- 1 tsp. ground turmeric

- ½ tsp. salt
- ¼ tsp. pepper
- 2 Tbsp. cooking oil
- 1 8-oz. can tomatoes, undrained and cut up
- ½ cup beef broth
- 2 cups chopped onions
- 2 cloves garlic, minced
- 1 bay leaf
- ½ tsp. dried thyme, crushed
- 4 medium carrots, cut into 1-inch pieces

◆◆◆

- ¼ cup all-purpose flour

1 Trim fat from meat. In a small bowl stir together the ginger, curry powder, turmeric, salt, and pepper. Rub over surface of meat. In a Dutch oven brown roast in hot oil. Drain off fat. Add the undrained tomatoes, beef broth, onions, garlic, bay leaf, and thyme to Dutch oven. Bring to boiling; reduce heat. Simmer, covered, for 1½ hours. Add carrots and simmer, covered, for 30 to 40 minutes more or till meat and vegetables are tender. Transfer meat and vegetables to a platter, reserving juices in Dutch oven. Keep meat and vegetables warm.

2 For gravy, measure juices; skim fat. If necessary, add enough *water* to equal 1½ cups. Return juices to Dutch oven. Combine flour and ½ cup *cold water.* Stir into juices. Cook and stir till thickened and bubbly. Cook and stir for 1 minute more. Serve gravy with meat and vegetables. Makes 6 servings.

Nutrition facts per serving: 362 cal., 16 g total fat (5 g sat. fat), 110 mg chol., 405 mg sodium, 15 g carbo., 3 g fiber, 38 g pro. *Daily values:* 116% vit. A, 15% vit. C, 4% calcium, 36% iron.

SPICED ORANGE POT ROAST

Prep: 20 min. ◆ Cook: 2 hr.

This recipe earned Harriet L. Weil of Takoma Park, Maryland, $200 in the magazine's monthly contest.

1 2½- to 3-lb. beef chuck pot roast
1 Tbsp. cooking oil
1 8-oz. can tomato sauce
½ cup chopped onion
1 clove garlic, minced
2 Tbsp. sugar
1 Tbsp. finely shredded orange peel
½ tsp. ground cinnamon
¼ tsp. ground cloves
⅛ tsp. pepper
   Dash salt
4 oranges, peeled and sectioned

1 Trim fat from meat. In a large pot brown meat on all sides in hot oil. Drain off fat. In a medium mixing bowl combine the tomato sauce, onion, garlic, sugar, orange peel, cinnamon, cloves, pepper, and salt. Stir in 1 of the peeled and sectioned oranges (cover and chill remaining orange sections for later). Pour tomato mixture over roast. Bring to boiling; reduce heat. Simmer, covered, for 2 to 2½ hours or till tender. Transfer meat to a serving platter. Keep meat warm.

2 For gravy, measure juices; skim fat. Bring juices to boiling; reduce heat. Simmer, uncovered, about 5 minutes or till juices are reduced to 1¼ cups. Stir in reserved orange sections; heat through. To serve, spoon gravy over roast; pass remainder. Makes 8 to 10 servings.

Nutrition facts per serving: 267 cal., 11 g total fat (4 g sat. fat), 93 mg chol., 255 mg sodium, 10 g carbo., 1 g fiber, 31 g pro. *Daily values:* 3% vit. A, 36% vit. C, 2% calcium, 26% iron.

PIZZA BURGERS

Prep: 15 min. ◆ Broil: 12 min.

1 egg
¼ cup rolled oats
2 Tbsp. catsup
¾ tsp. dried Italian seasoning, crushed
¼ tsp. garlic powder
¼ tsp. onion powder
¼ tsp. salt
12 oz. lean ground beef
4 oz. reduced-fat mozzarella cheese, sliced

◆◆◆

4 whole wheat buns or kaiser rolls, split and toasted
   Lettuce leaves (optional)
   Tomato slices (optional)
   Catsup (optional)

1 In a medium mixing bowl stir together the egg, oats, 2 tablespoons catsup, dried Italian seasoning, garlic powder, onion powder, and salt. Add ground beef; mix well. Shape mixture into four ¾-inch-thick patties.

2 Place patties on an unheated rack in a broiler pan. Broil 3 to 4 inches from heat for 12 to 14 minutes or till well-done, turning once. Top with cheese; broil about 1 minute more or till cheese is melted.

3 Serve hot pizza burgers on toasted buns or kaiser rolls. If desired, add lettuce, tomato slices, and additional catsup or other condiments. Makes 4 burgers.

Nutrition facts per serving: 370 cal., 15 g total fat (7 g sat. fat), 122 mg chol., 711 mg sodium, 28 g carbo., 3 g fiber, 30 g pro. *Daily values:* 5% vit. A, 2% vit. C, 26% calcium, 20% iron.

PORK AND LENTIL CASSOULET

Prep: 20 min. ◆ Cook: 4½ to 12 hr.

A slow-cooked cassoulet is a hearty relief when it awaits you at the end of the day. Ours uses lentils instead of the traditional white beans. (See the photograph on page 37.)

12 oz. boneless pork shoulder
1 large onion, cut into wedges
2 cloves garlic, minced
2 tsp. cooking oil
1 14½-oz. can tomatoes, undrained and cut up
4 medium carrots and/or parsnips, sliced ½ inch thick
2 stalks celery, thinly sliced
¾ cup lentils, rinsed and drained
1½ tsp. dried rosemary, crushed
1 tsp. instant beef bouillon granules
   Fresh rosemary sprigs (optional)

1 Trim fat from pork; cut meat into ¾-inch cubes. In a large nonstick skillet brown pork, onion, and garlic in hot oil. Transfer mixture to a 3½- to 4-quart crockery cooker. Add the undrained tomatoes, carrots and/or parsnips, celery, lentils, rosemary, bouillon, 2½ cups

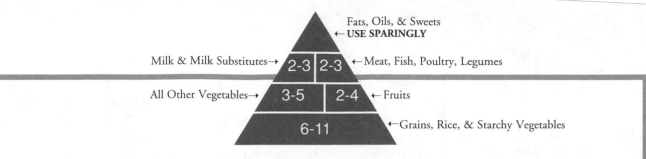

Fats, Oils, & Sweets
← **USE SPARINGLY**

Milk & Milk Substitutes→ 2-3 | 2-3 ←Meat, Fish, Poultry, Legumes

All Other Vegetables→ 3-5 | 2-4 ←Fruits

6-11 ←Grains, Rice, & Starchy Vegetables

PENNY-WISE, POUND-SMART STRATEGIES

Preparing healthful family meals that don't cost a bundle is easier than you think if you follow the right guidelines. The United States Department of Agriculture's (USDA) Food Guide Pyramid (see above) is the perfect place to start. Here are some strategies based on information from the Pyramid and professional health experts:

◆ Start at the bottom of the Food Guide Pyramid because the foods listed at the top—fats, oils, and sweets—can wreak havoc with both your diet and your budget if you overindulge. Not only are these items high in calories but they also tend to be high in cost. Enjoy them only sparingly.

◆ Moving up the pyramid: The bottom of the Food Guide Pyramid suggests six to 11 servings of breads, rice, pasta, and cereals. This makes sense from a health standpoint and also is very cost-effective. Extending high-cost meats, fish, and poultry with low-cost grains, rice, and pasta is an excellent way to stay within both your food and your calorie budget.

◆ Get a leg up on legumes: In the protein group, the little bean is the biggest nutrition bargain. Beans and other legumes (such as split peas and lentils) are delicious alternatives to meat, poultry, and fish. They are low-cost as well as low-fat. Each week, plan on serving a few meatless meals using beans and legumes. For even better value, use dried beans rather than canned. Although they take extra time to prepare, they are less expensive in the long run.

◆ Fit in 5-A-Day: Expert health organizations, such as the National Cancer Institute and the Produce for Better Health Foundation, urge everyone to eat at least five servings of fruits and vegetables each day. (A serving is one medium piece of fruit, ½ cup cut-up fruit, or ½ cup cooked vegetables.

To do this economically, take advantage of fresh fruits and vegetables in season. In the off-seasons, consider frozen or canned produce—it's about the same nutritionally as fresh.

◆ Easy does it at the dairy case: Dairy products can be a major source of calories from fat. Read labels and, when possible, use low-fat dairy items. Soy-based cheese substitutes also are a good bet. All of these products usually are comparable in price to regular dairy products.

◆ Stay light and lean: Go easy on the meat, fish, and poultry. Serve only 2 to 3 ounces of cooked meat per serving and opt for the leanest meat cuts. They're better for you and cost less per serving. For example, 90-percent lean ground beef usually costs more per pound than 85-percent lean ground beef. But you can get five to six servings per pound of 90-percent lean compared to four servings per pound for the 85-percent lean.

◆ Keep the use of the product in mind: When shape, uniformity of size, or color of a product is unimportant, use the thriftiest form. For example, canned mushroom stems and pieces are less expensive than canned sliced or whole mushrooms.

◆ Don't forget smart shopping: The oft-repeated warning to never go grocery shopping when you're hungry is worth heeding. Items bought on impulse tend to be snack foods rich in fats or sugars, which may end up replacing low-fat, high complex-carbohydrate foods in your diet. And, these foods are usually more expensive than fruits and vegetables.

water, ¼ teaspoon *salt,* and ¼ teaspoon *pepper.* Cover and cook on high-heat setting for 4½ to 5½ hours (12 hours if using the low-heat setting). If desired, garnish each serving with a fresh rosemary sprig. Makes 4 servings.

Nutrition facts per serving: 354 cal., 12 g total fat (3 g sat. fat), 37 mg chol., 641 mg sodium, 37 g carbo., 5 g fiber, 26 g pro.
Daily values: 167% vit. A, 37% vit. C, 8% calcium, 37% iron.

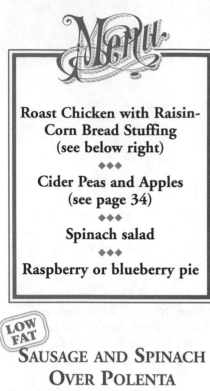

Roast Chicken with Raisin-
Corn Bread Stuffing
(see below right)

◆◆◆

Cider Peas and Apples
(see page 34)

◆◆◆

Spinach salad

◆◆◆

Raspberry or blueberry pie

LOW FAT

SAUSAGE AND SPINACH OVER POLENTA

Prep: 50 min. ◆ Bake: 20 min.
Chill: 3 to 24 hr.

For a more authentic country Italian flavor, use turkey sausage with fennel.

- 1 14½-oz. can reduced-sodium chicken broth
- 1¾ cups water
- 1¼ cups cornmeal
- ¾ cup shredded reduced-fat mozzarella cheese (3 oz.)

◆◆◆

- 12 oz. fully cooked smoked turkey sausage (95% fat free)
- 1 tsp. cooking oil
- 1 medium onion, cut into thin wedges
- 4 cloves garlic, minced
- ¼ to ½ tsp. crushed red pepper

◆◆◆

- 1 tsp. cornstarch
- 10 oz. fresh spinach, trimmed and coarsely chopped

1 Set aside ⅓ cup chicken broth. For polenta, in a 3-quart saucepan heat remaining chicken broth and water just till boiling. Slowly stir in cornmeal, ¼ cup at a time. Bring mixture to boiling; reduce heat to very low. Cook, covered, for 20 minutes, stirring often. Stir in ½ cup of the cheese. Spread on a baking sheet to a 10×8-inch rectangle. Cover and chill for 3 hours or overnight.

2 To serve, sprinkle chilled polenta with the remaining cheese. Bake, uncovered, in a 350° oven about 20 minutes or till hot. Meanwhile, bias-cut the sausage into ¼-inch-thick slices. In a large nonstick skillet heat oil; add sausage, onion, garlic, and red pepper. Cook mixture about 5 minutes or till onion is tender and sausage is heated through.

3 In a small mixing bowl stir together reserved chicken broth and cornstarch. Stir into mixture in skillet. Cook and stir till boiling; reduce heat. Add spinach, a little at a time, stirring constantly till all is wilted. To serve, cut the baked polenta into rectangles and arrange on plates. Top with sausage-spinach mixture. Makes 4 to 6 servings.

Nutrition facts per serving: 370 cal., 10 g total fat (6 g sat. fat), 94 mg chol., 1,249 mg sodium, 41 g carbo., 4 g fiber, 26 g pro.
Daily values: 48% vit. A, 86% vit. C, 29% calcium, 37% iron.

ROAST CHICKEN WITH RAISIN-CORN BREAD STUFFING

Prep: 25 min. ◆ Roast: 1¼ hr.

Extra stuffing can be baked separately in a covered casserole for the last 30 to 45 minutes of chicken roasting time.

- ½ cup finely chopped celery
- ½ cup finely chopped onion
- ¼ cup chicken broth
- ¼ cup raisins
- ¼ tsp. dried dillweed
- ¼ tsp. salt
- 2 cups coarsely crumbled corn bread
- 1 slightly beaten egg white Chicken broth

◆◆◆

- 1 2½- to 3-lb. whole roasting chicken

◆◆◆

Fresh herbs (optional)

1 In a small saucepan simmer the celery and onion in the ¼ cup chicken broth till tender. In a medium mixing bowl combine the undrained celery mixture, raisins, dillweed, and salt. Add the corn bread and beaten egg white; toss gently till mixed. Drizzle with desired amount of additional broth to moisten; toss gently to mix.

2 Rinse chicken; pat dry. Loosely spoon stuffing mixture into body cavity. Pull neck skin to back; fasten with a small skewer. Slip drumsticks under band of skin to secure or tie the drumsticks securely to tail. Twist wing tips under the back. Place chicken, breast side up, on a rack in a shallow roasting pan.

3 Roast chicken, uncovered, in a 375° oven for 1¼ to 1½ hours or till drumsticks move easily in their sockets and the thickest part feels soft when pressed, or till the meat is no longer pink. If using a meat thermometer, it should register 180° to 185° when placed in the center of the thigh.

4 When chicken is done, remove from the oven and cover with foil. Let stand 15 to 20 minutes before carving. Remove skin before serving. If desired, garnish with herbs. Makes 4 servings.

Nutrition facts per serving with skin removed: 355 cal., 12 g total fat (3 g sat. fat), 111 mg chol., 659 mg sodium, 30 g carbo., 1 g fiber, 32 g pro.
Daily values: 3% vit. A, 3% vit. C, 5% calcium, 15% iron.

Pasta with Ratatouille

Start to finish: 35 min.

Pasta dishes are more popular than ever—for all the right reasons. Pasta is the quintessential inexpensive health food. Just 20 percent of the calories in this fast noodle dish are from fat.

1 Tbsp. cooking oil
8 oz. ground raw chicken
1 large eggplant, cubed
2 onions, cut into wedges
2 medium green sweet peppers, cut into strips
2 cloves garlic, minced
♦♦♦
1 15-oz. can tomato sauce
1 14½-oz. can diced tomatoes, undrained
2 tsp. dried marjoram, crushed
¼ tsp. ground red pepper
♦♦♦
8 oz. wide egg noodles
 Fresh marjoram sprigs (optional)

1 For sauce, in a large pot heat oil and cook chicken till just browned. Add eggplant, onions, green sweet peppers, and garlic. Cook about 3 minutes more or till vegetables are crisp-tender, stirring occasionally.

2 Add the tomato sauce, undrained tomatoes, dried marjoram, and ground red pepper. Bring mixture just to boiling; reduce heat. Simmer, uncovered, 15 minutes, stirring occasionally.

3 Meanwhile, cook noodles according to the package directions. Drain well and top with sauce. If desired, garnish with fresh marjoram sprigs. Makes 4 servings.

Nutrition facts per serving: 403 cal., 9 g total fat (2 g sat. fat), 76 mg chol., 948 mg sodium, 63 g carbo., 8 g fiber, 19 g pro.
Daily values: 22% vit. A, 104% vit. C, 7% calcium, 36% iron.

Red Bean "Shepherd's Pie"

Prep: 25 min. ◆ Bake: 45 min.

This lamb-free version of the English classic satisfies both the shepherd and the sheep.

1 lb. small round red potatoes
♦♦♦
1 Tbsp. cooking oil
1 cup chopped onion
½ cup sliced celery
4 cloves garlic, minced
¼ tsp. cracked black pepper
1 15-oz. can garbanzo beans, drained and rinsed
1 15-oz. can small red beans, drained and rinsed
1 cup frozen peas
1 cup chopped green sweet pepper
1 10¾-oz. can condensed cream of potato soup
¼ cup skim milk
½ tsp. ground cumin
½ tsp. ground coriander
½ cup shredded reduced-fat Monterey Jack cheese

1 Scrub potatoes and thinly slice. Cook, covered, in enough boiling water to cover for 4 to 5 minutes or till nearly tender; drain. Run cold water over potatoes in colander. Drain and set aside.

2 In a large saucepan heat oil. Add onion, celery, garlic, and black pepper; cook about 5 minutes or till vegetables are tender. Mash ½ *cup* of the garbanzo beans; add to vegetable mixture along with the remaining garbanzo beans, red beans, peas, sweet pepper, soup, milk, cumin, and coriander. Gently stir to combine.

3 In a greased 2-quart casserole, place a single layer of potato slices. Spoon bean mixture on top and cover with remaining potato slices in layers, overlapping if necessary. Bake, covered, in 350° oven for 35 minutes. Uncover and sprinkle with cheese. Bake about 10 minutes more or till cheese melts. Makes 5 servings.

▪ TO MAKE AHEAD

Prepare the pie as directed at left, except do not bake or top with cheese. Cover tightly and chill overnight. To serve, bake, covered, in a 350° oven about 1 hour or till heated through. Uncover and sprinkle with the cheese. Bake, uncovered, 5 minutes more or till the cheese melts.

Nutrition facts per serving: 376 cal., 8 g total fat (2 g sat. fat), 11 mg chol., 1,073 mg sodium, 63 g carbo., 12 g fiber, 19 g pro.
Daily values: 6% vit. A, 41% vit. C, 16% calcium, 35% iron.

FOODS WITH "PHYTE"

Broccoli, grapefruit, soybeans—these and other plant foods are loaded with vitamins, minerals, and fiber, but they may offer even bigger bonuses.

Eating fruits, vegetables, and whole grains is a great way to ensure a healthful, low-fat diet in part because they contain compounds called phytochemicals ("phyto" is Greek for plant). Scientists speculate that these phytochemicals may be one reason people who eat plenty of fruits and vegetables are less likely to develop cancer. These naturally occurring and readily available substances also may reduce the risk of heart attacks and other chronic diseases.

PHYTOCHEMICALS FIGHT FOUR WAYS

The American Dietetic Association says that phytochemicals (also known as functional foods and neutriceuticals) "may have a beneficial role in health as part of a varied diet." The different phytochemicals (more than 600 have been identified) are diverse in their actions, but they can be grouped into four basic categories:

◆ **Antioxidants:** These phytochemicals scavenge renegade molecules known as "free radicals." Free radicals cause the kind of cellular damage that can lead to cancer, heart disease, arthritis, and aging.

◆ **Detoxifiers:** The phytochemicals in this category are believed to assist processes that allow a body to recognize and destroy or eliminate toxic components introduced into the body or produced by the body itself.

◆ **Hormone modulators:** Some phytochemicals, such as phytoestrogens, mimic the actions of certain hormones. This trait is a boon when the hormone in question is "overreacting" and triggering cell damage. For instance, estrogen has been linked to breast cancer in postmenopausal women.

Phytoestrogens, acting like less powerful replacements for estrogen, may help modulate the body's natural output of this potent hormone. Another way phytochemicals might modulate hormones such as estrogen is by inhibiting their production from the beginning, before they can instigate cellular damage.

◆ **Cell regulators:** The phytochemicals classified as cell regulators help control the rampant cell growth characteristic of tumors, which are a collection of cancer cells whose growth is out of control. Phytochemicals that can check this wild process could inhibit or even halt the growth of some types of cancer.

A SHOPPING LIST OF FOODS FILLED WITH "PHYTE"

All plant foods are rich in phytochemicals. Fruits and vegetables are especially loaded—one reason health authorities recommend eating at least five servings each of fruits and vegetables every day. Most phytochemicals also are heat-stable so they won't break down during cooking. You can enjoy these foods for taste while you boost your intake of phytochemicals.

◆ Broccoli, kale, cabbage, Brussels sprouts, and other cruciferous vegetables contain phytochemicals that change the metabolism of estrogen in a way that may lower breast cancer risk and help neutralize carcinogens. Research suggests eating these vegetables reduces colon cancer risk, too.

---

30 MIN. NO FAT

CIDER PEAS AND APPLES

Start to finish: 20 min.

Apple cider accents the sweet taste of peas in this simple recipe.

3 cups frozen peas
1 medium apple, cored and thinly sliced

◆◆◆

⅓ cup apple cider or apple juice
1 tsp. cornstarch

1 Place steamer basket in a saucepan and add water till just below the basket; bring to boiling. Add peas to steamer basket; cover and steam for 5 minutes. Add the apple slices; steam 2 to 4 minutes more or till apples are just tender.

2 Meanwhile, in a medium saucepan, combine apple cider and cornstarch. Cook and stir till mixture is thickened and bubbly.

Cook for 1 minute more, stirring often. Add peas and apples, tossing gently to evenly coat with sauce. Makes 4 servings.

Nutrition facts per serving: 102 cal., 0 g total fat, 0 mg chol., 82 mg sodium, 21 g carbo., 4 g fiber, 5 g pro.
Daily values: 6% vit. A, 18% vit. C, 2% calcium, 10% iron.

◆ Tomatoes and carrots contain high amounts of carotenoids, which give these and other vegetables their orange-red color. The most studied of these phytochemicals is beta-carotene. Carotenoids are powerful antioxidants. Lycopene, the predominant carotenoid in tomatoes, has been linked to reduced prostate cancer risk. Cooking tomatoes seems to help the body increase absorption of lycopene.

◆ Garlic, onions, leeks, chives, and shallots have groups of sulfur-containing phytochemicals called allyl sulfides. Such sulfur compounds show an ability to inhibit cancer development in laboratory animals and humans. Intake of these phytochemicals is associated with reduced stomach and colon cancer risk. Garlic, rich in allyl sulfide, has been used to treat many diseases and dysfunctions and is currently being studied for its potential to protect against heart disease by lowering both cholesterol and blood pressure.

◆ Oranges, grapefruit, lemons, limes, and other citrus fruits are rich in limonenes and liminoids, which may increase the activity of an enzyme that detoxifies certain carcinogens. Limonenes and liminoids also are thought to bind to mutated cells and help the body eliminate them before they become carcinogenic. Some researchers believe these phytochemicals hold the greatest promise for reducing the risk of cancer, especially colon cancer.

◆ Strawberries and raspberries are excellent sources of ellagic acid. Ellagic acid may inactivate carcinogens and inhibit free-radical formation, protecting the body from damage caused by tobacco smoke and air pollution.

◆ Soybeans and soyfoods (such as tofu and soymilk) have been enjoyed for centuries in Asia, but scientists only recently started uncovering the health properties of these legumes. They contain isoflavone, a phytoestrogen being studied for its possible role in protecting against cancer, particularly breast and prostate cancer. They affect enzymes that control the growth of tumor cells and also function as antioxidants to help prevent heart disease.

HOW MANY "PHYTE" FOODS SHOULD WE EAT?

There is no recommended dietary allowance for phytochemicals. Some companies have been promoting pill forms in the market but the best thing about phytochemicals is that they are already available in the inexpensive and great-tasting form of fruits, vegetables, grains, and beans.

Studies show that most Americans still eat only four servings of fruits and vegetables a day instead of the recommended five, and they also fail to include enough grains and beans in their diet. Phytochemicals can't help you fight cancer if they remain at the supermarket. Five servings of fruits and vegetables, 2 to 3 ounces of beans, and six to 11 servings of grains each day is more than just a low-fat diet—it's good food and good health you can count on.

By Mark Messina, Ph.D., former program director at the National Cancer Institute and coauthor of The Vegetarian Way *(Crown Publishing, 1996).*

---

30 MIN. NO FAT

STEAMED CHARD
Prep: 20 min. ◆ Cook: 5 min.

This quick and simple side dish served with steak and potatoes is vitamin-rich and prepared without fat or oil. If chard is not available, you may use another leafy green, such as kale or mustard greens.

**1 bunch Swiss chard
(about 12 oz.)
Salt**

1 Wash chard; shake dry. Cut leaves from stems; cut leaves into 1-inch strips. Place steamer basket in a saucepan or skillet; add water till just below the basket. Bring water to boiling. Place chard in the steamer basket. Cover and steam about 5 minutes or till chard is just tender. Season with salt to taste; serve immediately. Makes 4 servings.

Nutrition facts per serving: 18 cal., 0 g total fat, 0 mg chol., 190 mg sodium, 4 g carbo., 2 g fiber, 2 g pro.
Daily values: 27% vit. A, 26% vit. C, 4% calcium, 13% iron.

THAI PEANUT SOUP

Start to finish: 25 min.

This creamy soup blends flavors popular in Thai recipes, including peanuts, coconut, lemongrass, and a bit of ground red pepper for "heat." Serve small portions as an appetizer course or serve along with a salad for a full meal. (See the photograph on page 37.)

⅓ cup finely chopped onion
⅓ cup finely chopped celery
2 Tbsp. finely chopped red
    sweet pepper
1 Tbsp. margarine or butter
3 Tbsp. all-purpose flour
1 Tbsp. very finely chopped
    lemongrass (white portion
    only) or 1 tsp. finely
    shredded lemon peel
¼ tsp. ground red pepper
1 14½-oz. can chicken broth
1 13½-oz. can coconut milk
    (unsweetened)
♦♦♦
½ cup smooth peanut butter
1 Tbsp. soy sauce
    Chopped peanuts (optional)
    Snipped fresh cilantro
    (optional)
    Red sweet pepper strips
    (optional)

1 In a medium saucepan cook the finely chopped onion, celery, and red sweet pepper in hot margarine or butter about 4 minutes or till vegetables are tender, stirring occasionally. Stir in the flour, lemongrass or lemon peel, and ground red pepper. Add the chicken broth and coconut milk all at once. Cook and stir till the mixture is slightly thickened and bubbly. Cook and stir for 1 minute more.

2 Add peanut butter and soy sauce to the saucepan; stir till well blended and heated through. To serve, ladle soup into bowls. If desired, top each serving with chopped peanuts, cilantro, and red sweet pepper strips. Makes 8 side-dish servings.

Nutrition facts per serving: 268 cal., 24 g total fat (13 g sat. fat), 4 mg chol., 395 mg sodium, 8 g carbo., 1 g fiber, 7 g pro. *Daily values:* 2% vit. A, 5% vit. C, 1% calcium, 8% iron.

QUICK QUESADILLAS

As a quick snack, tortillas stack up great—literally. Quesadillas (keh-suh-DEE-yahs), popular Mexican "sandwiches" made with flour or corn tortillas, can be filled with almost anything and griddled or grilled *muy rápido*. Filling combinations are only limited by your imagination. To make quesadillas, lightly brush tortillas with cooking oil or spray cooking surface with nonstick coating.

Sprinkle ¼ to ½ cup shredded cheese evenly on a tortilla. Add other ingredients, spreading evenly over cheese. Top with second tortilla. Place quesadilla on heated surface and cook 1 to 2 minutes per side, or till cheese melts. Cut into wedges. If desired, serve topped with salsa or sour cream.

AUSTIN QUESADILLA

Sprinkle a white corn tortilla with shredded Monterey Jack cheese. Add 2 to 3 medium serrano peppers, cut into thin slices; a spoonful of chopped tomato; and fresh snipped cilantro leaves. Top with a second tortilla and cook on a griddle or grill.

NOGALES NOPALES QUESADILLA

This western quesadilla is made with two flour tortillas, soft Mexican white cheese or goat cheese, and chopped canned cactus leaves (nopales) or chopped green sweet pepper. Add browned and drained ground beef, if desired, and sprinkle lightly with ground cumin and chili powder. Add a pinch of crushed red pepper, if desired, before topping with the second tortilla and cooking.

CALIFORNIA QUESADILLA

This version uses two large flour tortillas, a generous helping of shredded cheddar cheese, chopped ripe avocado, sliced ripe olives, peeled roasted poblano pepper strips, cooked boneless chicken, and, if desired, jalapeño pepper slices. For a more authentic taste, make this quesadilla with shredded pieces of roasted chicken. It's good with turkey, too.

Top: *Thai Peanut Soup (page 36)*
Above: *Pork and Lentil Cassoulet (page 30)*

Top: *Peppered Chutney Roast (page 12)*
Right: *Sicilian Meat Roll (page 12)*
Above: *Dried Tomato-Pesto Spread (page 11)*

Top: *Greek Croustade (page 10)*
Above left: *Pork Chop Barbecue (page 13)*
Above right: *Orange-Hazelnut Blueberry Bread (page 48)*

Top: *Carrot and Fruit Salad (page 116)*
Above: *Flank Steak Salad with Cantaloupe (page 116)*

Top: *Moroccan Chicken with Cucumber-Melon Relish (page 138)*
Above left: *Grilled Vegetable Salad (page 111)*
Above right: *Jambalaya Salad (page 131)*
Left: *New Potato Salad with Fennel (page 133)*

Top: *Cardamom Ice Cream (page 144)*
Above: *Cranberry-Orange Punch (page 127)*

Top: *Champagne Fruit Bowl (page 143)*
Above: *Chocolate Malt-Peppermint Cooler (page 128)*
Right: *Italian Cream Tarts (page 143)*

Top: *Quick Bread Salad*
(page 108)
Above: *Garlic-Sauced Chicken*
over Pasta (page 115)
Left: *Beef Steak in Thai*
Marinade (page 137) and
Parsnip-Fruit Salad (page 132)

Left: *Middle Eastern Salad Plate (page 125)*
Below: *Scallops, Mussels, and Asparagus Salad (page 125)*

MIDDLE EASTERN SALAD PLATE

Start to finish: 25 min.

This universally popular dish is fast, easy to make, and high in fiber. (See the photograph on page 124.)

2 medium cucumbers
2 medium tomatoes
¼ cup snipped fresh parsley
2 Tbsp. white wine vinegar
3 Tbsp. olive oil
⅛ tsp. coarsely ground black pepper

◆◆◆

1 15-oz. can garbanzo beans
½ cup tahini*
4 cloves garlic, minced
1 Tbsp. lemon juice
8 large pita bread rounds
⅛ to ¼ tsp. ground red pepper

1 Peel cucumbers, if desired. Chop cucumbers and tomatoes; toss together with parsley, vinegar, *1 tablespoon* of the olive oil, black pepper, and ⅛ teaspoon *salt.* Cover and chill.

2 Meanwhile, for hummus, drain garbanzo beans, reserving liquid. In a food processor bowl combine beans, tahini, and garlic. Add *1 tablespoon* olive oil, lemon juice, and ¼ teaspoon *salt;* cover and process till smooth, adding enough bean liquid till consistency is like thick oatmeal.

3 Wrap pita rounds in foil; heat in a 350° oven 10 minutes or till warm. Cut pitas into wedges. Spoon hummus onto plates, drizzle with *1 tablespoon* olive oil, and sprinkle with red pepper. Serve with cucumber and tomato salad. Makes 6 side-dish servings.

***Note:** Tahini, a puree of sesame seeds, can be found in large supermarkets, specialty food stores, or Middle Eastern markets.

Nutrition facts per serving: 473 cal., 19 g total fat (3 g sat. fat), 0 mg chol., 802 mg sodium, 64 g carbo., 5 g fiber, 14 g pro. *Daily values:* 6% vit. A, 36% vit. C, 11% calcium, 33% iron.

SCALLOPS, MUSSELS, AND ASPARAGUS SALAD

Prep: 1 hr. ◆ Chill: 2 to 8 hr.

When purchasing live mussels, be sure they are moist and have tightly closed shells with no chips or cracks. (See the photograph on page 124.)

6 large or 12 small fresh mussels in shell

◆◆◆

8 oz. fresh asparagus spears, trimmed

◆◆◆

2 tsp. cooking oil
8 oz. fresh sea scallops
⅓ cup light dairy sour cream
½ tsp. finely shredded lime peel
2 tsp. lime juice
⅛ tsp. pepper
2 tsp. salmon roe or red caviar

◆◆◆

1 head Bibb lettuce
Fresh chives
Lime wedges

1 Scrub mussels under cold running water; remove beards and discard. Soak mussels in *cold salted water* for 15 minutes; drain and rinse. Repeat soaking, draining, and rinsing twice more. Cover clean mussels and set aside.

2 In a large saucepan bring 1 cup *water* just to boiling. Add the asparagus; cook, covered, for 4 to 6 minutes or till crisp-tender. *(Do not overcook.)* Remove asparagus, reserving water in saucepan. Rinse asparagus in cold water; cover and chill. Meanwhile, return water just to boiling. Add mussels to water and simmer, covered, about 5 to 7 minutes or till shells open. (Discard any mussels that do not open.) Drain and rinse mussels; cover and chill.

3 Heat oil in nonstick skillet. Cook scallops in hot oil for 1 to 3 minutes or till scallops are opaque. Remove scallops; cover and chill. In a small bowl combine sour cream, lime peel, lime juice, pepper, and *1 teaspoon* of the roe or caviar. Cover and chill.

4 Arrange chilled mussels, scallops, and asparagus on leaves of lettuce. Serve with sour cream mixture and remaining roe or caviar. Garnish salad with chives and lime wedges. Makes 2 main-dish servings.

Nutrition facts per serving: 305 cal., 12 g total fat (3 g sat. fat), 103 mg chol., 511 mg sodium, 16 g carbo., 2 g fiber, 35 g pro. *Daily values:* 25% vit. A, 51% vit. C, 15% calcium, 46% iron.

Menu

Lentil soup

◆◆◆

Middle Eastern Salad Plate (see left)

◆◆◆

Purchased or homemade baklava

◆◆◆

Iced water with lemon

LOBSTER AND ARTICHOKE SALAD

Prep: 25 min. ◆ Chill: 1 to 24 hr.

You can substitute peeled, cooked shrimp for the lobster meat in this recipe. Or, you can use a combination of the two.

- 1 Tbsp. refrigerated or frozen egg product, thawed
- 1 Tbsp. Dijon-style mustard
- 1 Tbsp. white wine vinegar
- ½ cup olive oil
- 2 Tbsp. finely chopped shallot
- 2 Tbsp. snipped fresh chives
- ¼ tsp. salt
- ⅛ tsp. ground white pepper
- 1 14-oz. can artichoke hearts, drained and halved
- 12 oz. cooked lobster meat, cut into 1-inch pieces
- 1 head Bibb lettuce or green or red leaf lettuce
- 4 hard-cooked eggs, cut into wedges
- 2 Tbsp. snipped fresh parsley Greek black olives (optional)

1 In a food processor bowl or blender container combine the egg product, Dijon-style mustard, and wine vinegar. Cover and process or blend till combined. With the processor or blender running slowly, add the olive oil in a thin steady stream, stopping and scraping the sides of the bowl or container as necessary.

2 Transfer the dressing to a medium mixing bowl. Stir in the shallot, chives, salt, and white pepper. Add the artichoke hearts and cooked lobster meat, tossing gently to coat. Cover and chill for 1 to 24 hours.

3 To serve, line a large platter with lettuce leaves. Arrange the lobster mixture atop. Add the egg wedges, sprinkle with the parsley, and, if desired, garnish with the Greek black olives. Makes 5 main-dish servings.

Nutrition facts per serving: 354 cal., 27 g total fat (4 g sat. fat), 219 mg chol., 646 mg sodium, 8 g carbo., 2 g fiber, 22 g pro. *Daily values:* 19% vit. A, 16% vit. C, 8% calcium, 11% iron.

30 MIN. LOW FAT

ORANGE-AND-BASIL-GLAZED SHRIMP

Start to finish: 30 min.

For more than glazed shrimp, stir-fry some fresh pea pods and add to the thickened sauce along with the shrimp and a small can of drained mandarin oranges.

- ½ cup orange juice
- ½ tsp. cornstarch
- 1 Tbsp. snipped fresh basil or ½ tsp. dried basil, crushed
- ¼ tsp. salt
- ¼ tsp. crushed red pepper
- 1 Tbsp. butter or margarine
- 1 tsp. peanut oil
- 1 lb. fresh or frozen medium shrimp, peeled and deveined
- 2 cloves garlic, minced

◆◆◆

- 1 Tbsp. vermouth (optional) Hot cooked rice

1 For sauce, in a small mixing bowl stir together the orange juice, cornstarch, basil, salt, and crushed red pepper. In a large skillet heat butter or margarine and peanut oil over medium-high

heat. Add shrimp and garlic; cook and stir for 2 to 3 minutes or till the shrimp turn pink. Remove shrimp from skillet.

2 If desired, carefully stir vermouth into skillet. Stir sauce; add to skillet. Cook and stir till thickened and bubbly. Cook and stir for 2 minutes more. Add shrimp and heat through. Serve over rice. Makes 4 servings.

Nutrition facts per serving: 118 cal., 5 g total fat (2 g sat. fat), 138 mg chol., 313 mg sodium, 4 g carbo., 3 g fiber, 14 g pro. *Daily values:* 95% vit. A, 29% vit. C, 2% calcium, 14% iron.

GINGER TROPICAL PUNCH

Prep: 30 min. ◆ Chill: 4 to 24 hr.

This recipe earned Shabri Moore of Frederick, Maryland, $200 in the magazine's monthly contest.

- 1½ cups water
- 1 cup sugar
- 2 Tbsp. chopped gingerroot
- 3 or 4 whole cloves
- 1 inch stick cinnamon

◆◆◆

- 1 6-oz. can frozen apple juice concentrate
- 1 6-oz. can frozen orange juice concentrate
- ½ cup freshly squeezed lemon juice
- 1 lemon, thinly sliced
- 1 orange, thinly sliced Orange peel curls (optional)

1 In a medium saucepan combine water, sugar, gingerroot, cloves, and stick cinnamon. Bring to boiling over medium heat, stirring constantly; reduce heat. Simmer, uncovered, for 5 minutes. Cool the mixture; cover and let steep in the refrigerator for several hours.

2 Meanwhile, prepare apple and orange juice concentrates according to package directions. In a large container combine the apple juice, orange juice, and lemon juice. Cover and chill.

3 To serve, strain the steeped ginger mixture. In a punch bowl stir together fruit juices and ginger mixture. Reserve 8 lemon or orange slices. Float remaining fruit slices in the punch. Ladle punch into punch cups or small glasses. Cut the reserved fruit slices in half. Garnish each cup with half a fruit slice and, if desired, an orange peel curl. Makes 16 (4-ounce) servings.

Nutrition facts per serving: 86 cal., 0 g total fat, 0 mg chol., 4 mg sodium, 22 g carbo., 0 g fiber, 1 g pro.
Daily values: 33% vit. C, 1% calcium, 1% iron.

CRANBERRY-ORANGE PUNCH

Start to finish: 10 min.

Pack this fruity beverage with more punch by adding a splash of rum. (See the photograph on page 120.)

3 cups cranberry juice cocktail
1 6-oz. can frozen orange juice concentrate, thawed

1 cup water
1 10- or 12-oz. bottle ginger-flavored carbonated beverage or ginger ale
Ice cubes
Mint leaves

1 In a bowl or large pitcher stir together the cranberry juice cocktail, orange juice concentrate, and water. Add the ginger-flavored carbonated beverage or ginger ale.

2 To serve, in punch glasses or other small glasses, pour punch over ice cubes. Garnish each serving with mint leaves. Makes 12 (4-ounce) servings.

Nutrition facts per serving: 67 cal., 0 g total fat, 0 mg chol., 5 mg sodium, 17 g carbo., 0 g fiber, 0 g pro.
Daily values: 73% vit. C, 1% iron.

KAHLÚA AND COFFEE SODAS

Start to finish: 15 min.

The old soda fountain favorite gets new life with the popular flavor combination of Kahlúa and coffee.

¼ cup whipping cream
¼ to ½ cup Kahlúa or other coffee liqueur
14- to 16-oz. (1¾ to 2 cups) sparkling water
1 pint coffee or chocolate ice cream
4 3-inch pieces stick cinnamon

1 In a small chilled mixing bowl beat the whipping cream with an electric mixer on low speed till stiff peaks form.

2 In each of four 8-ounce glasses, pour 1 to 2 tablespoons Kahlúa or other coffee liqueur. Add 1 tablespoon whipped cream and 2 tablespoons carbonated water; stir till foamy. Add a ½-cup scoop of ice cream to each glass. Pour in enough carbonated water to fill glasses. Spoon remaining whipped cream atop each and add a cinnamon stick stirrer. Makes 4 (8-ounce) servings.

Nutrition facts per serving: 242 cal., 13 g total fat (8 g sat. fat), 49 mg chol., 80 mg sodium, 24 g carbo., 0 g fiber, 3 g pro.
Daily values: 14% vit. A, 8% calcium.

THE CLEVER COOK

BRIDAL SHOWER MEMORIES

When my bridesmaids mailed shower invitations for me, they included a recipe card and requested that everyone submit a favorite chocolate recipe (knowing my fondness for chocolate!). At my shower they presented the recipes to me in a recipe box. With each guest's name on her recipe card, I now have a lasting memory of each friend.

Laura Bailey
Liverpool, New York

ICED COFFEE

Prep: 5 min. ◆ Cool: 2 hr.

For fun, make some coffee cubes, instead of plain ice cubes. Simply freeze regular-strength coffee in ice cube trays.

3 cups hot strong coffee

◆◆◆

2 to 3 Tbsp. sugar (optional)
Ice cubes
Orange wedges (optional)

1 Pour hot coffee into a non-metal container. Cover and cool to room temperature. (Do not refrigerate, as this causes coffee to become cloudy.)

2 Before serving, stir the desired amount of sugar into cooled coffee. Pour coffee over ice in tall glasses. If desired, garnish with the orange wedges. Makes 4 (6-ounce) servings.

Nutrition facts per serving: 0 cal., 0 g total fat (0 g sat. fat), 0 mg chol., 2 mg sodium, 0 g carbo., 0 g fiber, 0 g pro.

Iced Cappuccino: Add 1 teaspoon *vanilla* to cooled coffee. Sweeten to taste. Pour over ice in glasses. Pour about 3 tablespoons *half-and-half* or *light cream* into each glass. Makes 4 (6-ounce) servings.

Iced Cafe Mocha: Add ½ cup *half-and-half* or *light cream* and ¼ cup *chocolate-flavored syrup* to cooled coffee. Sweeten to taste. Serve over ice. Makes 4 (7-ounce) servings.

CHOCOLATE MALT-PEPPERMINT COOLER

Start to finish: 20 min.

This recipe earned Carol Gillespie of Chambersburg, Pennsylvania, $400 in the magazine's monthly contest.
(See the photograph on page 120.)

3 cups chocolate milk
1 qt. vanilla or chocolate ice cream
¼ cup malted milk powder
½ tsp. peppermint extract
⅛ tsp. ground cinnamon
Coarsely crushed hard peppermint candies
6 peppermint sticks

1 In a blender container place the chocolate milk, *half* of the ice cream, the malted milk powder, peppermint extract, and ground cinnamon. Cover and blend till mixture is smooth. Pour into 6 large, chilled glasses. Top each drink with a scoop of the remaining ice cream. Sprinkle with the crushed candy pieces. Place a peppermint stick in each glass. Makes 6 servings.

Nutrition facts per serving: 329 cal., 13 g total fat (8 g sat. fat), 49 mg chol., 199 mg sodium, 46 g carbo., 0 g fiber, 8 g pro. *Daily values:* 17% vit. A, 3% vit. C, 24% calcium, 3% iron.

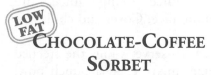

CHOCOLATE-COFFEE SORBET

Prep: 20 min. ◆ Freeze: 6 to 27 hr.

A refreshing sweet treat that gives you all the satisfaction of a cup of coffee, except the heat.

1½ cups chocolate ice cream
½ cup freshly brewed strong coffee
1 tsp. grated gingerroot
1 tsp. brown sugar
¼ tsp. ground cinnamon
¼ tsp. ground nutmeg

1 Place all ingredients in a food processor bowl or blender container. Cover and process or blend till smooth. Pour mixture into an 8×8×2-inch baking pan. Cover and freeze for 2 to 3 hours or till almost firm. Break mixture into small chunks; transfer to a chilled bowl. Beat with an electric mixer till smooth but not melted. Return to pan. Cover and freeze till firm. Makes 4 servings.

Nutrition facts per serving: 59 cal., 3 g total fat (2 g sat. fat), 8 mg chol., 20 mg sodium, 8 g carbo., 0 g fiber, 1 g pro. *Daily values:* 2% vit. A, 2% calcium, 2% iron.

JUNE
Sweet Days of Summer

30-minute recipes indicated in RED.
Low-fat and no-fat recipes indicated
with a ♥.
Photographs indicated in italics.

Flowers are in full bloom, songbirds in full voice, and life moves at full speed. Could June be sweeter? It could if you broke out the desserts. Sweet summer fruits are radiant in meal enders such as Peach and Double Berry Crisp, Strawberry and Cheese Crumble, and Champagne Fruit Bowl. They're also luscious served over Floribbean Pound Cake. Go ahead, you deserve a treat after a busy evening of early-summer yard work.

Fire up your barbecue grill for zesty Moroccan Chicken with Cucumber-Melon Relish or Beef Steak in Thai Marinade. Thirty days just isn't enough for such a delicious month.

Dried Tomato Spread

Prep: 20 min. ◆ Cook: 15min.
Chill: 4 to 24 hr.

This recipe earned De Anne Pearson of Austin, Texas, $400 in the magazine's monthly contest.

1 to 2 cloves garlic, minced
1 Tbsp. olive oil
⅓ cup dry white wine
½ cup dried tomatoes, snipped (not oil-packed)

◆◆◆

1 8-oz. pkg. cream cheese, softened
⅓ cup snipped fresh basil
3 Tbsp. grated Parmesan cheese
  Baguette-style French bread slices, toasted

1 In a medium skillet cook garlic in oil till light brown. Add wine and dried tomatoes. Cook, uncovered, over low heat 15 minutes. Remove from heat; let stand 10 minutes. Drain liquid.

2 Meanwhile, in a food processor bowl or blender container, combine the cream cheese, snipped basil, and Parmesan cheese. Cover and process or blend till smooth. Add tomato mixture; process till almost smooth. Transfer to a bowl. Cover and chill 4 to 24 hours. Before serving, let stand at room temperature for 30 minutes. Serve with baguette slices. If desired, garnish with additional *fresh basil.* Makes 1 cup.

Nutrition facts per teaspoon: 25 cal., 2 g total fat (1 g sat. fat), 6 mg chol., 36 mg sodium, 1 g carbo., 0 g fiber, 1 g pro.

Smoked Catfish Pâté

Prep: 30 min. ◆ Chill: 2 to 48 hr.

After smoking the catfish fillets on the grill, process them into an appetizer spread accented with lemon, garlic, and pepper. Your mini food processor is the perfect size for this amount of mixture.

1 lb. fresh or frozen skinless catfish fillets (about ¾ to 1 inch thick)*
1 cup hardwood chips, soaked in water about 1 hour

◆◆◆

1 3-oz. pkg. cream cheese, cut up
¼ cup milk
2 Tbsp. snipped fresh parsley
2 tsp. finely shredded lemon peel
2 Tbsp. lemon juice
2 cloves garlic, minced
¼ tsp. salt
¼ tsp. ground red pepper

◆◆◆

  Baguette-style French bread slices, toasted, or crackers (optional)
  Vegetable dippers, such as cooked asparagus spears, carrot sticks, and cherry tomatoes (optional)
  Lemon peel curls (optional)
  Fresh herb sprigs (optional)

1 Thaw fish, if frozen. In a grill with a cover arrange preheated coals around a foil drip pan. Test for medium heat above the pan. Drain wood chips and sprinkle over coals. Prick a few holes in a piece of heavy foil large enough to hold fish and place on rack above drip pan. Place the fish on foil. Cover and grill 8 to 12 minutes (about 4 to 6 minutes per ½-inch thickness of fish) or till fish begins to flake easily with a fork. Cool completely; break fish into pieces, removing any bones.

2 Place fish in a food processor bowl. Cover and process till nearly smooth. Add cream cheese, milk, parsley, lemon peel, lemon juice, garlic, salt, and red pepper. Cover and process till mixture is smooth. (Or, in a mixing bowl combine cream cheese, milk, parsley, lemon peel, lemon juice, garlic, salt, and red pepper with an electric mixer; beat till smooth. Flake the cooked fish and stir into the cream cheese mixture.)

3 Spoon mixture into a serving bowl and chill at least 2 hours or for up to 2 days. If desired, serve pâté as a spread for toasted baguette slices or crackers and as a dip for vegetables. If desired, garnish pâté with lemon peel and fresh herb sprigs. Makes about 2 cups.

Note: Instead of smoking the fish yourself, you can substitute ¾ pound *smoked, cooked catfish* for the fresh or frozen fillets. Look for smoked fish in fish markets or in mail-order catalogs. Simply flake the smoked catfish and mix with the cream cheese mixture as directed. If the catfish is seasoned, omit the salt.

Nutrition facts per tablespoon: 31 cal., 2 g total fat (1 g sat. fat), 12 mg chol., 37 mg sodium, 0 g carbo., 0 g fiber, 3 g pro. *Daily values:* 1% vit. A, 1% vit. C, 1% iron.

CREAM OF SPINACH AND BASIL SOUP

Start to finish: 40 min.

⅓ cup thinly sliced green onions
2 Tbsp. margarine or butter
2 14½-oz. cans reduced-sodium chicken broth
4 cups torn fresh spinach
1 cup torn fresh basil
    Dash pepper
    ◆◆◆
1 cup half-and-half or light cream
3 Tbsp. all-purpose flour
    Fresh basil (optional)

1 In a large saucepan cook green onions in margarine or butter till tender. Add broth; bring to boiling. Add spinach, the 1 cup basil, and pepper. Return to boiling; reduce heat. Simmer, covered, for 10 minutes. Remove from heat; cool slightly.

2 Transfer mixture to a food processor bowl or blender container. Cover and process or blend till smooth. Return to saucepan. Gradually stir half-and-half or light cream into flour till smooth; add to pan. Cook and stir till thickened and bubbly. Cook and stir for 1 minute more.

3 To serve, ladle soup into bowls. If desired, garnish each serving with fresh basil. Makes 8 side-dish servings.

Nutrition facts per serving: 92 cal., 7 g total fat (3 g sat. fat), 11 mg chol., 357 mg sodium, 5 g carbo., 1 g fiber, 3 g pro. *Daily values:* 27% vit. A, 14% vit. C, 5% calcium, 6% iron.

THE CLEVER COOK

NO GREASE STAINS

To keep your cookbook or magazine free of spills and spatters, slip it into a gallon-size clear plastic bag before you start cooking.

Joyce Rinehart
Richland, Washington

JAMBALAYA SALAD

Prep: 45 min. ◆ Chill: 4 to 24 hr.

Andouille sausage and crawfish tails give an authentic Cajun taste to this robust salad.
(See the photograph on page 119.)

2 cups long-grain rice
    ◆◆◆
8 oz. cooked andouille sausage or other cooked smoked sausage
1 Tbsp. olive oil
2 cups chopped onions
    ◆◆◆
1 lb. cooked and peeled crawfish tails or cooked, peeled, and deveined shrimp
2 medium tomatoes, chopped (1⅓ cups)
1½ cups chopped green, red, and/or yellow sweet pepper
½ cup snipped fresh parsley
1 recipe Citrus-Pepper Dressing (see right)
8 cups mixed salad greens, such as Swiss chard, kale, mustard greens, arugula, and/or leaf lettuce

1 In a large saucepan combine rice, 4 cups *water,* and ⅛ teaspoon *salt.* Bring to boiling; reduce heat. Simmer, covered, 15 minutes. Remove from heat. Rinse rice with cool water; drain. Set aside.

2 Bias-slice sausage into ½-inch pieces. In a large skillet brown sausage over medium-high heat 2 to 3 minutes. Drain off fat. Remove sausage from skillet. Add oil to skillet; cook onions in oil till tender, stirring occasionally.

3 In a very large bowl combine rice, sausage, onions, cooked crawfish tails or shrimp, tomatoes, sweet pepper, and parsley. Add Citrus-Pepper Dressing; toss well. Cover; chill 4 to 24 hours. To serve, arrange greens on a large platter; top with the chilled seafood mixture. Serves 16 to 20.

Citrus-Pepper Dressing: In a screw-top jar combine ⅓ cup *olive oil;* 2 teaspoons finely shredded *orange peel;* ⅓ cup *orange juice;* ¼ cup *lemon juice;* 1 tablespoon snipped *fresh thyme* or 1 teaspoon *dried thyme,* crushed; 4 cloves *garlic,* minced; ½ teaspoon *salt;* ¼ to ½ teaspoon *ground red pepper;* and ¼ teaspoon *ground black pepper.* Cover; shake well. Use immediately or chill. Shake before using.

◼ POTLUCK TIP ◼

Tote seafood mixture and mixed greens separately in a cooler. When ready to serve, spoon the seafood mixture atop a lettuce-lined platter.

Nutrition facts per serving: 237 cal., 11 g total fat (2 g sat. fat), 49 mg chol., 341 mg sodium, 25 g carbo., 1 g fiber, 11 g pro. *Daily values:* 8% vit. A, 57% vit. C, 4% calcium, 14% iron.

Grilled pork loin or chicken

◆◆◆

Mediterranean Salad Platter
(see below)

◆◆◆

Pita bread wedges

◆◆◆

Floribbean Pound Cake
(see page 142)

MEDITERRANEAN SALAD PLATTER

Start to finish: 1 hr.

For a stunning platter presentation, use assorted colors of sweet peppers, such as red, yellow, and orange, and both red and yellow tomatoes.

8 **large sweet peppers**
2 **large tomatoes, sliced**
 Chinese cabbage leaves and lettuce leaves (optional)
2 **Tbsp. olive oil**
1 **cup kalamata olives**
½ **cup crumbled feta cheese (2 oz.)**
1 **Tbsp. snipped fresh tarragon or basil (optional)**
 Fresh herb sprigs, such as tarragon or basil (optional)

1 Cut peppers in half lengthwise; remove stems, seeds, and membranes. Place, cut side down, on a large foil-lined baking sheet. Bake in a 450° oven for 15 to 20 minutes or till skins are blistered and bubbly. Fold up foil on baking pan around peppers to form a packet, sealing edges. Let stand 20 minutes to loosen skins. Peel peppers; cut into strips. Cover and chill till serving time.

2 To serve, arrange roasted pepper strips and tomato slices on a platter lined with Chinese cabbage leaves and lettuce leaves, if desired. Drizzle with olive oil and season with *salt* and *pepper.* Sprinkle olives, feta, and snipped herb over peppers. If desired, garnish with fresh herb sprigs. Makes 10 to 12 side-dish servings.

▐ **POTLUCK TIP** ▌

Assemble the salad platter at home and tote it tightly wrapped with clear plastic wrap in a cooler.

Nutrition facts per serving: 78 cal., 6 g total fat (1 g sat. fat), 5 mg chol., 129 mg sodium, 6 g carbo., 1 g fiber, 2 g pro. *Daily values:* 6% vit. A, 82% vit. C, 3% calcium, 3% iron.

PARSNIP-FRUIT SALAD

Prep: 30 min. ◆ Chill: 2 to 24 hr.

Adults will find the parsnip-tarragon intriguing, but children may like it better if it's made with snipped parsley. (See the photograph on page 122.)

2 **lb. parsnips**
1 **cup assorted dried fruit, such as cranberries, pineapple, apricots, and raisins**
¼ **cup lemon juice**
¼ **cup olive oil**
¼ **cup frozen pineapple or apple juice concentrate, thawed**
1 **Tbsp. snipped fresh tarragon or 2 Tbsp. snipped fresh parsley**
¼ **tsp. ground cinnamon**

1 Using a vegetable peeler, peel parsnips; bias-slice ½ inch thick. Cook parsnips in *lightly salted boiling water* 7 to 9 minutes or till crisp-tender; drain and cool. Meanwhile, if desired, coarsely chop larger pieces of dried fruit. In a large bowl stir together the dried fruits, lemon juice, olive oil, juice concentrate, tarragon or parsley, ¼ teaspoon *salt,* and cinnamon.

2 Add the parsnips to the fruit mixture, tossing to coat. Cover and chill at least 2 hours. Makes 8 to 10 side-dish servings.

Nutrition facts per serving: 219 cal., 7 g total fat (1 g sat. fat), 0 mg chol., 81 mg sodium, 40 g carbo., 7 g fiber, 2 g pro. *Daily values:* 4% vit. A, 40% vit. C, 4% calcium, 8% iron.

PRIZE TESTED RECIPE WINNER

SOUTHWESTERN SUMMER SALAD

Start to finish: 45 min.

This recipe earned Susan Burns of Trenton, New Jersey, $200 in the magazine's monthly contest.

1 **dried chipotle pepper**
1 **lb. fresh green beans, cut into 1-inch pieces, or one 16-oz. pkg. frozen cut green beans**
6 **fresh ears of corn or one 16-oz. pkg. frozen whole kernel corn**

◆◆◆

2 **cloves garlic, minced**
2 **Tbsp. white wine vinegar**
1 **Tbsp. balsamic vinegar**
1 **Tbsp. frozen orange juice concentrate, thawed**

½ cup loosely packed fresh
   basil leaves
¼ cup loosely packed fresh
   parsley
1 shallot, cut up
¼ cup olive oil
   ◆◆◆
1 large tomato, chopped
1 cup plain croutons

1 Rinse dried pepper in water; cut open and discard stem and seeds. Cut pepper into small pieces. Pour *boiling water* over pepper and soak 20 to 30 minutes to soften; drain well.

2 Meanwhile, in a saucepan cook fresh beans, if using, in a small amount of *boiling water,* covered, about 15 minutes or till crisp-tender; drain. If using fresh corn, cut the kernels off the cobs. Cook corn, covered, in *boiling water* about 4 minutes or till corn is tender; drain. (If using frozen beans and corn, cook according to package directions; drain.) Set vegetables aside to cool.

3 In a food processor bowl or blender container, combine pepper pieces, garlic, vinegars, juice concentrate, herbs, shallot, ¼ teaspoon *salt,* and ¼ teaspoon *pepper.* Cover; process till combined. Add oil in a thin stream, processing till nearly smooth. Pour *⅓ cup* dressing over vegetables. (Chill remaining dressing for another use.) Add tomato and croutons, tossing lightly. If desired, serve on a bed of *flowering kale.* Makes 6 to 8 side-dish servings.

Nutrition facts per serving: 188 cal., 6 g total fat (1 g sat. fat), 0 mg chol., 113 mg sodium, 33 g carbo., 5 g fiber, 5 g pro. *Daily values:* 11% vit. A, 37% vit. C, 4% calcium, 13% iron.

NEW POTATO SALAD WITH FENNEL

Prep: 30 min. ◆ Cool: 1 hr.
Chill: 2 to 24 hr.

See the photograph on page 118.

2 fennel bulbs
3 lb. whole tiny new potatoes,
   quartered
3 small yellow summer squash,
   sliced ¼ inch thick
   ◆◆◆
⅓ cup olive oil or salad oil
⅓ cup lemon juice
2 Tbsp. coarse-grain brown
   mustard
1 tsp. sugar
2 cloves garlic, minced
2 green onions, thinly sliced
   Watercress, curly endive, or
   other greens (optional)

1 Cut off and discard upper stalks from fennel bulbs. Remove tough outer layer of bulbs; cut off a thin slice from base. Cut fennel bulbs into thin wedges. In a covered large pot cook potatoes in *lightly salted boiling water* 7 minutes; add fennel wedges and squash slices. Cook for 1 to 2 minutes more or till potatoes are just tender and fennel is crisp-tender; drain well. Let cool 1 hour.

2 In a screw-top jar combine oil, lemon juice, mustard, sugar, garlic, ½ teaspoon *salt,* and ⅛ teaspoon *pepper;* cover and shake. Add to potato mixture along with green onions, gently tossing to combine. Cover and chill. If desired, serve salad atop watercress, curly endive, or greens. Makes 12 side-dish servings.

Nutrition facts per serving: 181 cal., 6 g total fat (1 g sat. fat), 0 mg chol., 142 mg sodium, 29 g carbo., 2 g fiber, 3 g pro.

SALAD WITH HERBED CROUTONS

Prep: 30 min. ◆ Bake: 45 min.

1 8½-oz. pkg. corn muffin mix
2 Tbsp. snipped fresh parsley
1 Tbsp. snipped fresh
   rosemary
1 Tbsp. snipped fresh cilantro
¼ cup butter or margarine,
   melted
¼ cup grated Parmesan cheese
   ◆◆◆
6 cups torn romaine
1½ cups torn arugula or spinach
⅓ cup snipped fresh cilantro
¼ cup sliced green onions (2)
½ cup bottled Italian salad
   dressing

1 Prepare corn bread in an 8×8×2-inch baking pan according to package directions, adding the parsley, rosemary, and 1 tablespoon cilantro with the liquid ingredients. Cool in pan 10 minutes. Remove from pan; cool completely. Cut into 1-inch cubes. Toss cubes with melted butter and Parmesan; spread in a 15×10×1-inch baking pan. Bake, in a 300° oven about 25 minutes or till crisp, stirring twice. Turn onto a piece of foil; cool completely. Place half the croutons in a freezer container or bag and freeze for another time.

2 In a large salad bowl combine romaine, arugula or spinach, ⅓ cup cilantro, and green onions. Toss with remaining half of croutons and Italian dressing. Makes 6 side-dish servings.

Nutrition facts per serving: 220 cal., 16 g total fat (5 g sat. fat), 12 mg chol., 357 mg sodium, 17 g carbo., 1 g fiber, 4 g pro. *Daily values:* 22% vit. A, 25% vit. C, 6% calcium, 7% iron.

TRIPLE CHEESE PASTA CASSEROLE

Prep: 25 min. ◆ Bake: 25 min.

Macaroni and cheese is all dressed up with extra cheese, fresh oregano, and a hint of nutmeg.

12　oz. tricolored rotelle
1　16-oz. pkg. frozen yellow, green, and red peppers and onion stir-fry vegetables

◆◆◆

3　Tbsp. all-purpose flour
2　Tbsp. snipped fresh oregano or basil; or 1 tsp. dried oregano or basil, crushed
¼　tsp. salt
¼　tsp. pepper
¼　tsp. ground nutmeg
3½　cups milk
2　cups shredded smoked Gouda cheese (8 oz.)

½　of an 8-oz. pkg. cream cheese, cut up
⅓　cup finely shredded Parmesan cheese

◆◆◆

Sliced plum tomatoes (optional)
Snipped fresh oregano or basil (optional)

1 Lightly grease a 3-quart rectangular baking dish; set aside. In a large pot cook rotelle pasta in *lightly salted boiling water* for 7 minutes. Add the frozen vegetables; return to boiling. Cook about 2 minutes more or till pasta is tender. Drain well.

2 In a screw-top jar combine flour, dried herb (if using), salt, pepper, nutmeg, and *1 cup* of the milk; shake well. Transfer to a large saucepan; add remaining milk. Cook and stir over medium-high heat till slightly thickened and bubbly. Gradually add the Gouda cheese, cream cheese, and Parmesan cheese stirring till melted. Stir in cooked pasta mixture and fresh herb (if using). Transfer to prepared baking dish.

3 Bake, covered, in a 350° oven about 25 minutes or till heated through. If desired, garnish with thinly sliced plum tomatoes and additional snipped fresh oregano or basil. Makes 16 side-dish servings.

POTLUCK TIP

Bake the casserole just before leaving home. Wrap the hot casserole in several layers of newspaper and a heavy towel; place the wrapped casserole in a large cardboard box or an insulated container to tote. It should stay warm for up to 2 hours. (Or, chill the unbaked casserole for up to 4 hours and tote it in a cooler. Bake the casserole once you arrive at your potluck site in a 350° oven for 35 to 40 minutes or till heated through; stir before garnishing and serving.)

Nutrition facts per serving: 202 cal., 8 g total fat (5 g sat. fat), 30 mg chol., 239 mg sodium, 22 g carbo., 1 g fiber, 10 g pro. *Daily values:* 29% vit. A, 15% vit. C, 17% calcium, 3% iron.

ASHEVILLE SALAD

Prep: 30 min. ◆ Chill: 4 to 24 hr.

Tastes do change over time, especially over 70 years. That's why we updated this salad using lower-fat ingredients and reduced-sodium soup while boosting the fresh flavors. Serve it with other salad offerings for a summer buffet or enjoy slices on the side with dinner.

1　envelope unflavored gelatin
⅓　cup cold water
6　oz. reduced-fat cream cheese (Neufchâtel), cut up
1　10¾-oz. can reduced-sodium condensed tomato soup
　　Several drops bottled hot pepper sauce
¼　cup plain fat-free yogurt
½　cup finely chopped green sweet pepper
½　cup finely chopped celery
¼　cup finely chopped green onions
¼　cup finely chopped pitted ripe olives

◆◆◆

Leaf lettuce
Sweet pepper strips (optional)

1 In medium mixing bowl stir together the gelatin and water; let stand for 5 minutes. Add the reduced-fat cream cheese. Beat with an electric mixer on low speed till well combined (mixture will be very thick but will thin when heated); transfer to a medium saucepan. Heat and stir over medium-low heat for 8 to 10 minutes or till cream cheese is melted and gelatin is dissolved. Using a whisk, blend in the tomato soup and hot pepper sauce till smooth. Remove from heat; cool slightly. Stir in yogurt; add chopped sweet pepper, celery, green onions, and olives.

2 Pour mixture into an 8×4×2½-inch loaf pan or small individual molds. Chill till thoroughly set. Unmold onto a platter or plates lined with lettuce leaves; slice loaf in ½-inch portions. If desired, garnish with pepper strips. Makes 8 side-dish servings.

Nutrition facts per serving: 103 cal., 6 g total fat (3 g sat. fat), 17 mg chol., 262 mg sodium, 8 g carbo., 0 g fiber, 4 g pro. *Daily values:* 10% vit. A, 38% vit. C, 3% calcium, 2% iron.

SUMMERTIME EGGPLANT AND HERBS

Start to finish: 35 min.

If you don't have bow tie pasta on hand, substitute any small to medium pasta, such as rotelle, gemelli, rigatoni, or penne.

6 oz. bow tie pasta
◆◆◆
1 medium eggplant, peeled and chopped
¼ cup chopped onion
2 cloves garlic, minced
2 Tbsp. olive oil
2 cups chopped tomatoes
1 cup cherry tomatoes, halved

Menu

Grilled tuna or swordfish steaks

◆◆◆

Summertime Eggplant and Herbs (see below)

◆◆◆

Toasted garlic bread

¼ cup slivered fresh basil
1 Tbsp. snipped fresh savory
◆◆◆
¼ cup finely shredded Parmesan or Romano cheese
2 Tbsp. pine nuts or slivered almonds, toasted

1 Cook pasta according to package directions; drain.

2 Meanwhile, in a large skillet cook and stir eggplant, onion, and garlic in hot oil till onion is tender. Add chopped tomatoes. Bring to boiling; reduce heat. Simmer, uncovered, for 5 minutes. Stir in the cherry tomatoes, basil, savory, ¼ teaspoon *salt,* and ⅛ teaspoon *pepper;* heat through.

3 To serve, toss vegetable mixture with hot pasta. Sprinkle with Parmesan or Romano and pine nuts or almonds. Makes 6 to 8 side-dish servings.

Nutrition facts per serving: 216 cal., 9 g total fat (1 g sat. fat), 28 mg chol., 158 mg sodium, 29 g carbo., 4 g fiber, 8 g pro. *Daily values:* 7% vit. A, 33% vit. C, 5% calcium, 14% iron.

HERBED POTATO CAKES

Prep: 15 min. ◆ Cook: 10 min.

Here's a great way to use up leftover mashed potatoes.

2 cups cold seasoned mashed potatoes*
1 slightly beaten egg
¼ cup finely chopped onion
2 Tbsp. finely snipped fresh parsley or chives
1 Tbsp. finely snipped fresh dill
◆◆◆
2 Tbsp. all-purpose flour
¼ tsp. seasoned salt
2 Tbsp. butter or margarine

1 In a large mixing bowl combine the mashed potatoes, egg, onion, parsley or chives, and dill. Mix well. Shape mixture into 6 patties, about ¾ inch thick.

2 In a shallow dish mix flour, seasoned salt, and ⅛ teaspoon *pepper.* Carefully coat patties with flour mixture. In a 12-inch skillet melt butter over medium-low heat; add potatoes patties. Cook, uncovered, about 5 minutes on each side. Remove from skillet; serve immediately. Serves 6.

*Note: For mashed potatoes, start with 1 to 1¼ pounds *potatoes.* Peel potatoes, cook in boiling water, drain, and mash. Add 2 tablespoons *butter or margarine* and enough *milk* (¼ to ½ cup) to make desired consistency. Season lightly with *salt* and *pepper.*

Nutrition facts per serving: 160 cal., 9 g total fat (5 g sat. fat), 57 mg chol., 173 mg sodium, 18 g carbo., 1 g fiber, 3 g pro. *Daily values:* 9% vit. A, 12% vit. C, 2% calcium, 4% iron.

COOL TIPS FOR HOT WEATHER

It's summertime and the bugs are multiplying. We're not talking about mosquitoes and black-flies, either. We're talking about those critters that sometimes contaminate meat, poultry, seafood, eggs, fresh fruits, and vegetables.

Disease-causing bacteria grow rapidly on warm food. That's why the incidence of foodborne illnesses increases with the temperature. Children, the elderly, pregnant women, and people with chronic health problems are especially susceptible to bacterial infections. You can help reduce your family's risks by taking some simple precautions.

Watch those temperatures. The bugs that cause food poisoning thrive at temperatures between 40° and 140°F—the danger zone. Food safety experts warn not to leave prepared food in that danger zone more than two hours. Those same foods are safe for only one hour if the temperature rises above 90°F, indoors or out. For family picnics, tote salads, dairy products, meat for the grill, and other perishable foods in an ice-filled cooler. Unless the food is kept cold (40°F or below) or hot (at least 140°F), bacteria will not hesitate to spread out and multiply. Remember: When in doubt, throw it out. Discard all perishable food left at room temperature more than two hours or at temperatures greater than 90° more than one hour.

You've heard this one before, too, but we'll say it again: Don't eat rare meat. Aim for a happy medium. A meat thermometer can help you figure out when your meat, fish, or poultry reaches the temperature necessary to kill those bugs that can cause food poisoning.

When is the meat done? Poultry should be cooked to an internal temperature of 180°F; red meat, ground meat, and ground poultry to 160°F. The juices of properly cooked ground meat and ground poultry run clear and no pink remains. Check the temperature by inserting the thermometer in the thickest part of meat or poultry, away from bone, if there is one.

Remember the thaw law. That law says never defrost food at room temperature. At that temperature, harmful bacteria can grow on the outer layer of food before the inside thaws. Instead, thaw frozen food in the refrigerator or wrap the food in a sealed plastic bag and place it in a large bowl of ice water. Change the water every 30 minutes until the food is thawed. Then cook the food immediately. When you're marinating food, seal the marinade and the food in a plastic bag and set it in the refrigerator until you're ready to cook it.

The egg and I. Like rare meat, raw eggs are out, too, because they may be contaminated with the wrong stuff. Get rid of that recipe for homemade ice cream if it contains raw eggs, unless you cook the egg mixture before freezing it. If you're making mayonnaise or a Caesar salad, use a pasteurized egg substitute in the dressing. You'll find refrigerated and frozen pasteurized egg substitutes at most grocery stores. In many recipes you can replace one large egg with ¼ cup of egg substitute.

Watch that catch. Properly cooked fish looks opaque and will just start to flake easily with a fork. The juices should be milky white. When grilling fish fillets, steaks, or kabobs, plan on cooking the fish to 160°F. This will take four to six minutes per ½-inch thickness of fish.

Although raw seafood and shellfish are considered treats by some, they can cause serious illness. Some raw oysters, for example, contain a bacteria that can cause flulike symptoms or even death, especially in those with chronic health problems such as liver disease, cancer, or diabetes, or people who are HIV-positive. "They should not be eating raw seafood of any type, particularly oysters and clams," says Mark Tamplin, Ph.D., food safety specialist at the University of Florida. Children, pregnant women, and the elderly also should heed that advice. Fully cooking all seafood to 160°F kills the bacteria.

Fruits and vegetables. Summer's the optimum time to pick fresh fruits and vegetables from the fields or the market. However, be cautious of buying produce, such as a melon, cut on unrefrigerated counters. Bacteria from hands and knives can easily be transferred to the cut fruits and vegetables. At warm temperatures, the bacteria can multiply and lead to a serious stomachache.

No matter what time of year, select fruits and vegetables that are free of mold, bruises, and cuts. Rinse fruits and vegetables in cold water and, if necessary, scrub well with a vegetable brush.

BEEF STEAK IN THAI MARINADE

Prep: 10 min. ◆ Marinate: 4 to 24 hr.
Grill: 12 min.

You may need to visit a specialty market to purchase a few of these marinade ingredients, but we think you'll find it's worth the trip. (See the photograph on page 122.)

2½ lb. boneless beef sirloin
   steak, cut 1 inch thick
½ cup unsweetened coconut
   milk
½ of a lemongrass stalk,
   trimmed and coarsely
   chopped, or ⅛ tsp. finely
   shredded lemon peel
3 Tbsp. lime juice
2 Tbsp. fish sauce or soy sauce
2 to 4 Tbsp. red curry paste
2 tsp. sugar

1 Trim fat from meat. Place meat in a plastic bag set in a shallow dish. For marinade, in a blender container or food processor bowl, combine coconut milk, lemongrass or lemon peel, lime juice, fish sauce or soy sauce, red curry paste, and sugar. Cover and blend or process till smooth. Pour marinade over meat. Close bag; chill for 4 to 24 hours, turning bag occasionally. Drain steaks, reserving marinade.

2 Grill the steak on the rack of an uncovered grill directly over medium coals for 12 to 15 minutes or to desired doneness, turning once and brushing once with reserved marinade halfway through. Discard any remaining marinade. Remove steak from grill; let stand for 5 minutes. Thinly slice meat across the grain. Makes 10 servings.

POTLUCK TIP

Keep the meat soaking in the marinade as you transport it on ice. Then grill the meat just before everyone gathers to eat. Remember to pack a long-handled brush (to brush on the marinade as meat cooks), long-handled tongs, and a knife.

Nutrition facts per serving: 233 cal., 12 g total fat (6 g sat. fat), 77 mg chol., 210 mg sodium, 3 g carbo., 0 g fiber, 26 g pro. *Daily values:* 3% vit. A, 2% vit. C, 1% calcium, 20% iron.

FRESH HERB SAUCE

Prep: 10 min. ◆ Cook: 17 min.

Jazz up the basics— chicken, pork, or fish—with this creamy herb sauce.

1 cup dry white wine
2 Tbsp. hazelnut liqueur
   (optional)
¼ cup thinly sliced leek
2 tsp. snipped fresh rosemary
½ tsp. snipped fresh tarragon
⅛ tsp. salt
⅛ tsp. ground white pepper
½ cup whipping cream

1 In a medium saucepan combine wine and, if desired, liqueur. Bring to boiling; reduce heat. Simmer, uncovered, 10 minutes or till reduced to ½ cup. Add leek, rosemary, tarragon, salt, and pepper. Simmer, uncovered, 5 minutes more. Add whipping cream; return to boiling. Boil gently, uncovered, 2 to 3 minutes more or till slightly thickened. Serve at once over hot cooked chicken, pork, or fish. Makes about ¾ cup.

Nutrition facts per tablespoon: 49 cal., 4 g total fat (2 g sat. fat), 14 mg chol., 27 mg sodium, 1 g carbo., 0 g fiber, 0 g pro.

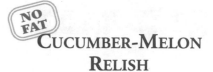

CUCUMBER-MELON RELISH

Prep: 20 min. ◆ Chill: up to 8 hr.

Our taste testers liked how this refreshing mix contrasted with the spiciness of the Moroccan Chicken (page 138). It also pairs well with grilled pork or fish. (See the photograph on page 119.)

1 medium cantaloupe (3 lb.),
   seeded, peeled, and
   chopped (3 cups)
½ of a small honeydew melon
   (1½ lb.), seeded, peeled,
   and chopped (1½ cups)
1 medium cucumber, seeded
   and chopped (1½ cups)
2 green onions, sliced (¼ cup)
2 Tbsp. lemon juice
2 Tbsp. snipped fresh mint
1 Tbsp. honey

1 In a large bowl combine the chopped cantaloupe, honeydew melon, cucumber, and green onions. In a small bowl combine the lemon juice, snipped mint, and honey; mix well. Pour the honey mixture over melon mixture, tossing gently to coat. Cover and chill relish for up to 8 hours.

2 Stir relish before serving. Using a slotted spoon, serve relish over grilled chicken. Makes about 4 cups.

Nutrition facts per ⅓ cup: 30 cal., 0 g total fat, 0 mg chol., 6 mg sodium, 7 g carbo., 1 g fiber, 1 g pro. *Daily values:* 13% vit. A, 41% vit. C, 2% iron.

PICNIC PLANNING

When it comes to safe picnicking, there's more to it than tossing some food in a basket, loading the children in the car, and driving to your favorite picnic spot. Follow the tips to help ensure a food-safe outing.

◆ When you're traveling and toting cold food, be sure to carry it in an insulated cooler. Wait until just before leaving home to pack your cooler and make sure you have plenty of ice or ice packs to surround your perishable foods.

◆ Take two coolers: one for drinks, the other for perishable foods. That way warm air won't get into the perishables each time someone reaches in for a drink.

◆ Once at the picnic site, keep the tightly closed coolers in a shady spot and not in the trunk of the car. Add ice often to the cooler, draining off the water as the ice melts.

◆ Wash hands before and after handling food. Soap and hot water are ideal, but bring along a jug of water and paper towels, just in case there are none available at the picnic site. Disposable moist towelettes are an easy-to-carry option, too.

MOROCCAN CHICKEN WITH CUCUMBER-MELON RELISH

Prep: 15 min.
Marinate: 4 to 24 hr. ◆ Grill: 35 min.

It's the kicky blend of seasonings that gives this grilled chicken its Moroccan roots. (See the photograph on page 119.)

½ cup lemon juice
⅓ cup olive oil
4 cloves garlic, minced
3 Tbsp. grated gingerroot
2 Tbsp. ground cumin
4 tsp. ground coriander
1 Tbsp. salt
1 Tbsp. ground cinnamon
1 Tbsp. paprika
2 tsp. ground red pepper
1½ tsp. ground black pepper
6 to 8 lb. meaty chicken pieces (skinned, if desired)
1 recipe Cucumber-Melon Relish (see page 137)

1 For marinade, in a small bowl stir together the lemon juice, oil, garlic, gingerroot, cumin, coriander, salt, cinnamon, paprika, red pepper, and black pepper. Place chicken into 2 large plastic bags set in 2 large bowls. Pour half of the marinade over chicken in each bag. Seal bags and turn several times to distribute the marinade. Marinate chicken in the refrigerator for 4 to 24 hours, turning bags occasionally. Drain chicken, discarding marinade.

2 Grill chicken on the rack of an uncovered grill directly over medium coals for 35 to 45 minutes or till chicken is no longer pink, turning once. Serve with Cucumber-Melon Relish. Makes 12 servings.

Confirm that grills will be available at your gathering. Then you can tote the marinating chicken on ice in your cooler. Keep the relish in a covered container on ice till you're ready to serve chicken. Another option is to grill the chicken at home and serve it chilled.

Nutrition facts per serving (without relish): 294 cal., 16 g total fat (4 g sat. fat), 104 mg chol., 360 mg sodium, 2 g carbo., 0 g fiber, 34 g pro. *Daily values:* 6% vit. A, 5% vit. C, 3% calcium, 16% iron.

PORK PINWHEELS WITH ROASTED GARLIC MAYONNAISE

Prep: 30 min. ◆ Roast: 45 min.
Cool: 30 min. ◆ Chill: 2 to 24 hr.

A single slice will do as an appetizer portion; two or three make a meal when partnered with other potluck favorites.

3 leeks, thinly sliced (1 cup)
1 Tbsp. olive oil
◆◆◆
¼ cup grated Parmesan or Romano cheese
1 cup snipped fresh parsley
2 Tbsp. snipped fresh thyme or 1 tsp. dried thyme, crushed
¼ tsp. salt
¼ tsp. pepper
3 Tbsp. olive oil or cooking oil
¼ cup chopped walnuts
◆◆◆
2 12-oz. pork tenderloins
1 recipe Roasted Garlic Mayonnaise (see page 139)

1 In a medium skillet cook leeks in the 1 tablespoon olive oil till tender; remove from heat.

2 In a blender container or food processor bowl, combine the Parmesan or Romano cheese, parsley, thyme, salt, and pepper. Cover and blend or process with several on-off turns till parsley is finely chopped. With the machine running, gradually add the 3 tablespoons olive oil or cooking oil; blend or process to the consistency of soft butter. Add leeks and walnuts; blend with several off-on turns till coarsely chopped. Set aside.

3 Remove fat and paper-thin membrane from surface of tenderloins. Using a sharp knife, cut each tenderloin lengthwise to, but not through, opposite side. Cover a tenderloin with clear plastic wrap. Using flat side of a meat mallet and working from center to edges, pound meat to a 12×8-inch rectangle. Remove wrap; repeat with remaining tenderloin.

4 Sprinkle tenderloins lightly with additional *salt* and *pepper*. Spread half the parsley mixture evenly over each tenderloin to within 1 inch of edges. Roll up each tenderloin from a short side. Tie rolls with kitchen string, if necessary. Insert a meat thermometer in center of a tenderloin. Place meat, seam side down, on rack in shallow roasting pan.

5 Roast, uncovered, in a 325° oven 45 to 60 minutes or till thermometer registers 160°. Cool 30 minutes at room temperature. Remove strings; cut rolls into slices ½ inch thick. Cover and chill. Serve with Roasted Garlic Mayonnaise. Makes 32 slices.

Herbed Pork Piccata over hot cooked linguine (see right)

♦♦♦

Salad with Herbed Croutons (see page 133)

♦♦♦

Frozen yogurt with fresh berries

Roasted Garlic Mayonnaise: Peel away outer skin from 1 medium head *garlic.* Cut off the pointed top portion with a knife, leaving the bulb intact but exposing the individual cloves. Place in a small baking dish; drizzle with 2 teaspoons *olive oil.* Bake, covered, alongside the meat, for 45 to 60 minutes or till cloves are very soft. Cool slightly. Press to remove garlic "paste" from individual cloves. Mash garlic with tines of a fork. Stir together garlic paste and ½ cup *light mayonnaise dressing or salad dressing.* Thin mixture with a little *milk,* if necessary. Cover and chill till serving.

POTLUCK TIP

Tightly wrap chilled pork slices in foil; pack the Roasted Garlic Mayonnaise in a covered container. Keep both on ice till it's time to serve.

Nutrition facts per slice with 1 teaspoon mayonnaise: 79 cal., 5 g total fat (1 g sat. fat), 16 mg chol., 82 mg sodium, 2 g carbo., 0 g fiber, 5 g pro.
Daily values: 1% vit. A, 5% vit. C, 1% calcium, 3% iron.

30 MIN. LOW FAT

HERBED PORK PICCATA

Start to finish: 25 min.

In Italy, veal and chicken are typically prepared piccata-style, but we found pork to be a delicious option.

- 1 lb. boneless pork loin roast
- ¼ tsp. salt
- ⅛ tsp. pepper
- 1 Tbsp. olive oil
- 1 Tbsp. butter or margarine

♦♦♦

- ¼ cup dry white wine
- ¼ cup chicken broth
- 1 Tbsp. lemon juice
- 1 Tbsp. snipped fresh parsley
- 1 Tbsp. snipped fresh basil
- 2 tsp. snipped fresh oregano
- 1 tsp. snipped fresh thyme

1 Using a sharp knife, slice pork about ¼ inch thick; season with the salt and pepper. In a 12-inch skillet heat olive oil and butter or margarine over medium-high heat. Add pork slices in a single layer; cook for 1 to 2 minutes or till browned; turn and cook 1 to 2 minutes more or till done. Remove to serving platter; cover and keep warm. Repeat with remaining pork.

2 Add white wine, chicken broth, lemon juice, parsley, basil, oregano, and thyme to skillet. Bring to boiling, stirring to scrape up browned bits; reduce heat. Simmer, uncovered, 2 to 3 minutes or till reduced to ⅓ cup. Spoon sauce over pork. Serve at once. Makes 6 servings.

Nutrition facts per serving: 136 cal., 9 g total fat (3 g sat. fat), 39 mg chol., 167 mg sodium, 0 g carbo., 0 g fiber, 11 g pro.
Daily values: 2% vit. A, 3% vit. C, 3% iron.

BUTTERMILK-PECAN BROWNIES WITH SOUR CREAM FROSTING

Prep: 20 min. ♦ Bake: 30 min.

You can count on brownies to do a quick disappearing act when they're part of a potluck menu.
(See the photograph on the cover.)

1 **cup butter or margarine**
¾ **cup granulated sugar**
¾ **cup packed brown sugar**
3 **eggs**
¼ **cup buttermilk or sour milk***
1 **tsp. vanilla**

♦♦♦

1⅓ **cups all-purpose flour**
½ **tsp. baking soda**
½ **cup finely chopped toasted pecans**
5 **oz. semisweet chocolate, melted and cooled**
½ **tsp. ground cinnamon**
1 **recipe Sour Cream Frosting (see top right) or sifted powdered sugar****
Chocolate curls (optional)

1 Grease a 13×9×2-inch baking pan; set aside. In a medium saucepan melt the butter or margarine over low heat. Cool slightly. Stir the granulated sugar and brown sugar into the melted butter. Add the eggs, 1 at a time, beating by hand just till combined. Stir in the buttermilk or sour milk and vanilla.

2 Stir together flour and baking soda. Add flour mixture to egg mixture; stir just till combined. Divide batter into 2 equal portions (about 1¾ cups each). Stir pecans into 1 portion and spread this batter into the prepared pan.

3 Bake in a 350° oven for 10 minutes. Stir the melted chocolate and cinnamon into the remaining batter; blend well. Spread the chocolate batter over partially baked brownies. Continue baking about 20 minutes or till a wooden toothpick inserted in center comes out clean. Cool on a wire rack. Frost with Sour Cream Frosting or sift with powdered sugar. If desired, garnish with chocolate curls. Makes 36 bars.

*Note: To make sour milk, place ½ teaspoon *lemon juice* in a glass measuring cup; add enough *milk* to make ¼ cup liquid total.

**Note: If you opt to simply sift powdered sugar over the brownies, lightly place a wire cooling rack over the brownies before topping with sugar; this adds an interesting design to the top of the brownies.

Nutrition facts per frosted bar: 174 cal., 10 g total fat (5 g sat. fat), 36 mg chol., 92 mg sodium, 22 g carbo., 0 g fiber, 2 g pro.

SOUR CREAM FROSTING

Prep: 10 min.

Spread this tangy white frosting over your favorite pan of brownies or sheet cake.

⅓ **cup dairy sour cream**
¼ **cup butter or margarine, softened**
1 **tsp. vanilla**
3 **cups sifted powdered sugar**

1 In a medium mixing bowl beat together the sour cream, butter or margarine, and vanilla with an electric mixer on low speed till smooth. Gradually add the powdered sugar, beating on low speed till smooth and spreadable. Makes 1½ cups.

FUDGY BROWNIES

Prep: 20 min. ♦ Bake: 30 min.

Plain or nutty? Frosted or topped with caramel? There are several ways you can dress this dessert, or you can add a cream cheese swirl before baking—follow the directions for Cheesecake Swirl Brownies on page 141.
(See the photograph on the cover.)

½ **cup butter or margarine**
3 **oz. unsweetened chocolate**

♦♦♦

1 **cup sugar**
2 **eggs**
1 **tsp. vanilla**

♦♦♦

⅔ **cup all-purpose flour**
¼ **tsp. baking soda**
½ **cup chopped nuts (optional)**

♦♦♦

1 **recipe Chocolate-Cream Cheese Frosting with Drizzles or Caramel Topping (see page 141) (optional)**

1 In a medium saucepan melt butter or margarine and unsweetened chocolate over low heat, stirring constantly. Remove from heat; cool.

2 Meanwhile, grease an 8×8×2- or 9×9×2-inch baking pan; set aside. Stir sugar into chocolate mixture in saucepan. Add the eggs, 1 at a time, beating by hand just till combined. Stir in the vanilla.

3 In a small mixing bowl stir together the flour and baking soda. Add flour mixture to chocolate mixture; stir just till combined. If desired, stir in nuts. Spread the batter into the prepared pan.

4 Bake in a 350° oven, allowing 30 minutes for an 8-inch pan or 25 minutes for a 9-inch pan. Cool on a wire rack.

5 If desired, frost with Chocolate-Cream Cheese Frosting, then spoon or pipe with Chocolate Drizzle and/or White Chocolate Drizzle. Or, drizzle with Caramel Topping. Makes 16 bars.

Nutrition facts per bar: 152 cal., 9 g total fat (5 g sat. fat), 42 mg chol., 86 mg sodium, 18 g carbo., 0 g fiber, 2 g pro. *Daily values:* 6% vit. A.

CHOCOLATE-CREAM CHEESE FROSTING WITH DRIZZLES

Prep: 15 min.

½ **cup semisweet chocolate pieces**
1 **3-oz. pkg. cream cheese, softened**

2 **to 4 Tbsp. powdered sugar**
1 **recipe Chocolate Drizzle and/or White Chocolate Drizzle (see below) (optional)**

1 In a small saucepan melt semisweet chocolate pieces over low heat, stirring constantly. Remove from heat; cool. In a small mixing bowl stir together the cream cheese and sugar. Stir in chocolate till smooth. Spread frosting over cooled brownies. Let frosting set. If desired, top with Chocolate Drizzle and/or White Chocolate Drizzle.

Chocolate Drizzle: In a small saucepan combine 1 ounce *unsweetened chocolate,* chopped; 2 tablespoons *margarine or butter;* and 2 tablespoons *milk.* Stir constantly over low heat till melted. Remove from heat. Stir in 1 cup sifted *powdered sugar* and ½ teaspoon *vanilla,* beating till smooth.

White Chocolate Drizzle: Prepare the Chocolate Drizzle as directed above except substitute ¼ cup *white baking chips* for the unsweetened chocolate.

CARAMEL TOPPING

Prep: 15 min.

Instead of frosting, add a gooey touch to chocolaty brownies.

12 **vanilla caramels**
1 **Tbsp. margarine or butter**
4 **tsp. milk**

1 In a small saucepan combine caramels, margarine or butter, and milk. Heat and stir over medium-low heat till smooth.

Remove from heat. Cut unfrosted brownies into bars; drizzle warm caramel mixture over bars. Allow caramel to set before serving.

CHEESECAKE SWIRL BROWNIES

Prep: 30 min. ◆ Bake: 40 min.

These simply delicious brownies unite two of America's favorites— chocolate and cheesecake. (See the photograph on the cover.)

1 **recipe Fudgy Brownies (see page 140)**
◆◆◆
2 **3-oz. pkg. cream cheese, softened**
1 **egg**

1 Grease an 8×8×2- or 9×9×2-inch baking pan; set aside. Prepare the batter for Fudgy Brownies as directed; set aside.

2 In a medium mixing bowl beat together cream cheese and egg. Spread two-thirds of the brownie batter into the prepared pan. Drizzle cream cheese mixture atop. Drop remaining brownie batter by spoonfuls on top of cream cheese batter. Using a knife, gently swirl to create a marbled effect.

3 Bake in a 350° oven, allowing 40 minutes for the 8-inch pan or 30 minutes for the 9-inch pan. Cool brownies on a wire rack. Makes 16 bars.

Nutrition facts per bar: 195 cal., 13 g total fat (7 g sat. fat), 67 mg chol., 122 mg sodium, 18 g carbo., 0 g fiber, 3 g pro.

Floribbean Pound Cake

Prep: 35 min. ◆ Bake: 55 min.

3 cups all-purpose flour
1½ tsp. baking powder

◆◆◆

1½ cups butter, softened
1½ cups sugar
6 eggs
4 to 5 tsp. finely shredded lime
    peel (about 3 limes)

◆◆◆

⅓ cup canned unsweetened
    coconut milk or milk

◆◆◆

½ cup sugar
⅓ cup lime juice

◆◆◆

½ to 1 cup coconut, toasted
    Assorted tropical fruits, such
    as mango slices and
    kiwifruit slices
    Whipped cream (optional)

1 Grease and flour a 10-inch fluted tube pan; set aside. Stir together the flour and baking powder; set aside.

2 In a large mixing bowl beat the butter with an electric mixer on medium speed for 30 seconds. Gradually add the 1½ cups sugar, 2 tablespoons at a time, beating on medium-high speed about 6 minutes total or till very light and fluffy. Add eggs, 1 at a time, beating 1 minute after each addition, scraping bowl often. Beat in the lime peel.

3 Gradually add flour mixture to butter mixture, beating on medium-low speed just till combined. Beat in coconut milk or regular milk. Spread batter evenly into the prepared pan. Bake in a 325° oven for 55 to 60 minutes or till a wooden toothpick inserted near center comes out clean. Cool cake in the pan on a wire rack for 10 minutes.

4 Meanwhile, for syrup, in a small saucepan combine the ½ cup sugar and lime juice. Cook and stir over medium heat to dissolve sugar. Remove from heat.

5 Invert cake onto a wire rack (place a sheet of waxed paper under the rack). Prick top and sides of cake with a toothpick and brush with the syrup. Immediately sprinkle with coconut; cool. Serve slices of cake with any remaining coconut, fresh fruit, and, if desired, whipped cream. Serves 18.

Nutrition facts per serving: 335 cal., 19 g total fat (11 g sat. fat), 112 mg chol., 212 mg sodium, 39 g carbo., 1 g fiber, 4 g pro. *Daily values:* 17% vit. A, 3% vit. C, 8% iron.

Pineapple Cooler

Prep: 10 min. ◆ Chill: 2 to 24 hr.

To dress up a pitcher of this simple beverage, freeze edible flowers and mints sprigs in ice cubes. Serve each with a Fruit Swizzle Stick.

1 12-oz. can frozen pineapple
    juice concentrate, thawed
1 6-oz. can frozen limeade
    concentrate, thawed
4 cups cold water
1 liter bottle club soda
    Ice cubes
    Fresh strawberries (optional)
    Fruit Swizzle Sticks (see
    right) (optional)

1 In a large pitcher combine the pineapple juice concentrate, limeade, and cold water. Chill well in the refrigerator.

2 To serve, add club soda and ice cubes. If desired, add fresh strawberries to juice mixture and serve with Fruit Swizzle Sticks. Makes 14 (6-ounce) servings.

Fruit Swizzle Sticks: On short (6-inch) wooden skewers, thread *assorted fruits, such as halved orange slices, halved lime slices, orange sections, raspberries, strawberries, sliced kiwifruit, and mint sprigs.*

Nutrition facts per serving: 66 cal., 0 g total fat, 0 mg chol., 17 mg sodium, 17 g carbo., 0 g fiber, 0 g pro. *Daily values:* 19% vit. C, 1% calcium, 1% iron.

Pineapple Rum Cooler: Prepare Pineapple Cooler as directed, except increase water to 6 cups, add 1½ cups *rum or tequila*, and omit the club soda.

Pineapple Rum Slush: Prepare Pineapple Rum Cooler as directed, except omit ice cubes. Pour mixture (without club soda) into one 13×9×2-inch pan or two 8×8×2-inch pans. Cover and freeze overnight. To serve, scrape the top of the frozen mixture with a spoon to form a slush and spoon into glasses. Serve plain with spoons or stir chilled club soda into the slush mixture, if desired.

ITALIAN CREAM TARTS

Prep: 45 min. ◆ Bake: 10 min.
Chill: up to 24 hr.

Berries, pastry, and cream—who can resist? The pastry cream is laced with mascarpone cheese, a soft cheese similar to cream cheese but more buttery tasting and smoother.
(See the photograph on page 121.)

⅓ cup sugar
¼ cup all-purpose flour
1 cup milk
3 beaten egg yolks
2 Tbsp. liqueur, such as clear crème de cacao, orange, or raspberry, or 1 tsp. vanilla

◆◆◆

1 17¼-oz. pkg. frozen puff pastry, thawed (2 sheets)
1 8-oz. carton mascarpone cheese (1 cup)
4 oz. semisweet chocolate, cut up
1 Tbsp. shortening
  Assorted fresh berries (optional)

1 For pastry cream, in a medium saucepan combine sugar and flour; gradually stir in milk. Add egg yolks, beating till smooth. Cook and stir over medium heat till thickened and bubbly. Remove from heat; stir liqueur or vanilla into pastry cream. Pour into a bowl and cover surface with clear plastic wrap. Cool and chill.

2 For tart shells, thaw pastry according to package directions. Unfold pastry sheets, 1 at a time, on a lightly floured surface. Roll lightly to minimize ridges. Using 2½- to 3-inch cookie cutters, cut out about 24 tarts (be sure to cut out an even number of each shape); place half of them on an ungreased baking sheet and prick each a few times with a fork. Using 1½- to 2-inch cutters (of the same design or round), cut the middle out of the remaining pastries, reserving cutouts.

3 Brush edges of the tarts on baking sheet with *water* and top with tarts that have the middles cut out; press gently to fuse layers together. Arrange small cutouts on another ungreased baking sheet. Bake pastries in 400° oven till puffed and golden, allowing 7 to 9 minutes for small cutouts and 10 to 12 minutes for larger tarts. Cool pastries completely.

4 Up to 1 hour before serving time, add mascarpone cheese to chilled pastry cream; beat with an electric mixer on low speed till smooth. Carefully spoon mixture into tart shells. In a small saucepan melt semisweet chocolate and shortening together over very low heat, stirring constantly. Remove from heat. Spread a thin layer of chocolate over tops of small cutouts. Pipe or drizzle remaining chocolate over the cream-filled tarts; refrigerate both till chocolate is set. To serve, arrange filled tarts and chocolate-glazed cutouts on large platter and surround with berries. Makes 12.

POTLUCK TIP

These tarts are best reserved for when the potluck is near home. That way, you can fill the pastry shells close to serving time, and the chocolate drizzle won't get messy en route to a faraway spot.

Nutrition facts per tart: 377 cal., 27 g total fat (8 g sat. fat), 79 mg chol., 176 mg sodium, 30 g carbo., 1 g fiber, 8 g pro.
Daily values: 9% vit. A, 2% calcium, 4% iron.

CHAMPAGNE FRUIT BOWL

Prep: 20 min. ◆ Chill: up to 2 hr.
See the photograph on page 120.

4 apples and/or pears, cored and cut up
¼ cup orange juice
2 Tbsp. lemon juice
4 cups assorted fruits, such as halved strawberries; melon balls; sliced nectarines, peaches, or plums; and seedless grapes
3 Tbsp. sugar
2 tsp. finely shredded orange peel

◆◆◆

1 187-ml bottle champagne or ¾ cup white grape juice, chilled
⅓ cup sliced almonds, toasted (optional)
  Edible geranium leaves and marigolds (optional)

1 Combine apples and/or pears with orange juice and lemon juice; toss gently. Add remaining fruit, sugar, and orange peel; toss again. Cover; chill up to 2 hours.

2 Just before serving, stir in champagne or grape juice; if desired, sprinkle with almonds and garnish with geranium leaves and marigolds. Serves 12.

POTLUCK TIP

Carry fruit mixture and champagne or grape juice on ice in a cooler. To serve, follow Step 2, above.

Nutrition facts per serving: 81 cal., 0 g total fat, 0 mg chol., 2 mg sodium, 16 g carbo., 2 g fiber, 1 g pro.
Daily values: 5% vit. A, 35% vit. C, 1% iron.

THE CLEVER COOK

THE SCOOP ON ICE CREAM

I attended a party where the hostess put scoops of ice cream in baking cups, placed them on a tray, and kept them in the freezer till dessert time. All she had to do for sundaes was pull the scooped ice cream out of the freezer and let guests decide the flavor they wanted.

Beth Russell
Campbell, California

FRESH FRUIT COMPOTE WITH BASIL

Prep: 25 min. ◆ Stand: 1 hr.

½ cup sugar
½ cup water
¼ cup honey
1 vanilla bean, split lengthwise, or 1 tsp. vanilla
2 tsp. cornstarch
1 Tbsp. water

◆◆◆

2 Tbsp. crème de cassis, almond or strawberry liqueur, or orange juice
4 cups assorted fresh fruit, such as strawberries; sliced peaches; sliced pears; blackberries; raspberries; blueberries; pitted sweet cherries; and/or sliced bananas*

⅓ cup shredded fresh basil
Lemon sherbet or French vanilla ice cream (optional)

1 In a small saucepan combine sugar, the ½ cup water, honey, and, if using, vanilla bean. Bring to boiling, stirring to dissolve sugar; reduce heat. Simmer, uncovered, 5 minutes. Combine the cornstarch and 1 tablespoon water; add to saucepan. Cook and stir till thickened and bubbly. Cook and stir for 2 minutes more. Cool slightly.

2 Remove vanilla bean, if used. Add liqueur or orange juice and, if using, the vanilla. Place fruit and basil in large bowl; pour syrup mixture over, stirring gently. Cover and let stand about 1 hour or till cooled to room temperature, or chill several hours, stirring once or twice. If desired, serve with a small scoop of sherbet or ice cream. Makes 6 servings.

*Note: If using bananas, slice and add just before serving.

Nutrition facts per serving: 184 cal., 0 g total fat, 0 mg chol., 3 mg sodium, 43 g carbo., 2 g fiber, 1 g pro.
Daily values: 39% vit. C, 1% calcium, 2% iron.

MINTY LEMON ICE

Prep: 25 min. ◆ Cool: 30 min.
Freeze: 8 to 28 hr.

A scoop of this refreshing, icy delight makes a perfect palate cleanser between courses.

2 cups water
1½ cups sugar
½ cup loosely packed fresh peppermint or mint leaves

1 tsp. finely shredded lemon peel
⅔ cup lemon juice
1 12-oz. can ginger ale

1 In a medium saucepan combine water, sugar, mint, lemon peel, and lemon juice. Bring to boiling, stirring to dissolve sugar; reduce heat. Simmer, covered, 5 minutes. Remove from heat; cool. Strain and discard solids. Stir in ginger ale.

2 Transfer liquid to an 8×8×2-inch baking pan. Cover and freeze 4 to 6 hours or till almost firm. Break mixture into small chunks; transfer to a chilled bowl. Beat with an electric mixer till smooth, but not melted. Return to pan. Cover and freeze for 4 to 24 hours or till firm. Makes 5 cups (10 servings).

Nutrition facts per ½-cup serving: 134 cal., 0 g total fat, 0 mg chol., 5 mg sodium, 34 g carbo., 0 g fiber, 0 g pro.
Daily values: 1% vit. A, 17% vit. C, 5% iron.

CARDAMOM ICE CREAM

Prep: 20 min. ◆ Chill: 4 to 24 hr.

Cardamom is an aromatic spice with a flowery sweet taste reminiscent of, but more subtle than, ginger. Serve the custardy ice cream in cups or cones. (See the photograph on page 120.)

1½ cups sugar
2 Tbsp. all-purpose flour
5 cups milk
4 beaten egg yolks
1 Tbsp. vanilla
1½ tsp. ground cardamom
1 tsp. finely shredded lemon peel

◆◆◆

3 cups whipping cream

1 In a large saucepan stir together the sugar and flour. Gradually stir in *2 cups* of the milk. Cook and stir over medium heat till thickened and bubbly. Cook and stir for 1 minute more. Stir about *1 cup* of the hot mixture into beaten egg yolks; return to remaining hot mixture in saucepan. Cook and stir just till mixture returns to boiling. Remove from heat. Stir in vanilla, cardamom, lemon peel, and remaining milk. Cool slightly. Cover the surface with clear plastic wrap. Refrigerate for several hours or till completely chilled.

2 Stir whipping cream into chilled mixture. Freeze in a 4- or 5-quart ice cream freezer according to manufacturer's directions. Makes 2 quarts (16 servings).

Nutrition facts per ¹/₂-cup serving: 286 cal., 19 g total fat (12 g sat. fat), 120 mg chol., 57 mg sodium, 25 g carbo., 0 g fiber, 4 g pro. *Daily values:* 32% vit. A, 1% vit. C, 10% calcium, 1% iron.

PRIZE TESTED RECIPE WINNER

VERY BERRY TRIFLE

Prep: 40 min. ◆ Chill: 4 to 24 hr.

This recipe earned Sandy Marshall of Virginia Beach, Virginia, $200 in the magazine's monthly contest.

1 **4-serving-size pkg. fat-free, sugar-free instant vanilla pudding mix**
2 **cups skim milk**
1 **8-oz. pkg. reduced-fat cream cheese (Neufchâtel), softened**

1 **8-oz. carton raspberry yogurt**

◆◆◆

8 **cups angel food cake cubes**
4 **cups strawberries, quartered**
2 **cups blueberries and/or raspberries**

◆◆◆

1 **recipe Berry Sauce (see below)**
Fresh mint (optional)

1 Prepare pudding mix according to package directions using the skim milk; set aside. In a large mixing bowl beat cream cheese and yogurt with an electric mixer on medium speed till smooth; stir in pudding.

2 To assemble the trifle, in a 3-quart glass bowl or two 1½-quart glass bowls, layer one-third of the cake cubes, one-third of the pudding mixture, and one-third of the berries. Repeat layers twice. Cover and chill 4 to 24 hours.

3 To serve, spoon the Berry Sauce onto individual serving plates; top with trifle. If desired, garnish with fresh mint. Makes 10 to 12 servings.

Berry Sauce: In a blender container or food processor bowl combine 2 cups *strawberries or raspberries,* 2 to 3 tablespoons *sugar,* and 1 tablespoon *raspberry liqueur, rum, or orange juice.* Cover and blend or process till smooth; sieve to remove seeds, if desired. Cover and chill till serving time. Makes 1 cup.

Nutrition facts per serving: 285 cal., 6 g total fat (4 g sat. fat), 20 mg chol., 301 mg sodium, 50 g carbo., 2 g fiber, 8 g pro. *Daily values:* 11% vit. A, 88% vit. C, 12% calcium, 2% iron.

STRAWBERRY AND CHEESE CRUMBLE

Prep: 35 min. ◆ Bake: 40 min.

½ **cup butter**
½ **cup packed brown sugar**
1¼ **cups all-purpose flour**
½ **cup finely chopped walnuts**

◆◆◆

2 **cups strawberries, hulled**
½ **cup granulated sugar**
1 **Tbsp. cornstarch**

◆◆◆

1 **8-oz. pkg. cream cheese, softened**
1 **egg**
1 **Tbsp. lemon juice**
1 **tsp. vanilla**

1 In a bowl beat butter 30 seconds. Beat in brown sugar till combined. Stir in flour and walnuts (mixture will be crumbly). Reserve *½ cup* of the mixture. Press remaining mixture into an 11×7×1½-inch baking pan. Bake in a 350° oven 10 minutes.

2 Mash strawberries; transfer to a small saucepan. Stir in *¼ cup* of the granulated sugar and the cornstarch. Cook and stir till thickened and bubbly. Cook and stir 2 minutes more. Cool slightly.

3 Beat cream cheese, remaining ¼ cup granulated sugar, egg, lemon juice, and vanilla till combined. Spoon atop crust. Spoon strawberry mixture over. Sprinkle with reserved crumbs. Return to oven. Bake for 30 minutes more. Serve slightly warm or chilled. Makes 15 servings.

Nutrition facts per serving: 229 cal., 14 g total fat (7 g sat. fat), 47 mg chol., 114 mg sodium, 23 g carbo., 1 g fiber, 3 g pro. *Daily values:* 12% vit. A, 19% vit. C, 2% calcium, 6% iron.

FAVORITE FRUIT CLAFOUTI

Prep: 15 min. ◆ Bake: 30 min.

This recipe earned Carolyn Ryba of Wixom, Michigan, $400 in the magazine's monthly contest.

 4 **slightly beaten egg whites**
 2 **slightly beaten eggs**
 ⅓ **cup granulated sugar**
 3 **Tbsp. honey**
 2 **Tbsp. fruit liqueur, such as orange or raspberry, or**
 ½ **tsp. rum extract plus**
 2 **Tbsp. orange juice**
 1 **tsp. vanilla**
    Dash salt
1½ **cups plain nonfat yogurt**
 1 **cup all-purpose flour**

◆◆◆

 3 **cups raspberries, blueberries, and/or sliced strawberries**
 2 **tsp. sifted powdered sugar**
    Additional raspberries (optional)
    Edible flowers (optional)

1 In a large bowl beat together the egg whites, whole eggs, granulated sugar, honey, liqueur or rum extract and orange juice, vanilla, and salt with a wire whisk or an electric mixer on low speed till light and frothy. Stir in the yogurt till mixture is smooth. Add flour; beat till combined and mixture is smooth.

2 Grease a 10-inch quiche dish; arrange desired berries in bottom of dish. Pour batter over

fruit. Bake in a 375° oven for 30 to 35 minutes or till center appears set when shaken. Cool on a wire rack for 30 minutes. Serve warm. Just before serving, sprinkle with powdered sugar and, if desired, garnish with additional raspberries and edible flowers. Makes 8 servings.

Nutrition facts per serving: 196 cal., 2 g total fat (0 g sat. fat), 54 mg chol., 93 mg sodium, 36 g carbo., 2 g fiber, 8 g pro. *Daily values:* 3% vit. A, 19% vit. C, 8% calcium, 7% iron.

PEACH AND DOUBLE BERRY CRISP

Prep: 20 min. ◆ Bake: 30 min.

Once baked, the once soft, buttery bread crumbs put the crunch into the crisp.

 3 **cups sliced, peeled peaches**
 1 **cup blueberries**
 1 **cup halved or quartered strawberries or whole raspberries**
 1 **Tbsp. lime juice**
 ⅓ **cup granulated sugar**
 2 **Tbsp. all-purpose flour**

◆◆◆

 ⅓ **cup butter or margarine**
 ½ **cup packed brown sugar**
 2 **Tbsp. all-purpose flour**
 ¼ **tsp. ground cinnamon**
 ¼ **tsp. ground ginger**
 2 **cups soft bread crumbs**
    Vanilla ice cream (optional)

1 In a 2-quart casserole combine peaches, blueberries, strawberries or raspberries, and lime juice. In a small mixing bowl stir together the granulated sugar and the 2 tablespoons flour; stir into fruit mixture. Set aside.

TEST KITCHEN TIP

PEELING THIN-SKINNED FRUIT

Some recipes call for peeled apricots, nectarines, peaches, or tomatoes. To peel these fruits easily, immerse them in boiling water for 20 seconds, then use a sharp paring knife to remove the thin skin. For food safety, avoid eating the skin of the following: avocado, banana, citrus (except when finely shredded), mango, melon, papaya, and pineapple.

2 In a medium saucepan melt butter or margarine; remove from heat. Stir in the brown sugar, the 2 tablespoons flour, the cinnamon, and ginger. Add bread crumbs, tossing to coat. Sprinkle atop fruit mixture.

3 Bake in a 350° oven for 30 to 35 minutes or till the topping is golden and syrup around edges is bubbly. Serve warm with ice cream, if desired. Makes 6 servings.

Nutrition facts per serving: 303 cal., 11 g total fat (6 g sat. fat), 27 mg chol., 187 mg sodium, 51 g carbo., 3 g fiber, 3 g pro. *Daily values:* 14% vit. A, 39% vit. C, 3% calcium, 8% iron.

JULY
All Hands on Deck

30-minute recipes indicated in RED.
Low-fat and no-fat recipes indicated
with a ♥.
Photographs indicated in italics.

Midsummer's heat is on, so who feels like working at a stove? It's time to linger longer on the deck with foods from the grill and from the garden. Hot, hearty meals? Their time will come again. But these are salad days—time to focus on freshness and eat later and lighter. Brighter, too: We know light fare is smart, but it's most appealing now. Consider dishes such as Southwestern Pasta and Bean Salad, Ravioli and Sweet Pepper Salad, Grilled Tomatoes with Pesto, Light Potato Salad, and Tropical Fiesta Steak. And what taste goes better with Independence Day than homemade ice cream? Treat yourself to scoops of Mocha Chip, Taffy Apple, Butter Pecan, and Lime and Lemon.

Menu

Mustard Chicken Barbecue
(see page 166)

◆◆◆

Grilled Tomatoes
with Pesto
(see page 149)

◆◆◆

Toasted Italian bread slices

◆◆◆

Sparkling water with
carambola (star fruit) slices

HERBED SEAFOOD BRUSCHETTA

Start to finish: 35 min.

This recipe earned Edwina Gadspy of Great Falls, Montana, $200 in the magazine's monthly contest.
(See the photograph on page 159.)

1 Tbsp. olive oil
1 Tbsp. lemon juice
1 Tbsp. snipped fresh chives
1 Tbsp. snipped fresh basil
1 Tbsp. snipped fresh mint
1 tsp. bottled minced garlic
6 oz. frozen crabmeat, thawed
   and drained, or one
   6½-oz. can crabmeat,
   drained, flaked, and
   cartilage removed
8 oz. peeled, deveined, and
   cooked shrimp, coarsely
   chopped
1 cup chopped plum tomatoes
½ cup finely chopped onion

◆◆◆

1 8-oz. loaf baguette-style
   French bread

2 Tbsp. olive oil
   Freshly ground pepper
   Fresh chives (optional)

1 In a mixing bowl stir together the 1 tablespoon olive oil, lemon juice, snipped chives, basil, mint, and garlic. Add crabmeat, shrimp, plum tomatoes, and onion; toss to coat.

2 Cut the bread into 48 thin slices. Brush 1 side of each slice with some of the 2 tablespoons olive oil; sprinkle lightly with pepper. Arrange bread, brushed side up, on baking sheet. Broil 3 to 4 inches from heat for 1 to 2 minutes till toasted. Turn and broil other side till toasted. Arrange, oiled side up, on a serving platter; spoon seafood mixture on top. If desired, garnish with additional chives. Serve at once. Makes 48 appetizer servings.

Nutrition facts per serving: 24 cal., 1 g total fat (0 g sat. fat), 12 mg chol., 39 mg sodium, 2 g carbo., 0 g fiber, 2 g pro. *Daily values:* 2% vit. C, 1% iron.

TOMATO-PESTO PIZZA

Prep: 15 min. ◆ Bake: 8 min.

1 3-oz. pkg. cream cheese,
   softened
2 Tbsp. purchased pesto
⅛ tsp. pepper
2 4-oz. Italian bread shells
   (Boboli)
2 plum tomatoes or 1 medium
   tomato, seeded and
   chopped
2 Tbsp. thinly sliced green
   onion (1)
½ cup shredded Monterey Jack
   cheese or mozzarella
   cheese (2 oz.)

1 In a small mixing bowl stir together cream cheese, pesto, and pepper. Spread the pesto mixture atop the Italian bread shells. Top with tomatoes and green onion. Sprinkle with cheese. Place pizzas on a baking sheet. Bake in a 450° oven for 8 to 10 minutes or till heated through. Cut into wedges. Makes 12 appetizer servings.

Nutrition facts per serving: 113 cal., 7 g total fat (2 g sat. fat), 13 mg chol., 170 mg sodium, 9 g carbo., 0 g fiber, 4 g pro. *Daily values:* 5% vit. A, 3% vit. C, 5% calcium, 3% iron.

MEXICAN SHRIMP COCKTAIL

Prep: 20 min. ◆ Chill: 2 to 4 hr.

This recipe earned Gail Popham of Donna, Texas, $400 in the magazine's monthly contest.
(See the photograph on page 159.)

¼ cup catsup
¼ cup lime juice
1 to 2 tsp. bottled hot pepper
   sauce
1 lb. fresh or frozen shrimp,
   peeled, deveined, and
   cooked
½ cup chopped tomato
¼ cup chopped onion
¼ cup snipped fresh cilantro
2 avocados, halved, seeded,
   peeled, and chopped
   Lime wedges (optional)
   Purple flowering kale
   (optional)

1 In a large bowl stir together catsup, lime juice, and hot pepper sauce. Add shrimp, tomato, onion, and cilantro; toss to coat. Cover and chill for 2 to 4 hours.

2 Just before serving, add avocados to the shrimp mixture; toss to coat. If desired, garnish with lime wedges and flowering kale. Makes 8 appetizer servings.

Nutrition facts per serving: 113 cal., 6 g total fat (1 g sat. fat), 65 mg chol., 183 mg sodium, 9 g carbo., 2 g fiber, 8 g pro. *Daily values:* 8% vit. A, 20% vit. C, 1% calcium, 9% iron.

GRILLED TOMATOES WITH PESTO

Prep: 15 min. ◆ Grill: 13 min.

Grilled tomatoes brighten up Mustard Chicken Barbecue (see recipe, page 166) or any barbecue dish. Use as a side dish or quick appetizer while folks are waiting for slower grilled meat dishes.

3 medium firm tomatoes, cored and halved crosswise
¼ cup purchased pesto
6 very thin onion slices

◆◆◆

½ cup shredded Monterey Jack cheese (2 oz.)
⅓ cup smoked almonds, chopped
2 Tbsp. snipped fresh parsley

1 Using a spoon, hollow out the top ¼ inch of tomato halves. Top each tomato half with 2 teaspoons of pesto sauce and an onion slice. Arrange tomatoes in 2 foil pie pans.

2 In a grill with a cover, arrange medium-hot coals around the edge of the grill. Test for medium heat in center of the grill. Place the foil pans containing the

tomatoes in the center of the grill rack, but not over the coals. Cover and grill for 8 to 10 minutes or till tomatoes are heated through.

3 In a small mixing bowl stir together the cheese, almonds, and snipped parsley. Sprinkle mixture over the tomatoes. Cover and grill about 5 minutes more or till cheese melts. If desired, season to taste with *salt* and *pepper*. Makes 6 servings.

Nutrition facts per serving: 170 cal., 14 g total fat (2 g sat. fat), 10 mg chol., 194 mg sodium, 7 g carbo., 2 g fiber, 6 g pro. *Daily values:* 7% vit. A, 23% vit. C, 8% calcium, 4% iron.

LIGHT POTATO SALAD

Prep: 30 min. ◆ Chill: 4 to 24 hr.

Enjoy this simple summer potato salad alongside the Chutney Spareribs (see recipe, page 168) or any hearty grilled meat dish.
(See the photograph on page 158.)

1 lb. whole tiny new potatoes

◆◆◆

¼ cup light dairy sour cream
¼ cup plain low-fat yogurt
¼ cup chopped red sweet pepper
¼ cup chopped yellow sweet pepper
¼ cup thinly sliced celery
¼ cup bite-size strips of carrot
¼ tsp. salt
⅛ tsp. white pepper

1 Scrub potatoes and place in a medium saucepan; add *water* to cover. Bring to boiling; reduce heat. Simmer, covered, about 15 minutes or till just tender. Drain well; cool slightly. Quarter potatoes, leaving skins on.

THE CLEVER COOK

VEGETABLES DO DOUBLE DUTY

After washing and peeling your vegetables for mealtime use, store the vegetable trimmings and peels in a large plastic bag in the freezer. When the bag is full, empty it into a large saucepan. Cover the peels with water, and simmer until the broth cooks down to a concentrated flavor. Strain the broth and use it in soups or sauces. Discard the trimmings or add them to your compost pile. Best veggies to use are carrots, celery, and onions.

Janice M. Owen-Thomas
Kittery Point, Maine

2 Meanwhile, for dressing, in a large mixing bowl combine the sour cream, yogurt, red sweet pepper, yellow sweet pepper, celery, carrot, salt, and white pepper. Carefully stir quartered potatoes into dressing mixture. Cover and chill for 4 to 24 hours. (If the potato salad seems thick after chilling several hours, gently stir in 1 tablespoon *milk* before serving.) Makes 6 side-dish servings.

Nutrition facts per serving: 95 cal., 1 g total fat (0 g sat. fat), 3 mg chol., 114 mg sodium, 19 g carbo., 1 g fiber, 3 g pro. *Daily values:* 25% vit. A, 43% vit. C, 3% calcium, 8% iron.

PREPARATION AND TIMINGS FOR GRILLED VEGETABLES

Asparagus: Snap off and discard tough bases of stems. Precook 2 minutes, then tie asparagus in bundles of 3 or 4 spears with strips of cooked green onion tops. Grill bundles 3 to 5 minutes or till vegetables are of desired doneness.

Small carrots: Cut off carrot tops; wash and peel. Precook 3 minutes. Grill 3 to 5 minutes.

Eggplant: Cut off top and blossom ends. Cut crosswise into ¾-inch-thick slices. Do not precook. Grill 6 to 8 minutes.

Fennel: Snip off feathery leaves. Cut off stems. Precook whole bulbs 8 minutes. Cut bulbs into 6 to 8 wedges and grill 8 to 10 minutes.

Sweet peppers: Remove stems. Quarter peppers and remove seeds and membranes. Cut peppers into 1-inch-wide strips. Do not precook. Grill 8 to 10 minutes.

Leeks: Cut off green tops; trim bulb roots and remove 1 or 2 layers of white skin. Precook 6 to 10 minutes, then halve leeks lengthwise and grill 5 minutes or till tender.

New potatoes: Halve potatoes. Precook 10 minutes or till almost tender. Grill 10 to 12 minutes.

Yellow squash (crookneck or straightneck) or zucchini: Wash; cut off ends. Cut each vegetable lengthwise into strips. Do not precook. Grill 6 to 8 minutes.

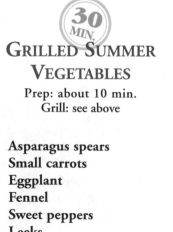

GRILLED SUMMER VEGETABLES

Prep: about 10 min.
Grill: see above

Asparagus spears
Small carrots
Eggplant
Fennel
Sweet peppers
Leeks
New potatoes
Baby zucchini or regular zucchini
Olive oil, melted margarine, or melted butter

1 Before grilling, rinse, trim, cut up, and precook vegetables as directed in "Preparations and Timings for Grilled Vegetables" (see above). To precook any one vegetable, in a saucepan bring a small amount of *water* to boiling; add desired vegetable and simmer, covered, for the time specified. Drain well.

2 To grill, brush vegetables with olive oil, margarine, or butter. Cook vegetables on grill rack directly over medium-hot coals till tender and slightly charred, turning occasionally. Use the timings above as a guide. (Actual timings will differ depending on thickness of vegetables, how hot the coals are, and how far the vegetables are from the coals.)

Nutrition facts per serving (1 new potato, 1 small carrot, 5 asparagus spears, brushed with 1 tablespoon olive oil): 195 cal., 14 g total fat (2 g sat. fat), 0 mg chol., 34 mg sodium, 16 g carbo., 3 g fiber, 3 g pro. *Daily values:* 108% vit. A, 46% vit. C, 2% calcium, 8% iron.

RABE WITH SHELL PASTA

Start to finish: 25 min.

4 oz. medium shell macaroni (2 cups)
8 oz. broccoli rabe
2 Tbsp. olive oil
¼ tsp. coarsely ground pepper
2 cloves garlic, minced
1 2-oz. jar sliced pimiento, drained
¼ cup dry white wine or chicken broth
2 Tbsp. snipped fresh thyme
1 Tbsp. margarine or butter

1 Cook pasta according to package directions. Drain; keep warm. Meanwhile, trim and rinse rabe; cut into small flowerets and short, leafy stems. In a large skillet heat oil over medium heat. Add rabe and pepper; cook and stir 1 minute. Add garlic; cook 1 minute. Add pimiento, wine, thyme, and ⅛ teaspoon *salt;* reduce heat. Simmer, covered, 1 minute or till rabe is tender. Remove from heat. Stir in margarine. Toss with pasta. Makes 4 to 6 side-dish servings.

Nutrition facts per serving: 198 cal., 7 g total fat (1 g sat. fat), 0 mg chol., 118 mg sodium, 26 g carbo., 2 g fiber, 5 g pro. *Daily values:* 32% vit. A, 81% vit. C, 4% calcium, 14% iron.

Parsley Pesto Pasta

Start to finish: 25 min.

Put some zing into your menu—add a side of this dilled pasta to grilled fish or poultry.

8 oz. fettuccine or linguine
1 cup frozen peas

◆◆◆

1 cup lightly packed fresh parsley leaves
2 Tbsp. snipped fresh dillweed or 1 tsp. dried dillweed
1 large clove garlic, quartered
½ of an 8-oz. pkg. reduced-fat cream cheese (Neufchâtel), cut up
⅓ cup light dairy sour cream
2 Tbsp. milk
½ tsp. salt
⅛ tsp. ground pepper

1 Cook pasta according to package directions in lightly *salted water,* adding peas during the last 1 minute of cooking. Drain well; return to saucepan.

2 Meanwhile, in a food processor bowl or blender container, combine parsley, dillweed, and garlic. Cover and process or blend with several on/off turns till finely chopped. Add cream cheese, sour cream, milk, salt, and pepper. Process or blend till well combined. In a small saucepan cook and stir sauce till heated through. Add the sauce to the hot cooked pasta; toss to coat. Makes 6 to 8 side-dish servings.

Nutrition facts per serving: 241 cal., 6 g total fat (3 g sat. fat), 17 mg chol., 296 mg sodium, 37 g carbo., 1 g fiber, 9 g pro. *Daily values:* 14% vit. A, 26% vit. C, 5% calcium, 16% iron.

Gemelli and Dried Tomato Salad

Start to finish: 25 min.

Gemelli is a small pasta that looks like twisted ropes. The corkscrew pasta known as rotini is a good option.

6 oz. gemelli or rotini pasta (1¾ cups)
¼ cup dried tomatoes (not oil-packed)
1 6 oz. jar marinated artichoke hearts

◆◆◆

¼ cup thinly sliced green onions (2)
¼ cup shredded fresh basil
¼ cup snipped fresh Italian parsley
¼ cup white wine vinegar
1 clove garlic, minced

1 Cook pasta according to package directions; drain. Rinse with cold water; drain again. Meanwhile, in a small bowl combine tomatoes and enough *boiling water* to cover; let stand 10 minutes or till softened. Drain; cut tomatoes into thin slivers. Drain artichoke hearts reserving liquid. Quarter artichoke hearts.

2 In a large bowl combine pasta, tomatoes, artichokes, green onions, basil, and parsley. In a screw-top jar combine artichoke liquid, vinegar, garlic, ¼ teaspoon *salt,* and ⅛ teaspoon *pepper;* cover and shake well. Add to pasta mixture; toss. Serve at once or cover and chill up to 24 hours. Makes 6 side-dish servings.

Nutrition facts per serving: 140 cal., 2 g total fat (0 g sat. fat), 0 mg chol., 226 mg sodium, 27 g carbo., 0 g fiber, 5 g pro. *Daily values:* 4% vit. A, 19% vit. C, 1% calcium, 10% iron.

Spinach Pasta Salad

Prep: 25 min. ◆ Chill: Up to 24 hr.

This recipe earned Patricia Sicilia of Newtown, Pennsylvania, $200 in the magazine's monthly contest.

8 oz. ziti pasta (2¼ cups)
1 cup lightly packed fresh spinach leaves
¼ cup lightly packed fresh basil leaves
2 Tbsp. finely shredded Parmesan cheese
2 cloves garlic, quartered
1 Tbsp. olive oil
½ cup light mayonnaise dressing or salad dressing

◆◆◆

¼ cup chopped prosciutto or cooked ham (1 oz.)
2 Tbsp. pine nuts, toasted

1 Cook pasta according to package directions; drain. Rinse with cold water; drain again. In a blender or food processor combine 1 cup spinach, basil, cheese, garlic, ⅛ teaspoon *salt,* and ⅛ teaspoon *pepper.* Add oil and 1 tablespoon *water;* cover and blend till nearly smooth and mixture forms a paste, scraping down sides. Combine mayonnaise and spinach mixture. Add to pasta; toss. Cover; chill up to 24 hours.

2 Serve in a *spinach and radicchio*-lined bowl. Sprinkle with prosciutto or ham and pine nuts. Makes 6 to 8 side-dish servings.

Nutrition facts per serving: 277 cal., 13 g total fat (2 g sat. fat), 2 mg chol., 310 mg sodium, 32 g carbo., 1 g fiber, 8 g pro. *Daily values:* 6% vit. A, 4% vit. C, 3% calcium, 13% iron.

THE CLEVER COOK

CREATE HERB MIX FROM LEFTOVERS

I love to cook with my fresh herbs but usually cut more than I need for a recipe. I can't bear to throw the extra herbs away, so I chop them and spread them on a plate to dry. When dry, I put them in a jar labeled "herb mix," and use them to season winter soups and stews.

Renee Pachta
Wamego, Kansas

CORN AND TOMATO PASTA SALAD

Prep: 25 min. ◆ Chill: 2 to 24 hr.

This recipe earned Jenny Spencer of Syracuse, New York, $400 in the magazine's monthly contest.

3 oz. farfalle pasta (bow ties) (1½ cups)

2 fresh ears of corn or 1 cup loose-pack frozen whole kernel corn

◆◆◆

1 cup shredded, cooked chicken

1 large tomato, seeded and chopped (about ¾ cup)

¼ cup olive oil

3 Tbsp. vinegar

2 to 3 Tbsp. purchased pesto

1 Tbsp. chicken broth or water

¼ tsp. salt

⅛ tsp. pepper

◆◆◆

Romaine leaves

2 Tbsp. finely shredded Parmesan cheese
Snipped fresh basil

1 Cook pasta according to package directions. Drain pasta. Rinse with cold water; drain again. Meanwhile, if using fresh corn, cut the kernels off the cobs. Cook corn, covered, in *boiling water* about 4 minutes or till tender; drain. If using frozen corn, cook according to package directions; drain. Let cool slightly.

2 In a large bowl combine pasta, corn, chicken, and tomato. In a screw-top jar combine the olive oil, vinegar, pesto, chicken broth or water, salt, and pepper. Cover and shake well. Pour over pasta mixture; toss gently to coat. Cover and chill 2 to 24 hours.

3 To serve, line a serving platter with romaine leaves. Arrange salad atop romaine. Sprinkle with Parmesan cheese and basil. Makes 8 side-dish servings.

Nutrition facts per serving: 194 cal., 12 g total fat (2 g sat. fat), 28 mg chol., 146 mg sodium, 14 g carbo., 1 g fiber, 9 g pro. *Daily values:* 3% vit. A, 9% vit. C, 2% calcium, 7% iron.

30 MIN. LOW FAT

SOUTHWESTERN PASTA AND BEAN SALAD

Start to finish: 30 min.

6 oz. wagon wheel pasta, rigatoni, or macaroni (2 cups)

1 cup loose-pack frozen whole kernel corn

1 15-oz. can black beans, rinsed and drained

½ cup shredded carrot

1 or 2 fresh jalapeño peppers, seeded and finely chopped*

½ of a medium red onion, thinly sliced and separated into rings

¼ cup picante sauce or salsa

2 Tbsp. vinegar

2 Tbsp. salad oil

2 tsp. sugar

½ tsp. ground cumin
Shredded leaf lettuce

2 Tbsp. snipped fresh cilantro

1 Cook pasta according to package directions, adding corn during the last 1 minute of cooking; drain. Rinse pasta and corn with cold water; drain again.

2 Combine pasta-corn mixture, beans, carrot, jalapeños, and red onion. Combine picante sauce, vinegar, oil, sugar, and cumin. Add to pasta mixture; toss to coat. Serve at once or cover and chill up to 8 hours. Serve atop lettuce; sprinkle with cilantro. Makes 8 side-dish servings.

*****Note:** Because hot peppers contain pungent oils, be sure to protect your hands when preparing them. Wear gloves or sandwich bags so your skin doesn't come in contact with the peppers. Always wash your hands and nails thoroughly in hot, soapy water after handling chili peppers.

Nutrition facts per serving: 179 cal., 4 g total fat (1 g sat. fat), 0 mg chol., 192 mg sodium, 31 g carbo., 3 g fiber, 7 g pro. *Daily values:* 25% vit. A, 18% vit. C, 3% calcium, 14% iron.

ZESTY PASTA SALAD

Start to finish: 30 min.

You can hold the tomatoes and chill the salad up to 24 hours. Before serving, let salad stand at room temperature 30 minutes, then toss in the tomatoes.

- 8 oz. rotini pasta (3⅓ cups)
- 1 9-oz. pkg. frozen Italian green beans
- 1 cup cubed fontina or provolone cheese (4 oz.)
- 1 cup cherry tomatoes, halved
- ¼ cup diced prosciutto or cooked ham (1 oz.)

◆◆◆

- ¼ cup balsamic vinegar
- 3 Tbsp. olive oil
- 2 tsp. Dijon-style mustard
- 2 cloves garlic, minced
- 1 tsp. dried oregano, crushed
- ½ tsp. crushed red pepper
- ⅛ tsp. ground black pepper
  Leaf lettuce

1 In a large pot cook pasta in *boiling water* for 5 minutes. Add green beans; return to boiling. Cook for 8 to 10 minutes more or till pasta is tender; drain. Rinse with cold water; drain again. In a large mixing bowl combine pasta-bean mixture, cheese, tomatoes, and prosciutto or ham.

2 In a screw-top jar combine vinegar, oil, mustard, garlic, oregano, red pepper, and black pepper. Cover and shake well. Drizzle over pasta mixture; toss. Serve on lettuce-lined plates. Makes 8 side-dish servings.

Nutrition facts per serving: 240 cal., 11 g total fat (3 g sat. fat), 16 mg chol., 218 mg sodium, 27 g carbo., 1 g fiber, 9 g pro. *Daily values:* 9% vit. A, 14% vit. C, 8% calcium, 11% iron.

RAVIOLI AND SWEET PEPPER SALAD

Prep: 30 min. ◆ Chill: 2 to 6 hr.

You can substitute one 9-ounce package of refrigerated cheese-filled ravioli for the dried ravioli.

- 1 cup dried miniature cheese-filled ravioli (about ½ of an 8-oz. pkg.)
- 1½ cups chopped red, yellow, and/or green sweet pepper
- 1 cup shredded fresh spinach
- ¼ cup thinly sliced green onions (2)
- ¼ cup sliced pitted ripe olives (optional)

◆◆◆

- 3 Tbsp. white wine vinegar
- 2 Tbsp. salad oil
- 2 tsp. honey
- 2 tsp. snipped fresh thyme or ½ tsp. dried thyme, crushed
- 1 clove garlic, minced
- ¼ tsp. dry mustard

1 Cook pasta according to package directions; drain. Rinse with cold water; drain again. In a large bowl combine pasta, sweet peppers, spinach, green onions, and, if using olives.

2 In a screw-top jar combine vinegar, oil, honey, thyme, garlic, mustard, and ¼ teaspoon *salt.* Cover and shake well. Pour over pasta mixture; toss to coat. Cover and chill 2 to 6 hours. If desired, let stand 30 minutes at room temperature before serving. Makes 6 side-dish servings.

Nutrition facts per serving: 193 cal., 10 g total fat (4 g sat. fat), 38 mg chol., 277 mg sodium, 20 g carbo., 0 g fiber, 7 g pro. *Daily values:* 15% vit. A, 65% vit. C, 9% calcium, 8% iron.

SHRIMP AND SCALLOP BROCHETTES

Prep: 20 min. ◆ Marinate: 2 to 4 hr. Grill: 6 min.

For summer fare, serve these lightly sweetened seafood morsels with a salad of spring greens, fresh melon, and crackerlike breadsticks.

- 1 lb. sea scallops
- ¼ cup cooking oil
- ¼ cup whiskey
- ¼ cup stone-ground mustard
- 2 Tbsp. honey
- 2 Tbsp. vinegar
- 1 Tbsp. soy sauce
- ½ tsp. bottled hot pepper sauce
- ¼ tsp. salt
- 1½ lb. fresh medium to large shrimp, peeled and deveined (about 40 pieces)

1 Halve large scallops (you should have about 40 pieces). In a 2- or 3-quart rectangular baking dish combine oil, whiskey, mustard, honey, vinegar, soy sauce, hot pepper sauce, and salt. Add the shrimp and scallops, stirring to coat. Cover and chill for 2 to 4 hours, stirring occasionally.

2 To serve, drain the shrimp and scallops, discarding the marinade. On long metal skewers alternately thread the shrimp and scallops. (Or, thread a scallop in the "curl" of each shrimp.) Grill the kabobs on rack of an uncovered grill directly over medium coals for 6 to 8 minutes or till scallops are opaque, turning once. Makes 8 servings.

Nutrition facts per serving: 116 cal., 3 g total fat (0 g sat. fat), 126 mg chol., 283 mg sodium, 2 g carbo., 0 g fiber, 19 g pro. *Daily values:* 4% vit. A, 2% vit. C, 5% calcium, 18% iron.

ROCK LOBSTER TAILS

Start to finish: 30 min.

To perk up your picnic, serve these succulent lobster tails with a dilled dipping sauce and a lightly dressed coleslaw.

4   medium (6 oz. each) fresh or frozen rock lobster tails, thawed

♦♦♦

1   lemon or lime
2   Tbsp. olive oil
2   cloves garlic, minced
1   tsp. chili powder

♦♦♦

½   cup light mayonnaise dressing or salad dressing
1   tsp. snipped fresh dillweed or ¼ tsp. dried dillweed
    Lemon or lime wedges
    Fresh tarragon sprigs (optional)

1 With kitchen shears or large sharp knife, cut through center of hard top shell and meat of lobster tail. Do not cut through under-shell. Spread tails open, butterfly style, to expose meat on top (see below). Set lobster aside.

2 Finely shred lemon or lime to make ½ teaspoon peel; set peel aside. Squeeze juice from lemon or lime to make 4 to 5 teaspoons juice. In a small bowl combine *half* the lemon or lime juice with the olive oil, garlic, and chili powder. Brush on exposed lobster meat, reserving extra sauce.

3 Grill lobster, meaty side down, on the rack of an uncovered grill directly over medium coals for 6 to 10 minutes or till meat is opaque, turning once halfway through cooking and brushing again with remaining sauce. *Do not overcook.*

4 Meanwhile, for dipping sauce, in a small bowl combine light mayonnaise dressing or salad dressing, dillweed, lemon or lime peel, and remaining lemon or lime juice. If desired, split lobster tails in half lengthwise. Serve with dill sauce and fresh lemon or lime wedges. If desired, garnish each plate with tarragon sprigs. Makes 4 servings.

Nutrition facts per serving: 272 cal., 18 g total fat (3 g sat. fat), 78 mg chol., 640 mg sodium, 5 g carbo., 0 g fiber, 22 g pro. *Daily values:* 5% vit. A, 4% vit. C, 5% calcium, 3% iron.

SPICY SHRIMP GAZPACHO

Prep: 20 min. ♦ Chill: 2 to 24 hr.

2   cups chopped, peeled tomatoes
2   cups tomato juice
1   cup beef or vegetable broth
2   medium peaches or nectarines, peeled and chopped (1½ cups)
½   cup chopped, seeded cucumber
¼   cup sliced green onions (2)
¼   cup snipped fresh cilantro
2   medium fresh jalapeño peppers, seeded and finely chopped*
2   Tbsp. lime juice
2   Tbsp. tequila (optional)
1   clove garlic, minced
1   tsp. sugar
    Several dashes bottled hot pepper sauce

♦♦♦

1   8-oz. pkg. frozen, peeled, cooked shrimp, thawed
    Tortilla chips (optional)
    Dairy sour cream (optional)

1 In a large mixing bowl stir together the tomatoes, tomato juice, broth, peaches or nectarines, cucumber, green onions, cilantro, jalapeño peppers, lime juice, tequila (if desired), garlic, sugar, and bottled hot pepper sauce. Cover and chill mixture 2 to 24 hours.

2 Just before serving, stir in shrimp. If desired, serve with tortilla chips and sour cream. Makes 4 to 6 main-dish servings.

***Note:** Because hot peppers contain pungent oils, be sure to protect your hands when preparing them. Wear gloves or sandwich bags over your hands so your skin doesn't come in contact with the peppers. Always wash your hands and nails thoroughly in hot, soapy water after handling chili peppers.

Nutrition facts per serving: 153 cal., 1 g total fat (0 g sat. fat), 111 mg chol., 761 mg sodium, 23 g carbo., 4 g fiber, 15 g pro. *Daily values:* 24% vit. A, 98% vit. C, 4% calcium, 22% iron.

FAT: HOW LOW SHOULD YOU GO?

You Don't Have to Count Every Fat Gram

Most health professionals agree that we Americans are still eating too much fat (about 34 percent of our total calorie intake). Dietary fat is important, but fear of eating fat has become nothing less than a cultural phobia.

Fat need not be a "four-letter word." An essential nutrient, dietary fat is needed for nerve coverings, transportation of certain vitamins, and cell structure. So what amount of fat should worry us?

30 Percent, or 20 Percent?

To lower risk of heart disease, the American Dietetic Association and the United States Department of Agriculture (USDA), through their dietary guidelines, recommend 30 percent of your total daily calories come from fat. That's about 67 grams fat in a 2,000-calorie-a-day diet—or the equivalent of less than 5 tablespoons of oil.

But some health and fitness experts, pointing to the epidemic of heart disease and diabetes in our country, recommend 20 percent or less, or 44 grams fat in a 2,000-calorie day.

Who's right? Both (30 percent and 20 percent) are good targets for their own reasons. However, the numbers are only that: targets to aim for, not absolutes. The three things that matter most when focusing on your fat intake are how healthy you are, the total number of fat calories you eat over time, and what your activity level is.

The Relaxed Approach

Mealtimes are meant for crunching food, not numbers, so here's the "skinny": The 30 percent target ought to suit you fine if you are moderately active (exercising a half-hour or more every day), have no diagnosed health problems, have normal blood cholesterol (200 mg or less), and have normal triglyceride levels (less than 150 mg).

Regardless of outside pressure—if you're active, healthy, and within normal weight limits for your height, you may not gain significant health benefit by following a strict, ultra-low-fat diet.

More and more research indicates that dietary fat has less of an adverse effect on active people with normal blood cholesterol than was previously believed. Some studies have gone so far as to suggest that, for some inactive people, a diet too low in fat could be detrimental. In the absence of fat, the body uses carbohydrates to make fat, which may lead to a rise in cholesterol.

Who Should Eat More Lean?

Fat intake has been linked to diseases such as diabetes, and breast, colon, and other cancers. Those at high risk for these diseases may want to lower the fat in their diet to 20 percent. Persons with diagnosed cardiovascular problems—including high cholesterol and triglycerides—also benefit from a 20 percent fat diet. Also, if you have a liver disease, your doctor may place you on a specialized low-fat diet.

A Question of Balance

The idea of balance—especially where it concerns diet—is that you allow for differences over time. An average of 30 percent calories from fat means some foods, or even whole days, can have more. Some can have less. For example, let's say you have a day where lunch is a cheeseburger and fries, and you can't keep your spoon out of the ice cream carton; you end the day with nearly half your calories having come from fat.

The following day you eat a salad for lunch, steamed chicken breast and veggies for dinner, and an apple for dessert—under 20 percent of calories from fat. The two-day average is 30 percent. If at the end of the week your total fat intake is around 30 percent, you're doing fine.

Separating Fat from Calories

Cutting fat, yet increasing calories—say, eating twice as many cookies as usual because they're fat-free—makes you gain weight. Studies show that this is precisely what happens when fat-bearing foods are "oversubstituted" with their fat-free versions. Putting more calories in your body—whether from fat, carbohydrates, or protein—than you use up with activity leads to weight gain.

Stay Active

Activity is vital: 30 minutes or more of exercise each day can do more to reduce disease risk than dropping fat intake by a few percentage points.

CURRIED SEA AND SHORE KABOBS

Prep: 25 min. ◆ Grill: 12 min.

Pork is leaner than ever, and you can find a bounty of high-quality shellfish in your supermarket. Our favorite version of surf-and-turf is lower in fat than traditional steak and lobster.
(See the photograph on page 157.)

8 oz. fresh or frozen jumbo
    shrimp in shells
2 Tbsp. cooking oil
2 Tbsp. finely chopped onion
¼ tsp. finely shredded lime
    peel
4 tsp. lime juice
¾ tsp. curry powder
1 clove garlic, minced
8 oz. boneless pork loin roast,
    cut into 1-inch cubes
¼ of a fresh pineapple cut into
    1-inch cubes (about 1 cup)
3 plums, pitted and quartered

◆◆◆

½ of a papaya, halved, seeded,
    peeled, and cut into 1- to
    1½-inch cubes
   Mixed salad greens
    (optional)

1 Thaw shrimp, if frozen. Peel and devein shrimp; set aside. For glaze, stir together cooking oil, onion, lime peel, lime juice, curry powder, and garlic. On four 8-inch skewers thread pork, pineapple, and plums. If desired, season with *salt* and *pepper*.

2 Grill kabobs on rack of uncovered grill directly over medium coals for 12 to 14 minutes or till meat is done, turning once. Use half of the glaze to occasionally brush kabobs.

3 Meanwhile, on 4 additional 8-inch skewers thread the shrimp and the papaya pieces. Grill the kabobs directly over medium coals for 10 to 12 minutes or till the shrimp turns opaque, occasionally brushing kabobs with remaining glaze and turning once. If desired, garnish with mixed salad greens. Makes 4 servings.

Nutrition facts per serving: 201 cal., 11 g total fat (2 g sat. fat), 91 mg chol., 96 mg sodium, 11 g carbo., 1 g fiber, 15 g pro. *Daily values:* 8% vit. A, 38% vit. C, 2% calcium, 10% iron.

**30 MIN.
LOW FAT**

SPEEDY SALMON FILLETS

Prep: 15 min. ◆ Grill: 8 min.

As long as you have the grill going, throw some summer vegetables on, too.
(See the photograph on page 157.)

1½ lb. boneless, skinless fresh
     salmon fillet or tuna,
     halibut, or swordfish
     steaks, about 1 inch thick
3   Tbsp. lemon juice
2   cloves garlic, minced
2   Tbsp. snipped fresh basil or
     1 tsp. dried basil, crushed
1   Tbsp. cooking oil
1   Tbsp. soy sauce
1   tsp. Worcestershire sauce
¼   tsp. pepper

◆◆◆

Ti leaves (optional)*
Lemon wedges (optional)
Grilled vegetables, such as
  asparagus, new potatoes,
  and sweet peppers (see
  page 150) (optional)

1 Rinse fish; pat dry. Cut fish into 6 serving-size pieces. In a small mixing bowl combine lemon juice, garlic, basil, oil, soy sauce, Worcestershire sauce, and pepper; brush mixture over fish.

2 Place fish fillets on the rack of an uncovered grill over medium coals or in a greased grill basket, turning thin ends under to make an even thickness. Grill fillets 4 to 6 minutes per ½-inch thickness or till fish flakes easily when tested with a fork, brushing occasionally with remaining sauce. (If fish is 1 inch or thicker, turn halfway through grilling.)

3 If desired, serve on ti leaves, with lemon wedges and grilled vegetables. Makes 6 servings.

***Note:** If using ti leaves, be sure they have not been sprayed or treated in a way that would make them unsafe for contact with food. Wash them thoroughly before using. Use leaves as garnish and wrappers for steaming and grilling food. They are not toxic, but they should not be eaten.

Nutrition facts per serving: 130 cal., 6 g total fat (1 g sat. fat), 20 mg chol., 248 mg sodium, 1 g carbo., 0 g fiber, 16 g pro. *Daily values:* 2% vit. A, 9% vit. C, 1% calcium, 6% iron.

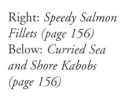

Right: *Speedy Salmon Fillets (page 156)*
Below: *Curried Sea and Shore Kabobs (page 156)*

Left: *Chutney Spareribs (page 168) and Light Potato Salad (page 149)*
Top: *Mexican Shrimp Cocktail (page 148)*
Above: *Herbed Seafood Bruschetta (page 148)*

Above: *Toasted Almond Ice Cream (page 173) and Miracle Mocha Chip Ice Cream (page 171)*
Left: *Cream Cheese Ice Cream (page 172)*

Opposite page:
Top left: *Peach-a-Berry Cobbler (page 174)*
Top right: *Taffy Apple Ice Cream (page 173)*
Bottom: *Lime and Lemon Ice Cream (page 171)*

Left: *Roasted Ratatouille (page 180)*
Below: *Lamb Kefta (page 182)*
Opposite: *Seafood Skewers (page 179)*

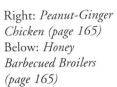

Right: *Peanut-Ginger Chicken (page 165)*
Below: *Honey Barbecued Broilers (page 165)*

PEANUT-GINGER CHICKEN

Prep: 25 min.
Marinate: 12 to 24 hr.
Grill: 50 min.

East meets West when we pair this Asian-style chicken with chilled fruit salsa and Napa Cabbage Slaw. (See the photograph on page 164.)

12 chicken thighs (about 3 lb.)

♦♦♦

½ cup water
½ cup creamy peanut butter
¼ cup bottled chili sauce
¼ cup soy sauce
2 Tbsp. salad oil
2 Tbsp. vinegar
4 cloves garlic, minced
1 Tbsp. grated gingerroot or
   ¾ tsp. ground ginger
¼ to ½ tsp. ground red pepper

♦♦♦

1 cup chopped fresh fruit,
   such as peeled peaches,
   nectarines, pears, or plums
1 cup chopped, seeded
   cucumber
2 Tbsp. thinly sliced green
   onion (1)
1 Tbsp. sugar
1 Tbsp. salad oil
1 Tbsp. vinegar

♦♦♦

1 recipe Napa Cabbage Slaw
   (optional) (see right)
   Peach, nectarine, pear, or
   plum wedges (optional)

1 If desired, remove skin from chicken. Rinse chicken and pat dry with paper towels. Place the chicken in a plastic bag set in a shallow bowl.

2 For marinade, in a medium mixing bowl gradually stir water into peanut butter. (The mixture will stiffen at first.) Stir in chili sauce, soy sauce, the 2 tablespoons salad oil, the 2 tablespoons vinegar, the garlic, gingerroot or ginger, and red pepper. Pour over chicken. Seal bag; turn to coat chicken with marinade. Chill for 12 to 24 hours; turn occasionally.

3 For salsa, in a medium mixing bowl combine chopped fruit, cucumber, green onion, sugar, the 1 tablespoon oil, and the 1 tablespoon vinegar. Cover and chill for 1 to 2 hours.

4 In a grill with a cover, arrange medium-hot coals around a drip pan. Test for medium heat above the pan. Remove chicken from marinade; discard marinade. Place chicken on the grill rack over the drip pan but not over the coals. Cover and grill chicken for 50 to 60 minutes or till tender and no longer pink. Spoon salsa onto plates; serve chicken atop salsa. If desired, serve with Napa Cabbage Slaw and garnish with fruit wedges. Makes 6 servings.

Napa Cabbage Slaw: In a large mixing bowl combine 3 cups finely shredded *Napa cabbage,* 1 cup finely shredded *bok choy,* and 2 to 3 tablespoons of very thin *red sweet pepper strips.* In a small mixing bowl stir together ¼ cup *seasoned rice vinegar or white vinegar* and 1 tablespoon *toasted sesame oil.* Immediately toss dressing with the salad mixture. Makes 6 side-dish servings.

Nutrition facts per serving of chicken and salsa: 455 cal., 30 g total fat (7 g sat. fat), 103 mg chol., 715 mg sodium, 12 g carbo., 2 g fiber, 34 g pro.
Daily values: 10% vit. A, 8% vit. C, 2% calcium, 14% iron.

HONEY BARBECUED BROILERS

Prep: 15 min. ♦ Chill: 2 hr.
Grill: 50 min.

This simple recipe from nearly 30 years ago has been updated slightly to reduce fat and intensify flavor. (See the photograph on page 164.)

1 2½- to 3-lb. broiler-fryer
   chicken, quartered
4 cloves garlic, minced
1½ tsp. dried marjoram, crushed
1 tsp. dry mustard
¼ tsp. salt
¼ tsp. freshly ground pepper
2 Tbsp. honey
2 Tbsp. balsamic vinegar
   Torn mixed greens (optional)

1 If desired, remove skin from chicken. Rinse chicken and pat dry with paper towels. Stir together garlic, marjoram, mustard, salt, and pepper; rub mixture into chicken pieces. Combine honey and vinegar; lightly brush over entire surface of chicken pieces. Cover and chill at least 2 hours.

2 In a grill with a cover, arrange medium-hot coals around a drip pan. Test for medium heat above the pan. Place chicken pieces, bone side down, on the grill rack over the drip pan but not over the coals. Cover and grill for 50 to 60 minutes or till chicken is tender and no longer pink. If desired, serve chicken atop torn mixed greens. Makes 4 servings.

Nutrition facts per serving: 316 cal., 15 g total fat (4 g sat. fat), 99 mg chol., 227 mg sodium, 12 g carbo., 0 g fiber, 31 g pro.
Daily values: 5% vit. A, 4% vit. C, 2% calcium, 13% iron.

MUSTARD CHICKEN BARBECUE

Prep: 20 min. ◆ Marinate: 4 to 24 hr.
Grill: 50 min.

Experiment with various flavored mustards to add a different spin to this simple glaze.

4 **chicken legs (thigh-drumstick piece) or 4 each drumsticks and thighs (about 3 lb. total) or 4 chicken breast halves (about 2 lb. total)**
◆◆◆
½ **cup Dijon-style mustard**
3 **Tbsp. vinegar**
4 **tsp. Worcestershire sauce**
1 **tsp. snipped fresh thyme or ⅛ tsp. dried thyme, crushed**
◆◆◆
2 **Tbsp. light-flavored molasses**

1 If desired, remove skin from chicken. Rinse chicken and pat dry with paper towels. Place chicken in a plastic bag in a shallow dish; set aside.

2 For marinade, stir together mustard, vinegar, Worcestershire sauce, and thyme till smooth. Pour marinade over the chicken. Seal the bag and turn to coat the chicken with marinade. Chill for 4 to 24 hours, turning the bag occasionally. Drain the chicken, reserving marinade. Measure ⅓ cup marinade; set aside to use to make the sauce.

3 In a grill with a cover, arrange medium-hot coals around a drip pan. Test for medium heat above the drip pan. Place the chicken pieces, bone side down, on the grill rack over the drip pan but not over the coals. Cover and grill for 50 to 60 minutes or till tender and no longer pink, brushing occasionally with remaining marinade. *(Do not brush during the last 5 minutes of grilling.)*

4 Meanwhile, in a small saucepan, combine the ⅓ cup reserved marinade and the molasses. Heat to boiling; reduce heat. Simmer, covered, for 5 minutes. Pass sauce with chicken. Makes 4 servings.

Nutrition facts per serving: 327 cal., 17 g total fat (4 g sat. fat), 103 mg chol., 904 mg sodium, 10 g carbo., 0 g fiber, 31 g pro. *Daily values:* 4% vit. A, 14% vit. C, 3% calcium, 15% iron.

TROPICAL FIESTA STEAK

Prep: 30 min. ◆ Marinate: 12 to 24 hr. ◆ Grill: 18 min.

For a quick side dish, partially cook 2 medium yams, let cool, then cut into ½-inch-thick slices. Grill with onion wedges for 7 to 9 minutes on each side.

¼ **cup frozen orange juice concentrate, thawed**
3 **Tbsp. cooking oil**
2 **Tbsp. honey**
1 **Tbsp. spicy brown mustard or Dijon-style mustard**
1 **Tbsp. sliced green onion**
1 **tsp. snipped fresh mint or ¼ tsp. dried mint, crushed**
Several dashes bottled hot pepper sauce
1½ **lb. boneless beef sirloin steak, cut 1 to 1½ inches thick**
◆◆◆
½ **cup chopped red sweet pepper**
½ **cup chopped red apple**
½ **cup chopped pear**
½ **cup chopped, peeled peach**
¼ **cup chopped celery**
2 **Tbsp. sliced green onion (1)**
2 **tsp. lemon juice**
◆◆◆
Romaine leaves (optional)
Grilled sliced yams (optional)
Grilled red onion wedges (optional)

1 For marinade, in a small mixing bowl stir together orange juice concentrate, cooking oil, honey, mustard, 1 tablespoon sliced green onion, mint, and hot pepper sauce. Set aside ¼ cup of the mixture to make the relish; cover and chill till needed. Place the steak in a plastic bag set in a shallow bowl. Pour the remaining

HOW HOT IS HOT?

Some foods need to be grilled hot and fast, some low and slow. To gauge how hot the coals in your grill are, hold the palm of your hand a few inches over the center of the grill rack. If you can hold your hand there two seconds or less, the coals are hot; three seconds would be medium-hot, four for medium, and five for medium-slow coals.

When grilling indirectly, hot coals will provide medium-hot heat at the cooking site, and medium-hot coals will provide medium heat.

marinade over meat. Seal the bag and turn to coat the meat with marinade. Chill for 12 to 24 hours, turning bag occasionally.

2 For relish, in a medium bowl combine reserved ¼ cup marinade, sweet pepper, apple, pear, peach, celery, the 2 tablespoons green onion, and the lemon juice. Cover and chill for up to 24 hours.

3 Remove the steak from the plastic bag, reserving marinade. Grill steak on the rack of an uncovered grill directly over medium coals to desired doneness, turning once and brushing occasionally with marinade till the last 10 minutes of grilling. Allow 18 to 22 minutes for medium doneness for a 1-inch-thick steak or 36 to 40 minutes for medium doneness for a 1½-inch-thick steak.

4 To serve, bias-slice steak into thin strips. If desired, arrange strips of steak on romaine leaves. Top steak with fruit relish. If desired, serve with yam slices and onion wedges. Makes 6 servings.

Nutrition facts per serving: 300 cal., 16 g total fat (5 g sat. fat), 76 mg chol., 91 mg sodium, 13 g carbo., 1 g fiber, 27 g pro. *Daily values:* 8% vit. A, 51% vit. C, 1% calcium, 20% iron.

INDONESIAN SATÉ

Prep: 25 min. ◆ Marinate: 4 to 24 hr.

Grill: 12 min.

Saté (pronounced sah-TAY), grilled skewers of meat served with peanut sauce, is an Indonesian favorite.

1   lb. boneless beef round steak or sirloin steak, cut into 1½-inch cubes
1   lb. lean boneless lamb, cut into 1½-inch cubes
8   oz. skinless, boneless turkey breast, cut into 1½-inch cubes

◆◆◆

1   cup purchased unsweetened coconut milk
1   small onion, finely chopped
2   cloves garlic, minced
2   tsp. dry mustard
2   tsp. ground coriander
½   tsp. ground turmeric
¼   tsp. salt
¼   tsp. ground cumin

◆◆◆

10 green onions, trimmed and each cut into 4 pieces

◆◆◆

1   recipe Peanut Sauce (see page 168)
    Hot rice pilaf (optional)
    Grilled split sugarcane* (optional)

1 Place the cubed beef, lamb, and turkey in a plastic bag set in a shallow bowl. Set aside.

2 For marinade, in a mixing bowl combine coconut milk, onion, garlic, dry mustard, coriander, turmeric, salt, and cumin; mix well. Pour marinade over the meat. Seal the bag and turn to coat meat with marinade. Chill for several hours or overnight, turning the bag occasionally. Drain the meat, reserving the marinade.

3 On twenty 8-inch skewers, alternately thread beef, lamb, turkey, and green onion pieces. Grill kabobs on rack of uncovered grill directly over medium coals for 12 to 16 minutes for medium doneness for beef and lamb and till turkey is no longer pink; brush with marinade during first half of grilling and turn once.

4 To serve, arrange 2 kabobs on each of 10 dinner plates. Serve kabobs with Peanut Sauce. If desired, serve with pilaf and garnish plates with sugarcane. Makes 10 servings.

*Note: To grill sugarcane, saw the cane into 2- to 3-inch sections, then very carefully split each section lengthwise with a sharp knife. Spray the open side lightly with nonstick spray coating and grill, split side down, for 1 to 2 minutes.

Nutrition facts per serving, without sauce: 189 cal., 9 g total fat (6 g sat. fat), 62 mg chol., 108 mg sodium, 2 g carbo., 0 g fiber, 23 g pro. *Daily values:* 2% vit. A, 4% vit. C, 1% calcium, 15% iron.

Safety First And Always

You can't match the fun of a backyard barbecue, but you will need to "match" the coals—and that's where you'll be playing with fire. Here are a few tips to keep you from having too hot a time at your next grill fest:

◆ Use only fire starters certified for use on outdoor grills. Never use gasoline, kerosene, or other flammable or nonfoodsafe liquids to start your coals.

◆ Don't store gas cylinders, starter fluids, and other flammable substances indoors or near sources of heat. Be sure gas cylinder connectors and regulators are in good condition and hooked up according to the manufacturer's instructions.

◆ Even though the weather is hot, short-sleeved clothing isn't the safest apparel to wear when using a grill. Lightweight long sleeves and slacks, plus a long apron protects you from spatters and singes. Watch for loosely hanging apron strings, sleeves, and shirttails.

◆ Keep a water-filled spray bottle nearby to douse minor flareups and baking soda for grease flare-ups. Make sure a fire extinguisher is readily available. Don't move a grill when it is hot or flaming.

◆ Always use the right tools for the job: long-handled barbecue forks and tongs, fireproof mitts, and barbecue baskets for smaller foods.

◆ Don't leave a lit grill unattended. Children should never be allowed to operate a grill.

PEANUT SAUCE
Start to finish: 20 min.

Some like it hot! If you want to turn up the "burn" on this peanut sauce recipe, stir in a little ground red pepper to taste.

2 Tbsp. sliced green onion (1)
1 clove garlic, minced
¾ cup reduced-sodium chicken broth or beef broth
1 Tbsp. reduced-sodium soy sauce
½ tsp. finely shredded lemon peel
1 Tbsp. lemon juice
1 to 1½ tsp. chili powder
½ tsp. brown sugar
⅓ cup peanut butter
1 Tbsp. grated gingerroot or ¾ tsp. ground ginger

◆◆◆

Purchased unsweetened coconut milk (optional)

1 In a small saucepan cook green onion and garlic in the broth, covered, about 2 minutes or till onion is tender. Add soy sauce, lemon peel, lemon juice, chili powder, and brown sugar. Bring to boiling; reduce heat. Simmer sauce, uncovered, for 5 minutes, stirring the mixture frequently. Stir in the peanut butter and the gingerroot or ginger; let mixture heat gently through without boiling.

2 If desired, thin sauce with a little unsweetened coconut milk. Serve at room temperature. Cover and chill the peanut sauce to store. Makes about 1½ cups.

Nutrition facts per tablespoon: 35 cal., 3 g total fat (1 g sat. fat), 0 mg chol., 90 mg sodium, 2 g carbo., 0 g fiber, 2 g pro. Daily values: 1% vit. C.

Chutney Spareribs
(see below)

◆◆◆

Light Potato Salad
(see page 149)

◆◆◆

Corn on the cob

◆◆◆

Chocolate pound cake with fresh fruit and sweetened whipped cream

CHUTNEY SPARERIBS
Prep: 15 min. ◆ Cook: 1 hr.
Grill: 15 min.

Our first barbecue story in 1941 dubbed spareribs "the most satisfactory cut of fresh pork for this type of cooking." Some things never change. (See the photograph on page 158.)

3 to 4 lb. meaty pork spareribs or loin back ribs

◆◆◆

1 cup snipped chutney
¼ cup bottled chili sauce
2 Tbsp. vinegar
1 Tbsp. Worcestershire sauce
1 tsp. dry mustard
½ tsp. onion powder
Several dashes bottled hot pepper sauce

◆◆◆

Fresh thyme sprigs (optional)

1 Cut ribs into serving-size pieces. Place ribs in a large pot. Add enough *water* to cover ribs. Bring to boiling; reduce heat. Simmer, covered, about 1 hour or till meat is tender. Drain ribs; sprinkle lightly with *salt*.

2 For sauce, in a medium saucepan combine the chutney, chili sauce, vinegar, Worcestershire sauce, dry mustard, onion powder, hot pepper sauce, and 1 tablespoon *water*. Cook and stir over medium heat till heated.

3 Place ribs, meaty side down, on rack of an uncovered grill directly over medium coals. Grill 10 minutes. Turn ribs meaty side up; brush with some of the sauce. Grill 5 minutes more. If desired, garnish ribs with fresh thyme sprigs. Pass remaining warmed sauce. Makes 6 servings.

Nutrition facts per serving: 421 cal., 23 g total fat (9 g sat. fat), 70 mg chol., 297 mg sodium, 29 g carbo., 1 g fiber, 23 g pro. *Daily values:* 4% vit. A, 13% vit. C, 4% calcium, 14% iron.

OUTDOOR BURGERS

Prep: 15 min. ◆ Grill: 14 min.

Our updated version of the perennially favorite outdoor hamburger uses 90-percent lean beef. The Basil-Mozzarella Cheeseburger version is the same burger dressed up, Italian-style.

- ¼ **cup finely chopped onion**
- 2 **Tbsp. fine dry bread crumbs**
- 2 **Tbsp. finely chopped green sweet pepper (optional)**
- 2 **Tbsp. catsup**
- 1 **Tbsp. prepared horseradish**
- 1 **Tbsp. prepared mustard**
- ¼ **tsp. salt**
- ¼ **tsp. ground black pepper**
- 1 **lb. extra-lean ground beef**
- 4 **whole wheat hamburger buns, split and toasted**
  Shredded radicchio (optional)
  Fresh dillweed (optional)

THE CLEVER COOK

NONSTICK GRILLING

To prevent food from sticking to the grill, spray the food, rather than the grill, with nonstick cooking spray. It works especially well with foods that tend to stick or fall apart such as vegetables, fish, or poultry.

Mary A. Campbell
Condon, Oregon

Red and yellow cherry tomato halves (optional)

1 In a medium mixing bowl combine onion, bread crumbs, and, if desired, green pepper. Add catsup, horseradish, mustard, salt, and black pepper. Add ground beef; mix well. Shape the meat mixture into four ¾-inch-thick patties.

2 Grill patties on the rack of an uncovered grill directly over medium coals for 14 to 18 minutes or till no pink remains, turning once halfway through grilling.

3 Serve burgers on toasted whole wheat buns. If desired, top with shredded radicchio, fresh dillweed, and cherry tomato halves. Makes 4 servings.

Nutrition facts per serving: 336 cal., 13 g total fat (5 g sat. fat), 71 mg chol., 632 mg sodium, 27 g carbo., 1 g fiber, 25 g pro. *Daily values:* 4% vit. C, 6% calcium, 24% iron.

Basil-Mozzarella Cheeseburgers: Prepare burgers as directed, except add 1 slice *smoked or regular mozzarella cheese* to each patty during the last 2 minutes of grilling.

Serve on toasted whole wheat buns with *fresh basil leaves* and 1 tablespoon *Red Sweet Pepper Relish* (see recipe, below).

30 MIN. LOW FAT

RED SWEET PEPPER RELISH

Prep: 10 min.

With just 1 gram of fat per tablespoon, this relish makes an excellent low-fat condiment for grilled burgers.

- ½ **cup purchased roasted red sweet pepper strips**
- 1 **Tbsp. finely chopped pitted ripe olives**
- 2 **tsp. olive oil**
- 2 **tsp. snipped fresh thyme or ½ tsp. dried thyme, crushed**
- ¼ **tsp. ground black pepper**

1 In a food processor bowl combine red sweet pepper strips, ripe olives, olive oil, fresh or dried thyme, and black pepper. Cover and process with several on-off turns till coarsely chopped. Cover and chill till ready to serve. Makes about ⅔ cup.

Nutrition facts per tablespoon: 10 cal., 1 g total fat (0 g sat. fat), 0 mg chol., 4 mg sodium, 1 g carbo., 0 g fiber, 0 g pro. *Daily values:* 3% vit. A, 31% vit. C.

STRAWBERRY GELATO

Prep: 1 hr. ◆ Chill: 4 to 24 hr.
Ripen: 4 hr.

*Italian gelato is made with milk
rather than cream, resulting
in a lower fat content than most
other ice creams.*

3 cups cut-up strawberries

◆◆◆

6 cups milk
1⅓ cups sugar
12 beaten egg yolks
**Several drops red food
coloring (optional)**

1 Place berries in a blender container or food processor bowl. Cover and blend or process till nearly smooth; set aside.

2 In a large saucepan combine *3 cups* of the milk, the sugar, and egg yolks. Cook and stir over medium heat till mixture coats a spoon. (Dip a spoon into the custard and draw a line with your finger through the coating. The custard is done when the edges along the line keep their shape.) Remove from heat. Stir in the remaining milk, the berries, and, if desired, food coloring.

3 Cover surface of gelato mixture with plastic wrap and refrigerate several hours or overnight. (Or, place saucepan in a sink of ice water to chill quickly.) Freeze in a 4- or 5-quart ice-cream freezer according to the manufacturer's directions. Ripen 4 hours. Makes 2½ quarts (20 servings).

Nutrition facts per serving: 130 cal., 5 g total fat (2 g sat. fat), 133 mg chol., 41 mg sodium, 19 g carbo., 0 g fiber, 4 g pro. *Daily values:* 23% vit. A, 22% vit. C, 8% calcium, 3% iron.

BUTTER PECAN ICE CREAM

Prep: 50 min. ◆ Ripen: 4 hr.

*This scrumptious ice cream
is buttery rich with lightly
toasted pecans.*

1 cup coarsely chopped pecans
½ cup granulated sugar
2 Tbsp. butter or margarine

◆◆◆

**4 cups half-and-half or light
cream**
2 cups packed brown sugar
4 tsp. vanilla
4 cups whipping cream

1 In a heavy 8-inch skillet combine pecans, granulated sugar, and butter or margarine. Cook mixture over medium heat, stirring constantly, for 6 to 8 minutes or till sugar melts and turns a rich brown color. Remove from heat and spread nuts on a buttered baking sheet or foil; separate into clusters. Set aside and allow to cool completely. Break the clusters into small chunks, setting aside ¼ cup to sprinkle on top of ice cream.

2 In a large bowl combine half-and-half or light cream, brown sugar, and vanilla; stir till sugar is dissolved. Stir in the pecan mixture and whipping cream. Freeze in a 4- or 5-quart ice-cream freezer according to manufacturer's directions. Ripen 4 hours. Serve with reserved broken pecan clusters. Makes about 3½ quarts (28 servings).

Nutrition facts per serving: 259 cal., 20 g total fat (11 g sat. fat), 61 mg chol., 39 mg sodium, 19 g carbo., 0 g fiber, 2 g pro. *Daily values:* 20% vit. A, 5% calcium, 2% iron.

ROCKY ROAD ICE CREAM

Prep: 40 min. ◆ Chill: 2 to 4 hr.
Ripen: 4 hr.

*Serve as a sundae in 4-inch wafer
ice-cream cups with fudge topping,
miniature chocolate pieces,
chopped nuts, whipped cream, and
a cherry on top.*

**2 oz. unsweetened chocolate,
chopped**
**1 14-oz. can (1¼ cups)
sweetened condensed milk**
1 cup water
2 cups whipping cream
1 cup chopped walnuts
1 tsp. vanilla
**1⅓ cups tiny marshmallows,
halved**

1 In a medium saucepan melt the chocolate over medium-low heat, stirring constantly. Gradually stir in sweetened condensed milk till combined. Gradually stir in the water. Remove from heat. Pour half the mixture into a blender container. Cover and blend till smooth. Transfer to a bowl. Repeat with other half of mixture. Cover surface of mixture with plastic wrap and refrigerate till chilled thoroughly.

2 Stir whipping cream, walnuts, and vanilla into the chilled mixture. Freeze in a 4- or 5-quart ice-cream freezer according to the manufacturer's directions. Stir in marshmallows before ripening. Ripen 4 hours. Makes about 1 quart (8 servings).

Nutrition facts per serving: 524 cal., 39 g total fat (19 g sat. fat), 98 mg chol., 91 mg sodium, 40 g carbo., 1 g fiber, 8 g pro. *Daily values:* 31% vit. A, 3% vit. C, 16% calcium, 7% iron.

LIME AND LEMON ICE CREAM

Prep: 40 min. ◆ Ripen: 4 hr.

For citrus curls, use a zester to cut the lemon or lime peel into long strips. Wrap strips around a chopstick or drinking straw and let sit for 30 minutes. Cut to desired lengths. (See the photograph on page 161.)

4 cups whole milk
1½ cups sugar
1 cup whipping cream
1 tsp. finely shredded lemon peel
⅓ cup lemon juice
1 tsp. finely shredded lime peel
3 Tbsp. lime juice
 Several drops yellow food coloring (optional)

◆◆◆

Lemon and/or lime slices and curls (optional)

1 In a large mixing bowl thoroughly combine milk, sugar, whipping cream, lemon peel, lemon juice, lime peel, lime juice, and, if desired, food coloring. (Mixture may appear curdled.)

2 Freeze in a 3- to 4-quart ice-cream freezer according to the manufacturer's directions. Ripen 4 hours. If desired, garnish with lemon and lime slices and curls. Makes 2 quarts (16 servings).

Nutrition facts per serving: 164 cal., 8 g total fat (5 g sat. fat), 29 mg chol., 36 mg sodium, 23 g carbo., 0 g fiber, 2 g pro. *Daily values:* 8% vit. A, 6% vit. C, 6% calcium.

MIRACLE MOCHA CHIP ICE CREAM

Prep: 50 min. ◆ Chill: 4 to 24 hr.
Ripen: 4 hr.

The "miracle" is in the way the melted chocolate forms chips after it is stirred into the cooled custard mixture. (See the photograph on page 160.)

2½ cups sugar
¼ cup cornstarch
3 Tbsp. instant coffee powder or crystals
½ tsp. salt
8 cups half-and-half or light cream

◆◆◆

6 slightly beaten eggs
2 Tbsp. vanilla

◆◆◆

3 oz. unsweetened chocolate, chopped

◆◆◆

Chocolate shavings (optional)
Melted chocolate (optional)

1 In a large saucepan combine sugar, cornstarch, coffee powder or crystals, and salt. Stir in *4 cups* of the half-and-half or light cream. Cook and stir over medium heat till mixture is thickened and bubbly.

2 Gradually stir 1 cup of the hot mixture into the eggs; return to hot mixture in saucepan. Cook and stir 2 minutes more. Cover surface of mixture with plastic wrap and refrigerate till chilled thoroughly. Stir in remaining cream and the vanilla.

WHAT IS RIPENING?

"Ripening" means allowing the newly made ice cream to firm up undisturbed in the ice-cream maker. It improves both the flavor and texture of the finished product. To ripen, drain off excess liquid from the freezer bucket. Remove dasher from canister; cover canister with waxed paper, plastic wrap, or foil and replace the lid. Plug the hole in the lid with a cork. Push the can back down into the ice. Using 4 parts ice to 1 part rock salt, pack additional layers of ice and rock salt into the freezer to cover the top of the can. Cover the freezer with newspapers or a heavy cloth to keep it cold. Allow to stand, out of direct sunlight, at least 4 hours, repacking with additional ice and rock salt as needed.

3 In a small heavy saucepan melt the unsweetened chocolate over low heat, stirring constantly. While chocolate is still hot, pour it very slowly into chilled mixture, stirring constantly.

4 Freeze in a 5-quart ice-cream freezer according to manufacturer's directions. Ripen 4 hours. If desired, garnish with chocolate shavings and melted chocolate. Makes about 1 gallon (32 servings).

Nutrition facts per serving: 177 cal., 10 g total fat (5 g sat. fat), 63 mg chol., 71 mg sodium, 21 g carbo., 0 g fiber, 3 g pro. *Daily values:* 8% vit. A, 5% calcium, 2% iron.

ICE-CREAM-MAKING TIPS

To ensure that your ice cream turns out as delicious as it did in the Better Homes and Gardens® Test Kitchen, follow these hints:

Use only rock salt, a very coarse, unrefined salt usually found in bags next to the rest of the salt in your grocery store. In some communities, however, it's sold in hardware stores. It's important to use rock salt because its larger crystals melt the ice more slowly with the result that the ice cream freezes more evenly.

Mix the rock salt and ice in a ratio of 6 parts crushed ice or very small cubes to 1 part salt. For ripening use 4 parts ice to 1 part salt. On hot days, when the temperature is above 75 degrees, plan on changing the salt and ice mixture about two hours into the ripening process. Don't try to ripen ice cream in a home freezer; it's not cold enough to get the ice cream sufficiently hard.

Use only the milk products called for; ice cream is an indulgence and should be treated that way. Unless called for in the recipe, don't substitute one dairy product with a similar but lower fat product; substituting will produce an icy, watery result.

TOASTED COCONUT ICE CREAM

Prep: 40 min. ◆ Chill: 1½ to 2 hr.
Ripen: 4 hr.

Chewy toasted coconut turns vanilla ice cream into a sweet tropical snowball.

2 12-oz. cans (3 cups total) evaporated milk
1 cup sugar
4 tsp. vanilla
2 cups whipping cream
1⅓ cups flaked coconut, toasted*
    Coconut shell cups** and coconut curls (optional)

1 In a small saucepan combine evaporated milk and sugar. Cook and stir till sugar dissolves; remove from heat. Stir in vanilla. Cool slightly. Cover surface with plastic wrap and refrigerate 1½ to 2 hours or till well chilled. Stir in whipping cream and coconut. Freeze in a 3- to 4-quart ice-cream freezer according to manufacturer's directions. Ripen 4 hours. If desired, serve in coconut cups and garnish with coconut curls. Makes 1½ quarts (12 servings).

*Note: To toast coconut, spread in a single layer in a shallow baking pan. Bake in a 350° oven for 5 to 10 minutes or till light golden brown, stirring occasionally.

**Note: To make coconut shell cups, locate the three soft eyes at top of coconut. Pierce eyes and drain coconut milk. Lay coconut on side and with a hammer, tap firmly till nut begins to crack. Rotate one quarter turn and tap

again. Continue turning and tapping till coconut cracks into pieces; use as serving bowls.

For curls, separate meat from shell in large pieces. Cut slices from a long edge, using a vegetable peeler. Arrange slices on a baking sheet. Bake in a 350° oven for 2 to 3 minutes or till edges just start to brown. Cool in pan on wire rack. Store in a tightly covered shallow container.

Nutrition facts per serving: 339 cal., 23 g total fat (12 g sat. fat), 73 mg chol., 101 mg sodium, 28 g carbo., 0 g fiber, 6 g pro. *Daily values:* 22% vit. A, 2% vit. C, 15% calcium, 2% iron.

CREAM CHEESE ICE CREAM

Prep: 50 min. ◆ Chill: 4 to 24 hr.
Ripen: 4 hr.

This thick and sinfully delicious ice cream really does taste just like a slice of creamy cheesecake.
(See the photograph on page 160.)

5 cups half-and-half or light cream
2½ cups sugar
4 beaten eggs
3 8-oz. pkg. cream cheese or reduced-fat cream cheese (Neufchâtel), softened
◆◆◆
1 tsp. finely shredded lemon peel
2 Tbsp. lemon juice
2 tsp. vanilla
    Fresh blueberries, nectarines, and/or dark cherries (optional)

1 In a large saucepan combine *3 cups* of the half-and-half or light cream, the sugar, and eggs. Cook and stir over medium heat just till boiling. In a large mixing bowl beat cream cheese with an electric mixer till smooth; gradually beat in hot mixture. Cover surface with plastic wrap and refrigerate till chilled thoroughly.

2 Stir in remaining half-and-half, lemon peel, lemon juice, and vanilla. Freeze in a 4- or 5-quart ice-cream freezer according to manufacturer's directions. Ripen 4 hours. If desired, garnish with choice of fresh fruit. Makes about 3 quarts (24 servings).

Nutrition facts per serving: 260 cal., 17 g total fat (10 g sat. fat), 85 mg chol., 116 mg sodium, 24 g carbo., 0 g fiber, 5 g pro. *Daily values:* 20% vit. A, 1% vit. C, 6% calcium, 3% iron.

TOASTED ALMOND ICE CREAM
Prep: 1 hr. ◆ Chill: 1 to 2 hr.
Ripen: 4 hr.

Pair with a scoop of Miracle Mocha Chip Ice Cream, page 171, and add chocolate curls, melted chocolate, or chocolate sauce.
(See the photograph on page 160.)

½ **cup sugar**
2 **cups milk**
◆◆◆
2 **cups whipping cream**
½ **cup sugar**
4 **slightly beaten egg yolks**
½ **tsp. almond extract**
◆◆◆
¾ **to 1 cup toasted almonds, chopped**
Fresh raspberries (optional)
Chocolate curls* (optional)
Chocolate sauce (optional)

1 In a small heavy saucepan cook the ½ cup sugar over medium-high heat till sugar begins to melt, shaking the skillet occasionally to heat the sugar evenly. *Do not stir.* Once the sugar starts to melt, reduce heat to low and cook about 5 minutes more or till all of the sugar is melted and golden, stirring as needed with a wooden spoon. Remove from heat.

2 In a small saucepan heat the 2 cups milk till bubbles just form around edge of liquid. *Do not allow to boil.* Gradually stir warmed milk into cooked sugar. Cook and stir over medium heat till sugar is dissolved.

3 In a medium bowl combine whipping cream, ½ cup sugar, and egg yolks. Stir in 1 cup of the warmed milk mixture. Return to saucepan. Cook and stir over medium heat till mixture just comes to a boil; remove from heat. Stir in almond extract. Cover and chill for 1 to 2 hours or till mixture is cooled completely.

4 Freeze in a 4- to 5-quart ice-cream freezer according to manufacturer's directions. Stir in nuts. Ripen 4 hours. If desired, garnish with raspberries, chocolate curls, and chocolate sauce. Makes 1½ quarts (12 servings).

*Note: To make chocolate curls, warm a chocolate bar in your hand, then carefully shave curls from the bar with a sharp vegetable peeler.

Nutrition facts per serving: 290 cal., 21 g total fat (11 g sat. fat), 128 mg chol., 61 mg sodium, 22 g carbo., 1 g fiber, 5 g pro. *Daily values:* 30% vit. A, 1% vit. C, 8% calcium, 3% iron.

TAFFY APPLE ICE CREAM
Prep: 45 min. ◆ Chill: 4 to 24 hr.
Ripen: 4 hr.

Granny Smith or other tart apples work best in this flavorful ice cream. (See the photograph on page 161.)

1 **cup granulated sugar**
½ **cup packed brown sugar**
2 **12-oz. cans (3 cups total) evaporated milk**
1 **Tbsp. molasses**
4 **beaten eggs**
2 **cups whipping cream**
3 **cups peeled, cored, and finely chopped apples**
1 **tsp. vanilla**
Apple slices (optional)
Caramel ice-cream topping (optional)

1 In a medium saucepan combine granulated sugar, brown sugar, evaporated milk, and molasses. Cook and stir over medium heat till sugar dissolves; remove from heat. Slowly stir 1 cup of hot milk mixture into the beaten eggs; return to hot mixture in saucepan. Cook and stir over low heat just till bubbling; *do not boil.* Remove from heat. Cool slightly. Cover surface with plastic wrap and refrigerate till chilled.

2 Stir whipping cream, apples, and vanilla into chilled mixture. Freeze in a 4- or 5-quart ice-cream freezer according to manufacturer's directions. Ripen 4 hours. If desired, garnish with apple slices and caramel topping. Makes about 2 quarts (16 servings).

Nutrition facts per serving: 272 cal., 16 g total fat, (9 g sat. fat), 108 mg chol., 79 mg sodium, 28 g carbo., 0 g fiber, 5 g pro. *Daily values:* 19% vit. A, 3% vit. C, 13% calcium, 3% iron.

PEACH-A-BERRY COBBLER

Prep: 30 min. ◆ Bake: 35 min.

For a taste of summer during the winter months, substitute frozen berries and canned peaches for the fresh, using ½ cup peach syrup in place of the cold water.
(See the photograph on page 161.)

1 cup all-purpose flour
½ cup granulated sugar
1½ tsp. baking powder
½ cup milk
¼ cup butter or margarine, softened

◆◆◆

¼ cup packed brown sugar
1 Tbsp. cornstarch
½ cup cold water
3 cups sliced fresh peaches
1 cup fresh blueberries
1 Tbsp. butter or margarine
1 Tbsp. lemon juice
2 Tbsp. coarse granulated sugar
¼ tsp. ground nutmeg or cinnamon

1 For topping, combine flour, ½ cup granulated sugar, and baking powder. Add milk and ¼ cup butter all at once. Stir till smooth.

2 For filling, in a medium saucepan stir together brown sugar and cornstarch; stir in water. Add fruit; cook and stir over medium heat till thickened and bubbly. Add 1 tablespoon butter and lemon juice; stir till butter melts. Pour into a 1½-quart ungreased casserole. Spoon topping in mounds over hot filling; spread evenly over filling. Sprinkle with a mixture of coarse sugar and nutmeg. Place on a shallow baking pan in oven.

THE CLEVER COOK

MEMORY GAME

Keep summer fun with a memory game that kids can make and play. Clean frozen juice lids. Place stickers on the lids, making sure each has a partner. Arrange the lids sticker side down. The kids overturn two lids at a time, remembering where the partner for each lid is.

Gail Lainhart
Spokane, Washington

---

3 Bake cobbler in a 350° oven about 35 minutes or till bubbly and a wooden toothpick inserted into crust comes out clean. If desired, serve warm with *vanilla ice cream.* Makes 6 servings.

Nutrition facts per serving: 328 cal., 10 g total fat (6 g sat. fat), 27 mg chol., 203 mg sodium, 58 g carbo., 3 g fiber, 4 g pro. *Daily values:* 14% vit. A, 16% vit. C, 10% calcium, 9% iron.

PINEAPPLE-SOUR CREAM PIE

Prep: 35 min. ◆ Bake: 15 min.
Cool: 1 hr. ◆ Chill: 3 to 6 hr.

3 egg whites
½ cup sugar
2 Tbsp. all-purpose flour
1 20-oz. can crushed pineapple, undrained
1 8-oz. carton dairy sour cream
3 slightly beaten egg yolks
1 baked 9-inch pastry shell (see recipe, page 190)
½ tsp. vanilla
¼ tsp. cream of tartar
6 Tbsp. sugar

1 Let egg whites stand at room temperature for 30 minutes. Meanwhile, for filling, in a 1½-quart saucepan combine the ½ cup sugar and flour. Stir in undrained pineapple and sour cream. Cook and stir over medium heat till thickened and bubbly; reduce heat. Cook and stir for 2 minutes more. Gradually stir 1 cup of the hot filling into egg yolks; return all to saucepan. Bring to a gentle boil. Cook and stir for 2 minutes more. Pour hot filling into baked pie shell.

2 For meringue, add vanilla and cream of tartar to egg whites in bowl. Beat with an electric mixer on medium speed about 1 minute or till soft peaks form (tips curl). Gradually add the 6 tablespoons sugar, 1 tablespoon at a time, beating on high speed about 4 minutes or till mixture forms stiff, glossy peaks and sugar is dissolved.

3 Immediately spread the meringue onto hot filling, pushing meringue into the pastry edge so the pie is completely sealed. Bake in a 350° oven for at least 15 minutes or till meringue is golden. Cool for 1 hour on a wire rack. Chill for 3 to 6 hours. Cover loosely and chill for longer storage. Makes 8 servings.

Nutrition facts per serving: 365 cal., 17 g total fat (6 g sat. fat), 92 mg chol., 107 mg sodium, 50 g carbo., 1 g fiber, 6 g pro. *Daily values:* 19% vit. A, 11% vit. C, 4% calcium, 9% iron.

AUGUST
Along Country Roads

30-minute recipes indicated in RED.
Low-fat and no-fat recipes indicated
with a ♥.
Photographs indicated in italics.

*T*ake a weekend drive in the country and visit roadside stands ripe with fresh produce. Amble among the booths at a farmers' market and follow the menu cues that abound. You can add an international flavor to your local fare with recipes for Insalata Mista, Mediterranean Cucumber Yogurt-Mint Soup, Farfalle with Spinach and Mushrooms, and Oriental Chicken Salad. Summertime state fairs showcase the pride of farmers and gardeners and exhibit blue-ribbon baking. Follow their lead at home with Almond Macaroons, a refreshing Nectarine-Pistachio Tart, and prize-tested White Chocolate-Banana Cream Pie.

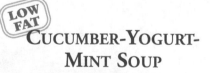

CUCUMBER-YOGURT-MINT SOUP

Prep: 15 min. ◆ Chill: 2 to 24 hr.

The combination of ingredients used here is a Mediterranean mainstay that shows up in soups, salads, and sauces.

1 large cucumber

❖❖❖

1 8-oz. carton plain low-fat yogurt
1 Tbsp. lime juice
1 tsp. honey
½ tsp. ground cumin

¼ tsp. salt
2 Tbsp. milk (optional)
⅓ cup snipped fresh mint
Fresh mint sprigs

1 Peel cucumber; cut in half lengthwise. Scoop out seeds and discard. Cut the cucumber into ½-inch-thick slices (1½ cups).

2 In a blender container or food processor combine cucumber, yogurt, lime juice, honey, cumin, and salt. Cover and blend or process till smooth. If desired, blend in milk. Stir in snipped mint. Cover and chill soup 2 to 24 hours. Stir before serving. Garnish with fresh mint sprigs. Makes 4 side-dish servings.

Nutrition facts per serving: 56 cal., 1 g total fat (1 g sat. fat), 3 mg chol., 176 mg sodium, 8 g carbo., 1 g fiber, 4 g pro. *Daily values:* 4% vit. A, 17% vit. C, 10% calcium, 11% iron.

INSALATA MISTA (MIXED GREENS SALAD)

Prep: 20 min.

Fresh mozzarella, also called buffalo mozzarella, has a sweet flavor and soft texture. Find it in Italian markets, cheese shops, and specialty delis. (See the photograph on page 203.)

4 cups torn mixed greens, such as radicchio, spinach, arugula, and/or chicory
1 cup yellow and/or red cherry tomatoes, halved
½ cup Greek black olives
¼ cup snipped fresh basil
1 recipe Italian Vinaigrette (see above right)
3 oz. thinly sliced fresh mozzarella cheese

1 In a large salad bowl toss together the mixed greens, tomatoes, olives, and snipped basil. Drizzle Italian Vinaigrette over salad and toss to coat. Top with mozzarella cheese. Makes 4 side-dish servings.

Italian Vinaigrette: In a screw-top jar combine 2 tablespoons *olive oil or salad oil*, 2 tablespoons *balsamic vinegar*, 2 teaspoons *snipped fresh oregano or basil*, ⅛ teaspoon *salt*, and ⅛ teaspoon *pepper*. Cover and shake well. Serve immediately or cover and chill for up to 2 weeks. Shake before serving.

Nutrition facts per serving: 169 cal., 14 g total fat (4 g sat. fat), 16 mg chol., 255 mg sodium, 7 g carbo., 2 g fiber, 6 g pro. *Daily values:* 28% vit. A, 34% vit. C, 13% calcium, 9% iron.

COUSCOUS-ARTICHOKE SALAD

Prep: 20 min.

In Morocco, a special two-tiered pot is used to cook couscous, the country's national dish. We've simplified the method but retained the flavors. (See the photograph on page 202.)

1½ cups chicken broth
1 cup couscous
⅓ cup finely chopped onion
1 to 2 Tbsp. finely chopped fresh jalapeño pepper*
¼ tsp. ground cinnamon
¼ tsp. ground black pepper

❖❖❖

1 9-oz. pkg. frozen artichoke hearts, thawed and cut up
1⅓ cups cut up tomato
¾ cup finely chopped green sweet pepper

¼ cup raisins
¼ cup olive oil
¼ cup balsamic vinegar

1 In a medium saucepan bring broth to boiling. Add couscous and onion. Remove from heat. Cover and let stand 5 minutes. Stir in jalapeño pepper, cinnamon, and black pepper; cool.

2 In a large bowl combine couscous mixture with artichoke hearts, tomato, sweet pepper, and raisins. Whisk together the olive oil and balsamic vinegar; pour over couscous, tossing gently to coat. Makes 8 side-dish servings.

*Note: Because hot peppers contain pungent oils, be sure to protect your hands when preparing them. Wear gloves or sandwich bags so your skin doesn't come in contact with the peppers. Always wash your hands and nails thoroughly in hot, soapy water after handling chili peppers.

Nutrition facts per serving: 209 cal., 7 g total fat (1 g sat. fat), 0 mg chol., 189 mg sodium, 31 g carbo., 7 g fiber, 6 g pro. *Daily values:* 4% vit. A, 56% vit. C, 2% calcium, 10% iron.

GREEK SALAD

Start to finish: 15 min.

Feta cheese—a key ingredient in Greek cooking—gets its sharp, salty flavor from the brine in which it is cured. (See the photograph on page 203.)

3 medium tomatoes, cut into wedges
1 medium cucumber, halved lengthwise and thinly sliced

1 small red onion, cut into thin wedges
1 recipe Greek Vinaigrette (see below)
8 to 10 Greek black olives
½ cup crumbled feta cheese (2 oz.)

1 In a salad bowl combine the tomatoes, cucumber, and red onion. Add Greek Vinaigrette; toss to coat. Sprinkle with Greek olives and feta cheese. Makes 4 side-dish servings.

Greek Vinaigrette: In a screw-top jar combine 2 tablespoons *olive oil or salad oil;* 2 tablespoons *lemon juice;* 2 teaspoons snipped *fresh oregano* or ½ teaspoon *dried oregano,* crushed; ⅛ teaspoon *salt;* and ⅛ teaspoon *pepper.* Cover and shake well.

Nutrition facts per serving: 143 cal., 12 g total fat (3 g sat. fat), 12 mg chol., 273 mg sodium, 9 g carbo., 2 g fiber, 4 g pro. *Daily values:* 9% vit. A, 43% vit. C, 8% calcium, 5% iron.

30 MIN.
LOW FAT

SUMMER SQUASH-CARROT MEDLEY

Prep: 20 min. ◆ Cook: 5 min.

See the photograph on page 199.

2 medium carrots, thinly sliced
2 small yellow summer squash, halved lengthwise and sliced ¼ inch thick
2 small zucchini, halved lengthwise and sliced ¼ inch thick
◆◆◆
1 Tbsp. lemon juice
1 Tbsp. olive oil
1 Tbsp. snipped fresh dillweed or 1 tsp. dried dillweed

THE CLEVER COOK

TOO MANY TOMATOES?

When your tomato plants have been especially prolific, just wash and dry the extra tomatoes, core them, and pop them whole into self-seal plastic bags in the freezer. When you're ready to use tomatoes in sauces, chili, soups, or stews, dip the frozen whole tomato in warm water for a few seconds. The peel slips right off. Thaw tomatoes in a bowl before cutting and using them.

Hazel Bergerson
Sisseton, South Dakota

1 In a medium saucepan cook carrots, covered, in a small amount of *boiling water* for 2 minutes. Add summer squash and zucchini. Cook for 3 to 5 minutes more or till crisp-tender; drain. Transfer vegetables to a serving bowl.

2 Meanwhile, combine the lemon juice, olive oil, dillweed, and ¼ teaspoon *salt.* Pour over the vegetables and toss lightly to coat. Makes 6 side-dish servings.

Nutrition facts per serving: 45 cal., 2 g total fat (0 g sat. fat), 0 mg chol., 106 mg sodium, 6 g carbo., 2 g fiber, 1 g pro. *Daily values:* 58% vit. A, 9% vit. C, 1% calcium, 2% iron.

RISOTTO WITH LEEKS AND RADICCHIO

Prep: 20 min. ◆ Cook: 20 min.

Be sure to stir in the radicchio at the last minute. Its brilliant ruby coloring fades quickly when mixed with the warm rice.
(See the photograph on page 200.)

2 medium leeks, white part only, cleaned and thinly sliced (about ⅔ cup)
2 cloves garlic, minced
1 Tbsp. olive oil
1 cup Arborio rice or short-grain rice
◆◆◆
3 cups reduced-sodium chicken broth
◆◆◆
½ cup radicchio or curly endive, finely shredded
¼ cup freshly shredded Parmesan cheese
3 Tbsp. snipped Italian parsley or curly-leaf parsley
Green onions (optional)
Cracked black pepper

1 In a large saucepan cook leeks and garlic in hot oil till tender. Add uncooked rice. Cook and stir over medium heat for 5 minutes.

2 Meanwhile, in another saucepan bring broth to boiling; reduce heat and simmer. Slowly add *1 cup* of the hot broth to the rice mixture, stirring constantly. Continue to cook and stir over medium heat till liquid is absorbed. Add another *½ cup* of the broth to the rice mixture, stirring constantly. Continue to cook and stir till liquid is absorbed. Add another *1 cup* broth, ½ cup at a time, stirring constantly till broth has been absorbed. (This should take about 15 minutes.)

3 Stir in the remaining ½ cup broth. Cook and stir till rice is slightly creamy and just tender (add additional broth, if necessary, and cook till rice is just tender). Stir in the shredded radicchio or endive, Parmesan cheese, and parsley. If desired, garnish with green onions. Serve immediately. Pass cracked pepper. Makes 6 side-dish servings.

Nutrition facts per serving: 178 cal., 4 g total fat (0 g sat. fat), 3 mg chol., 380 mg sodium, 29 g carbo., 2 g fiber, 6 g pro. *Daily values:* 1% vit. A, 8% vit. C, 5% calcium, 12% iron.

FARFALLE WITH SPINACH AND MUSHROOMS

Start to finish: 25 min.

If you're using spinach that hasn't been washed, be sure to rinse it well because it often is very sandy.
(See the photograph on page 203.)

6 oz. farfalle pasta (bow ties) (3 cups)
◆◆◆
1 Tbsp. margarine or butter
¾ cup chopped onion
1 cup sliced fresh mushrooms, such as portobello, chanterelle, shiitake, and/or cremini
2 cloves garlic, minced
4 cups thinly sliced fresh spinach or 2 cups thinly sliced sorrel and 2 cups thinly sliced fresh spinach
1 tsp. snipped fresh thyme
⅛ tsp. pepper

1 Tbsp. licorice liqueur (optional)
2 Tbsp. finely shredded Parmesan cheese

1 Cook farfalle pasta according to package directions. Drain.

2 Meanwhile, in a large skillet melt the margarine or butter over medium heat. Add onion, mushrooms, and garlic. Cook and stir for 2 to 3 minutes or till mushrooms are nearly tender. Stir in spinach or sorrel and spinach, thyme, and pepper; cook about 1 minute or till heated through and spinach is slightly wilted. Stir in cooked pasta and, if desired, liqueur; toss gently to mix. Sprinkle with Parmesan cheese. Makes 4 side-dish servings.

Nutrition facts per serving: 214 cal., 6 g total fat (1 g sat. fat), 39 mg chol., 127 mg sodium, 33 g carbo., 2 g fiber, 9 g pro. *Daily values:* 42% vit. A, 29% vit. C, 8% calcium, 24% iron.

GOLDEN ITALIAN FLATBREAD

Prep: 20 min. ◆ Chill: 1 hr.
Bake: 20 min.

Escape the routine by cutting this flatbread into triangles or diamond shapes instead of squares. Better yet, experiment with your family's favorite cookie cutters.

1½ cups milk
2 Tbsp. margarine or butter
¾ cup milk
½ cup quick-cooking farina
¼ tsp. salt
1 beaten egg
⅓ cup grated Parmesan cheese

1 Line a 13×9×2-inch baking pan with foil; grease foil. Set aside.

2 In a medium saucepan bring the 1½ cups milk and the margarine or butter to boiling. Meanwhile, stir together the ¾ cup milk, the farina, and salt; slowly add to boiling milk, stirring constantly. Cook and stir for 3 to 4 minutes or till very thick and mixture just begins to bubble. Remove from heat; gradually stir hot mixture into egg. Stir in the Parmesan cheese. Pour mixture into prepared baking pan; spread evenly. Cool; cover surface with plastic wrap and chill at least 1 hour or till firm.

3 Remove plastic wrap. Carefully invert pan to remove mixture onto a lightly floured surface. Cut into 8 pieces. Place on a well-greased baking sheet. Bake in a 450° oven about 20 minutes or till golden. Makes 4 servings.

Nutrition facts per serving: 256 cal., 12 g total fat (5 g sat. fat), 70 mg chol., 440 mg sodium, 24 g carbo., 0 g fiber, 12 g pro. *Daily values:* 20% vit. A, 2% vit. C, 24% calcium, 8% iron.

SEAFOOD SKEWERS

Prep: 30 min. ◆ Marinate: 2 hr.
Grill: 8 min.

Garlic lovers throughout the neighborhood will be drawn by the aroma of this seafood combination. (See the photograph on page 163.)

1 lb. skinless fresh or frozen
　fish fillets, 1 inch thick,
　such as salmon, halibut,
　sea bass, and/or red
　snapper
8 oz. fresh or frozen medium
　shrimp in shells

2 medium fennel bulbs
◆◆◆
¼ cup olive oil
3 Tbsp. lemon juice
4 cloves garlic, minced
3 Tbsp. snipped fresh oregano
¼ tsp. salt

1 Thaw fish and shrimp, if frozen. Rinse fish and pat dry with paper towels. Cut fish into 1-inch cubes. Peel and devein shrimp, leaving the tails intact. Rinse shrimp; pat dry. Set aside.

2 Cut off and discard upper stalks of fennel, reserving some of the leafy tops. Snip 2 tablespoons of the tops for use in the marinade. Remove any wilted outer layers from fennel bulbs; cut off a thin slice from base of each bulb. Wash and cut each bulb lengthwise into 6 wedges. Cook wedges, covered, in a small amount of *boiling water* about 5 minutes or till nearly tender. Drain.

3 Place fennel wedges, fish cubes, and shrimp in a plastic bag set in a deep bowl. For marinade, stir together olive oil, lemon juice, garlic, oregano, salt, and the 2 tablespoons snipped fennel tops. Pour over seafood and fennel wedges. Close bag and turn to coat with marinade. Chill for 2 hours, turning occasionally.

4 Drain seafood and fennel, discarding marinade. On skewers alternately thread fennel wedges and seafood.* Grill on a greased rack of an uncovered grill directly over medium coals for 8 to 12 minutes or till fish flakes with a fork and shrimp turn pink. Makes 6 servings.

THE FLAVOR OF PARMESAN

No cheese says "Italian" like Parmesan cheese. Its rich, salty taste enhances the flavor of many dishes, Italian or not.

Cheese connoisseurs can tell the difference between true Italian Parmigiano-Reggiano and its closely related cousin Parmesan, which is made outside Italy. Production of Parmigiano-Reggiano is strictly regulated to maintain its unique taste. The cheese typically is aged from two to four years there, compared to about 14 months in the United States.

Both domestic and imported cheeses are found in many supermarkets, as well as in specialty cheese shops and Italian markets. Its rising popularity has pushed manufacturers to offer the cheese already shredded in packages or in chunks for you to grate at home.

You'll also find a mild, domestic Parmesan in a drier, grated form available in shakers at most grocery stores.

*****Note:** If you're using bamboo skewers, soak them in water for 30 minutes before assembling the kabobs.

Nutrition facts per serving: 185 cal., 12 g total fat (2 g sat. fat), 57 mg chol., 199 mg sodium, 4 g carbo., 0 g fiber, 16 g pro. *Daily values:* 3% vit. A, 13% vit. C, 3% calcium, 8% iron.

Rosemary Chicken
(see right)

◆◆◆

Summer Squash-Carrot
Medley
(see page 177)

◆◆◆

Crusty bread or toasted
bread slices

◆◆◆

White wine or sparkling
water with lemon

LOW FAT

ROASTED RATATOUILLE

Prep: 20 min. ◆ Roast: 28 min.

*Eggplant, zucchini, sweet pepper,
and tomatoes are key ingredients in this
dish, but you can vary the vegetables
according to your taste.
(See the photograph on page 162.)*

1 **small zucchini or yellow
summer squash, cubed
(1 cup)**
1 **small eggplant, cubed
(3½ cups)**
1 **medium yellow sweet pepper,
cut into 1-inch strips**
1 **large onion, chopped
(1 cup)**
2 **Tbsp. snipped fresh Italian
parsley or curly-leaf
parsley**

◆◆◆

2 **cloves garlic, minced**
1 **Tbsp. olive oil**
⅛ **tsp. salt**
⅛ **tsp. ground black pepper**

---

2 **large tomatoes, chopped
(2 cups)**
1½ **tsp. lemon juice**

◆◆◆

1 **recipe Golden Italian
Flatbread (see page 178)**
2 **Tbsp. finely shredded
Parmesan cheese**

1 In a greased 15×10×1-inch
baking pan combine the zucchini
or summer squash, eggplant,
sweet pepper, onion, and parsley.

2 In a small bowl stir together
the garlic, olive oil, salt, and pepper. Drizzle mixture over vegetables and toss gently to coat.

3 Roast vegetables, uncovered, in a 450° oven about
20 minutes or till vegetables are
tender and lightly browned, stirring once halfway through roasting. Stir in tomatoes and lemon
juice. Return to oven for 8 to 10
minutes more or till tomatoes are
very soft and starting to juice out.

4 To serve, spoon vegetable
mixture atop pieces of Golden
Italian Flatbread. Sprinkle with
Parmesan cheese. Makes 4 main-
dish servings.

*Nutrition facts per serving without
flatbread:* 120 cal., 5 g total fat (1 g sat. fat),
2 mg chol., 141 mg sodium, 18 g carbo.,
4 g fiber, 4 g pro.
Daily values: 10% vit. A, 189% vit. C, 6%
calcium, 7% iron.

LOW FAT

ROSEMARY CHICKEN

Prep: 15 min. ◆ Grill: 35 min.

Marinate: 6 to 24 hr.

*Even though rosemary grows like a
weed in the Mediterranean, it's one of
the region's favorite herbs.
(See the photograph on page 199.)*

2 **to 2½ lb. meaty chicken
pieces (breasts, thighs, and
drumsticks)**

◆◆◆

½ **cup dry white wine**
2 **Tbsp. olive oil**
4 **cloves garlic, minced**
4 **tsp. snipped fresh rosemary**
1 **Tbsp. finely shredded lemon
peel**
¼ **tsp. salt**
¼ **tsp. pepper**

◆◆◆

Rosemary sprigs (optional)

1 If desired, skin chicken.
Rinse chicken and pat dry with
paper towels. Place chicken in a
plastic bag set in a shallow dish.

2 For marinade, in a blender
container or food processor bowl,
combine the white wine, olive oil,
garlic, snipped rosemary, lemon
peel, salt, and pepper. Cover and
blend or process about 15 seconds
or till well mixed. Pour over
chicken in bag. Close bag, turning
to coat chicken with marinade.
Chill for 6 hours or overnight,
turning the bag occasionally.

3 Drain chicken, reserving
marinade. Place the chicken, bone
side up, on the rack of an uncovered grill. Grill directly over medium coals for 35 to 45 minutes or
till chicken is tender and no
longer pink, turning once and
brushing with marinade halfway

---

through grilling. Discard any remaining marinade. Remove the chicken from the grill to a serving platter. If desired, garnish with rosemary sprigs. Makes 6 servings.

Nutrition facts per serving: 192 cal., 10 g total fat (3 g sat. fat), 69 mg chol., 93 mg sodium, 0 g carbo., 0 g fiber, 22 g pro. *Daily values:* 2% vit. A, 1% vit. C, 1% calcium, 6% iron.

ORIENTAL CHICKEN SALAD

Prep: 25 min. ◆ Broil: 10 min.

The dressing softens the uncooked noodles to make pseudo croutons. (See the photograph on page 203.)

4 **cups torn mixed greens, such as spinach, romaine, Napa cabbage, and/or leaf lettuce**

2 **cups fresh vegetables, such as bean sprouts; pea pods, halved crosswise; and/or cucumber strips**

1 **cup coarsely chopped red cabbage**

¼ **cup thinly sliced green onions (2)**

1 **3-oz. pkg. ramen noodles (do not need seasoning packet)**

◆◆◆

4 **medium skinless, boneless chicken breast halves (12 oz. total)**
Nonstick spray coating

3 **Tbsp. reduced-sodium soy sauce**

2 **tsp. grated gingerroot**

◆◆◆

1 **recipe Pineapple-Sesame Dressing (see below right)**

2 **tsp. sesame seed**
Chive blossom flowers (optional)

1 In a large bowl toss together the mixed greens, assorted fresh vegetables, red cabbage, and green onions. Break uncooked ramen noodles into small pieces; add to salad, tossing to mix.

2 To prepare chicken, rinse chicken breasts; pat dry with paper towels. Halve chicken breasts lengthwise. Spray the rack of a broiler pan with nonstick coating. Place chicken breast halves on broiler rack. Stir together soy sauce and gingerroot; brush onto chicken. Broil 4 inches from heat for 10 to 12 minutes or till no longer pink, turning once and brushing with soy mixture. Cool chicken slightly.

3 Cut chicken into bite-size strips; add to vegetable mixture. Pour Pineapple-Sesame Dressing over the salad and toss to coat. Sprinkle sesame seed over all. If desired, garnish with chive

blossom flowers. Serve immediately. Makes 4 main-dish servings.

Pineapple-Sesame Dressing: In a screw-top jar combine ⅓ cup *unsweetened pineapple juice,* ¼ cup *rice vinegar* or *white vinegar,* 1 tablespoon *water,* 1 tablespoon *reduced-sodium soy sauce,* 2 teaspoons *sugar,* 1½ teaspoons *toasted sesame oil,* and ¼ teaspoon *pepper.* Cover and shake dressing mixture well.

Nutrition facts per serving: 205 cal., 6 g total fat (1 g sat. fat), 48 mg chol., 677 mg sodium, 17 g carbo., 3 g fiber, 22 g pro. *Daily values:* 30% vit. A, 84% vit. C, 7% calcium, 23% iron.

LAMB KEFTA

Prep: 20 min. ◆ Grill: 10 min.

Kefta is the Moroccan word for ground meat. These patties, laced with aromatic herbs and spices, are traditionally placed on skewers and then grilled. (See the photograph on page 162.)

3 Tbsp. grated onion
2 Tbsp. snipped fresh parsley
2 Tbsp. snipped fresh cilantro
½ tsp. ground cumin
½ tsp. ground cinnamon
¼ tsp. salt
¼ tsp. ground red pepper
1 lb. ground lamb or a mixture of ground lamb and ground beef

◆◆◆

Thinly sliced cucumber (optional)
Chicory leaves (optional)
Grilled lemon wedges (optional)

1 In a medium mixing bowl combine the onion, parsley, snipped cilantro, cumin, cinnamon, salt, and red pepper. Add meat and mix well. Shape about ¼ cup of the mixture into an oval about ¾ inch thick; repeat to make 8 patties total.

2 Grill patties on the rack of an uncovered grill directly over medium coals for 10 to 12 minutes or till no pink remains, turning once. (Or, to broil, place patties on the unheated rack of a broiler pan. Broil patties 3 to 4 inches from the heat for 10 to 12 minutes or till no pink remains, turning once.)

TEST KITCHEN TIP

FRESH HERBS

An assortment of fresh herbs are essential to Mediterranean cooks. Although fresh herbs impart a vibrant flavor, you can substitute dried herbs in a pinch. For strong-flavored herbs such as rosemary, tarragon, and thyme, substitute ½ teaspoon dried herb for each tablespoon of fresh herb. For mild-flavored herbs such as basil, mint, and oregano, use about 1 teaspoon dried herb for each tablespoon of fresh herb.

3 To serve, if desired, place on a bed of cucumber slices, garnish with chicory, and serve with grilled lemon wedges. Makes 4 servings.

Nutrition facts per serving: 232 cal., 16 g total fat (6 g sat. fat), 76 mg chol., 199 mg sodium, 2 g carbo., 0 g fiber, 20 g pro. *Daily values:* 1% vit. A, 5% vit. C, 2% calcium, 13% iron.

PRIZE TESTED RECIPE WINNER

PESTO-PACKED PORK CHOPS

Prep: 25 min. ◆ Grill: 35 min.

This recipe earned Shirley DeSantis of Bethlehem, Pennsylvania, $400 in the magazine's monthly contest.

3 Tbsp. crumbled feta cheese
4 to 5 Tbsp. purchased pesto
1 Tbsp. pine nuts, toasted
2 Tbsp. jalapeño jelly

---

1 Tbsp. balsamic vinegar

◆◆◆

4 pork loin chops or boneless pork loin chops, cut 1¼ inches thick

◆◆◆

1 tsp. minced garlic
1 tsp. ground black pepper
½ tsp. ground red pepper
½ tsp. celery seed
½ tsp. fennel seed, crushed
¼ tsp. dried thyme, crushed
¼ tsp. ground cumin

◆◆◆

Fresh basil leaves (optional)

1 For filling, in a small mixing bowl stir together feta cheese, *2 tablespoons* of the pesto, and the pine nuts. Set aside. For glaze, in a small saucepan melt jelly over low heat. Stir in the remaining 2 to 3 tablespoons pesto and the balsamic vinegar; heat through. Set aside.

2 Trim fat from meat. Make a pocket in each chop by cutting horizontally from the fat side almost to the bone or the opposite side. Spoon filling into each pocket. If necessary, secure the opening with a wooden pick.

3 For rub, in a small mixing bowl combine garlic, black pepper, red pepper, celery seed, fennel seed, thyme, and cumin. Rub evenly onto all sides of meat.

4 In a grill with a cover arrange preheated coals around a drip pan for indirect grilling. Test for medium heat above the pan. Place the chops on the grill rack over the drip pan. Cover; grill for 35 to 40 minutes or till juices run clear, turning once and brushing occasionally with glaze during the

Pesto-Packed Pork Chops
(see page 182)

❖❖❖

Buttered green beans

❖❖❖

Tomato slices

❖❖❖

**Ice cream or frozen yogurt
and oatmeal cookies**

last 10 minutes of grilling. If desired, garnish with basil. Makes 4 servings.

Nutrition facts per serving: 427 cal., 28 g total fat (7 g sat. fat), 101 mg chol., 322 mg sodium, 12 g carbo., 0 g fiber, 30 g pro. *Daily values:* 2% vit. A, 4% vit. C, 7% calcium, 13% iron.

ORANGE AND ROSEMARY MARINATED CHOPS

Prep: 15 min. ◆ Marinate: 4 to 24 hr.
Grill: 35 min.

2 tsp. finely shredded orange peel
½ cup orange juice
2 Tbsp. olive oil or cooking oil
2 Tbsp. white wine Worcestershire sauce
1 Tbsp. snipped fresh rosemary or 1 tsp. dried rosemary, crushed
1 Tbsp. light-flavored molasses
2 tsp. sugar
¼ tsp. salt
⅛ tsp. pepper

❖❖❖

4 boneless pork loin chops, cut 1½ inches thick

1 For marinade, combine orange peel, orange juice, olive oil or cooking oil, white wine Worcestershire sauce, rosemary, molasses, sugar, salt, and pepper.

2 Trim fat from chops. Place chops in a plastic bag set in a shallow dish. Add marinade. Seal bag and turn to coat chops with marinade. Chill for 4 to 24 hours, turning bag occasionally. Remove the chops from bag, reserving the marinade.

3 In a grill with a cover arrange preheated coals around a drip pan for indirect grilling. Test for medium heat above the pan. Place chops on the grill rack over the drip pan. Cover and grill for 35 to 40 minutes or till juices run clear, turning once and brushing with reserved marinade after 20 minutes of grilling. Makes 4 servings.

Nutrition facts per serving: 371 cal., 22 g total fat (6 g sat. fat), 102 mg chol., 276 mg sodium, 11 g carbo., 2 g fiber, 33 g pro. *Daily values:* 1% vit. A, 30% vit. C, 2% calcium, 11% iron.

LIME SALSA CHOPS

Prep: 25 min. ◆ Marinate: 2 to 4 hr.
Grill: 8 min.

If all of this light and lively salsa doesn't get snatched up for supper, chill the leftovers and serve it with tortilla chips as a snack.

¼ cup finely chopped red onion
¼ cup lime juice
2 fresh serrano or jalapeño peppers, seeded and finely chopped
1 Tbsp. toasted sesame oil
1 tsp. cumin seed, crushed

6 boneless pork loin chops, cut ¾ inch thick

❖❖❖

4 plum tomatoes, chopped
1 small cucumber, seeded and chopped
¼ cup sliced green onions (2)
2 Tbsp. snipped fresh cilantro
1 Tbsp. honey

❖❖❖

3 tablespoons jalapeño jelly

1 For marinade, combine red onion, lime juice, serrano or jalapeño peppers, sesame oil, and cumin seed. Reserve 2 tablespoons mixture. Trim fat from chops; place chops in a plastic bag set in a shallow dish. Add remaining marinade. Seal bag and turn to coat chops with marinade. Chill for 2 to 4 hours, turning the bag occasionally.

2 For salsa, to reserved marinade add tomatoes, cucumber, onion, cilantro, and honey. Cover and chill till serving time.

3 Drain chops, reserving marinade; transfer marinade to a small saucepan. Add jalapeño jelly; cook and stir till mixture boils. Remove from heat; set aside.

4 Grill pork chops on the rack of an uncovered grill directly over medium coals for 8 to 11 minutes or till juices run clear, turning once and brushing with jelly mixture during the last 5 minutes of grilling. Serve with salsa. Serves 6.

Nutrition facts per serving: 211 cal., 10 g total fat (3 g sat. fat), 51 mg chol., 46 mg sodium, 14 g carbo., 1 g fiber, 17 g pro. *Daily values:* 4% vit. A, 27% vit. C, 1% calcium, 8% iron.

drip pan for indirect grilling. Test for medium heat above the pan. Place ribs on grill over drip pan. Cover and grill for 1½ hours.

2 Meanwhile, for sauce, in a small saucepan combine cranberry sauce, steak sauce, brown sugar, mustard, lemon peel, and celery seed. Cook and stir till combined; remove from heat. Brush some of sauce on ribs. Grill 15 to 30 minutes more or till ribs are tender and no pink remains, brushing once or twice with remaining sauce. Makes 4 servings.

Nutrition facts per serving: 374 cal., 17 g total fat (6 g sat. fat), 105 mg chol., 269 mg sodium, 25 g carbo., 2 g fiber, 29 g pro. *Daily values:* 5% vit. C, 2% calcium, 10% iron.

CRANBERRY-SAUCED COUNTRY-STYLE RIBS

Prep: 15 min. ◆ Grill: 1¾ hr.

There's a little flavor magic that happens when you alter the variety of mustard used in the sauce. Try regular, Dijon-style, coarse-grain brown, peppercorn, or stone-ground mustard.

2 to 2½ lb. pork country-style
     ribs
     ◆◆◆
1 8-oz. can jellied cranberry
     sauce
2 Tbsp. steak sauce
2 tsp. brown sugar
2 tsp. prepared mustard
½ tsp. finely shredded lemon
     peel
¼ tsp. celery seed

1 In a grill with a cover arrange preheated coals around a

PLUM-GLAZED SPARERIBS

Prep: 15 min. ◆ Grill: 1¼ hr.

1 16-oz. can whole, unpitted
     purple plums
2 Tbsp. orange juice
     concentrate
2 Tbsp. bottled hoisin sauce
1 Tbsp. soy sauce
1 tsp. grated gingerroot
¼ tsp. pepper
2 Tbsp. sesame seed, toasted
     ◆◆◆
4 lb. pork spareribs, cut into
     serving-size pieces

1 Drain plums, reserving liquid. Pit plums. In food processor bowl or blender container, combine pitted plums and their reserved liquid, orange juice concentrate, hoisin sauce, soy sauce, gingerroot, and pepper. Cover and process or blend till mixture is nearly smooth. Transfer mixture

to saucepan. Bring to boiling; reduce heat. Simmer, uncovered, about 15 minutes or till slightly thickened. Stir in sesame seed.

2 Sprinkle ribs with *salt* and *pepper*. In a grill with a cover arrange preheated coals around a drip pan for indirect cooking. Test for medium heat above pan. Place ribs on grill over drip pan. Cover and grill for 1¼ to 1½ hours or till ribs are tender and no pink remains, brushing with sauce the last 10 minutes of grilling. Heat any remaining sauce and pass with ribs. Makes 6 servings.

Nutrition facts per serving: 428 cal., 27 g total fat (10 g sat. fat), 103 mg chol., 372 mg sodium, 18 g carbo., 1 g fiber, 26 g pro. *Daily values:* 2% vit. A, 15% vit. C, 4% calcium, 16% iron.

ORIENTAL-STYLE BARBECUED RIBS

Prep: 20 min. ◆ Cool: 30 min.
Marinate: 3 to 8 hr. ◆ Grill: 1 hr.

Carry through your menu with the Oriental theme and serve these tender ribs with a side of rice that's seasoned with a sprinkling of finely shredded orange peel and a dash of cloves.

½ cup water
4 cloves garlic, minced
2 star anise
1 tsp. onion powder
     Dash ground cinnamon
¼ cup rice wine
3 Tbsp. soy sauce
2 tsp. sugar
     ◆◆◆
2½ to 3 lb. pork loin back ribs

1 In a small saucepan combine water, garlic, star anise, onion powder, and cinnamon. Bring to boiling; reduce heat.

Simmer, covered, for 5 minutes. Stir in rice wine, soy sauce, and sugar; cool to room temperature.

2 Meanwhile, cut ribs into 2-rib pieces. Place ribs in a large plastic bag set in a shallow dish. Pour marinade over meat. Seal and turn to coat with marinade. Chill 3 to 8 hours, turning bag occasionally. Drain meat.

3 In a grill with a cover arrange preheated coals around a drip pan for indirect grilling. Test for medium heat above the drip pan. Place ribs, bone side down, on grill rack over drip pan. Cover and grill for 1 to 1¼ hours or till meat is tender, brushing with marinade occasionally during the first hour of grilling. Add more coals as necessary during grilling to maintain heat. Makes 4 servings.

Nutrition facts per serving: 329 cal., 16 g total fat (6 g sat. fat), 81 mg chol., 446 mg sodium, 2 g carbo., 0 g fiber, 39 g pro. *Daily values:* 1% vit. C, 1% calcium, 10% iron.

SOUTHWESTERN RIBS WITH A RUB

Prep: 20 min. ♦ Cook: 25 min. Grill: 1¼ hr.

This recipe earned Robert A. Kowalewski of Berwyn, Illinois, $200 in the magazine's monthly contest.

4 cups mesquite chips
1 cup catsup
½ cup light-colored corn syrup
¼ cup white vinegar
¼ cup packed brown sugar
¼ cup finely chopped onion

Menu

Southwestern Ribs with a Rub
(see below)

♦♦♦

Coleslaw

♦♦♦

Baked beans

♦♦♦

Ice-cold beer or iced tea

2 Tbsp. prepared mustard
1½ tsp. Worcestershire sauce
2 cloves garlic, minced
½ tsp. coarse black pepper
½ tsp. bottled hot pepper sauce
¼ tsp. ground cumin or chili powder
⅛ tsp. ground red pepper

♦♦♦

1 recipe Rib Rub (see right)
4 lb. pork loin back ribs

1 At least 1 hour before grilling, cover chips with *water* and soak; drain before using. In a 1½-quart saucepan combine the remaining ingredients except for Rib Rub and pork loin back ribs. Bring to boiling; reduce heat. Simmer, uncovered, for 25 to 30 minutes or till mixture is thickened, stirring occasionally.

2 Cut the ribs in serving-size pieces. Pat Rib Rub evenly onto all sides of meat.

3 In a grill with a cover arrange preheated coals around a drip pan. Test for medium heat above pan. Put some of the drained wood chips onto coals. Place ribs on grill rack over the drip pan. Cover and grill 1¼ to

1½ hours or till ribs are tender and no pink remains, adding charcoal and chips as needed. Brush with some of the sauce the last 10 minutes of grilling. Pass any additional sauce. Serves 6.

Rib Rub: In a blender container or small food processor bowl, combine 2 teaspoons each *dried rosemary,* crushed; *dried thyme,* crushed; *dried minced onion; dried minced garlic;* 1 teaspoon *coarse salt;* and ¾ teaspoon *pepper.* Blend or process till coarsely ground.

Nutrition facts per serving: 497 cal., 17 g total fat (6 g sat. fat), 84 mg chol., 1,057 mg sodium, 44 g carbo., 1 g fiber, 42 g pro. *Daily values:* 5% vit. A, 20% vit. C, 5% calcium, 26% iron.

CINNAMON ORANGE SLICES

Prep: 10 min. plus chilling

This barely qualifies as a recipe, but one taste will show you why it's nearly impossible to improve upon the wonderful, fresh flavor of this traditional Moroccan dessert. (See the photograph on page 201.)

2 large oranges
Ground cinnamon

1 Peel oranges, removing white pith. Cut fruit horizontally into thin slices; remove seeds. Place in a storage container and chill. When ready to serve, arrange orange slices on serving plate. Sprinkle slices lightly with cinnamon. Makes 2 or 3 servings.

Nutrition facts per serving: 62 cal., 0 g total fat, 0 mg chol., 0 mg sodium, 16 g carbo., 3 g fiber, 1 g pro. *Daily values:* 2% vit. A, 116% vit. C, 4% calcium, 1% iron.

MIGRAINES: THE NUTRITION CONNECTION

There are headaches—and then there are headaches. Migraines—those crippling, chronic headaches that feel as if you stopped a freight train with your brain—affect 45 million Americans each year, according to Suzanne Simons, director of the National Headache Foundation.

About 70 percent of those who suffer these atomic skull-splitters are female. Costwise, consumers annually spend billions of dollars on headache medications, even though most provide little relief for migraines. Businesses lose 157 million worker-days because of absenteeism from this condition. And this doesn't include decreased productivity by those of us who, feeling too guilty to call in sick "with a headache," suffer through the workday with a migraine.

ARE YOUR HEADACHES REAL MIGRAINES?

Symptoms of true migraine headaches can include any or all of the following:
- a throbbing or dull ache on one or both sides of head
- sensitivity to light, smells, and/or noise
- fatigue, dizziness, confusion, and/or forgetfulness
- nausea (with or without vomiting)

These symptoms typically last from 4 to 24 hours or more, and usually are worsened by physical activity.

THE NUTRITION LINK

The causes of most headaches in general—and migraines or cluster headaches in particular—are as varied as the people who get them. And no matter who gets the migraine, everyone involved with the victim suffers. Although migraines are a largely inherited affliction, everything from allergies to odors have been investigated as sources. One highly suspect dietary cause of migraine headaches is tyramine—an amino acid found in cheddar cheese, chocolate, and pickles.

Other foods currently experiencing close scientific scrutiny are:
- caffeine (in excess)
- red wine
- aged cheeses
- preserved, pickled, and marinated foods
- nitrates, monosodium glutamate (MSG)
- beans, nuts, or other legumes (i.e.,: peanuts)
- brewer's yeast

THE CAFFEINE CONNECTION

Coffee, tea, and cola drinks are stimulants, causing constrictions of tiny blood vessels in the brain. Whereas this reaction could actually help in the case of an acute headache, it can initiate a "cranial cataclysm" in persons prone to chronic headaches. Drinks with caffeine taken on a regular basis also can disrupt your sleep cycle, reducing both the quantity and the quality of sleep. This, too, may precipitate migraines.

On the other hand, withdrawal from caffeine also can cause traumatizing headaches that mimic migraines. Be sure to pace yourself and taper off your intake if you are decaffeinating your life. Should you still incur migrainelike reactions, there are several things you can do to help relieve your suffering. Drink plenty of water, exercise regularly, and eat balanced meals. Plus, be sure to get plenty of sleep. Fortunately, caffeine withdrawal headaches usually last no more than a week or so.

WHAT YOU CAN DO

Not only do migraines often have more than one single source, combinations of situations such as stress, allergies and intolerances, sleep deficit, medication, or other factors can combine to cause one monster of a headache. The most important thing to do if you suffer from repetitious and relentless headaches is to seek professional help from your primary care provider, a headache specialist, or a neurologist.

Chronic headache sufferers who are unsure if the cause is allergies, intolerances, or just plain stress can rule out suspected catalysts by keeping a diary of the foods they eat and the occurrence and durations of their headaches. Providing a diary to your headache specialist also will be a big help in pinning down a culprit.

Once you have a list of possible items, you can gradually eliminate or avoid one prospective headache initiator at a time. However, Simons cautions, "Not all of the suspected substances cause headaches in all sufferers, all the time."

For instance, if you believe that caffeine or red wine is responsible, don't cut out coffee and wine. First, taper off on all sources of caffeine—coffee, tea, soft drinks, and over-the-counter medications containing caffeine—from your diet. Should the eliminated substances lead to a decrease in the number or duration of your headaches after several weeks, you may have discovered your nemesis. In the event that this doesn't help, you can then target the wine or other presumed offender.

FOODS THAT MAY HELP

Omega-3 fatty acids—the kind of fats found in fish oils—have been gaining some attention lately as possible therapy for some migraines. Already famous for helping reduce risk of heart disease, in one study these readily available compounds were found deficient in many subjects with frequent and severe migraine headaches.

Increasing omega-3 fatty acids in migraine sufferers' diets by about 10g per day led to a decrease in both the number and severity of their  headaches. Although doctors may not yet be ready to advise you to "take two herring and call me in the morning," it looks as if what's been good for your heart also may be good for your head.

VITAMIN AND MINERAL THERAPY

Deficiencies of certain vitamins, such as the B-complex vitamins and antioxidants, are another possible cause of migraines. Although preliminary, some clinical studies are showing that supplementation with these vitamins may reduce the severity of migraine headaches.

Magnesium supplements also could prove promising in fighting migraines. The supplements mitigated most symptoms in studies with women who had migraines with their menstrual periods.

IMPROVING DIET AND OTHER STRATEGIES

For whatever reason you suffer from headaches, the most important dietary changes you can make are to eat healthfully, enjoy a variety of fresh foods, and don't skip meals.

Breakfast, the most important meal of the day, is doubly so for migraine endurers. In a poll of chronic sufferers, the majority skipped breakfast on a regular basis. It could be the subjects were susceptible to the influences of caffeine as outlined on page 186 (drinking their morning coffee on an empty stomach). Or, maybe they had no time to eat because they got little sleep at night and rushed out the next day without breakfast.

Then again, they could have just been under a stress in general. All three—caffeine, lack of sleep, and stress—are suspected migraine triggers, but one thing is certain: The folks in question did not get a good meal before dashing out to face the day.

To get free information, call the National Headache Foundation at 800/843-2256 or visit its Internet site at http://www.headaches.org.

DO ARTIFICIAL FLAVORING AND PRESERVATIVES CAUSE HEADACHES?

Most wines, pickles, and preserved foods contain natural or added sulfites—a common trigger of crushing headaches. Artificial sweeteners abound in thousands of foods and beverages, especially those boasting reduced calories or bearing "diet" and "light" labels. Scientific studies support the idea that some people may have intolerances to foods containing sulfites, sweeteners, preservatives, artificial flavors and enhancers (especially monosodium glutamate), or additives, making them susceptible to typically throbbing, migraine-like head pains after eating foods containing these compounds. "Intolerances"—which, unlike true allergies, do not involve the immune system—can cause reactions other than headaches, such as sneezing and breathing distress. Avoiding these substances can be difficult since they appear in many packaged and processed food products.

ALMOND MACAROONS

Prep: 15 min. ◆ Bake: 18 min.

*To keep the parchment paper
from sliding on the cookie sheet while
you're working, lightly grease the cookie
sheet before placing parchment on top.
You should be able to find parchment
paper in the cookware department
of most major department stores
or at cookware shops.
(See the photograph on page 201.)*

Parchment paper
◆◆◆
2 **egg whites**
½ **tsp. vanilla**
⅔ **cup sugar**
◆◆◆
1 **8-oz. can almond paste
    (made without syrup or
    liquid glucose)**
◆◆◆
30 **unblanched whole almonds**

1 Line large cookie sheets with parchment paper; grease the top of the paper. Set aside.

2 In a medium mixing bowl beat egg whites and vanilla with an electric mixer on high speed till soft peaks form (tips curl). Gradually add sugar, about 1 tablespoon at a time, beating on high speed till stiff peaks form (tips stand straight).

3 Crumble the almond paste into a small bowl. Add the crumbled almond paste to the egg white mixture, a small amount at a time, beating till combined (mixture will appear grainy).

4 Drop the macaroon mixture by rounded teaspoons 2 inches apart on the parchment-lined cookie sheets. Place a whole unblanched almond in the center of each cookie.

5 Bake in a 325° oven for 18 to 20 minutes or till the edges of the macaroons are lightly browned. Cool cookies on the cookie sheet for 1 minute. Transfer the cookies to a wire rack and let cool. Makes about 30 cookies.

Nutrition facts per cookie: 60 cal., 3 g total fat (0 g sat. fat), 0 mg chol., 5 mg sodium, 8 g carbo., 0 g fiber, 1 g pro.
Daily values: 1% calcium, 2% iron.

YOGURT MYTHS AND TRUTHS

Since ancient times, folks have valued yogurt as a health food, and even as a cure for many ills. But can it cure? We'll help you sort out the truths and myths regarding this internationally renowned dairy product.

Myth: All yogurts are low in fat and calories.
Truth: Dieters and the fat conscious, beware. Not all yogurts are created equal. The amount of fat and calories in yogurt depends on the amount of milk fat used. By law, a carton that's just labeled "yogurt" (also known as whole-milk yogurt) contains at least 3.25 percent milk fat. Low-fat yogurt contains between 0.5 and 2 percent milk fat; nonfat yogurt must have less than 0.5 percent milk fat. That means the amount of fat for one 8-ounce container of yogurt varies from 0 grams for the nonfat version to about 7 grams for whole-milk yogurt.

Additional ingredients, such as fruit, granola, and sweeteners, also boost the calories in yogurt. To minimize calories, add your own unsweetened fruit or fruit spread to flavor plain yogurt.

Myth: Yogurt ensures longevity, helps control diarrhea, reduces the incidence of vaginal infections, and lowers blood cholesterol levels.
Truth: Although all of the above health claims have been researched, none of them is generally accepted by experts at this time.

Scientists do agree on several points. Yogurt is an excellent source of calcium, riboflavin, and protein. Also, because active cultures help the body digest lactose, yogurts with active cultures are easier than other dairy products for lactose-intolerant people to digest.

Myth: All yogurts contain active cultures.
Truth: Active cultures are required to turn milk into yogurt during fermentation. After fermentation, some yogurt products are heat-treated to make them stay fresh longer. This kills the active cultures. If you are counting on live cultures for easier digestion of lactose, then make sure the carton states active (or living) yogurt cultures or contains active cultures.

FRESH FRUIT WITH MINTED YOGURT

Prep: 15 min. plus chilling

With summer produce at its peak, you'll have no trouble finding your favorite fruits to mix and match in this "plum good" dessert. (See the photograph on page 1.)

1 16-oz. carton plain low-fat yogurt
3 Tbsp. honey
2 Tbsp. snipped fresh mint

♦♦♦

4 medium plums, pitted and thinly sliced (about 3 cups)*
3 cups assorted berries, such as blueberries, raspberries, and strawberries
Fresh mint sprigs (optional)

1 In a small mixing bowl stir together the yogurt, honey, and snipped mint. Cover and chill till ready to serve.

2 To serve, in a medium bowl combine the plums and assorted berries. Divide the fruit mixture among 6 individual dessert bowls. Spoon minted yogurt on top. If desired, garnish with fresh mint sprigs. Makes 6 servings.

*Note: You can substitute thinly sliced nectarines or peaches for the plums.

Nutrition facts per serving: 144 cal., 1 g total fat (0 g sat. fat), 1 mg chol., 56 mg sodium, 31 g carbo., 3 g fiber, 5 g pro. *Daily values:* 3% vit. A, 52% vit. C, 11% calcium, 5% iron.

NECTARINE-PISTACHIO TART

Prep: 40 min. ◆ Bake: 18 min.

Leaving the bright-colored peels on the nectarines and sprinkling them with colorful green pistachios makes this dessert a brilliant feast for the eyes. (See the photograph on page 2.)

1 cup all-purpose flour
⅓ cup finely chopped pistachio nuts
2 Tbsp. granulated sugar
⅓ cup cold butter
3 to 5 Tbsp. ice water

♦♦♦

½ of an 8-oz. pkg. cream cheese, softened
⅓ cup sifted powdered sugar
⅓ cup whipping cream
2 medium nectarines, thinly sliced, or peaches, peeled and thinly sliced (about 2 cups)

♦♦♦

⅓ cup peach or apricot preserves
1 Tbsp. honey
2 Tbsp. chopped pistachio nuts

1 In a medium mixing bowl stir together flour, the ⅓ cup nuts, and granulated sugar. Using a pastry blender, cut butter into flour mixture till pieces are the size of small peas. Gradually add water, 1 tablespoon at a time, to flour mixture, tossing with a fork till dry ingredients are moistened. Form dough into a ball. If necessary, cover dough with plastic wrap and chill 30 to 60 minutes or till dough is easy to handle.

2 On a lightly floured surface, flatten pastry dough slightly. Roll dough from center to edges, forming an 11- to 12-inch circle.

To transfer pastry, wrap it around the rolling pin. Then unroll the pastry onto a 9½- to 10-inch fluted tart pan with a removable bottom. Ease the pastry into the tart pan, being careful not to stretch it. Fold edges in and press pastry against fluted sides of the tart pan.

3 Line pastry shell with a double thickness of foil. Bake in a 375° oven 10 minutes. Remove foil. Bake shell 8 to 10 minutes more or till golden. Completely cool shell in pan on a wire rack.

4 For the filling, in a medium mixing bowl beat together cream cheese and the powdered sugar with an electric mixer on medium speed till fluffy. Stir in *1 tablespoon* of the whipping cream. In a small, chilled mixing bowl beat remaining whipping cream till soft peaks form; fold into cheese mixture. Spread filling into the cooled tart shell. Arrange the nectarine or the peach slices in a circular pattern, overlapping slices slightly, on top of the filling.

5 In a small saucepan combine peach or apricot preserves and honey; heat and stir just till melted. Press through sieve, discarding solids. Carefully brush or spoon the glaze over the nectarine or peach slices. Sprinkle with the 2 tablespoons chopped pistachio nuts. Chill up to 1 hour. Gently remove side of the tart pan; carefully transfer the tart to a serving platter. Makes 8 to 10 servings.

Nutrition facts per serving: 335 cal., 20 g total fat (11 g sat. fat), 50 mg chol., 126 mg sodium, 36 g carbo., 2 g fiber, 5 g pro. *Daily values:* 20% vit. A, 4% vit. C, 3% calcium, 10% iron.

PASTRY FOR SINGLE-CRUST PIE

Prep: 15 min.
Bake: 13 min. (baked shell only)

Butter-flavored shortening also works well in this recipe.

1¼ cups all-purpose flour
¼ tsp. salt
⅓ cup shortening
4 to 5 Tbsp. cold water

1 Stir together flour and salt. Using a pastry blender, cut in shortening till pieces are the size of small peas. Gradually add water, 1 tablespoon at a time, to flour mixture, tossing with a fork till dry ingredients are moistened. Form the dough into a ball.

2 On a lightly floured surface, use your hands to slightly flatten dough. Roll dough from center to edges into a circle about 12 inches in diameter. To transfer pastry, wrap it around the rolling pin. Unroll pastry into a 9-inch pie plate. Ease pastry into pie plate, being careful not to stretch pastry. Trim pastry to ½ inch beyond edge of pie plate. Fold under extra pastry. Crimp edge as desired. *Do not prick pastry.* Bake as directed in individual recipes. Serves 8.

Food Processor Directions: Prepare pastry as above, except place steel blade in food processor bowl. Add flour, shortening, and salt. Cover and process with on/off turns till most of mixture resembles cornmeal, but a few larger pieces remain. With food processor running, quickly add *3 tablespoons* water through feed tube. Stop processor as soon as all water is added; scrape down sides. Process with 2 on/off turns (mixture may not all be moistened). Remove dough from bowl; shape into a ball.

Baked Pastry Shell: Prepare as at left, except generously prick bottom and sides of pastry in pie plate with a fork. Prick all around where bottom and sides meet. Line pastry with a double thickness of foil. Bake in a 450° oven for 8 minutes. Remove foil. Bake 5 to 6 minutes more or till golden. Cool on a wire rack.

Nutrition facts per serving: 141 cal., 9 g total fat (2 g sat. fat), 0 mg chol., 67 mg sodium, 14 g carbo., 0 g fiber, 2 g pro. *Daily values:* 5% iron.

CINNAMON-CHOCOLATE TART

Prep: 35 min. ◆ Chill: 3 to 4 hr.

Dress up the presentation of this chocolaty cream-filled tart by sprinkling powdered sugar over the plate and adding a twist or two of orange alongside.

1 recipe Pastry for Single-Crust Pie (see left)

◆◆◆

¼ cup sugar
2 Tbsp. cornstarch
¼ tsp. ground cinnamon
2 cups half-and-half, light cream, or milk
3 oz. semisweet chocolate, chopped
1 slightly beaten egg
1 Tbsp. margarine or butter
1 tsp. vanilla

◆◆◆

Whipped cream (optional)
Ground cinnamon (optional)

1 On a lightly floured surface, flatten pastry dough slightly. Roll dough from center to edges, forming an 11- to 12-inch circle. To transfer pastry, wrap it around the rolling pin. Then unroll the pastry onto a 9- to 10-inch fluted tart pan with a removable bottom. Ease the pastry into the tart pan, being careful not to stretch it. Trim pastry to edge of tart pan. *Do not prick.* Line pastry with a double thickness of foil. Bake in a 450° oven for 8 minutes. Remove foil. Bake 5 to 6 minutes more or till golden. Set aside to cool.

2 Meanwhile, in a medium saucepan combine the sugar, cornstarch, and ¼ teaspoon cinnamon. Gradually stir in the half-and-half. Stir in the chocolate. Cook and stir over medium-high heat till thickened and bubbly. Cook and stir 2 minutes more. Remove from heat. Gradually stir about *half* of the hot mixture into the egg. Return all mixture to the saucepan. Cook and stir till nearly bubbly, but *do not boil.* Reduce heat; cook and stir for 2 minutes more. Remove from heat. Stir in margarine or butter and vanilla.

3 Pour filling into the baked tart shell. Cover and chill 3 to 4 hours or till set. If desired, top each serving with whipped cream and sprinkle with additional cinnamon. Makes 10 servings.

Nutrition facts per serving: 261 cal., 17 g total fat (7 g sat. fat), 39 mg chol., 94 mg sodium, 25 g carbo., 1 g fiber, 4 g pro. *Daily values:* 8% vit. A, 5% calcium, 7% iron.

CANDY-CUSTARD TART

Prep: 35 min. ◆ Bake: 38 min.

1 recipe Pastry for
   Single-Crust Pie
   (see recipe, page 190)

◆◆◆

1 egg
⅓ cup light-colored corn syrup
¼ cup sugar
1 Tbsp. margarine or butter,
   melted
½ tsp. vanilla
½ cup semisweet chocolate
   pieces

◆◆◆

2 eggs
3 Tbsp. sugar
⅛ tsp. salt
1¼ cups milk
½ tsp. vanilla

1 On lightly floured surface, flatten pastry dough slightly. Roll dough from center to edges, forming an 11-inch circle. To transfer pastry, wrap it around the rolling pin. Unroll pastry onto a 9- to 10-inch fluted tart pan with removable bottom. Ease the pastry into tart pan, being careful not to stretch it. Trim pastry to edge of tart pan. *Do not prick.* Line pastry with a double thickness of foil. Bake in a 450° oven 8 minutes. Remove foil. Bake 4 to 5 minutes more or till set and dry.

2 For candy layer, in a medium bowl lightly beat together the 1 egg, the corn syrup, the ¼ cup sugar, melted margarine or butter, and ½ teaspoon vanilla. Pour the mixture into the partially baked tart shell. Sprinkle chocolate pieces evenly atop. Bake in a 450° oven 8 to 10 minutes or till just barely set.

3 Meanwhile, for custard layer, in the same bowl lightly beat together the 2 eggs, the 3 tablespoons sugar, and salt using a wire whisk or fork. Beat in milk and the ½ teaspoon vanilla just till combined.

4 Reduce oven temperature to 325°. Carefully pour custard mixture over first layer. Bake in the 325° oven 30 to 35 minutes or till custard is set and a knife inserted near center comes out clean. Cool on a wire rack for 1 hour before slicing; serve warm. Serves 8.

Nutrition facts per serving: 334 cal., 16 g total fat (3 g sat. fat), 83 mg chol., 170 mg sodium, 44 g carbo., 1 g fiber, 6 g pro. *Daily values:* 7% vit. A, 5% calcium, 13% iron.

WHITE CHOCOLATE-BANANA CREAM PIE

Prep: 30 min. ◆ Chill: 4 hr.

This recipe earned Bernice V. Janowski of Stevens Point, Wisconsin, $200 in the magazine's monthly contest.

40 chocolate wafers
⅓ cup butter or margarine,
   melted

◆◆◆

½ cup granulated sugar
¼ cup cornstarch
2½ cups milk
3 slightly beaten egg yolks
4 oz. white chocolate baking
   squares, finely chopped
1¼ tsp. vanilla

◆◆◆

4 medium bananas
1 cup whipping cream
2 Tbsp. sifted powdered sugar
   Milk chocolate and white
   chocolate curls (optional)

1 Crush *30* of the chocolate wafers into fine crumbs (1½ cups). In a bowl combine crumbs and melted butter or margarine; toss to mix well. Spread into a 9-inch pie plate. Press onto bottom and sides to form a firm, even crust; cover and chill.

2 For filling, in a saucepan combine granulated sugar, cornstarch, and ¼ teaspoon *salt.* Stir in milk. Cook and stir over medium heat till thickened and bubbly. Cook and stir 2 minutes more. Remove from heat. Gradually stir *1 cup* of hot filling into yolks. Return all mixture to saucepan. Bring just to boiling. Reduce heat; cook and stir 2 minutes more. Remove from heat. Stir in chopped white chocolate and *1 teaspoon* of the vanilla. Stir till chocolate has melted.

3 Slice *2* bananas onto the chilled crust. Spread *half* of the filling over all. Layer remaining chocolate wafers on filling. Chop 2 remaining bananas and place on chocolate wafers. Cover with remaining filling. Cover and chill at least 4 hours. Before serving, combine whipping cream, powdered sugar, and remaining ¼ teaspoon vanilla in a chilled bowl. Beat with an electric mixer on medium speed till stiff peaks form. Spread whipped cream over pie. If desired, top with white and milk chocolate curls. Makes 10 servings.

Nutrition facts per serving: 422 cal., 24 g total fat (13 g sat. fat), 131 mg chol., 210 mg sodium, 47 g carbo., 1 g fiber, 6 g pro.
Daily values: 30% vit. A, 8% vit. C, 10% calcium, 4% iron.

LEMON-BLUEBERRY CREAM PIE

Prep: 20 min. ◆ Chill: 5 hr.

This recipe earned Catherine Schott of Needham, Massachusetts, $400 in the magazine's monthly contest.

1   cup sugar
3   Tbsp. cornstarch
1   cup milk
3   beaten egg yolks
¼   cup butter or margarine
1   Tbsp. finely shredded lemon
     peel
¼   cup lemon juice
1   8-oz. carton dairy sour
     cream
2   cups fresh blueberries
1   9-inch baked pastry shell
     (see recipe, page 190)
     Sweetened whipped cream
     (optional)
     Lemon slices (optional)

1 In a saucepan combine the 1 cup sugar and cornstarch. Add milk, egg yolks, butter or margarine, and lemon peel. Cook and stir over medium heat till thickened and bubbly; cook and stir 2 minutes more. Remove from heat; stir in lemon juice. Transfer to a bowl; cover surface with plastic wrap and chill. When cool, stir the sour cream into mixture, then fold in blueberries; pour mixture into pastry shell. Cover and chill at least 4 hours. If desired, garnish with whipped cream lemon slices. Makes 8 servings.

Nutrition facts per serving: 420 cal., 23 g total fat (10 g sat. fat), 110 mg chol., 161 mg sodium, 50 g carbo., 2 g fiber, 5 g pro. *Daily values:* 26% vit. A, 16% vit. C, 7% calcium, 7% iron.

GINGERED LEMON PIE

Prep: 40 min. ◆ Bake: 20 min.
Cool: 1 hr. ◆ Chill: 3 to 6 hr.

1¼   cups finely crushed
       gingersnaps
⅓   cup melted butter

◆◆◆

1½   cups sugar
3   Tbsp. all-purpose flour
3   Tbsp. cornstarch
3   eggs, separated
2   Tbsp. butter
1   tsp. finely shredded lemon
     peel
⅓   cup lemon juice
¼   cup finely chopped
     crystallized ginger
1   recipe Meringue for Pie (see
     below right)

1 Combine gingersnaps and butter. Spread into a 9-inch pie plate. Press onto bottom and sides to form a firm, even crust. Bake in a 375° oven for 5 minutes. Cool on wire rack.

2 In a saucepan combine sugar, flour, cornstarch, and dash *salt*. Add 1½ cups *water*. Cook and stir over medium-high heat till thickened and bubbly. Reduce heat; cook and stir 2 minutes. Remove from heat. Slightly beat egg yolks; gradually stir about *1 cup* hot filling into yolks. Return all mixture to saucepan. Bring to a gentle boil. Cook and stir 2 minutes. Remove from heat. Stir in 2 tablespoons butter, peel and juice, and ginger. Keep filling warm; prepare Meringue for Pie.

3 Pour warm filling into crust. Spread meringue over filling; seal to edge. Bake in a 350° oven 15 minutes. Cool 1 hour. Chill 3 to 6 hours before serving. Serves 8.

MAKING A PERFECT MERINGUE

For a meringue with great volume, let the egg whites stand at room temperature for a full 30 minutes before beating.

Be sure to use the size bowl called for in your recipe. Copper, stainless-steel, and glass bowls work best. Also make sure your electric mixer beaters are clean.

Begin to gradually add the sugar (about 1 tablespoon at a time) as soon as soft peaks form (tips bend over slightly).

After adding all of the sugar, continue beating until stiff peaks form and sugar is completely dissolved (rub a little meringue between your fingers; it should feel smooth).

Meringue for Pie: In a large mixing bowl combine the 3 *egg whites,* ½ teaspoon *vanilla,* and ¼ teaspoon *cream of tartar.* Beat with an electric mixer on medium speed about 1 minute or till soft peaks form (tips curl). Gradually add 6 tablespoons *sugar,* 1 tablespoon at a time, beating on high speed about 4 minutes or till mixture forms stiff, glossy peaks (tips stand straight) and the sugar completely dissolves.

Nutrition facts per serving: 423 cal., 14 g total fat (5 g sat. fat), 94 mg chol., 260 mg sodium, 70 g carbo., 0 g fiber, 8 g pro. *Daily values:* 13% vit. A, 10% vit. C, 2% calcium, 13% iron.

SEPTEMBER
Shifting Gears

IN THIS CHAPTER

30-minute recipes indicated in RED.
Low-fat and no-fat recipes indicated
with a ♥.
Photographs indicated in italics.

The first taste of autumn comes in the morning, when the dew is heavy and the air unexpectedly brisk. It's a brilliant season: By day, skies are bluer; by night, stars are brighter. And by now, families are adjusting to the busy back-to-school rhythm. That adjustment is easier with a little advance focus on meals. Hungry families and busy cooks will be equally satisfied by recipes that can be prepared well ahead of mealtimes: Roasted Turkey Calzones, Italian Shepherd's Pie, Lamb and Polenta Bake, Comforting Cassoulet-Style Stew, Chicken and Vegetable Lasagna, Lentil-Pumpkin Soup, and Ciao Down Ravioli.

Green Relish

Prep: 45 min. ◆ Chill: 24 hr.
Process: 5 or 10 min.

6 medium green tomatoes,
   cored and cut up (about
   4 cups chopped)
8 oz. cabbage, cored and cut
   up (about 3 cups chopped)
3 medium green sweet
   peppers, seeded and cut
   up (about 2¼ cups
   chopped)
2 medium red sweet peppers,
   seeded and cut up (about
   1½ cups chopped)
1 large onion, cut up (about
   1 cup chopped)
2 Tbsp. pickling salt

◆◆◆

1¼ cups sugar
2 tsp. mustard seed
1 tsp. celery seed
½ tsp. ground turmeric
1¼ cups cider vinegar
½ cup water

1 Use a food processor to finely chop green tomatoes, cabbage, sweet peppers, and onion a portion at a time, using several on/off turns. (Or, finely chop by hand.) Place vegetables in a large bowl. Sprinkle with the pickling salt; stir well. Cover and chill overnight. Rinse well in colander under running water; drain.

2 In a large pot stir together sugar, mustard seed, celery seed, and turmeric. Stir in vinegar and water. Bring to boiling, stirring to dissolve sugar. Stir in vegetables. Return mixture to boiling, stirring frequently. Remove from heat. Ladle hot relish into hot, sterilized half-pint or pint canning jars, leaving a ½-inch headspace. Wipe jar rims and adjust

lids. Process in boiling water canner for 5 minutes for half-pints or 10 minutes for pints (start timing when water begins to boil). Makes 6 to 7 half-pints or 3 to 4 pints.

Nutrition facts per tablespoon: 15 cal., 0 g total fat, 0 mg chol., 68 mg sodium, 4 g carbo., 0 g fiber, 0 g pro.
Daily values: 2% vit. A, 13% vit. C.

Lentil-Pumpkin Soup

Prep: 10 min. ◆ Cook: 20 min.

4 cups reduced-sodium
   chicken broth
1 15-oz. can pumpkin
1 cup dry lentils, rinsed and
   drained
1 cup chopped onion
1 cup water
½ tsp. dried thyme, crushed
¼ tsp. dried marjoram, crushed
⅛ tsp. ground pepper

1 In a large saucepan stir together broth, pumpkin, lentils, onion, water, thyme, marjoram, and pepper. Bring to boiling; reduce heat. Simmer soup, covered, for 20 to 25 minutes or till lentils and onion are tender, stirring occasionally. Makes 6 side-dish servings.

TO MAKE AHEAD

Prepare soup as directed; cool. Place in a 2-quart freezer container and freeze. To reheat, place frozen soup in a large saucepan. Cook, covered, over medium-low heat 20 minutes or till heated, stirring occasionally.

Nutrition facts per serving: 175 cal., 1 g total fat (0 g sat. fat), 0 mg chol., 434 mg sodium, 31 g carbo., 3 g fiber, 12 g pro.
Daily values: 156% vit. A, 9% vit. C, 3% calcium, 31% iron.

Ciao Down Ravioli

Prep: 20 min. ◆ Bake: 20 min.

1 10-oz. pkg. frozen chopped
   spinach
½ cup sliced fresh mushrooms
1 Tbsp. margarine or butter
1 14½-oz. can diced tomatoes
   with herbs, undrained
1 8-oz. can low-sodium tomato
   sauce
¼ cup dry red wine
½ tsp. pepper
¼ tsp. fennel seed, crushed

◆◆◆

1 9-oz. pkg. refrigerated meat-
   or cheese-filled ravioli
¼ cup finely shredded
   Parmesan cheese

1 Thaw and drain spinach. Press out excess liquid; set aside. In large skillet cook mushrooms in margarine 5 minutes or till tender, stirring often. Add undrained tomatoes, tomato sauce, wine, pepper, and fennel seed. Bring to boiling; reduce heat. Simmer, covered, over low heat for 5 minutes.

2 Cook ravioli according to package directions; drain. Toss ravioli with tomato mixture and spinach. Transfer to an ungreased 1½-quart casserole. Top with cheese. Bake, uncovered, in a 350° oven 20 minutes or till heated. Makes 4 main-dish servings.

TO MAKE AHEAD

Prepare casserole as directed; cover and chill up to 24 hours. Bake, covered, in a 350° oven about 40 minutes or till hot.

Nutrition facts per serving: 325 cal., 13 g total fat (6 g sat. fat), 69 mg chol., 875 mg sodium, 35 g carbo., 1 g fiber, 16 g pro.
Daily values: 54% vit. A, 48% vit. C, 26% calcium, 17% iron.

FABULOUS-LOOKING FOOD

Simple ideas presented well can have a stunning effect at the dinner table. When you're short on time, but you long for a ravishing look, remember some of these easy presentation tips:

Garnishing food can be as simple as adding a sprig of fresh herb to a plate. Look for interesting varieties of familiar herbs, such as variegated sage or purple basil.

Cut foods into different shapes: bias-slice carrots, thinly slice cucumbers and peppers, shred radishes, and so forth.

Instead of coating the entire recipe with a special sauce, pool the sauce under the food or spoon it on top. Pass any remaining sauce at the table.

Just when you think you're ready to serve, look again. Would a sprinkle of pepper, ground spice, or chopped nuts add that extra flourish?

Keep it simple. Food that's overdressed can lose its appeal. Use only two or three of these ideas on any one dish and let the food, not the garnish, be the star.

GARNISHING TECHNIQUES

Scored cucumbers: Run tines of a fork lengthwise down a cucumber, pressing to break skin. Repeat at regular intervals around cucumber. Slice or bias-slice. Use with salads and dips.

Fluted vegetables: Use a fluted vegetable knife to decoratively cut vegetables or fruits for salads, stir-fries, and dipping.

Strawberry fans: Use fresh berries with the green tops attached. Slice berries from tips almost all the way to the stem ends; fan out the berry slices. Use to garnish desserts and fruit salads.

Citrus twists: Thinly slice lemons, limes, and oranges. Cut into center of each slice; twist ends in opposite directions. Use with fish and citrus or cream pies.

Citrus peel curls: Use a fruit zester to remove the peel from lemons, limes, and oranges (avoid getting any of the bitter white membrane immediately beneath it). Tie the peel into knots or wrap long pieces around a long skewer and immerse in ice water to hold the spiral twist; drain. Use to garnish fish or citrus and chocolate desserts.

Piping: Pipe whipped cream, cake frosting, or melted chocolate from a decorating bag fitted with a plain or fancy tip (a variety of styles is available). Fill bag (with tip in place) about half full. Next, fold corners over and roll bag down to filling. With your writing hand, grip bag near the roll above the frosting level. Then apply pressure from the palm of your hand, forcing frosting toward the tip. Use your other hand to guide the tip of the bag. With a little practice, you'll learn to control the flow by changing pressure. Pipe rosettes, a border, or a single special design, or completely cover your dessert with piped decorations.

Stenciling: Use a purchased doily, a purchased stencil, or make your own stencil from lightweight cardboard. Place the stencil on top of the dessert surface. Sift powdered sugar or cocoa powder over stencil. Then, carefully lift off the stencil. Stenciling works best on cakes, tortes, and pastries with flat surfaces. For other desserts, try stenciling a design directly on the serving plate.

Chocolate curls: Use a chocolate bar at room temperature. Carefully draw a vegetable peeler across chocolate, making thin strips that curl. Use to garnish cakes, tortes, custards, and ice cream.

GARNISHING WITH EDIBLE FLOWERS

Top almost any dessert with naturally colorful, edible flowers. Scatter small flowers or flower petals over cakes, tortes, mousses, or puddings. Before garnishing food with flowers, make sure the flowers are not a poisonous variety and are pesticide-free. To find flowers for decorating food, look no farther than your own garden, provided that neither you nor your neighbors use chemical fertilizers or pesticides. Pick the flowers just before using; rinse and gently pat dry. Also look for edible flowers in the produce sections of some supermarkets. Flowers from a florist usually are treated with chemicals and should not be used with food. Below are some common edible flowers and what they taste and/or smell like:

◆ Pansies: lettuce
◆ Squash Blossoms: sweet nectar
◆ Roses: floral
◆ Violets: very floral
◆ Carnations: bland and somewhat bitter
◆ Bachelor's Buttons: bland
◆ Lilacs: light floral
◆ Lavender: lemon perfume
◆ Nasturtiums: pepper, radish, watercress

TORTELLINI ALFREDO WITH ROASTED PEPPERS

Start to finish: 25 min.

Use a combination of regular and spinach tortellini for a dish that showcases the Italian colors of red, green, and white.
(See the photograph on page 197.)

1 **9-oz. pkg. refrigerated meat- or cheese-filled tortellini**
½ **of a 7-oz. jar roasted red sweet peppers (½ cup)**

◆◆◆

½ **cup refrigerated light alfredo sauce**

◆◆◆

½ **cup shredded fresh basil**
¼ to ½ tsp. coarsely ground black pepper

1 Prepare the tortellini according to package directions; drain. Meanwhile, drain the roasted sweet peppers and cut into ½-inch-wide strips.

2 In a large saucepan heat the alfredo sauce. Add the cooked and drained tortellini. Reduce heat; add the sweet pepper strips. Simmer, uncovered, for 5 minutes, stirring often.

3 To serve, stir *half* of the basil into the pasta mixture. Spoon mixture into shallow pasta bowls or onto dinner plates. Sprinkle with ground black pepper and the remaining basil. Makes 3 main-dish servings.

Nutrition facts per serving: 362 cal., 12 g total fat (5 g sat. fat), 61 mg chol., 710 mg sodium, 50 g carbo., 1 g fiber, 16 g pro. *Daily values:* 19% vit. A, 113% vit. C, 13% calcium, 14% iron.

FETTUCCINE WITH SWEET PEPPERS AND ONIONS

Start to finish: 20 min.

This fast Italian pasta dish is low in fat, high in protein, and packed with vitamins A and C.
(See the photograph on page 197.)

12 **oz. skinless, boneless chicken breasts**
½ **cup chicken broth**
1 **tsp. cornstarch**

◆◆◆

1 **16-oz. pkg. frozen yellow, green, and red peppers, and onion (stir-fry vegetables)**
1 **9-oz. pkg. refrigerated fettuccine or linguine**
1 **Tbsp. olive oil**

◆◆◆

2 **tsp. bottled minced garlic**
¼ to ½ tsp. crushed red pepper

◆◆◆

½ **cup chopped tomatoes**
¼ **cup snipped fresh basil**
Romano cheese

1 Rinse chicken and pat dry with paper towels. Cut chicken into bite-size pieces; set aside. Stir together the chicken broth and cornstarch; set aside.

2 Bring a large pot of *salted water* to boiling. Add frozen pepper mixture and pasta. Return to boiling; cook 2 minutes or till pasta is just tender. Drain and return mixture to saucepan. Add *1 teaspoon* of the olive oil, tossing to coat. Keep pasta warm.

3 Meanwhile, in a large skillet heat remaining olive oil over medium-high heat. Add chicken, garlic, and crushed red pepper.

Cook and stir for 2 to 3 minutes or till chicken is no longer pink. Push chicken to sides of skillet. Stir cornstarch mixture; add to center of skillet. Cook and stir till thickened and bubbly. Stir all ingredients to coat with sauce.

4 Add chicken mixture to cooked pasta mixture. Add tomatoes and basil; toss to mix. Serve with curls of Romano cheese. Makes 4 main-dish servings.

Nutrition facts per serving: 389 cal., 9 g total fat (1 g sat. fat), 96 mg chol., 261 mg sodium, 46 g carbo., 1 g fiber, 28 g pro. *Daily values:* 83% vit. A, 67% vit. C, 9% calcium, 12% iron.

TEST KITCHEN TIP

PICK A PASTA

Stash refrigerated pasta products in the fridge for those days when you need a swift supper. Toss the pasta of your choice with snipped fresh basil, garlic butter, and shaved Parmesan or Romano cheese.

Or, mix and match varieties of fresh pasta with purchased sauces. Some fun combos to try: chicken ravioli with alfredo sauce; tomato and herb linguine with red bell pepper sauce; and spinach tagliatelle with a garlic-herb butter.

You'll find pastas to suit just about any occasion and palate. Tortellini and ravioli stuffed with meat or maybe cheese, or even trendier flavors such as Gorgonzola cheese and walnuts or prosciutto and herbs.

Top: *Tortellini Alfredo with Roasted Peppers (page 196)*
Above: *Fettuccine with Sweet Peppers and Onions (page 196)*

Page 199: *Rosemary Chicken (page 180) and Summer Squash-Carrot Medley (page 177)*
Top left: *Smoked Salmon Pizza (page 212)*
Top right: *Mustard Shrimp in Potato Nests (page 211)*
Bottom left: *Turkey Sausage Brunch Pie (page 210)*
Bottom right: *Lamb and Polenta Bake (page 213)*

Below: *Smoked Trout Appetizers (page 251)*
Right: *Mosaic Potatoes (page 252)*
Bottom: *Carrot-Spinach Terrine (page 254)*
Page 283: *Crown Roast (page 258)*

Fruit Tarts (page 285)

Fruit Tarts

Prep: 1 hr. ◆ Bake: 7 min.
Chill: Up to 2 days

To avoid last-minute scurrying to get this delicious dessert ready, start it up to two days ahead and make it in stages.
(See the photograph on page 284.)

1 recipe Candied Pecans (see right)
1 recipe Crème Fraîche (see right)
½ cup sugar
½ cup water
1 cup cranberries
1 tangerine or orange, peeled and sectioned
   ◆◆◆
1 Tbsp. cold water
2 tsp. cornstarch
   ◆◆◆
6 Tbsp. unsalted butter, melted
6 sheets frozen phyllo dough (about 17×12-inch rectangles), thawed

1 Prepare Candied Pecans and Crème Fraîche; set aside.

2 For cranberry sauce, in a medium saucepan combine sugar and the ½ cup water. Bring to boiling, stirring to dissolve sugar. Boil rapidly for 5 minutes. Add the cranberries. Return to boiling; reduce heat. Boil gently, uncovered, over medium heat for 3 to 4 minutes or till the skins pop, stirring occasionally. Stir in the tangerine or orange sections.

3 Meanwhile, in a small bowl stir together the 1 tablespoon water and the cornstarch. Stir into cranberry mixture. Return to boiling; reduce heat. Cook and stir for 1 minute more. Remove from heat; set aside to cool. Cover and chill. (If desired, this sauce can be made up to 2 days ahead and refrigerated.)

4 To make pastry cups, lightly brush twelve 2½-inch muffin cups with some of the melted butter; set aside. Lightly brush a sheet of phyllo with melted butter. Place another sheet of phyllo on top of it; brush with melted butter. (Cover remaining phyllo with plastic wrap or a slightly damp towel to keep it from drying out.)

5 Cut phyllo stack into twelve 4-inch squares. Place one phyllo square on top of a second square, followed by a third square, setting each at a slight angle to create a star shape. Gently press the 6-layer stack into a muffin cup, leaving the points sticking up or drooping slightly. Repeat process with phyllo and butter to form 12 cups total.

6 Bake in a 375° oven for 7 to 9 minutes or till golden and crisp. Cool completely in pan on a wire rack. Carefully remove cups from pan. Store in a dry place up to several hours.

7 To assemble, spoon about 1 tablespoon of Crème Fraîche into each pastry shell. Spoon 1 tablespoon cranberry sauce on top of crème mixture. Top with Candied Pecans. Makes 12 tarts.

Candied Pecans: Line a baking sheet with foil. Butter the foil; set baking sheet aside. In a small heavy skillet combine ½ cup coarsely chopped *pecans*, ¼ cup *sugar*, and 1 tablespoon *butter or margarine*. Cook over medium-high heat, shaking skillet occasionally, till sugar begins to melt. (*Do not stir.*) Reduce heat to low; continue cooking till sugar is golden brown, stirring occasionally. Remove skillet from heat. Pour nut mixture onto the prepared baking sheet. Cool completely. Break into small chunks. Store in an airtight container for up to 1 week.

Crème Fraîche: Up to 1 week before serving, in a small mixing bowl stir together ½ cup *whipping cream* and ½ cup *dairy sour cream*. Cover with plastic wrap. Let stand at room temperature for 2 to 5 hours or till mixture thickens. When thickened, cover and refrigerate for up to 1 week. About 1 hour before serving, stir in ¼ cup sifted *powdered sugar* and 1 teaspoon finely shredded *tangerine or orange peel*.

Nutrition facts per tart: 238 cal., 16 g total fat (8 g sat. fat), 35 mg chol., 66 mg sodium, 23 g carbo., 1 g fiber, 2 g pro. *Daily values:* 13% vit. A, 6% vit. C, 2% calcium, 3% iron.

FESTIVE HOLIDAY BISCOTTI

Prep: 30 min.
Bake: 36 min. plus cooling

½ cup butter or margarine
1⅓ cups sugar
2 tsp. finely shredded lemon peel
2 tsp. finely shredded orange peel
2½ tsp. baking powder
½ tsp. baking soda
3 eggs
1 tsp. vanilla
3 cups all-purpose flour
1 cup dried cranberries
1 cup chopped pistachio nuts
♦♦♦
1 6-oz. pkg. white chocolate baking squares, cut up
4 tsp. shortening

1 In a large mixing bowl beat butter with an electric mixer on medium speed 30 seconds. Add sugar, lemon and orange peels, baking powder, and soda; beat till combined. Beat in eggs and vanilla. Beat in as much of the flour as you can. Stir in any remaining flour, the cranberries, and pistachio nuts. Shape dough into three 12×2-inch rolls. Place rolls on ungreased cookie sheets; flatten slightly. Bake in a 375° oven about 20 minutes or till a wooden toothpick inserted near center comes out clean. Cool on baking sheet for 1 hour.

2 Cut each roll crosswise into ½-inch-thick slices. Place slices, cut side down, on cookie sheet. Bake in a 325° oven for 8 minutes; turn and bake 8 minutes more or till crisp and light brown. Transfer to a wire rack to cool.

3 In a small saucepan over low heat stir white chocolate and shortening just till chocolate is melted. Drizzle atop cooled cookies. Let stand a few minutes at room temperature till set. Makes about 72 biscotti.

Nutrition facts per biscotti: 77 cal., 3 g total fat (2 g sat. fat), 13 mg chol., 40 mg sodium, 11 g carbo., 0 g fiber, 1 g pro. *Daily values:* 1% vit. A, 1% calcium, 2% iron.

CRANBERRY-PECAN PINWHEELS

Prep: 40 min. ♦ Chill: 4 hr.
Bake: 10 min. per batch

½ cup butter
¾ cup granulated sugar
¼ tsp. baking powder
1 egg yolk
1 tsp. vanilla
1¾ cups all-purpose flour
♦♦♦
½ cup finely chopped cranberries
½ cup finely chopped pecans
1 tsp. finely shredded orange peel
♦♦♦
2 tsp. milk
3 Tbsp. packed brown sugar

1 In a mixing bowl beat butter with an electric mixer on medium speed 30 seconds. Beat in granulated sugar and baking powder till combined. Beat in egg yolk and vanilla till combined. Beat in as much of the flour as you can with the mixer. Stir in any remaining flour. Cover and chill 1 to 2 hours or till easy to handle.

2 Meanwhile, for filling, in a small mixing bowl stir together the cranberries, pecans, and orange peel; set aside.

3 On a lightly floured surface roll dough to a 12-inch square. Brush dough with milk and sprinkle with brown sugar, leaving ½-inch edge on all sides. Sprinkle with cranberry mixture. Roll up tightly. Cover and chill dough for 3 hours or till firm. Cut roll into ¼-inch-thick slices. Place slices on a greased cookie sheet about 2 inches apart. Bake cookies in a 375° oven for 10 to 12 minutes or till lightly browned. Remove and cool on a wire rack. Makes about 42 cookies.

Nutrition facts per cookie: 64 cal., 3 g total fat (1 g sat. fat), 11 mg chol., 25 mg sodium, 8 g carbo., 0 g fiber, 1 g pro. *Daily values:* 2% vit. A 1% iron.

DECEMBER
Comfort and Joy

*H*oliday foods offer a comfortable connection to our heritage and a joyful tie to family and friends. They are expressions of love—and not chosen lightly. We would be honored if your holiday table included some of our recipes this year, from Capon with Macadamia Nut Stuffing and Smoked Salmon and Eggs in Puff Pastry to a celebration of cookie classics including Chocolate-Mint Creams, Kris Kringles, and Scandinavian Almond Bars. It's a season of tradition, so bring along the old and create some new; they may become the traditions that your descendants will cherish.

30-minute recipes indicated in RED.
Low-fat and no-fat recipes indicated with a ♥.
Photographs indicated in italics.

SMOKED SALMON AND EGGS IN PUFF PASTRY

Prep: 30 min. ◆ Bake: 25 min.

Your holiday brunch will be merrier if you prepare this dish the night before and bake it in the morning.
(See the photograph on page 318.)

½ of a 17¼-oz. pkg. frozen
    puff pastry (1 sheet)
8 eggs or 4 eggs plus
    1 cup refrigerated or
    frozen egg product, thawed
½ cup skim milk
¼ tsp. salt
¼ tsp. pepper
1 Tbsp. margarine or butter
½ of an 8-oz. tub cream cheese
    with chive and onion
½ tsp. dried dillweed

◆◆◆

3 oz. thinly sliced smoked
    salmon (lox-style)
⅓ cup shredded mozzarella
    cheese
1 slightly beaten egg
1 recipe Puff Pastry Stars (see
    below right) (optional)

1 Thaw puff pastry according to package directions. Lightly grease a baking sheet; set aside.

2 In a bowl beat together 8 eggs or eggs plus egg product, milk, salt, and pepper. In a large skillet melt margarine over medium heat; pour in egg mixture. Cook without stirring till mixture begins to set on bottom and around edge. Using a spatula, lift and fold partially cooked eggs so uncooked portion flows underneath. Continue cooking 2 minutes or till eggs are just set. Remove from heat. Dot with cream cheese; sprinkle with dillweed. Fold till combined.

3 Unfold pastry on a lightly floured surface; roll into a 17×12-inch rectangle. Place on prepared baking sheet (short sides may extend over side of sheet). Arrange the smoked salmon crosswise down the center one-third of the pastry to within 1 inch of the top and bottom edges. Spoon scrambled eggs over salmon. Sprinkle with mozzarella. Combine the 1 beaten egg with 1 tablespoon *water.* Brush edges of pastry with egg mixture. Fold a short side of pastry over filling. Fold remaining short side over top; seal. Seal ends well and brush top of the pastry with egg mixture. If desired, top with about 10 to 12 Puff Pastry Stars, and brush with egg mixture.

4 Bake in a 375° oven about 25 minutes or till pastry is golden brown. Makes 6 servings.

TO MAKE AHEAD

Assemble and chill the unbaked, filled pastry for up to 24 hours. To serve, bake, uncovered, in a 375° oven for 35 to 40 minutes or till pastry is golden brown and filling is hot.

Puff Pastry Stars: Thaw remaining sheet of *puff pastry.* Unfold on a lightly floured surface. Roll into a 10-inch square. Using a 1-inch star-shaped cutter, cut out stars. Place 10 to 12 stars on unbaked, filled pastry. Place remaining stars on an ungreased baking sheet. Bake in a 375° oven 12 to 15 minutes or till golden. Makes about 40 stars.

Nutrition facts per serving (with whole eggs): 417 cal., 30 g total fat (7 g sat. fat), 347 mg chol., 580 mg sodium, 18 g carbo., 0 g fiber, 17 g pro. *Daily values:* 23% vit. A, 10% calcium, 8% iron.

GINGERED FRUIT

Prep: 15 min. ◆ Cook: 40 min.

Baking intensifies the flavor of the fruits and makes this gingery breakfast dish a fuss-free favorite.
(See the photograph on page 318.)

½ cup dried tart red cherries
½ cup water
1 tsp. finely shredded orange
    peel
½ cup orange juice
¼ cup packed brown sugar
1 tsp. grated gingerroot
5 cups assorted thinly sliced
    fruit, such as peeled
    mangoes, peaches, pears,
    apples, and/or unpeeled
    nectarines
1 Tbsp. margarine or butter

◆◆◆

Orange peel (optional)

1 In a 1½-quart casserole combine dried cherries, water, the 1 teaspoon shredded orange peel, orange juice, brown sugar, and gingerroot. Stir in desired fruit; dot with margarine or butter.

2 Bake fruit, covered, in a 375° oven for 40 to 45 minutes or till fruit is tender, stirring gently after 30 minutes. Serve warm. If desired, garnish with additional orange peel. Makes 6 side-dish servings.

Nutrition facts per serving: 162 cal., 2 g total fat (0 g sat. fat), 0 mg chol., 26 mg sodium, 37 g carbo., 3 g fiber, 1 g pro. *Daily values:* 25% vit. A, 42% vit. C, 1% calcium, 2% iron.

SEASON'S EATINGS TO ALL

Ahh ... the golden turkey with buttery mashed potatoes and gravy. Ohh ... the vegetables drizzled with cheese sauce. Mmm ... the pumpkin pie and whipped cream. Argh ... the calories, cholesterol, and fat.

Contrary to public opinion, the annual foray into season's eatings can bring pleasure without adding pounds. Our favorite yuletide treats can indeed stay on the holiday menu, nutrition experts say. Moderation is the key.

"All foods can fit into a healthy-eating plan. There really are no bad foods, whether it's holiday time or the rest of the year," says Edith Howard Hogan, registered dietitian and spokesperson for the American Dietetic Association (ADA). But before you head for the fridge to forage for that leftover roast duck to nibble while you're sipping a mug of hot buttered rum, heed some advice from the ADA. This page has some of the association's best tips to get you through the holiday season without discarding those good eating habits you've cultivated all year.

Keep an Eye on Your Food Bank

Just as you balance your checkbook, you need to balance your nutritional account. If you know you're going to a dinner or party where extra calories cry out for attention, plan to eat low-fat or fat-free foods the rest of the day or week. The day of the event, eat a light breakfast and lunch. Or, fix yourself a bowl of oatmeal to quell your appetite before a party. One cup of oatmeal cooked with water contains only 2 grams of fat and 146 calories. It just might fill you up enough to prevent you from reaching for a second piece of pumpkin pie with whipped cream, which has 16 grams of fat and 315 calories per slice.

Focus on Flavor

There are plenty of flavors that add flair to your holiday festivities without adding fat and calories.

◆ Offer gingerbread cookies or sugar cookies instead of pies or cakes for dessert. One 5- or 6-inch gingerbread boy has 157 calories and 6 grams of fat compared to a piece of pecan pie at 541 calories and 30 grams of fat.

◆ Fix a lighter version of traditional eggnog by combining purchased low-fat eggnog with skim milk. Or, serve hot spiced cider instead of eggnog.

◆ Substitute refrigerated or frozen cholesterol-free egg products and low-fat turkey sausage when you're fixing a holiday breakfast.

◆ Satisfy cravings for rich food by searching out more healthful recipes such as low-fat cheesecake with reduced-fat cream cheese and refrigerated or frozen egg product.

◆ Bake or poach pears until tender and drizzle with a chocolate-flavored syrup (most syrups are even fat-free). Serve warm for an elegant dessert.

◆ Go ahead and splurge occasionally on whipped cream, but use a teaspoon of whipped cream to top off each dessert instead of one tablespoon. One teaspoon of whipped cream contains 9 calories; a tablespoon has 27.

◆ Stir a bit of your favorite liqueur into low-fat or nonfat whipped topping and float it on a steaming mug of coffee. Serve it with a gingersnap cookie for a simple finale to a cozy winter dinner.

Create a Help-Yourself Shelf

Encourage healthful snacking, even when decadent temptations abound, with some of these simple ideas:

Instead of discouraging your family from gobbling up the goodies you've prepared in advance for a special gathering, encourage them to grab a healthy snack. Set aside a help-yourself shelf in the refrigerator entirely for grazing. Keep the shelf stocked with fresh fruit, low-fat yogurt, reduced-fat cheeses, and raw veggies. You can even keep pretzels, gingersnaps, and individual boxes of cereal in the fridge, so they're handy for nibbling.

Or display some healthful, edible decor, such as a big bowl of shiny red apples and gorgeous golden pears, throughout the living areas of your home. Encourage your family and holiday visitors to sample the edible art.

Take a Hike

After a holiday dinner that leaves you with a tranquil smile on your face, push yourself away from the table, put the food away, and convince your family and friends to take a stroll around the neighborhood. A brisk 15-minute walk in the invigorating fresh air will perk you up as well as burn about 85 calories (almost the amount in a dinner roll).

Bear in mind that an occasional indulgence isn't all bad. Sometimes it's nice to be naughty. Just don't make a habit of it.

ROOT VEGETABLES AND RAISINS

Start to finish: 30 min.

After trimming and peeling, use a mandoline—a hand-operated slicer and shredder—to save time when cutting carrots and parsley roots or parsnips into thin strips.

½ cup orange juice
1 tsp. brown sugar
1 tsp. cornstarch
◆◆◆
2½ cups julienned carrots
1 medium onion, cut into thin wedges
2 Tbsp. margarine or butter
2½ cups julienned parsley roots or parsnips
¼ cup golden raisins
Fresh parsley

1 For glaze, in a small mixing bowl stir together the orange juice, brown sugar, and cornstarch; set aside.

2 In a large skillet over medium-high heat cook and stir carrot and onion in hot margarine or butter for 2 minutes. Add parsley roots or parsnips and cook 5 minutes more or till vegetables are crisp-tender.

3 Stir the glaze. Carefully add the glaze to the vegetables in the skillet. Cook and stir till glaze is thickened and bubbly. Cook and stir for 1 minute more. Remove from heat. Stir in raisins. Garnish with parsley. Serve immediately. Makes 8 side-dish servings.

Nutrition facts per serving: 117 cal., 3 g total fat (1 g sat. fat), 0 mg chol., 69 mg sodium, 22 g carbo., 4 g fiber, 2 g pro.
Daily values: 111% vit. A, 27% vit. C, 3% calcium, 5% iron.

CRIMSON GREENS WITH PAPAYA SEED DRESSING

Start to finish: 25 min.

Coarsely ground papaya seeds add a peppery kick to the dressing in contrast to the soothing sweetness of the fresh fruit.

1 large papaya
◆◆◆
7 cups torn red-tip leaf lettuce and/or mixed salad greens
1 cup shredded radicchio
1 small red onion, thinly sliced and separated into rings
¼ cup snipped fresh cilantro
◆◆◆
3 Tbsp. salad oil
1 Tbsp. toasted sesame oil*
2 Tbsp. lemon juice
2 Tbsp. rice wine vinegar or white wine vinegar
1 Tbsp. sugar
⅛ tsp. salt

1 Peel, seed, and slice the papaya, reserving 1 tablespoon of the seeds for the dressing.

2 In a large salad bowl combine the papaya, salad greens, radicchio, red onion, and cilantro; toss gently to mix.

3 For dressing, in a blender container or food processor bowl, combine salad oil, sesame oil, lemon juice, vinegar, sugar, and salt. Cover and blend or process till smooth. Add the reserved papaya seeds and blend or process till the seeds are the consistency of coarsely ground pepper. Pour dressing over salad. Toss lightly to coat. Makes 8 side-dish servings.

Menu

Capon with Macadamia Nut Stuffing
(see below)
◆◆◆
Root Vegetables and Raisins
(see left)
◆◆◆
Crimson Greens with Papaya Seed Dressing
(see left)
◆◆◆
Assorted breads and rolls
◆◆◆
Fruit pie

*Note: If toasted sesame oil is unavailable, increase the salad oil to ¼ cup.

Nutrition facts per serving: 87 cal., 7 g total fat (1 g sat. fat), 0 mg chol., 40 mg sodium, 6 g carbo., 1 g fiber, 1 g pro.
Daily values: 12% vit. A, 36% vit. C, 3% calcium, 4% iron.

CAPON WITH MACADAMIA NUT STUFFING

Prep: 10 min. ◆ Roast: 2½ hr.

Although somewhat smaller than a traditional turkey, capon is a succulent, flavorful option that offers more breast meat per pound.

1 5- to 7-lb. capon
Salt (optional)
1 recipe Macadamia Nut Stuffing (see page 293)
◆◆◆
1 Tbsp. cooking oil
1 clove garlic, minced

½ **tsp. grated gingerroot or**
    ⅛ **tsp. ground ginger**

♦♦♦

Fresh variegated sage sprigs
    (optional)
Fresh rosemary sprigs
    (optional)
Kumquats (optional)

1 Rinse capon on the outside as well as inside body and neck cavities; pat dry with paper towels. If desired, season the body cavity with salt. Spoon some of the Macadamia Nut Stuffing loosely into the body cavity. Pull the neck skin to the back; fasten with a skewer.

2 Place capon, breast side up, on a rack in a shallow roasting pan. In a small bowl stir together the cooking oil, garlic, and gingerroot or ginger. Brush the mixture over the capon. Insert a meat thermometer into the center of one of the inside thigh muscles. The bulb should not touch bone. Cover capon loosely with foil.

3 Roast in a 325° oven for 2½ to 3 hours or till the meat thermometer registers 180°, uncovering capon for the last 30 minutes of roasting time. Baste capon occasionally with pan drippings. When the capon is done, the drumsticks should move easily in their sockets. The stuffing should be at least 165°.

4 Remove capon from oven. Cover and let stand 10 minutes before carving. Use a spoon to remove stuffing from capon; place in a serving bowl. Carve capon. If

desired, garnish platter with sage, rosemary, and kumquats. Makes 10 to 14 servings.

Nutrition facts per serving (without stuffing): 260 cal., 14 g total fat (4 g sat. fat), 93 mg chol., 53 mg sodium, 0 g carbo., 0 g fiber, 31 g pro.
Daily values: 2% vit. A, 1% calcium, 10% iron.

MACADAMIA NUT STUFFING

Prep: 30 min. ♦ Bake: 30 min.

The rich flavor and crunch of macadamia nuts accent this seasonal specialty. It's OK to make the stuffing ahead and refrigerate it so it's ready to go, but don't stuff the capon, or other poultry, until just before you roast it.

3 **cups sliced fresh mushrooms,**
    such as shiitake or oyster
¾ **cup sliced green onions**
    with tops
2 **cloves garlic, minced**
¼ **cup margarine or butter**
1½ **tsp. ground sage**
1 **to 1½ tsp. grated gingerroot**
    or ½ tsp. ground ginger
½ **tsp. salt**
¼ **tsp. pepper**

♦♦♦

8 **cups dried ½-inch cubes of**
    Hawaiian sweet bread
    (about ¾ of a 1-lb. loaf)
    or soft French bread*
1 **cup coarsely chopped**
    macadamia nuts
½ **cup snipped dried mangoes**
    or dried apricots
½ **to ¾ cup reduced-sodium**
    chicken broth or water

1 In a medium saucepan cook mushrooms, green onions, and garlic in margarine or butter till

tender but not brown. Remove from heat. Stir in sage, gingerroot, salt, and pepper.

2 In a large bowl combine bread cubes, macadamia nuts, and dried mangoes or apricots; add onion mixture. Drizzle with ¼ *cup* of the broth to moisten, tossing lightly.

3 Use some of the stuffing to stuff one 5- to 7-pound capon. Place any remaining stuffing in a casserole.** Drizzle with remaining ¼ to ½ cup chicken broth. Cover and chill.

4 Bake casserole with stuffing in a 325° oven alongside capon during the last 30 to 45 minutes of roasting time or till heated through. Makes 10 to 14 side-dish servings.

*Note: To make dry bread cubes for stuffing, cut bread into ½-inch cubes. (You'll need 12 to 14 slices of bread for 8 cups of dry bread cubes.) Spread in a single layer in a 15½×10½×2-inch baking pan. Bake in a 300° oven for 10 to 15 minutes or till dry, stirring twice; cool.

**Note: If desired, place all of the stuffing in a 3-quart casserole. Drizzle with the remaining ¼ to ½ cup chicken broth. Bake stuffing, covered, in a 325° oven for 40 to 45 minutes or till stuffing is heated through.

Nutrition facts per serving (without capon): 268 cal., 17 g total fat (3 g sat. fat), 12 mg chol., 291 mg sodium, 26 g carbo., 3 g fiber, 6 g pro.
Daily values: 11% vit. A, 4% vit. C, 2% calcium, 12% iron.

SUPER SOUP BASE

Start to finish: 20 min.

For a less hectic holiday, make up a double batch of this soup starter and pop it in the refrigerator up to three days before your holiday buffet. Use half for Shrimp and Scallop Chowder (see below) and the other half for the Curried Broccoli-Potato Soup (see far right).

1 cup chopped onion
1 clove garlic, minced
1 Tbsp. olive oil or cooking oil
1 10¾-oz. can condensed cream of celery soup

1 In a large saucepan cook the onion and garlic in hot oil till tender but not brown. Stir in the soup. Use immediately to make Shrimp and Scallop Chowder or Curried Broccoli-Potato Soup. Or, cover and refrigerate up to 3 days till ready to prepare one of the soups.

SHRIMP AND SCALLOP CHOWDER

Prep: 15 min. ◆ Cook: 3 min.

The seafood combination makes this soup doubly delicious. However, if you desire, use one pound of the seafood of your choice.

8 oz. fresh or frozen shrimp
8 oz. fresh or frozen scallops

◆◆◆

1 recipe Super Soup Base (see above)
1½ cups milk

Shrimp and Scallop Chowder (see below left)

◆◆◆

Shortcut Olive Flatbread (see page 295)

◆◆◆

Vegetable crudites

◆◆◆

Holiday cookies or candies

1 Tbsp. snipped fresh basil or 1 tsp. dried basil, crushed
¼ tsp. pepper
¼ cup dry white wine

◆◆◆

Fresh basil sprigs

1 Thaw shrimp and scallops, if frozen. Peel and devein shrimp; halve shrimp lengthwise. Set seafood aside.

2 In a large saucepan combine Super Soup Base with milk, basil, and pepper. Heat till bubbly. Add shrimp and scallops. Return to boiling; reduce heat. Simmer, covered, for 3 to 5 minutes or till seafood turns opaque. Stir in wine; heat through.

3 To serve, ladle soup into bowls. Garnish each serving with basil sprigs. Makes 3 or 4 main-dish servings.

Nutrition facts per serving: 298 cal., 13 g total fat (3 g sat. fat), 130 mg chol., 1,044 mg sodium, 18 g carbo., 1 g fiber, 25 g pro. Daily values: 13% vit. A, 8% vit. C, 21% calcium, 22% iron.

CURRIED BROCCOLI-POTATO SOUP

Prep: 15 min. ◆ Cook: 20 min.

You can be sure your family will stay toasty warm when you serve this spiced-up vegetable soup. Vary the spiciness by using more or less curry powder.

1 recipe Super Soup Base (see recipe, far left)
2 cups milk
8 small whole tiny new potatoes, cut into quarters (about 2½ cups)
2 medium carrots, sliced
1 to 2 tsp. curry powder
¼ tsp. pepper
¼ tsp. ground cumin
2 cups broccoli flowerets

◆◆◆

Carrot strips (optional)

1 In a large saucepan combine Super Soup Base with milk. Heat till bubbly. Add potatoes, carrots, curry powder, pepper, and cumin. Bring to boiling; reduce heat. Simmer, covered, for 10 minutes. Add broccoli; cover and simmer for 10 minutes more or till vegetables are tender.

2 To serve, ladle soup into bowls. If desired, garnish each serving with carrot strips. Makes 4 side-dish servings.

Nutrition facts per serving: 283 cal., 10 g total fat (3 g sat. fat), 18 mg chol., 687 mg sodium, 42 g carbo., 6 g fiber, 10 g pro. Daily values: 104% vit. A, 113% vit. C, 20% calcium, 21% iron.

SHORTCUT OLIVE FLATBREAD

Prep: 25 min. ◆ Rise: 30 min.
Bake: 15 min.

When baking both breads at once, switch placement of baking sheets in the oven halfway through the baking. Or, bake one flatbread at a time, keeping the unbaked bread covered in the refrigerator while the other bread is baking.

1　16-oz. pkg. hot roll mix
1　egg
2　Tbsp. olive oil or cooking oil
¼　cup snipped fresh basil or
　　2 tsp. dried basil, crushed

◆◆◆

⅔　cup finely chopped onion
3　Tbsp. olive oil or cooking oil
¾　cup pitted kalamata olives,
　　drained and chopped
½　cup crumbled feta cheese
　　(2 oz.)

1 Lightly grease 2 large baking sheets; set aside.

2 Prepare hot roll mix according to package directions for basic dough, using the 1 egg and substituting the 2 tablespoons olive oil or cooking oil for margarine. Stir in *1 tablespoon* of the fresh basil or *½ teaspoon* of the dried basil. Knead dough and allow to rest as directed. Divide dough in half. On a lightly floured surface, roll each portion into a 12- or 13-inch round. Place on prepared baking sheets.

3 In a skillet cook onion and remaining basil in 3 tablespoons oil till onion is tender but not

brown. With fingertips, press indentations every inch or so in dough rounds. Top dough evenly with onion mixture. Sprinkle with chopped olives and cheese. Cover and let rise in a warm place till dough is nearly double in size (30 to 40 minutes).

4 Bake in a 375° oven for 15 to 20 minutes or till golden. Remove from oven. Transfer rounds to a wire rack; cool. Makes 16 servings.

Nutrition facts per serving: 166 cal., 7 g total fat (1 g sat. fat), 16 mg chol., 237 mg sodium, 22 g carbo., 0 g fiber, 5 g pro. *Daily values:* 1% vit. A, 2% calcium, 5% iron.

Ginger-Sesame Flatbread: Prepare as above, omitting the basil, olives, and cheese. Stir 1 teaspoon *grated gingerroot* into the cooked onion mixture; top dough with onion mixture. Sprinkle 1 tablespoon *white sesame seed* and 1 tablespoon *black sesame seed* atop dough. Proceed as directed.

PRIZE TESTED RECIPE WINNER

PESTO PINWHEELS

Prep: 25 min. ◆ Rise: 45 min.
Bake: 30 min.

This recipe earned Grace A. Eckstorm of Chandler, Arizona, $200 in the magazine's monthly contest.

1　cup packed fresh basil
¾　cup pine nuts or almonds
2　Tbsp. olive oil
2　large cloves garlic, minced
½　tsp. salt
¼　tsp. pepper

½　cup grated fresh Parmesan
　　cheese
½　cup grated fresh Romano
　　cheese
⅓　cup diced pimiento

◆◆◆

2　1-lb. loaves frozen bread
　　dough, thawed
1　Tbsp. olive oil

1 In a blender container or food processor bowl, combine the basil, pine nuts or almonds, 2 tablespoons olive oil, garlic, salt, and pepper. Cover and blend or process till mixture is finely minced. Place mixture in a bowl. Stir in Parmesan cheese, Romano cheese, and pimiento; set aside.

2 Lightly grease a 13×9×2-inch baking pan. Roll each of the thawed loaves into an 8×8-inch square. Brush squares lightly with the 1 tablespoon olive oil. Spread half of the filling onto each of the squares. Roll up each square, jelly-roll style; seal seams. Slice each roll into 8 equal pieces (16 total). Place pinwheels in the prepared pan. Cover and let rise till nearly double (45 minutes to 1 hour).

3 Bake in a 375° oven about 30 minutes or till golden. Cool slightly; remove from pan. Serve warm. Makes 16 pinwheels.

Nutrition facts per pinwheel: 224 cal., 8 g total fat (1 g sat. fat), 5 mg chol., 147 mg sodium, 26 g carbo., 0 g fiber, 7 g pro. *Daily values:* 1% vit. A, 5% vit. C, 9% calcium, 5% iron.

Fruited Christmas Wreath

Prep: 40 min. ◆ Rise: 1½ hr.
Bake: 30 min.

4¾ to 5¼ cups all-purpose flour
1 pkg. active dry yeast
½ tsp. ground nutmeg
1 cup milk
⅓ cup granulated sugar
⅓ cup butter or margarine
2 eggs

◆◆◆

1 6-oz. pkg. mixed dried fruit
   bits (1½ cups)
½ cup orange juice
¾ cup chopped pecans
1 pear, peeled and chopped
¼ cup granulated sugar
2 tsp. finely shredded lemon
   peel
1 tsp. ground cinnamon

◆◆◆

2 Tbsp. butter or margarine,
   melted
1 recipe Powdered Sugar Glaze
   (see right)

1 In a large mixing bowl combine *2 cups* of the flour, yeast, and nutmeg; set aside. In a medium saucepan heat and stir milk, ⅓ cup granulated sugar, ⅓ cup butter or margarine, and ½ teaspoon *salt* just till warm (120° to 130°) and butter almost melts. Add milk mixture to flour mixture; add eggs. Beat with an electric mixer on low to medium speed 30 seconds, scraping bowl. Beat on high speed 3 minutes. Using a spoon, stir in as much of the remaining flour as you can.

2 Turn dough onto a floured surface. Knead in enough remaining flour to make a moderately soft dough that is smooth and elastic (3 to 5 minutes total).

Shape dough into a ball. Place dough in a greased bowl; turn once. Cover; let rise in a warm place till double (about 1 hour).

3 Meanwhile, for filling, in a saucepan combine fruit and orange juice. Heat to boiling; remove from heat. Cover and let stand for 10 minutes; drain. Stir together fruit, pecans, pear, ¼ cup granulated sugar, lemon peel, and cinnamon. Cover; chill till needed.

4 Punch dough down. Cover and let rest 10 minutes. Grease a 12-inch pizza pan. Divide dough in half. On lightly floured surface, roll each portion of dough into a 12-inch circle. Place a round in the prepared pan. Brush with some of the melted butter. Spread fruit mixture atop. Top with the second round. Place a 2-inch glass on top of center of dough to use as a guide. Cut dough into 16 wedges, cutting from the edge just to the glass. Remove the glass. Twist each wedge 2 times. Brush

with the melted butter. Cover and let rise in a warm place till nearly doubled (30 to 40 minutes).

5 Bake in a 350° oven about 30 minutes or till golden and bread sounds hollow when gently tapped. If necessary, cover with foil the last 10 minutes of baking, to prevent overbrowning. Cool slightly. Drizzle with Powdered Sugar Glaze. Makes 16 servings.

Powdered Sugar Glaze: In a medium bowl stir together 1 cup sifted *powdered sugar* and enough *milk* (1 to 2 tablespoons) to make glaze easy to drizzle.

Nutrition facts per serving: 315 cal., 10 g total fat (4 g sat. fat), 42 mg chol., 144 mg sodium, 52 g carbo., 2 g fiber, 6 g pro. *Daily values:* 9% vit. A, 8% vit. C, 3% calcium, 13% iron.

PRIZE TESTED RECIPE WINNER

Cranberry Bread With a Twist

Prep: 30 min. ◆ Rise: 1½ hr.
Bake: 25 min.

This recipe earned Stefin Preboski of Snohomish, Washington, $400 in the magazine's monthly contest. (See the photograph on page 319.)

2¾ to 3 cups all-purpose flour
1 pkg. active dry yeast
½ cup milk
¼ cup water
2 Tbsp. granulated sugar
2 Tbsp. butter or margarine
½ tsp. salt
1 egg

◆◆◆

½ cup finely chopped
   cranberries

¼ cup packed brown sugar

2 Tbsp. finely chopped pecans

1½ tsp. finely shredded orange peel

¼ tsp. ground cinnamon

¼ tsp. ground nutmeg

⅛ tsp. ground cloves

♦♦♦

1½ tsp. butter or margarine, melted

♦♦♦

Orange Icing (see right)

1 In a large bowl combine *1 cup* of the all-purpose flour and yeast; set aside. In a medium saucepan heat and stir milk, water, granulated sugar, the 2 tablespoons butter, and salt till warm (120° to 130°) and butter almost melts. Add milk mixture to flour mixture; add egg. Beat with an electric mixer on low speed 30 seconds, scraping sides of bowl. Beat on high speed 3 minutes. Using a wooden spoon, stir in as much of the remaining flour as you can.

2 Turn dough out onto a floured surface. Knead in enough remaining flour to make a soft dough that is smooth and elastic (3 to 5 minutes total). Shape into a ball. Place in a lightly greased bowl; turn once. Cover and let rise in a warm place till double in size (1 to 1½ hours).

3 Meanwhile, for filling, in a small mixing bowl stir together the cranberries, brown sugar, pecans, orange peel, cinnamon, nutmeg, and cloves; set aside.

4 Punch dough down. Turn out onto lightly floured surface. Cover and let rest for 10 minutes. Grease a baking sheet. Roll dough into a 14×10-inch rectangle.

Brush with the melted butter. Spread cranberry filling over dough. Roll up, jelly-roll style, starting from a long side. Seal seam. Cut roll in half lengthwise. Turn cut sides up. Loosely twist halves together, keeping cut sides up. Pinch ends to seal. Place loaf on the prepared baking sheet. Cover; let rise in a warm place till nearly double (about 30 minutes).

5 Bake in a 375° oven about 25 minutes or till golden. Remove loaf from baking sheet and cool on a wire rack. Drizzle with Orange Icing. Makes 18 servings.

Orange Icing: In a small mixing bowl combine ½ cup sifted *powdered sugar* and enough *orange juice* (1 to 3 teaspoons) to make icing easy to drizzle.

Nutrition facts per serving: 67 cal., 2 g total fat (1 g sat. fat), 10 mg chol., 47 mg sodium, 12 g carbo., 1 g fiber, 2 g pro. *Daily values:* 1% vit. A, 1% calcium, 3% iron.

CREAM CHEESE AND RASPBERRY COFFEE CAKE

Prep: 15 min. ♦ Bake: 30 min.

You can readily change the flavor of this time-honored recipe by substituting different fruit preserves—such as strawberry or blackberry— for the raspberry.

1 8-oz. pkg. cream cheese or reduced-fat cream cheese (Neufchâtel), softened*

1 cup granulated sugar

½ cup butter or margarine, softened*

1¾ cups all-purpose flour

2 eggs

¼ cup milk

½ tsp. vanilla

1 tsp. baking powder

½ tsp. baking soda

¼ tsp. salt

♦♦♦

½ cup seedless raspberry preserves

♦♦♦

Sifted powdered sugar
Fresh mint leaves (optional)
Fresh raspberries (optional)

1 Grease and flour a 13×9×2-inch baking pan; set aside. In a large mixing bowl beat cream cheese, granulated sugar, and butter or margarine with an electric mixer on medium speed till fluffy. Add *half* of the flour, the eggs, milk, vanilla, baking powder, baking soda, and salt. Beat about 2 minutes or till well mixed. Beat in remaining flour on low speed till well mixed.

2 Spread batter evenly into the prepared baking pan. Spoon preserves in 8 to 10 portions on top of batter. With a knife, swirl preserves into batter to marble.

3 Bake in a 350° oven for 30 to 35 minutes or till a wooden toothpick inserted in the center comes out clean. Cool slightly on a wire rack. Sift powdered sugar atop. Cut into squares; serve warm. If desired, garnish with fresh mint and raspberries. Makes 24 servings.

***Note:** Do not use fat-free cream cheese. Also, use real butter or margarine, not a spread.

Nutrition facts per serving: 157 cal., 8 g total fat (3 g sat. fat), 28 mg chol., 144 mg sodium, 20 g carbo., 0 g fiber, 2 g pro. *Daily values:* 9% vit. A, 2% calcium, 4% iron.

CHOCOLATE CHALLAH

Prep: 40 min. ◆ Rise: 2½ hr.
Bake: 35 min.

Jewish holidays that fall on a Sabbath often include a sweet challah (HAH-luh) in their celebration, as a symbolic way of ensuring a sweet year.

2¾ to 3¼ cups all-purpose flour
⅓ cup unsweetened cocoa
    powder
1 pkg. active dry yeast

◆◆◆

¾ cup milk
½ cup sugar
¼ cup margarine
½ tsp. salt
1 egg
½ cup chopped pecans
¼ cup chopped pitted dates
1 Tbsp. finely shredded orange
    peel

◆◆◆

1 recipe Three Glazes (see
    below right)

1 In a large mixing bowl stir together *1 cup* of the flour, cocoa powder, and yeast; set aside.

2 In a medium saucepan heat milk, sugar, margarine, and salt just till warm (120° to 130°) and margarine almost melts. Add milk mixture to flour mixture. Add egg; beat with an electric mixture on low to medium speed for 30 seconds, scraping sides of bowl. Beat on high speed 3 minutes. Using a wooden spoon, stir in pecans, dates, and orange peel. Stir in as much of the remaining flour as you can.

3 Turn dough out onto a lightly floured surface. Knead in enough of the remaining flour to make a moderately soft dough that is smooth and elastic (3 to 5 minutes). Shape dough into a ball. Place in a greased bowl; turn once. Cover; let rise in a warm place till double (about 1½ hours).

4 Punch dough down. Turn onto a lightly floured surface. Divide dough into thirds. Cover and let dough rest 10 minutes. Lightly grease a baking sheet. Shape each portion of dough into a 16-inch-long rope (3 ropes total). Place ropes on prepared baking sheet about 1 inch apart.

5 Starting in the middle of ropes, loosely braid by bringing left rope under center rope. Next bring right rope under new center rope. Repeat to the end. On the other end, braid by bringing alternate ropes over center rope. Press ends together to seal; tuck under. Cover; let rise in a warm place till nearly double (about 1 hour).

6 Bake in 325° oven 35 minutes or till bread sounds hollow when tapped (if necessary, cover bread loosely with foil the last 10 minutes to prevent overbrowning). Remove from baking sheet. Cool. Drizzle with Three Glazes. Makes 1 loaf (24 servings).

Three Glazes: In a mixing bowl stir together 1½ cups sifted *powdered sugar* and 4 teaspoons softened *margarine*. Add 1 to 2 tablespoons *warm water* till icing is of drizzling consistency. Divide evenly into 3 portions.

To 1 portion, stir in 1 teaspoon *unsweetened cocoa powder,* adding more *warm water* 1 drop at a time, if necessary, till icing is easy to drizzle.

THE HANUKKAH STORY

More than 2,100 years ago, a small band of Jewish soldiers overthrew Syrians who had seized, desecrated, and destroyed the holy temple in Jerusalem. The miracle of Hanukkah is that a single day's worth of sacramental oil kept the restored lamp of eternal light burning for eight days until more oil could be prepared. The eight candles of the Hanukkah candelabra (called a menorah or hanukkiah) represent the eight days of this miracle of lights. The ninth candle, called the shammash (servant), is used to light the other candles.

Food is an integral part of ritual in every culture. Whether it's a favorite cookie recipe handed down, the invention of a new recipe for family gatherings, or the simple act of baking bread together, good things to eat help create fond family memories—especially at holiday times.

Other rich traditions are recalled during Hanukkah. Hand out chocolate coins, spin dreidels with the children, and retell the Hanukkah story over plates of cookies, doughnuts, and challah.

For another portion, combine ¼ teaspoon *instant coffee crystals* and a few drops of *hot water* till coffee is dissolved. Add coffee mixture to sugar mixture, adding more *warm water* a drop at a time, if necessary, till icing is easy to drizzle. Leave third portion white.

Nutrition facts per serving: 144 cal., 5 g total fat (1 g sat. fat), 9 mg chol., 81 mg sodium, 23 g carbo., 1 g fiber, 3 g pro.

SUFGANYOT

Prep: 40 min. ◆ **Rise:** 1 hr.
Fry: 1 min. each

During Hanukkah in some Israeli communities, vendors sell sufganyot by the basketful. The community takes on a block-party atmosphere as neighbors mill about eating, listening to music, and chatting while the children play tag, their fingers dusted with powdered sugar and sticky from the filling.

3¼ to 3½ **cups all-purpose flour**
2 **pkg. active dry yeast**
½ **tsp. ground cinnamon**
◆◆◆
1 **cup water**
⅓ **cup granulated sugar**
2 **Tbsp. cooking oil**
1 **egg**
½ **tsp. vanilla**
◆◆◆
¼ **cup fruit preserves, such as raspberry, blueberry, or blackberry; or chocolate-hazelnut spread**
Cooking oil for deep-fat frying
Sifted powdered sugar

1 In a large mixing bowl stir together *1¼ cups* of the flour, the yeast, and cinnamon; set aside. In a saucepan heat and stir water, granulated sugar, cooking oil, and ½ teaspoon *salt* just till warm (120° to 130°). Add oil mixture to flour mixture; add egg and vanilla. Beat with an electric mixer on low to medium speed for 30 seconds, scraping sides of bowl. Beat on high speed 3 minutes. Stir in as much of the remaining flour as you can.

2 Turn dough out onto a lightly floured surface. Knead in enough of the remaining flour to make a moderately soft dough

that is smooth and elastic (3 to 5 minutes total). Shape dough into a ball. Place dough in a lightly greased bowl; turn once. Cover and let rise in a warm place till double in size (about 1 hour).

3 Punch dough down. Turn dough out onto a lightly floured surface. Divide in half. Cover and let rest for 10 minutes. Roll dough, 1 portion at a time, to ¼-inch thickness. Cut dough with a floured 2½-inch biscuit cutter, dipping cutter into flour between cuts. Place about ½ teaspoon preserves or chocolate spread onto the centers of half of the circles. Lightly moisten edges of circles; top with remaining circles. Press edges together to seal. Repeat with remaining dough and fillings. Reroll and cut trimmings.

4 Fry filled doughnuts, 2 or 3 at a time, in deep hot oil (365°) about 1 minute on each side or till golden, turning once with a slotted spoon. Remove from oil; drain on paper towels. Sprinkle with powdered sugar. Cool on wire racks. Makes about 24.

Nutrition facts per preserve-filled sufganyot: 117 cal., 4 g total fat (1 g sat. fat), 9 mg chol., 48 mg sodium, 19 g carbo., 1 g fiber, 2 g pro. Daily values: 5% iron.

HAZELNUT COOKIES

Prep: 30 min. ◆ **Chill:** 3 hr.
Bake: 8 min. per batch

When selecting a margarine for baking, be sure it contains no less than 60 percent vegetable oil. You'll find this information on the product label.

1¾ **cups all-purpose flour**
½ **cup finely ground hazelnuts (filberts)**

1 **tsp. poppy seed (optional)**
½ **tsp. baking powder**
◆◆◆
¾ **cup margarine, softened**
¾ **cup sugar**
1 **egg**
1 **tsp. vanilla**
◆◆◆
1 **recipe Apple Icing (see below)**

1 In a bowl combine flour, hazelnuts, poppy seed (if using), and baking powder; set aside.

2 In a large mixing bowl beat margarine and sugar with an electric mixer on medium to high speed till fluffy. Add egg and vanilla; beat till combined. Add flour mixture; beat on low speed till combined. Cover; chill dough 3 hours or till easy to handle.

3 On a lightly floured surface, roll the chilled dough to ⅛- to ¼-inch thickness. Using 2-inch cookie cutters, cut dough into desired shapes. Place cutouts about 2 inches apart on an ungreased cookie sheet. Bake in a 375° oven for 8 to 10 minutes or till golden. Cool on a wire rack. Decorate cookies with Apple Icing. Makes 36 cookies.

Apple Icing: In a medium mixing bowl stir together 2 cups sifted *powdered sugar*, 1 teaspoon *vanilla*, and enough *apple juice* (2 to 3 tablespoons) to make a glaze. Divide in half. Tint half of the icing with *blue food coloring*; leave other half white.

Nutrition facts per cookie: 105 cal., 5 g total fat (1 g sat. fat), 6 mg chol., 52 mg sodium, 14 g carbo., 0 g fiber, 1 g pro.

CHOCOLATE-MINT CREAMS

Prep: 25 min. ◆ **Chill:** 1 to 2 hr.
Bake: 10 min. per batch

Good shippers, these cookies have been delighting recipients since they first appeared in Better Homes and Gardens® *magazine in 1985. Look for the mints at candy shops, department store candy counters, or food gift shops. (See the photograph on page 317.)*

1¼ **cups all-purpose flour**
½ **tsp. baking soda**
⅔ **cup packed brown sugar**
6 **Tbsp. butter or margarine**
1 **Tbsp. water**
1 **6-oz. pkg. (1 cup) semisweet chocolate pieces**

◆◆◆

1 **egg**

◆◆◆

8 **to 12 oz. pastel cream mint kisses**

1 Stir together flour and baking soda; set aside. In a medium saucepan cook and stir brown sugar, butter or margarine, and water over low heat till butter is melted. Add chocolate pieces. Cook and stir till chocolate is melted. Pour into a large mixing bowl; let stand for 10 to 15 minutes or till cool.

2 Using a wooden spoon, beat egg into chocolate mixture. Stir in the flour mixture till well mixed. (Dough will be soft.) Cover and chill for 1 to 2 hours or till dough is easy to handle.

3 Shape dough into 1-inch balls. Place 2 inches apart on ungreased cookie sheets. Bake in a 350° oven for 8 minutes. Remove from oven and immediately top each cookie with a mint kiss.

Return to the oven and bake about 2 minutes more or till edges are set. Swirl the melted mints with a knife to "frost" cookies. Transfer cookies to wire racks; let cool till mints are firm. Makes about 48 cookies.

Nutrition facts per cookie: 76 cal., 4 g total fat (2 g sat. fat), 8 mg chol., 34 mg sodium, 10 g carbo., 0 g fiber, 1 g pro.
Daily values: 1% vit. A, 1% calcium, 2% iron.

KRIS KRINGLES

Prep: 25 min. ◆ **Chill:** 1 hr.
Bake: 20 min. per batch

Orange and lemon peel bring a welcome taste of sunshine to these nut-covered cookies. (See the photograph on page 317.)

½ **cup butter or margarine**
¼ **cup sugar**
1 **egg yolk**
1 **tsp. finely shredded lemon peel (set aside)**
1 **tsp. lemon juice**
1 **cup all-purpose flour**
1 **Tbsp. finely shredded orange peel**
Dash salt

◆◆◆

1 **slightly beaten egg white**
⅔ **cup finely chopped walnuts**
13 **whole candied red or green cherries, halved**

1 In a medium mixing bowl beat butter or margarine with an electric mixer on medium to high speed for 30 seconds. Add the sugar and beat till combined. Beat in egg yolk and lemon juice till combined. Stir in flour, orange peel, salt, and lemon peel. Cover and chill for 1 hour or till dough is easy to handle.

2 Grease cookie sheets; set aside. Shape dough into 1-inch balls. Dip balls in egg white and then roll in walnuts. Place on prepared cookie sheets. Press a cherry half into each ball. Bake cookies in a 325° oven about 20 minutes or till lightly browned. Transfer cookies to wire racks; let cool. Makes about 26 cookies.

Nutrition facts per cookie: 85 cal., 6 g total fat (2 g sat. fat), 18 mg chol., 46 mg sodium, 8 g carbo., 0 g fiber, 1 g pro.
Daily values: 3% vit. A, 1% vit. C, 2% iron.

MOCHA LOGS

Prep: 25 min.
Bake: 10 min. per batch

When you're after a cookie with a sophisticated flavor, try these tiny chocolate-dipped logs.

1 **cup butter or margarine**
¾ **cup sugar**
4 **tsp. instant espresso coffee powder**

STORING COOKIES

The recipes in this book offer several storage options: You can refrigerate or freeze dough before baking, or store baked cookies at room temperature, in the refrigerator, or in the freezer.

Mix Now, Bake Later

Most cookie doughs can be mixed, then refrigerated or frozen for baking later. The exceptions are bar-cookie batters, and meringue or macaroon mixtures.

Pack dough into freezer containers, or shape slice-and-bake dough into rolls and wrap in foil. Store in a tightly covered container in the refrigerator up to one week, or freeze up to six months.

Before baking, thaw frozen dough in the container in refrigerator. If dough is too stiff to work with, let it stand at room temperature to soften.

Storing Baked Cookies

Follow these four basic rules for storing cookies after baking:

◆ Make sure cookies are completely cooled before storing.

◆ Store cookies unfrosted; frosting may cause sticking. Also, cookies tend to absorb moisture from the frosting and lose their crispness.

◆ Store crisp and soft cookies separately. Stored together, they all become soft.

◆ Use covered containers or sealed plastic bags.

You can store cookies at room temperature up to three days. Store bar cookies tightly covered in a container or in their own baking pan.

Cookies with a frosting or filling that contains cream cheese or yogurt must be stored in the refrigerator.

Freezing Cookies

Most drop, sliced, bar, and shaped cookies freeze well. If the cookies are to be frosted or glazed, wait until they are thawed. Freeze cookies in layers separated by a sheet of waxed paper. To thaw, let the cookies stand about 15 minutes in the container at room temperature.

If you plan to freeze bar cookies, line the baking pan with foil, leaving 2 inches extra foil at each end. Add the batter, bake, and cool in the lined pan. Then lift the foil to remove the cooled cookie. Wrap in foil, seal, and freeze. Frost and cut after thawing.

Cookies by Mail

Crisp cookies stay fresher during shipping than moist ones. Slice-and-bake cookies and most drop and uncut bar cookies are good travelers. Frosted and filled cookies are not good for shipping because they may stick to each other or to the wrappings. For cutout cookies, choose simple shapes; shapes with points or narrow areas tend to break easily during shipping.

Package gifts in plastic- or foil-lined heavy boxes. Make generous cushions of filler, such as plastic bubble wrap, foam packing pieces, or crumpled tissue paper.

Wrap cookies with plastic wrap individually or in back-to-back pairs. Form layers with the sturdiest cookies on the bottom, then a layer of filler. Continue layering, and end with more filler to prevent shifting. Insert a card with the recipient's address. Tape the box shut with strapping tape and mark it "perishable." Cover the outside address with transparent tape.

½ tsp. salt
¼ tsp. baking powder
1 egg
1 tsp. vanilla
2⅓ cups all-purpose flour

◆◆◆

8 oz. semisweet chocolate, melted and cooled
1½ cups finely chopped pecans

1 In a mixing bowl beat butter with an electric mixer on medium to high speed 30 seconds. Add sugar, coffee powder, salt, and baking powder. Beat till combined. Beat in egg and vanilla. Beat in flour till combined.

2 Using a star plate in a cookie press, press dough into 3-inch-long strips onto ungreased cookie sheets. Bake in a 375° oven 10 to 12 minutes. Transfer cookies to wire racks; let cool. Dip ends of cookies in melted chocolate. Sprinkle pecans over chocolate. Makes about 72 cookies.

Nutrition facts per cookie: 75 cal., 5 g total fat (2 g sat. fat), 10 mg chol., 43 mg sodium, 7 g carbo., 0 g fiber, 1 g pro. *Daily values:* 2% vit. A, 2% iron.

HICKORY NUT MACAROONS

Prep: 25 min.
Bake: 15 min. per batch

With just three ingredients, these chewy holiday treats reflect the flavor of the nut that's used.

- 4 **egg whites**
- 4 **cups sifted powdered sugar**
- 2 **cups chopped hickory nuts, black walnuts, or toasted pecans**

1 Grease cookie sheets; set aside. In a large mixing bowl beat egg whites with an electric mixer on high speed till stiff, but not dry, peaks form. Gradually add powdered sugar, about ¼ cup at a time, beating at medium speed just till well combined. Beat 1 to 2 minutes more or till well combined. By hand, fold in the nuts.

2 Drop mixture by rounded teaspoons 2 inches apart on prepared cookie sheets. Bake in a 325° oven about 15 minutes or till edges are very lightly browned. Transfer cookies to wire racks; let cool. Makes about 36 cookies.

Note: These cookies often split around the edges as they bake.

Nutrition facts per cookie: 86 cal., 4 g total fat (0 g sat. fat), 0 mg chol., 6 mg sodium, 12 g carbo., 1 g fiber, 1 g pro.

CRANBERRY-PECAN TASSIES

Prep: 25 min. ◆ **Bake:** 30 min.

Tassie is a word the Scottish use for "small cup." This festive version contrasts a sweet filling with the tartness of the cranberries. (See the photograph on page 317.)

- ½ **cup butter or margarine, softened**
- 1 **3-oz. pkg. cream cheese, softened**
- 1 **cup all-purpose flour**

◆◆◆

- 1 **egg**
- ¾ **cup packed brown sugar**
- 1 **tsp. vanilla**
  Dash salt
- ⅓ **cup finely chopped cranberries**
- 3 **Tbsp. chopped pecans**

1 For pastry, in a mixing bowl beat the butter and cream cheese till well combined. Stir in flour. If desired, chill 1 hour. Shape into 24 balls; place in ungreased 1¾-inch muffin pans. Press dough evenly against bottom and up sides of each muffin cup.

2 For filling, in a mixing bowl beat together egg, brown sugar, vanilla, and salt just till smooth. Stir in cranberries and pecans. Spoon into pastry-lined muffin cups. Bake in a 325° oven for 30 to 35 minutes or till pastry is golden brown. Cool in pans on wire racks. Remove from pans by running a knife around the edges. Makes 24 cookies.

Nutrition facts per cookie: 94 cal., 6 g total fat (3 g sat. fat), 23 mg chol., 59 mg sodium, 10 g carbo., 0 g fiber, 1 g pro.
Daily values: 5% vit. A, 2% iron.

TEST KITCHEN TIP

HOW MUCH FLOUR DO YOU NEED TO ROLL COOKIES?

It's a fine line: Too little flour on the work surface and the dough sticks; too much and the dough absorbs flour, making cookies hard or tough. Use just enough to prevent sticking.

You will need less flour if you use a pastry cloth and slip the rolling pin into a stockinette cover.

When you're rolling sugar cookies, one way to prevent tough rerolled cookies is to combine equal amounts of powdered sugar and flour to sprinkle on the pastry cloth.

SUGAR COOKIES

Prep: 25 min.
Bake: 7 min. per batch

Have some fun and make small, medium, and large versions of the same holiday cookie shapes. Package them as a threesome for a unique gift. To save decorating time, dip the tops of the cooled mini cutouts in the frosting.

- ⅓ **cup butter or margarine**
- ⅓ **cup shortening**
- ¾ **cup granulated sugar**
- 1 **tsp. baking powder**
  Dash salt
- 1 **egg**
- 1 **tsp. vanilla**
- 2 **cups all-purpose flour**

◆◆◆

1 recipe Powdered Sugar Icing
(see below right)
(optional)
Small multicolored
decorative candies
(optional)

1 In a large mixing bowl beat butter or margarine and shortening with an electric mixer on medium to high speed for 30 seconds. Add granulated sugar, baking powder, and salt. Beat till combined, scraping bowl. Beat in egg and vanilla. Beat in as much of the flour as you can with the mixer. Stir in remaining flour. Divide dough in half. If necessary, cover and chill dough for 3 hours or till easy to handle.

2 On a lightly floured surface, roll half of the dough at a time ⅛ inch thick (¼ inch thick if using 1½-inch mini cookie cutters). Using cookie cutters, cut dough into desired shapes, dipping cutters into flour every few cuts. Place cookies on ungreased cookie sheets.

3 Bake in a 375° oven for 7 to 8 minutes (5 to 7 minutes for mini cookies) or till edges are firm and bottoms are very lightly browned. Transfer cookies to a wire rack; cool. If desired, frost with Powdered Sugar Icing and sprinkle with decorative candies before icing dries. Makes about 120 mini (1½-inch) cookies, 36 to 48 medium (2½-inch) cookies, or 20 large (5-inch) cookies.

THE CLEVER COOK

ICING FOR SANTA'S BOOTS

Need black icing for accents on holiday cakes and cookies? Start with chocolate frosting and then add black food coloring until you get just the right shade. You'll use less color than if you start with white frosting, and your treats won't have that tell-tale food coloring taste.

Terri Newton
Marshall, Texas

Powdered Sugar Icing: In a mixing bowl combine 2 cups sifted *powdered sugar,* ½ teaspoon *vanilla,* and 2 tablespoons *milk.* Stir in additional *milk,* 1 teaspoon at a time, till icing is easy to spread. If desired, tint with *food coloring.* Makes about 1 cup.

Nutrition facts per medium cookie: 95 cal., 4 g total fat (2 g sat. fat), 11 mg chol., 33 mg sodium, 15 g carbo., 0 g fiber, 1 g pro. *Daily values:* 1% vit. A, 1% calcium, 2% iron.

LEMON BARS DELUXE

Prep: 15 min. ◆ Bake: 45 min.

We gave these classics more lemon flavor by adding some shredded peel. (See the photograph on page 317.)

2 cups all-purpose flour
½ cup sifted powdered sugar
1 cup butter or margarine

◆◆◆

4 beaten eggs
1½ cups granulated sugar
1 to 2 tsp. finely shredded
    lemon peel (set aside)
⅓ cup lemon juice
¼ cup all-purpose flour
½ tsp. baking powder

◆◆◆

Sifted powdered sugar
Citrus peel strips (optional)

1 Stir together the 2 cups flour and the ½ cup powdered sugar. Cut in butter till mixture clings together. Press into bottom of a 13×9×2-inch baking pan. Bake in a 350° oven for 20 to 25 minutes or till lightly browned.

2 Meanwhile, beat together eggs, granulated sugar, and lemon juice. Combine the ¼ cup flour and the baking powder; stir into egg mixture along with the lemon peel. Pour over baked crust.

3 Bake bars in a 350° oven for 25 minutes more. Cool in pan on a wire rack. Sprinkle with additional powdered sugar. Cut into bars or into 2×1¾-inch diamonds. If desired, garnish with strips of citrus peel. Makes 30 bars.

Nutrition facts per bar: 141 cal., 7 g total fat (4 g sat. fat), 45 mg chol., 77 mg sodium, 19 g carbo., 0 g fiber, 2 g pro. *Daily values:* 6% vit. A, 2% vit. C, 1% calcium, 3% iron.

CHEWY NOELS

Prep: 15 min. ◆ Bake 20 min.

Any holiday message is sweeter when written on these bar cookies.
(See the photograph on page 317.)

⅓ cup all-purpose flour
⅛ tsp. baking soda
⅛ tsp. salt
¾ cup packed brown sugar
1 cup chopped nuts
2 slightly beaten eggs
2 Tbsp. butter or margarine, melted
1 tsp. vanilla

◆◆◆

Sifted powdered sugar (optional)
1 recipe Powdered Sugar Icing (see below)

1 Grease and flour an 11×7×1½-inch baking pan. In a medium mixing bowl stir together flour, baking soda, and salt. Stir in brown sugar and nuts. Stir in eggs, melted butter or margarine, and vanilla. Spread mixture into the prepared baking pan.

2 Bake in a 350° oven 20 to 25 minutes or till golden brown. Cool in pan on a wire rack. If desired, sift the powdered sugar over cookie. Cut into 24 bars. Fit a pastry bag with a small writing tip and fill with Powdered Sugar Icing. (Or, fill a self-sealing plastic bag with icing and snip off one corner.) Pipe the word "NOEL" with frosting on each bar. Makes 24 bars.

Powdered Sugar Icing: In a mixing bowl combine 1 cup sifted *powdered sugar*, 1 tablespoon *milk*, and ¼ teaspoon *vanilla*. Stir in additional *milk*, 1 teaspoon at a

TEST KITCHEN TIP

ROUND ROLLS

Wrap rolls of dough in clear plastic wrap; twist the ends tightly to seal. Place the wrapped rolls in tall drinking glasses before chilling so the rolls will not flatten from resting on the refrigerator shelf.

time, to make an icing that's easy to pipe. Tint green with several drops *green food coloring.*

Nutrition facts per bar: 90 cal., 4 g total fat (1 g sat. fat), 20 mg chol., 35 mg sodium, 12 g carbo., 0 g fiber, 1 g pro.
Daily values: 1% vit. A, 1% calcium, 2% iron.

SCANDINAVIAN ALMOND BARS

Prep: 15 min. ◆ Bake: 12 min.

These bars, which first appeared in Better Homes and Gardens® magazine in 1985, have a rich almond flavor enhanced by a drizzle of Almond Icing.

1¾ cups all-purpose flour
2 tsp. baking powder
¼ tsp. salt
½ cup butter or margarine
1 cup sugar
1 egg
½ tsp. almond extract

◆◆◆

Milk
½ cup sliced almonds, coarsely chopped

◆◆◆

1 recipe Almond Icing (see right) (optional)

1 In a bowl stir together flour, baking powder, and salt; set aside. In a large mixing bowl beat butter or margarine with an electric mixer on medium to high speed for 30 seconds. Add sugar and beat till well combined. Add egg and almond extract and beat well. Add flour mixture and beat till well mixed.

2 Divide dough into four equal portions. Form each into a 12-inch-long roll. Place 2 rolls 4 to 5 inches apart on an ungreased cookie sheet. Using your hands, flatten each till 3 inches wide. Repeat with remaining rolls on another cookie sheet. Brush flattened rolls with milk and sprinkle with almonds.

3 Bake in a 325° oven for 12 to 15 minutes or till edges are lightly browned. While cookies are still warm and soft on the cookie sheet, cut them crosswise at a diagonal into 1-inch-wide strips. Transfer strips to wire racks; let cool. If desired, drizzle cookies with Almond Icing. Makes 48 cookies.

Almond Icing: In a small bowl stir together 1 cup sifted *powdered sugar*, ¼ teaspoon *almond extract*, and enough *milk* (3 to 4 teaspoons) to make an icing that is easy to drizzle.

Nutrition facts per cookie: 58 cal., 3 g total fat (1 g sat. fat), 10 mg chol., 47 mg sodium, 7 g carbo., 0 g fiber, 1 g pro.
Daily values: 1% vit. A, 1% calcium, 1% iron.

SANTA'S WHISKERS

Prep: 20 min. ◆ Chill: 2 to 24 hr.
Bake: 8 min. per batch

The "whiskers" are the shreds of coconut that give these holiday favorites their name. Flaked coconut won't give the cookies the same appearance. (See the photograph on page 317.)

¾ cup butter or margarine
¾ cup sugar
1 Tbsp. milk
1 tsp. vanilla
2 cups all-purpose flour
¾ cup finely chopped candied
   red and/or green cherries
⅓ cup finely chopped pecans
¾ cup shredded coconut

1 In a large mixing bowl beat the butter or margarine with an electric mixer on medium to high speed for 30 seconds. Add the sugar and beat till combined, scraping sides of bowl. Beat in milk and vanilla till combined. Beat in as much of the flour as you can with the mixer. Stir in any remaining flour. Stir in candied cherries and pecans. Shape into two 8-inch-long rolls. Roll in coconut. Wrap rolls in plastic wrap or waxed paper; chill for 2 to 24 hours.

2 Cut into ¼-inch-thick slices. Place slices 1 inch apart on ungreased cookie sheets. Bake in a 375° oven for 8 to 10 minutes or till edges are golden brown. Transfer cookies to wire racks; let cool. Makes about 60 cookies.

Nutrition facts per cookie: 59 cal., 3 g total fat (2 g sat. fat), 6 mg chol., 24 mg sodium, 8 g carbo., 0 g fiber, 1 g pro.
Daily values: 2% vit. A, 1% iron.

THE CLEVER COOK

A CASE FOR CANDY CANES

Use any extra candy canes after Christmas to turn chocolate chip cookies into minty chocolate chip sensations. Grind up candy canes in your food processor until they are a fine powder. Substitute ½ cup of candy-cane sugar for the ½ cup of granulated sugar called for in your cookie recipe. Mix and bake cookies as usual. Extra candy-cane sugar can be stored in an airtight container for use in future recipes.

Rebecca Waszak
Kalamazoo, Michigan

BROWN SUGAR-HAZELNUT ROUNDS

Prep: 25 min. ◆ Chill: 4 to 48 hr.
Bake: 8 min. per batch

1 cup butter
1¼ cups packed brown sugar
½ tsp. baking soda
1 egg
1 tsp. vanilla
¾ cup toasted ground
   hazelnuts (filberts) or
   pecans
2½ cups all-purpose flour

◆◆◆

1 6-oz. pkg. (1 cup) semisweet
   chocolate pieces
2 Tbsp. shortening
1 recipe Powdered Sugar Icing
   (see right) (optional)

Toasted, finely chopped
   hazelnuts (filberts) or
   pecans (optional)

1 In a large mixing bowl beat butter with an electric mixer on medium to high speed for 30 seconds. Add brown sugar, soda, and ⅛ teaspoon *salt;* beat till combined. Beat in egg and vanilla. Beat in ground nuts and as much of the flour as you can with the mixer. Stir in any remaining flour. Shape into two 10-inch-long rolls. Wrap in plastic wrap or waxed paper; chill 4 to 48 hours.

2 Cut rolls into ¼-inch-thick slices. Place slices 1 inch apart on ungreased cookie sheets. Bake in a 375° oven for 8 to 10 minutes or till edges are firm. Transfer cookies to wire racks; let cool.

3 In a small heavy saucepan heat chocolate pieces and shortening over low heat just till melted, stirring occasionally. Dip half of each cookie into chocolate mixture. Place on waxed paper and let stand till chocolate is set. (Or, drizzle cookies with melted chocolate mixture.) If desired, drizzle with Powdered Sugar Icing and sprinkle with chopped nuts. Makes 60 cookies.

Powdered Sugar Icing: In a small bowl stir together ½ cup sifted *powdered sugar,* ¼ teaspoon *maple flavoring or vanilla,* and enough *milk* (2 to 3 teaspoons) to make icing easy to drizzle.

Nutrition facts per cookie: 86 cal., 5 g total fat (2 g sat. fat), 12 mg chol., 48 mg sodium, 9 g carbo., 0 g fiber, 1 g pro.
Daily values: 3% vit. A, 2% iron.

BAKING WITH KIDS

Baking cookies is a great way for children to have fun as they learn to cook. Here are some tips for making cookie baking a happy experience for both you and your young baker:

◆ Let the child choose his job and how much he wants to help. Don't be surprised if his attention wanders before all the cookies are baked.

◆ Clear a large work area. Find an apron or an old shirt to protect the child's clothes.

◆ Keep paper towels at hand to wipe up spills promptly.

◆ When a school-age child is helping, read through the recipe together before you begin. Get out all the ingredients and utensils before starting to bake.

◆ When a young child is only helping shape cookies, mix the dough ahead of time so the child won't lose interest before you're ready for help.

◆ Good jobs for a young first-time baker are placing chocolate candies in the center of a cookie after baking or decorating already baked cookies.

◆ Provide icings, sprinkles, and candies for decorating. Allow children to be as artistic as they wish.

◆ Supervise difficult or hazardous steps such as beating with an electric mixer, transferring cookie sheets to or from a hot oven, and chopping nuts.

◆ Appliances can be handled by an older child who learns the dos and don'ts. That includes a reminder to unplug the mixer when putting in or taking out the beaters. Explain the importance of keeping wet hands away from appliances and electrical outlets.

◆ Start developing good kitchen habits early. Have a youngster pitch in with cleanup.

2 Divide each color of dough into 4 equal portions. On a lightly floured surface, roll each portion into a ½-inch-diameter rope. Place a red, a green, and a plain rope side by side. Twist together. Repeat with remaining ropes. Chill twisted ropes for 30 minutes. Cut ropes into ½-inch-thick slices for larger cookies or ¼-inch-thick slices for smaller ones. Carefully roll into balls, blending colors as little as possible. Place balls about 2 inches apart on ungreased cookie sheets.

3 Flatten each ball to ¼-inch thickness with the bottom of a glass dipped in additional sugar. Repeat with remaining dough. Bake in a 375° oven till edges are set (allow 8 to 10 minutes for larger cookies or 6 to 8 minutes for smaller ones). Transfer cookies to wire racks; let cool. Makes about 72 (2½-inch) cookies or 144 (1¼-inch) cookies.

Nutrition facts per larger cookie: 46 cal., 3 g total fat (2 g sat. fat), 10 mg chol., 29 mg sodium, 5 g carbo., 0 g fiber, 0 g pro. *Daily values:* 2% vit. A, 1% iron.

SWIRLED MINT COOKIES

Prep: 25 min. ◆ Chill: 1½ hr.
Bake: 8 min. per batch

These dainty cookies are crisp and light enough to be served after the heartiest holiday feast.
(See the photograph on page 317.)

2 **cups all-purpose flour**
½ **tsp. baking powder**
1 **cup butter or margarine**
1 **cup sugar**
1 **egg**
1 **tsp. vanilla**
½ **tsp. peppermint extract**
10 **drops red food coloring**
10 **drops green food coloring**

◆◆◆

Sugar

1 Stir together flour and baking powder; set aside. In a large mixing bowl beat butter or margarine with an electric mixer on medium to high speed for 30 seconds. Add the 1 cup sugar and beat till fluffy. Add egg, vanilla, and peppermint extract; beat well. Add flour mixture; beat till well mixed. Divide into 3 equal portions. Stir red food coloring into a portion, stir green food coloring into another, and leave remaining portion plain. Cover each portion and chill about 1 hour or till easy to handle.

FARMYARD FRIENDS

Prep: 1 hr. ◆ Chill: 2 hr.
Bake: 18 min. per batch

Mold a merry menagerie with this peppermint dough.

4 **cups all-purpose flour**
1 **Tbsp. baking powder**
¼ **tsp. salt**

◆◆◆

¾ **cup butter or margarine**
⅔ **cup shortening**
1½ **cups sugar**

2 eggs

1 tsp. peppermint extract

❖❖❖

Paste or liquid food coloring

1 In a medium mixing bowl stir together flour, baking powder, and salt; set aside.

2 In a large mixing bowl beat the butter or margarine and shortening with an electric mixer on medium to high speed for 30 seconds. Add sugar and beat till fluffy. Add eggs and peppermint extract; beat well. Beat in as much of the flour mixture as you can with the mixer. Stir in remaining flour mixture (dough should be stiff). Cover and chill dough for at least 2 hours.

3 To color and shape dough, divide dough into portions— 1 for each color that you want to use. Knead food coloring into each portion, adding it slowly till dough becomes desired color.

4 On an ungreased cookie sheet, form dough into animal shapes about ¼ inch thick (see shaping directions, right). Working with the dough as you would clay, start by molding the animal's body. Decorate as suggested. Arrange cookies about 1 inch apart on cookie sheets.

5 Bake in a 300° oven 18 to 20 minutes or till edges are firm and cookies look set, but bottoms are not brown. Transfer cookies to wire racks; let cool. Makes about 25 (3-inch cookies), but yield will vary depending on animals made.

Shaping Directions for the Farmyard Friends:

Striped Pig: For the body, flatten a ¾-inch colored ball of dough to about 2½ inches. For the white stripe down the middle of the body, shape a ¾-inch-wide, very thin strip of untinted dough. Roll a small colored ball for head. Use colored and untinted doughs to make legs, tail, ears, eyes, and snout. Attach these pieces by pressing them gently onto the body and head. (For spotted pig, shape body with white dough and add spots with black or other dark-colored dough.)

Roly-Poly Lamb: For the body, roll untinted dough into small balls (varying sizes) and lay on cookie sheet, touching each other. Use a small round ball of tinted dough for head and small ovals for the feet.

Holly Horse: For the body, flatten a 1-inch oval of untinted dough horizontally to about 2½ inches across. For the neck and head, place a heart-shaped piece of dough upside down next to the body. For the neck wreath, twist together two ⅛-inch-thick ropes of colored dough. Use colored and untinted doughs to make legs, tail, mane, spots, and eye. Use the tines of a fork to mark mane and tail.

Lucky Duck: For body, flatten a ¾-inch oval of dough horizontally to 2 inches across, shaping the back top corner into a slight point. Attach neck and head in the same color dough. Use 2 or 3 different colors of dough for eye, beak, feet, and neck ribbon.

Merry Cow: For the body, flatten a 1-inch oval of colored dough horizontally to about 2½ inches across. Roll colored dough into a log, ½ inch wide and 2½ inches long. Cut into 3 equal pieces for legs and head; attach to body. For spots, udder, eyes, and nose, roll untinted dough into small circles; flatten till thin. Roll colored dough into a rope for the tail and into 2 small dots for the nostrils.

Rainbow Rooster: For body, flatten a 1-inch oval of dough vertically to about 2¾ inches long, making slight curves in the 2 sides at 1 end to form the head. Roll 5 logs of dough, about ¼ inch wide and 1 inch long (use different colors). For the crown, attach a log to head, horizontally, using a knife to make the grooves in top. Use the other 4 logs for tail feathers. Use tinted dough to make beak, eye, beard, and legs.

Polka-Dot Cat: For body, flatten a round, 2-inch ball of tinted dough. Attach a smaller ball of the same color dough for the head. For legs and tail, roll dough into 3 thin logs, each about 1¼ inches long; attach to body. Attach tinted spots as directed for cow. Use tinted dough for ears, eyes, nose, and whiskers.

Nutrition facts per 3-inch cookie: 217 cal., 12 g total fat (5 g sat. fat), 32 mg chol., 126 mg sodium, 26 g carbo., 0 g fiber, 2 g pro.
Daily values: 5% vit. A, 3% calcium, 6% iron.

BAKING DAY HELPERS

You'll notice at once if your oven is running hotter than the temperature you set because cookies will brown too fast. A temperature that is too low causes pale cookies that are coarse-textured and dry.

Home economists in the Better Homes and Gardens® Test Kitchen keep thermometers in their ovens at all times so they can note the temperature and be sure the baking times given in our recipes are accurate. You don't need to monitor oven temperature constantly, but do check your oven temperature occasionally.

You can buy an oven thermometer at a hardware store. Set the oven at 350° and let it heat for at least 10 minutes. Place the thermometer in the oven. Close the door and leave the thermometer in the oven for at least 5 minutes.

If the thermometer reads higher than 350°, reduce oven setting by number of degrees difference when you bake. If thermometer reads lower than 350°, increase setting by the number of degrees difference.

If your oven is more than 50 degrees off in either direction, you should have the thermostat adjusted by an appliance service person.

CHILL COOKIE DOUGH PROPERLY

Almost all recipes for cutout or sliced cookies call for chilling dough. The chilling time given in a recipe is optimum time for easy rolling and cutting or slicing, except for cookie dough made with 100-percent-corn-oil margarine. Chill these doughs in the freezer.

For faster chilling of any dough, divide it in half before chilling. Then work with one portion at a time, keeping the other portion chilled. Or, chill any dough in the freezer. About 20 minutes of chilling in the freezer is equal to one hour of chilling in the refrigerator.

Chilling dough too long, or chilling butter doughs in the freezer, will make dough too firm to work with. Overchilling is easy to fix; let dough stand at room temperature until soft enough to work with.

Well-chilled dough absorbs less flour during rolling, so it's less likely to become tough. It's a good idea to chill the scraps again before rerolling.

If your drop cookies spread too much during baking, try chilling the dough before you add extra flour, which often makes the cookies hard or dry and less flavorful.

MAKING COOKIES MORE HEALTHFUL

With all the low-fat and fat-free commercial products available, it's tempting to reduce or make substitutions for the sugar and fat in your own recipes to make cookies more healthful. This is risky, because any change in ingredient proportions also changes the texture and flavor of the cookies, and the results may not be what you expect.

Besides adding flavor, sugar and fat make cookies crisp and tender. Reducing sugar and fat makes cookies less crisp and more cakelike. Substituting an artificial sweetener or a lower-fat product will not yield an acceptable cookie.

Here's what you can do to make cookies healthier:

◆ Substitute rolled oats or whole wheat flour for one-fourth of the all-purpose flour to make cookies higher in fiber.

◆ Add fruits or vegetables such as raisins or dried fruit bits, shredded or chopped apple, or shredded carrot to add fiber.

◆ Use refrigerated or frozen egg product instead of a whole egg, or use two egg whites in place of one whole egg.

◆ Reduce the amount of nuts and finely chop them. For bar cookies, sprinkle nuts over the surface where they show rather than stirring them into the batter.

◆ Substitute mini semisweet chocolate pieces for the regular-size pieces and use half as many. You'll still get chocolate in every bite.

◆ Substitute applesauce or fruit puree for half the fat in some bar cookies.

CRANBERRY-PEAR PIE

Prep: 35 min. ◆ Bake: 55 min.

A sprinkling of coarse sugar on the crust shimmers like glistening snow on this pie that's made doubly delicious with a cranberry-pear combination. (See the photograph on page 320.)

1 recipe Pastry for Double-Crust Pie (see below right)

◆◆◆

1 cup sugar
¼ cup water
4 cups thinly sliced, peeled, and cored pears
2 cups cranberries

◆◆◆

3 Tbsp. cornstarch
¼ cup cold water
½ tsp. aniseed, crushed (optional)

◆◆◆

1 beaten egg white
1 Tbsp. water
Coarse sugar

1 Prepare pastry and roll out half of it into a circle 12 inches in diameter. Transfer rolled-out pastry to a 9-inch pie plate. Cover remaining pastry; set aside.

2 In a large saucepan combine sugar and ¼ cup water. Bring to boiling, stirring to dissolve sugar; reduce heat. Simmer, uncovered, 5 minutes. Add pears and cranberries. Return to boiling; reduce heat. Simmer fruit mixture, uncovered, over medium-high heat 3 to 4 minutes or till cranberries pop, stirring occasionally.

3 In a small bowl stir together the cornstarch and ¼ cup cold water. Stir cornstarch mixture into the cranberry mixture. Bring to boiling; reduce heat. Simmer,

uncovered, for 2 minutes, stirring occasionally. Remove from heat. If desired, stir in aniseed.

4 Transfer cranberry mixture to the pastry-lined pie plate. Trim pastry to edge of pie plate. Roll remaining pastry into a circle about 12 inches in diameter. With a 1-inch holiday cookie cutter, cut shapes from the center of pastry, reserving cutouts. Or, cut slits in pastry if not using cookie cutters.

5 Place pastry on filling and seal. Crimp edge as desired. Combine egg white and 1 tablespoon water; brush onto pastry. Sprinkle with coarse sugar. Top with holiday cutouts, if used. Brush cutouts with egg white mixture. To prevent overbrowning, cover edge of pie with foil.

6 Bake in a 375° oven for 25 minutes. Remove foil. Bake for 30 to 35 minutes more or till the top is golden. Cool on a wire rack. Serve warm or at room temperature. Makes 8 servings.

Pastry for Double-Crust Pie: Stir together 2 cups *all-purpose flour* and ½ teaspoon *salt*. Cut in ⅔ cup *shortening* till pieces are the size of small peas. Using 6 to 7 tablespoons total *cold water*, sprinkle 1 tablespoon water over part of the mixture; gently toss with a fork. Push to side of bowl. Repeat till all is moistened. Divide dough in half.

Nutrition facts per serving: 435 cal., 18 g total fat (4 g sat. fat), 0 mg chol., 142 mg sodium, 67 g carbo., 4 g fiber, 4 g pro. *Daily values:* 11% vit. C, 1% calcium, 10% iron.

DATE PUDDING

Prep: 15 min. ◆ Bake: 30 min.

Use shallow bowls to serve this old-fashioned dessert that makes its own sweet sauce.

1 cup all-purpose flour
¾ cup packed light brown sugar
1 tsp. baking powder
½ cup milk
1 cup chopped pitted dates

◆◆◆

1¼ cups boiling water
1 cup chopped pecans or walnuts
¾ cup packed light brown sugar
1 Tbsp. margarine or butter
1 tsp. vanilla

◆◆◆

Unsweetened whipped cream (optional)

1 Grease a 2-quart rectangular baking dish; set aside. In a large mixing bowl stir together flour, ¾ cup brown sugar, and baking powder. Add milk; mix well. Stir in the dates and spread into the prepared dish.

2 In a medium mixing bowl stir together boiling water, nuts, ¾ cup brown sugar, margarine or butter, and vanilla. Pour over the date mixture in the dish.

3 Bake mixture, uncovered, in a 350° oven about 30 minutes or till set. If desired, serve warm with unsweetened whipped cream. Makes 12 to 16 servings.

Nutrition facts per serving: 244 cal., 7 g total fat (1 g sat. fat), 1 mg chol., 57 mg sodium, 45 g carbo., 2 g fiber, 2 g pro. *Daily values:* 1% vit. A, 6% calcium, 9% iron.

CHEESECAKE TREASURES

Prep: 15 min. ◆ Bake: 20 min.
Cool: 30 min. ◆ Chill: 4 to 24 hr.

Neufchâtel cheese mimics cream cheese in taste, but has a lower milk fat content and contains slightly more moisture. That means these individual desserts are high in flavor and lower in fat.

Nonstick spray coating
3 Tbsp. finely crushed vanilla wafers or graham cracker crumbs
12 oz. reduced-fat cream cheese (Neufchâtel), softened
¾ cup sugar
1 Tbsp. all-purpose flour
1½ tsp. vanilla
1 4-oz. carton refrigerated or frozen egg product, thawed (about ½ cup)
1½ tsp. finely shredded lemon or orange peel

◆◆◆

¾ to 1 cup peeled and sliced kiwifruit; halved strawberries or grapes; whole raspberries; and/or orange sections
Mint leaves (optional)
Lime slices, halved (optional)

1 Spray bottom and sides of twelve 2½- or 2¾-inch muffin cups with nonstick coating. Sprinkle with crushed vanilla wafers; set aside. In a mixing bowl beat cream cheese with an electric mixer on medium speed till smooth. Add sugar, flour, and vanilla. Beat on medium speed till fluffy. Add egg product; beat on low speed just till combined. *(Don't overbeat.)* Stir in peel. Divide mixture evenly among muffin cups.

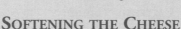

SOFTENING THE CHEESE

To ensure a smooth, creamy cheesecake, be sure to allow time for the cream cheese to soften before preparing the filling. To speed the softening, unwrap the cream cheese and cut each block into 10 cubes. Allow cheese cubes to stand at room temperature for 1 hour.

2 Bake in a 325° oven about 20 minutes or till set. Cool in pan on a wire rack about 30 minutes or till firm. Loosen edges and carefully remove cheesecakes from muffin cups. Cover and chill for 4 to 24 hours. Just before serving, spoon fresh fruit atop. If desired, garnish with mint leaves and lime slices. Makes 12 servings.

Nutrition facts per serving: 156 cal., 8 g total fat (4 g sat. fat), 23 mg chol., 135 mg sodium, 17 g carbo., 0 g fiber, 4 g pro. *Daily values:* 15% vit. A, 6% vit. C, 2% calcium, 2% iron.

HAZELNUT CAKE ROLL

Prep: 25 min. ◆ Bake: 12 min.

A traditional cake roll gets gussied up with the addition of a hazelnut-laced cream cheese filling. For a special treat, serve it by the fireside with a cup of coffee or hot chocolate.

½ cup all-purpose flour
1 tsp. baking powder

◆◆◆

4 egg yolks

½ tsp. vanilla
⅓ cup granulated sugar

◆◆◆

4 egg whites
½ cup granulated sugar

◆◆◆

Sifted powdered sugar

◆◆◆

1 recipe Cream Cheese Icing (see page 309)
1 cup chopped toasted hazelnuts (filberts) or almonds
1 recipe Chocolate Glaze (see page 309)
Sifted powdered sugar
Hazelnuts (filberts) or almonds (optional)
Sliced kumquats (optional)
Fresh raspberries (optional)

1 Grease and lightly flour a 15×10×1-inch jelly-roll pan; set pan aside. Stir together flour and baking powder; set aside.

2 In a medium mixing bowl beat egg yolks and vanilla with an electric mixer on high speed for 5 minutes or till mixture is thick and lemon-colored. Gradually add the ⅓ cup granulated sugar, beating on high speed till sugar is almost dissolved.

3 Thoroughly wash the beaters. In another bowl beat egg whites on medium speed till soft peaks form (tips curl). Gradually add the ½ cup granulated sugar, beating till stiff peaks form (tips stand straight). Fold egg yolk mixture into beaten egg whites. Sprinkle flour mixture over egg mixture; fold in gently just till combined. Spread batter evenly in the prepared pan.

4 Bake in a 375° oven for 12 to 15 minutes or till cake springs back when lightly touched. Immediately loosen edges of cake from pan and turn cake out onto a towel sprinkled with powdered sugar. Roll up towel and cake, jelly-roll style, starting from one of the cake's short sides. Cool on a wire rack. Unroll cake; remove towel.

5 Spread cake with Cream Cheese Icing to within 1 inch of edges. Sprinkle with 1 cup chopped hazelnuts. Roll up cake. Cover and chill till serving time. To serve drizzle with Chocolate Glaze and sift powdered sugar over top. If desired, garnish with hazelnuts, kumquats, and raspberries. Slice to serve. Makes 10 servings.

Cream Cheese Icing: In a small mixing bowl beat *half* of an 8-ounce package *cream cheese,* softened, with an electric mixer on medium speed till light and fluffy. Gradually beat in 1 cup sifted *powdered sugar* and 1½ teaspoons *dark rum or hazelnut liqueur* till smooth.

Chocolate Glaze: Melt 1 ounce *semisweet chocolate,* cut up, and 1 tablespoon *butter or margarine* over low heat, stirring frequently. Remove from heat. Stir in ½ cup sifted *powdered sugar,* 1 tablespoon *light-colored corn syrup,* and 1 teaspoon *hot water.* Stir in additional *hot water,* 1 teaspoon at a time, if needed, to make glaze easy to drizzle.

Nutrition facts per serving: 321 cal., 15 g total fat (5 g sat. fat), 101 mg chol., 109 mg sodium, 43 g carbo., 1 g fiber, 6 g pro. *Daily values:* 18% vit. A, 6% calcium, 8% iron.

PEPPERMINT-EGGNOG PUNCH

Start to finish: 10 min.

Santa would love to find this frothy ice cream-eggnog drink awaiting him while he makes his rounds on Christmas Eve. It's a perfect refresher for a dessert buffet, too.

1 qt. peppermint ice cream
1 qt. dairy eggnog
1 cup rum (optional)
4 12-oz. cans ginger ale, chilled
Candy canes (optional)

1 Reserve 2 or 3 scoops of ice cream in the freezer to use for garnish. In a large chilled bowl stir remaining peppermint ice cream till softened. Gradually stir in eggnog and, if using, rum. Transfer to a punch bowl; add ginger ale. Float scoops of reserved ice cream on top.

2 To serve, immediately ladle punch into punch glasses or other glasses. If desired, serve punch with candy canes. Makes about 28 (4-ounce) servings.

Nutrition facts per serving: 100 cal., 5 g total fat (1 g sat. fat), 8 mg chol., 41 mg sodium, 13 g carbo., 0 g fiber, 2 g pro. *Daily values:* 3% vit. A, 4% calcium.

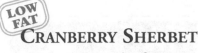

CRANBERRY SHERBET

Prep: 10 min. plus freezing

Here's another quick-to-fix make-ahead marvel that can be brought out and served with sugar cookies to delight your family and visitors.

1 12-oz. can (1½ cups) evaporated milk
1 12-oz. can frozen cranberry juice cocktail concentrate, thawed
1 tsp. finely shredded orange peel

◆◆◆

Cranberries (optional)
Variegated mint leaves (optional)

1 Stir together the evaporated milk, cranberry juice cocktail concentrate, and orange peel. Pour into a 2-quart square baking dish. Cover and freeze for 2 to 4 hours or till mixture is almost firm.

2 Break mixture into chunks. Transfer chunks to a chilled mixing bowl. Beat with an electric mixer on medium speed till fluffy, but not melted. Return to pan. Cover and freeze till firm.

3 To serve, scoop sherbet into dessert dishes. If desired, garnish with cranberries and mint leaves. Makes 6 to 8 servings.

Nutrition facts per serving: 101 cal., 4 g total fat (3 g sat. fat), 16 mg chol., 60 mg sodium, 12 g carbo., 0 g fiber, 4 g pro. *Daily values:* 4% vit. A, 52% vit. C, 12% calcium.

On the day of a gathering at our house, I change the message on our answering machine to include important details of the event, such as time, directions to the house, and what to bring. That way, I don't spend all day answering the phone and repeating the same information. I let the answering machine do the work for me.

Denise Jacobs
Dallas, Texas

30 MIN. NO FAT

APRICOT-APPLE SIPPER

Prep: 10 min. ◆ Cook: 10 min.

Get another jump on your holiday brunch by fixing this spiced fruit drink a day early, then refrigerating it. Reheat the cider and pour it into an electric crockery cooker. The cider will keep warm on the low-heat setting for up to 4 hours. (See the photograph on page 319.)

4 **cups apple cider or apple juice***

4 **cups apricot nectar**

2 **Tbsp. lemon juice**

2 **Tbsp. honey**

1 **tsp. whole cloves**

1 **tsp. whole allspice**

4 **inches stick cinnamon, broken**

◆◆◆

Cinnamon sticks (optional)

1 In a large saucepan combine apple cider or juice, apricot nectar, lemon juice, and honey. For spice bag, place cloves, allspice, and broken stick cinnamon on a double-thickness, 6-inch square of 100-percent-cotton cheesecloth. Bring corners together and tie with a clean string. Add bag to cider mixture.

2 Bring mixture to boiling; reduce heat. Simmer, covered, for 10 minutes. Discard spice bag. To serve, ladle mixture into cups. If desired, serve with cinnamon sticks. Makes about 10 (6-ounce) servings.

***Note:** If desired, substitute 4 packets *spiced cider instant apple flavor drink mix* (each packet is about ¾ oz.) and 4 cups *water* for the apple juice or cider and whole spices. Stir together; bring all ingredients to boiling. There is no need to simmer for 10 minutes before serving.

Nutrition facts per serving: 120 cal., 0 g total fat, 0 mg chol., 6 mg sodium, 32 g carbo., 1 g fiber, 0 g pro.
Daily values: 13% vit. A, 59% vit. C, 1% calcium, 5% iron.

30 MIN. LOW FAT

SOUTHEASTERN CAFÉ

Start to finish: 10 min.

Desired amount ground coffee (to make a 10-cup pot of coffee)

2 **inches stick cinnamon**

1 **1-inch piece gingerroot, thinly sliced**

2 **whole cloves**

¼ **tsp. whole cardamom seed (or 1 pod)**

⅓ **cup sweetened condensed milk, or half-and-half or light cream plus sugar to taste**

1 Measure coffee into filter-lined coffeemaker basket. Add cinnamon stick, gingerroot, cloves, and cardamom. Pour *cold water* into water compartment of coffeemaker to make 10 cups. Place pot on heating element; let water drip through basket. When coffee is finished dripping, remove basket; discard grounds and spices. Pour coffee into cups. For each serving, stir in 1 to 2 teaspoons sweetened condensed milk, or half-and-half or cream and sugar to taste. Makes 10 servings.

Nutrition facts per serving: 36 cal., 1 g total fat (1 g sat. fat), 3 mg chol., 16 mg sodium, 6 g carbo., 0 g fiber, 1 g pro.
Daily values: 1% vit. A, 2% calcium.

PRIZE TESTED RECIPE WINNER

HOT MINTY COCOA

Start to finish: 10 min.

This recipe earned Ellen Hardy of Salt Lake City, Utah, $200 in the magazine's monthly contest.

4 **cups milk**

¾ **cup sugar**

½ **cup unsweetened cocoa powder**

1 **tsp. peppermint extract or ¼ to ½ cup peppermint schnapps**

1 **pint mint-chocolate chip ice cream**

Chocolate-flavored syrup

8 **candy canes or peppermint sticks**

1 In a large saucepan combine milk, sugar, cocoa powder, and peppermint extract, if using. Heat over medium heat till hot; do not boil. Add schnapps, if using; heat through. Pour into 8 large mugs. Float a scoop of ice cream in each mug. Drizzle with chocolate-flavored syrup. Serve with candy canes or peppermint sticks. Makes 8 servings.

Nutrition facts per serving: 263 cal., 8 g total fat (5 g sat. fat), 22 mg chol., 84 mg sodium, 42 g carbo., 0 g fiber, 7 g pro. *Daily values:* 9% vit. A, 1% vit. C, 18% calcium, 7% iron.

HAZELNUT HOT COCOA

Start to finish: 10 min.

1 cup white baking pieces
⅓ cup hazelnut-flavored liquid nondairy creamer
1½ cups milk
2 cups hot brewed hazelnut-flavored coffee
Whipped cream
Ground nutmeg (optional)
Cinnamon sticks (optional)

1 In a medium saucepan melt baking pieces over low heat, stirring till smooth. Stir in liquid creamer and continue to cook and stir over low heat till smooth. Add milk and heat through. Stir in hot coffee; pour into mugs. Top with whipped cream and, if desired, sprinkle with nutmeg and serve each with a cinnamon stick. Makes 4 to 6 servings.

Nutrition facts per serving: 416 cal., 24 g total fat (17 g sat. fat), 39 mg chol., 119 mg sodium, 42 g carbo., 0 g fiber, 7 g pro. *Daily values:* 10% vit. A, 1% vit. C, 14% calcium.

SPICED CAPPUCCINO

Start to finish: 10 min.

1 cup hot brewed espresso
¼ cup flavored liquid nondairy creamer, such as amaretto, Irish creme, or French vanilla
Dash ground cinnamon
½ cup vanilla ice cream
Dash ground cardamom
2 cinnamon sticks (optional)

1 In a glass measure stir together the espresso, creamer, and cinnamon. Pour into 2 mugs. Add a scoop of ice cream to each and sprinkle with cardamom. If desired, serve with cinnamon sticks. Makes 2 servings.

Nutrition facts per serving: 189 cal., 10 g total fat (8 g sat. fat), 15 mg chol., 59 mg sodium, 26 g carbo., 0 g fiber, 1 g pro. *Daily values:* 3% vit. A, 3% calcium.

CANDY BAR COCOA

Start to finish: 10 min.

1 cup prepared hot cocoa
1 Tbsp. cream of coconut
Few drops almond extract
Whipped cream
Chopped desired candy bar

1 In a large mug stir together cocoa, cream of coconut, and almond extract. Top with whipped cream and sprinkle with candy bar. Makes 1 serving.

Nutrition facts per serving: 370 cal., 22 g total fat (14 g sat. fat), 53 mg chol., 146 mg sodium, 35 g carbo., 3 g fiber, 11 g pro. *Daily values:* 17% vit. A, 4% vit. C, 28% calcium, 7% iron.

FROTHY MOCHA SEVILLE

Start to finish: 15 min.

This recipe earned Josephine B. Piro of Easton, Pennsylvania, $400 in the magazine's monthly contest. (See the photograph on page 319.)

½ cup packed brown sugar
4 oz. semisweet chocolate, cut up
2 oz. unsweetened chocolate, cut up
3 tsp. finely shredded orange peel
½ tsp. ground cinnamon
4 cups hot brewed coffee
1 cup half-and-half or light cream, warmed
1 recipe Whipped Topping (see below)

1 Place sugar, chocolates, peel, and cinnamon in blender container. Cover; blend till chocolate is finely chopped. Remove *half* the mixture; set aside. Add *2 cups* coffee to blender; blend till chocolate is melted. Add *½ cup* cream; blend till frothy. Pour into cups. Repeat with reserved chocolate mixture and remaining coffee and cream. Pour into cups. Top each with Whipped Topping and, if desired, *orange peel.* Serves 8.

Whipped Topping: Beat ½ cup *whipping cream,* 1 tablespoon *honey,* and, if desired, 1 tablespoon *orange liqueur* till soft peaks form.

Nutrition facts per serving: 245 cal., 17 g total fat (7 g sat. fat), 32 mg chol., 24 mg sodium, 27 g carbo., 1 g fiber, 3 g pro. *Daily values:* 10% vit. A, 2% vit. C, 5% calcium, 8% iron.

Casual Weekend Breakfast

Pick a weekend morning to sleep late, then rise to enjoy an easy-to-fix café-style breakfast.

Up-and-Down Biscuits (page 22)
◆◆◆
Ham and Swiss Skillet (page 104)
◆◆◆
Fresh Fruit with Minted Yogurt (page 189)
◆◆◆
Coffee and/or fruit juice

30 minutes before:
◆ Make and bake biscuits.
◆ Prepare yogurt mixture; cover and chill.

15 minutes before:
◆ Combine fruit; divide among dessert bowls.

Just before serving:
◆ Prepare Ham and Swiss Skillet.
◆ Prepare coffee and/or fruit juice.
◆ Top fruit with yogurt.

Taste-of-the-Tropics Barbecue

When the sun's blazing down and your backyard is in full bloom, gather your family for a tropical barbecue—sizzling flavors from the grill teamed with cool and crisp side dishes.

Peanut-Ginger Chicken (page 165)
◆◆◆
Napa Cabbage Slaw (page 165)
◆◆◆
Crusty rolls of bread
◆◆◆
Floribbean Pound Cake (page 142)
◆◆◆
Beer or iced tea with lemon

The day before:
◆ Prepare marinade. Pour over chicken; chill.

Several hours before:
◆ Make and bake pound cake. Add syrup and coconut; chill.
◆ Prepare iced tea, if serving.

2 hours before:
◆ Prepare salsa; cover and chill.

1 hour before:
◆ Grill chicken.

Just before serving:
◆ Prepare slaw.
◆ Pour beer or iced tea.

Between courses:
◆ Cut cake and top with fruit and whipped cream.

Lunch with the Kids

Cherish the times when little hands like to help and spend some you-and-me time preparing and eating lunch together.

Pizza Burgers (page 30)

◆◆◆

Chips with Zip (page 90)

◆◆◆

Cut up assorted fresh fruits

◆◆◆

Chocolate-Covered Cherry Cookies (page 26)

◆◆◆

Milk

Up to 3 days before:
◆ Bake chips and cookies; cool and store at room temperature in airtight containers.

30 minutes before:
◆ Cut up fresh fruits.
◆ Prepare and broil burgers.

Just before serving:
◆ Assemble sandwiches.

Friends and Family Picnic

Wait for the perfect weather weekend, then head outdoors to enjoy sun, fun, and great picnic food.

Pork Pinwheels with Roasted Garlic Mayonnaise (page 138)

◆◆◆

Gemelli and Dried Tomato Salad* (page 151)

◆◆◆

Light Potato Salad* (page 149)

◆◆◆

Assorted fresh breads

◆◆◆

Buttermilk-Pecan Brownies with Sour Cream Frosting (page 140)

◆◆◆

Toasted Almond Ice Cream (page 173)

The day before:
◆ Prepare pasta salad; cover and chill.
◆ Prepare brownies; do not frost.
◆ Prepare Pork Pinwheels; cover and chill.

Up to 5 hours before:
◆ Make and freeze ice cream; ripen.
◆ Prepare Roasted Garlic Mayonnaise; cover and chill.
◆ Frost brownies.

Just before serving:
◆ Slice breads and arrange in a basket.

*If you're serving a larger crowd, you may want to double these recipes.

Simple Pasta Supper

*With a meal as easy as this, you can take time to do as they do in Italy—
savor good conversation over good food.*

**Fettuccine with Sweet Peppers
and Onions (page 196)**

◆◆◆

Insalata Mista (page 176)

◆◆◆

Italian bread with olive oil for dipping

◆◆◆

**Toasted Hazelnut Bars (page 220) with
frozen vanilla yogurt or ice cream**

Up to 2 weeks before:
◆ Prepare vinaigrette; cover and chill.

Up to 2 days before:
◆ Make and bake bars; cool, cut, cover, and chill.

30 minutes before:
◆ Prepare salad (do not add vinaigrette).

Just before serving:
◆ Prepare pasta.
◆ Toss vinaigrette with salad.

Between courses:
◆ Top bars with frozen yogurt or ice cream.

A Meal of Comfort Food

Treat a special someone to a dinner of old-fashioned favorites.

**Corned Beef and Cabbage
Dinner (page 60)**

◆◆◆

Dill Bread (page 236)

◆◆◆

**Mixed green salad topped with
apple slices, toasted pecans, and
poppyseed dressing**

◆◆◆

Chocolate Cookie Cake (page 246)

Several hours before:
◆ Make and bake the bread.
◆ Make filling and frosting; assemble cake
(do not garnish).
◆ Cover and store cake in the refrigerator.

3 hours before:
◆ Prepare Corned Beef and Cabbage Dinner.

Just before serving:
◆ Prepare salad.
◆ Remove cake from refrigerator.

Between courses:
◆ Garnish cake; cut into wedges.

Summertime Salad Supper

When the farmers markets are bursting with ripe fruits, fill your basket, then showcase them in this fabulous, fresh meal.

Flank Steak Salad with Cantaloupe (page 116)

♦♦♦

Light Bread or Pan Rolls (page 22)

♦♦♦

Nectarine-Pistachio Tart (page 189) with sweetened whipped cream

♦♦♦

Chilled white wine or sparkling water

Up to 3 months before:
♦ Make and bake bread or rolls; cool, cover, and freeze.

The day before:
♦ Marinate meat; cover and chill.

3 hours before:
♦ Begin preparing tart.
♦ Thaw bread or rolls at room temperature.

15 minutes before:
♦ Grill steak.
♦ Cook green beans; toss together salad mixture.

Just before serving:
♦ Arrange salad on plates.

Between courses:
♦ Whip the cream.
♦ Cut tart into wedges; top each wedge with whipped cream.

Holiday Morning Brunch

Whatever the holiday may be, Mother's Day or Christmas, bring together those who are dear for a memorable morning meal.

Smoked Salmon and Eggs in Puff Pastry (page 288)

♦♦♦

Gingered Fruit (page 288)

♦♦♦

Salad of mixed greens and tomato wedges

♦♦♦

Apricot-Apple Sipper (page 310)

The day before:
♦ Assemble pastry, prepare Sipper; cover and chill.

4 hours before:
♦ Pour Apricot-Apple Sipper into an electric crockery cooker on low setting.

1 hour before:
♦ Prepare and bake fruit.

45 minutes before:
♦ Bake pastry.

Just before serving:
♦ Arrange salad on plates.

Tree-Trimming Appetizer Buffet

After the tree is trimmed, share laughter of the season over fancy foods and flavorful spirits.

Smoked Trout Appetizers (page 251)

◆◆◆

**Chilled Artichokes with
Two Dips (page 85)**

◆◆◆

Ricotta Puffs (page 10)

◆◆◆

Wrap-and-Roll Basil Pinwheels (page 90)

◆◆◆

Pickled Carambola (page 268)

◆◆◆

Candied Orange Pecans (page 269)

◆◆◆

Assorted holiday cookies

◆◆◆

**Glacier Punch or All-Ages Glacier
Punch (page 250)**

Up to 1 month before:
◆ Prepare pecans; cover and store.

Up to 2 weeks before:
◆ Prepare Pickled Carambola; chill.

The day before:
◆ Prepare Curry Dip and Dilly Crab Dip;
cover and chill.
◆ Cook artichokes; cover and chill.
◆ Prepare Raspberry Brittle; freeze.

4 hours before:
◆ Prepare pinwheels; cover and chill.
◆ Bake pastry cups for Smoked
Trout Appetizers; cool.

2 hours before:
◆ Assemble Smoked Trout Appetizers;
cover and chill.

1 hour before:
◆ Make and bake Ricotta Puffs.

Just before serving:
◆ Prepare punch.
◆ Arrange appetizers on platters and in bowls.

Top: *Chocolate-Mint Creams (page 298)*
Above: *Chewy Noels (page 302)* and *Swirled Mint Cookies (page 304)*

Top: *Cranberry-Pecan Tassies (page 300)* and *Lemon Bars Deluxe (page 301)*
Above: *Kris Kringles (page 298)* and *Santa's Whiskers (page 303)*

Top: *Cranberry Bread with a Twist*
(page 294)
Above: *Frothy Mocha Seville (page 311)*
Left: *Smoked Salmon and Eggs in Puff*
Pastry (page 288), Gingered Fruit
(page 288), and *Apricot-Apple Sipper*
(page 310)

Cranberry-Pear Pie (page 307)

GLOSSARY

Andouille sausage: Like many Cajun foods, this spicy, smoked sausage has its roots in France. A traditional ingredient in gumbos and jambalayas, creative cooks throughout the country add andouille to soups, stews, and many other dishes to impart a smokey flavor. For an appetizer, slice andouille and add to a cheese and meat tray. Look for andouille at large supermarkets or specialty stores. If you can't find andouille, kielbasa makes a good substitute.

Bread flour: When it comes to bread making, all flours are not the same. Bread flour is made from a hard wheat giving it a higher protein and gluten content than all-purpose flour. When used in bread doughs, the extra protein and gluten provides superior structure and height. Bread flour is available in most grocery stores. Store in an airtight container in a cool, dry place for up to 5 months or freeze for up to 1 year.

Brie cheese: Mild, yet robust in flavor, savor Brie cheese as a delicious snack or use it in cooking. A snowy white, edible rind envelopes a pale yellow cheese. Made from cow's milk, a surface mold ripens the cheese from the outside in. If your preference runs to milder cheeses, choose a young Brie. This cheese will be creamy and mild-tasting and hold a cut edge when sliced. For a stronger cheese, look for a ripe Brie that will ooze when cut. When buying Brie, press down on the cheese with your finger to determine its age. If the cheese bounces back, the Brie is young. If your finger leaves an indentation, then the Brie is ripe. Another sign of ripe Brie is a slightly bulging package. Avoid buying Brie that gives off the smell of ammonia.

Chili peppers: Chili peppers are taking American cooking by storm, adding hotness and spunk to exotic as well as everyday foods. Both sweet and hot peppers are fruits of plants in the capsicum family. The term chili peppers refers to the hot ones. Several varieties are available in fresh and dried forms in most grocery stores. Some of the less common peppers can be found in Latin or Asian markets.

The jalapeño is the hot pepper of choice for most Americans. If it proves too fiery for your liking, replace it with a milder green chili, such as the New Mexico or Anaheim. The serrano pepper is more potent than the jalapeño and the habanero is hottest of all peppers. Fresh peppers should have bright colors and good shapes. Avoid shriveled, bruised, or broken peppers. Cover and store fresh peppers in your refrigerator for up to 5 days.

Ancho, mulato, and chipotle are some of the varieties of dried chili peppers. When buying dried peppers look for ones that are clean, unbroken, and have a deep or brilliant, uniform color. Store in airtight containers in a cool, dark place for up to 1 year.

Coconut milk: Coconut milk is a product made from water and coconut pulp. It is not the clear liquid in the center of the coconut. Canned unsweetened coconut milk is available in Asian markets and some supermarkets. Do not confuse unsweetened coconut milk with sweetened coconut cream often used to make mixed drinks.

Crawfish: Whether you call them crawfish, crayfish, or crawdads, these freshwater shellfish taste like shrimp only sweeter. Buy whole crawfish live (they look like small lobsters) or boiled. Cooked, peeled tails also are available either fresh or frozen. Like lobster and crab, whole crawfish should be cooked live in boiling water. When cooked, crawfish turn a bright red. Eat only those with curled tails, discarding any with straight tails. A curled tail means the crawfish was alive up until it was cooked. All of the meat is found in the tail. Plan 1 pound of crawfish per serving, which yields 3 to 4 ounces of meat.

Cremini mushrooms: Of the many mushroom varieties popping up in grocery stores, cremini are one of the most versatile. Earthy but mild in flavor, use cremini mushrooms anywhere you would use white mushrooms. Look for firm mushrooms that are plump and have no bruises or moistness. Avoid spotted or slimy mushrooms. Store fresh cremini mushrooms, unwashed, in the refrigerator for up to 2 days. Store prepackaged mushrooms in the package. Loose mushrooms or those in open packages should be stored in a paper bag or in a damp cloth bag in the refrigerator. This allows them to breathe so they stay firmer longer. To clean mushrooms, wipe them with a clean, damp cloth or rinse them lightly, then dry gently with paper towels.
continued

Curry paste: Often the culprit responsible for the fire in Asian and Indian dishes, this seasoning is made from a combination of herbs and spices. The paste comes in three colors. Red curry paste contains dried red chili peppers, green contains fresh green chilies, and yellow contains turmeric. Green curry paste is the hottest (use it sparingly) and yellow is the mildest. Look for cans or jars of curry paste in Asian grocery stores. After opening, store it in the refrigerator.

Fennel: Enjoy this delightful vegetable by itself or add it to other dishes where it bestows a subtle licoricelike flavor. To prepare fennel, cut off and discard the stalks, reserving some of the feathery, bright green leaves for a garnish. Cut the bulb into wedges or strips. Raw fennel has a light licoricelike flavor and celerylike texture. When cooked, the flavor becomes more delicate and the texture softens. Look for firm, smooth bulbs without cracks and brown spots. Stalks should be crisp and the leaves should be bright green and fresh. Fennel is available September through April.

Gluten flour: Adding just a small amount of gluten flour to breads can spell the difference between success and failure. This wheat product, sometimes called wheat gluten, is made by removing most of the starch from a high-protein, hard-wheat flour. It is frequently added to whole-wheat or rye breads made in bread machines to increase the gluten content, thus stabilizing the structure. If you can't find gluten flour at your supermarket, look for it at a health-food store. Store in an airtight container in a cool dry place for up to 5 months or freeze for up to 1 year.

Guava paste: With the taste of lime, kiwi, bananas, and berries all rolled into one, guava paste brings a taste of the tropics to your table. This thick red jelly is made by cooking down puréed guavas. In Mexico, guava paste is sliced and eaten with a knife and fork but here it is more frequently used as an ingredient in desserts. Look for guava paste in Latin American or Mexican markets. After opening, store guava paste in a plastic bag in the refrigerator.

Jamaican jerk seasoning: This snappy seasoning blend contains salt, sugar, allspice, thyme, cinnamon, onion, and red pepper. Rub Jamaican jerk seasoning onto poultry, pork, and fish, or add it to marinades and salad dressings. You'll find it on the spice shelf of most supermarkets.

Lemongrass: A staple in Asian cuisines, this vegetable looks like a green onion and tastes like a lemon. The leaves and stems are tough and fibrous, and sprout from a white, juicy, slightly bulbous base. When buying lemongrass, choose firm and unbroken stalks. Use only the tender inner portions of the white bulb. Chop the inner section and add to meat and vegetable dishes. Store lemongrass in the refrigerator for up to 3 weeks or freeze in a moisture- and vapor-proof container. If you can't find lemongrass, substitute lemon peel (½ teaspoon of lemon peel for 1 tablespoon chopped lemongrass).

Masa harina tortilla flour: This special flour is the principal ingredient in both corn tortillas and tamales. The flour is made from corn kernels that are cooked in lime water, dried, and ground into flour. Look for masa harina tortilla flour in the ethnic foods section of some grocery stores and Mexican markets.

Mascarpone cheese: Best known for its role in the classic Italian dessert, tiramisu, this ultrarich cheese pairs well with fruit, such as strawberries or pear slices, or spread over delicate crackers. Mascarpone cheese tastes like a cross between whipped butter and cream cheese. You'll find this cheese sold in plastic containers in the cheese section of your grocery store or a specialty food shop.

Mussels: This mildly to moderately flavored shellfish is instantly recognized by its bluish black shells. The cooked meat ranges in color from orange to tan. Mussels are sold live in the shell or freshly shucked. When buying live mussels, look for tightly closed shells that are moist and intact, and not chipped. If any of the shells are open, tap them lightly. If the mussels are alive, the shells will close. Mussels should smell like the sea and not have a strong odor. Refrigerate live mussels, covered with a moist cloth in an open container, for up to 3 days. Before cooking, discard any mussels that aren't alive. To clean, scrub shells with a stiff brush under cold water. Pull off the beard visible between the two shells. (Remove the beards just before cooking because the mussels will die once they are debearded.)

Napa cabbage: Crunchier and sweeter than head cabbage, napa cabbage makes a delicious addition to Asian stir-fries, salads, sandwiches, egg rolls, spring rolls, and wontons. Napa cabbage has elongated, tightly curled leaves with large white ribs and slightly frilly, pale green tips. Select fresh looking heads with crisp leaves. Avoid those with discolored, wilted leaves. To store, refrigerate in a plastic bag for up to 4 days. When napa cabbage isn't available, try substituting smaller amounts of head cabbage.

Pancetta: Often referred to as the Italian version of bacon, pancetta is made from the belly or *pancia* of a hog. Like bacon, pancetta has deep pink stripes of flesh. Unlike bacon, pancetta is not smoked. Instead, pancetta is seasoned with pepper and other spices and cured with salt. Look for pancetta, which is available flat or in a sausagelike roll, in some supermarkets, Italian grocery stores, or specialty food shops. Use this spiced meat to flavor sauces, vegetables, or meats.

Pepperoncini salad peppers: No antipasto platter would be complete without these pickled, small green peppers. When raw the peppers have a mild sweet flavor. When packed in vinegar and bottled, they make a pungent addition to salads as well as a tasty garnish. Look for them with other pickles in larger grocery stores or in Italian markets.

Phyllo dough: Many Greek desserts, appetizers, and main dishes feature layers of this paper-thin pastry. Although phyllo can

be made at home, a frozen commercial product is available and much more handy to use. Allow frozen phyllo dough to thaw while it is still wrapped. Once unwrapped, sheets of phyllo dough quickly dry out and become unusable. To preserve phyllo sheets, keep the stack of dough covered with plastic wrap while you're preparing your recipe. Rewrap any remaining sheets of the dough and return them to your freezer.

Plantains: It looks like a banana, but acts like a vegetable. This tropical fruit resembles a banana with a thick, green skin and a longer, more squared-off shape. Unlike bananas, plantains must be cooked to be enjoyed. Look for plump, undamaged plantains, but don't be too concerned about slight bruises. The tough skin absorbs most of the bumps. Ripen plantains at room temperature. It takes 1 week for them to turn from totally green to yellow-brown and another week or two until the plantains are black and fully ripe. They can be cooked at various stages of ripeness.

Portobello mushrooms: These giants of the mushroom family are actually mature brown mushrooms. Their large size makes them ideal for grilling. In fact, cooking enhances the hearty beef flavor. Look for fresh portobellos, whole or sliced, in most supermarkets. Choose those that are firm with dry gills, and with no soft spots on the caps. Refrigerate them unwashed and in paper bags or with a paper towel in a porous plastic bag. They will keep for several days to a week.

Shiitake mushrooms: These Oriental mushrooms are easy to recognize by their large floppy caps; tough slender stems; and a smoky, woodsy flavor. Cook only the caps; remove and discard the stems before using. Look for fresh or dried shiitake mushrooms in larger grocery stores. Store unwashed fresh mushrooms in the refrigerator for up to 2 days. Soak dried mushrooms in warm water; rinse well, and remove stems before using.

Squid: A relative of the octopus, squid is a saltwater shellfish also known by its Italian name, calamari. The firm, white meat is mild and generally takes in the flavor of ingredients with which it's cooked. Fresh squid is available whole or processed into tubes, rings, or strips. Frozen squid is sold cleaned. Squid also can be found smoked and dried.

Star anise: Although it is not related to anise seed, this star-shaped spice has a similar licorice-like flavor. A perfect star anise is an eight-pointed star, but most frequently you'll find the pod broken into pieces. Star anise is one of the spices used to make five-spice powder. Look for star anise in Asian grocery stores and larger supermarkets.

Thai fish sauce: This bold, salty condiment is used to season foods at the table and during cooking. The thin brown liquid is made from fermented fish. A little goes a long way, so add it judiciously to Thai and other Asian dishes. Look for fish sauce with the ethnic foods in larger supermarkets and Asian grocery stores.

INDEX

EMERGENCY SUBSTITUTIONS

IF YOU DON'T HAVE:	SUBSTITUTE:
1 teaspoon baking powder	½ teaspoon cream of tartar plus ¼ teaspoon baking soda
1 tablespoon cornstarch (for thickening)	2 tablespoons all-purpose flour
1 package active dry yeast	1 cake compressed yeast
1 cup buttermilk	1 tablespoon lemon juice or vinegar plus enough milk to make 1 cup (let stand 5 minutes before using); or 1 cup plain yogurt
1 cup whole milk	½ cup evaporated milk plus ½ cup water; or 1 cup water plus ⅓ cup nonfat dry milk powder
1 cup light cream	1 tablespoon melted butter or margarine plus enough whole milk to make 1 cup
1 cup dairy sour cream	1 cup plain yogurt
1 whole egg	2 egg whites, 2 egg yolks, or 3 tablespoons frozen egg product, thawed
1 cup margarine	1 cup butter; or 1 cup shortening plus ¼ teaspoon salt, if desired
1 ounce semisweet chocolate	3 tablespoons semisweet chocolate pieces; or 1 ounce unsweetened chocolate plus 1 tablespoon granulated sugar
1 ounce unsweetened chocolate	3 tablespoons unsweetened cocoa powder plus 1 tablespoon cooking oil or shortening, melted
1 cup corn syrup	1 cup granulated sugar plus ¼ cup liquid
1 cup honey	1¼ cups granulated sugar plus ¼ cup liquid
1 cup molasses	1 cup honey
1 cup granulated sugar	1 cup packed brown sugar or 2 cups sifted powdered sugar
1 cup beef broth or chicken broth	1 teaspoon or 1 cube instant beef or chicken bouillon plus 1 cup hot water
2 cups tomato sauce	¾ cup tomato paste plus 1 cup water
1 cup tomato juice	½ cup tomato sauce plus ½ cup water
¼ cup fine dry bread crumbs	¾ cup soft bread crumbs, ¼ cup cracker crumbs, or ¼ cup cornflake crumbs
1 small onion, chopped (⅓ cup)	1 teaspoon onion powder or 1 tablespoon dried minced onion
1 clove garlic	½ teaspoon bottled minced garlic or ⅛ teaspoon garlic powder
1 teaspoon lemon juice	½ teaspoon vinegar
1 teaspoon poultry seasoning	¾ teaspoon dried sage, crushed, plus ¼ teaspoon dried thyme or marjoram, crushed
1 teaspoon dry mustard (in cooked mixtures)	1 tablespoon prepared mustard
1 tablespoon snipped fresh herb	½ to 1 teaspoon dried herb, crushed
1 teaspoon dried herb	½ teaspoon ground herb
1 teaspoon grated gingerroot	¼ teaspoon ground ginger
1 teaspoon apple pie spice	½ teaspoon ground cinnamon plus ¼ teaspoon ground nutmeg, ⅛ teaspoon ground allspice, and dash ground cloves or ginger
1 teaspoon pumpkin pie spice	½ teaspoon ground cinnamon plus ¼ teaspoon ground ginger, ¼ teaspoon ground allspice, and ⅛ teaspoon ground nutmeg

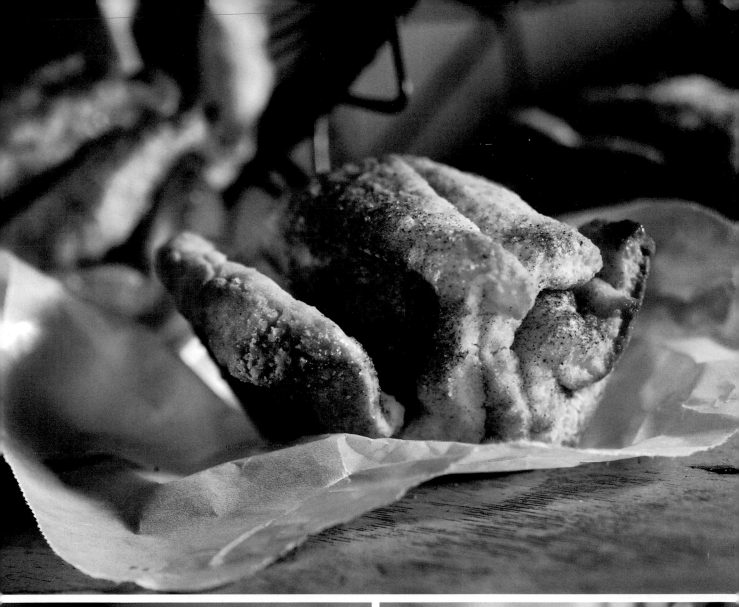

Top: *Up-and-Down Biscuits (page 22)*
Above left: *Apple-Walnut Cobbler (page 25)*
Above right: *Pumpkin-Pecan Pie (page 25)*

Chocolate-Covered Cherry Cookies (page 26)

Left: *Chocolate Cream Cheese Cake (page 24)*
Below: *White Chocolate Cream Cheese Cake (page 24)*

Left: *Easy Peach Crisp*
(page 22)
Below: *Linguine with*
Mixed Nuts and
Gorgonzola (page 45)

JERK CHICKEN SALAD

Prep: 20 min. ◆ Grill: 20 min.

Jerk seasoning—a blend of chili, thyme, garlic, onion, and ginger— derives its name from Jerk Island, near Jamaica in the Caribbean.

⅓ cup olive oil

2 Tbsp. lime juice

2 tsp. snipped fresh thyme or ½ tsp. dried thyme, crushed

1 tsp. honey

1 lb. skinless, boneless chicken breast halves

1 plantain, 2 red bananas, or 1 large yellow banana, sliced

◆◆◆

2 Tbsp. Jamaican jerk seasoning

1 medium red or yellow sweet pepper, cut into strips

◆◆◆

6 cups torn mixed greens

1 medium avocado, halved, seeded, peeled, and cut into thin wedges

1 medium mango, peeled and cut into thin wedges

1 In a screw-top jar combine oil, lime juice, thyme, and honey; cover and shake well. Remove 1 tablespoon dressing. Set remaining dressing aside. Rinse chicken; pat dry. Brush the chicken and plantain or red bananas with the 1 tablespoon reserved dressing.

2 Rub jerk seasoning onto chicken. Grill chicken on the rack of an uncovered grill directly over medium coals 12 to 15 minutes or till no longer pink, turning once. Remove chicken from grill; cut into strips and set aside. Grill plantain or red bananas (if using yellow banana, do not grill) and

pepper strips over medium coals about 8 minutes or till tender.

3 In a large bowl toss together greens and remaining dressing. Divide among 4 plates. Top each with chicken, plantain or banana, peppers, avocado, and mango. Makes 4 main-dish servings.

Nutrition facts per serving: 492 cal., 29 g total fat (5 g sat. fat), 59 mg chol., 364 mg sodium, 38 g carbo., 7 g fiber, 26 g pro. *Daily values:* 84% vit. A, 131% vit. C, 8% calcium, 25% iron.

GRILLED VEGETABLE SALAD

Prep: 20 min. ◆ Grill: 8 min.

Vegetables may need more or less grilling time depending on their thickness and the heat of the coals. (See the photograph on page 119.)

1 medium red onion, cut into ¾-inch-thick slices

1 medium eggplant, cut crosswise into 1-inch-thick slices

2 large red sweet peppers, cut into ¾-inch-thick rings

6 fresh thin asparagus spears, trimmed

1 medium zucchini, sliced lengthwise into ¼-inch slices

1 medium yellow squash, sliced lengthwise into ¼-inch slices

¼ cup olive oil

◆◆◆

6 cups torn mixed greens

¼ cup balsamic vinegar

¼ cup snipped fresh basil

1 Brush vegetables with olive oil and, if desired, sprinkle each

"TLC" FOR SALAD GREENS

The different leaf lettuce varieties, such as romaine and green leaf, can be washed ahead of time and stored for several days. Remove the core and pull apart the separate leaves. (Do not cut away stems and ribs till ready to prepare salad.)

Remove any brown-edged, bruised, wilted, or old leaves. Wash greens first under cold running water, then separate leaves and rinse them in a colander under cold water.

Shake washed lettuce greens dry. If they're very sandy or gritty, repeat washing and rinsing steps. Layer leaves on paper towels and store in a sealed container or sealable plastic bag. Cleaned lettuce will keep this way for a week.

side with *freshly ground pepper* and *salt*. Lay vegetables perpendicular to wires on rack of an uncovered grill directly over medium to medium-hot coals. Grill onion, eggplant, and pepper rings for 8 to 10 minutes. Grill asparagus, zucchini, and yellow squash for 5 to 6 minutes or till crisp-tender, turning occasionally. Arrange vegetables on mixed greens. Drizzle with vinegar and sprinkle with basil. Makes 6 side-dish servings.

Nutrition facts per serving: 139 cal., 9 g total fat (1 g sat. fat), 0 mg chol., 24 mg sodium, 13 g carbo., 4 g fiber, 3 g pro. *Daily values:* 38% vit. A, 101% vit. C, 3% calcium, 11% iron.

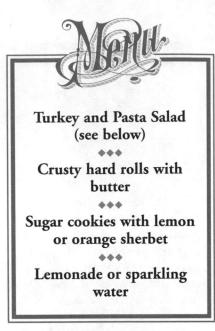
**30 MIN.
LOW FAT**

TURKEY AND PASTA
SALAD

Start to finish: 30 min.

*This healthful salad is low in fat
and packed with plenty of B vitamins,
vitamin C, and protein.*

6 oz. radiatore or rotelle pasta
1 medium apple, cored and cut
   into very thin slices
1 Tbsp. lime juice or lemon
   juice
8 oz. fully cooked smoked
   turkey, cut into bite-size
   pieces
1 cup fresh strawberries,
   quartered
½ cup sliced celery

♦♦♦

¼ cup plain fat-free yogurt
2 Tbsp. fat-free mayonnaise
   dressing or salad dressing
2 Tbsp. skim milk
4 tsp. Dijon-style mustard
¼ tsp. celery seed
1 Tbsp. fresh marjoram leaves

1 Cook pasta according to
package directions; rinse with
cold water and drain well. Toss

apple slices with lime or lemon
juice to coat. In a large mixing
bowl toss together the cooked
pasta, apple, turkey, strawberries,
and celery.

2 For dressing, in a small mixing bowl combine yogurt, mayonnaise dressing or salad dressing,
milk, mustard, and celery seed.
Drizzle dressing over pasta mixture, tossing gently to coat. Top
with marjoram. Makes 8 side-dish
or 4 main-dish servings.

Nutrition facts per side-dish serving:
140 cal., 1 g total fat (0 g sat. fat), 12 mg
chol., 415 mg sodium, 23 g carbo., 1 g
fiber, 10 g pro.
Daily values: 21% vit. C, 3% calcium,
7% iron.

THAI TURKEY KABOBS

Prep: 40 min. ♦ Broil: 12 min.

*This recipe earned Lisa Keys of
Middlebury, Connecticut, $400 in the
magazine's monthly contest.*

1 cup soft bread crumbs
¼ cup chopped green onions
2 Tbsp. Thai fish sauce or soy
   sauce
1 egg white
1 Tbsp. snipped fresh cilantro
1 large clove garlic, minced
1 tsp. ground ginger
1 lb. ground raw turkey
2 red sweet peppers, cut into
   1½-inch pieces

♦♦♦

¼ cup pepper jelly
1 Tbsp. margarine or butter
   Hot cooked rice (optional)
   Bottled plum sauce
   (optional)

1 In a medium mixing bowl
combine bread crumbs, green
onions, fish sauce or soy sauce,
egg white, cilantro, garlic, and
ginger. Add ground turkey; mix
well. Shape into 30 meatballs.*
On 12 metal skewers, alternately
thread meatballs and red pepper
pieces, leaving ¼-inch space
between each piece. Spray a broiler pan with *nonstick spray coating.*
Place skewers on the unheated
rack of the broiler pan.

2 Meanwhile, in a small
saucepan, combine the pepper
jelly and margarine or butter.
Cook and stir over low heat till
jelly melts. Brush *half* of the jelly
mixture over meatballs and peppers. Broil 4 to 6 inches from the
heat for 6 minutes. Turn kabobs;
brush with remaining jelly mixture. Broil 6 to 8 minutes more or
till meat is no longer pink. If
desired, serve over hot rice with
plum sauce. Makes 6 servings.

*Note: For 30 meatballs of
equal size, on waxed paper shape
meat mixture into a 6×5-inch rectangle. Cut into 1-inch squares;
roll each square into a ball.

Nutrition facts per serving: 180 cal., 8 g
total fat (2 g sat. fat), 30 mg chol., 292 mg
sodium, 15 g carbo., 1 g fiber, 12 g pro.
Daily values: 21% vit. A, 71% vit. C.

**LOW
FAT**

CHICKEN MARSALA

Prep: 25 min. ♦ Cook: 10 min.

*In the traditional recipe, the chicken
breasts are left whole. By cutting the
chicken into bite-size pieces, we reduced
the cooking time by more than half.*

12 oz. skinless, boneless chicken
   breast halves

3 Tbsp. all-purpose flour
½ tsp. seasoned salt
⅛ tsp. pepper

◆◆◆

1 Tbsp. cooking oil
8 oz. fresh button mushrooms, quartered
½ cup reduced-sodium chicken broth

◆◆◆

½ cup dry marsala wine or reduced-sodium chicken broth
1 Tbsp. all-purpose flour
Hot cooked linguine
Snipped fresh parsley

1 Rinse chicken; pat dry. Cut chicken into bite-size pieces. In a shallow dish stir together the 3 tablespoons flour, seasoned salt, and pepper. Add chicken pieces, tossing to coat.

2 In a large skillet, cook chicken in hot oil over medium heat 5 minutes or till chicken is tender and no longer pink, stirring occasionally. (Add more oil if necessary to prevent sticking.) Remove from skillet. Add mushrooms and ½ cup broth to skillet. Bring to boiling; reduce heat. Simmer, covered, for 3 to 5 minutes or till mushrooms are tender.

3 Stir together the wine or broth and 1 tablespoon flour. Add to skillet. Cook and stir over medium heat till thickened and bubbly. Cook and stir 1 minute more. Add chicken; heat through. Serve chicken with pasta. Sprinkle with parsley. Makes 4 servings.

Nutrition facts per serving: 333 cal., 7 g total fat (1 g sat. fat), 45 mg chol., 283 mg sodium, 39 g carbo., 3 g fiber, 23 g pro. *Daily values:* 3% vit. C, 25% calcium, 25% iron.

CHICKEN PAPRIKA

Start to finish: 35 min.

12 oz. skinless, boneless chicken breast halves
Nonstick spray coating

◆◆◆

¾ cup chicken broth
½ cup chopped onion
½ cup chopped green sweet pepper
½ cup chopped, seeded tomato
2 cloves garlic, minced
2 tsp. paprika
⅛ tsp. ground black pepper

◆◆◆

1 8-oz. carton plain yogurt
2 Tbsp. all-purpose flour
Hot cooked rice

1 Rinse chicken; pat dry. Cut chicken into bite-size pieces. Spray a cold large skillet with nonstick coating. Heat over medium-high heat. Add chicken. Cook and stir 3 to 4 minutes or till chicken is no longer pink. Remove from skillet; set aside.

2 Add broth, onion, green pepper, tomato, and garlic to skillet. Bring to boiling; reduce heat. Simmer, covered, about 5 minutes or till vegetables are tender. Stir in paprika and black pepper.

3 Stir together the yogurt and flour. Add to the mixture in the skillet. Cook and stir over medium heat till thickened and bubbly. Cook and stir 1 minute more. Stir in chicken; heat through. Serve over rice. Makes 4 servings.

Nutrition facts per serving: 271 cal., 4 g total fat (1 g sat. fat), 48 mg chol., 230 mg sodium, 34 g carbo., 9 g fiber, 23 g pro. *Daily values:* 10% vit. A, 28% vit. C, 11% calcium, 15% iron.

TEST KITCHEN TIP

PICK A PEPPERCORN

When ground from the whole dried berry, pepper's natural sweetness comes through its heat. Pepper, the world's most popular spice, is used in many salad recipes to accent the fresh flavor of the springtime greens. Peppercorns come in black, green, and white, each with a different flavor and intensity.

Black, green, and white peppercorns are actually berries from the *Piper nigrum* vine. Pepper's strong flavor comes from volatile oils in the berry. Over time, the flavors from these oils dissipate and only the heat remains. Keep pepper in tightly sealed containers and discard any pepper older than six months.

Black: The berries used (for black pepper) are harvested while slightly underripe, then sun-dried. These are the strongest and most aromatic of the three peppercorns.

Green: These soft green berries are picked while still immature, giving them a mild flavor. They are available freeze-dried or packed in brine.

White: These mild-tasting peppercorns come from mature berries. The outer skins are removed, leaving the white peppercorns inside. They are sold whole or ground.

TERIYAKI CHICKEN WITH CUCUMBERS

Prep: 20 min. ◆ Marinate: 30 min.
Cook: 10 min.

This recipe earned Christina Nguyen of Houston, Texas, $200 in the magazine's monthly contest.

 4 large skinless, boneless
    chicken breast halves
    (about 1 lb.)
 1 Tbsp. teriyaki sauce
 2 tsp. toasted sesame oil
 ½ tsp. grated gingerroot
 1 clove garlic, minced
 ½ tsp. sugar
         ◆◆◆
 3 medium cucumbers, thinly
    bias-sliced (about 4 cups)
 2 Tbsp. cider vinegar
 1½ tsp. sugar
 ¾ tsp. salt
 ½ tsp. crushed red pepper
         ◆◆◆
 2 tsp. cooking oil
    Fresh red serrano peppers
    (optional)

1 Rinse chicken; pat dry. Place chicken in a plastic bag set in a shallow dish. For marinade, in a small bowl stir together teriyaki sauce, sesame oil, gingerroot, garlic, and ½ teaspoon sugar. Pour over chicken in bag; close bag. Marinate in the refrigerator for 30 minutes, turning bag occasionally. Drain chicken, discarding marinade.

2 Meanwhile, in a medium bowl combine cucumbers, vinegar, 1½ teaspoons sugar, salt, and crushed red pepper. Cover and chill till serving time.

3 In a large nonstick skillet cook chicken in hot oil over medium heat 10 to 12 minutes or till chicken is tender and no longer pink, turning once. Remove and cut chicken into bite-size strips.

4 To serve, arrange cucumbers on a plate. Top with chicken. If desired, garnish with red peppers. Makes 4 servings.

Nutrition facts per serving: 180 cal., 7 g total fat (1 g sat. fat), 59 mg chol., 573 mg sodium, 6 g carbo., 1 g fiber, 23 g pro. *Daily values:* 4% vit. A, 9% vit. C, 2% calcium, 7% iron.

STROGANOFF-STYLE CHICKEN

Start to finish: 50 min.

 12 oz. skinless, boneless chicken
     breast halves
 ½ tsp. ground coriander
 ½ tsp. dried thyme, crushed
 ¼ tsp. dried oregano, crushed
 ¼ tsp. dried basil, crushed
 ⅛ tsp. ground nutmeg
 ⅛ tsp. pepper
     Nonstick spray coating
         ◆◆◆
 1 Tbsp. cooking oil
 2 cups sliced fresh mushrooms
 ½ cup chopped onion
 2 cloves garlic, minced
         ◆◆◆
 1 14½-oz. can reduced-sodium
    chicken broth
 ½ of an 8-oz. package reduced-
    fat cream cheese
    (Neufchâtel), cut up

 2 Tbsp. grated Parmesan
    cheese
 ½ cup skim milk
 2 Tbsp. all-purpose flour
    Hot cooked noodles
    Snipped fresh parsley

1 Rinse chicken; pat dry. Cut into bite-size pieces. In a shallow dish stir together the coriander, thyme, oregano, basil, nutmeg, and pepper. Add chicken pieces, tossing to coat well.

2 Spray a cold large skillet with nonstick coating. Heat over medium-high heat. Add chicken; cook and stir for 3 to 4 minutes or till chicken is tender and no longer pink. Remove chicken from skillet. Add oil to skillet. Heat over medium-high heat. Add mushrooms, onion, and garlic. Cook and stir for 3 to 4 minutes or till vegetables are tender.

3 Carefully add chicken broth to skillet. Bring to boiling; reduce heat. Boil gently, uncovered, about 15 minutes or till broth is reduced by half. Stir in cream cheese and Parmesan cheese. In a screw-top jar shake together the milk and flour till combined. Add to skillet. Cook and stir till thickened and bubbly. Cook and stir 1 minute more. Add chicken; heat through. Serve over hot cooked noodles. Sprinkle with parsley. Makes 4 servings.

Nutrition facts per serving: 413 cal., 16 g total fat (6 g sat. fat), 107 mg chol., 520 mg sodium, 38 g carbo., 4 g fiber, 29 g pro. *Daily values:* 13% vit. A, 5% vit. C, 11% calcium, 18% iron.

GARLIC-SAUCED CHICKEN OVER PASTA

Prep: 25 min. ◆ Cook: 41 min.

Wow—15 to 20 garlic cloves sounds like a lot! You'll find that after cooking, the garlic sweetly mellows. (See the photograph on page 123.)

2 lb. meaty chicken pieces
⅓ cup all-purpose flour
♦♦♦
1 Tbsp. olive oil
15 to 20 garlic cloves, peeled
1¼ cups rosé wine
¾ cup water
1 tsp. paprika
½ tsp. poultry seasoning
¼ tsp. pepper
♦♦♦
¼ cup water
2 Tbsp. all-purpose flour
1 Tbsp. snipped fresh basil or
   1 tsp. dried basil, crushed
   Hot cooked penne pasta

1 Skin chicken, if desired. Rinse chicken; pat dry. Place the ⅓ cup flour in a plastic bag. Add a few chicken pieces at a time to the flour, shaking to coat.

2 In a 12-inch nonstick skillet heat olive oil. Add chicken and garlic cloves to skillet. Cook, uncovered, over medium heat for 10 minutes, turning to brown evenly. Reduce heat; carefully add the wine, ¾ cup water, paprika, poultry seasoning, pepper, and ¼ teaspoon *salt*. Bring to boiling; reduce heat. Simmer, covered, about 30 minutes or till chicken is tender and no longer pink. Remove chicken; keep warm.

3 Skim fat from drippings. Crush garlic with the tines of a fork. Stir together the ¼ cup water, the 2 tablespoons flour, and basil; stir into pan drippings. Cook and stir till thickened and bubbly. Cook and stir for 1 minute more. Serve chicken and sauce over hot cooked pasta. If desired, garnish with additional *fresh basil*. Makes 6 servings.

Nutrition facts per serving: 419 cal., 12 g total fat (3 g sat. fat), 69 mg chol., 156 mg sodium, 40 g carbo., 2 g fiber, 29 g pro. *Daily values:* 4% vit. A, 4% vit. C, 3% calcium, 22% iron.

SHEPHERD'S PIE

Prep: 40 min. ◆ Bake: 15 min.

Need a hearty, Sunday-style meal for during the week? Try this easy-to-make, sure-to-please, potato-topped casserole.

12 oz. ground beef
1 cup thinly sliced carrots
½ cup chopped onion
½ cup chopped green sweet pepper
2 cloves garlic, minced
1 14½-oz. can undrained tomatoes, cut up
1 10¾-oz. can condensed tomato soup
1 Tbsp. brown sugar
1 Tbsp. Dijon-style mustard
1 Tbsp. balsamic vinegar
½ tsp. Worcestershire sauce
⅛ tsp. ground black pepper
1 cup frozen cut green beans
♦♦♦
3 medium potatoes, peeled and cut up
1 cup shredded cabbage
⅛ tsp. ground black pepper
   Milk
¾ cup shredded cheddar cheese

1 In a large skillet cook beef, carrots, onion, green pepper, and garlic till beef is no longer pink. Drain off fat. Stir in *undrained* tomatoes, tomato soup, brown sugar, Dijon-style mustard, vinegar, Worcestershire sauce, and ⅛ teaspoon pepper. Bring to boiling; add beans. Return to boiling; reduce heat. Simmer, covered, for 10 minutes. Uncover and simmer about 5 minutes more or till slightly thickened.

2 Meanwhile, cook potatoes, covered, in boiling *salted water* for 15 minutes. Add cabbage and cook for 5 to 10 minutes more or till potatoes are tender; drain. Mash with a potato masher or beat with an electric mixer on low speed. Beat in ⅛ teaspoon pepper and enough milk to make fluffy. Stir in *½ cup* of the cheese.

3 Spoon beef mixture into a 2-quart square baking dish. Spoon potato mixture into 4 mounds atop beef mixture. Bake, uncovered, in a 350° oven 15 minutes. Sprinkle potato mounds with remaining cheese. Let stand for 5 minutes. Makes 4 servings.

Nutrition facts per serving: 485 cal., 20 g total fat (9 g sat. fat), 77 mg chol., 1,018 mg sodium, 51 g carbo., 4 g fiber, 28 g pro. *Daily values:* 100% vit. A, 147% vit. C, 22% calcium, 31% iron.

Menu

Garlic-Sauced Chicken Over Pasta
(see left)
♦♦♦
Sautéed zucchini and yellow summer squash
♦♦♦
French bread
♦♦♦
White wine or beer

How Many Does a Recipe Serve?

With each recipe in this book, we suggest the number of servings. These servings are based on satiety value (not on the Food Guide Pyramid portion sizes). When planning menus and selecting recipes, keep in mind that appetites and accompanying foods affect how far a recipe will stretch. A family with two adults and two children, for instance, may find a recipe that "serves four" is exactly right; another family with two parents and a teenage son may find the same recipe barely feeds three. If you have young children who eat small portions or family members who tend to snack throughout the day, you'll probably serve more people than a recipe suggests. On the other hand, men, teenage boys, athletes, or pregnant women need more calories, so you probably won't have many leftovers.

Flank Steak Salad With Cantaloupe

Prep: 10 min. ◆ Marinate: 12 to 24 hr.
Grill: 12 min.

The green beans in this salad can be left uncooked, if desired. Choose crisp, dark green beans that stand up straight and snap easily.
(See the photograph on page 117.)

1 8-oz. bottle Italian salad
   dressing
2 tsp. finely shredded lemon
   peel

1 lb. beef flank steak
   Lemon-pepper seasoning
   ◆◆◆
8 oz. fresh haricots vert or
   other young, tender green
   beans, trimmed
5 cups torn leaf lettuce
3 cups watercress or arugula
   ◆◆◆
1 medium cantaloupe, cut into
   wedges
   Teardrop or other cherry
   tomatoes (optional)

1 Mix salad dressing and lemon peel. Sprinkle steak with lemon-pepper seasoning. Place steak in a plastic bag set in a glass dish; pour ¾ *cup* of the dressing mixture over meat. Seal bag and marinate in refrigerator for 12 to 24 hours, turning occasionally. At serving time, remove steak from bag; discard excess marinade. Grill steak on rack of an uncovered grill directly over medium-hot coals 12 to 14 minutes or till desired doneness, turning once.

2 Meanwhile, in a medium saucepan add beans to *boiling water*. Simmer, covered, about 2 minutes or till crisp-tender. Drain; rinse in cold water and set aside. In a large mixing bowl toss the green beans with the lettuce and watercress or arugula. Arrange tossed salad mixture on individual dinner plates.

3 Thinly slice the flank steak across the grain. Arrange slices on top of the greens. Serve with cantaloupe wedges and, if desired, garnish with tomatoes. Drizzle salad with remaining ¼ cup dressing. Makes 6 main-dish servings.

Nutrition facts per serving: 248 cal., 15 g total fat (4 g sat. fat), 35 mg chol., 245 mg sodium, 12 g carbo., 1 g fiber, 16 g pro. *Daily values:* 37% vit. A, 76% vit. C, 4% calcium, 14% iron.

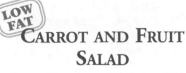

Carrot and Fruit Salad

Prep: 15 min. ◆ Chill: 4 to 24 hr.

This carrot salad will stay fresh and crisp for two to three days if refrigerated in a tightly covered container.
(See the photograph on page 117.)

2 medium carrots, peeled
1½ cups fresh pineapple chunks
   or one 15-oz. can
   pineapple chunks, drained
¼ cup raisins
¼ cup pecan pieces
½ cup plain low-fat yogurt
1 Tbsp. frozen orange juice
   concentrate, thawed
   ◆◆◆
1 medium peach or nectarine
1½ cups torn sorrel leaves

1 Using a vegetable peeler, cut carrots lengthwise into thin strips (you should have about 2 cups). In a medium bowl combine carrot strips, pineapple chunks, raisins, and pecans. Stir together yogurt and orange juice concentrate. Stir yogurt dressing into carrot mixture. Cover and chill thoroughly.

2 Cut peach or nectarine into thin wedges; toss with carrot salad. Serve on sorrel-lined plates. Makes 4 side-dish servings.

Nutrition facts per serving: 164 cal., 5 g total fat (1 g sat. fat), 2 mg chol., 61 mg sodium, 28 g carbo., 4 g fiber, 4 g pro. *Daily values:* 102% vit. A, 43% vit. C, 8% calcium, 9% iron.

½ cup packed brown sugar
½ tsp. mustard seed
¼ tsp. ground turmeric
¼ tsp. celery seed

1 In a small glass or ceramic bowl combine zucchini, onion, garlic, and pickling salt. Add about 2 inches of cracked ice or cover with cold water. Refrigerate for 3 hours; drain well.

2 In a small saucepan combine the vinegar, brown sugar, mustard seed, turmeric, and celery seed. Bring to boiling; reduce heat. Simmer, uncovered, for 3 minutes. Allow to cool; pour over zucchini mixture. Marinate overnight in the refrigerator. (Mixture will keep up to 3 days in the refrigerator.) Makes about 2 cups (16 servings).

*Note: For crisper zucchini, cut into 1½-inch-long sticks.

Nutrition facts per serving: 11 cal., 0 g total fat, 0 mg chol., 134 mg sodium, 3 g carbo., 0 g fiber, 0 g pro.
Daily values: 1% vit. C, 1% iron.

PICKLED ONIONS

Prep: 40 min. plus chilling

4 cups water
12 oz. pearl onions or shallots or 2½ cups frozen small whole onions, thawed
1 Tbsp. pickling salt
♦♦♦
2 bay leaves
1 tsp. juniper berries or 1 Tbsp. gin
1 cup white vinegar
3 Tbsp. sugar
1 tsp. pickling salt

1 tsp. dried whole mixed peppercorns
1 small fresh hot red chili pepper or jalapeño pepper

1 In a medium saucepan bring the 4 cups of water to boiling. Peel onions or shallots. Immerse the whole fresh onions or shallots, if using, in boiling water for 3 minutes; drain. (Omit this step if using frozen onions.) Trim off the root ends of onions or shallots and gently press to slip off the skins. Place onions or shallots in a medium glass or ceramic bowl. Sprinkle with the 1 tablespoon pickling salt. Add enough *cold water* to just cover onions; let stand overnight in refrigerator.

2 The next day, rinse onions or shallots and drain well. Tie the bay leaves and, if using, juniper berries in a 6-inch square of 100% cotton cheesecloth. (Do not tie bay leaves in cheesecloth if using gin.) In a medium saucepan combine the cheesecloth bag of herbs (or the bay leaves and gin), the vinegar, sugar, 1 teaspoon pickling salt, peppercorns, and chili pepper. Bring the vinegar mixture to boiling; reduce heat. Simmer, covered, for 5 minutes. Add onions or shallots; return to boiling and reduce heat. Simmer, uncovered, for 2 to 3 minutes or till crisp-tender. Remove and discard cheesecloth bag or bay leaves. Transfer onions and liquid to hot clean screw-top jars. Cover; refrigerate for at least 1 week (or up to 3 months) before using. Makes about 2½ cups (20 servings).

Nutrition facts per serving: 16 cal., 0 g total fat, 0 mg chol., 267 mg sodium, 4 g carbo., 0 g fiber, 0 g pro.
Daily values: 3% vit. C, 1% iron.

CANDIED ORANGE PECANS

Prep: 10 min. ♦ Cook: 35 min.

5 cups pecan halves, toasted
♦♦♦
1¼ cups sugar
¾ cup half-and-half or light cream
2 Tbsp. finely shredded orange peel
2 tsp. orange juice
Dash salt

1 To toast pecans, spread pecan halves in a single layer in a shallow baking pan. Bake in a 350° oven for 5 to 10 minutes or till golden brown; cool.

2 Line a baking sheet with foil. Butter foil; set aside. Place cooled, toasted pecans in an extra-large bowl.

3 In a 1½-quart saucepan combine sugar, half-and-half, orange peel, orange juice, and salt. Cook and stir over medium-high heat till mixture comes to boiling. Clip candy thermometer to pan. Reduce heat to medium-low; continue boiling at a moderate, steady rate, stirring occasionally, till thermometer registers 234°, soft-ball stage (about 25 minutes). Remove from heat. Pour over pecan halves, stirring to coat. Immediately spread pecan mixture onto prepared baking sheet. Cool completely; break into pieces. Store in an airtight container at room temperature up to 1 month. Makes 12 servings.

Nutrition facts per serving: 402 cal., 32 g total fat (4 g sat. fat), 6 mg chol., 18 mg sodium, 30 g carbo., 3 g fiber, 4 g pro.
Daily values: 2% vit. A, 4% vit. C, 2% calcium, 6% iron.

WHOLE WHEAT BISCUIT MIX

Prep 20 min. ◆ Bake: 8 or 15 min.

One batch of mix makes about 48 biscuits. Keep the mix on your kitchen shelf for up to 6 weeks or in the freezer for 6 months.

6 cups all-purpose flour
4 cups whole wheat flour
⅓ cup baking powder
¼ cup sugar
2 tsp. salt
2 cups shortening

1 In an extra-large bowl stir together all-purpose flour, whole wheat flour, baking powder, sugar, and salt. Using a pastry blender, cut in shortening till mixture resembles coarse crumbs. Place mixture in a freezer container. Cover and store in the freezer.

2 To use, bring mix to room temperature. Spoon mix lightly into a measuring cup; level off with a spatula. Continue as directed in variations below and at right. Makes about 12 cups.

Basic Biscuits: Stir together 1 cup *Whole Wheat Biscuit Mix* and ¼ cup *milk* just till dough clings together. On a floured surface, knead dough gently 10 to 12 strokes. Roll to ½-inch thickness. Cut with a 2½-inch biscuit cutter. Place on an ungreased baking sheet. Bake in a 450° oven for 8 to 10 minutes or till biscuits are golden. Makes 4 biscuits.

Nutrition facts per Basic Biscuit: 174 cal., 9 g total fat (2 g sat. fat), 1 mg chol., 218 mg sodium, 20 g carbo., 2 g fiber, 3 g pro.
Daily values: 11% calcium, 8% iron.

Drop Biscuits: Prepare Basic Biscuits, except increase milk to ⅓ cup. Do not knead, roll, or cut dough. Drop dough from a tablespoon onto a greased baking sheet. Bake as directed. Makes 4 biscuits.

Buttermilk Biscuits: Prepare Drop Biscuits or Basic Biscuits, except stir ¼ teaspoon *baking soda* into the flour mixture in a bowl and substitute *buttermilk* for the milk. Makes 4 biscuits.

Mexican-Style Biscuits: Prepare Drop Biscuits, except stir ¼ cup well-drained canned *whole kernel corn with sweet peppers,* ½ cup shredded *Monterey Jack cheese with jalapeño peppers* (2 ounces), and ⅛ teaspoon *ground cumin* into the flour mixture in a mixing bowl along with the ⅓ cup milk. Makes 5 biscuits.

Cherry and Orange Biscuits: Prepare Drop Biscuits, except add ⅓ cup *dried tart red cherries,* 3 tablespoons *sugar,* 2 tablespoons chopped *pecans,* and ½ teaspoon finely shredded *orange peel* to the flour mixture. Bake in a 400° oven about 15 minutes or till golden (this is a lower oven temperature than the standard recipe). Makes 5 biscuits.

Pesto Biscuits: Prepare Drop Biscuits, except stir in 1 tablespoon *pesto* with the ⅓ cup milk. If desired, also stir in ¼ cup chopped *ripe olives.* Makes 4 biscuits.

RICE FLOUR BREAD

Prep: 20 min. ◆ Rise: 1½ hr.
Bake: 35 min.

This wheat-free bread uses rice flour, tapioca flour, and xanthan gum. Look for them at a health-food store or ask your grocer to stock them.

1¾ cups white or brown rice flour
¼ cup tapioca flour
1 pkg. active dry yeast
2 tsp. xanthan gum
◆◆◆
1½ cups buttermilk
¼ cup sugar
3 Tbsp. margarine
1 tsp. salt
2 eggs
½ cup packaged instant mashed potato flakes or buds
◆◆◆
2 tsp. cornmeal

1 In a large mixing bowl combine *1 cup* of the rice flour, the tapioca flour, yeast, and xanthan gum. Set aside.

2 In a medium saucepan heat and stir the buttermilk, sugar, margarine, and salt over low heat just till warm (120° to 130°) and the margarine almost melts. Add buttermilk mixture to the flour mixture. Add the eggs. Beat with an electric mixer on low to medium speed for 30 seconds, scraping sides of bowl constantly. Beat on high speed for 2 minutes more. Using a wooden spoon, stir in the potato flakes or buds and the remaining ¾ cup rice flour to make a soft dough. Cover and let dough rise in a warm place till double in size (1 to 1¼ hours).

3 Lightly grease a 1½-quart soufflé dish or casserole or an 8×4×2-inch loaf pan. Lightly sprinkle dish or pan with cornmeal. Stir down dough and spread evenly in prepared casserole or pan. Cover and let rise till nearly double in size (30 to 45 minutes).

4 Bake in a 375° oven for 35 to 40 minutes or till center of bread springs back when touched. If necessary, cover bread with foil during the last 15 minutes of baking to prevent overbrowning. Remove bread from casserole or pan. Cool bread on a wire rack. Makes 1 loaf (16 servings).

Nutrition facts per serving basic bread: 131 cal., 3 g total fat (1 g sat. fat), 27 mg chol., 193 mg sodium, 21 g carbo., 1 g fiber, 3 g pro.
Daily values: 4% vit. A, 2% vit. C, 2% calcium, 3% iron.

Herb Bread: Stir in ¾ teaspoon dried dillweed, basil, or sage, crushed, along with potato flakes or buds.

Fruit 'n' Spice Bread: Add ¾ teaspoon *ground cardamom or cinnamon* to the rice flour mixture. Stir in ¾ cup *golden raisins, dried cherries, snipped dates, or mixed dried fruit bits* along with the potato flakes or buds.

Orange and Nut Bread: Stir 1½ teaspoons finely shredded *orange peel* into the rice flour mixture. Stir in ½ cup finely chopped *toasted pecans or almonds* with the potato flakes or buds.

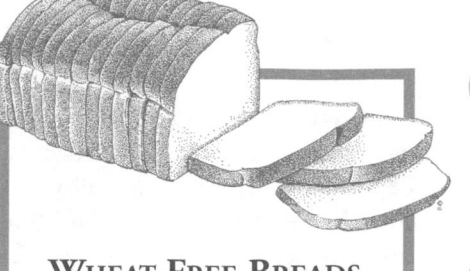

WHEAT-FREE BREADS

When the doctor says "no more bread" because you have an intolerance to gluten, don't be cheated out of one of life's pleasures. Fresh-baked bread need not be a dim memory. The yeast bread recipe on page 270, which is made with gluten-free rice flour, is delicious and easy. Plus, with just this one basic recipe, you can enjoy it plain or try one of the three different flavor variations.

Before you begin making wheat-free breads, take a trip to a health food store to pick up the following ingredients.

Rice flour: Rice flour is milled from rice. You can choose from brown and white rice flour. Use brown rice flour if you prefer a texture that is similar to whole wheat bread.

Tapioca flour: Milled from the cassava root, tapioca flour is used as a thickening agent. It is sweet with a sticky texture. Use tapioca flour in combination with other flours.

Xanthan gum: This corn product is used as a binder, thickener, stabilizer, and emulsifier. Use it sparingly in your baking.

30 MIN. LOW FAT

BACKWOODS RICE

Prep: 15 min. ◆ Cook: 15 min.

When presenting this fruit-and-nut-studded rice mix as a gift, be sure to include the cooking directions.

- 4 **cups uncooked long-grain rice**
- ½ **cup snipped dried apricots**
- ½ **cup dried tart red cherries**
- ½ **cup chopped toasted walnuts or pecans**
- 2 **Tbsp. instant chicken bouillon granules**
- 1 **Tbsp. instant minced onion**
- ½ **tsp. ground cinnamon (optional)**
- ¼ **tsp. pepper**

1 In a large bowl stir together the rice, apricots, cherries, walnuts or pecans, bouillon granules, onion, cinnamon (if using), and pepper; mix well.

2 Divide rice mixture evenly among 4 clean and dry decorative jars. Seal and label. Store in refrigerator. Makes four 1¼-cup jars.

To make rice: In a medium saucepan stir together *rice mix,* 1¾ cups *water,* and 1 tablespoon *butter.* Bring to boiling; reduce heat. Simmer, covered, for 15 to 20 minutes or till rice is tender and liquid is absorbed. Fluff rice with a fork. Makes 4 servings.

Nutrition facts per serving: 218 cal., 3 g total fat (0 g sat. fat), 0 mg chol., 330 mg sodium, 44 g carbo., 1 g fiber, 4 g pro.
Daily values: 5% vit. A, 1% calcium, 15% iron.

RUM AND EGGNOG CAKES

Prep: 35 min. ◆ Bake: 30 or 55 min.
Chill or freeze: 1 to 2 days

1½ cups butter
3 eggs
1¼ cups dairy eggnog
2¼ cups all-purpose flour
2 tsp. baking powder
¾ tsp. ground nutmeg
1 cup diced mixed candied
    fruits and peels
½ cup golden raisins
½ cup chopped pecans
2 Tbsp. all-purpose flour

◆◆◆

1 cup sugar
1 to 1½ cups rum or 1½ cups
    orange juice plus ½ tsp.
    rum extract

◆◆◆

1 recipe Eggnog Glaze (see
    right)

1 Let butter, eggs, and eggnog stand at room temperature for 30 minutes. Grease and flour twelve 1-cup or one 10-inch (12- cup) fluted tube pan(s). Stir together 2¼ cups flour, baking powder, and nutmeg. Toss together fruits, raisins, nuts, and 2 tablespoons flour; set aside.

2 In a large bowl beat butter with an electric mixer on medium speed 30 seconds. Slowly add sugar; beat 10 minutes or till light and fluffy. Add eggs, 1 at a time, beating 1 minute after each. Add flour mixture and eggnog alternately to egg mixture, beating on low speed after each just till combined. *(Do not overbeat.)* Stir in ¼ cup rum or ¼ cup orange juice and rum extract. Fold in fruit mixture. Pour into prepared pan(s).

3 Bake in a 350° oven till a wooden toothpick inserted near center comes out clean, allowing 30 minutes for small pans or 55 to 60 minutes for large pan. Cool in pan(s) on a wire rack for 10 minutes for small pans or 15 minutes for large pan. Remove from pan(s); cool completely on rack.

4 Poke holes in cake(s). Soak a 100-percent-cotton cheesecloth with rum or orange juice, using *1 cup* rum or juice for small cakes and *½ cup* rum or juice for large cake. Wrap cake(s) in rum- or orange juice-moistened cheesecloth. Wrap tightly in foil or seal in plastic storage bags.

5 Store cake(s) in the freezer or in the refrigerator 1 to 2 days to mellow flavors. After 1 day, drizzle with *¼ cup* rum or juice. Rewrap for another day, or serve. Before serving, drizzle with Eggnog Glaze. Serves 24 to 30.

Eggnog Glaze: In a small mixing bowl stir together 1 cup *sifted powdered sugar,* 1 tablespoon *dairy eggnog,* 1 tablespoon *light-colored corn syrup,* and ½ teaspoon *light rum* or ¼ teaspoon *rum extract.* Add more *eggnog,* a teaspoon at a time, till icing is easy to glaze.

TO MAKE AHEAD

Freeze the cakes for up to 3 months. To thaw, let stand in the refrigerator. Drizzle cakes with additional rum or juice and glaze as directed.

Nutrition facts per serving: 290 cal., 15 g total fat (8 g sat. fat), 65 mg chol., 163 mg sodium, 33 g carbo., 1 g fiber, 3 g pro. *Daily values:* 13% vit. A, 4% calcium, 5% iron.

PRALINE-SURPRISE COFFEE CAKE

Prep: 20 min. ◆ Bake: 45 min.

⅓ cup packed brown sugar
⅓ cup dark-colored corn syrup
2 Tbsp. butter or margarine
3 Tbsp. water
⅔ cup chopped pecans
¼ cup all-purpose flour

◆◆◆

2½ cups all-purpose flour
2 tsp. baking powder
½ tsp. baking soda
½ tsp. ground nutmeg
¼ tsp. salt
⅓ cup butter or margarine
¾ cup packed brown sugar
½ cup granulated sugar
3 eggs
¾ cup condensed tomato soup
¼ cup buttermilk
1 tsp. vanilla

1 Grease a 13×9×2-inch baking pan. In a medium saucepan combine ⅓ cup brown sugar, the corn syrup, 2 tablespoons butter, and the water. Cook and stir over low heat till well combined. Increase heat to medium-high; bring mixture to boiling. Boil, uncovered, 1 minute; remove from heat. Stir in pecans and ¼ cup flour; set aside.

2 Combine 2½ cups flour, baking powder, soda, nutmeg, and salt; set aside. In a mixing bowl beat ⅓ cup butter 30 seconds. Gradually beat in ¾ cup brown sugar and ½ cup granulated sugar till well combined. Add eggs, 1 at a time, beating well after each addition. Combine soup, buttermilk, and vanilla. Add soup mixture and flour mixture alternately to egg mixture; mix well.

MAPLE SYRUP Q&A

Q. How is maple syrup made?
A. Pure maple syrup comes from collecting and boiling down the sap of the sugar maple tree. It is produced only in North America, with the largest U.S. supply coming from Vermont. Harvest time is late February through early April.

Q. What are the different grades and variations?
A. Pure maple syrup is graded based on color, clarity, and flavor. The first of these grades, Grade A Light (also called Fancy), is light in color and delicate in taste. Consecutively, the grades get darker in color and fuller in maple flavor, including Grade A Medium Amber (a good syrup for pancakes), Grade A Dark Amber (hearty flavor, good for cooking), and Grade B (seldom sold at retail). Grade A Medium Amber and Dark Amber are the most available grades.

Q. How long can you keep pure maple syrup?
A. Unopened, pure maple syrup keeps indefinitely when stored in a cool, dry place. Even opened, it keeps about a year. Cover opened syrup tightly and chill.

Q. What is the difference between pure maple syrup and maple-flavored pancake syrup?
A. To be labeled pure maple syrup, 100 percent of the syrup must come from the sap of maple trees. Maple-flavored syrups usually contain little or no real maple syrup. Instead, they are primarily sugar syrups, made with maple flavoring. Maple-flavored syrups usually are much less expensive. As for flavor, pure maple syrup has a more delicate and distinctly maple taste, whereas maple-flavored syrups have a much sweeter flavor and a thicker consistency.

Q. How much does pure maple syrup cost, and where can you purchase this specialty syrup?
A. It takes 40 gallons of sap and a substantial amount of time and labor to make 1 gallon of pure maple syrup. That's why it costs almost four times more than maple-flavored pancake syrup. To purchase pure maple syrup, look near the pancake mixes or in the gourmet aisle of your local grocery store. Or, try a specialty foods shop or health-food store.

---

3 Spoon batter into the prepared pan. Spoon praline mixture over batter; swirl gently with a knife. Bake in a 325° oven 45 to 50 minutes or till a wooden toothpick inserted near the center comes out clean. Serve warm. Makes 12 servings.

Nutrition facts per serving: 350 cal., 13 g total fat (5 g sat. fat), 72 mg chol., 370 mg sodium, 55 g carbo., 1 g fiber, 5 g pro. *Daily values:* 9% vit. A, 8% calcium, 17% iron.

AUTUMN MAPLE CAKE
Prep: 20 min. ◆ Bake: 40 min.

1½ **cups all-purpose flour**
 1 **tsp. baking powder**
 ½ **tsp. baking soda**
 ¼ **tsp. salt**
 ◆◆◆
 1 **beaten egg**

1½ **cups peeled, cored, and chopped baking apples**
 ½ **cup sugar**
 ½ **cup pure maple syrup**
 ½ **cup raisins**
 ⅓ **cup applesauce**
 ⅓ **cup cooking oil**
1½ **tsp. grated orange peel**
 Pure maple syrup
 1 **recipe Maple Cream (see right)**

1 Spray an 8×8×2-inch baking pan with *nonstick spray coating*. Combine the flour, baking powder, baking soda, and salt.

2 Combine egg and apples. Stir in sugar, the ½ cup maple syrup, raisins, applesauce, oil, and orange peel. Add flour mixture; stir just till combined. Spread batter into the prepared pan.

3 Bake in a 350° oven 40 to 45 minutes or till a toothpick inserted near the center comes out clean. Brush the warm cake with additional maple syrup and cool slightly. Serve warm or at room temperature with Maple Cream. Makes 9 servings.

Maple Cream: In a chilled bowl beat ½ cup *whipping cream* with chilled beaters of an electric mixer on medium speed till stiff peaks form. Stir together ½ cup *dairy sour cream* and ¼ cup *pure maple syrup;* fold into whipped cream. Serve immediately.

Nutrition facts per serving: 384 cal., 16 g total fat (6 g sat. fat), 47 mg chol., 161 mg sodium, 58 g carbo., 2 g fiber, 4 g pro.

ORANGE-CAPPUCCINO CREAMS

Prep: 30 min. ◆ Chill: 20 min.

This recipe earned Miriam Baroga of Fircrest, Washington, $400 in the magazine's monthly contest.
(See the photograph on page 277.)

1½ lb. white chocolate, chopped
½ cup whipping cream
1 Tbsp. finely shredded orange peel
1 Tbsp. orange liqueur or orange juice
1 tsp. orange extract
½ cup finely chopped walnuts
◆◆◆
About 72 small paper or foil candy cups (1¼- to 1½-inch size)
◆◆◆
¼ cup whipping cream
4 tsp. instant espresso coffee powder or instant coffee crystals
8 oz. semisweet chocolate
White chocolate curls (optional)
Orange peel (optional)

1 For filling, in a large saucepan combine white chocolate, the ½ cup whipping cream, orange peel, orange liqueur or juice, and orange extract. Stir over low heat till white chocolate is just melted. Remove from heat and stir in walnuts. Cool slightly.

2 Place the white chocolate mixture in a self-sealing plastic bag. Make a small opening by snipping off a bottom corner of the bag. Squeeze mixture through hole to fill candy cups about two-thirds full. Chill for 20 minutes.

3 In a medium saucepan heat the ¼ cup whipping cream and espresso powder or coffee crystals over low heat till dissolved. Add semisweet chocolate, stirring over low heat 3 to 4 minutes or till chocolate melts. Spoon ½ teaspoon of semisweet chocolate mixture onto each white chocolate cream. If desired, top with white chocolate curls and orange peel. Store in refrigerator; serve at room temperature. Makes about 72 candies.

Nutrition facts per candy: 84 cal., 5 g total fat (3 g sat. fat), 7 mg chol., 11 mg sodium, 8 g carbo., 0 g fiber, 1 g pro.
Daily values: 1% vit. A, 1% calcium.

TIRAMISU CHARLOTTE

Prep: 40 min. ◆ Chill: 45 min. plus overnight

To prepare the sugared kumquat and strawberry garnish, first dip the fruit in light-colored corn syrup, then into granulated sugar.
(See the photograph on page 279.)

3 tsp. unflavored gelatin
⅓ cup cold water
◆◆◆
½ of a 10¾-oz. pkg. frozen or fresh pound cake, thawed if necessary and cut into ¼-inch-thick slices, or 24 ladyfingers
2 to 3 Tbsp. Marsala or apple juice
◆◆◆
1 8-oz. container mascarpone cheese* or one 8-oz. pkg. cream cheese, softened
1 Tbsp. powdered sugar
¼ cup Marsala or apple juice
◆◆◆
4 egg yolks
⅓ cup granulated sugar
◆◆◆
1½ cups whipping cream
2 Tbsp. instant espresso coffee powder
1 vanilla bean, split, or 1 tsp. vanilla
◆◆◆
1 cup whipping cream
◆◆◆
Sugared kumquats (optional)
Sugared strawberries (optional)
Orange peel curls (optional)

1 In a 1-cup glass measure sprinkle the gelatin over cold water and let stand for 5 minutes. In a small saucepan bring a small amount of water to boiling. Place glass measure with gelatin in saucepan; heat and stir till gelatin dissolves. Remove from heat; set aside to cool.

2 Meanwhile, line bottom of a 6-cup bowl with plastic wrap. Line bottom of bowl with pound cake slices or ladyfingers, trimming to fit as necessary. To line sides, press cake or ladyfingers against each other around side of bowl; trim to fit. Using a spoon or small shaker bottle, sprinkle cake with the 2 to 3 tablespoons Marsala or apple juice.

3 For the mascarpone mixture, in a small bowl mix mascarpone or cream cheese, powdered sugar, and *2 tablespoons* of the cooled gelatin mixture. Stir in the ¼ cup Marsala or apple juice. Set mixture aside.

4 For the espresso mixture, in a medium mixing bowl beat egg yolks and granulated sugar with an electric mixer on medium speed about 2 minutes or till thick. Set egg yolks aside.

5 In a medium saucepan place the 1½ cups whipping cream, instant espresso powder, and, if using, vanilla bean; bring to a simmer. Remove vanilla bean and discard. Pour *1 cup* of the hot mixture into the egg yolk mixture. Return all to the saucepan. Cook and stir over medium heat till thickened and just bubbly. Reduce heat; cook and stir for 2 minutes more. Stir in vanilla, if using, and remaining gelatin mixture. Transfer to a large bowl. Cover and chill for 45 to 60 minutes or till mixture cools and starts to mound.

6 In a medium mixing bowl beat the 1 cup whipping cream with an electric mixture on medium speed till soft peaks form. Fold the whipped cream into the espresso mixture.

7 Pour *half* of the espresso mixture into the bowl with the pound cake or ladyfingers. Spread mascarpone mixture atop. Top with the remaining espresso mixture. Cover with plastic wrap and chill overnight.

8 To serve, uncover and invert onto a serving plate. Remove remaining plastic wrap. If desired, garnish with sugared kumquats and strawberries and orange peel curls. Makes 10 servings.

*Note: Mascarpone is a rich Italian cream cheese often served with fruit for dessert. You can buy it at the cheese counter of your local supermarket.

Nutrition facts per serving: 449 cal., 39 g total fat (22 g sat. fat), 196 mg chol., 87 mg sodium, 20 g carbo., 0 g fiber, 9 g pro. *Daily values:* 39% vit. A, 4% calcium, 2% iron.

FESTIVE CRANBERRY TORTE

Prep: 35 min. plus freezing

This make-ahead frozen torte has been a popular dessert since it was first published in the magazine in 1979. This time around the recipe is updated for safety's sake using powdered egg whites instead of raw egg whites.

1½ **cups graham cracker crumbs**
½ **cup finely chopped pecans**
¼ **cup sugar**
⅓ **cup margarine or butter, melted**

♦♦♦

1 **12-oz. pkg. cranberries**
¾ **cup sugar**
1 **Tbsp. frozen orange juice concentrate, thawed**
1 **tsp. vanilla**

♦♦♦

Powdered egg whites equivalent to 3 egg whites
⅓ **cup sugar**

♦♦♦

1 **cup whipping cream**

♦♦♦

Cranberry Glaze (see right)

1 Stir together graham cracker crumbs, pecans, the ¼ cup sugar, and melted margarine or butter. Press mixture onto bottom and 2 inches up sides of an 8-inch springform pan; chill.

2 Set aside ¾ *cup* of the cranberries for glaze. In a food processor bowl process remaining cranberries till coarsely ground. (Or, finely chop using a knife.) In a large bowl combine ground cranberries, the ¾ cup sugar, the juice concentrate, and vanilla; set aside.

3 Reconstitute powdered egg whites according to package directions. In a medium mixing bowl beat reconstituted egg whites to soft peaks with an electric mixer on low to medium speed. Gradually add the ⅓ cup sugar, beating to stiff peaks. Fold into ground cranberry mixture.

4 With an electric mixer on medium speed beat whipping cream to soft peaks; fold into ground cranberry mixture. Spread into crust. Cover and freeze till firm. To serve, use a spatula to loosen torte from pan; remove sides from pan. Spoon Cranberry Glaze over each serving. Makes 12 servings.

Cranberry Glaze: In a small saucepan stir together ½ cup *sugar* and 1 tablespoon *cornstarch;* stir in ½ cup *water* and the ¾ cup reserved *cranberries.* Cook and stir till thickened and bubbly. Cook and stir for 2 minutes more. Cover surface with plastic wrap. Cool, but do not chill.

Nutrition facts per serving: 297 cal., 16 g total fat (6 g sat. fat), 27 mg chol., 132 mg sodium, 37 g carbo., 2 g fiber, 2 g pro. *Daily values:* 15% vit. A, 10% vit. C, 2% calcium, 4% iron.

RASPBERRY-CHOCOLATE CAKE

Prep: 35 min. ◆ Bake: 30 min.

The bright flavor of raspberries brings a touch of summer to the holidays. (See the photograph on page 277.)

2¼ cups all-purpose flour
1 tsp. baking powder
¾ tsp. baking soda
¼ tsp. salt
◆◆◆
⅔ cup butter or margarine*
1¾ cups sugar
2 eggs
3 oz. unsweetened chocolate, melted and cooled
1 tsp. vanilla
1¼ cups water
◆◆◆
3 Tbsp. raspberry liqueur (optional)
◆◆◆
½ cup seedless raspberry jam
1 recipe Raspberry Chocolate Frosting (see right)
◆◆◆
   Fresh raspberries (optional)
   Fresh mint sprigs (optional)

1 Grease and lightly flour two 9×1½-inch round baking pans; set aside. Stir together flour, baking powder, baking soda, and salt; set aside.

2 In a large mixing bowl beat the butter or margarine with an electric mixer on medium to high speed for 30 seconds. Add sugar; beat till well mixed. Add eggs, 1 at a time, beating well after each. Beat in chocolate and vanilla. Add flour mixture and the 1¼ cups water alternately to beaten mixture, beating on low speed after each addition just till combined.

Pour batter into the prepared pans; spread evenly.

3 Bake in a 350° oven for 30 to 35 minutes or till a wooden toothpick inserted near centers comes out clean. Cool cake layers in pans on wire racks for 10 minutes. Remove cakes from pans. Cool thoroughly on racks.

4 To assemble, split cake layers in half horizontally to make 4 layers. If desired, drizzle each layer with liqueur.

5 Place a cake layer, cut side up, on serving plate; spread with *half* of the raspberry jam. Top with second cake layer, cut side down. Spread with about ⅔ *cup* Raspberry-Chocolate Frosting. Place another cake layer, cut side up, on top of frosting; spread with remaining jam and top with last cake layer, cut side down. Frost top and sides with remaining frosting. If desired, garnish with raspberries and mint sprigs. Store any leftover cake in the refrigerator. Makes 14 servings.

***Note:** For best results with margarine, use only products labeled as containing not less than 80 percent vegetable oil (the nutrition label should say 100 calories per tablespoon). A lower oil content will result in a tougher, flatter cake.

Nutrition facts per serving for cake with Raspberry-Chocolate Frosting: 556 cal., 28 g total fat (12 g sat. fat), 89 mg chol., 247 mg sodium, 76 g carbo., 1 g fiber, 5 g pro. *Daily values:* 21% vit. A, 6% vit. C, 6% calcium, 19% iron.

RASPBERRY-CHOCOLATE FROSTING

Prep: 25 min. ◆ Chill: 2 hr.

This truffle-style, whipped frosting performs the holiday miracle of being simultaneously light and rich.

1 10-oz. pkg. frozen red raspberries in syrup, thawed
1 envelope unflavored gelatin
◆◆◆
1 12-oz. pkg. (2 cups) semisweet chocolate pieces
¼ cup light-colored corn syrup
◆◆◆
1½ cups whipping cream
1 tsp. vanilla

1 Press undrained raspberries through a sieve; discard seeds. (You should have about 1 cup puree.) In a heavy medium saucepan combine the raspberry puree and gelatin; let stand 5 minutes. Cook and stir till gelatin is dissolved; set aside.

2 Meanwhile, in another saucepan heat and stir chocolate pieces over low heat till smooth. Stir in corn syrup till smooth.

3 Stir whipping cream and vanilla into chocolate mixture till smooth. Stir in raspberry mixture; heat and stir till smooth and no flecks of chocolate remain. Transfer to a large mixing bowl. Cover and refrigerate about 2 hours or till thoroughly chilled, stirring occasionally. Beat with an electric mixer till fluffy. Makes about 4 cups (enough to fill and frost a 2-layer cake).

Top: *Orange-Cappuccino Creams (page 274)*
Above: *Raspberry-Chocolate Cake (page 276)*

Top: *Truffle Oil Salad (page 256)*
Above left: *Glacier Punch (page 250)*
Above right: *Tiramisu Charlotte (page 274)*
Page 278: *Mushroom-Stuffed Beef (page 257)*

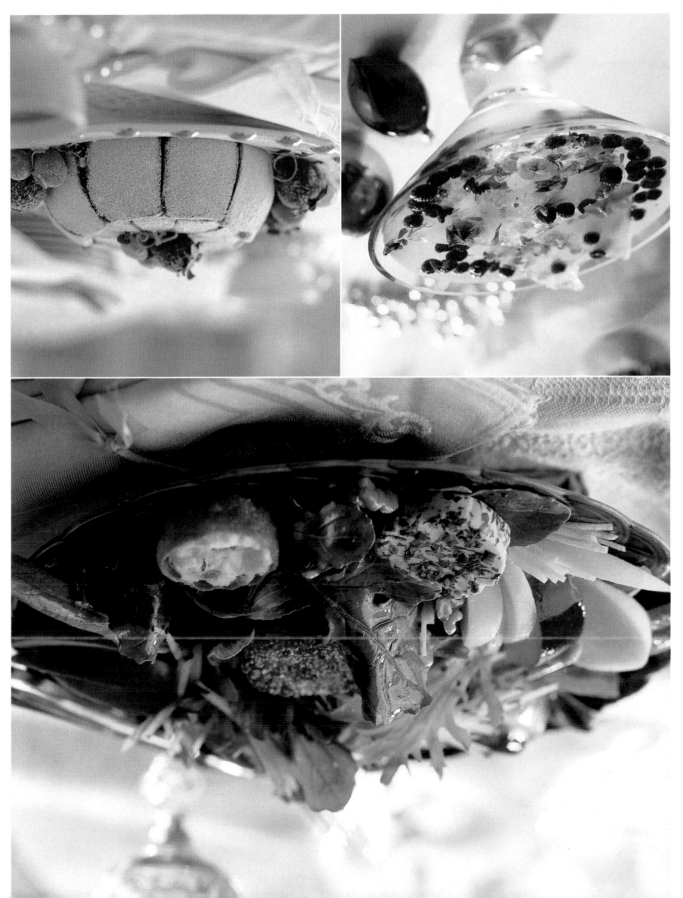

Top: *Nut-Crusted Turkey (page 260)*
Above: *Wild-Rice-Stuffed Squash (page 255)*
Right: *Glazed Roasted Vegetables (page 254)*

30 MIN.

LINGUINE WITH MIXED NUTS AND GORGONZOLA

Start to finish: 15 min.

See the photograph on page 44.

1 9-oz. pkg. refrigerated
    linguine or fettuccine
    ◆◆◆
¾ cup chopped hazelnuts
    (filberts), pecans, and/or
    pine nuts
1 Tbsp. butter
1 Tbsp. olive oil
½ cup crumbled Gorgonzola or
    blue cheese (2 oz.)
¼ cup shredded Parmesan
    cheese
2 Tbsp. snipped fresh basil
    Fresh basil (optional)

1 Cook pasta in boiling water according to package directions; drain. Return to pan; keep warm.

2 Meanwhile, in a medium skillet cook the hazelnuts, pecans, or pine nuts in butter and olive oil till toasted and butter begins to brown, stirring frequently. Add nut mixture to pasta. Add the Gorgonzola or blue cheese, Parmesan cheese, and the snipped basil, tossing gently to coat. Transfer to a serving platter. If desired, garnish with fresh basil. Makes 6 side-dish servings.

Nutrition facts per side-dish serving: 298 cal., 19 g total fat (4 g sat. fat), 23 mg chol., 212 mg sodium, 25 g carbo., 1 g fiber, 9 g pro.
Daily values: 4% vit. A, 8% calcium, 5% iron.

TEST KITCHEN TIP

NITTY-GRITTY ON NUTS

Almonds: Almonds are light-colored and have a rich but mild flavor that goes well in many foods. Unshelled almonds (with skin on) may be whole or sliced. Blanched unshelled almonds (skin removed) may be whole, slivered, or ground.

Brazil nuts: These have a thin, brown skin and an oily, rich flavor. They're not used much in cooking, but often are mixed with other salted nuts for a snack.

Cashews: Cashews have a rich, buttery flavor and often are used in cashew-nut butter, stir-fries, and snack mixes.

Hazelnuts: Also known as filberts, hazelnuts have a mild, sweet flavor. This nut is being rediscovered as a cooking nut.

Macadamias: These tropical nuts taste rich, sweet, and buttery. Consider using them as you would cashews. Most macadamia nuts are sold already shelled, roasted in oil, or dry-roasted.

Peanuts: The popular peanut is often mistakenly called a nut. It's actually a legume. Peanuts have a buttery, nutty flavor when roasted. Unshelled peanuts can be raw or roasted. Shelled peanuts may be raw, roasted in oil, or dry-roasted, and may be salted or unsalted.

Pecans: Pecans have a delicate flavor. Many classic dishes, such as rice dressing, pecan pie, and pralines, evolved in the South where pecan trees are abundant.

Pine nuts: The pine nut, also known as pignolia or piñon, has a sweet, faint pine flavor. The small, creamy white nut can be slender and pellet-shaped or more triangular. Pine nuts frequently are used in Italian dishes, such as pasta sauces, pesto, risotto, and cookies.

Pistachios: These nuts are actually the seed of the fruit of a small evergreen tree. Their shells are naturally beige, but often are dyed red or green. The thin, oval shell, which is split at one end, encases a ½-inch-long nut with a paper-thin brown skin. Pistachios have a mild, sweet flavor similar to almonds.

Walnuts: Walnuts are the seeds of either English (Persian) walnut trees or native North American black walnut trees. The English walnut is mild in flavor. The black walnut is smaller than the English walnut and has a richer, more intense flavor. The walnut is perhaps the most widely used nut in American cooking.

ROASTED GARLIC MASHED POTATOES

Start to finish: 50 min.

Fluffy mashed potatoes make the perfect companion to steak or other red meat. The savory flavor of sweet roasted garlic lets you use less margarine or butter which means fewer total calories.

10 to 12 cloves garlic
1 tsp. cooking oil

◆◆◆

4 medium potatoes
    (1 to 1½ lb.)
2 tsp. margarine or butter
½ tsp. salt
¼ tsp. pepper
¼ cup milk

1 Place garlic cloves in a custard cup; drizzle with oil. Bake in a 350° oven about 20 minutes or till garlic is very soft; cool. When cool enough to handle, peel garlic, discarding skins and reserving oil.

2 Meanwhile, peel and cut up potatoes. Cook, covered, in boiling *salted water* for 20 to 25 minutes or till tender; drain. Transfer potatoes to a large mixing bowl. Mash potatoes with a potato masher or beat with an electric mixer on low speed. Add the garlic, reserved oil, margarine or butter, salt, and pepper. Gradually beat in enough of the milk to make light and fluffy. Serve immediately. Makes 4 servings.

Nutrition facts per serving: 175 cal., 4 g total fat (1 g sat. fat), 1 mg chol., 316 mg sodium, 31 g carbo., 2 g fiber, 3 g pro. *Daily values:* 4% vit. A, 21% vit. C, 3% calcium, 4% iron.

CREAMY PASTA SALAD

Start to finish: 25 min.

We call it creamy because of the dressing, but there's no cream in the recipe and only a gram of fat per serving.

2 cups small pasta, such as
    wagon wheels, corkscrews,
    or elbow macaroni
2 medium carrots, thinly
    sliced or crinkle cut
    (about 1 cup)
1 cup frozen peas

◆◆◆

¼ cup fat-free mayonnaise or
    salad dressing
¼ cup plain low-fat yogurt
1 tsp. sugar
½ tsp. salt
⅛ tsp. white or black pepper

1 In a large saucepan cook the pasta according to package directions, adding carrots to the water for the last 7 minutes of cooking. Drain pasta and carrots well. Stir in the peas; rinse with cold water to chill quickly. Drain again; transfer to a serving bowl. Cover and chill till ready to serve.

2 For dressing, stir together the mayonnaise or salad dressing, yogurt, sugar, salt, and pepper. Pour dressing over pasta and vegetables, tossing gently to coat. Makes 6 servings.

Nutrition facts per serving: 152 cal., 1 g total fat (0 g sat. fat), 1 mg chol., 344 mg sodium, 31 g carbo., 2 g fiber, 6 g pro. *Daily values:* 54% vit. A, 4% vit. C, 2% calcium, 10% iron.

CITRUS-JICAMA SALAD

Start to finish: 25 min.

To enjoy this Southwestern-style salad at its best, use only the firmest jicama available.

2 Tbsp. orange juice
1 Tbsp. lemon juice
1 Tbsp. honey
1 tsp. Dijon-style mustard
⅓ cup salad oil

◆◆◆

Lettuce leaves
1 medium grapefruit, peeled
    and sectioned
2 medium oranges, peeled and
    sectioned
1 medium jicama, peeled and
    cut into thin bite-size
    strips (about 2 cups)
Cracked black pepper

1 For dressing, in a blender container combine the orange juice, lemon juice, honey, and Dijon-style mustard. Cover and blend till smooth. With blender running, slowly add oil through hole in lid in a thin, steady stream. Continue blending till mixture is thickened. Cover and chill till serving time.

2 In 4 lettuce-lined salad bowls arrange the grapefruit sections, orange sections, and jicama. Drizzle *half* the dressing over salads, reserving remainder for another use. Sprinkle salads with cracked black pepper. Makes 4 servings.

Nutrition facts per serving: 178 cal., 9 g total fat (1 g sat. fat), 0 mg chol., 18 mg sodium, 23 g carbo., 3 g fiber, 2 g pro. *Daily values:* 3% vit. A, 128% vit. C, 3% calcium, 5% iron.

In a Jam? Try Fruitful Tricks

Mindful of our health and figures, many of us are determined to cut down on fat and calories but not on flavor. Mission impossible? An answer to our prayers is waiting in the wings—jamming our cupboards in the guise of jellies, jams, and preserves. The intense, fruity flavor packed into each teaspoon of these toppings is too versatile to spend its life solely atop a slice of toast. Stirred into saucy toppings, glazes, marinades, and relishes, jams and jellies contribute less than 20 calories per teaspoon while often usurping the role of fat. Here are cooking ideas that are sure to jam pizzazz into stale recipes while preserving healthful eating.

◆ Toss strawberry jelly with half as much balsamic vinegar or fruit juice to make a light salad dressing. Or, drizzle the mixture over fresh fruit, such as strawberries or peaches, for a dessert that is refreshingly light.

◆ Add two parts orange marmalade, currant jelly, or apricot preserves to one part apple cider or dark beer to liven your next barbecue. Brush on meats before and during grilling if grilling time is short or during the last 15 minutes for longer grilling times. Try the orange marmalade mixture on pork or duck and the currant or apricot combos with turkey or chicken.

◆ Dress up cooked fish or chicken with a sweet salsa. Simply combine apple-mint jelly with chopped onion, sweet and hot peppers, and your pick of tropical fruits such as pineapple or mango.

◆ Spread jam or jelly, instead of frosting, between layers of a cake.

◆ Stir a rounded spoonful of raspberry jelly and a few mint leaves into servings of iced tea.

◆ Add oomph to smoothies by blending together a couple of tablespoons of your favorite preserve with low-fat yogurt and ripe fruit. Try a triple-blueberry combo using fresh berries, blueberry jam, and blueberry yogurt or an apricot-lemon-banana blend. Sip it now or freeze the mixture in a paper cup with a stick inserted for a nutritious frozen treat.

◆ Top pancakes, waffles, or French toast with a spoonful of strawberry or blueberry preserves. (The preserves also can double as a delicious topping for ice-cream sundaes.) If you're serving crepes for breakfast, spread preserves on the crepes, then roll into a loose cylinder and sprinkle with powdered sugar.

◆ Dilute preserves with a compatible liqueur and spoon the mixture over chunks of fresh fruit. Enjoy this dessert solo or serve it atop slices of pound cake or angel food cake.

◆ Spread some spicy jalapeño pepper jelly on top of a round of Brie cheese and bake or microwave until the cheese is slightly softened. Serve with crusty bread or crackers for a quick-to-fix appetizer.

◆ Create a yogurt fruit dip as a low-fat snack and serve with slices of your favorite fruits. Simply combine a few tablespoons of peach preserves with a carton of plain yogurt and a sprinkling of cinnamon. Chill at least an hour before serving.

Sunflower Green Salad with Thyme Vinaigrette

Start to finish: 20 min.

Serve this refreshing salad of greens and vegetables with the shepherd's pie on page 33. The dressing recipe can be made with different herbs or a combination of herbs to suit your taste.

1 small carrot
4 cups torn romaine or other greens
½ cup thinly sliced radishes
⅓ cup finely shredded green or red cabbage
3 Tbsp. toasted shelled sunflower seeds

◆◆◆

¼ cup cider vinegar
3 Tbsp. salad oil
½ tsp. dried thyme, crushed
¼ tsp. pepper

1 Peel carrot and shave thin slices with peeler. Toss together carrot shavings, greens, radishes, cabbage, and sunflower seeds.

2 In a screw-top jar combine vinegar, oil, thyme, and pepper. Cover and shake well. Toss salad with dressing. Makes 5 servings.

Nutrition facts per serving: 117 cal., 11 g total fat (1 g sat. fat), 0 mg chol., 11 mg sodium, 5 g carbo., 2 g fiber, 2 g pro. *Daily values:* 52% vit. A, 27% vit. C, 2% calcium, 7% iron.

ORANGE-HAZELNUT BLUEBERRY BREAD

Prep: 15 min.
Bake: per manufacturer's directions

Before making this bread, be sure the capacity of your bread machine pan is 10 cups or more—this loaf is too lofty for smaller pans. (See the photograph on page 40.)

1 cup milk
2 Tbsp. butter or margarine
1 egg
3⅓ cups bread flour
1 Tbsp. finely shredded orange peel
1 tsp. salt
3 Tbsp. brown sugar
½ cup dried blueberries
⅓ cup toasted chopped hazelnuts (filberts)
2 tsp. bread machine yeast or active dry yeast
1 recipe Orange Icing (optional) (see below)

1 Add the ingredients to bread machine according to the manufacturer's directions. Select light setting, if available. If desired, when bread is cool, drizzle loaf with Orange Icing. Makes one 1½-pound loaf (16 servings).

Orange Icing: In a small mixing bowl stir together ½ cup *sifted powdered sugar* and enough *orange juice* to make an icing that's easy to drizzle.

Nutrition facts per serving: 174 cal., 4 g total fat (1 g sat. fat), 114 mg chol., 163 mg sodium, 29 g carbo. 1 g fiber, 5 g pro. *Daily values:* 3% vit. A, 1% vit. C, 2% calcium, 10% iron.

TOMATO AND CHEESE BREAD

Prep: 15 min.
Bake: per manufacturer's directions

¾ cup water
1 egg
4 tsp. margarine or butter
2¾ cups bread flour
¾ cup shredded cheddar cheese (3 oz.)
¼ cup oil-packed dried tomatoes, well-drained and snipped
1 Tbsp. sugar
1 tsp. salt
1 tsp. dried Italian seasoning, crushed
1 tsp. bread machine yeast or active dry yeast

1 Add ingredients to bread machine according to manufacturer's directions. Makes one 1½-pound loaf (16 servings).

Nutrition facts per serving: 127 cal., 4 g total fat (1g sat. fat), 19 mg chol., 187 mg sodium, 19 g carbo. 1 g fiber, 5 g pro. *Daily values:* 3% vit. A, 2% vit. C, 3% calcium, 8% iron.

GOOD SEED BREAD

Prep: 15 min.
Bake: per manufacturer's directions

This recipe earned K. Janiene Oliver of Golden, Colorado, $200 in the magazine's monthly contest.

1¼ cups water
2 Tbsp. honey
4 tsp. canola oil or cooking oil
1½ cups whole wheat flour
1¼ cups bread flour
⅓ cup rolled oats
4 tsp. gluten flour*
¼ cup shelled sunflower seeds
¼ cup pumpkin seed
¼ cup sesame seed
2 Tbsp. poppy seed
2 tsp. flax seed*
¾ tsp. anise seed
¾ tsp. salt
1¼ tsp. active dry yeast

1 Add ingredients to bread machine (with a capacity of at least 10 cups) according to manufacturer's directions. Select the basic or whole wheat cycle, medium color setting. Makes one 1½-pound loaf (16 servings).

***Note:** Health food stores typically carry these items.

Nutrition facts per serving: 150 cal., 6 g total fat (1 g sat. fat), 0 mg chol., 103 mg sodium, 21 g carbo., 3 g fiber, 5 g pro. *Daily values:* 2% calcium, 12% iron.

MULTIGRAIN BREAD

Prep: 25 min. ◆ Rise: 1½ hr.
Bake: 35 min.

This recipe makes two loaves, so enjoy one loaf now and freeze one for later.

¼ cup warm water (105° to 115°)
2 pkg. active dry yeast
½ cup honey
⅓ cup cooking oil
2 eggs
1 tsp. salt
1 cup nonfat dry milk powder
½ cup rolled oats
½ cup cornmeal
½ cup toasted wheat germ

◆◆◆

3¼ to 3¾ cups all-purpose flour
2 cups whole wheat flour
1 cup rye flour

❖❖❖

1 Tbsp. margarine or butter

1 In a large mixing bowl stir together warm water and yeast. Add honey, oil, eggs, and salt; beat with an electric mixer on medium speed till combined. Add the dry milk powder, oats, cornmeal, and wheat germ; beat till combined.

2 Add *1 cup* of the all-purpose flour and all of the whole wheat flour; beat on low speed for 30 seconds, scraping the bowl constantly. Beat on high speed for 3 minutes. Using a wooden spoon, stir in rye flour and as much remaining all-purpose flour as you can.

3 Turn dough out onto a lightly floured surface. Knead in enough remaining all-purpose flour to make a moderately stiff dough that is smooth and elastic (6 to 8 minutes). Shape into a ball. Place in a lightly greased bowl; turn once to grease surface. Cover and let rise in a warm place till double (1 to 1¼ hours).

4 Grease two 8×4×2-inch loaf pans. Punch dough down. Turn out onto a lightly floured surface. Divide in half. Cover and let rest for 10 minutes. Shape each half into a loaf. Place in the prepared loaf pans. Cover; let rise in a warm place till nearly double (30 to 45 minutes).

5 Bake in a 375° oven for 35 to 40 minutes or till bread sounds hollow when tapped. If necessary, cover with foil the last 20 minutes to prevent overbrowning. Remove from pans; place on a wire rack. Brush with margarine or butter. Cool completely. Makes 2 loaves (32 servings).

Nutrition facts per slice: 153 cal., 4 g total fat (1 g sat. fat), 14 mg chol., 88 mg sodium, 26 g carbo., 2 g fiber, 5 g pro. *Daily values:* 2% vit. A, 3% calcium, 10% iron.

Multigrain Cloverleaf Rolls: Prepare dough as directed through first rising and resting. Divide each half into 36 pieces. Shape each into a ball, pulling edges under to make smooth tops. Lightly grease 24 muffin cups. Place 3 balls in each cup, smooth side up. Let rise in a warm place till nearly double (about 30 minutes). Bake in a 375° oven 12 to 15 minutes or till tops are golden brown. Remove from pans; place on a wire rack. Brush with margarine or butter. Serve warm. Makes 24.

SPREAD IS THE WORD

As low-fat substitutes for butter on your bread or make-ahead companions for melba rounds, bagel chips, or toast, these spreads are quick, tasty, and as formal or casual as you want them to be. Set out a ramekin of each and pass around the crackers. You can prepare both spreads ahead of time and store them in the refrigerator.

RAISIN-SPICE SPREAD

In a large skillet cook ¼ cup chopped onion in 1 tablespoon cooking oil till tender. Add ½ cup raisins, ½ cup dry red wine, ¼ cup snipped, oil-packed dried tomatoes (drained), and ⅛ teaspoon ground cloves. Bring to boiling. Reduce heat and simmer, uncovered, till liquid is reduced to about 1 tablespoon and raisins are soft. Transfer to food processor bowl and process till almost smooth. Transfer to serving or storage container. Serve warm or chilled. Makes about ½ cup.

Nutrition facts per tablespoon raisin spread: 62 cal., 2 g total fat, 0 mg chol., 20 mg sodium.

OLIVE AND SWEET PEPPER SPREAD

In a food processor bowl combine ¼ cup pitted ripe olives, ¼ cup pimiento-stuffed green olives, ¼ cup purchased roasted sweet pepper, 1 teaspoon olive oil, 1 teaspoon snipped fresh oregano, and ¼ teaspoon ground pepper. Cover and process with several on-off turns till coarsely chopped. (Or, coarsely chop olives and sweet pepper by hand. Stir in oil, oregano, and ground pepper.) Transfer to serving dish and chill, covered, before serving. Makes about ½ cup.

Nutrition facts per tablespoon tapenade: 15 cal., 0 g total fat, 2 mg chol., 100 mg sodium.

RASPBERRY-ALMOND ROLLS

Prep: 20 min.
Rise: machine rise plus 30 min.
Bake: 18 min.

This recipe earned Nancy Ceronsky of Oxford, Connecticut, $100 in the magazine's monthly contest.

1 cup water
1 egg
2 Tbsp. cooking oil, or margarine or butter, cut up
3½ cups bread flour
¼ cup granulated sugar
½ tsp. salt
½ tsp. almond extract
1 pkg. active dry yeast
3 Tbsp. raspberry or blackberry jam
1 8-oz. can almond paste*

♦♦♦

1 recipe Powdered Sugar Icing (see above right)

1 Add first 8 ingredients to bread machine (with a capacity of at least 10 cups) according to manufacturer's directions. Select dough cycle. When cycle is complete, remove dough from machine. Punch down. Cover; let rest 10 minutes. On a floured surface, roll dough into a 12×10-inch rectangle. Spread jam over dough. Crumble almond paste and sprinkle over dough. Roll up dough, jelly-roll style, starting from a long side; seal seams. Slice into twelve 1-inch-thick slices. Place rolls, cut side down, 2 inches apart on greased baking sheets for individual rolls, or arrange in a greased 13×9×2-inch baking pan.

Cover; let rise till nearly double (about 30 minutes).

2 Bake in a 350° oven till golden brown, allowing 18 minutes for individual rolls or about 30 minutes for rolls in pan. Cool on a wire rack 5 minutes; transfer to a serving platter. Drizzle with Powdered Sugar Icing. Serve warm. Makes 12 rolls.

Powdered Sugar Icing: In a medium mixing bowl stir together 1 cup *sifted powdered sugar,* 1 tablespoon *milk,* and ¼ teaspoon *vanilla.* Stir in additional *milk,* ½ teaspoon at a time, till icing is of drizzling consistency.

*Note: For best results, use an almond paste made without syrup or liquid glucose.

Nutrition facts per roll: 321 cal., 9 g total fat (1 g sat. fat), 18 mg chol., 99 mg sodium, 54 g carbo., 1 g fiber, 8 g pro. *Daily values:* 4% calcium, 15% iron.

APPLE BUTTER COFFEE CAKE

Prep.: 15 min. ♦ Bake : 25 min.

1 8½-oz. pkg. corn muffin mix
¼ cup toasted or untoasted wheat germ
1 beaten egg or ¼ cup frozen egg product, thawed
½ cup apple butter
⅓ cup milk
¾ tsp. pumpkin pie spice or apple pie spice

♦♦♦

¼ cup packed brown sugar
¼ cup toasted or untoasted wheat germ
¼ cup apple butter

♦♦♦

Powdered sugar (optional)
Apple butter (optional)

1 Grease an 8×8×2-inch baking pan; set aside. In a medium mixing bowl combine muffin mix and the ¼ cup wheat germ. In another bowl combine the egg or the egg product, ½ cup apple butter, milk, and pumpkin or apple pie spice. Add egg mixture all at once to wheat germ mixture, stirring just till combined. Pour the batter into the prepared pan.

2 For topping, stir together brown sugar, ¼ cup wheat germ, and ¼ cup apple butter. Spoon mixture in small mounds atop batter in pan. Using a knife, marble the mixture through batter. Bake in a 350° oven for 25 to 30 minutes or till a wooden toothpick inserted near center comes out clean. Cool slightly.

3 Cut cake into 8 or 9 wedges. If desired, sift powdered sugar over each and serve with additional apple butter. Serve warm. Makes 8 or 9 servings.

Nutrition facts per serving: 237 cal., 5 g total fat (0 g sat. fat), 27 mg chol., 226 mg sodium, 45 g carbo., 1 g fiber, 5 g pro. *Daily values:* 2% vit. A, 1% vit. C, 4% calcium, 12% iron.

DATE-GINGER CAKE

Prep: 20 min. ♦ Bake: 30 min.

Use kitchen shears to cut dates, dipping the shears in water between snips to keep the dates from sticking.

1 cup all-purpose flour
1 tsp. baking powder
¼ tsp. baking soda

♦♦♦

⅓ **cup butter or margarine,**
  softened
1 **tsp. grated fresh gingerroot**
  or ½ tsp. ground ginger
½ **cup sugar**
1 **egg**
½ **cup orange or lemon yogurt**
2 **Tbsp. milk**
  ♦♦♦
1 **cup pitted whole dates,**
  snipped
2 **Tbsp. all-purpose flour**
  ♦♦♦
1 **recipe Orange Sauce (see**
  below)

1 Grease and flour an 8×8×2-inch baking pan; set aside. In a bowl stir together the 1 cup flour, baking powder, and baking soda; set aside.

2 In a medium mixing bowl beat butter or margarine and gingerroot or ginger with an electric mixer on medium speed for 30 seconds. Add sugar; beat till fluffy. Add egg; beat well. Stir in yogurt and milk. Add flour mixture, beating on low to medium speed till combined. Toss the dates with 2 tablespoons flour; fold into batter. Spread batter evenly in the prepared pan.

3 Bake in a 350° oven for 30 to 35 minutes or till a wooden toothpick inserted in the center comes out clean. Cool slightly (about 30 minutes). Cut into squares. Serve warm with Orange Sauce. Makes 9 servings.

Orange Sauce: In a saucepan stir ¼ cup *sugar*, 2½ teaspoons *cornstarch*, 1 teaspoon grated *gingerroot* or ½ teaspoon *ground ginger*, and ¼ teaspoon finely shredded *orange peel*. Stir in ¾ cup

orange juice. Cook and stir over medium heat till the mixture is thickened and bubbly; cook and stir 2 minutes more. Remove pan from heat. Stir in 1 tablespoon *margarine or butter*, cut up, till melted. Cover pan and cool slightly. Serve warm. Makes a scant 1 cup.

Nutrition facts per serving: 277 cal., 9 g total fat (5 g sat. fat), 43 mg chol., 176 mg sodium, 48 g carbo., 2 g fiber, 3 g pro. *Daily values:* 9% vit. A, 17% vit. C, 6% calcium, 7% iron.

WALNUT-MOCHA TORTE
Prep: 30 min. ♦ Bake: 20 min.

Short in height, but tall with flavor, this typical nut torte uses very finely ground nuts as part of the flour. The layers are on the skinny side, so pile them high with the creamy mocha frosting.

1 **cup walnuts or pecans**
2 **Tbsp. all-purpose flour**
2½ **tsp. baking powder**
4 **eggs**
¾ **cup sugar**
  ♦♦♦
1 **recipe Mocha Frosting (see**
  right)
  Chocolate curls (optional)
  Edible rose petals (optional)

1 Grease and lightly flour two 8×1½-inch round baking pans; set aside. In a medium bowl combine the walnuts or pecans, flour, and baking powder. In a food processor bowl or blender container process or blend eggs and sugar till smooth. Add nut mixture; process till smooth. Spread cake batter in prepared pans.

2 Bake in a 350° oven for 20 to 25 minutes or till cake

THE CLEVER COOK

COCOA COATS THE CAKE

Instead of flouring the cake pan and turning chocolate cake white on the outside, grease and "cocoa" the pan, using sifted unsweetened cocoa powder.

Vera B. Sweeney
Bedminster, New Jersey

springs back when lightly touched (center may dip slightly). Cool in pans for 10 minutes on wire racks. Remove from the pans; cool completely.

3 Split each cake layer in half. Spread Mocha Frosting between layers and on top and sides of cake. Chill frosted cake several hours before serving. To serve, cut into wedges; if desired, top with chocolate curls and garnish with rose petals. Makes 8 servings.

Mocha Frosting: In a small chilled mixing bowl dissolve 1 teaspoon crushed *instant coffee crystals* in 1 cup *whipping cream;* beat with an electric mixer on low speed till slightly thickened. Add ⅓ cup *sugar* and ¼ cup *unsweetened cocoa powder;* beat till stiff peaks form. Makes 2½ cups.

Nutrition facts per serving: 360 cal., 23 g total fat (8 g sat. fat), 147 mg chol., 158 mg sodium, 34 g carbo., 1 g fiber, 7 g pro. *Daily values:* 18% vit. A, 1% vit. C, 15% calcium, 9% iron.

APRICOT-ALMOND TART

Prep: 35 min. ◆ Bake: 44 min.

*A bit of whipped cream
adds a perfect touch to this treat.*

6 Tbsp. cold butter
1¼ cups all-purpose flour
1 beaten egg yolk
2 to 3 Tbsp. ice water

◆◆◆

½ cup snipped dried apricots
2 beaten eggs
⅔ cup light-colored corn syrup
⅓ cup sugar
2 Tbsp. butter, melted
1 cup sliced almonds

◆◆◆

Whipped cream (optional)

1 In a medium bowl, using a pastry blender, cut cold butter into flour till pieces are the size of small peas. In a small bowl combine the egg yolk and *1 tablespoon* of the ice water. Gradually stir the yolk mixture into flour mixture. Sprinkle 1 more tablespoon ice water over mixture, gently tossing with a fork. Repeat with the remaining ice water till all of mixture is moistened. Gently knead the dough just till a ball forms.

2 On a lightly floured surface, flatten dough with hands. Roll dough from center to edges, forming a circle about 11 inches in diameter.

3 To transfer pastry, roll it around the rolling pin. Unroll pastry into a 9-inch tart pan with a removable bottom or a 9-inch pie plate. Ease the pastry into pan, being careful not to stretch pastry. Trim edges of pastry even with the pan or plate. Line the pastry shell with a double thickness of foil to prevent it from puffing. Bake in 450° oven for 10 minutes. Remove foil; bake for 4 to 5 minutes more or till pastry is nearly done. Remove from oven. Reduce oven temperature to 325°.

4 For the filling, in a small saucepan combine the snipped dried apricots and enough *water* to cover. Bring mixture to boiling; reduce heat. Simmer, covered, for 5 minutes. Remove from heat; drain. In a medium mixing bowl stir together the beaten eggs, corn syrup, sugar, and melted butter. Gently stir in the drained apricots and almonds.

5 Place the baked crust on a baking sheet. Carefully spoon almond filling into the crust. Bake in the 325° oven for 30 to 35 minutes or till a knife inserted near the center comes out clean. Place the tart pan or pie plate on a wire rack and cool completely.

6 If using the tart pan, remove sides of pan. To serve, cut tart into wedges. If desired, top each serving with whipped cream. Makes 10 servings.

Nutrition facts per serving: 318 cal., 16 g total fat (7 g sat. fat), 88 mg chol., 122 mg sodium, 40 g carbo., 2 g fiber, 6 g pro. *Daily values:* 18% vit. A, 5% calcium, 17% iron.

TEST KITCHEN TIP

QUICK AND NUTTY IDEAS

A sprinkling of nuts turns an ordinary recipe into something extra-special, adding big crunch and great nutty flavor. Try these quick and easy hints.

◆ Top cookies and cakes. Sprinkle toasted, chopped, or ground nuts onto frosted cakes or cookies. First shake the chopped nuts in a sieve to remove the fine nut dust that comes from chopping.

◆ Switch nuts. Substitute a different kind of nut in your favorite recipe. Turn a pecan bar into a tropical macadamia bar or traditional banana nut bread into a hazelnut bread.

◆ Show off a simple salad. Sprinkle toasted nuts over tossed greens and fruit; do so just before serving so the nuts don't lose their crunch.

◆ Go meatless. Toss a few nuts into your next stir-fry as a protein to replace some or all of the meat. Remember, nuts have nutrition benefits and are cholesterol-free, but they are not low in fat.

◆ Jazz up pie pastry. Stir ⅓ cup finely chopped nuts into the flour mixture for pie pastry.

◆ Crown your casseroles. Sprinkle chopped nuts atop your favorite casserole the last 10 minutes of baking; and bake, uncovered, to develop a toasty flavor and extra crunch.

◆ Top off oatmeal. Sprinkle a few nuts onto a bowlful of hot oatmeal just before serving.

MARCH
Cooking at the Speed of Life

*L*ife accelerates in March: things to do, plans to make, seeds to order. Spring cleaning waits behind all the chores that come with winter's end. Quicker meals and lighter fare come as naturally as the season's first songbirds. Bring new meaning to fast food at home with 30-minute recipes for Sesame Chicken, Fettuccine and Salmon, Peppered Pork Chops and Pilaf, or Caesar Shrimp and Asparagus Salad. Many low-fat dishes, such as Chicken and Shrimp Tortilla Soup, can be put together so quickly that a few minutes spent in the kitchen today repays you with healthier tomorrows—for all those things you want to do at the speed of life.

30-minute recipes indicated in RED.
Low-fat and no-fat recipes indicated
with a ♥.
Photographs indicated in italics.

SESAME CHICKEN

Start to finish: 30 min.

The appealing nutty flavor of these quick-to-fix chicken breasts comes from both sesame seed and toasted sesame oil.

6 medium skinless, boneless
   chicken breast halves
½ cup all-purpose flour
1½ tsp. lemon-pepper seasoning
⅓ cup sesame seed
   ◆◆◆
2 cups sliced fresh shiitake or
   button mushrooms
¼ cup finely chopped onion
2 tsp. olive oil
1½ cups milk
1 Tbsp. Dijon-style mustard
1 Tbsp. snipped fresh parsley
   ◆◆◆
⅓ cup milk
1 Tbsp. olive oil
1 tsp. toasted sesame oil

1 Rinse chicken; pat dry with paper towels. Set aside. In a shallow bowl stir together the flour, lemon-pepper seasoning, and ¾ teaspoon *salt*. Reserve *2 tablespoons* flour mixture. Stir sesame seed into remaining flour mixture; set aside.

2 For sauce, in a medium saucepan cook mushrooms and onion in the 2 teaspoons olive oil till tender. Stir the reserved 2 tablespoons flour mixture into mushrooms-and-onion mixture till blended. Add 1½ cups milk all at once. Cook and stir till mixture is thickened and bubbly. Cook and stir 1 minute more. Stir in the mustard and parsley. Keep warm.

3 Meanwhile, dip chicken in the ⅓ cup milk; roll in sesame-seed-and-flour mixture. In a 12-inch skillet heat 1 tablespoon olive oil and the sesame oil over medium-high heat. Cook chicken in hot oil about 6 minutes or till tender and no longer pink, turning once. Serve sauce with chicken. Makes 6 servings.

Nutrition facts per serving: 362 cal., 14 g total fat (3 g sat. fat), 65 mg chol., 702 mg sodium, 30 g carbo., 2 g fiber, 30 g pro. *Daily values:* 5% vit. A, 20% vit. C, 11% calcium, 23% iron.

COBB SALAD

Start to finish: 30 min.

For easier preparation, we suggest you use your favorite purchased French salad dressing instead of the original Brown Derby dressing that was included with the recipe in 1964.

½ of a large head lettuce,
   shredded (about 6 cups)
4 medium skinless, boneless
   chicken breast halves,
   cooked, chilled, and
   cubed; or 3 cups diced
   cooked chicken
2 medium tomatoes, chopped
3 hard-cooked eggs, chopped
6 slices bacon, crisp-cooked,
   drained, and crumbled
¾ cup crumbled blue cheese
   (3 oz.)
   ◆◆◆
1 or 2 medium avocados,
   halved, seeded, peeled, and
   cut into wedges
1 small head Belgian endive
1 Tbsp. snipped fresh chives or
   thinly sliced green onion
   tops (optional)
½ cup French salad dressing

1 On 4 individual salad plates or on a large platter, arrange the shredded lettuce. On top of the lettuce, arrange a row each of chicken, tomatoes, eggs, bacon, and blue cheese. If desired, cover and chill overnight.

2 Just before serving, tuck avocado wedges and endive leaves around the edges of the plates or platter. If desired, sprinkle with chives or green onion tops. Serve with dressing. Makes 4 to 6 main-dish servings.

Nutrition facts per serving: 508 cal., 34 g total fat (10 g sat. fat), 238 mg chol., 815 mg sodium, 18 g carbo., 4 g fiber, 34g pro. *Daily values:* 20% vit. A, 42% vit. C, 8% calcium, 18% iron.

For a lower-fat version: Use a low-fat or low-calorie French salad dressing in place of the regular salad dressing and omit or reduce the amount of bacon and avocado you use.

Chicken and Shrimp Tortilla Soup

Start to finish: 30 min.

This citrusy Mexican-style soup is simple to fix and deliciously nutritious.

6 oz. fresh or frozen peeled, deveined medium shrimp
1 large onion, chopped
1 tsp. cumin seed
1 Tbsp. cooking oil
4½ cups reduced-sodium chicken broth
1 14½-oz. can Mexican-style stewed tomatoes
3 Tbsp. snipped fresh cilantro
2 Tbsp. lime juice
10 oz. shredded, cooked chicken breast (about 1⅔ cups)
1 recipe Crisp Tortilla Shreds (see below right)
Snipped fresh cilantro (optional)

1 Thaw shrimp, if frozen. In a large saucepan cook the onion and cumin seed in hot oil about 5 minutes or till onion is tender, stirring occasionally. Carefully add the chicken broth, tomatoes, 3 tablespoons snipped cilantro, and lime juice. Bring to boiling; reduce heat. Simmer, covered, for 8 minutes. Add the shrimp and chicken. Cook about 3 minutes more or till shrimp turn pink, stirring occasionally.

2 To serve, ladle soup into bowls. Top each serving with Crisp Tortilla Shreds. If desired, garnish with fresh cilantro. Makes 6 main-dish servings.

Brown-Bag Ideas

Tired of unhealthy, expensive grab-and-go lunches? You'll have better lunches in the bag with the following brown-bag ideas. These lunches will provide a fresh-tasting break from the usual midday meal routine.

Fiesta! Lunch
Spice up your chicken salad. Substitute salsa and a little low-fat sour cream for mayonnaise. Roll salad up with a lettuce leaf in a soft flour tortilla. A small bag of baked tortilla chips and a container of black bean dip, plus some toasted pumpkin seeds (pepitas), make lunch a fiesta.

"Ciao" Down
For this totable Italian concerto, mix soft-style chive-and-onion-flavored cream cheese with a pinch or two of dried basil. Sandwich between Italian bread slices with strips of red and green sweet pepper and sliced ripe olives. Shredded zucchini tossed with low-fat Italian dressing makes a *bellissimo* salad. For dessert, try biscotti.

It's All Greek
Stir some sliced black olives, a dash of lemon juice, and a pinch of oregano into your favorite tuna salad. Spoon into pita halves and top with diced cucumbers and tomatoes. For a more Mediterranean flavor, add some feta cheese. Stay light with an apricot bar or splurge with a piece of baklava for dessert.

Paris, Texas
Hearty Southwest flavors on crusty French bread—voilà, Pardner! Stack slices of smoked turkey on a baguette and blazon with barbecue sauce, pickled jalapeño slices, sweet relish, and Dijon-style mayonnaise. Pack a side of tomato slices for the sandwich, and add a bag of baked white corn tortilla chips. A slice of banana bread satisfies the sweet tooth to round out this Paris-meets-Texas lunch.

English Garden
Paper-thin cucumber slices and alfalfa sprouts on whole wheat bread refresh cold poached salmon. Dress with chopped watercress stirred into a little low-fat mayonnaise; salt and pepper to taste. When accompanied by baby carrots and celery sticks, plus fresh strawberries for "afters" (dessert to the British), this becomes a "simply smashing" take-to-the-office lunch.

Crisp Tortilla Shreds: Brush four 5½-inch *corn tortillas* with 1 tablespoon *cooking oil.* In a small bowl combine ½ teaspoon *salt* and ⅛ teaspoon *pepper.* Sprinkle salt mixture over tortillas. Cut tortillas in half. Next, cut each half into thin shreds. On a baking sheet arrange tortilla shreds in a single layer. Bake in a 350° oven 8 minutes or till crisp.

Nutrition facts per serving: 160 cal., 5 g total fat (1 g sat. fat), 80 mg chol., 794 mg sodium, 8 g carbo., 0 g fiber, 21 g pro. *Daily values:* 7% vit. A, 22% vit. C, 2% calcium, 10% iron.

SHRIMP, PRAWNS, OR SCAMPI

Large or jumbo shrimp, prawns, and scampi are so similar that many seafood markets often use the names interchangeably.

Shrimp: Widely available across the United States, shrimp comes in a variety of sizes. Most markets categorize this shellfish by the number per pound or with descriptive names such as colossal.

Prawns: This seafood has a thin abdomen and long legs and is usually sold about six to 10 per pound, heads on. Because of its large size and sweet, lobsterlike flavor, the prawn is often served stuffed.

Scampi: In the United States this term refers to shrimp sautéed in garlic butter (shrimp scampi). Authentically, scampi is the Mediterranean term for a small lobster.

---

30 MIN. LOW FAT

ITALIAN-STYLE SHRIMP AND RICE

Start to finish: 30 min.

- 1 Tbsp. olive oil
- 1 clove garlic, minced
- ¾ cup long-grain rice
- 1 14½-oz. can chicken broth
- 12 oz. fresh or frozen, peeled, deveined medium shrimp
- 1 14½-oz. can Italian-style stewed tomatoes
- 1 medium zucchini, halved lengthwise and thinly sliced
- ¼ cup thinly sliced green onions
- 2 Tbsp. snipped fresh basil or 1 tsp. dried basil, crushed
- ¼ cup shredded mozzarella cheese or finely shredded Parmesan cheese (1 oz.)

1 In a large skillet heat oil; add garlic and rice. Cook and stir 2 minutes. Carefully add broth. Bring to boiling; reduce heat. Simmer, covered, 15 minutes or till rice is tender and water is absorbed. Stir in shrimp, tomatoes, zucchini, onions, basil, and ⅛ teaspoon *pepper.* Return to boiling; reduce heat. Cook, covered, 2 to 3 minutes or till shrimp turn pink. Remove from heat. Sprinkle with cheese. Cover and let stand 2 minutes. Serves 4.

Nutrition facts per serving: 294 cal., 6 g total fat (2 g sat. fat), 135 mg chol., 871 mg sodium, 37 g carbo., 1 g fiber, 22 g pro. *Daily values:* 18% vit. A, 30% vit. C, 9% calcium, 28% iron.

CAESAR SHRIMP AND ASPARAGUS SALAD

Start to finish: 20 min.

- 12 oz. fresh asparagus spears
- 4 green onions, sliced
- ½ cup bottled Caesar salad dressing
- ½ tsp. finely shredded lemon peel
- 6 cups purchased torn mixed salad greens
- 1 lb. cooked, peeled, and deveined large or jumbo shrimp (with tails left on)
- 1 cup Herb Croutons (see recipe, below) Finely shredded Parmesan cheese (optional)

1 Rinse asparagus. Snap woody bases from spears and discard. In a saucepan cook asparagus spears, covered, in a small amount of boiling water for 4 to 6 minutes or till crisp-tender; drain. Set aside; keep warm.

2 Meanwhile, in a small skillet cook green onions, covered, in 2 tablespoons *water* for 2 to 3 minutes or till tender. Stir in the salad dressing, lemon peel, and ¼ teaspoon *pepper;* heat through.

3 Divide greens among 4 dinner plates. Arrange asparagus spears, cooked shrimp, and Herb Croutons among greens. Spoon warm dressing mixture over salads. If desired, sprinkle with finely shredded Parmesan cheese. Serve salad immediately. Makes 4 main-dish servings.

Herb Croutons: In a large skillet melt ¼ cup *margarine or butter.* Remove from heat. Stir in ½ teaspoon *dried thyme,* crushed, and ⅛ teaspoon *garlic powder.* Add 2 cups *French or sourdough bread cubes;* stir till cubes are coated with margarine mixture. Spread in a single layer in a baking pan. Bake in a 300° oven about 15 minutes or till dry and crisp, stirring twice; cool. Tightly cover and store at room temperature up to 1 week.

Nutrition facts per serving: 387 cal., 27 g total fat (3 g sat. fat), 174 mg chol., 407 mg sodium, 12 g carbo., 2 g fiber, 22 g pro. *Daily values:* 40% vit. A, 51% vit. C, 7% calcium, 28% iron.

SALMON IN PANCETTA CREAM SAUCE

Prep: 20 min. ◆ Broil: 4 min.

1 lb. fresh or frozen skinless salmon fillets, about ½ inch thick and cut into 4 portions
1 small zucchini, cut into thin bite-size strips (1¼ cups)
1 small yellow summer squash, cut into thin bite-size strips (1¼ cups)
1 medium carrot, cut into thin bite-size strips (½ cup)

◆◆◆

1 oz. pancetta, sliced, or 2 strips bacon
¼ cup sliced green onions
¾ cup whipping cream
2 Tbsp. snipped fresh basil

◆◆◆

Fresh basil leaves (optional)

1 Thaw fish, if frozen. In a steamer basket over, but not touching, boiling water, steam strips of zucchini, yellow squash, and carrot about 3 minutes or till crisp-tender. Keep warm.

2 For sauce, in a small skillet cook pancetta or bacon till crisp. Remove pancetta, reserving *1 tablespoon* drippings in skillet. Set aside remaining drippings. Coarsely crumble pancetta or bacon; set aside. Cook green onions in reserved drippings about 2 minutes or till tender. Carefully stir in whipping cream. Bring to boiling; reduce heat. Boil gently, uncovered, 4 to 5 minutes or till reduced and slightly thickened (you should have about ½ cup). Stir in snipped basil. Remove from heat; keep warm.

3 Rinse fish and pat dry with paper towels. Place fish on the greased unheated rack of a broiler pan. Tuck under thin edges of fish. Brush with reserved drippings; sprinkle with *pepper*. Broil 4 inches from heat for 4 to 6 minutes or till fish just begins to flake easily. To serve, divide sauce among 4 dinner plates. Place fish atop sauce. Add vegetables and crumbled pancetta. If desired, garnish with basil leaves. Serves 4.

Nutrition facts per serving: 296 cal., 22 g total fat (12 g sat. fat), 84 mg chol., 147 mg sodium, 6 g carbo., 2 g fiber, 19 g pro. *Daily values:* 65% vit. A, 10% vit. C, 5% calcium, 8% iron.

FETTUCCINE AND SALMON

Start to finish: 20 min.

1 lb. fresh or frozen skinless salmon fillet, cut into 4 portions

◆◆◆

Nonstick spray coating
⅓ cup finely chopped onion
1½ cups skim milk
1½ tsp. cornstarch
6 oz. reduced-fat cream cheese, (Neufchâtel), cubed and softened
½ cup finely shredded smoked Gouda cheese (2 oz.)
1 Tbsp. snipped fresh chives
¼ to ½ tsp. coarsely ground pepper

◆◆◆

½ of a 9-oz. pkg. refrigerated linguine and ½ of a 9-oz. pkg. refrigerated spinach fettuccine, or one 9-oz. pkg. refrigerated linguine or spinach fettuccine

Fettuccine and Salmon
(see below left)

◆◆◆

Buttered yellow summer squash slices

◆◆◆

Garlic bread

◆◆◆

Heavenly Baked Apples
(see page 69)

1 Thaw fish, if frozen. In a large skillet bring 2 cups *water* to boiling. Measure thickness of fish. Add fish to skillet. Return to boiling; reduce heat. Simmer, covered, till fish flakes easily, allowing 4 to 6 minutes per ½-inch thickness. Drain; keep warm.

2 Meanwhile, spray a medium saucepan with nonstick coating. Add onion and cook till tender. Stir together the milk and cornstarch. Add to saucepan. Cook and stir till slightly thickened and bubbly. Cook and stir 2 minutes more. Add cream cheese and Gouda cheese. Cook and stir till melted. Stir in snipped chives and coarsely ground pepper.

3 Meanwhile, cook pasta according to package directions; drain. Divide hot pasta among 4 dinner plates; place salmon atop pasta. Spoon sauce over salmon. If desired, garnish with *chives with blossoms*. Makes 4 servings.

Nutrition facts per serving: 566 cal., 26 g total fat (13 g sat. fat), 131 mg chol., 579 mg sodium, 43 g carbo., 0 g fiber, 40 g pro. *Daily values:* 25% vit. A, 3% vit. C, 33% calcium, 18% iron.

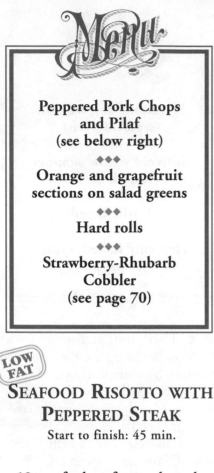

Menu

Peppered Pork Chops
and Pilaf
(see below right)

◆◆◆

Orange and grapefruit
sections on salad greens

◆◆◆

Hard rolls

◆◆◆

Strawberry-Rhubarb
Cobbler
(see page 70)

LOW FAT

SEAFOOD RISOTTO WITH PEPPERED STEAK

Start to finish: 45 min.

12 oz. fresh or frozen cleaned
squid;* bay scallops;
and/or peeled, deveined
shrimp, halved lengthwise
8 oz. beef top loin steak or
tenderloin, cut 1 inch
thick
1 tsp. olive oil or cooking oil
1 tsp. coarsely ground pepper
¾ tsp. dried thyme, crushed

◆◆◆

2 small shallots, finely
chopped
4 cloves garlic, minced
1 Tbsp. margarine or butter
1 cup Arborio or short-grain
rice
½ cup dry white wine or
chicken broth
½ tsp. dried thyme, crushed

◆◆◆

1 14½-oz. can chicken broth

1 Thaw seafood, if frozen. Rub both sides of steak with oil.

Sprinkle both sides of steak with pepper and ¾ teaspoon thyme, pressing into surface. Cover and chill steak till needed.

2 In a medium saucepan cook shallots and garlic in hot margarine till tender. Add uncooked rice. Cook and stir 2 minutes more. Carefully add wine or broth and ½ teaspoon thyme. Cook and stir till most wine is absorbed.

3 Meanwhile, in a 1-quart saucepan bring the can of broth and 1¼ cups *water* to boiling. Add ½ *cup* broth mixture to the rice mixture, stirring constantly over low heat till rice has absorbed most of the broth. Continue adding the broth, ½ cup at a time, stirring constantly for 15 minutes. Add seafood. Cook and stir about 5 minutes more or till rice is tender and seafood turns opaque.

4 Place steak on the unheated rack of a broiler pan. Broil 3 to 4 inches from heat 10 to 12 minutes for medium rare, turning meat over once halfway through.

5 To serve, cut beef across grain into very thin slices; season to taste with *salt*. Fan the steak slices on 6 dinner plates. Spoon risotto-rice mixture atop. If desired garnish with *fresh chives* and *Parmesan cheese* shavings. Makes 6 servings.

*Note: If cleaned squid is not available, here's how to clean it: Pull head and tentacles out of the body. Cut the head off the tentacles. Reserve tentacles; discard head. Remove and discard any entrails that remain in the body. Pull out and discard the clear car-

tilage "pen" running down the back of the body. With your fingers, peel skin off outside of the body, leaving body whole. Rinse body; pat dry. Using a sharp knife, cut body and tentacles crosswise into ½- to 1-inch rings.

Nutrition facts per serving: 267 cal., 6 g total fat (2 g sat. fat), 96 mg chol., 315 mg sodium, 29 g carbo., 0 g fiber, 19 g pro. *Daily values:* 7% vit. A, 5% vit. C, 4% calcium, 23% iron.

PEPPERED PORK CHOPS AND PILAF

Start to finish: 25 min.

See the photograph on page 81.

4 boneless pork loin chops, cut
¾ inch thick
1 Tbsp. herb-pepper seasoning
2 Tbsp. olive oil
2 cups cut-up salad-bar
vegetables, such as sweet
peppers, carrots,
mushrooms, onion, and/or
broccoli
1 14½-oz. can chicken broth
2 cups quick-cooking brown
rice
¼ cup chopped roasted red
sweet pepper

1 Sprinkle both sides of meat with *2 teaspoons* of the herb-pepper seasoning. In a large skillet cook chops in *1 tablespoon* of the olive oil for 5 minutes. Turn chops. Cook for 5 to 7 minutes more or till slightly pink in center and juices run clear.

2 Meanwhile, cut vegetables into bite-size pieces. In a saucepan heat the remaining 1 tablespoon olive oil. Add vegetables and cook for 2 minutes. Carefully add broth. Bring to boiling. Stir in uncooked rice, roasted sweet pepper, and remaining 1 teaspoon herb-pepper seasoning. Return to boiling. Simmer, covered, for 5 minutes. Remove from heat. Let stand 5 minutes. Serve chops with rice. Makes 4 servings.

Nutrition facts per serving: 431 cal., 20 g total fat (5 g sat. fat), 77 mg chol., 408 mg sodium, 34 g carbo., 5 g fiber, 31 g pro. *Daily values:* 48% vit. A, 99% vit. C, 2% calcium, 16% iron.

ROAST PORK TANGERINE

Prep: 25 min. ◆ Roast: 2¼ hr.

1 4- to 5-lb. pork loin center rib roast, backbone loosened
1 tsp. dry mustard
1 tsp. dried marjoram, crushed

◆◆◆

2 tsp. finely shredded tangerine or orange peel
½ cup tangerine or orange juice
1 Tbsp. brown sugar

◆◆◆

Chicken broth or beef broth
⅔ cup chicken broth
3 Tbsp. all-purpose flour
⅛ tsp. dry mustard
⅛ tsp. dried marjoram, crushed
3 tangerines or 2 oranges, peeled, sectioned, and seeded

1 Place pork, rib side down, in a shallow roasting pan. In a small bowl combine 1 teaspoon dry mustard, 1 teaspoon marjoram, and ½ teaspoon *salt;* rub over meat. Insert a meat thermometer. Roast, uncovered, in a 325° oven for 1¾ hours.

2 Stir together the peel, juice, and brown sugar; spoon over meat. Roast about 30 minutes more or till thermometer registers 155°, spooning pan juices over meat once or twice. Transfer meat to platter. Let stand, covered, 10 minutes before slicing.

3 Meanwhile, strain pan juices. Skim off fat. Measure juices; add enough broth to juices to equal ¾ *cup* liquid. Place the liquid in a medium saucepan. In a screw-top jar combine the ⅔ cup broth and the flour; shake well. Add to saucepan along with ⅛ teaspoon dry mustard and ⅛ teaspoon marjoram. Cook and stir till thickened and bubbly. Cook and stir for 1 minute more. Season with *salt* and *pepper.* Stir in tangerine sections; heat through. Serve with pork. Serves 10.

Nutrition facts per serving: 197 cal., 9 g total fat (3 g sat. fat), 61 mg chol., 245 mg sodium, 7 g carbo., 1 g fiber, 20 g pro. *Daily values:* 3% vit. A, 20% vit. C, 1% calcium, 6% iron.

THAI BEEF STIR-FRY

Start to finish: 45 min.

You can buy bottles of fish sauce in Asian markets.

12 oz. boneless beef sirloin steak, cut ¾ inch thick
½ cup catsup
3 Tbsp. fish sauce or soy sauce
1 Tbsp. brown sugar
1 Tbsp. lime juice

◆◆◆

½ cup beef broth
2 tsp. grated gingerroot
1½ tsp. cornstarch
½ to 1 tsp. crushed red pepper

◆◆◆

1 Tbsp. cooking oil
1 clove garlic, minced
2 medium carrots, thinly sliced
2 green onions, cut into ½-inch pieces
1 medium cucumber, halved lengthwise, seeded, and thinly sliced
½ of a medium red sweet pepper, cut into bite-size strips
¼ cup chopped peanuts
2 cups hot cooked rice

1 Partially freeze beef. Thinly slice across the grain into bite-size strips. Combine catsup, fish sauce or soy sauce, brown sugar, and lime juice. Add beef strips, tossing to coat. Let stand at room temperature for 30 minutes, stirring once. Drain beef, reserving marinade. Stir broth, gingerroot, cornstarch, and crushed red pepper into reserved marinade; set aside.

2 Pour oil into a wok or large skillet. (Add more oil, if necessary, during cooking.) Preheat over medium-high heat. Stir-fry garlic in hot oil 15 seconds. Add carrots; stir-fry 3 minutes. Add onions, cucumber, and sweet pepper; stir-fry 1 to 2 minutes more or till crisp-tender. Remove from wok. Add beef to hot wok. Stir-fry 2 to 3 minutes or to desired doneness. Stir broth mixture; add to wok. Cook and stir till thickened and bubbly. Stir in vegetables; heat through. Stir peanuts into rice. Serve beef and vegetables over rice mixture. If desired, garnish with *carrot strips.* Makes 4 servings.

Nutrition facts per serving: 410 cal., 16 g total fat (4 g sat. fat), 60 mg chol., 787 mg sodium, 41 g carbo., 3 g fiber, 26 g pro. *Daily values:* 97% vit. A, 45% vit. C, 4% calcium, 27% iron.

The mealtime ritual helps build family bonds that will endure, but schedule conflicts make it a challenge to get together around the table. Here's how you and your family can make it happen.

It's coming up on 6:30 p.m.—what used to be the traditional family dinner hour—and as usual, the dinner table at the Alquist home in suburban Los Angeles is deserted.

Brian, 9, is just getting out of his tae kwon do class and is waiting for his ride home; Amanda, 13, will be in her dance class until 7:30; father Chuck, a police detective, has an investigation that's running late and still hasn't started his 90-minute commute; mom Linda is stuck at the office meeting a late deadline.

Despite what seem like insurmountable obstacles, they still manage to have dinner together this evening, just as they do four or five nights a week. What's their secret? "We eat really late," says Linda Alquist, a newspaper editor, who says she makes sure her kids get a "really solid snack" after school to tide them over until dinner, which is usually served sometime after 8 p.m.

But families like the Alquists, who work hard to preserve an important family ritual, are facing ever-higher hurdles and that's a problem, say experts. When we miss family dinners, we miss the chance to demonstrate our support for one another, which, when combined with the restorative powers of food, is the glue that holds family relationships together and makes life a little better.

"The world can be so cruel, it's nice coming home to a family where they say 'How was your day?'" says Fredric Medway, a professor of psychology at the University of South Carolina and an expert on rituals, such as mealtimes, that nurture the human spirit. "It's a time for a family to talk, reflect on activities during the week, find out what everyone is doing; it allows everyone to interact."

While more than half of all families manage to eat dinner together five or more times a week, there are still many barriers to assembling the clan around the table: A poll of 1,000 people by the National Pork Producers Council found that conflicting schedules are the major obstacle to regular mealtimes for 64 percent of those interviewed. Other reasons: no time to cook and no interest from family members.

Sometimes there are seemingly unavoidable conflicts. Many employers are imposing mandatory overtime, and some parents have to hold down two jobs just to make ends meet. In the pork council poll, 42 percent of those surveyed cited work schedules as the reason they can't eat together.

But time has to be found, say experts, because mealtime is often the only opportunity parents and children have to interact for an uninterrupted hour. It's also a good way to stay tuned in to your family's well-being, Medway says.

The first step in getting the family together at mealtime is to make it the number one priority, say time management experts. "If you're going to get

CORNED BEEF AND CABBAGE DINNER

Prep: 25 min. ◆ Cook : 2½ hr.

Corned beef got its name before refrigeration, when meat was preserved using coarse grains of salt, called "corn." Today, beef is corned with spices strictly for flavor and not for preservation, so the meat must be refrigerated. A bit of updating hasn't changed the allure of this all-American favorite.
(See the photograph on page 80.)

1 2- to 2½-lb. corned beef brisket*
2 bay leaves
1 tsp. whole black pepper

◆◆◆

3 medium carrots, quartered lengthwise
2 medium parsnips or 1 medium rutabaga, peeled and cut into chunks

2 medium red onions, cut into wedges
10 to 12 whole, tiny new potatoes (1 lb.)
1 small cabbage, cut into 6 wedges (1 lb.)

1 Trim fat from meat. Place in a 4- to 6-quart pot; add juices and spices from package of beef. Add enough *water* to cover meat. Add bay leaves and pepper. Bring to

together for dinner, write it on the calendar as if it were an appointment. It sounds far-fetched, but do it," says Jeffrey J. Mayer, author of *Time Management for Dummies* (IDG Books Worldwide, $16.99). "It's about taking control. If it's important to get home for dinner, then you'll do it."

Mayer's advice is simple when it comes to activities that interfere with mealtimes: Drop them. "Many times mom and dad schedule so many things for kids they've run them ragged," he says.

Here are some other ways to help you get your family to the table:

◆ If you never eat together, set aside one day of the week for family meals: The best day is one when there are no scheduling conflicts; if there are, cancel the conflicting activity.

◆ Ignore family members' protests: We live in an age when individuality is given precedence over family and social obligations, but once family members get into the swing of eating together, they'll thank you.

◆ Start young: When children get into the habit early, family mealtime becomes a ritual they'll rely on when they enter their teen years.

◆ Make snacks: When you have to eat late, take a tip from the Alquists and supply afternoon snacks to keep appetites tamed until dinnertime, either by sending the food you want along to the kids' after-school day-care centers or having some healthy snacks waiting in the refrigerator at home.

An easy way to do this is to double up when making lunches. If you're making one sandwich anyway, make two and set one aside for a snack.

◆ Look beyond dinner: Scheduling breakfast or brunch on weekends can be a good way to get family members to eat together. And because everyone won't be tired and frazzled, the meal just might be more lively.

◆ Involve everyone: Assign tasks to each family member. When everyone pitches in, the whole enterprise goes much more quickly and seems less like drudgery.

◆ Turn off the television: A lot of families watch TV throughout the dinner hour, but having it on makes communication almost impossible and defeats the purpose of getting together.

◆ Buy a slow cooker: You can often get one for less than $30. With a little advance planning, slow cookers or crockery cookers allow you to put dinner on the table with a minimum of fuss. (You can make it a bit easier by relying on a cookbook—a good bet is *Better Homes and Gardens® Crockery Cookbook*, $14.95.)

◆ Keep it simple: There's no need to make a major production out of mealtime. It's not necessary to serve seven courses, polish the heirloom silverware, and set out finger bowls to promote family togetherness. Everyone is there to eat, but what's more important is that you're bringing your family together to share what led you to create a family in the first place: love.

---

boiling; reduce heat. Simmer, covered, about 2 hours or till meat is almost tender.

2 Add carrots, parsnips or rutabaga, and onions to meat. Return to boiling; reduce heat. Simmer, covered, for 10 minutes. Scrub potatoes; halve or quarter. Add the potatoes and cabbage to pot. Cover and cook about 20 minutes more or till the vegetables and meat are tender. Discard bay leaves. Remove meat from pot.

3 To serve, slice the meat across the grain. Transfer the meat and vegetables to a serving platter. Makes 6 servings.

*Note: If your brisket comes with an additional packet of spices, add it instead of the pepper and bay leaves called for in the ingredients list.

Nutrition facts per serving: 319 cal., 15 g total fat (5 g sat. fat), 74 mg chol., 895 mg sodium, 30 g carbo., 6 g fiber, 17 g pro. *Daily values:* 57% vit. A, 74% vit. C, 5% calcium, 22% iron.

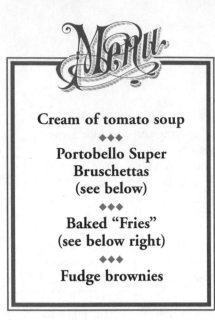

Cream of tomato soup

♦♦♦

**Portobello Super
Bruschettas
(see below)**

♦♦♦

**Baked "Fries"
(see below right)**

♦♦♦

Fudge brownies

PORTOBELLO SUPER BRUSCHETTAS

Prep: 30 min. ♦ Bake: 10 min.

*Serve hot from the oven.
(See the photograph on page 79.)*

¼ cup chopped onion
2 cloves garlic, minced
2 tsp. olive oil
½ cup diced, peeled eggplant
¼ tsp. salt
⅛ tsp. ground red pepper
½ of a 19-oz. can cannellini
    beans, rinsed and drained
    (about 1 cup)
1 medium tomato, seeded and
    chopped

♦♦♦

2 portobello mushrooms
    Olive oil
4 ¾-inch-thick slices Italian
    bread, toasted
2 to 3 Tbsp. pesto
4 slices mozzarella cheese
    (6 oz.)
    Chopped red onion
    (optional)
    Snipped fresh basil
    (optional)

1 In a medium skillet cook onion and garlic in the 2 tea-spoons hot olive oil till onion is tender. Add eggplant, salt, and red pepper. Cook and stir for 2 to 3 minutes or till eggplant is almost tender. Stir in beans and tomato. Remove from heat.

2 Clean mushrooms; discard stems. Halve mushrooms cross-wise. Rub gently with some olive oil. Place mushrooms, gill sides up, on a baking sheet. Bake in a 350° oven for 5 minutes. Remove from oven. Spread each slice of bread generously with pesto; place each mushroom half on a slice of Italian bread. Spoon bean mixture onto mushrooms. Top each mushroom with a slice of cheese. Return to oven and bake for 5 to 10 minutes more or till cheese bubbles and bean mixture is heated through. If desired, garnish with chopped red onion and snipped basil. Makes 4 servings.

Nutrition facts per serving: 339 cal., 17 g total fat (5 g sat. fat), 25 mg chol., 668 mg sodium, 32 g carbo., 5 g fiber, 19 g pro. *Daily values:* 9% vit. A, 15% vit. C, 26% calcium, 18% iron.

BAKED "FRIES"

Prep: 10 min. ♦ Bake: 30 min.

Spray the wedges with nonstick coating so the seasonings stick. This also helps the potatoes crisp in the oven.

   Nonstick spray coating
2 large baking potatoes (about
    1 lb.)
¼ cup grated Parmesan cheese
½ tsp. paprika
⅛ tsp. pepper

1 Lightly spray a 15×10×1-inch baking pan with nonstick coating; set aside. Cut potatoes lengthwise into thin wedges. Place in a plastic bag. Spray potato wedges with nonstick coating. Combine the Parmesan cheese, paprika, and pepper; add to bag. Close bag and shake to coat pota-toes with the seasonings.

2 Arrange potatoes in a single layer on prepared baking sheet. Bake in a 425° oven about 30 minutes or till crisp and fork-tender, turning once. Season with *salt.* Makes 4 servings.

Nutrition facts per serving: 148 cal., 2 g total fat (1 g sat. fat), 5 mg chol., 126 mg sodium, 27 g carbo., 1 g fiber, 5 g pro. *Daily values:* 2% vit. A, 28% vit. C, 8% calcium, 10% iron.

LOW FAT
RISOTTO WITH SAUSAGE AND ARTICHOKES

Start to finish: 35 min.

8 oz. ground turkey sausage
⅓ cup finely chopped onion
2 cloves garlic, minced
1 cup Arborio or short-grain
    rice
⅛ tsp. crushed red pepper

♦♦♦

2½ cups water
1   14½-oz. can reduced-sodium
     chicken broth
1   9-oz. pkg. frozen artichoke
     hearts, thawed
¼   cup snipped fresh basil

1 Crumble turkey sausage into a large saucepan. Add onion and garlic. Cook and stir till sausage is brown. Drain off fat, if necessary. Add uncooked rice and red pepper to sausage mixture; cook and stir for 1 minute.

2 Meanwhile, in a medium saucepan heat water and broth to simmering. Slowly add *1 cup* of the hot broth mixture to rice mixture, stirring constantly. Cook and stir over medium heat till liquid is absorbed. Continue to add broth mixture, ½ cup at a time, cooking and stirring till rice is tender and slightly creamy. Stir in artichokes and basil; heat. Makes 6 side-dish servings.

Nutrition facts per serving: 221 cal., 5 g total fat (2 g sat. fat), 14 mg chol., 528 mg sodium, 31 g carbo., 3 g fiber, 13 g pro. *Daily values:* 1% vit. A, 8% vit. C, 3% calcium, 17% iron.

HAZELNUT AND CURRENT RICE PILAF

Prep: 20 min. ◆ Cook: 45 min.

1½ **cups sliced fresh mushrooms, such as cremini, shiitake, or button**
2 **shallots, finely chopped**
1 **clove garlic, minced**
1 **Tbsp. olive oil**
1 **cup regular brown rice**
2 **cups beef broth**
1 **tsp. snipped fresh tarragon or ¼ tsp. dried tarragon, crushed (optional)**
¼ **cup toasted chopped hazelnuts (filberts)**
¼ **cup currants**

1 In a medium saucepan cook mushrooms, shallots, and garlic in hot oil till tender. Add uncooked rice; cook and stir 2 minutes more. Carefully add broth, dried tarragon (if using), and ⅛ teaspoon *pepper*. Bring to boiling; reduce heat. Simmer, covered, 45 minutes. Stir in the fresh tarragon (if using), hazelnuts, and currants. Cover; let stand 5 minutes. Makes 6 side-dish servings.

BASICALLY BALSAMIC

Balsamic vinegar's intriguing flavor is one that gives ordinary meats, salads, and sauces a distinct and subtly luxurious Mediterranean accent. Traditionally, true balsamic vinegar is made by boiling the juice of white grapes into a sweet concentrate. The thick juice is poured into wooden barrels where it slowly ages—for weeks, years, or even lifetimes. As more and more of the remaining vinegar evaporates, it is poured into smaller and smaller casks. The barrels' wood contributes flavor and color until a deep mahogany syrup is achieved.

This extensive processing, taking so much time and so many grapes to produce each small bottle, makes balsamic more costly than wine vinegars. But because it is so intensely flavored, it is best rationed by the drop so it can contribute its pungent, sweet-sour resonance to dishes.

Commercially produced balsamic vinegar is processed more quickly, sometimes within five years. It's also more readily available, and its flavor is fine for home use. You'll find balsamic among the flavored vinegars on your grocer's shelves or in Italian or European specialty markets. Each balsamic vinegar maker's version boasts its own distinct flavor—some sweeter, some sharper—so shop around to see which brand best suits your taste buds. Here are some suggestions for letting the balsamic genie out of those bottles.

◆ Add a few drops to an oil-and-vinegar dressing to spark salads of mixed greens, meats, pasta, or fruit. It's especially classy in a spinach and fruit salad.

◆ For a really light salad "dressing," sprinkle greens with balsamic and top with grated Parmesan cheese and freshly ground black pepper.

◆ Enliven beef, veal, roasts, steaks, and chops by stirring a spoonful into pan juices at the end of the preparation; long cooking times dissipate the vinegar's remarkable aroma.

◆ Tomato-based pasta sauces and risotto dishes gain a more pronounced depth of flavor from balsamic essence; stir it in just before serving to retain its special zest.

◆ Create a distinctive dessert by sprinkling a teaspoon per serving over sweetened fresh strawberries; this tasting-is-believing trick even invests paler strawberries with a more fully ripened flavor.

◆ Drizzle balsamic vinegar atop omelets and frittatas; be sure to let the egg dishes sit a minute or two before serving to absorb the vinegar's flavor.

◆ Refresh thirsty guests with an Italian spritzer: Add a few drops of balsamic vinegar to sparkling tonic water on ice.

Nutrition facts per serving: 198 cal., 6 g total fat (1 g sat. fat), 0 mg chol., 265 mg sodium, 31 g carbo., 3 g fiber, 5 g pro. *Daily values:* 8% vit. A, 3% vit. C, 2% calcium, 9% iron.

BULGUR PILAF

Prep: 25 min. ◆ Cook: 15 min.

This recipe earned Bonnie Burgard of Bozeman, Montana, $400 in the magazine's monthly contest.

- 1   cup bulgur
- ½   cup chopped onion
- ½   cup sliced celery
- 2   Tbsp. margarine or butter
- 1½ cups finely shredded carrots
- ¾   cup long-grain rice
- 1   4-oz. can mushroom pieces, drained
- 2   tsp. instant chicken bouillon granules
- ¾   tsp. dried dillweed
- ¾   tsp. dried oregano, crushed
- ¼   tsp. pepper
- 3   cups water
- ¼   cup sliced, pitted ripe olives

1 In a large skillet cook bulgur, onion, and celery in margarine or butter over medium-low heat about 8 minutes or till vegetables are tender and bulgur is toasted. Add carrots, rice, mushrooms, bouillon granules, dillweed, oregano, and pepper. Stir in water. Bring to boiling; reduce heat. Simmer, covered, about 15 minutes or till rice is tender and liquid is absorbed. Stir in *2 tablespoons* of the olives. Garnish with remaining olives. Makes 10 side-dish servings.

Nutrition facts per serving: 138 cal., 3 g total fat (1 g sat. fat), 0 mg chol., 280 mg sodium, 25 g carbo., 4 g fiber, 3 g pro. *Daily values:* 49% vit. A, 3% vit. C, 2% calcium, 8% iron.

RISOTTO-STYLE BARLEY AND VEGETABLES

Start to finish: 30 min.

- 1   Tbsp. olive oil or cooking oil
- ⅔   cup thinly sliced zucchini
- ⅓   cup chopped onion
- ⅓   cup chopped carrot
- ¼   tsp. dried rosemary, crushed
- ⅛   tsp. pepper
- ⅔   cup quick-cooking barley

◆◆◆

- 1   14½-oz. can reduced-sodium chicken broth
- ¼   cup evaporated milk, half-and-half, or light cream

1 Heat oil in a medium saucepan; add zucchini, onion, carrot, rosemary, and pepper. Cook and stir till vegetables are just tender; stir in barley.

2 Meanwhile, in a small pan heat broth till simmering. Carefully stir *1 cup* hot broth into the barley mixture. Cook and stir over medium heat till liquid is absorbed. Add remaining broth, about ½ cup at a time, cooking and stirring till broth is absorbed. (This will take 15 to 20 minutes.) Stir in evaporated milk or cream; cook and stir 2 minutes more. Season to taste with *salt* and *pepper.* Makes 4 side-dish servings.

Nutrition facts per serving: 188 cal., 6 g total fat (1 g sat. fat), 5 mg chol., 317 mg sodium, 29 g carbo., 3 g fiber, 6 g pro. *Daily values:* 28% vit. A, 3% vit. C, 4% calcium, 4% iron.

FESTIVE RICE

Prep: 30 min. ◆ Bake: 20 min.

This recipe earned Lynn Lombardi of Poughkeepsie, New York, $200 in the magazine's monthly contest.

- 1   cup chopped red, yellow, and/or green sweet pepper
- ½   cup chopped onion
- 2   to 3 medium fresh jalapeño peppers, seeded and finely chopped
- 2   cloves garlic, minced
- 1   Tbsp. cooking oil
- 1½ cups chopped plum tomatoes
- 2   to 3 Tbsp. snipped fresh cilantro
- ¼   tsp. salt
- 2   cups cooked brown rice (⅔ cup uncooked rice)
- 1   15-oz. can garbanzo beans, rinsed and drained
- 1   cup shredded Monterey Jack cheese (4 oz.)

1 In a large saucepan cook sweet pepper, onion, jalapeños, and garlic in hot oil about 5 minutes or till tender, stirring occasionally. Stir in tomatoes, cilantro, and salt. Simmer, uncovered, for 5 minutes. Add cooked rice, garbanzo beans, and *½ cup* of the cheese, stirring gently to combine. Turn into a 1½-quart casserole. Sprinkle with remaining cheese. Bake, covered, in a 350° oven for 20 minutes or till hot. Makes 8 side-dish servings.

Nutrition facts per serving: 189 cal., 8 g total fat (3 g sat. fat), 13 mg chol., 347 mg sodium, 24 g carbo., 4 g fiber, 8 g pro. *Daily values:* 7% vit. A, 47% vit. C, 11% calcium, 12% iron.

JEWELED RICE

Prep: 15 min. ◆ Cook: 45 min.

See the photograph on page 82.

1 Tbsp. margarine or butter
½ cup regular brown rice
1 14½-oz. can chicken broth
⅔ cup water
¼ tsp. ground cardamom
½ cup long-grain white rice
¼ cup snipped dried apricots
  and/or golden raisins
¼ cup chopped red or green
  sweet pepper
¼ cup sliced green onions
1 Tbsp. honey
2 Tbsp. sliced almonds,
  toasted

1 In a medium saucepan melt margarine or butter; add uncooked brown rice. Cook and stir 2 minutes. Carefully add broth, water, and cardamom. Bring to boiling; reduce heat. Simmer, covered, 30 minutes. Stir in uncooked white rice, apricots and/or raisins, sweet pepper, and green onions. Return to boiling; reduce heat. Simmer, covered, 15 minutes or till rice is tender. Stir in honey. Sprinkle with almonds. Makes 4 to 6 side-dish servings.

Nutrition facts per serving: 269 cal., 6 g total fat (1 g sat. fat), 0 mg chol., 366 mg sodium, 47 g carbo., 3 g fiber, 7 g pro. *Daily values:* 15% vit. A, 19% vit. C, 3% calcium, 14% iron.

LIGHT POPOVERS

Prep: 10 min. ◆ Bake: 40 min.

A popover pan creates the classic tall shape with a puffed top. Custard cups work, but popovers are shorter and wider.

Nonstick spray coating
1 egg
2 egg whites
1 cup skim milk
1 Tbsp. cooking oil
1 cup all-purpose flour

1 Spray a popover pan or six 6-ounce custard cups with nonstick spray coating. Place cups on a baking pan; set aside. Beat egg and egg whites; beat in milk and oil. Add flour and ¼ teaspoon *salt;* beat till blended but still lumpy. Fill cups half full. Bake in a 400° oven till firm, allowing 35 minutes for pans or 40 minutes for cups. Turn off oven. Prick popovers with a fork. Leave in oven for 5 to 10 minutes more or till crispy. Serve warm. Makes 6.

Nutrition facts per popover: 126 cal., 4 g total fat (1 g sat. fat), 36 mg chol., 139 mg sodium, 17 g carbo., 1 g fiber, 6 g pro.

A TOAST TO ROASTING

Roasted vegetables have become the darling of restaurant chefs. Yet, good home cooks from Italy to Iowa have been roasting veggies since potatoes and heat first met. The high, dry heat of roasting creates a deep, intense flavor and heightens each vegetable's natural sweetness, while the alluring caramel color snares diners even before they dig in.

GET THE MOST FROM YOUR ROAST

Select the freshest vegetables in the bin. Peel and trim them as you normally would. Cut large vegetables, such as eggplant, in half lengthwise, or cube or slice. Slice round or oval vegetables into halves or quarters, depending on their size. Others, such as asparagus, mushrooms, and small zucchini, can be roasted whole.

Brush vegetables with olive oil or cooking oil. Place in baking pans, allowing plenty of room around each piece so vegetables will roast and brown, not steam. Roast vegetables on the middle rack of your preheated oven, using tongs to turn them halfway through baking. Higher oven temperatures brown roasted vegetables most successfully, but we've also provided timings for a lower setting. The roasting time will depend on the vegetables; they're ready to eat when tender but still firm. If you're cooking a mixture, add the faster-cooking vegetables toward the end.

Serve roasted vegetables hot or chilled. Enjoy them plain, or drizzle with additional oil and sprinkle with salt, pepper, lemon juice, and/or snipped fresh herbs.

VEGETABLE ROASTING CHART

Vegetable	425°	350°
Asparagus, whole	15 min.	30 min.
Carrot, 1½-inch chunks, halved	20 min.	50 min.
Eggplant, 1-inch slices, quartered	15 min.	30 min.
Fennel bulb, quartered	30 min.	45 min.
Mushroom, whole	15 min.	25 min.
Onion, 1-inch wedges	20 min.	35 min.
Potato, baking, 1½-inch chunks	25 min.	45 min.
Potato, tiny new, halved	25 min.	50 min.
Sweet pepper, quartered	20 min.	30 min.
Tomato, halved	15 min.	25 min.
Zucchini, 1½-inch chunks, halved	15 min.	30 min.

ROASTED SWEET ONION AND GARLIC SPREAD

Prep: 10 min. ◆ Bake: 30 min.

2 **medium sweet onions**
2 **tsp. olive oil**
2 **tsp. honey**
4 **large cloves garlic, peeled**
   French bread or toast points

1 Peel and quarter onions. In a bowl combine oil and honey. Add onions and garlic, stirring to coat. Transfer mixture to a greased 2-quart square baking dish. Bake, uncovered, in a 350° oven 30 to 40 minutes, stirring occasionally. Remove from oven; cool. Place in food processor bowl. Add ⅛ teaspoon *salt;* cover and process till smooth. Serve spread on crusty French bread or toast points. Store any leftovers, covered, in the refrigerator up to 1 week. Makes about ½ cup.

Nutrition facts per teaspoon: 15 cal., 0 g fat, 0 mg chol., 12 mg sodium, 3 g carbo., 0 g fiber, 0 g pro.

PEANUT WAFFLES WITH BUTTERSCOTCH SAUCE

Prep: 30 min. ◆ Bake: 3 min. each

1¾ **cups all-purpose flour**
2 **Tbsp. granulated sugar**
1 **Tbsp. baking powder**
2 **eggs, separated**
1¾ **cups milk**
½ **cup cooking oil**
½ **cup chopped peanuts**
◆◆◆
1 **recipe Butterscotch Sauce**
   (see page 67)
   Fresh or frozen berries
   (optional)

1 In a mixing bowl stir together the flour, sugar, baking powder, and ¼ teaspoon *salt*. In another bowl lightly beat the egg yolks with the milk and oil; stir into dry ingredients all at once, stirring just till combined but still slightly lumpy. Stir the chopped peanuts into the batter; set aside. In a small mixing bowl beat the egg whites with an electric mixer on medium speed till stiff peaks form (tips stand straight). Gently fold the egg whites into batter. Do not overmix; leave a few fluffs of egg white in the batter.

2 Pour about 1 cup of batter onto grids of a preheated, lightly greased waffle baker. Close lid quickly; do not open during baking. Bake according to manufacturer's directions. When done, use a fork to lift waffle off grid. Repeat with remaining batter.

3 Serve waffles hot with Butterscotch Sauce and top with berries, if desired. Makes 12 (4-inch) waffles.

Butterscotch Sauce: In a medium saucepan stir together 1¼ cups packed *brown sugar*, ⅔ cup *light-colored corn syrup*, ¼ cup *milk,* and ¼ cup *margarine or butter.* Bring just to boiling; reduce heat. Simmer for 20 minutes, stirring occasionally. Serve sauce warm. Refrigerate any remaining sauce; reheat in saucepan over low heat.

Nutrition facts per waffle with 2 tablespoons sauce: 375 cal., 18 g total fat (3 g sat. fat), 39 mg chol., 279 mg sodium, 50 g carbo., 1 g fiber, 6 g pro.
Daily values: 8% vit. A, 00% vit. C, 14% calcium, 15% iron.

STUFFED FRENCH TOAST

Prep: 20 min. ◆ Chill: 6 to 24 hr.
Bake: 30 min.

Plan to prepare the Cranberry-Pear Sauce while the strata-style French toast bakes.
(See the photograph on page 79.)

24 ¾-inch-thick slices Italian bread, about 3 inches in diameter
12 very thin slices cooked ham
12 very thin slices cooked turkey
2 medium pears, peeled, cored, and thinly sliced
12 thin slices provolone cheese

❖❖❖

4 beaten eggs
1 cup milk
¼ tsp. ground nutmeg
1 recipe Cranberry-Pear Sauce (see below right)

1 Arrange *half* of the bread slices in the bottom of a greased 3-quart rectangular baking dish. Top each bread slice in dish with a slice of ham, a slice of turkey, some of the pears, and a slice of cheese (cut and/or fold meat and cheese as necessary to fit on bread slices). Top with remaining bread.

2 Combine eggs, milk, and nutmeg; slowly and evenly pour over sandwiches in dish. Press sandwiches down lightly with back of spoon so they absorb liquid. Cover with plastic wrap. Chill for 6 to 24 hours. Bake, uncovered, in a 350° oven about 30 minutes or till top is lightly browned. Let stand 10 minutes before serving. Serve with warm Cranberry-Pear Sauce. If desired, garnish with shredded *orange peel.* Makes 12 main-dish servings.

HOW TO USE AN EGG SEPARATOR

The American Egg Board advises that the best and safest way to separate an egg is with an egg separator. Separating the egg yolk from the egg white by passing the yolk from shell to shell is not considered safe. Because bacteria found on the eggshell are so tiny, some may remain in the pores of the eggshell even after rinsing with water. By using an egg separator, you avoid letting the egg yolk and egg white touch the outer shell.

To use, place the separator onto a small cup. Break the egg into the separator. The separator holds the yolk as the white slips out into the cup.

Cranberry-Pear Sauce: In a small saucepan combine 1½ cups *cranberry juice cocktail* and 2 tablespoons *cornstarch.* Add 1 tablespoon *brown sugar,* 1 teaspoon finely shredded *orange peel,* ⅛ teaspoon *ground cinnamon,* and, if desired, 1 drop *red food coloring.* Cook and stir over medium heat till thickened and bubbly. Cook and stir for 2 minutes more. Stir in 2 *pears,* peeled, cored, and chopped.

Nutrition facts per serving: 246 cal., 8 g total fat (4 g sat. fat), 95 mg chol., 631 mg sodium, 29 g carbo., 2 g fiber, 15 g pro.
Daily values: 8% vit. A, 28% vit. C, 14% calcium, 10% iron.

MAPLE PECAN BREAD PUDDING

Prep: 25 min. ◆ Bake: 45 min.

This delightful homespun dessert tastes as if it's straight from Grandma's kitchen, yet it's easy enough for any '90s cook to put together.

    4 cups French bread cubes
    3 eggs
 1½ cups half-and-half or light
       cream
    ½ cup sugar
    1 tsp. finely shredded orange
       peel
    1 tsp. vanilla
       ◆◆◆
    ½ cup orange juice
    ½ cup pure maple syrup or
       maple-flavored syrup
    3 inches stick cinnamon
    ½ tsp. whole allspice
    ¼ tsp. whole cloves
    ⅓ cup small pecan halves,
       toasted

1 Place bread cubes in a 15×10×1-inch baking pan. Bake in a 350° oven for 10 to 15 minutes or till toasted, stirring twice. In a mixing bowl beat eggs; stir in half-and-half or light cream, sugar, orange peel, and vanilla just till combined. Divide bread cubes evenly among 4 individual 8- to 10-ounce au gratin dishes or individual casseroles. Pour the egg mixture evenly over the bread cubes. Bake in a 325° oven about 35 minutes or till a knife inserted near center comes out clean. Cool bread pudding slightly.

2 Meanwhile, in a small saucepan combine orange juice, maple syrup, cinnamon, allspice, and cloves. Heat to boiling; reduce heat. Simmer, covered, for 10 minutes. Remove spices with slotted spoon. Simmer, uncovered, about 8 minutes more or till reduced to ½ cup. Stir in pecans. Cool slightly. Spoon sauce atop warm bread pudding. Serve immediately. Makes 4 servings.

Nutrition facts per serving: 543 cal., 21 g total fat (8 g sat. fat), 193 mg chol., 297 mg sodium, 79 g carbo., 1 g fiber, 11 g pro. *Daily values:* 19% vit. A, 28% vit. C, 12% calcium, 14% iron.

MARBLED GINGERBREAD

Prep: 25 min. ◆ Bake: 45 min.

This variation of the old-time classic is distinctive because of its bold fresh ginger flavor and its luscious cream cheese swirl. (See the photograph on page 80.)

    2 3-oz. pkg. cream cheese,
       softened
    3 Tbsp. granulated sugar
    1 egg
       ◆◆◆
 1½ cups all-purpose flour
    1 tsp. ground cinnamon
    1 tsp. grated gingerroot
    ¾ tsp. baking soda
    ½ tsp. baking powder
       ◆◆◆
    ½ cup margarine or butter,
       softened
    ¼ cup packed brown sugar
    1 egg
    ½ cup dark-colored molasses
    ½ cup buttermilk or sour milk*
       ◆◆◆
       Coarse sugar (optional)

1 Lightly grease and flour an 8×8×2-inch baking pan; set aside. For filling, in a mixing bowl beat softened cream cheese with an electric mixer on medium speed till smooth. Beat in granulated sugar and 1 egg. Set aside.

2 For the gingerbread batter, in another bowl stir together the all-purpose flour, cinnamon, gingerroot, baking soda, and baking powder. Set mixture aside.

3 In a large mixing bowl beat margarine or butter with an electric mixer on medium speed for 30 seconds. Add brown sugar; beat till fluffy. Add egg and molasses; beat the mixture for 2 minutes more. Add flour mixture and buttermilk or sour milk alternately to margarine mixture, beating on low speed after each addition till combined.

4 Spread *half* of the gingerbread batter in the prepared baking pan. Pour the cream cheese filling over batter in pan. Top with remaining batter. Swirl the batter and cream cheese filling using a small spatula or bread knife to create a marbled effect.

5 Bake in a 350° oven about 45 minutes or till a wooden toothpick inserted near the center of the gingerbread comes out clean. Cool on a wire rack for 30 minutes. Cut into squares; serve warm. If desired, sprinkle each serving with a little coarse sugar. Makes 9 servings.

*Note: To make sour milk, combine 1½ teaspoons *vinegar or lemon juice* with enough *milk* to make ½ cup liquid. Let stand 5 minutes.

Nutrition facts per serving: 329 cal., 18 g total fat (7 g sat. fat), 69 mg chol., 334 mg sodium, 37 g carbo., 1 g fiber, 5 g pro. *Daily values:* 22% vit. A, 8% calcium, 15% iron.

HEAVENLY BAKED APPLES

Prep: 15 min. ◆ Bake: 40 min.

1¼ cups apricot nectar
⅓ cup snipped dried apricots
2 Tbsp. dried tart red cherries
    or cranberries

◆◆◆

4 medium baking apples, such
    as Rome or Winesap
2 Tbsp. sugar
¼ tsp. ground nutmeg
⅛ tsp. ground cardamom
½ tsp. vanilla
    Edible flowers (optional)

1 In a small saucepan combine apricot nectar, apricots, and cherries. Bring to boiling; remove from heat. Let stand 5 minutes. Drain fruit, reserving liquid.

2 Meanwhile, core apples almost through to bottom. Peel a strip about 1 inch wide around the middle of each. Use the tines of a fork to make a crisscross pattern in the peeled area. Place apples in a 2-quart square baking dish. Combine drained fruit mixture, sugar, and nutmeg. Spoon into centers of apples. Combine reserved liquid, cardamom, and vanilla; pour over and around apples. Bake, covered, in a 350° oven 20 minutes. Uncover; bake 20 to 25 minutes more or till apples are tender, basting occasionally with cooking liquid. Before serving, spoon liquid over apples. Serve warm. If desired, garnish with edible flowers. Makes 4 servings.

Nutrition facts per serving: 142 cal., 0 g total fat, 0 mg chol., 4 mg sodium, 36 g carbo., 3 g fiber, 1 g pro. *Daily values:* 20% vit. A, 49% vit. C, 1% calcium, 6% iron.

DANISH PASTRY APPLE BARS

Prep: 30 min. ◆ Bake: 50 min.

Our taste testers agree that this 25-year-old recipe is worth sharing one more time. The ideal pastry—so tender and so flaky—tops off the perfectly spiced apple filling. "Serve warm" was the unanimous recommendation. (See the photograph on page 81.)

2½ cups all-purpose flour
1 tsp. salt
1 cup shortening
1 egg yolk
    Milk

◆◆◆

1 cup cornflakes
8 to 10 tart baking apples,
    such as Cortland, Rome,
    Beauty, or Granny Smith,
    peeled and sliced (8 cups)
½ cup sugar
1 tsp. ground cinnamon
1 egg white
1 Tbsp. water
    Sifted powdered sugar or
    whipped cream (optional)

1 In a large mixing bowl stir together the flour and salt. Using a pastry blender, cut in shortening till mixture resembles coarse crumbs. Lightly beat egg yolk in a glass measuring cup. Add enough milk to egg yolk to make ⅔ cup liquid total; mix well. Stir egg yolk mixture into flour mixture; mix well. Divide dough in half.

2 On a floured surface, roll *half* the dough to an 18×12-inch rectangle; fit into and up sides of a 15×10×1-inch baking pan. Sprinkle with cornflakes; top with apples. Combine sugar and cinnamon; sprinkle over apples. Roll remaining dough to a 16×12-inch rectangle; place over apples. Seal edges; cut slits in top for steam to escape. Beat egg white and water; brush over pastry. Bake in a 375° oven about 50 minutes or till golden. Cool on a wire rack. Serve warm or cool, topped with powdered sugar or whipped cream, if desired. Makes 32 bars.

Nutrition facts per bar: 128 cal., 7 g total fat (2 g sat. fat), 7 mg chol., 80 mg sodium, 16 g carbo., 1 g fiber, 1 g pro.
Daily values: 2% vit. A, 2% vit. C, 3% iron.

Strawberry-Rhubarb Cobbler

Prep: 30 min. ◆ Bake: 20 min.

Orange liqueur lends elegance to this old-fashioned dessert.

1 cup sugar
4 tsp. cornstarch
2 Tbsp. orange liqueur or orange juice
4 cups sliced fresh rhubarb
1 cup all-purpose flour
2 Tbsp. sugar
1½ tsp. baking powder
¼ cup margarine or butter
1 egg
2 Tbsp. milk
1 pint fresh strawberries, halved
Whipped cream, half-and-half, light cream, or ice cream (optional)

1 In a large saucepan combine the 1 cup sugar and cornstarch. Stir in liqueur or orange juice. Add rhubarb. Cook and stir till thickened and bubbly. Remove from heat. Keep hot.

2 In a medium bowl stir together 1 cup flour, 2 tablespoons sugar, and baking powder. Cut in the margarine or butter till mixture resembles coarse crumbs. Stir together egg and milk; add to flour mixture, stirring just to moisten. Turn out onto lightly floured surface. Knead 5 or 6 times. Roll dough to an 11×4-inch rectangle. Cut lengthwise into ½-inch-wide strips.

3 Stir the strawberries into rhubarb mixture. Turn hot fruit mixture into a 2-quart rectangular or oval baking dish. Weave dough strips atop fruit mixture to make a lattice top, trimming strips to fit dish. Place baking dish on a foil-lined baking sheet. Bake in a 400° oven for 20 to 25 minutes or till fruit is tender and lattice top is golden. Serve warm with whipped cream, if desired. Serves 6 to 8.

Nutrition facts per serving: 350 cal., 9 g total fat (2 g sat. fat), 36 mg chol., 198 mg sodium, 63 g carbo., 3 g fiber, 4 g pro. *Daily values:* 12% vit. A, 57% vit. C, 14% calcium, 10% iron.

Pineapple and Banana-Nut Sundaes

Prep: 15 min. ◆ Bake: 18 min.
Chill: 1 to 24 hr.

½ cup all-purpose flour
⅓ cup chopped macadamia nuts or slivered almonds
¼ cup butter or margarine, melted
3 Tbsp. brown sugar
1 20-oz. can crushed pineapple (juice pack)
1 Tbsp. brown sugar
1½ tsp. cornstarch
1 Tbsp. rum or ¼ tsp. rum flavoring
2 medium bananas
3 cups vanilla ice cream or frozen yogurt

1 In a bowl combine the flour, nuts, butter or margarine, and 3 tablespoons brown sugar. Spread evenly in an 8×8×2-inch baking pan. Bake in a 350° oven for 18 to 20 minutes or until golden, stirring occasionally. Cool.

2 Drain pineapple, reserving juice (you should have ⅔ cup juice). Transfer juice to a small saucepan; stir in the 1 tablespoon brown sugar and cornstarch. Cook and stir till thickened and bubbly. Cook and stir 2 minutes more. Remove from heat. Stir in the pineapple and rum. Transfer to bowl; cover and chill.

3 Just before serving, peel and cut banana into ½-inch slices. Stir banana into pineapple mixture. Top ice cream with pineapple sauce and sprinkle with the nut crumble. Makes 6 servings.

Nutrition facts per serving: 406 cal., 21 g total fat (10 g sat. fat), 50 mg chol., 135 mg sodium, 54 g carbo., 2 g fiber, 5 g pro. *Daily values:* 15% vit. A, 19% vit. C, 9% calcium, 8% iron.

Guava Bars

Prep: 20 min. ◆ Bake: 30 min.

See the photograph on page 80.

1½ cups all-purpose flour
1½ cups quick-cooking rolled oats
1 cup packed brown sugar
1 tsp. baking powder
¾ cup butter or margarine
½ of a 22-oz. can guava paste, cut into slices, or 1 cup apricot preserves

1 Grease a 13×9×2-inch baking pan. In a bowl combine flour, oats, brown sugar, baking powder, and ⅛ teaspoon *salt.* Cut in butter till crumbly. Pat ⅔ of the mixture into the prepared baking pan. Top with the guava slices or spoon on apricot preserves. Sprinkle the remaining crumb mixture atop. Bake in a 375° oven for 30 to 35 minutes or till crumbs are golden. Cool on wire rack. Cut into bars. Makes 30 bars.

Nutrition facts per bar: 130 cal., 5 g total fat (3 g sat. fat), 12 mg chol., 69 mg sodium, 21 g carbo., 1 g fiber, 1 g pro. *Daily values:* 5% vit. A, 5% vit. C, 1% calcium, 6% iron.

PERFECTLY PINEAPPLE

Think of it as the friendly fruit. In the Caribbean West Indies, pineapples dangling in doorways have long been a sign of welcome. Using the exotic fruit as a symbol of hospitality spread to Europe and parts of the United States, where its familiar shape often is found today on gateposts, in doorways, or on tableware.

There's nothing more hospitable than serving up sweet wedges of fresh pineapple. Many people must agree because it's among the most popular of all tropical fruits. Come spring, fresh pineapples appear in greater numbers in the supermarkets—although they're available year-round. A quick trip through the produce section reveals rows of whole fresh pineapples alongside ready-to-eat fresh pineapple that is peeled, cut, and packaged.

SQUEEZE AND SNIFF

Don't be shy when shopping for pineapple. Look for the ones that are plump; the larger the fruit, the greater the proportion of edible meat. The leaves (the crown) should be bright and fresh, with a deep green color. Contrary to popular lore, the ease with which a leaf can be pulled out is not a sign of ripeness. Gently squeeze the fruit; it should be slightly soft to the touch, yet firm, with no leaks. Sniff the base of the fruit, too; it should have a sweet, fragrant aroma. The peel color is an indication not of ripeness or maturity, but of variety. Avoid fruit that looks old or bruised, has brown leaves, or has soft or brown spots on the peel.

SERVING—THE SOONER, THE BETTER

Unlike most fruits, a pineapple does not continue to ripen or sweeten after it is picked because it has no starch reserve to convert into sugar. Use pineapple as soon as possible after purchase. You can store the whole fruit at cool room temperature for three or four days, but for best results, store it in the refrigerator. Refrigerate cut pineapple, covered with plastic wrap, for up to three days. A medium pineapple weighs about 3 pounds and yields about 3 cups of cut-up, peeled fruit. Go ahead, dig in! One cup of pineapple contains only about 50 calories.

Peeling is a snap. To peel a pineapple, start by twisting or cutting off the top. Using a sharp knife, cut off the stem and the bottom ends on a cutting board. Stand the fruit upright and slice off the prickly outer peel from top to bottom.

The peeled pineapple will be studded with "eyes" that lie in diagonal spirals around the fruit. Make V-shaped cuts along the spiral rows of eyes, then lift out and discard the strips, removing a row of eyes at a time. This is an easy way to remove the eyes with minimal waste. Halve or quarter the pineapple vertically, or cut it horizontally into thin or thick slices.

In modern varieties of pineapples, the cores are only a little harder than the surrounding flesh and can be eaten, especially if thinly sliced. However, if you think the core is too hard, remove it.

Kitchen shops carry handy little gadgets that peel and core at the same time; the eyes still must be trimmed with a knife. An alternative method is to cut off the crown and base, slice the pineapple into wedges, then cut away the peel. Of course, there also is the option of buying the pineapple already peeled and cut.

TRY IT WITH CINNAMON

In Hawaii, you'll find pineapple in almost every dish, from curries and salsas to sandwiches, seafood, and desserts. At home, slip some pineapple cubes onto seafood skewers before grilling or broiling, or grill thick wedges alongside chicken. Stir some chopped fruit into a rice pilaf just before serving. Good flavor matches include brown sugar, mint, cinnamon, cloves, and allspice. In Asia, it is common to sprinkle a little salt on fresh pineapple.

Fresh pineapple contains a natural enzyme that prevents gelatin from setting. For gelatin salads or desserts with a taste of pineapple, use canned pineapple instead.

IS IT A COUSIN OF THE APPLE?

In most languages, the word pineapple is based on *nana* or *anana*, which means "excellent fruit" or "fragrance" in the Brazilian Tupi Indian language. The original home of the pineapple, in fact, was the lowlands of Brazil, but the fruit spread throughout the tropics, including to Guadeloupe in the French West Indies, where Christopher Columbus discovered it in 1493. The Spanish explorers gave this fruit the name *s*, which means "pinecone" in Spanish, because of its resemblance to a pinecone. The English added "apple" to associate it with juicy sweet fruit.

LOW FAT

HAMANTASCHEN AND RUGALACH

Prep: 40 min. for each recipe
Chill: 2 hr. ◆ Bake: 10 or 12 min.

Purim, celebrated by the Jewish people more than 2,500 years, is a time for giving traditional gift packages of cookies. Use this basic recipe for both hamantaschen and rugalach cookies.

½ **cup margarine or butter**
¼ **cup granulated sugar**
¼ **cup packed brown sugar**
2 **tsp. baking powder**
1 **tsp. vanilla**
⅛ **tsp. salt**
2 **eggs**
2 **teaspoons finely shredded orange peel (for hamantaschen only)**
¼ **cup orange juice**
2¾ **cups all-purpose flour**

1 In a large mixing bowl beat the margarine or butter with an electric mixer on medium speed for 30 seconds or till softened. Add the granulated sugar, brown sugar, baking powder, vanilla, and salt, beating till light and fluffy. Beat in eggs, 1 at a time, till well combined. Slowly add orange juice (mixture may appear curdled). Beat in as much of the flour as you can with the mixer.

2 Using a wooden spoon, stir in the remaining flour. Cover and chill dough about 2 hours or till easy to handle. Use 1 recipe of the dough for either hamantaschen or rugalach.

For hamantaschen: Prepare dough as directed above, adding the 2 teaspoons finely shredded orange peel with the orange juice.

Divide dough in half. For filling, use ½ cup *cake and pastry filling* (such as poppy seed, prune, apricot, or cherry). On a lightly floured surface, roll out 1 portion of the dough to ⅛-inch thickness. Using a fluted biscuit or cookie cutter, cut into 2¼- to 2½-inch circles, rerolling scraps as necessary. Brush edge of circles with *water*. Spoon ½ teaspoon desired filling onto center of each circle.

Bring 2 of the circle's opposing edges together toward top to make a "V" and pull the unfolded edge up, pinching the edges together to form a shape like a three-cornered hat. Leave center slightly open to expose filling. Place cookies on an ungreased cookie sheet.

Repeat with the remaining dough and filling. Bake in a 350° oven for 10 to 12 minutes or till cookies are lightly browned. Remove from cookie sheet and cool on a wire rack. Makes about 60 hamantaschen.

Nutrition facts per poppy seed cookie:
51 cal., 2 g total fat (0 g sat. fat), 7 mg chol., 39 mg sodium, 7 g carbo., 0 g fiber, 1 g pro.
Daily values: 2% vit. A, 1% vit. C, 1% calcium, 2% iron.

For rugalach: Prepare and chill basic dough as directed at left. Divide the chilled dough into 5 portions. Soak 1 cup *raisins* in 1½ cups *boiling water* for 10 to 15 minutes. Drain raisins, discarding liquid. In a food processor bowl combine raisins with ½ cup toasted *pistachio nuts and/or walnuts,* 1 tablespoon *honey,* 1 tablespoon *orange juice,* 1 teaspoon *ground cinnamon,* and ⅛ teaspoon *ground cloves;* process the mixture till coarsely chopped.

THE CLEVER COOK

CARROTS LIVEN UP COOKIES

Adding some grated—or finely shredded—carrots to oatmeal cookie batter gives not only extra crunch but extra vitamins to your cookies. A half-cup of finely shredded carrots works well in a recipe that yields about 48 cookies.

John Shepherd
Mantachie, Mississippi

On a lightly floured surface, roll out 1 portion of dough to an 8-inch circle, ⅛ inch thick. Spread about 2 tablespoons of the raisin filling on the circle of dough and cut the circle into 12 equal wedges. Starting from the wide end of each wedge, roll up toward the point. Place, point up, on an ungreased cookie sheet. Bake in a 350° oven for 12 to 15 minutes or till lightly browned. Remove from cookie sheet and cool on a wire rack. Repeat with remaining dough and filling. Makes 60 rugalach.

Nutrition facts per cookie: 57 cal., 2 g total fat (0 g sat. fat), 7 mg chol., 37 mg sodium, 8 g carbo., 0 g fiber, 1 g pro.
Daily values: 2% vit. A, 1% vit. C, 1% calcium, 2% iron.

PARADISE PUDDING PARFAITS

Prep: 20 min. ◆ Chill: 1 to 4 hr.

For a lower-fat version of this tropical dessert, use fat-free, sugar-free instant pudding mix.

1   8-oz. can crushed pineapple, drained
1   medium banana, peeled and chopped
1   mango, seeded, peeled, and chopped
1   cup milk
½   cup coconut milk or milk
½   cup frozen pineapple-orange-banana juice concentrate, thawed
1   4-serving-size pkg. instant vanilla pudding mix

◆◆◆

¼   cup flaked coconut, toasted
    Fresh mint leaves (optional)

1 In a medium bowl combine pineapple, banana, and mango; set aside. In a large mixing bowl stir together milk, coconut milk, and thawed juice concentrate. Add pudding mix to milk mixture; beat with an electric mixer on low speed for 2 minutes.

2 To assemble, spoon half of the pudding mixture into 4 or 5 parfait glasses or wine glasses. Top with half of the fruit. Repeat layers. Sprinkle each serving with some of the coconut. Cover and chill for 1 to 4 hours. If desired, garnish with mint leaves. Makes 4 or 5 servings.

Nutrition facts per serving: 336 cal., 7 g total fat (6 g sat. fat), 5 mg chol., 388 mg sodium, 67 g carbo., 2 g fiber, 4 g pro. *Daily values:* 24% vit. A, 96% vit. C, 8% calcium, 5% iron.

MANGO MOUSSE

Prep: 25 min. ◆ Chill: 6 hr.

This recipe earned Minerva V. Pratt of Manassas, Virginia, $200 in the magazine's monthly contest.

2   ripe mangoes, seeded, peeled, and cut up

◆◆◆

¼   cup granulated sugar
1   tsp. unflavored gelatin
¼   cup cold water

◆◆◆

1   cup whipping cream
2   Tbsp. sifted powdered sugar

◆◆◆

1   ripe kiwifruit, peeled and sliced (optional)
¼   cup coconut, toasted (optional)

1 In a food processor bowl or blender container, process or blend the mangoes till smooth (you should have about 1 cup of mango puree).

2 In a medium saucepan combine the granulated sugar and gelatin. Stir in water. Cook and stir over low heat till gelatin is dissolved. Remove from heat. Stir in mango puree. Cover and chill till mixture is partially set (the consistency of unbeaten egg whites), about 2 hours.

3 In a medium chilled mixing bowl beat whipping cream and powdered sugar with an electric mixer on low speed till soft peaks form. Fold mango mixture into whipped cream. Chill again till mixture mounds when spooned.

MANAGING A MANGO

Since the meat from a mango holds tightly to the seed, an easy way to remove the meat is to make a cut through the mango, sliding a sharp knife next to the seed along one side of the mango. Repeat on other side of the seed, resulting in two large pieces. Then cut away all of the meat that remains around the seed. Remove the peel on all pieces and cut up or puree the meat.

Or, to remove the meat from the peel and cut it into pieces at the same time, work with one of the large pieces at a time. Make cuts in crosshatch fashion through the meat just to the peel. Bend the peel back and carefully slide the knife between the peel and the meat to separate. Discard the peel.

4 To assemble, spoon mango mixture into dessert dishes. Cover and chill 4 hours or till set. If desired, garnish with kiwifruit and toasted coconut. Serves 6.

Nutrition facts per serving: 248 cal., 15 g total fat (9 g sat. fat), 54 mg chol., 18 mg sodium, 30 g carbo., 2 g fiber, 2 g pro. *Daily values:* 58% vit. A, 48% vit. C, 3% calcium, 1% iron.

ROSE-MANGO CREPES

Start to finish: 50 min.

¼ cup sugar
3 Tbsp. water
2 Tbsp. rose petals,* cleaned
   and rinsed (1 rose) or
   2 drops rose water
2 mangoes, seeded, peeled, and
   finely chopped
2 Tbsp. orange juice

♦♦♦

2 beaten eggs
1¼ cups milk
1 cup all-purpose flour
2 Tbsp. sifted powdered sugar
1 tsp. baking powder
1 tsp. vanilla
¼ tsp. salt

♦♦♦

Whipped cream (optional)
Powdered sugar (optional)

1 For filling, in a small saucepan combine the ¼ cup sugar and water; cook and stir till sugar is dissolved. Meanwhile, if using rose petals, cut into small strips. Stir strips into sugar mixture. Cook and stir 1 to 2 minutes or till petals just start to lose their color. Stir mangoes, orange juice, and rose water, if using, into sugar mixture. Cook and stir till heated through. Set aside to cool slightly.

2 Meanwhile, in a medium mixing bowl combine the eggs, milk, flour, 2 tablespoons powdered sugar, baking powder, vanilla, and salt. Beat with a rotary beater or wire whisk till smooth. Heat a lightly greased 6-inch skillet over medium heat; remove from heat. Spoon about 3 tablespoons crepe mixture into skillet; lift and tilt skillet to spread batter. Return to heat; brown on 1 side

only. Invert skillet over paper towels; remove crepe. Repeat with remaining crepe batter, greasing skillet occasionally.

3 To serve, spoon about 3 tablespoons filling down the center of the unbrowned side of each crepe; roll up. If desired, top with whipped cream and sprinkle with powdered sugar. Makes about 12 crepes.

*Note: Choose a rose that has been grown without the use of pesticides or other chemicals.

Nutrition facts per crepe: 105 cal., 2 g total fat (1 g sat. fat), 37 mg chol., 99 mg sodium, 20 g carbo., 1 g fiber, 3 g pro. *Daily values:* 16% vit. A, 18% vit. C, 5% calcium, 4% iron.

PRIZE
TESTED
RECIPE
WINNER

MANGO CREAM PIE

Prep: 40 min. ♦ Bake: 20 min.
Chill: 3 to 6 hr.

This recipe earned Diane Halferty of Tucson, Arizona, $400 in the magazine's monthly contest. (See the photograph on page 81.)

1 cup all-purpose flour
½ cup finely chopped toasted
   macadamia nuts
⅓ cup butter
1 beaten egg

♦♦♦

4 oz. cream cheese, softened
   (½ of an 8-oz. pkg.)
⅓ cup sifted powdered sugar
⅓ cup whipping cream
2 large mangoes, seeded,
   peeled, and thinly sliced
⅓ cup granulated sugar

4 tsp. cornstarch
1 tsp. finely shredded orange
   peel
¾ cup peach nectar
1 tsp. lemon juice
   Chopped toasted macadamia
   nuts

1 In a medium mixing bowl combine the flour and ½ cup toasted nuts; cut in butter till mixture forms coarse crumbs. Add egg; stir till combined. Form into a ball. On a lightly floured surface, roll out dough to a 12-inch circle. Line a 9-inch pie plate with pastry. Trim pastry to ½ inch beyond edge of pie plate. Fold edge under and flute. Prick well. Bake in a 350° oven 20 minutes or till golden brown; cool.

2 In a bowl beat together cream cheese and powdered sugar. Stir in *1 tablespoon* of the whipping cream. Beat remaining cream till soft peaks form; fold into cheese mixture. Spread in pie shell. Overlap mango slices in circles on top, reserving a few mango slices for garnish.

3 In a saucepan combine granulated sugar, cornstarch, and orange peel. Stir in peach nectar and lemon juice. Cook and stir till thick and bubbly. Cook and stir 2 minutes more. Remove from heat; cool slightly. Spoon mixture evenly over mango slices. Chill 3 to 6 hours. Garnish with reserved mango slices and additional nuts. Makes 10 servings.

Nutrition facts per serving: 297 cal., 19 g total fat (9 g sat. fat), 61 mg chol., 108 mg sodium, 31 g carbo., 2 g fiber, 4 g pro. *Daily values:* 31% vit. A, 21% vit. C, 2% calcium, 6% iron.

74 BETTER HOMES AND GARDENS ANNUAL RECIPES 1997

APRIL
A Fresh Start

*D*aylight comes earlier, brighter, and cheerier in the dewy mornings of April. Little wonder we're more eager for breakfast. Zesty Lemon Scones can be ready in less time than it takes to rouse some sleepy teenagers. And when there's time to linger over breakfast, Brunch Seafood Strata will tempt all at the table.

Enjoy a pleasant April evening dining al fresco with a menu of appetizers including Brie-Pecan Quesadillas and Chilled Artichokes with Two Dips. For dessert? A luscious slice of Chocolate Cream Tortilla Torte or Sunburst Sundae Cups filled with fresh fruit and frozen yogurt can put a little spring in your step anytime.

30-minute recipes indicated in RED.
Low-fat and no-fat recipes indicated
with a ♥.
Photographs indicated in italics.

Chocolate Cream Tortilla Torte

Prep: 45 min. ◆ Chill: 3 to 13 hr.

This delectable tortilla dessert easily makes the transition from flat to fantastic. Chocoholics might want to drizzle fudge topping over the torte in place of the raspberry sauce.
(See the photograph on page 77.)

¾ cup sugar
⅓ cup unsweetened cocoa
　　powder
2 Tbsp. cornstarch
1 tsp. ground cinnamon
2⅔ cups milk
4 beaten egg yolks
1 oz. semisweet chocolate,
　　grated
1 Tbsp. margarine or butter
1½ tsp. vanilla
◆◆◆
¾ cup whipping cream
◆◆◆
10 8-inch flour tortillas
1 cup chopped pecans
1 recipe Raspberry Sauce
　　(optional) (see right)
　　Fresh raspberries (optional)

1 For pudding, in a heavy medium saucepan combine sugar, cocoa powder, cornstarch, and cinnamon. Stir in milk. Cook and stir over medium heat till mixture is thickened and bubbly. Cook and stir 2 minutes more. Remove mixture from heat. Gradually stir about *1 cup* of the hot mixture into the egg yolks. Return all of the mixture to saucepan. Bring mixture to a gentle boil; reduce heat. Cook and stir 2 minutes more. Remove from heat. Stir in grated chocolate, margarine or butter, and vanilla. Pour the pudding into a bowl. Cover the surface of the pudding with clear plastic wrap; chill 1 hour.

2 In a chilled bowl beat whipping cream with chilled beaters of an electric mixer on medium speed till soft peaks form.

3 To assemble torte, place a tortilla on a serving plate. Spread ⅔ cup of the pudding over tortilla. Top with a second tortilla. Spread ⅓ cup of the whipped cream over tortilla; sprinkle with 2 to 3 tablespoons nuts. Repeat layers, alternating chocolate pudding with whipped cream and nuts, ending with nuts. Cover and chill 2 to 12 hours. (Cover and chill remaining pudding to serve another time.) Cut into wedges. If desired, drizzle Raspberry Sauce over top and garnish with fresh raspberries. Makes 10 servings.

Raspberry Sauce: Place 1½ cups *fresh raspberries* (if using frozen berries, thaw but do not drain) in a blender container or food processor bowl. Cover and blend or process till berries are smooth. Press berries through a fine-mesh sieve; discard seeds. Repeat with another 1½ cups *fresh raspberries.* (You should have about ½ cup of sieved puree from each 1½ cups berries.)

In a medium saucepan stir together ⅓ cup *sugar* and 1 teaspoon *cornstarch.* Add berry puree. Cook and stir over medium heat till thickened and bubbly. Cook and stir for 2 minutes more. Remove from heat. Cool to room temperature before serving. Store, covered, in the refrigerator.

Nutrition facts per serving: 381 cal., 22 g total fat (7 g sat. fat), 115 mg chol., 176 mg sodium, 40 g carbo., 1 g fiber, 7 g pro. *Daily values:* 26% vit. A, 1% vit. C, 14% calcium, 13% iron.

Sunburst Sundae Cups

Start to finish: 45 min.

Wow your family and friends with this stunning but simple dessert.
(See the photograph on page 77.)

8 6- to 7-inch flour tortillas
　　Cooking oil for deep-fat
　　frying
◆◆◆
2 Tbsp. sugar
½ tsp. ground cinnamon
1 qt. peach frozen yogurt
2 cups fresh blueberries, sliced
　　strawberries, or other fruit

1 Cut tortillas into sun shapes. In a large heavy saucepan heat 2 inches oil to 360°. Cook tortillas, 1 at a time, 30 to 45 seconds or till crisp, using a ladle to hold tortillas down in center, forming a cup. Empty ladle and remove from pan. Remove tortillas with a slotted spatula, draining excess oil from tortilla cup back into pan; transfer tortilla cup to paper towels. Repeat with remaining tortillas.

2 Combine sugar and cinnamon; sprinkle over cooked tortilla cups while warm. To assemble sundaes, place a scoop of frozen yogurt in each tortilla cup. Top with fresh fruit. Serve immediately. Makes 8 servings.

█ TO MAKE AHEAD █

Prepare tortilla cups as directed; cool completely. Loosely cover and store at room temperature for up to 1 day.

Nutrition facts per serving: 356 cal., 17 g total fat (3 g sat. fat), 0 mg chol., 135 mg sodium, 44 g carbo., 1 g fiber, 6 g pro. *Daily values:* 21% vit. C, 11% calcium, 7% iron.

Top: *Chocolate Cream Tortilla Torte (page 76)*
Above: *Sunburst Sundae Cups (page 76)*

Left: *Simple Chicken Stew (page 93)*
Top: *Portobello Super Bruschettas (page 62)*
Above: *Stuffed French Toast (page 67)*

Top: *Corned Beef and Cabbage Dinner (page 60)*
Above left: *Marbled Gingerbread (page 68)*
Above right: *Guava Bars (page 70)*

Top: *Peppered Pork Chops and Pilaf (page 58)*
Above left: *Mango Cream Pie (page 74)*
Above right: *Danish Pastry Apple Bars (page 69)*

Top: *Wrap-and-Roll Basil Pinwheels (page 90)*
Above: *Jeweled Rice (page 65)*
Right: *Pork and Plantain Fajitas (page 95)*

Top Left: *Chilled Artichokes with Two Dips (page 85)*
Top Right: *Spicy Southwestern Scones (page 99)*
Above: *Brunch Seafood Strata (page 92)*

CHILLED ARTICHOKES WITH TWO DIPS

Prep: 20 min. ◆ Cook: 20 min.

For a fresh and fanciful presentation, just before serving, spoon each of the dips into halved sweet peppers. (See the photograph on page 84.)

2 to 4 large artichokes
1 recipe Curry Dip (see below)
1 recipe Dilly Crab Dip
   (see right)

1 Trim and cook artichokes as directed on page 86. Serve warm or at room temperature. Or, cover and chill thoroughly.

2 To serve, pull off all outer leaves and arrange on a serving platter with both dips. Discard sharp inner artichoke leaves and fuzzy choke. Slice artichoke heart (the bottom) and add to platter or reserve for another use.

CURRY DIP

Prep: 10 min. ◆ Chill: 2 to 24 hr.

Look for curry paste in the Asian section of your supermarket or in ethnic markets. Or, for a less intense flavor, use curry powder.

1 8-oz. carton plain yogurt
½ cup light mayonnaise
   dressing or salad dressing
1 Tbsp. lemon juice or cider
   vinegar
2 to 3 tsp. curry paste or 1 to
   2 tsp. curry powder
2 tsp. prepared horseradish
2 tsp. grated onion
   Slivered green onion top
   (optional)

ODE TO THE ARTICHOKE

Springtime is prime time to play with, and enjoy, fresh artichokes. Although artichokes are available year round, more than half the crop is harvested between March and May. Another crop peaks in October.

The artichoke was introduced to this country by French settlers in Louisiana and by the Spanish in California. Italian immigrants, though, are credited with firmly establishing artichoke production in California–where most artichokes are grown–some 100 years ago.

The artichoke is actually a thistle; the part you eat is the flower's bud. The fibrous leaves and fuzz in the center of a mature bud are the choke and must be scraped away before you can eat the prized succulent heart or bottom of the artichoke.

1 In a small mixing bowl stir together the yogurt, light mayonnaise dressing or salad dressing, lemon juice or vinegar, curry paste or powder, horseradish, and onion. Cover and refrigerate for 2 hours or overnight. If desired, garnish dip with green onion. Serve with warm or chilled *artichokes.* Makes about 1½ cups.

Nutrition facts per tablespoon: 23 cal., 2 g total fat (0 g sat. fat), 1 mg chol., 48 mg sodium, 1 g carbo., 0 g fiber, 1 g pro. *Daily values:* 1% calcium.

DILLY CRAB DIP

Prep: 15 min. ◆ Chill: 2 to 24 hr.

You can use frozen or canned crabmeat, although for garnishing purposes, the frozen meat is prettiest. Crab-flavored, flaked fish (surimi) makes a less expensive and almost as tasty choice.

½ cup mayonnaise or salad
   dressing
½ cup dairy sour cream
1 cup flaked, cooked crabmeat
   (cartilage removed)
2 tsp. finely chopped onion or
   green onion
1 tsp. dried dillweed
½ tsp. finely shredded lime
   peel
1 tsp. lime juice
   Dash bottled hot pepper
   sauce
   Dash ground red pepper
   (optional)

1 In a small mixing bowl stir together the mayonnaise or salad dressing, sour cream, ⅔ *cup* of the flaked crabmeat, the onion, dillweed, lime peel, lime juice, hot pepper sauce, and, if desired, ground red pepper. Season to taste with *salt* and *pepper.* Cover and refrigerate for 2 hours or overnight. Just before serving, sprinkle dip with reserved crabmeat. Serve with warm or chilled *artichokes.* Makes about 1½ cups.

Nutrition facts per tablespoon: 49 cal., 5 g total fat (1 g sat. fat), 10 mg chol., 45 mg sodium, 0 g carbo., 0 g fiber, 1 g pro. *Daily values:* 1% vit. A, 1% calcium.

ARTICHOKE TIDBITS

Look for artichokes that are compact, firm, and heavy for their size. Size can range from baby to jumbo, and the shape can be round or conical. Those with tightly packed leaves and an even green color are fresher.

Young, fresh, baby artichokes (2 to 3 ounces each) are the most tender and are almost entirely edible; only the outer leaves and stems need to be trimmed.

Size is not an indication of age; it where the artichoke grew on the plant. The largest artichokes grow at the top of the stem in the center of the plant. Baby artichokes grow at the bottom of the plant, where they are protected from the sun. Artichoke hearts also come canned or frozen and with or without a marinade.

KEEPING IT FRESH

Sprinkle a fresh artichoke with a little water, then put it in an airtight plastic bag and refrigerate for up to a week. An artichoke is best if used soon after purchase.

TRIMMING

Rinse an artichoke under cold running water, flushing out any dirt between the leaves. Pull off and discard lower petals. Trim stem to one inch or less. Cut off the top quarter or third of artichoke.

Trim the leaf tips, if desired. Immediately rub the cut surfaces with a piece of lemon and drop the artichoke into a bowl of water with 1 or 2 tablespoons lemon juice added to help prevent browning. To minimize discoloration, use a stainless steel knife or scissors to trim the vegetable.

To use just the bottom or heart of the artichoke, remove all the outer leaves, then scrape away the prickly inner petals and the fuzzy choke.

For baby artichokes, peel off the tough outer green leaves to reveal a tender inner core where the leaves are half green (at the top) and half yellow. Cut off the top green part of the artichoke. Cut the stem flush with the base, and cut away any fibrous green outer layer covering the base. The rest is edible; there is no need to scrape out the choke, which is not developed. Leave whole, or halve or quarter. Immediately put trimmed artichokes in a bowl of water with 1 or 2 tablespoons lemon juice added to help prevent browning.

COOKING

To boil: Cook, covered, in a large amount of boiling salted water for 20 to 30 minutes (depending on size) or till a leaf pulls out easily. (Allow about 15 minutes for baby artichokes.) Invert artichoke to drain. To prevent discoloration, do not use aluminum or cast-iron pans; use stainless steel, nonstick-lined or enamel-coated cookware.

To micro-cook: Place one artichoke in a microwave-safe container; add an inch of water. Cover with wet paper towels or heavy-duty plastic wrap, venting a corner. Microwave on high for 7 to 9 minutes or till a leaf pulls out easily, turning once. (Allow 6 to 9 minutes for baby artichokes.)

HOW TO EAT AN ARTICHOKE

It will take you about 20 minutes to eat a whole artichoke, making it truly a case of delayed gratification.

Pull off the leaves (petals) one at a time, and draw each one between your teeth to remove the soft edible portion, then discard the leaf. (A plate for the discards is a nice touch.) Continue until you reach the prickly, purple-tipped leaves in the center. Scrape out the sharp leaves and fuzzy center (the choke) at the base and discard. The bottom (or heart) is entirely edible. Cut it into small pieces to eat it.

The leaves and the heart are usually served with a sauce or melted butter for dipping. Artichokes also can be marinated or stuffed with a filling of meat, vegetables, or salad. Serve them hot or cold.

ARTICHOKES WITH VEGETABLE STUFFING

Prep: 45 min. ♦ Bake: 15 min.

2 large artichokes

♦♦♦

3 Tbsp. margarine or butter
¾ cup finely shredded carrot
½ cup chopped onion
2 Tbsp. snipped fresh parsley
1 Tbsp. snipped fresh basil or
   1 tsp. dried basil, crushed
2 cloves garlic, minced
1½ cups soft bread crumbs
   (2 slices)

1 Trim and cook artichokes as directed on page 86; drain. When cool enough to handle, halve each artichoke lengthwise. Pull out prickly purple-tipped leaves in center of each artichoke to expose fuzzy choke. Using a small spoon, scrape out the choke and discard.

2 In a saucepan melt margarine. Add carrot, onion, parsley, dried basil (if using), garlic, and ¼ teaspoon *pepper*. Cook over medium heat till tender, stirring occasionally. Remove from heat. Stir in bread crumbs and fresh basil, if using. Spoon mixture into centers of artichoke halves.

3 Place artichokes in a 2-quart square baking dish. Pour *boiling water* around artichokes to depth of ½ inch. Cover loosely with foil. Bake in a 400° oven 15 to 20 minutes or till heated through. Remove artichokes with a slotted spoon; place on plates. Makes 4 side-dish servings.

Nutrition facts per serving: 170 cal., 9 g total fat (2 g sat. fat), 0 mg chol., 253 mg sodium, 19 g carbo., 3 g fiber, 4 g pro. *Daily values:* 70% vit. A, 19% vit. C, 10% iron.

CREAMY BABY ARTICHOKES

Start to finish: 50 min.

1 cup water
1 Tbsp. lemon juice
8 baby artichokes (about 1 lb.)

♦♦♦

1 onion, cut into thin wedges
2 Tbsp. margarine or butter
1 cup reduced-sodium chicken
   broth
¼ cup dry white wine

♦♦♦

2 Tbsp. whipping cream
1 Tbsp. Dijon-style mustard
1 Tbsp. snipped fresh dill

1 In a bowl combine the water and lemon juice; set aside. Remove tough outer green leaves from baby artichokes, leaving the inner, greenish yellow leaves intact. Snip off about 1 inch from leaf tops, cutting where the green meets the yellow. Trim artichoke stems. Quarter the artichokes lengthwise and place in the bowl of water; set aside.

2 In a medium skillet cook onion wedges in hot margarine or butter till tender. Drain baby artichokes. Add artichokes, chicken broth, and wine to skillet. Bring to boiling; reduce heat. Simmer, covered, about 10 minutes or till artichokes are tender.

3 Using a slotted spoon, remove artichokes; set aside. Boil cooking liquid, uncovered, about 10 minutes or till reduced to about ⅓ cup. Stir in whipping cream, mustard, and ¼ teaspoon *pepper*. Simmer, uncovered, 2 to 3 minutes or till sauce is slightly thickened. Return artichokes to skillet; heat through, spooning

sauce over artichokes. Sprinkle with snipped fresh dill. Makes 4 side-dish servings.

Nutrition facts per serving: 157 cal., 9 g total fat (3 g sat. fat), 10 mg chol., 427 mg sodium, 14 g carbo., 6 g fiber, 5 g pro. *Daily values:* 12% vit. A, 19% vit. C, 5% calcium, 95% iron.

BRIE-PECAN QUESADILLAS

Start to finish: 20 min.

When time allows, freeze the Brie for 30 minutes to make it easier to chop.

3 oz. Brie cheese, chopped
   (about ¾ cup)
2 8- or 9-inch flour tortillas
2 Tbsp. chopped pecans or
   walnuts, toasted
2 Tbsp. snipped fresh Italian
   parsley or parsley
¼ cup dairy sour cream

1 Sprinkle cheese over half of each tortilla. Top with nuts and parsley. Fold tortillas in half, pressing gently. In a lightly greased 10-inch skillet cook quesadillas over medium heat 2 to 3 minutes or till lightly browned, turning once. Cut quesadillas into wedges. Serve with sour cream and, if desired, garnish with *parsley sprigs*. Makes 4 servings.

Nutrition facts per serving: 170 cal., 12 g total fat (6 g sat. fat), 27 mg chol., 202 mg sodium, 9 g carbo., 0 g fiber, 6 g pro. *Daily values:* 8% vit. A, 4% vit. C, 6% calcium, 5% iron.

Gouda and Ham Quesadillas: Substitute 1 cup shredded *Gouda or smoked mozzarella cheese* (4 ounces) for Brie and ½ cup chopped *smoked ham* for nuts.

TORTILLA TIPS

You can prepare any of the recipes in this book using homemade or purchased tortillas. Homemade tortillas take some time to prepare, but their fresh flavor is sure to garner rave reviews.

When making tortillas with colored dough, as in the Chili Tortillas or Tomato Tortillas, roll out the dough between sheets of waxed paper rather than on a pastry cloth, which may discolor.

A tortilla press is great for making corn tortillas, but a rolling pin is recommended for flour tortillas. When using a press for corn tortillas, be sure to first place the dough between sheets of waxed paper.

Regular or nonstick skillets work well for cooking tortillas, and cast-iron pans or griddles create excellent results. If using a cast-iron griddle, reduce heat to medium.

Tortillas can be made ahead and stored in the refrigerator or freezer. To store, stack each cooled tortilla between two pieces of waxed paper. Wrap the stack well in plastic wrap and seal in a self-sealing plastic bag. Tortillas will keep for five days in the refrigerator, or up to six months in the freezer. Remove tortillas as needed from freezer bag; thaw completely before using.

LOW FAT

HOMEMADE FLOUR TORTILLAS

Start to finish: 1½ hr.

Lend new taste and color dimensions to the basic recipe with spinach, pepper, tomato, or whole wheat versions.

2 cups all-purpose flour
1 tsp. baking powder
½ tsp. salt
2 Tbsp. shortening
½ cup warm water

1 In a medium mixing bowl combine flour, baking powder, and salt. Using a pastry blender, cut in shortening till well combined. Add warm water, 1 tablespoon at a time, tossing till dough can be gathered into a ball (if necessary, add additional water, 1 tablespoon at a time). On a lightly floured surface knead dough 15 to 20 times. Let dough rest for 15 minutes.

2 For 8-inch tortillas, divide dough into 12 equal portions; shape into balls. (For 10-inch tortillas, divide dough into 8 equal portions; shape into balls.)

3 On a lightly floured surface flatten a ball of dough. Roll from center to edges into an 8-inch (or 10-inch) circle. Repeat with remaining dough. As you work, stack rolled-out tortillas between sheets of waxed paper.

4 Preheat a 10- or 12-inch ungreased skillet or griddle over medium-high heat. Remove a sheet of waxed paper from a tortilla and place the tortilla, paper side up, in the hot pan. As tortilla begins to heat, carefully peel off remaining waxed paper. Cook tortilla about 30 seconds or till puffy. Turn and cook about 30 seconds more or till edges curl up slightly. Wrap the tortillas in foil while making additional tortillas. Use tortillas immediately or cool and store (see Tortilla Tips, at left). Makes 12 (8-inch) or 8 (10-inch) tortillas.

Nutrition facts per 8-inch flour tortilla: 89 cal., 2 g total fat (1 g sat. fat), 0 mg chol., 120 mg sodium, 15 g carbo., 1 g fiber, 2 g pro.
Daily values: 2% calcium, 6% iron.

Spinach Tortillas: Prepare tortilla dough as directed at left, except add ⅓ cup very finely chopped, well-drained, *cooked spinach* with the flour.

Chili Tortillas: Prepare tortilla dough as directed at left, except add 1 tablespoon *ancho chili powder or regular chili powder* to the flour mixture. Add additional *water,* if necessary.

Tomato Tortillas: Prepare tortilla dough as directed at left, except add ¼ cup *tomato paste* to the flour mixture after cutting in the shortening.

Whole Wheat Tortillas: Prepare tortilla dough as directed at left, except substitute 1 cup *whole wheat flour* for 1 cup of the all-purpose flour. Add additional *water,* if necessary.

HOMEMADE CORN TORTILLAS

Start to finish: 1½ hr.

The first tortillas were made from masa—corn kernels simmered in water till soft, then ground by hand. Today masa harina (dehydrated masa) tortilla flour often is used instead.

2 cups masa harina tortilla flour
¼ tsp. salt (optional)
1¼ cups warm water

1 In a medium mixing bowl combine the tortilla flour and, if desired, the salt; add water. Stir mixture together with your hands till dough is firm but moist (if necessary, add additional water, 1 tablespoon at a time). Let dough rest for 15 minutes.

2 Divide dough into 12 equal portions; shape into balls. Use a tortilla press or a rolling pin to make tortillas. If using a tortilla press, place dough between 2 sheets of waxed paper on the press; press to a 6-inch circle. If using a rolling pin, flatten dough between 2 sheets of waxed paper. Roll from center to edges into a 6-inch circle. Repeat with remaining dough.

3 Preheat an 8-inch ungreased skillet or griddle over medium-high heat. Remove a sheet of waxed paper from a tortilla and place the tortilla, paper side up, in the hot pan. Carefully peel off remaining waxed paper. Cook, turning every 30 seconds, about 2 minutes or till tortilla is dry and light brown (tortilla should still be soft). Keep tortillas wrapped in foil while making additional tortillas to prevent them from drying out. Use tortillas immediately or cool and store (see Tortilla Tips, page 88). Makes 12 (6-inch) tortillas.

Nutrition facts per tortilla: 70 cal., 1 g total fat (0 g sat. fat), 0 mg chol., 2 mg sodium, 15 g carbo., 1 g fiber, 2 g pro.
Daily values: 2% calcium, 9% iron.

TRI-PEPPER NACHOS

Start to finish: 25 min.

Your family will love the bright colors in this updated nacho snack. Add even more color by using your own homemade spinach or tomato tortillas.

5 6- to 7-inch corn or flour tortillas, or 4 cups tortilla chips (about 4 oz.)
♦♦♦
1 cup canned black beans, rinsed and drained
½ cup salsa
♦♦♦
2 cups shredded Monterey Jack, cheddar, queso quesadilla, Chihuahua, and/or asadero cheese (8 oz.)
½ cup roasted red sweet peppers, cut into thin bite-size strips
2 to 4 Tbsp. fresh or canned sliced jalapeño peppers, drained
6 pepperoncini salad peppers, drained
Salsa (optional)

1 To make chips, stack tortillas and cut into wedges using scissors or a sharp knife. Place wedges in a single layer on an ungreased baking sheet. Bake in a 350° oven for 10 to 12 minutes or till light golden brown. Remove the chips from oven. Arrange the tortilla chips 1 layer deep, overlapping slightly, on an 11- or 12-inch ovenproof platter.

2 In a saucepan combine the black beans and the ½ cup salsa. Cook and stir over medium heat just till heated through. Remove from heat; spoon bean mixture over chips.

3 Sprinkle the cheese, red peppers, and jalapeño peppers over the bean mixture on chips. Using a small sharp knife, slit pepperoncini peppers; remove stems and seeds. Cut into strips; sprinkle over nachos. Bake in a 425° oven for 3 to 5 minutes or till cheese is melted. If desired, serve immediately with additional salsa. Makes about 12 appetizer servings.

Nutrition facts per serving: 180 cal., 8 g total fat (4 g sat. fat), 17 mg chol., 350 mg sodium, 19 g carbo., 2 g fiber, 8 g pro.
Daily values: 9% vit. A, 36% vit. C, 15% calcium, 9% iron.

TEST KITCHEN TIP

PEPPER TIPS

Because hot peppers contain oils that can burn your eyes, lips, and skin, protect yourself when working with the peppers by covering one or both hands with plastic bags (or wear plastic gloves). Be sure to wash your hands thoroughly before touching your eyes or face.

CHIPS WITH ZIP

Prep: 10 min. ◆ Bake: 8 min.

Fresh from the oven, these flavored chips make terrific munching. Try mixing homemade or purchased chips of different hues and flavors.

½ tsp. paprika
⅛ to ¼ tsp. salt
⅛ to ¼ tsp. pepper
2 Tbsp. olive oil or cooking oil
4 7- to 8-inch flour tortillas
Salsa (optional)

1 In a small bowl combine the paprika, salt, and pepper. Brush the oil over tortillas; sprinkle with paprika mixture. Cut each tortilla into 8 wedges. Spread on an ungreased 15×10×1-inch baking pan. Bake in a 350° oven for 8 to 10 minutes or till chips are crisp and edges are lightly browned. If desired, serve with salsa. Makes about 4 cups (8 servings).

Nutrition facts per serving: 75 cal., 5 g total fat (1 g sat. fat), 0 mg chol., 93 mg sodium, 7 g carbo., 0 g fiber, 1 g pro.
Daily values: 1% calcium, 3% iron.

Focaccia-Style Chips: In a small skillet cook ⅔ cup finely chopped *onion* in 2 tablespoons melted *margarine or butter* for 3 to 5 minutes or till tender. Stir in 1 teaspoon *dried Italian seasoning,* crushed. Carefully brush the onion mixture evenly over 1 side of tortillas. Cut each tortilla into 8 wedges, place in pan, and bake as directed above. Makes about 4 cups (8 servings).

Nutrition facts per serving: 105 cal., 7 g total fat (1 g sat. fat), 0 mg chol., 127 mg sodium, 9 g carbo., 0 g fiber, 1 g pro.
Daily values: 4% vit. A, 1% vit. C, 1% calcium, 4% iron.

WRAP-AND-ROLL BASIL PINWHEELS

Prep: 20 min. ◆ Chill: 2 to 24 hr.

Use plain, whole wheat, or colorful spinach or tomato tortillas to wrap up these unique bundles of flavor. (See the photograph on page 82.)

3 7- to 8-inch flour tortillas
1 5.2-oz. carton Boursin cheese or one 5-oz. container semisoft cheese with garlic and herb
12 large fresh basil leaves
½ of a 7-oz. jar roasted red sweet peppers, cut into ¼-inch strips
4 oz. thinly sliced cooked roast beef, ham, or turkey
1 Tbsp. mayonnaise or salad dressing

◆◆◆

Fresh basil leaves (optional)

1 Spread each flour tortilla with ⅓ of the Boursin cheese or semisoft cheese. Add a layer of the large fresh basil leaves to cover cheese. Divide roasted red sweet pepper strips between tortillas, arranging pepper strips over basil leaves 1 to 2 inches apart. Top with meat slices. Spread 1 teaspoon mayonnaise or salad dressing over meat on each tortilla. Roll up tortillas tightly, jelly-roll style, enclosing filling. Wrap each roll in plastic wrap. Chill rolls in the refrigerator 2 to 4 hours to blend flavors.

2 To serve, remove plastic wrap from tortilla rolls; cut each roll into 1-inch slices (make diagonal slices, if desired). If desired, skewer each cut tortilla roll on a frilly pick or short decorative

Menu

Shrimp-Tortilla Soup
(see below)

◆◆◆

Salad of fresh spinach and
sliced pears

◆◆◆

Chocolate cake with vanilla
frozen yogurt

skewer. Garnish with additional fresh basil, if desired. Makes about 24 pinwheels.

Nutrition facts per pinwheel: 52 cal., 4 g total fat (2 g sat. fat), 5 mg chol., 58 mg sodium, 2 g carbo., 0 g fiber, 2 g pro.
Daily values: 1% vit. A, 14% vit. C, 2% iron.

SHRIMP-TORTILLA SOUP

Start to finish: 45 min.

5 6-inch corn tortillas
Cooking oil for deep-fat frying

◆◆◆

2 medium carrots, cut into thin bite-size strips
4 green onions, sliced
3 cloves garlic, minced
2 14½-oz. cans reduced-sodium chicken broth
1 14½-oz. can diced tomatoes
¼ cup snipped fresh cilantro

◆◆◆

8 oz. fresh or frozen shrimp in shells, thawed, peeled, and deveined
1 cup shredded Monterey Jack cheese or crumbled queso fresco (4 oz.) (optional)
Chopped avocado (optional)
Cilantro sprigs (optional)

1 Cut tortillas into ½-inch-wide strips. In a large skillet pour cooking oil to a depth of ¼ inch; heat over medium-high heat. Fry tortilla strips, a few at a time, in hot oil about 1½ minutes or till browned and crisp. Using a slotted spoon, transfer the strips to paper towels to drain thoroughly.* Set aside.

2 In a pot heat *1 tablespoon* cooking oil. Cook carrots, onions, and garlic in hot oil for 5 minutes, stirring frequently. Stir in broth, undrained tomatoes, snipped cilantro, and ¼ teaspoon *pepper.* Bring to boiling; reduce heat. Simmer, covered, 10 minutes.

3 Meanwhile, place half of the tortilla strips in a food processor bowl; cover and process till tortilla strips are finely crushed. Stir crushed tortillas into the soup; cover and cook 5 minutes more.

4 Stir in shrimp; cook 1 to 3 minutes or till shrimp turn pink. If desired, stir in cheese till melted. Top soup with remaining tortilla strips. If desired, garnish with avocado and cilantro sprigs. Makes 4 main-dish servings.

*****Note:** If you prefer not to fry the tortilla strips, place strips on an ungreased baking sheet. Bake in a 350° oven about 15 minutes or till crisp, stirring once.

Nutrition facts per serving (with fried tortillas): 254 cal., 13 g total fat (2 g sat. fat), 65 mg chol., 967 mg sodium, 25 g carbo., 2 g fiber, 12 g pro.
Daily values: 96% vit. A, 34% vit. C, 9% calcium, 16% iron.

GRILLED SALMON SALAD
Start to finish: 1 hr.

Your own homemade tortilla bowls create a dramatic presentation for this delectable meal-in-one salad.

- **8 oz. fresh or frozen salmon fillets or firm white fish fillets**
- **1 Tbsp. olive oil or cooking oil**
- **1 Tbsp. lime juice or lemon juice**
- **1 to 1½ tsp. Cajun seasoning or Jamaican jerk seasoning**

♦♦♦

- **6 cups torn mixed greens, such as sorrel, spinach, romaine, radicchio, or leaf lettuce**
- **2 medium oranges, peeled and sectioned**
- **1 cup strawberries, halved**
- **1 medium avocado, halved, seeded, peeled, and sliced**
- **1 medium mango, seeded, peeled, and sliced**
- **¼ cup chopped macadamia nuts or almonds, toasted**
- **1 recipe Tortilla Bowls (see right) or purchased tortilla bowls**
- **1 recipe Tarragon-Buttermilk Dressing (see right)**
  Lime peel curls (optional)

1 Thaw fish if frozen. Brush fish with oil; sprinkle with lime juice and Cajun seasoning. Arrange fish fillets in a well-greased grill basket. Grill on the rack of an uncovered grill directly over medium coals 4 to 6 minutes for each ½ inch of thickness or till fish flakes easily, turning once. (Or, place fish on the unheated rack of a broiler pan. Broil 4 inches from heat for 4 to 6 minutes for each ½ inch of thickness or till fish flakes easily.) Tear fish into bite-size pieces.

2 In a large mixing bowl combine greens, oranges, strawberries, avocado, mango, and nuts; toss gently to mix. Spoon into the Tortilla Bowls and drizzle with Tarragon-Buttermilk Dressing. If desired, garnish each serving with a lime peel curl. Makes 4 main-dish servings.

Tortilla Bowls: Lightly brush four 9- to 10-inch *flour tortillas* with a small amount of *cooking oil,* or spray *nonstick spray coating* onto 1 side of each tortilla. Spray *nonstick spray coating* into four taco salad molds or small oven-safe bowls. Press tortillas, coated sides up, into molds or bowls. Place a ball of foil in each mold. Bake in a 350° oven 15 to 20 minutes or till light brown. Remove foil; cool. Remove tortillas from molds. Fill bowls with Grilled Salmon Salad or salad of your choice; serve immediately. If not using immediately, store Tortilla Bowls in an airtight container for up to 5 days. Makes 4 bowls.

Tarragon-Buttermilk Dressing: In a small bowl stir together ⅓ cup *buttermilk;* 2 tablespoons *light mayonnaise or salad dressing;* and 1 teaspoon snipped *fresh tarragon or dill,* or ¼ teaspoon *dried tarragon or dillweed,* crushed. Use immediately or cover and chill up to 1 week.

Nutrition facts per serving: 496 cal., 26 g total fat (5 g sat. fat), 11 mg chol., 369 mg sodium, 54 g carbo., 9 g fiber, 16 g pro.
Daily values: 58% vit. A, 159% vit. C, 15% calcium, 27% iron.

Brunch Seafood Strata

Prep: 30 min. ◆ Chill: 8 to 24 hr.
Bake: 45 min.

See the photograph on page 84.

Nonstick spray coating
2 **Tbsp. margarine or butter**
3 **leeks, sliced (white part only) or 1 cup chopped onion**
4 **7- to 8-inch flour tortillas**
4 **oz. cooked, peeled, and deveined shrimp***
4 **oz. flaked cooked crabmeat (½ cup)***
¾ **cup shredded Swiss cheese (3 oz.)**
½ **cup shredded mozzarella cheese (2 oz.)**
1 **Tbsp. chopped fresh dill or ¾ tsp. dried dillweed**

◆◆◆

3 **eggs**
1½ **cups milk**
1 **Tbsp. all-purpose flour**
¼ **tsp. pepper**
Additional cooked, peeled, and deveined shrimp (optional)
Fresh dill (optional)

1 Spray a 2-quart rectangular baking dish with nonstick coating. In a medium skillet melt margarine or butter. Add leeks or onions; cook 3 minutes or till tender. Tear tortillas into bite-size pieces. In the baking dish layer half of the tortilla pieces, half of the leeks, half of the shrimp and crab, half of the cheeses, and half of the chopped dill. Repeat layers.

2 In a bowl beat together eggs, milk, flour, and pepper till smooth. Pour the egg mixture over the layers in dish; cover and chill overnight.

3 Bake, uncovered, in a 350° oven for 45 to 50 minutes or till a knife inserted near center comes out clean and top is golden brown. Let stand 5 minutes. Cut into squares and serve. If desired, garnish with shrimp and fresh dill. Makes 6 servings.

*Note: You can substitute 8 ounces *crab-flavored flake-style fish pieces* for shrimp and crab.

Nutrition facts per serving: 301 cal., 15 g total fat (6 g sat. fat), 185 mg chol., 369 mg sodium, 20 g carbo., 2 g fiber, 21 g pro. *Daily values:* 20% vit. A, 7% vit. C, 29% calcium, 17% iron.

Thai Chicken Wraps

Start to finish: 50 min.

To get this dish from kitchen to table even more quickly, use prepared peanut sauce you can find in ethnic food sections of most grocery stores.

4 **skinless, boneless chicken breast halves (about 1 lb.)**
4 **cloves garlic, minced**
1 **tsp. sugar**
1 **tsp. pepper**

◆◆◆

1 **red onion, cut into thin wedges**
2 **tsp. cooking oil**
1 **cup finely shredded green cabbage or Chinese cabbage**
1 **cup shredded carrots**
4 **green onions, sliced**
1 **Tbsp. grated gingerroot**
2 **large cloves garlic, minced**

◆◆◆

12 **7- to 8-inch Spinach Tortillas (see recipe, page 88) or purchased flour tortillas**
3 **cups warm cooked rice**

1 **recipe Peanut Sauce (see page 93) or ¾ cup purchased peanut sauce**
Fresh mint leaves (optional)
1 **small red onion, cut into thin wedges (optional)**

1 Rinse chicken; pat dry with paper towels. Stir together the 4 cloves minced garlic, sugar, pepper, and ¼ teaspoon *salt;* rub over chicken. Place chicken on the unheated rack of a broiler pan. Broil 4 to 5 inches from heat for 12 to 15 minutes or till chicken is no longer pink and juices run clear, turning once. Let chicken stand for 5 minutes. Cut the chicken into thin strips.

2 In medium skillet cook onion wedges in hot oil over medium heat for 3 to 5 minutes or till tender. Add cabbage, carrots, green onions, gingerroot, and the 2 cloves minced garlic. Cook for 2 to 3 minutes or till vegetables are tender. Keep warm.

3 Meanwhile, wrap tortillas tightly in foil. Heat in a 350° oven about 10 minutes or till heated.

4 To assemble, spread about ¼ cup rice down the center of each tortilla to within 1½ inches of the edge. Top with chicken strips, vegetable mixture, and about 1½ teaspoons Peanut Sauce. Make a wrap by folding opposite sides of tortilla in, then rolling it up tightly to encase the filling. Or, simply fold tortilla over. If desired, garnish with fresh mint and red onion wedges. Serve immediately with remaining Peanut Sauce. Makes 6 servings.

Peanut Sauce: In a small saucepan combine ¼ cup *creamy peanut butter,* ¼ cup *sugar,* 3 tablespoons *soy sauce,* 3 tablespoons *water,* 2 tablespoons *cooking oil,* and 4 cloves minced *garlic.* Heat mixture to dissolve sugar, stirring often. Cool and serve.

Nutrition facts per serving: 497 cal., 17 g total fat (3 g sat. fat), 40 mg chol., 881 mg sodium, 62 g carbo., 3 g fiber, 24 g pro. *Daily values:* 53% vit. A, 21% vit. C, 7% calcium, 24% iron.

CHICKEN AND CORN ENCHILADAS

Prep: 40 min. ◆ Stand: 45 min.
Bake: 25 min.

2 **to 3 dried ancho chili peppers, seeded and cut up, or 1 tsp. crushed red pepper**
1 **14½-oz. can tomatoes**
1 **medium onion, cut up**
1 **clove garlic, quartered**
½ **tsp. ground cumin**
½ **cup whipping cream**

◆◆◆

3 **cups shredded cooked chicken or turkey**
1 **8¾-oz. can whole kernel corn, drained**
¼ **cup snipped fresh oregano or 2 tsp. dried oregano, crushed**

◆◆◆

3 **tsp. cooking oil**
8 **6-inch corn tortillas**

◆◆◆

1 **cup crumbled queso fresco or shredded Monterey Jack cheese (4 oz.)**
1 **fresh serrano pepper, cut in ¼-inch strips (optional)**
 Snipped fresh oregano (optional)

1 For sauce, in a small bowl place ancho chili peppers (if using) and cover with *boiling water.* Let stand for 45 to 60 minutes; drain. In a food processor bowl or blender container combine drained chili peppers or crushed red pepper, undrained tomatoes, onion, garlic, cumin, and ¼ teaspoon *salt.* Cover and process or blend till mixture is smooth. Transfer mixture to a medium saucepan. Bring to boiling; reduce heat. Simmer sauce, uncovered, about 10 minutes or till slightly thickened (you should have about 1⅔ cups). Remove from heat. Stir in whipping cream; season to taste with *salt* and *pepper.* Set aside.

2 For filling, in a medium mixing bowl combine the shredded chicken or turkey, drained corn, ¼ cup oregano or dried oregano, and ⅔ *cup* of the sauce.

3 In a small skillet heat *1 teaspoon* of the cooking oil. Place 1 tortilla into hot oil about 10 seconds or just till limp, turning once. Repeat with remaining tortillas, adding remaining 2 teaspoons of oil as necessary. Drain tortillas on paper towels.

4 Grease a 2-quart rectangular baking dish. To assemble, divide filling equally among the tortillas, spooning near an end of each; roll up and place, seam side down, in prepared dish. Pour remaining sauce over enchiladas. Cover and bake in a 350° oven about 25 minutes or till heated through. Uncover and sprinkle the enchiladas with cheese. Bake, uncovered, for 4 to 5 minutes more or till cheese is melted. If desired,

garnish with serrano pepper strips and oregano. Makes 8 enchiladas.

Nutrition facts per enchilada: 319 cal., 17 g total fat (7 g sat. fat), 84 mg chol., 458 mg sodium, 20 g carbo., 1 g fiber, 23 g pro. *Daily values:* 16% vit. A, 17% vit. C, 12% calcium, 13% iron.

SIMPLE CHICKEN STEW

Start to finish: 35 min.

See the photograph on page 78.

1 **cup chopped onion**
1 **clove garlic, minced**
1 **Tbsp. cooking oil**
1 **cup thinly sliced carrots**
¾ **cup chicken broth**
2 **Tbsp. catsup**
⅛ **tsp. ground nutmeg**
1½ **cups milk**
4 **tsp. cornstarch**
2 **cups chopped cooked chicken**
1 **cup frozen peas, thawed**
½ **cup whipping cream**
½ **cup grated Parmesan cheese**
2½ **cups hot cooked rice**

1 In a saucepan cook onion and garlic in hot oil till tender. Add carrots, broth, catsup, nutmeg, and ⅛ teaspoon *pepper.* Bring to boiling; reduce heat. Simmer, covered, 5 minutes. Stir together milk and cornstarch till smooth. Add milk mixture to broth mixture. Cook and stir till thickened and bubbly; cook and stir 2 minutes more. Stir in chicken, peas, cream, and cheese; heat through. Serve over rice. Serves 5.

Nutrition facts per serving: 470 cal., 21 g total fat (10 g sat. fat), 100 mg chol., 521 mg sodium, 40 g carbo., 2 g fiber, 29 g pro. *Daily values:* 84% vit. A, 10% vit. C, 23% calcium, 17% iron.

Menu

**Plum Wonderful Chicken
(see below)**

◆◆◆

Rice noodles

◆◆◆

Cooked snow peas

◆◆◆

Papaya or mango wedges

PRIZE TESTED RECIPE WINNER

PLUM WONDERFUL CHICKEN

Prep: 35 min. ◆ Bake: 40 min.

This recipe earned Norma J. Keleher of Pacific Grove, California, $200 in the magazine's monthly contest.

2½ to 3 lb. meaty chicken pieces, skinned
2 Tbsp. olive oil or cooking oil
¼ cup chopped onion
1 clove garlic, minced
1 tsp. grated gingerroot
⅓ cup bottled plum sauce
¼ cup frozen lemonade concentrate
¼ cup bottled chili sauce
2 Tbsp. soy sauce
1 Tbsp. lemon juice
1 tsp. dry mustard

1 In a skillet cook chicken in hot oil over medium heat about 10 minutes, turning often to brown evenly. Remove chicken and place in a 3-quart rectangular baking dish. Drain all but 1 tablespoon fat in skillet; add onion, garlic, and gingerroot. Cook till onion is tender.

2 Combine remaining ingredients. Carefully stir into onion mixture. Bring to boiling; reduce heat. Simmer, covered, for 5 minutes; spoon over chicken in dish. Bake, uncovered, in a 350° oven 40 to 45 minutes or till chicken is done, spooning sauce over chicken occasionally. Serves 6.

Nutrition facts per serving: 239 cal., 9 g total fat (2 g sat. fat), 77 mg chol., 556 mg sodium, 14 g carbo., 0 g fiber, 26 g pro. *Daily values:* 3% vit. A, 9% vit. C, 1% calcium, 8% iron.

GREEK-STYLE CHICKEN

Prep: 30 min. ◆ Bake: 40 min.

4 medium chicken breast halves (about 1½ lb. total)
8 cloves garlic, minced
2 Tbsp. olive oil

◆◆◆

1 8-oz. can tomato sauce
½ cup water
1 Tbsp. red wine vinegar
¼ tsp. salt
¼ tsp. pepper
Dash ground cloves
6 oz. frozen small whole onions (about 1½ cups)
1 cup orzo (rosamarina)

◆◆◆

Grated Parmesan cheese

1 Skin chicken, if desired. Rinse chicken; pat dry. In a large pot cook chicken and garlic in hot oil 15 minutes or till chicken is lightly browned, turning often to brown evenly. Drain off fat.

2 Meanwhile, stir together tomato sauce, water, vinegar, salt, pepper, and cloves. Stir in onions. Pour sauce over chicken. Bring to boiling; reduce heat. Simmer, covered, 35 to 40 minutes or till chicken is tender and no longer pink. Cook orzo according to package directions; drain.

3 Use a slotted spoon to transfer chicken to a serving platter; keep warm. Simmer sauce, uncovered, 5 to 10 minutes more or till thickened. Serve sauce over chicken and orzo. Sprinkle with Parmesan cheese. Serves 4.

Nutrition facts per serving: 506 cal., 17 g total fat (4 g sat. fat), 104 mg chol., 578 mg sodium, 42 g carbo., 2 g fiber, 44 g pro. *Daily values:* 9% vit. A, 20% vit. C, 4% calcium, 25% iron.

PRIZE TESTED RECIPE WINNER

BASIL CHICKEN IN COCONUT-CURRY SAUCE

Prep: 30 min. ◆ Marinate: ½ to 2 hr.

This recipe earned Neeraja Narayanan of New York, New York, $400 in the magazine's monthly contest.

4 skinless, boneless chicken breast halves (about 1 lb.)
½ tsp. ground coriander
½ tsp. ground cumin
½ tsp. ground cloves
½ tsp. ground cinnamon
½ tsp. ground cardamom
½ tsp. cracked black pepper
¼ tsp. chili powder
¼ tsp. ground turmeric

◆◆◆

1 large red onion, chopped
5 cloves garlic, minced
2 fresh jalapeño peppers,
   seeded and finely chopped
1 Tbsp. olive oil or cooking oil
1 14-oz. can coconut milk
2 tsp. cornstarch
3 Tbsp. snipped fresh basil
1 Tbsp. finely chopped
   gingerroot
   Hot cooked rice (optional)

1 Rinse chicken; pat dry. Cut into 1-inch pieces; place chicken in a medium bowl. In a small bowl stir together the coriander, cumin, cloves, cinnamon, cardamom, black pepper, chili powder, turmeric, and ½ teaspoon *salt*. Sprinkle over chicken; toss to coat well. Cover and let stand at room temperature 30 minutes or chill for 1 to 2 hours.

2 In a skillet cook onion, garlic, and jalapeños in hot oil over medium-high heat for 2 minutes. Remove vegetables, reserving drippings in skillet. Add half of the chicken. Cook and stir for 2 to 3 minutes or till chicken is tender and no longer pink. Remove chicken from skillet. Repeat with remaining chicken. Remove chicken from skillet. Combine coconut milk and cornstarch. Carefully add to skillet. Cook and stir till thick and bubbly. Add chicken mixture, basil, and gingerroot. Cook and stir for 2 minutes more. If desired, serve over hot rice and garnish with *red onion wedges* and *fresh basil*. Makes 4 servings.

Nutrition facts per serving: 365 cal., 25 g total fat (18 g sat. fat), 59 mg chol., 350 mg sodium, 10 g carbo., 1 g fiber, 24 g pro. *Daily values:* 1% vit. A, 23% vit. C, 3% calcium, 17% iron.

PORK AND PLANTAIN FAJITAS

Prep: 30 min. ◆ Marinate: ½ to 2 hr.

Plantains look like big bananas, but you have to cook them before eating. We used homemade Chili Tortillas for these fajitas, but any tortilla will do. (See the photograph on page 82.)

12 oz. lean boneless pork
½ cup pineapple juice
1 Tbsp. soy sauce
3 cloves garlic, minced
1 tsp. five-spice powder
¼ to ½ tsp. crushed red pepper
   ◆◆◆
8 8- or 10-inch Chili Tortillas
   (see recipe, page 88)
   ◆◆◆
2 ripe plantains or large firm
   bananas, peeled
2 Tbsp. cooking oil
1 cup red, yellow, and/or green
   sweet pepper, cut into
   bite-size strips
8 green onions, cut into 1-inch
   pieces (about ⅔ cup)
   ◆◆◆
   Bottled sweet-and-sour sauce
   Mango and orange slices
   (optional)

1 Partially freeze pork; slice across grain into thin strips. Place pork in a plastic bag set in a shallow dish. Combine pineapple juice, soy sauce, garlic, five-spice powder, and crushed red pepper; pour over pork. Seal bag. Cover

and let stand at room temperature for 30 minutes or chill for 2 hours, turning bag occasionally to redistribute marinade.

2 Wrap tortillas tightly in foil. Heat in a 350° oven about 10 minutes or till heated through. Keep warm.

3 Cut plantains or bananas in half lengthwise; slice crosswise into ½-inch slices. In a large skillet cook plantains (not bananas) in *1 tablespoon* of the cooking oil over medium-high heat 2 to 3 minutes or till golden brown, turning occasionally. Remove from skillet. Add pepper strips and onions to skillet; cook and stir 2 minutes or till vegetables are crisp-tender. Remove vegetables from skillet.

4 Drain pork well; discard marinade. Add the remaining 1 tablespoon oil to the skillet. Add pork; cook and stir over medium-high heat for 2 to 3 minutes or till no pink remains.

5 Return vegetable mixture to skillet. Stir in ⅓ *cup* sweet-and-sour sauce. Add plantains or bananas; cook and stir 1 minute or till heated through. To serve, fill warm tortillas with pork mixture; roll up. If desired, serve with additional sweet and sour sauce and slices of mango and orange. Makes 4 servings.

Nutrition facts per serving: 600 cal., 20 g total fat (5 g sat. fat), 38 mg chol., 718 mg sodium, 88 g carbo., 4 g fiber, 20 g pro. *Daily values:* 30% vit. A, 99% vit. C, 10% calcium, 30% iron.

TEA REMEDIES

TEA IS BACK

Well, tea never actually left—it's still the most popular drink in the world. Consumed in record amounts, tea is now riding the coattails of the espresso boom into the limelight in the United States. Aiding its popularity is its perception as a healthful beverage. Often "prescribed" for illnesses such as headaches, premenstrual tension, colds, and flu, scientific research does, in fact, show that tea contains elements that may make it a disease fighter.

Tea and the health connection. Enjoyed for thousands of years, tea has always played a key role in medicinal folklore. Scientists now know tea contains disease-fighting compounds called phytochemicals. The phytochemicals in tea may reduce the risk of cancer of the stomach, esophagus, breast, pancreas, and lungs. Tea may even help lower blood pressure and reduce heart disease.

Enjoying tea. There are only three kinds of true tea: green, black, and oolong. The difference between them is in the processing. With green tea the leaves are steamed right after plucking. Black and oolong tea leaves are crushed and dried after plucking. (Orange pekoe, the most popular tea in America, is actually a black tea.)

Tea can be enjoyed in nontraditional ways without forfeiting any health benefits related to it. You can use it in cooking, where it imparts flavor to soups and sauces. Strong tea, like Darjeeling, or smoky tea, such

as Lapsang Souchong, enhances soups or chilis when used in place of broth. Earl Grey tea is a black tea with a pronounced lavender flavor. It can be used as an ingredient in everything from cakes to custards. Green tea adds a sublime note to sweet desserts, especially ice creams. You can also make iced teas with different types of tea, or add herbs and spices, such as mint, jasmine, clove, or cinnamon.

How much tea should you drink? According to Dr. John Weisburger, director emeritus and leading researcher in tea and health at the American Health Foundation, there's no set amount of tea you should drink. As Dr. Weisburger explains, the greatest health benefit of tea is derived from its antioxidants and other phytochemicals. These useful compounds have no established recommended dietary amounts, but Dr. Weisburger says that 2 to 5 cups of tea provide the phytochemical "equivalent" of 1 to 2 servings of vegetables. (Fruits and vegetables are the primary source of phytochemicals.)

Of course, tea is no substitute for fresh fruits and vegetables. Plain tea has no calories and is not an alternative for food. Also, where research originally suggested that green tea and black tea have different anticancer effects, newer studies show no such difference between them, even when they are in the form of instant tea.

What about caffeine? Although the jury is still out about possible negative effects of caffeine, a cup of strong brewed black, orange, or green tea (often mistakenly believed to be caffeine-free) has only a third as much caffeine as a cup of coffee. Also most, but not all, herbal preparations are devoid of caffeine.

TEA OR NOT TEA

Hot herbal drinks are commonly called "tea," but only drinks from the *Camellia sinensis* plant are truly "tea." As occasional beverages, there's no problem with the majority of herbal drinks. But, if used daily or taken in excess concentrations, some could turn harmful.

Herbal safety. Many herbal drinks are probably safe. But some could trigger allergic or other adverse reactions. For example, chamomile and echinacea are both related to ragweed. This doesn't mean everyone should avoid these drinks, but if you have plant sensitivities, these or similar preparations could set them off.

Approach with caution. Drinks from plants such as ephedra (also called ma huang) contain the stimulant ephedrine. If consumed in large amounts or on a continual basis (for example, as a diet aid or for increased stamina), these drinks could pose a danger.

These, and other herbals, have been known to cause symptoms that range from mild discomfort and flushing to erratic heartbeat, respiratory distress, and, in extreme cases, death. Dr. Varro Tyler, professor emeritus of pharmacognosy at Purdue University in Indiana, points out that there is little, if any, scientific evidence these products are effective weight reducers. He stresses, however, that when used sensibly, most herbal beverages are completely harmless for an average, healthy adult.

What you see may not always be what you get. Most serious complications from taking herbal concoctions are attributable to contaminants that get mixed in during picking and processing. Regulations are in place for products making specific structure and function claims, but no regulations exist to control for the efficacy or concentration of herbal products claiming to control weight or provide extra energy.

The Food and Drug Administration is exploring regulatory measures against some of these ingredients (ma huang, for example). In 1995, their scientific advisory committee recommended more appropriate labeling for so-called "cleansing" or "dieters" teas.

Tea and maternity. Dr. Tyler notes that "infusions from herbs similar to food plants (for example, chamomile) can be considered safe during pregnancy. Drinks made from mint, ginger, or fennel are often recommended for nausea. They are harmless and can help relieve the morning sickness that's associated with pregnancy. Other herbals may be better left alone.

Dr. Tyler cautions, "It's wise for pregnant women to avoid exotic herbs, such as senna, cascara, and other stimulating or laxative herbs, which are closer to drugs than foods. Some of these have an effect on the smooth muscles and might adversely affect the uterine walls in pregnant women."

Herbal health. Like tea, herbs and spices contain disease-fighting phytochemicals, but not always in the same concentration. Since there is such a wide variety of herbs that are used as beverages, establishing a single specific health benefit for all herbal products is difficult. Lest you find yourself in hot water over an herbal preparation, use only reputable sources, such as brand-name products.

ZEN AND THE ART OF TEA

Tea also provides some psychological benefits. The word "tea" comes from *tai*, an ancient Chinese word for peace. The tea break assumes a different social connotation from a coffee break: You down a cup of "joe" to boost your energy level and get back to work; you break for a cup of tea to relax. In the eighteenth century, the Chinese emperor Ch'ien Lung declared tea a "miracle beverage," claiming it would "drive away the five causes of sorrow," and poet Ralph Waldo Emerson said one finds "a great deal of poetry and fine sentiment" in tea. To brew the perfect cup of tea (according to the Tea Council of the U.S.A.), start with fresh, cold water brought just to boiling. Preheat the teapot and, when the water is ready, bring the teapot to the water. Use 1 teaspoon or 1 tea bag of the best quality tea leaves per cup and brew for 3 to 5 minutes. Remove tea leaves from the pot before serving.

Mint-Rubbed Leg of Lamb
(see below)

◆◆◆

Buttered new potatoes

◆◆◆

**Steamed asparagus and
baby carrots**

◆◆◆

Whole wheat rolls

◆◆◆

Pound cake with berries

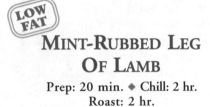

MINT-RUBBED LEG OF LAMB

Prep: 20 min. ◆ Chill: 2 hr.
Roast: 2 hr.

Though lamb is often paired with mint jelly, this roasted leg lets you leave the jelly jar in the pantry. Serve the roast medium-rare to medium, in its own juices, with a simple arrangement of spring vegetables.

1 **5-lb. whole leg of lamb
    (bone in)**
8 **cloves garlic**

◆◆◆

2 **Tbsp. dried mint, crushed**
1 **Tbsp. coarsely ground black
    pepper**
½ **tsp. salt**
3 **Tbsp. honey**

◆◆◆

  Fresh mint sprigs (optional)

1 Trim excess fat from meat. Cut ½-inch-wide slits into lamb leg in 16 different places. Cut the garlic cloves in half lengthwise and insert each half-clove deep into each slit.

2 Combine the dried mint, pepper, and salt; rub mixture over entire surface of lamb leg. Drizzle honey over lamb leg and rub to coat. Place on a rack in a shallow roasting pan. Cover lamb loosely with plastic wrap and refrigerate for 2 hours.

3 Remove plastic wrap. Insert a meat thermometer into the thickest part of meat without touching bone. Roast, uncovered, in a 325° oven for 2 to 3½ hours or till the meat thermometer registers 140° for medium-rare doneness or 155° for medium doneness. Remove from oven.

4 Cover meat loosely with foil and let stand for 15 minutes before carving. (The meat's temperature will rise 5° during the time it stands.) If desired, garnish with mint sprigs. Makes about 10 to 12 servings.

Nutrition facts per serving: 198 cal., 7 g total fat (2 g sat. fat), 80 mg chol., 169 mg sodium, 6 g carbo., 0 g fiber, 26 g pro. *Daily values:* 5% vit. C, 1% calcium, 17% iron.

ASPARAGUS AND CHEESE BUNDLES

Prep: 30 min. ◆ Bake: 10 min.

The cheese of your choice oozes over the crisp-tender vegetables tucked inside these tortilla pouches. It could be love at first bite when you introduce them at your next spring gathering.

6 **oz. asparagus spears**
2 **medium carrots, cut into
    thin strips**

◆◆◆

1 **8-oz. pkg. cream cheese,
    softened**
1 **egg**
2 **Tbsp. snipped fresh basil or
    1 tsp. dried basil, crushed**
½ **cup crumbled blue cheese or
    feta cheese (2 oz.)**

◆◆◆

8 **7- to 8-inch flour tortillas**
2 **Tbsp. milk**
2 **tsp. toasted sesame seed**

1 Snap off and discard the woody bases from asparagus spears; cut the spears into 2-inch pieces. Steam the asparagus and the carrots over gently boiling water for 4 to 6 minutes or till the vegetables are crisp-tender; drain.

2 In a medium mixing bowl beat together cream cheese, egg, and basil till smooth. Stir in crumbled cheese. Arrange asparagus and carrots in the center of a tortilla. Spoon 2 rounded tablespoons of cheese mixture on top of vegetables. Fold the bottom half of the tortilla up and over the filling; fold the left and right edges to the center. Fold the top half over the filling envelope-style.

3 Place the bundle, seam side down, on an ungreased baking sheet. Repeat the procedure with each of the remaining tortillas and the remaining filling. Brush each of the packets with milk; sprinkle them with sesame seed. Bake in a 425° oven for 10 to 12 minutes or till golden brown and heated through. Makes 8 bundles.

Nutrition facts per bundle: 245 cal., 16 g total fat (9 g sat. fat), 65 mg chol., 344 mg sodium, 18 g carbo., 1 g fiber, 8 g pro. *Daily values:* 57% vit. A, 7% vit. C, 10% calcium, 11% iron.

MEDITERRANEAN BISCUITS

Prep: 25 min. ◆ Bake: 10 min.

This recipe earned Valerie Donaldson of Rohnert, California, $200 in the magazine's monthly contest.

 2 **cups all-purpose flour**
 1 **Tbsp. baking powder**
 1 **Tbsp. sugar**
 1 **tsp. dried basil, crushed**
 ¼ **tsp. salt**
 6 **Tbsp. butter or margarine**
 ¾ **cup crumbled feta cheese (3 oz.)**
 ¼ **cup pitted and chopped Greek black olives**
 3 **Tbsp. oil-packed dried tomatoes, drained and snipped**
 ¾ **cup half-and-half or light cream**

◆◆◆

 1 **egg yolk**
 1 **Tbsp. half-and-half or light cream**
    Whole Greek black olives (optional)

1 In a medium mixing bowl stir together flour, baking powder, sugar, basil, and salt. Using a pastry blender, cut in butter or margarine till mixture resembles coarse crumbs. Stir in feta cheese, chopped olives, and tomatoes. Make a well in center of dry mixture. Add the ¾ cup half-and-half or light cream all at once. Using a fork, stir just till moistened.

2 Turn dough out onto a lightly floured surface. Quickly knead dough by gently folding and pressing dough 10 to 12 strokes or till nearly smooth. Lightly roll out dough to a 10×8-inch rectangle, about ½ inch thick. Cut into 2-inch squares. Place biscuits 1 inch apart on an ungreased baking sheet.

3 Combine egg yolk and 1 tablespoon half-and-half or light cream. Brush tops of biscuits with egg yolk mixture. Bake in a 450° oven 10 to 12 minutes or till golden. Remove from baking sheet. If desired, serve warm with whole olives. Makes 20 biscuits.

Nutrition facts per biscuit: 120 cal., 7 g total fat (4 g sat. fat), 32 mg chol., 237 mg sodium, 11 g carbo., 0 g fiber, 3 g pro. *Daily values:* 7% vit. A, 1% vit. C, 9% calcium, 4% iron.

SPICY SOUTHWESTERN SCONES

Prep: 25 min. ◆ Bake: 20 min.

See the photograph on page 84.

 1½ **cups all-purpose flour**
 ¼ **cup yellow cornmeal**
 2 **tsp. baking powder**
 1 **tsp. chili powder**
 ¼ **tsp. garlic salt**
 ⅓ **cup margarine or butter**
 1 **egg**
 ¼ **cup shredded cheddar cheese (1 oz.)**
 ¼ **cup half-and-half, light cream, or milk**
 ¼ **cup sliced green onions**
 ¼ **cup chunky salsa**
 2 **Tbsp. finely chopped, seeded fresh jalapeño pepper**

1 Lightly grease a large baking sheet; set aside. In a large mixing bowl stir together the flour, cornmeal, baking powder, chili powder, and garlic salt. With pastry blender, cut in margarine or butter till mixture resembles coarse crumbs. In a small bowl combine egg, cheese, half-and-half, green onions, salsa and jalapeño. Add to dry mixture. With a fork, stir till moistened.

2 Turn out onto a lightly floured surface. Quickly knead dough by gently folding and pressing dough 10 to 12 strokes. Pat dough into an 8-inch circle on prepared baking sheet. Cut circle into eight wedges. Separate wedges slightly. Bake in a 400° oven 20 minutes or till golden. Remove from baking sheet; serve warm. Makes 8 scones.

Nutrition facts per scone: 200 cal., 11 g total fat (6 g sat. fat), 54 mg chol., 297 mg sodium, 22 g carbo., 1 g fiber, 5 g pro. *Daily values:* 13% vit. A, 14% vit. C, 10% calcium, 10% iron.

THE CLEVER COOK

SPICE LIST AT A GLANCE

Make a list on a recipe card of all the spices you have in your pantry. Store this list in the front of your recipe box. When you pull out a recipe, just glance at the spice card to determine if you have all the spices you need. You won't have to fumble through your spice racks to be sure you have the right spices on hand.

Lynda Tart
Durham, North Carolina

IRISH SODA SCONES

Prep: 15 min. ◆ Bake: 20 min.

1¼ cups whole wheat flour
¾ cup all-purpose flour
⅓ cup quick-cooking rolled oats
3 Tbsp. brown sugar
¼ tsp. baking soda
¼ cup butter or margarine
½ cup chopped raisins or pitted dates
1 cup buttermilk

◆◆◆

1 Tbsp. buttermilk or milk
2 Tbsp. brown sugar

1 Lightly grease a baking sheet; set aside. In a mixing bowl combine flours, oats, 3 table-spoons brown sugar, soda, and ¼ teaspoon *salt.* Using a pastry blender, cut in butter till mixture resembles coarse crumbs. Stir in raisins. Add the 1 cup buttermilk; stir just till moistened.

2 Turn dough out onto a lightly floured surface. Quickly knead 10 to 12 strokes or till nearly smooth. On the prepared baking sheet, pat dough into a 7-inch circle, 1 inch thick. Cut into 8 wedges; separate wedges slightly. Brush with 1 tablespoon buttermilk and sprinkle with the 2 tablespoons brown sugar. Bake in a 400° oven about 20 minutes or till edges are golden. Remove from baking sheet; cool slightly. Makes 8 scones.

Nutrition facts per scone: 232 cal., 7 g total fat (4 g sat. fat), 17 mg chol., 203 mg sodium, 40 g carbo., 3 g fiber, 6 g pro. *Daily values:* 5% vit. A, 1% vit. C, 4% calcium, 11% iron.

ZESTY LEMON SCONES

Prep: 20 min. ◆ Bake: 12 min.

1¾ cups all-purpose flour
⅓ cup granulated sugar
2 tsp. baking powder
½ tsp. finely shredded lemon peel
¼ tsp. salt
⅛ tsp. baking soda
⅓ cup butter or margarine
3 Tbsp. half-and-half or light cream
2 Tbsp. lemon juice
1 egg
1 egg yolk

◆◆◆

1 egg white
1 Tbsp. water
2 tsp. coarse sugar or granulated sugar
¾ cup lemon curd (optional)

1 In a large mixing bowl com-bine flour, the ⅓ cup granulated sugar, baking powder, lemon peel, salt, and baking soda. Using a pas-try blender, cut in butter or mar-garine till mixture resembles coarse crumbs. In a small bowl combine half-and-half, lemon juice, whole egg, and egg yolk (mixture may appear curdled); add to dry mixture. Using a fork, stir just till moistened.

2 Turn dough out onto a lightly floured surface. Quickly knead 10 to 12 strokes or till dough is nearly smooth. Pat dough to ½-inch thickness. Cut with a 2-inch round biscuit cutter. Place 2 inches apart on an ungreased baking sheet. Brush tops with mixture of egg white and water; sprinkle tops with coarse sugar. Bake in a 400° oven for 12 to 15 minutes or till gold-en. Remove from baking sheet; cool slightly. If desired, split scones and spread bottom halves with lemon curd; replace tops. Makes 10 to 12 servings.

Nutrition facts per scone: 178 cal., 8 g total fat (4 g sat. fat), 61 mg chol., 218 mg sodium, 24 g carbo., 1 g fiber, 4 g pro. *Daily values:* 10% vit. A, 2% vit. C, 6% calcium, 7% iron.

PUMPKIN PRALINE BRUNCH BISCUITS

Prep: 20 min. ◆ Bake: 12 min.

2½ cups all-purpose flour
2 tsp. baking powder
1 tsp. pumpkin pie spice
¼ tsp. baking soda
½ cup butter or margarine
½ cup chopped, toasted pecans

◆◆◆

¾ cup canned pumpkin
⅔ cup milk
⅓ cup packed brown sugar
1 Tbsp. butter or margarine
⅓ cup packed brown sugar

3 Tbsp. half-and-half or light
   cream
¼ tsp. pumpkin pie spice
⅔ cup sifted powdered sugar
¼ cup finely chopped, toasted
   pecans

1 Grease a baking sheet; set aside. In a large mixing bowl combine flour, baking powder, the 1 teaspoon pumpkin pie spice, soda, and ⅛ teaspoon *salt*. Using a pastry blender, cut in the ½ cup butter or margarine till mixture resembles coarse crumbs. Stir in the ½ cup pecans. Make a well in the center of the dry mixture.

2 In another bowl combine canned pumpkin, milk, and ⅓ cup brown sugar; add all at once to dry mixture. Using a fork, stir just till moistened. Drop dough onto prepared baking sheet, forming 16 mounds. Bake in a 400° oven for 12 to 15 minutes or till golden. Remove from baking sheet.

3 In a small saucepan melt 1 tablespoon butter or margarine over medium heat. Stir in ⅓ cup brown sugar, half-and-half, and ¼ teaspoon pumpkin pie spice. Bring mixture just to boiling; reduce heat and boil gently for 2 minutes. Remove from heat; stir in powdered sugar. Beat till smooth. If necessary, let stand a few minutes to thicken slightly. Drizzle over warm biscuits. Sprinkle with finely chopped pecans. Serve warm. Makes 16.

Nutrition facts per biscuit: 213 cal., 11 g total fat (5 g sat. fat), 19 mg chol., 157 mg sodium, 28 g carbo., 1 g fiber, 3 g pro. *Daily values:* 32% vit. A, 1% vit. C, 6% calcium, 9% iron.

PRIZE TESTED RECIPE WINNER

DOUBLE CHOCOLATE SCONES

Prep: 20 min. ♦ Bake: 18 min.

This recipe earned Honee Aylmer of Lemoore, California, $400 in the magazine's monthly contest.

2 cups all-purpose flour
⅓ cup unsweetened cocoa
   powder
⅓ cup packed brown sugar
2 tsp. baking powder
¾ tsp. baking soda
⅛ tsp. salt
½ cup butter or margarine
♦♦♦
1 beaten egg yolk
1 8-oz. carton plain yogurt
½ cup miniature semisweet
   chocolate pieces
♦♦♦
1 recipe Powdered Sugar Glaze
   (see right)
Powdered sugar (optional)

1 In a large bowl stir together flour, cocoa powder, brown sugar, baking powder, baking soda, and salt. Using a pastry blender, cut in butter or margarine till mixture resembles coarse crumbs. Make a well in the center of dry mixture. In another bowl combine egg yolk and yogurt; add to dry mixture. Add chocolate pieces. Using a fork, stir just till moistened.

2 Turn dough out onto a lightly floured surface. Quickly knead dough 10 to 12 strokes or till dough is nearly smooth. Roll or pat dough into a 9-inch circle; cut into 10 wedges. Place the wedges 1 inch apart on an ungreased baking sheet.

STORING BISCUITS AND SCONES

Tender flaky biscuits and scones, warm from the oven, make a terrific addition to breakfast, brunch, lunch, or dinner.

So you're not hurried with last-minute baking hassles, you can make biscuits and scones ahead and have them waiting in your freezer.

Place the cool, unglazed baked biscuits or scones in a freezer container or bag and freeze for up to 3 months. Just before serving, wrap the frozen biscuits or scones in foil and bake in a 300° oven for 20 to 25 minutes or till warm. Glaze or sprinkle with sugar, as desired.

3 Bake in a 375° oven about 18 minutes or till bottoms are lightly browned. Remove from baking sheet; cool slightly. Drizzle with Powdered Sugar Glaze. If desired, dust tops of glazed scones with powdered sugar. Serve warm. Makes 10 scones.

Powdered Sugar Glaze: In a small mixing bowl stir together ½ cup sifted *powdered sugar*, 1 tablespoon melted *butter or margarine*, 1 teaspoon *milk*, and 1 teaspoon *vanilla*. Add more milk, ¼ teaspoon at a time, till glaze is of a drizzling consistency.

Nutrition facts per scone: 289 cal., 14 g total fat (7 g sat. fat), 50 mg chol., 317 mg sodium, 37 g carbo., 1 g fiber, 5 g pro. *Daily values:* 13% vit. A, 13% calcium, 13% iron.

CHOCOLATE-ALMOND SCONES

Prep: 20 min. ◆ Bake: 15 min.

For the bake shop look, add a drizzle of chocolate and a sprinkle of powdered sugar just before serving.

- 2 cups all-purpose flour
- ¼ cup sugar
- 1 Tbsp. baking powder
- ¼ tsp. ground cinnamon (optional)
- 6 Tbsp. butter or margarine
- ¼ cup finely chopped almonds
- 1 beaten egg
- ½ cup buttermilk
- 1 tsp. vanilla
- 1 oz. semisweet chocolate, melted and cooled

◆◆◆

- 1 Tbsp. buttermilk
- ¼ cup sliced almonds

1 In a large mixing bowl combine the flour, sugar, baking powder, and, if desired, cinnamon. Using a pastry blender, cut in butter or margarine till mixture resembles coarse crumbs. Stir in chopped nuts. In another bowl combine the egg, ½ cup buttermilk, and vanilla; add to dry mixture. Add melted chocolate. Stir just till moistened.

2 Turn dough onto a floured surface. Quickly knead dough 12 to 15 strokes or till nearly smooth. Pat into an 8-inch circle. Using a sharp knife, cut into 8 wedges. Place wedges on an ungreased baking sheet. Brush with 1 tablespoon buttermilk; sprinkle with sliced almonds. Bake in a 400° oven for 15 to 18 minutes or till bottoms are lightly browned. Remove scones from baking sheet; cool slightly. Makes 8 scones.

Nutrition facts per scone: 282 cal., 14 g total fat (7 g sat. fat), 50 mg chol., 250 mg sodium, 33 g carbo., 2 g fiber, 6 g pro. *Daily values:* 9% vit. A, 15% calcium, 14% iron.

LEMON MERINGUE PIE

Prep: 45 min. ◆ Bake: 15 min.
Cool: 1 hr. ◆ Chill: 3 to 6 hr.

Bakers sometimes notice their meringue "weeps" after baking (liquid forms where the meringue and the pie filling meet). The key is to spread the meringue over the filling while the filling is still hot.

- 1 9-inch Baked Pastry Crust (see recipe, right)
- 1½ cups sugar
- 3 Tbsp. cornstarch
- 3 Tbsp. all-purpose flour
- 1½ cups water
- 3 slightly beaten egg yolks
- 2 Tbsp. butter, cut up
- ½ to 2 tsp. finely shredded lemon peel
- ⅓ cup lemon juice

◆◆◆

- 3 egg whites
- 1 tsp. lemon juice
- 6 Tbsp. sugar

1 Prepare Baked Pastry Crust. In a medium saucepan stir together the 1½ cups sugar, the cornstarch, and flour; gradually stir in water. Bring to boiling, stirring constantly. Reduce heat; cook and stir over medium heat for 2 minutes. Remove from heat. Gradually stir about *1 cup* of the hot mixture into beaten egg yolks; pour yolk mixture into remaining hot mixture in saucepan. Bring to a gentle boil; cook for 2 minutes more, stirring constantly. Remove from heat; stir in butter and shredded lemon peel. Slowly stir in the ⅓ cup lemon juice. Keep filling warm while preparing the lemon meringue.

2 For meringue, in a large mixing bowl beat egg whites and 1 teaspoon lemon juice with an electric mixer on medium speed about 1 minute or till soft peaks form. Gradually add 6 tablespoons sugar, beating on high speed about 4 minutes or till stiff peaks form and sugar dissolves. Pour warm filling into cooled crust. Immediately spread meringue over filling, carefully sealing to edge of crust to prevent shrinkage. Bake in a 350° oven for 15 minutes. Cool on wire rack 1 hour. Chill 3 to 6 hours before serving. Makes 8 servings.

Baked Pastry Crust: In a medium mixing bowl stir together 1¼ cups *all-purpose flour* and ¼ teaspoon *salt*. Using a pastry blender, cut in ⅓ cup *shortening* till pieces are pea-size. Using 4 to 5 tablespoons *cold water*, sprinkle 1 tablespoon at a time over flour-shortening mixture till all the dough is moistened. Form dough into a ball.

On a lightly floured surface, roll dough to a 12-inch circle. Ease pastry into 9-inch pie plate, being careful not to stretch pastry. Trim and flute edge. Prick bottom and sides well with fork. Line pastry with double thickness of foil. Bake in a 450° oven 8 minutes. Remove foil; bake 5 to 6 minutes more or till golden. Cool.

Nutrition facts per serving: 395 cal., 14 g total fat (5 g sat. fat), 88 mg chol., 139 mg sodium, 65 g carbo., 1 g fiber, 5 g pro.

M AY
Sneak Previews

30-minute recipes indicated in RED.
Low-fat and no-fat recipes indicated
with a ♥.
Photographs indicated in italics.

*I*n spirit, summer arrives with weekends in May. These busy Saturdays and Sundays are appetizers, tastes of all the fun we'll pack into the months ahead.

Menus emphasize freshness, and salads reestablish themselves as meals. The prospect of swimwear drives a frantic search for new low-fat foods, especially quick-fix dinners such as Turkey and Pasta Salad or Orange-and-Basil-Glazed Shrimp.

After months of sipping hot tea and coffee, beverages take a cool place in our menu planning with tasty mugs of Ginger Tropical Punch, Cranberry-Orange Punch, and an old soda-fountain favorite, Kahlúa and Coffee Sodas.

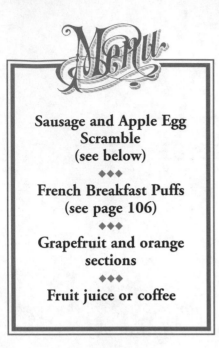

Menu

Sausage and Apple Egg Scramble
(see below)

◆◆◆

French Breakfast Puffs
(see page 106)

◆◆◆

Grapefruit and orange sections

◆◆◆

Fruit juice or coffee

SAUSAGE AND APPLE EGG SCRAMBLE

Start to finish: 30 min.

Choose either apple or potato to stir into this tasty morning starter.

4   oz. ground turkey sausage
½   cup chopped onion
1   cup chopped apple, such as Red Delicious or Granny Smith, or 1 medium potato, chopped

◆◆◆

6   eggs
2   Tbsp. milk
¼   tsp. salt
¼   tsp. dry mustard
    Dash pepper
    Snipped fresh parsley

1 In a large skillet cook the sausage over medium-high heat till no longer pink, stirring occasionally. Remove from skillet. Drain; reserve *1 tablespoon* of pan drippings (add *cooking oil* if necessary). In reserved drippings cook onion about 4 minutes or till tender, stirring occasionally. Add the potato, if using. Cook and stir over medium-high heat for 4 to 5 minutes or till the potato is tender, stirring constantly. Stir in the cooked sausage.

2 Meanwhile, in a medium mixing bowl beat together the eggs, milk, salt, dry mustard, and pepper. Pour over sausage mixture. Cook over medium heat, without stirring, till mixture begins to set on bottom and around edge.

3 Using a spatula or large spoon, lift and fold the partially cooked egg mixture so the uncooked portion flows underneath. Continue cooking over medium heat about 4 minutes or till eggs are cooked through, but are still glossy and moist. Stir in apple, if using. Sprinkle with snipped parsley. Serve immediately. Makes 4 servings.

Nutrition facts per serving: 214 cal., 11 g total fat (4 g sat. fat), 331 mg chol., 452 mg sodium, 11 g carbo., 1 g fiber, 7 g pro. *Daily values:* 15% vit. A, 12% iron.

HAM AND SWISS SKILLET

Start to finish: 30 min.

You'll need to make this recipe in an ovenproof skillet to melt the cheese under the broiler.

1   cup sliced fresh mushrooms
2   Tbsp. sliced green onion (1)
1   Tbsp. margarine or butter
¾   cup finely chopped zucchini
¾   cup finely chopped fully cooked ham

◆◆◆

6   eggs
¼   tsp. dried thyme, crushed
¼   tsp. caraway seed
    Dash salt
    Dash pepper
½   cup shredded Swiss cheese (2 oz.)
    Snipped fresh chives

1 In a 10-inch nonstick or well-seasoned ovenproof skillet, cook the mushrooms and green onion in margarine or butter over medium-high heat about 5 minutes or till tender. Add zucchini; cover and cook over medium-low heat 2 to 3 minutes, stirring occasionally. Stir in ham.

2 In a medium mixing bowl beat eggs till blended but not foamy. Stir in thyme, caraway seed, salt, and pepper. Pour egg mixture over vegetables. Cook over medium heat, without stirring, till mixture begins to set on the bottom and around the edge.

3 Using a spatula or large spoon, lift and fold the partially cooked egg mixture so the uncooked portion flows underneath. Continue cooking and lifting edge till mixture is almost set. Sprinkle with Swiss cheese. Broil 5 inches from heat for 1 to 2 minutes or till eggs are just set and cheese is melted. Sprinkle with chives. To serve, cut into wedges; serve from skillet. Makes 4 to 6 servings.

Nutrition facts per serving: 241 cal., 16 g total fat (6 g sat. fat), 347 mg chol., 547 mg sodium, 3 g carbo., 1 g fiber, 21 g pro. *Daily values:* 22% vit. A, 15% calcium.

HAM AND POTATO SKILLET

Prep: 40 min. ◆ Bake: 30 min.

Here are all the breakfast favorites—hash browns, eggs, sausage, and cheese—in one pan.

3 cups frozen loose-pack hash brown potatoes with onion and peppers

◆◆◆

¼ cup chopped onion
1 cup chopped red apple, such as Jonathan
2 Tbsp. water
1 tsp. dried sage, crushed
1 cup diced fully cooked ham

◆◆◆

1½ cups skim milk
1 cup frozen egg product, thawed, or 4 beaten eggs
½ cup shredded reduced-fat cheddar cheese (2 oz.)
¼ tsp. salt
Fresh sage (optional)

1 Thaw potatoes for 30 minutes. Press between paper towels to remove moisture; set aside.

2 In a 10-inch ovenproof skillet cook the onion, apple, water, and sage over medium heat about 5 minutes or till the onion is tender. Remove from heat. Stir in hash brown potatoes and ham.

3 In a medium mixing bowl combine the milk, egg product or eggs, the cheddar cheese, and salt. Pour egg mixture into skillet. *Do not stir.*

4 Bake, uncovered, in a 350° oven for 30 to 35 minutes or till the center appears just set. If desired, garnish with fresh sage. Makes 6 servings.

Nutrition facts per serving: 254 cal., 12 g total fat (4 g sat. fat), 21 mg chol., 561 mg sodium, 21 g carbo., 2 g fiber, 16 g pro. *Daily values:* 10% vit. A, 16% vit. C, 15% calcium, 12% iron.

---

30 MIN. LOW FAT

SAUSAGE AND EGG PANCAKES

Prep: 15 min. ◆ Bake: 11 min.

Forget the phrase "flat as a pancake." This puffs while baking.

¼ cup light dairy sour cream
¼ tsp. lemon-pepper seasoning
⅛ tsp. ground cumin

◆◆◆

4 oz. ground turkey sausage

◆◆◆

½ cup frozen egg product, thawed, or 2 beaten eggs
½ cup skim milk
½ cup all-purpose flour
¼ tsp. dried oregano, crushed
⅛ tsp. salt
Dash pepper
Nonstick spray coating
2 Tbsp. thinly sliced green onion (1)
¼ cup shredded reduced-fat cheddar cheese (1 oz.)
Chopped tomato (optional)
Sliced green onion (optional)

1 In a small mixing bowl stir together the sour cream, lemon-pepper seasoning, and cumin. Cover and chill till serving time.

2 In a medium skillet cook sausage till brown; drain off fat.

3 Combine egg product or eggs, milk, flour, oregano, salt, and pepper; beat till smooth. Spray four 4½-inch tart pans with nonstick coating. Add the batter, sausage, and the 2 tablespoons green onion.

4 Bake, uncovered, in a 425° oven for 10 to 13 minutes or till puffed and light brown. Top with cheese. Return to oven about 1 minute or till cheese is melted. Serve immediately. Top each with sour cream mixture. If desired, sprinkle with chopped tomato and additional green onion. Makes 4 main-dish servings.

Nutrition facts per serving: 218 cal., 9 g total fat (3 g sat. fat), 19 mg chol., 496 mg sodium, 18 g carbo., 1 g fiber, 15 g pro. *Daily values:* 11% vit. A, 13% vit. C, 11% calcium, 13% iron.

FRENCH BREAKFAST PUFFS

Prep: 20 min. ◆ Bake: 20 min.

The name for this recipe may sound more uptown than downhome, but many readers claim this prizewinner is one of the most delicious muffins they've ever tasted.

1½ **cups all-purpose flour**
½ **cup sugar**
1½ **tsp. baking powder**
¼ **tsp. ground nutmeg**
⅛ **tsp. salt**
◆◆◆
1 **egg**
½ **cup milk**
⅓ **cup butter or margarine, melted**
◆◆◆
¼ **cup sugar**
½ **tsp. ground cinnamon**
¼ **cup butter or margarine, melted**

1 Lightly grease twelve 2½-inch muffin cups; set aside. In a large mixing bowl combine flour, the ½ cup sugar, baking powder, nutmeg, and salt. Make a well in the center of the dry ingredients.

2 In another bowl beat egg slightly; stir in milk and ⅓ cup melted butter or margarine. Add egg mixture to flour mixture. Stir just till moistened (the batter may be lumpy).

3 Fill prepared muffin cups about two-thirds full with batter. Bake in a 350° oven for 20 to 25 minutes or till golden.

4 Meanwhile, in a shallow bowl combine the ¼ cup sugar and cinnamon. Immediately dip tops of hot muffins into the ¼ cup melted butter or margarine, then into the cinnamon-sugar mixture till coated. Serve warm. Makes 12 muffins.

Nutrition facts per muffin: 191 cal., 10 g total fat (6 g sat. fat), 42 mg chol., 169 mg sodium, 24 g carbo., 0 g fiber, 2 g pro. *Daily values:* 9% vit. A, 5% calcium, 5% iron.

SPRING-GREEN ASPARAGUS SOUP

Prep: 25 min. ◆ Cook: 25 min.

Pick spears that are crisp, straight, and firm with tightly closed buds. Fresh asparagus spears can be refrigerated for up to four days. Just wrap them in wet paper towels and seal them in a plastic bag. When ready to use the asparagus, snap off stem ends and rinse clean.

3 **cups water**
1 **Tbsp. instant chicken bouillon granules**
2 **large stalks fresh lemongrass, cut into 2-inch pieces, or 2 tsp. finely shredded lemon peel**
2 **Tbsp. snipped fresh cilantro**
¼ **tsp. ground white pepper**
◆◆◆
1 **lb. fresh asparagus, trimmed and cut into 2-inch pieces**
◆◆◆
1 **12-oz. can (1½ cups) evaporated skim milk**
2 **Tbsp. cornstarch**
◆◆◆
Dairy sour cream (optional)

1 In a medium saucepan stir together water, bouillon granules, fresh lemongrass or lemon peel,

SWEET HOMINY

They're not just for grits anymore, those treated dried kernels of white or yellow corn. Now, hominy's mild flavor lends a gentle antebellum accent to salads, soups, and stews. Dried hominy is prepared the same way as dried beans—best if soaked before boiling. Hominy is more commonly available canned, and you'll find it next to the canned beans in your supermarket. Yellow hominy has a roasted corn taste. White hominy has a more subtle flavor. The cool side-dish salad on page 107 combines the simple, south-of-the-Mason-Dixon tastes of hominy, beans, and cabbage, spiked with hot pepper.

fresh cilantro, and white pepper. Bring to boiling; reduce heat to low. Simmer, covered, for 15 minutes. Strain the liquid, discarding the solids; return the liquid to the saucepan.

2 Return liquid to boiling. Set aside a few of the asparagus tips for garnish. Add the remaining asparagus to saucepan. Reduce heat to low. Simmer, uncovered, for 8 to 10 minutes or till asparagus is tender. Remove from heat; cool slightly.

3 Carefully transfer the asparagus-broth mixture to a blender container. Cover and blend till smooth; set aside.

4 In the same saucepan gradually stir the evaporated milk into the cornstarch. Cook and stir over medium heat till thickened and bubbly. Cook and stir for 2 minutes more. (The mixture may be slightly foamy.) Gradually add the asparagus mixture, stirring constantly. Heat through.

5 To serve, ladle the asparagus soup into soup bowls. If desired, swirl a little dairy sour cream into each serving and top with the reserved asparagus tips. Makes 6 side-dish servings.

Nutrition facts per serving: 131 cal., 4 g total fat (1 g sat. fat), 3 mg chol., 581 mg sodium, 15 g carbo., 1 g fiber, 8 g pro. *Daily values:* 18% vit. A, 21% vit. C, 21% calcium, 5% iron.

HOMINY HOEDOWN SALAD

Prep: 20 min. ◆ **Chill: 2 to 24 hr.**

No longer restricted to Southern breakfasts, hominy shows off in this side dish.

1 15-oz. can hominy, rinsed and drained
1 15-oz. can black beans, rinsed and drained
1 cup shredded red cabbage
1 cup reduced-calorie Italian salad dressing
1 fresh serrano pepper or jalapeño pepper

◆◆◆

⅓ cup roasted red sweet peppers, thinly sliced

1 In separate small mixing bowls place the hominy, black beans, and cabbage with ⅓ *cup* of the Italian dressing for each. Toss

each mixture gently to coat; cover and refrigerate till thoroughly chilled. Remove stem and seeds from serrano or jalapeño pepper and cut into thin strips.*

2 Arrange hominy, beans, and cabbage in three strips on salad plates. Garnish with roasted sweet peppers, and arrange serrano or jalapeño strips on top. Makes 4 to 6 side-dish servings.

*****Note:** Because hot peppers contain oils that can burn eyes, lips, and skin, protect yourself when working with the peppers by wearing plastic gloves or by covering one or both of your hands with plastic bags. Be sure to wash your hands thoroughly in hot, soapy water after handling hot peppers.

Nutrition facts per serving: 192 cal., 7 g total fat (1 g sat. fat), 4 mg chol., 884 mg sodium, 30 g carbo., 6 g fiber, 8 g pro. *Daily values:* 13% vit. A, 78% vit. C, 4% calcium, 11% iron.

ORIENTAL CABBAGE SLAW

Prep: 25 min. ◆ **Chill: 4 to 24 hr.**

Chinese cabbage (also called napa cabbage) is a long, pale yellow-green cabbage with a tightly packed head. The leaves are crisp and wrinkly, and the flavor is mild and faintly sweet.

1 medium cucumber, halved lengthwise and thinly sliced
1 cup fresh pea pods, halved

◆◆◆

¼ cup rice vinegar

THE CLEVER COOK

KEEP COLESLAW CRISP

To keep coleslaw from becoming soupy, stir in a little dry plain gelatin after adding the dressing. Use 1½ teaspoons for each pint of slaw.

Eloise McDonald
Federal Way, Washington

1 Tbsp. salad oil
2 tsp. toasted sesame oil
½ tsp. sugar
½ tsp. red chili paste (optional)
⅛ tsp. salt

◆◆◆

4 cups shredded Chinese cabbage
½ cup coarsely chopped honey-roasted peanuts

1 In a large mixing bowl combine the cucumber and pea pods. For dressing, in a small mixing bowl stir together the rice vinegar, salad oil, sesame oil, sugar, red chili paste (if desired), and salt. Pour over cucumber and pea pods, stirring to coat. Cover and chill for 4 to 24 hours.

2 Just before serving, stir in the cabbage and peanuts. Makes 8 side-dish servings.

Nutrition facts per serving: 85 cal., 6 g total fat (1 g sat. fat), 0 mg chol., 61 mg sodium, 6 g carbo., 2 g fiber, 3 g pro. *Daily values:* 6% vit. A, 40% vit. C, 3% calcium, 5% iron.

QUICK BREAD SALAD

Start to finish: 20 min.

In Italy, day-old bread is put to good use as a replacement for croutons. The large cubes of sourdough bread hold the dressing as croutons can't. (See the photograph on page 123.)

- ¼ cup olive oil
- 3 Tbsp. red wine vinegar
- 3 Tbsp. snipped fresh oregano
- ½ tsp. sugar
- ¼ tsp. salt
- ¼ tsp. pepper

◆◆◆

- 4 oz. whole wheat sourdough or other country-style bread, cut into 1½-inch cubes
- ½ of a 10-oz. pkg. purchased torn Italian-style mixed salad greens (about 5 cups)
- 1 medium tomato, cut into thin wedges
- ¼ cup halved yellow cherry tomatoes or yellow sweet pepper, cut into ½-inch squares
- ½ cup Greek black olives or other olives

1 In a screw-top jar combine the olive oil, wine vinegar, oregano, sugar, salt, and pepper. Cover tightly and shake well.

2 In a large salad bowl combine bread cubes, mixed greens, tomato wedges, yellow cherry tomatoes or sweet pepper, and olives. Add dressing, tossing to mix. Makes 6 side-dish servings.

Nutrition facts per serving: 151 cal., 11 g total fat (1 g sat. fat), 0 mg chol., 238 mg sodium, 13 g carbo., 1 g fiber, 2 g pro. *Daily values:* 7% vit. A, 15% vit. C, 3% calcium, 7% iron.

"TEXAS CAVIAR" SALAD

Prep: 20 min. ◆ Chill: up to 24 hr.

If you want this Southwestern salad to pack more punch, use extra jalapeños. Serve with baked tortilla chips for some crunch in your lunch.

- 1 Tbsp. cooking oil
- 2 small yellow summer squash, thinly sliced (about 1½ cups)
- 1 to 2 fresh jalapeño peppers, seeded and chopped (about 2 Tbsp.)*
- 2 cloves garlic, minced
- ½ tsp. cumin seed, crushed

◆◆◆

- 1 15-oz. can black-eyed peas, rinsed and drained
- 1 green onion, sliced (2 Tbsp.)
- 1 tsp. snipped fresh cilantro
- ¼ tsp. salt
- 2 medium tomatoes, cut into thin wedges

1 In a medium skillet heat the cooking oil. Add the yellow squash, jalapeño peppers, garlic, and cumin seed. Cook, uncovered, about 8 minutes or till squash is tender, stirring occasionally. Remove from heat; let cool.

2 In a large bowl stir together the squash mixture, black-eyed peas, green onion, cilantro, and salt. Cover and chill for up to 24 hours.

3 Before serving, add the tomato wedges to the chilled mixture, tossing to coat. Makes 4 side-dish servings.

*****Note:** Because hot peppers contain oils that can burn eyes, lips, and skin, protect yourself

---

HYDROPONIC TOMATOES

When shopping for tomatoes, you've probably noticed the red, luscious-looking tomatoes in your grocery store labeled "hydroponic." This means they were grown in a greenhouse in a nutrient solution instead of soil. What can you expect from these greenhouse gems?

Better flavor: Vine-ripening develops more flavor. Hydroponics are vine-ripened, then shipped to nearby markets. Most other tomatoes are picked green for long-distance shipping, then ripened with gas.

Fewer pesticides: By growing hydroponic produce indoors, the growers can successfully use fewer pesticides, together with nonchemical controls.

Higher price: The cost of intensive labor and greenhouses with controlled environments increases the price.

---

when working with the peppers by wearing plastic gloves or by covering one or both of your hands with plastic bags. Be sure to wash your hands thoroughly in hot, soapy water after handling hot peppers.

Nutrition facts per serving: 163 cal., 5 g total fat (1 g sat. fat), 0 mg chol., 447 mg sodium, 24 g carbo., 7 g fiber, 7 g pro. *Daily values:* 6% vit. A, 44% vit. C, 4% calcium, 6% iron.

SALAD GREENS

SORREL (SOR-UHL)
Similar to spinach, sorrel has smaller and narrower leaves that are lighter green in color. It is often cooked in soups, but when used raw in salads, sorrel contributes a fresh flavor that expresses hints of citrus.

RADICCHIO (RUH-DEE-KEE-OH)
Resembling a small red cabbage, this tangy relative of chicory has a slightly bitter, nutlike flavor. Shredding it into salads adds a unique flavor as well as bright color.

CURLY ENDIVE
This is another member of the chicory family. Its filigreed edges and pungent bite add texture and flavor to basic salad. The younger baby endive has leaves that are more tender and less bitter than a mature curly endive.

GREEN LEAF LETTUCE
This popular lettuce has crisp edges and soft leaves, yet subtle flavor. The heart of this variety is sweet and can be cut up and included in salads for extra crunch.

ROMAINE
The lettuce of Caesar salads, romaine is bold and crisp and adds snap to any salad. It can also be "wilted" with heated dressing for warm salads. Hearts of romaine make an excellent side dish when cooked with minced garlic and fresh pepper in a little olive oil.

RED LEAF LETTUCE
The leaves of this head lettuce are much softer than its green leaf cousin and have an almost buttery flavor. Clean this lettuce carefully, though, as it is difficult to spot any brown edges along its deep red-tipped leaves. You'll also need to use this lettuce quickly, as it is not as hardy as some of the other varieties.

WATERCRESS
The best watercress has dark green leaves, sometimes with hints of red or purple. Its flavor is reminiscent of pepper and peaches. Clean watercress carefully, discarding any yellowing leaves. Rinse it well to remove any clinging mud. Refrigerate watercress, loosely covered, upright in a cup with an inch of fresh water on the bottom.

BIBB LETTUCE
Also called Boston, butternut, or butterhead lettuce, Bibb is prized for its soft leaves and sweet taste. An added plus is that there is usually very little waste with this variety.

ARUGULA (UH-ROO-GUH-LUH)
This Mediterranean green has a spicy flavor and is delicious either fresh or steamed. You'll find arugula year-round, although spring and early summer are prime time. Look for slender, dark green leaves. The older and larger leaves have more of a bite.

SIMPLY SUPER SALADS

To toss a great salad, start with crisp, well-chilled greens and a flavorful dressing. Next, stir in simplicity and inspiration—two critical ingredients found in these easy salad ideas.

Berried apples: Prepare an oil-vinegar dressing using raspberry vinegar; chill. In a large bowl toss together torn leaf lettuce, slices of red and green apples, broken toasted walnuts, and enough of the dressing to moisten. Spoon onto plates; top each serving with fresh raspberries.

Best tomatoes: Line salad plates with leaf lettuce or spinach, then arrange slices of ripe tomatoes on top. Stir enough milk into cream cheese with chives to make it the consistency of salad dressing. Drizzle cream cheese over the tomatoes. Sprinkle each plate with snipped fresh chives and coarsely cracked pepper.

Cuke 'n' oranges: In a bowl toss together equal amounts of cucumber slices and mandarin orange sections; add enough bottled cucumber ranch dressing to coat. Serve on lettuce-lined plates; sprinkle each serving with poppy seed.

Red-dotted potato salad: Cook, drain, and chill new potatoes. Slice the potatoes; gently toss with ham strips, chopped red sweet pepper, and bottled ranch salad dressing.

Gingered fruits: Arrange orange slices, halved grapes, and sliced plums on plates. Stir a little grated gingerroot into vanilla yogurt; spoon over fruit.

Tropical taste: Slice an avocado and a ripe papaya; place slices atop spinach-lined plates. Stir a little curry powder into equal parts of mayonnaise and plain yogurt; spoon over each salad. Finish each salad with a few cooked, chilled shrimp.

Springtime salad: Steam and chill asparagus spears and thin carrot strips. Arrange the vegetables on salad plates and sprinkle with a few toasted sliced almonds. Drizzle with bottled green goddess salad dressing.

Flowering endive: Place torn curly endive on salad plates; sprinkle with edible flowers (such as borage petals) and toasted pine nuts. Drizzle with a fruit-flavored vinegar.

Santa Fe flavors: Prepare a vinaigrette dressing, adding a few dashes bottled hot pepper sauce. Toss together mixed greens, kidney beans, sliced avocado, chopped tomato, and toasted pumpkin seed; drizzle with the dressing.

BARLEY AND WILD RICE TOSS

Prep: 1 hr. ◆ Chill: 2 to 24 hr.

To make a more exotic version of this dish, use porcini or other mushrooms.

⅓ **cup pearl barley**
¼ **cup wild rice**
1 **14½-oz. can chicken broth**
♦♦♦
1 **Tbsp. olive oil or salad oil**
8 **oz. fresh small button mushrooms**
1 **small onion, chopped (⅓ cup)**
1 **clove garlic, minced**
1 **green onion, sliced (2 Tbsp.)**
♦♦♦
¼ **cup white wine vinegar**
¼ **cup olive oil or salad oil**
2 **tsp. snipped fresh thyme**
⅛ **tsp. pepper**
6 **cups torn fresh spinach**
Mint blossoms (optional)

1 Rinse barley and wild rice. In a saucepan combine barley and rice with chicken broth. Bring to boiling; reduce heat. Simmer, covered, about 45 minutes or till liquid is absorbed.

2 In a large skillet heat the 1 tablespoon olive oil or salad oil. Add the mushrooms, chopped onion, and garlic; cook about 7 minutes or till mushrooms are cooked through, stirring occasionally. In a large mixing bowl combine barley and rice with the mushroom mixture and green onion. Cover and chill.

3 Just before serving, in a screw-top jar combine the wine vinegar, ¼ cup olive oil or salad oil, thyme, and pepper. Cover tightly and shake well. Add dressing to barley mixture, tossing to coat. Serve barley mixture on spinach-lined plates. If desired, garnish with mint blossoms. Season to taste with *salt* and *pepper*. Makes 6 side-dish servings.

Nutrition facts per serving: 196 cal., 12 g total fat (2 g sat. fat), 0 mg chol., 265 mg sodium, 18 g carbo., 4 g fiber, 6 g pro. *Daily values:* 38% vit. A, 30% vit. C, 5% calcium, 20% iron.

Left: *Risotto with Leeks and Radicchio (page 178)*
Top: *Beef and Mushrooms in Puff Pastry (page 214)*
Above: *Cinnamon Orange Slices (page 185) and
Almond Macaroons (page 188)*

Right: *Pasta and Portobello Mushroom Salad (page 205)*
Below: *Marinated Chicken Breasts with Mozzarella (page 205)*

Menu

Marinated Chicken Breasts with Mozzarella
(see right)

◆◆◆

Salad of Bibb lettuce with dried tomatoes and nuts

◆◆◆

Hard rolls

◆◆◆

Biscotti

TORTELLINI, GREEN AND SIMPLE

Start to finish: 20 min.

1 9-oz. pkg. refrigerated meat- or cheese-filled tortellini
½ cup frozen peas
½ cup broccoli flowerets
¼ cup shredded fontina or Swiss cheese (1 oz.)
1 Tbsp. olive oil
2 tsp. snipped fresh oregano or ½ tsp. dried oregano, crushed
¼ tsp. crushed red pepper

1 Prepare pasta according to package directions, adding peas and broccoli to water with pasta; drain. Add cheese, oil, oregano, and crushed red pepper to the pasta-vegetable mixture; toss to mix. If desired, garnish with *plum tomato wedges* and *oregano sprigs*. Makes 3 main-dish servings.

Nutrition facts per serving: 359 cal., 14 g total fat (4 g sat. fat), 51 mg chol., 410 mg sodium, 43 g carbo., 1 g fiber, 17 g pro. *Daily values:* 10% vit. A, 27% vit. C, 18% calcium, 16% iron.

PASTA AND PORTOBELLO MUSHROOM SALAD

Prep: 25 min. ◆ Chill: 4 hr.

The delicate flavor and soft texture of fresh mozzarella is unmatched, but if it's not available, use smaller cubes of another mild white cheese. (See the photograph on page 204.)

1 16-oz. pkg. frozen herb-seasoned or Italian-style pasta and vegetable mix

◆◆◆

3 Tbsp. olive oil
5 oz. fresh portobello mushrooms, sliced (about 2 cups)
½ tsp. crushed red pepper
8 oz. fresh mozzarella cheese, cubed
3 Tbsp. balsamic vinegar or red wine vinegar

◆◆◆

3 cups fresh torn mixed greens

1 Prepare pasta mix according to package directions; drain. Transfer pasta to a bowl; cover and chill 4 hours.

2 In a large nonstick skillet heat *1 tablespoon* of the oil. Add mushrooms and red pepper; cook and stir for 2 minutes. Add the mushroom mixture to the chilled pasta along with cheese, vinegar, and remaining oil; toss to mix.

3 To serve, divide mixed greens among 4 dinner plates or 6 salad plates. Spoon pasta mixture atop greens. Makes 4 main-dish or 6 side-dish servings.

Nutrition facts per serving: 400 cal., 27 g total fat (11 g sat. fat), 53 mg chol., 663 mg sodium, 24 g carbo., 5 g fiber, 18 g pro. *Daily values:* 44% vit. A, 26% vit. C, 29% calcium, 14% iron.

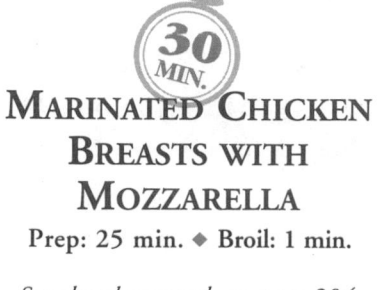

MARINATED CHICKEN BREASTS WITH MOZZARELLA

Prep: 25 min. ◆ Broil: 1 min.

See the photograph on page 204.

1 6-oz. pkg. long-grain and wild rice pilaf mix
¼ cup thinly sliced green onions (2)
1 cup broccoli flowerets

◆◆◆

4 Italian-style or butter-garlic marinated boneless chicken breast halves
2 tsp. olive oil
1 medium tomato, halved and thinly sliced
2 slices part-skim mozzarella cheese, halved (3 oz.)

1 Prepare rice according to package directions, adding green onions the last 5 minutes of cooking. In a saucepan bring ½ cup *water* to boiling; add broccoli. Cook, covered, 3 minutes or till crisp-tender; drain and set aside.

2 In a large cast-iron skillet cook chicken breasts in hot oil over medium heat 8 to 10 minutes or till no longer pink, turning once. Overlap halved tomato slices atop chicken breasts. Spoon cooked broccoli atop tomato slices; cover each with a half-slice of cheese. Broil chicken 3 to 4 inches from heat 1 minute or till cheese is melted and bubbly. Serve atop hot rice. Makes 4 servings.

Nutrition facts per serving: 377 cal., 12 g total fat (4 g sat. fat), 22 mg chol., 1,532 mg sodium, 38 g carbo., 2 g fiber, 31 g pro. *Daily values:* 14% vit. A, 60% vit. C, 16% calcium, 8% iron.

CHICKEN AND VEGETABLE LASAGNA

Prep: 30 min. ◆ Bake: 35 min.

- 10 dried lasagna noodles

  ◆◆◆

- 1 10¾-oz. can condensed cream of chicken soup
- 1 cup low-fat cottage cheese, drained
- ½ cup grated Parmesan or Romano cheese
- ¼ cup water
- 3 Tbsp. finely snipped fresh basil or 2 tsp. dried basil, crushed

  ◆◆◆

- 1½ cups coarsely shredded carrots (3 medium)
- ¾ cup chopped red or green sweet pepper, chopped
- 1 9-oz. pkg frozen artichoke hearts, thawed, drained, and coarsely chopped
- 1 cup sliced fresh mushrooms
- 12 oz. skinless, boneless chicken breast halves, cooked and cut into bite-size strips
- 2 cups shredded mozzarella or provolone cheese (8 oz.)

1 Cook lasagna noodles according to package directions. Drain and rinse with cold water. Drain well; set aside.

2 In a medium mixing bowl stir together the cream of chicken soup, cottage cheese, Parmesan or Romano cheese, water, and basil.

3 To assemble, layer *half* of the noodles in the bottom of a greased 3-quart rectangular baking dish. Sprinkle carrots, sweet pepper, artichoke hearts, mushrooms, and chicken atop noodles.

Menu

Chicken and Vegetable Lasagna (at left)

◆◆◆

Romaine leaves with bottled Caesar dressing

◆◆◆

Italian bread

◆◆◆

Pound cake topped with sweetened ricotta cheese and chocolate pieces

Spoon *half* of the soup mixture over chicken and vegetables. Sprinkle with *half* the shredded mozzarella. Arrange remaining noodles atop cheese. Spoon remaining soup mixture on top of the noodles.

4 Bake, covered, in a 375° oven for 35 to 40 minutes or till heated through. Uncover and sprinkle with remaining cheese. Let stand for 10 minutes before serving. Makes 10 servings.

TO MAKE AHEAD

Prepare lasagna as directed, except do not bake. Cover and chill for up to 24 hours. To serve, bake, covered, in a 350° oven for 50 to 60 minutes or till heated through. Sprinkle with cheese and let lasagna stand for 10 minutes before serving.

Nutrition facts per serving: 279 cal., 9 g total fat (4 g sat. fat), 39 mg chol., 585 mg sodium, 27 g carbo., 2 g fiber, 22 g pro. *Daily values:* 64% vit. A, 26% vit. C, 22% calcium, 13% iron.

FIVE-SPICE CHICKEN

Prep: 15 min. ◆ Bake: 15 min.

The skin of this chicken should have a dark, lacquered look and give off a rich, spicy aroma.

- ⅓ cup bottled hoisin sauce*
- 1 to 1½ tsp. five-spice powder**
  Orange juice
- 1 1½- to 2-lb. purchased warm deli-roasted chicken

  ◆◆◆

- 2 3-oz. pkg. ramen noodles

  ◆◆◆

  Fresh red chili peppers, sliced*** (optional)
  Steamed pea pods (optional)
  Orange slices (optional)

1 In a small bowl stir together the hoisin sauce, five-spice powder, and enough orange juice (1 to 2 tablespoons) to thin mixture for brushing. Brush about *half* of the mixture over entire chicken. Place chicken on a rack in a shallow roasting pan.

2 Bake the warm chicken, uncovered, in a 400° oven for 15 to 18 minutes or till heated through and glazed. Stir *1 to 2 tablespoons* additional orange juice into remaining hoisin mixture till easy to drizzle. Place in a small saucepan; heat through.

3 Remove seasoning packet from ramen noodles; discard or reserve for another use. Cook and drain noodles according to package directions.

4 To serve, carve the chicken. Arrange some of the chicken slices and ramen noodles on each dinner plate. Spoon half of the sauce over the chicken; pass the remaining sauce. If desired, garnish each serving with chili peppers. If desired, serve with pea pods and orange slices. Makes 4 servings.

*Note: Hoisin sauce is a thick, soy-based sweet and spicy sauce that's used in Asian cooking. Look for it in large supermarkets or Asian specialty stores.

**Note: You also can find the five-spice seasoning in Asian specialty stores or most supermarkets. Or, to prepare your own, in a spice grinder or blender combine 3 tablespoons *ground cinnamon,* 6 *star anise* or 2 teaspoons *aniseed,* 1½ teaspoons *fennel seed,* 1½ teaspoons *whole Szechwan peppers or whole black peppers,* and ¾ teaspoon *ground cloves.* Cover and blend spices to a fine powder. Store in a tightly covered container for up to 2 months. Makes about ¼ cup.

***Note: Because chili peppers contain very pungent oils, be sure to protect your hands when preparing them. Put plastic gloves or sandwich bags over your hands so your skin doesn't come in contact with the peppers. Always wash your hands and nails thoroughly in hot, soapy water after handling chili peppers.

Nutrition facts per serving: 317 cal., 16 g total fat (4 g sat. fat), 125 mg chol., 926 mg sodium, 20 g carbo., 1 g fiber, 24 g pro. *Daily values:* 4% vit. A, 6% vit. C, 0% calcium, 7% iron.

HAWAIIAN-STYLE CHICKEN ROLLS

Prep: 45 min. ◆ Bake: 30 min.

To shorten the last-minute preparation of this company-special chicken dish, prepare the stuffing up to a day ahead and chill until ready to use.

- 8 oz. bulk pork sausage
- 1 cup finely chopped onion
- ½ cup finely chopped celery
- ⅓ cup finely chopped red sweet pepper
- 2 tsp. grated gingerroot or ½ tsp. ground ginger
- 3 cups dry bread cubes*
- 1 medium mango or papaya, peeled, seeded, and chopped
- ¾ cup macadamia nuts, chopped
- 1 beaten egg
- 1 Tbsp. milk
- ¼ tsp. ground black pepper
- ⅛ tsp. salt

◆◆◆

- 8 large skinless, boneless chicken breast halves, (about 2 lb. total)
- ¼ cup fine dry bread crumbs
- 1 Tbsp. butter or margarine, melted
- 1 beaten egg
- 1 Tbsp. water

1 In a large skillet cook sausage, onion, celery, sweet pepper, and gingerroot or ginger over medium heat till vegetables are tender and sausage is done; drain. Stir bread cubes, mango or papaya, *½ cup* of the nuts, 1 egg, milk, ground black pepper, and salt into sausage mixture in skillet.

2 Rinse chicken and pat dry with paper towels. Place each breast half between 2 pieces of plastic wrap. Using the flat side of a meat mallet, lightly pound each piece into a rectangle about ¼ inch thick, working from center to edges. Remove plastic wrap.

3 To assemble rolls, spoon sausage stuffing mixture onto the center of each chicken breast. Roll up jelly-roll style, starting at a short side. Secure with wooden toothpicks; set aside.

4 In a blender container or food processor bowl, combine the bread crumbs and the remaining nuts. Cover and blend or process till mixture is fine crumbs. Stir in melted butter or margarine. Combine the 1 egg and water. Dip chicken rolls in egg mixture and then in crumb mixture. Place the rolls, seam side down, in a 3-quart rectangular baking dish. Bake in a 350° oven for about 30 minutes or till chicken is tender and no longer pink. Makes 8 servings.

*Note: For a slightly sweeter stuffing, use sweet Hawaiian bread in place of regular bread when making the bread cubes.

To make the dry bread cubes, cut bread into ½-inch-square pieces. (You'll need 4 to 5 slices for 3 cups of dry cubes.) Spread in a single layer in a baking pan. Bake in a 300° oven for 10 to 15 minutes or till dry, stirring twice; cool. (Bread will continue to dry and crisp as it cools.) Or, let stand, loosely covered, at room temperature for 8 to 12 hours.

Nutrition facts per serving: 381 cal., 20 g total fat (5 g sat. fat), 128 mg chol., 421 mg sodium, 21 g carbo., 3 g fiber, 29 g pro. *Daily values:* 18% vit. A, 27% vit. C, 5% calcium, 14% iron.

CHICKEN ENCHILADAS

Prep: 35 min. ◆ Bake: 33 min.

*Each enchilada contains half the fat
of the traditional version.*

2½ cups cut-up fresh tomatillos
     or one 18-oz. can
     tomatillos undrained
1   4-oz. can whole green chili
     peppers, rinsed and seeded
¼   cup cut-up onion
¼   cup fresh cilantro leaves
½   tsp. sugar
¼   tsp. ground cumin
½   to 1 cup reduced-sodium
     chicken broth
     ◆◆◆
1½ cups finely chopped cooked
     chicken or turkey
1   15¼-oz. can whole kernel
     corn, drained
⅓   cup tub cream cheese
¼   cup fat-free or light dairy
     sour cream
¼   cup sliced green onions (2)
     ◆◆◆
     Nonstick spray coating
8   8-inch flour tortillas
     ◆◆◆
¾   cup shredded reduced-fat
     Monterey Jack cheese
     (3 oz.)

1 For sauce, in a blender container combine fresh or undrained canned tomatillos, peppers, onion, cilantro, sugar, and cumin. Add 1 cup broth for fresh tomatillos or ½ cup broth for canned. Cover; blend till smooth. Transfer to a saucepan. Bring to boiling; reduce heat. Simmer, uncovered, 10 minutes.

2 For filling, in a bowl stir together the chicken or turkey, corn, cream cheese, sour cream, and green onions.

3 Spray a 3-quart rectangular baking dish with nonstick coating. Spray 1 side of a flour tortilla. Place tortilla, sprayed side down, in a large skillet over medium heat for 30 seconds; remove. Spoon about ⅓ *cup* filling onto uncooked side; roll up. Repeat.

4 Arrange tortillas, seam side down, in dish. Pour sauce atop. Bake, covered, in a 350° oven about 30 minutes or till hot. Uncover; add cheese. Bake 3 minutes more or till cheese melts. If desired, top with *salsa, sour cream,* and *cilantro.* Makes 8 servings.

Nutrition facts per enchilada: 258 cal., 11 g total fat (4 g sat. fat), 42 mg chol., 429 mg sodium, 26 g carbo., 1 g fiber, 16 g pro. *Daily values:* 6% vit. A, 21% vit. C, 12% calcium, 11% iron.

RED BANANA CHICKEN

Prep: 40 min. ◆ Cook: 27 min.

Red Jamaican bananas, red Jamaican beer—all you need now is a red sunset over Montego Bay.

2½ to 3 lb. meaty chicken pieces
1   Tbsp. cooking oil
2   large onions, sliced and
     separated into rings
1   12-oz. bottle red beer*
2   Tbsp. brown sugar
¼   to ½ tsp. ground red pepper
¼   tsp. salt
5   medium red bananas or
     unripe Cavendish bananas,
     bias-sliced into ¾-inch-
     thick pieces
1   Tbsp. cornstarch

1 Rinse chicken; pat dry with paper towels. In a 12-inch skillet heat oil; add chicken. Cook, uncovered, over medium heat for 10 minutes. Turn chicken; add

COOKING WITH BANANAS

There are more than 100 kinds of bananas in the world. Cavendish (the standard, yellow banana so familiar to us) and finger bananas are bred for handheld snacking. But some bananas actually taste better when cooked.

Cooking varieties, such as the plantain and churro banana, have a higher starch content and hold up better when subjected to high-heat cooking, such as frying, stir-frying, and stewing. If you are cooking with Cavendish or finger bananas, use them only while they are still fairly green. Cook plantains and other varieties at any stage of ripeness before they turn soft.

Plantains, churros, red bananas, and other hardy varietal bananas last longer than yellow Cavendish bananas and can be kept for up to 10 days or more in the refrigerator once they have begun to ripen.

onions and cook 5 minutes more or till chicken and onions are lightly browned. Drain off fat.

2 Carefully add 1¼ *cups* of the beer, brown sugar, red pepper, and salt to chicken in skillet. Bring to boiling; reduce heat. Simmer, covered, for 15 minutes. Uncover; add bananas and cook for 12 minutes more or till chicken is tender and no longer pink.

3 Using a slotted spoon remove chicken, onions, and bananas to a platter; cover to keep warm. Measure remaining liquid and, if necessary, add *water* to measure 1 cup.

4 Return liquid mixture to skillet. Combine remaining ¼ cup beer and cornstarch; add to skillet. Cook and stir over medium heat till thickened and bubbly; cook for 2 minutes more. If desired, serve chicken and sauce over hot *rice*. Makes 6 servings.

***Note:** Red beer adds a distinctive malty taste and rich color to the sauce, but any beer will work well in this recipe.

Nutrition facts per serving: 390 cal., 14 g total fat (4 g sat. fat), 86 mg chol., 175 mg sodium, 35 g carbo., 3 g fiber, 28 g pro. *Daily values:* 4% vit. A, 18% vit. C, 2% calcium, 11% iron.

STUFFED WHEAT BREAD

Prep: 30 min. ◆ Rise: 30 min.
Bake: 25 min.

Thaw dough and prepare and chill the filling the night before. The next day you'll need only to fill and shape the bread before popping it in the oven.

- 12 oz. ground raw chicken breast or ground raw chicken
- ⅓ cup chopped fresh fennel
- ¼ cup chopped onion
- 1 Tbsp. olive oil or cooking oil
- 1 8-oz. tub cream cheese with chive and onion
- ½ of a 10-oz. pkg. frozen chopped spinach, thawed and drained
- ⅓ cup purchased pesto
- ¼ cup fine dry bread crumbs

- 1 16-oz. loaf frozen whole wheat bread dough, thawed
- 2 tsp. margarine or butter, melted

1 For filling, in a large skillet cook chicken, fennel, and onion in hot oil till chicken is browned and vegetables are tender. Remove from heat; stir in cream cheese, spinach, pesto, and bread crumbs.

2 On a lightly floured surface, roll dough into a 12×9-inch rectangle; transfer to a greased baking sheet. Spread filling lengthwise in a 3-inch-wide strip down center of rectangle to within 1 inch of ends. Along both sides make 3-inch cuts from edges toward center at 1-inch intervals. Moisten end of each cut strip with *water*. Starting on an end, alternately fold opposite strips of dough at an angle across filling, sealing ends in center. Cover; let rise in a warm place till nearly double (about 30 minutes).

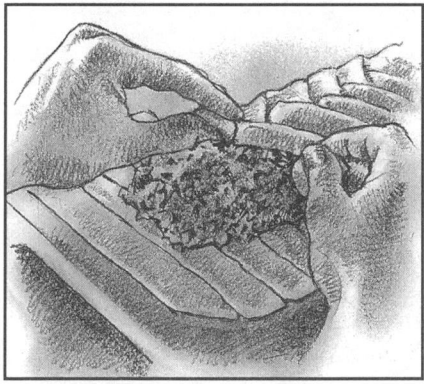

3 Bake in a 350° oven about 25 minutes or till golden brown. Brush top with melted margarine. Cool slightly before cutting. Makes 10 main-dish servings.

Nutrition facts per serving: 325 cal., 18 g total fat (5 g sat. fat), 43 mg chol., 447 mg sodium, 28 g carbo., 3 g fiber, 15 g pro.

KNOW YOUR BANANAS

Although more than 100 varieties of bananas are being produced, few are commonly available on the shelves at the supermarket. This information will help you identify varieties that are growing in popularity:

Plantains: These giants are salmon pink inside and have a flowery aroma and flavor. Plantains—a favorite ingredient in African and Caribbean cuisine—are usually fried or simmered. Use them when the skin is green or yellow going to brown (some varieties of plantain never turn yellow). The riper you let them get, the sweeter they will be. Plantains can be eaten uncooked when the skin has turned black.

Burro Bananas: These square bananas have a lemony flavor and are thick-skinned on the outside, creamy yellow on the inside. Burro bananas are ripe when they have brown patches. They can be eaten even after the skin turns completely brown. Churros are similar but slightly smaller; manzanas are large.

Red Bananas: A newly popular import, these can be eaten raw or cooked, but you should wait till skin is turning dark and flesh is slightly soft if you are not cooking them. Red bananas hail mostly from Jamaica and are orange-pink inside with an aroma reminiscent of honey.

Finger Bananas: These are available in many varieties, in colors from red to gold to bright yellow. Finger bananas have thin skins, and their aroma is strong and sweet. They are ready to eat when skin starts to turn brown.

TURKEY SAUSAGE BRUNCH PIE

Prep: 30 min. ◆ Bake: 42 min.

You can experiment with different types of sausage for a greater variety of flavors. (See the photograph on page 198.)

½ of a 15-oz. pkg. folded refrigerated unbaked piecrust (1 crust)

◆◆◆

2 medium onions, cut into eighths and thinly sliced
⅛ tsp. coarsely ground pepper
1 Tbsp. margarine or butter
1 8-oz. carton refrigerated or frozen egg product, thawed
¾ cup milk
¼ tsp. dried Italian seasoning, crushed
8 oz. cooked, smoked lean turkey sausage, halved lengthwise and thinly sliced
½ cup shredded cheddar cheese (2 oz.)
1 tsp. all-purpose flour

◆◆◆

Assorted cut fresh fruit (optional)

1 Prepare the piecrust in a 9-inch pie plate according to package directions; line with a double thickness of foil. Bake in a 450° oven for 8 minutes. Remove foil. Bake for 4 to 5 minutes more or till edges are golden. Remove from oven. Reduce oven temperature to 325°.

2 Meanwhile, in a large skillet cook onions and ground pepper in margarine or butter till onions

TEST KITCHEN TIP

THE SAUSAGE LINK

If you crave the flavor of sausage but are watching your calorie intake, you can substitute low-fat turkey sausage for pork sausage. One ounce of low-fat turkey sausage typically contains about 57 calories and 4 grams of total fat (1 gram of saturated fat) compared to one ounce of pork sausage, which has about 96 calories and 8 grams of total fat (3 grams of saturated fat).

are tender. Remove from heat; set aside. In a large mixing bowl combine egg product, milk, and Italian seasoning. Stir in the sausage and the onion mixture. Toss together shredded cheese and flour; stir into the egg mixture. Spoon mixture into piecrust.

3 Bake in the 325° oven for 30 to 35 minutes or till a knife inserted near the center comes out clean. If necessary, cover edge of crust with foil to prevent overbrowning. Let pie stand 10 minutes before cutting into 6 wedges. If desired, serve with fresh fruit. Makes 6 servings.

Nutrition facts per serving: 319 cal., 19 g total fat (4 g sat. fat), 59 mg chol., 643 mg sodium, 21 g carbo., 0 g fiber, 16 g pro. *Daily values:* 15% vit. A, 35% vit. C, 13% calcium, 11% iron.

ROASTED TURKEY CALZONES

Prep: 30 min. ◆ Bake: 18 min.

Make a batch of these sandwiches to keep in the freezer for those days when overwhelmed is an understatement.

12 oz. boneless cooked turkey breast, chopped (about 2¼ cups)
2 cups chopped fresh spinach
1 cup shredded 4-cheese pizza cheese (4 oz.)
1 8-oz. can pizza sauce
2 10-oz. pkg. refrigerated pizza dough

◆◆◆

Milk

◆◆◆

Grated Parmesan or Romano cheese (optional)

1 Grease a baking sheet; set aside. In a large mixing bowl combine turkey, spinach, pizza cheese, and ½ *cup* of the pizza sauce. On a lightly floured surface, roll *one package* of pizza dough out to a 12×10-inch rectangle. Cut into three 10×4-inch rectangles.

2 Place about ½ *cup* of the turkey mixture onto half of each rectangle to within about 1 inch of edge. Moisten edges of dough with *water* and fold over, forming a square. Pinch or press with a fork to seal edges. Prick tops of calzones with a fork; brush with milk and place on the prepared baking sheet. Repeat with remaining dough and turkey mixture.

3 If desired, sprinkle the top of each calzone with about ½ *teaspoon* of the grated Parmesan or Romano cheese.

CHEESE WITH CONVENIENCE

Check out the latest shredded-cheese combinations in your supermarket dairy case. You can count on them to be real timesavers. Not only do they come shredded and ready to use, but some combinations are already seasoned for faster family favorites. Tacos and nachos can be made lickety-split with a seasoned cheese blend and taco shells or chips. Other cheese combos make ideal pizza toppings or delicious toss-togethers with pasta and cooked vegetables.

4 Bake calzones in a 375° oven about 18 minutes or till golden brown. Serve with remaining pizza sauce. Makes 6 calzones.

TO MAKE AHEAD

Prepare and bake calzones as directed. Cool, wrap, label, and chill overnight or freeze up to 3 months. To serve, thaw frozen calzones in refrigerator overnight. Unwrap and place on baking sheet. Bake, calzones uncovered, in a 350° oven for 15 to 18 minutes or till heated through.

Nutrition facts per calzone: 344 cal., 10 g total fat (3 g sat. fat), 57 mg chol., 1,338 mg sodium, 41 g carbo., 2 g fiber, 23 g pro.
Daily values: 23% vit. A, 24% vit. C, 13% calcium, 23% iron.

MUSTARD SHRIMP IN POTATO NESTS

Prep: 20 min. ◆ Bake: 22 min.

Simple shredded potatoes hold succulent, dressed shrimp for an easy-to-make dish with an unexpected touch of class. (See the photograph on page 198.)

12 oz. fresh or frozen peeled and deveined medium shrimp with tails left on, if desired
 2 Tbsp. olive oil
⅛ tsp. dried dillweed

◆◆◆

1½ cups refrigerated shredded hash brown potatoes
 ¼ cup soft bread crumbs
 2 Tbsp. thinly sliced green onion (1)
 1 slightly beaten egg
 1 Tbsp. horseradish mustard
 2 tsp. olive oil
 ½ tsp. bottled minced garlic
 ⅛ tsp. ground red pepper
   Nonstick spray coating

◆◆◆

 3 Tbsp. light mayonnaise dressing
 1 Tbsp. horseradish mustard
 1 Tbsp. dry white wine
 ½ tsp. dried dillweed
   Fresh dill sprigs (optional)

1 Thaw shrimp, if frozen. Toss shrimp with the 2 tablespoons olive oil and the ⅛ teaspoon dillweed; set aside.

2 In a bowl combine potatoes, soft bread crumbs, onion, egg, 1 tablespoon horseradish mustard, 2 teaspoons oil, garlic, and red pepper. Spray a baking sheet with nonstick coating.

SAUCE FOR MINI PIZZA

Freeze leftover pizza sauce or spaghetti sauce in ice cube trays. For a hot lunch or quick dinner, pop out however many cubes you need. Thaw and heat the frozen cubes in a microwave oven; spread sauce on an English muffin, and top with cheese for a quick mini pizza.

Debbie Lokanc
San Diego, California

3 For each potato nest, pat ⅓ *cup* of the potato mixture into a thick patty on the baking sheet. Depress center of each patty with the back of a spoon, forming a 4-inch-round nest shape. Bake in a 425° oven for 10 minutes. Spoon shrimp filling in center and bake 12 to 15 minutes more or till crust is golden and shrimp are cooked. Remove from oven; let stand for 5 minutes.

4 Meanwhile, in a small mixing bowl combine mayonnaise dressing, 1 tablespoon horseradish mustard, wine, and the ½ teaspoon dillweed. Spoon sauce over each filled shell. If desired, garnish each serving with a fresh dill sprig. Makes 5 servings.

Nutrition facts per serving: 219 cal., 12 g total fat (2 g sat. fat), 147 mg chol., 306 mg sodium, 13 g carbo., 1 g fiber, 14 g pro.
Daily values: 6% vit. A, 83% vit. C, 2% calcium, 14% iron.

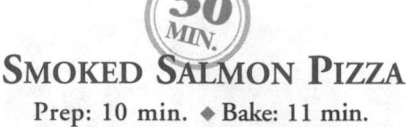

SMOKED SALMON PIZZA

Prep: 10 min. ◆ Bake: 11 min.

*For a flavor variation, top this
pizza with roasted garlic.
(See the photograph on page 198.)*

1 16-oz. Italian bread shell
   (Boboli)
2 medium tomatoes, very
   thinly sliced
3 oz. thinly sliced smoked
   salmon (lox-style)
4 oz. sliced provolone cheese
½ cup crumbled semisoft goat
   cheese or garlic-and-herb
   feta cheese
   Fresh marjoram sprigs
   (optional)

1 Place bread shell on a baking sheet. Arrange tomatoes,
salmon, and provolone on top.
Sprinkle with goat or feta cheese.
Bake in a 400° oven for 11 to 13
minutes or till heated. If desired,
garnish with fresh marjoram
sprigs. Cut into 6 to 8 wedges.
Makes 6 to 8 main-dish servings.

Nutrition facts per serving: 358 cal., 16 g
total fat (6 g sat. fat), 38 mg chol., 812 mg
sodium, 35 g carbo., 2 g fiber, 20 g pro.
Daily values: 10% vit. A, 13% vit. C, 20%
calcium, 13% iron.

PORK CHOPS WITH ONION-RAISIN CHUTNEY

Prep: 25 min. ◆ Marinate: 4 to 24 hr.
Grill: 11 min.

4 4-oz. boneless pork top loin
   chops, cut ¾ inch thick
½ of a 12-oz. bottle lemon-
   pepper or herb and garlic
   marinade
1 Tbsp. margarine or butter
½ cup finely chopped onion

THE CLEVER COOK

DESSERT ON THE GRILL

While you've got the grill
going, you can use it to prepare dessert. Wash, dry, and
core cooking apples. Fill centers with brown sugar and
butter; wrap each apple in
foil and place in small foil pie
tins on the grill. When the
apples are tender, unwrap
them and serve.

Betty Clark
Hot Springs, Arkansas

½ cup finely chopped red sweet
   pepper
¼ cup raisins
¼ tsp. ground cloves
¼ cup red wine vinegar
2 Tbsp. brown sugar
2 Tbsp. finely chopped toasted
   walnuts

◆◆◆

Fresh sage sprigs (optional)
Steamed fresh green beans
   (optional)

1 Place the pork chops in a
bag set in a bowl; add marinade.
Seal bag and chill 4 to 24 hours,
turning bag occasionally. Drain
chops, discarding marinade.

2 Grill pork chops on rack of
an uncovered grill directly over
medium coals 8 to 11 minutes or
till juices run clear, turning once.

3 Meanwhile, for chutney, in
a medium skillet heat margarine

or butter. Add onion, sweet pepper, raisins, and cloves. Cook and
stir about 4 minutes or till onion
is tender. Add vinegar and sugar;
reduce heat. Simmer, uncovered,
about 5 minutes or till liquid is
nearly evaporated. Stir in nuts.
Remove from heat; cover and let
stand for 10 minutes.

4 Serve pork chops topped
with some of the chutney. If
desired, garnish with sage sprigs
and serve with steamed fresh
green beans on the side. Pass
remaining chutney. Serves 4.

Nutrition facts per serving: 273 cal., 14 g
total fat (5 g sat. fat), 59 mg chol.,
1,270 mg sodium, 20 g carbo., 1 g fiber,
18 g pro.
Daily values: 12% vit. A, 37% vit. C, 1%
calcium, 8% iron.

ITALIAN SHEPHERD'S PIE

Prep: 30 min. ◆ Bake: 50 min.

*This recipe earned Betty A. Powell of
Leesburg, Virginia, $400 in the
magazine's monthly contest.*

1 lb. bulk pork sausage
½ cup green onions sliced in
   1-inch pieces
1 14½-oz. can stewed
   tomatoes, undrained
3 beaten eggs
1 cup shredded cheddar cheese
¾ tsp. dried oregano, crushed
1 9-inch unbaked pastry shell

◆◆◆

4 servings prepared instant
   mashed potatoes
½ cup shredded cheddar cheese
   Paprika

1 In a large skillet cook sausage and green onions till sausage is browned; drain. Stir undrained tomatoes, eggs, 1 cup cheese, and oregano into mixture in skillet. Spoon sausage mixture into unbaked pastry shell. Place on a foil-lined baking sheet.

2 Stir together the prepared potatoes and the ½ cup cheese. Pipe or spoon potato mixture around edge of pie. Sprinkle with paprika. Bake in a 375° oven for 50 to 55 minutes or till set. Let stand 15 minutes before cutting into wedges. Makes 8 servings.

◼ TO MAKE AHEAD ◼

Prepare pie up to the point of placing on a foil-lined baking sheet. Cover edge of pie with foil. Bake in a 375° oven for 25 minutes. Remove foil; bake pie 20 to 25 minutes more or till set. Cool on a wire rack. Wrap and freeze.

To serve, thaw pie overnight in the refrigerator. Unwrap and cover loosely with foil. Bake in a 350° oven for 1 hour. Combine prepared potatoes and the ½ cup cheese. Uncover pie. Pipe or spoon potato mixture around edge of pie. Bake, uncovered, about 20 minutes more or till heated through. Let stand 5 to 10 minutes. Cut into wedges.

Nutrition facts per serving: 410 cal., 27 g total fat (10 g sat. fat), 125 mg chol., 846 mg sodium, 25 g carbo., 1 g fiber, 16 g pro. *Daily values:* 13% vit. A, 10% vit. C, 16% calcium, 13% iron.

TEST KITCHEN TIP

MAKE IT QUICK

Shrink meal preparation time by taking advantage of packaged fresh or frozen produce. Pick portobello mushrooms that already are sliced; snatch up spinach that's been cleaned and sorted; or reach for a bag of frozen chopped onions that won't leave you crying at the kitchen sink.

LAMB AND POLENTA BAKE

Prep: 35 min. ◆ Bake: 30 min.

See the photograph on page 198.

12 oz. ground lamb
1 medium onion, chopped
1 small fennel bulb, chopped
4 cloves garlic, minced
1 Tbsp. snipped fresh oregano or 1 tsp. dried oregano, crushed
½ tsp. coarsely ground pepper
1 14½-oz. can whole Italian-style tomatoes, undrained and cut up

◆◆◆

1 16-oz. pkg. cooked polenta
1 cup crumbled feta or garlic-and-herb feta cheese

◆◆◆

1 cup Italian-style tomato sauce

1 In a large skillet cook lamb, onion, fennel, garlic, oregano, and pepper till lamb is browned and onion is tender; drain. Add undrained tomatoes to mixture in skillet. Bring to boiling; reduce heat. Simmer, uncovered, for 10 to 15 minutes or till most liquid is evaporated, stirring occasionally.

2 Meanwhile, slice polenta about ½ inch thick. Press or crumble *half* of the slices into the bottoms of four 10- to 12-ounce greased casseroles or soufflé dishes, overlapping slices as necessary.

3 Divide lamb mixture among casseroles atop polenta. Sprinkle cheese over lamb mixture, reserving ¼ cup cheese. Firmly press or crumble remaining polenta on top. Bake in a 375° oven about 30 minutes or till heated through. Let stand 10 minutes.

4 Meanwhile, in a saucepan heat tomato sauce just till boiling. Loosen edges of casseroles and invert onto serving plates; gently remove dish. Spoon sauce around casserole. Sprinkle remaining cheese atop. If desired, garnish with *cherry tomato quarters* and *parsley sprigs*. Makes 4 servings.

◼ TO MAKE AHEAD ◼

Prepare casseroles as directed, except do not bake. Cover; freeze up to 3 months. Thaw casseroles overnight in refrigerator. To serve, bake, covered with foil, in a 350° oven 45 to 50 minutes or till heated through, uncovering the last 10 minutes of baking. Let stand 10 minutes before loosening edges and inverting onto plates.

Nutrition facts per serving: 414 cal., 18 g total fat (9 g sat. fat), 82 mg chol., 1,551 mg sodium, 39 g carbo., 13 g fiber, 24 g pro. *Daily values:* 19% vit. A, 43% vit. C, 17% calcium, 15% iron.

COMFORTING CASSOULET-STYLE STEW

Prep: 50 min. ◆ Stand: 1 hr.
Cook: 1¾ hr.

This recipe earned Maral Mahdasian of Newton, Massachusetts, $200 in the magazine's monthly contest.

1 lb. dry navy beans
6 cups water

◆◆◆

1 meaty lamb shank (1 to 1½ lb.)
1 Tbsp. olive oil or cooking oil
2 cups chopped celery (include leaves)
2 medium unpeeled potatoes, coarsely chopped
¾ cup coarsely chopped carrot
¾ cup coarsely chopped parsnip
3 cloves garlic, minced
7 cups water
3 cups sliced fresh mushrooms
1¼ cups dry black-eyed peas, rinsed and drained
½ cup dry red wine or beef broth
2 tsp. salt
½ tsp. pepper

◆◆◆

1 28-oz. can diced tomatoes
2 Tbsp. snipped fresh thyme
1 Tbsp. snipped fresh rosemary
Fresh rosemary sprigs (optional)

1 Rinse beans. In a saucepan combine the 6 cups water and the beans. Bring to boiling; reduce heat. Simmer, uncovered, for 2 minutes. Remove from heat. Cover and let stand for 1 hour. Drain and rinse beans.

THE CLEVER COOK

PROTECTING NONSTICK PANS

If you stack your coated frying pans to save space, you can protect the nonstick surfaces by putting paper plates between the pans. They can be cut to fit and are easy to replace when worn.

Patti Harrington
Celina, Texas

2 In an 8- to 10-quart pot brown lamb shank in hot oil. Add celery, potatoes, carrot, parsnip, and garlic. Cook over medium-high heat for 5 minutes, stirring frequently. Add the 7 cups water, mushrooms, black-eyed peas, wine or broth, salt, pepper, and soaked beans. Bring to boiling; reduce heat. Simmer, covered, about 1½ hours or till the beans and peas are tender. Remove shank; let cool.

3 Add the tomatoes, thyme, and snipped rosemary to beans. Remove meat from shank; chop meat and add to stew. Simmer, covered, for 15 minutes more. To serve, ladle stew into bowls. If desired, garnish stew with fresh rosemary sprigs. Makes 12 main-dish servings.

■ **TO MAKE AHEAD** ■

Prepare stew as directed. Let cool for 30 minutes. Place stew in freezer containers and freeze for up to 3 months. To serve, place frozen stew in a saucepan. Heat, covered, over medium-low heat about 45 minutes or till heated through, stirring occasionally and breaking apart.

Nutrition facts per serving: 287 cal., 4 g total fat (1 g sat. fat), 14 mg chol., 553 mg sodium, 46 g carbo., 5 g fiber, 18 g pro. *Daily Values:* 24% vit. A, 29% vit. C, 36% iron.

BEEF AND MUSHROOMS IN PUFF PASTRY

Prep: 40 min. ◆ Bake: 20 min.

For a decorative touch, top pies with grated cheese just before serving. (See the photograph on page 201.)

½ of a 17¼-oz. pkg. frozen puff pastry (1 sheet)
Nonstick spray coating

◆◆◆

2 cloves garlic, minced
1 medium red onion, cut in bite-size pieces
2 small zucchini, halved lengthwise and thinly sliced (about 2 cups)

◆◆◆

12 oz. boneless beef sirloin steak, cut into ½-inch cubes
1 12-oz. jar lower-fat mushroom-and-wine or mushroom gravy
1 Tbsp. snipped fresh marjoram or thyme or 1 tsp. dried marjoram or thyme, crushed
¼ tsp. pepper

1 Thaw pastry according to package directions. On a lightly floured surface, roll puff pastry sheet to a 14-inch square. Cut into 4 equal squares. Fill four 10-ounce casseroles or custard cups with crumpled foil; invert onto a large baking sheet. (The foil will raise the casserole dish off the baking sheet and make a deeper pastry shell.) Spray outsides of cups with nonstick spray coating.

2 Drape pastry squares over inverted cups (see below), pinching sides to fit around the cups.

3 Bake pastry squares in a 375° oven for 20 minutes or till golden brown. Remove from oven and let cool for several minutes. Carefully pull the shells from the outsides of the casseroles. Invert shells onto individual plates.

4 Spray a large nonstick skillet with nonstick coating. Stir-fry garlic for 15 seconds; add onion and stir-fry 1 minute more. Add the zucchini; stir-fry for 2 to 3 minutes more or till vegetables are crisp-tender. Remove the vegetables from the skillet.

5 Add the beef to the hot skillet; stir-fry for 3 to 4 minutes or to desired doneness. Return vegetables to the skillet. Add the gravy, marjoram or thyme, and pepper; cook and stir about 1 minute more or till heated through. Carefully spoon beef and vegetable mixture into each baked pastry shell. Makes 4 main-dish servings.

Nutrition facts per serving: 450 cal., 27 g total fat (3 g sat. fat), 57 mg chol., 699 mg sodium, 30 g carbo., 1 g fiber, 22 g pro. *Daily values:* 1% vit. A, 6% vit. C, 1% calcium, 16% iron.

LOW FAT

BEEF AND BEAN BURRITOS

Prep: 25 min. ◆ Bake: 20 min.

*Black or pinto beans replace
some of the meat, lowering the fat
and adding fiber.*

8   **8-inch flour tortillas**

◆◆◆

8   **oz. lean ground beef**
1   **cup chopped onion**
2   **cloves garlic, minced**

1   **15-oz. can black beans or
    pinto beans, rinsed and
    drained**
½   **cup salsa**
2   **tsp. chili powder
    Several dashes bottled hot
    pepper sauce**

◆◆◆

1   **cup shredded reduced-fat
    cheddar cheese (4 oz.)**

◆◆◆

1½ **cups shredded fresh spinach**
1½ **cups shredded lettuce
    Salsa (optional)
    Sour cream (optional)**

1 Stack tortillas; wrap tightly in foil. Heat in a 350° oven for 10 minutes to soften.

2 Meanwhile, for filling, in a large skillet cook ground beef, onion, and garlic till beef is brown and onion is tender. Drain off fat. Stir in beans, salsa, chili powder, and pepper sauce. Heat through.

3 Spoon about ⅓ cup filling onto each tortilla; top with *1 tablespoon* cheese. Fold bottom edge up and over filling, just till covered. Fold in opposite sides. Roll up, tucking in sides. Secure with wooden picks. Arrange tortillas, seam side down, on a foil-lined baking sheet; cover with foil. Bake in a 350° oven about 10 minutes or till heated through.

4 Serve burritos atop a mixture of spinach and lettuce. Sprinkle with remaining cheese. If desired, serve with additional salsa and sour cream. Makes 8 burritos.

Nutrition facts per burrito: 268 cal., 9 g total fat (3 g sat. fat), 28 mg chol., 484 mg sodium, 31 g carbo., 3 g fiber, 17 g pro. *Daily values:* 16% vit. C, 15% calcium, 18% iron.

BE A LUNCH-BOX HERO

Break out the lunch boxes, the kids are heading off to school. Packing healthful lunches for your pride and joy needn't be a hassle. A few simple yet creative tactics will make your job easier while getting the kids involved in the lunch-making process. They'll also learn the importance of good food to good health—and good fun.

PACK THE PYRAMID

Boosting the quality of the brown-bag lunch is easy if you "pack the Pyramid." (See page 31 for information on The Food Guide Pyramid.) All you have to do is follow nutrition guidelines explained in Key Kid Nutrients, below. These guidelines were developed by the United States Department of Agriculture (USDA) to guide you to foods that supply key nutrients for children.

The secret to building a successful Pyramid-based lunch is the same as for building any important structure: Start with a strong base. Select one or more foods from each of the three bottom levels of the Pyramid—grains; fruits and vegetables; and meat, beans, and dairy products—to have a solid nutritional base and earn an "A+" in balanced brown-bag nutrition.

KEY KID NUTRIENTS

Grains and grain products from the base of the Pyramid supply the B-vitamins, fiber,  iron, and zinc. Kid-friendly grain foods include bagels, crackers, muffins, pasta salads, pretzels, and tortillas. When it comes to bread, opt for whole-grain versions if possible. But if your offspring insist on white bread, don't feel like a bad parent: Most white breads are fortified with iron and other essential nutrients.

Vegetables and fruits, the second level of the Pyramid, are primary sources of essential vitamins and minerals. Pack one or two foods from this level to help make a nutritionally complete lunch. Cucumber slices and cherry tomatoes are popular vegetables, but some kids prefer their veggies disguised. In these cases, chop them up and mix them into "user-friendly" sandwich fillings.

When it comes to fruit, does the apple you so carefully packed come home still in the bag, looking as if it were used for softball practice instead of dessert? Substitute fruit roll-ups or dried cherries. Also, pure fruit juices count, as do dried fruits.

Kids get protein, plus calcium and other important minerals, at the third level of the Pyramid. Needs for dietary zinc and iron (recognized as key problem nutrients in children) are high in growing kids, and meat and eggs are the best sources.

For young vegetarians, dried fruit, whole grains, and fortified juices are good providers of important minerals. Your children also need to eat at least three daily servings of calcium-rich foods, such as milk, yogurt, and cheese.

To complete the basics for the Pyramid-positive lunch, include protein in the form of a 2-ounce serving of meat, poultry, fish, cheese, yogurt, peanut butter, nuts, or beans.

No need to avoid fats and sweets at the tip of the Pyramid: These add flavor and appeal to lunches and provide extra calories kids need for energy and growth. Best bets include fruit-filled cookies, oatmeal cookies, granola bars, or even sweetened cereals to split the difference between healthful snacks and empty calories. Including some fun food treats, such as cake or cookies, keeps kids from feeling deprived.

There are healthful options for salty snacks, too. Young ones like potato or tortilla chips, and there's no denying the convenience of tossing a packet of chips into the lunch bag. But instead of plain chips, try multigrain chips or pretzels.

THE INCLUSION FACTOR

Registered Dietitian Michelle Barth sends her tots off to school with a variety of nutritious foods. "But," she admits, "I know they trade what they don't like with their friends, or lunch comes home still in the bag."

Yet even kindergartners can grasp the need to have energy for the playground and be instructed about healthy eating. Involve youngsters in menu planning: Present several choices for each course, then let your wee ones build their own menu.

Choices from groups of related items—for example, between carrot sticks, celery sticks, and sweet pepper strips—put kids in the driver's seat while guaranteeing good nutrition choices. Young people are more likely to eat foods they've chosen, even if the choice is from a group of foods they would normally reject.

Like you, your children have their own specific likes and dislikes. Working mother Joy Colangelo doesn't worry about the lunches she packs for her two children, Alex, 7, and Dakota, 9. "I always pack one of the three foods I know they'll eat," she says. "Peanut butter, jelly, and peanut butter and jelly."

Kids often get attached to a single food or food combination, but there's no cause for alarm since such food fads rarely last long. When they do happen, be like Joy: Don't panic. Pack what you know your boys and girls will eat, but don't forget to encourage them to add at least one new or different food for each lunch.

BEAT BROWN-BAG BOREDOM

For young people who haven't tried a new vegetable or fruit since they started on solid foods—or even those who have—plan a "fun food day" each week. Some fresh ideas are:

Fuzzy kiwi fruit—an excellent source of vitamin C—will have your child hopping like a kangaroo. Kiwi taste like a mixture of strawberries, bananas, melon, and lime. Cut them in half and pack a plastic spoon for scooping out the inside.

Sunny mango slices always surprise with their rich, sweet taste. Mangoes are loaded with vitamins A and C, and potassium.

Rainbows of orange, purple, yellow, and red sweet peppers, cut into strips, are great finger-food veggies that keep their crunch till lunch. Brilliant yellow cherry tomatoes are fun and attractive, but taste familiar and have lots of vitamin C.

Fresh snow pea pods and snap peas are an unexpected favorite of the younger set. They are sweet and crunchy and keep well in the bag.

Jicama, peeled and cut french-fry style, is another sweet and crunchy vegetable kids will enjoy. Squeeze fresh lime juice over the strips to keep them fresh and provide extra vitamin C.

Chunks of fresh coconut meat make for a tropical brown-bag hit when packed as a dessert or even just a quick calorie booster for between-classes snacking.

Food safety is every bit as important as nutrition. Your safest bet is to pack foods in insulated lunch boxes. Or, find out if the school has facilities where brown-bag lunches can be refrigerated. If these options don't exist, steer clear of foods containing easily spoiled ingredients, such as poultry, soft fruits, or products containing eggs. Wherever possible, use airtight plastic resealable containers. Remind your children to stash their lunches in a cool, dry spot—under their desk or in their locker—till they're ready to dive in.

CLEAN BREAK WITH SODA

Great-grandmother didn't clean compact disks with baking soda, but you can. She did use it to scrub the house from top to bottom. Today, even with manufactured specialty cleaners touting improved formulas, baking soda still shines.

Cleaning compact disks is just one new job for the little box of sodium bicarbonate. Soda is popular because its tiny crystals dissolve easily and leave no residue. Just follow these easy directions.

Polishing paste: In a jar, mix equal parts of baking soda and warm water. Use the paste to clean tarnished silverware, bathtubs, stainless-steel sinks, and toilets. (Do not use soda on aluminum surfaces because the metal will react and turn black.) To store, cover with plastic wrap.

Liquid cleaner: In a squirt bottle or plastic container with a tight lid, mix 2 tablespoons of baking soda with 1 pint of warm water. Use this solution to mop vinyl floors, clean compact disks, or wash windows.

Sponging: Sprinkle baking soda onto a damp sponge. Wipe scuffs, stains, or crayon marks from painted walls, laminated countertops, tile surfaces, and appliances, such as the microwave oven, stove top, and refrigerator. Dry them with a clean cloth.

Carpet deodorizer: Put baking soda into a sprinkle-top container. To test colorfastness, sprinkle a small amount directly onto carpet or upholstery in an out-of-sight spot. Let stand for 15 minutes before vacuuming or brushing off. Once you know the fabric is colorfast, shake soda onto the affected areas.

Air freshener: After you've cleaned, use baking soda as a natural deodorizer. Leave an open box in your refrigerator, clothes hamper, or closet. Change it every few months for maximum benefit.

A final note: Do not mix baking soda in cleaning solutions with acids, such as vinegar or lemon juice, because they will neutralize the soda and diminish its cleaning ability.

PRIZE TESTED RECIPE WINNER

APPLE-CRISP COOKIES

Prep: 25 min. ◆ Bake: 12 min.

This recipe earned Kimberly Kurkovic of Jefferson, Ohio, $200 in the magazine's monthly contest.

- 1 cup shortening
- ½ cup margarine or butter
- 1½ cups packed brown sugar
- 1 cup granulated sugar
- 1 0.7-oz. pkg. instant spiced apple-flavored drink mix
- 1 Tbsp. ground cinnamon
- 1½ tsp. baking powder
- 1½ tsp. baking soda
- ½ tsp. salt
- 3 eggs
- 2 tsp. vanilla
- 3 cups all-purpose flour
- 3 cups quick-cooking rolled oats
- 1½ cups raisins
- 1½ cups chopped dried apple pieces

1 In an extra-large mixing bowl beat together the shortening and margarine or butter with an electric mixer on medium to high speed for 30 seconds. Add brown sugar, granulated sugar, instant drink mix, cinnamon, baking powder, baking soda, and salt. Beat till combined, scraping the sides of bowl occasionally. Beat in eggs and vanilla till combined. Beat in as much flour as you can with the mixer. Using a wooden spoon, stir in any remaining flour, oats, raisins, and dried apples.

2 Drop dough from a rounded teaspoon 2 inches apart on an ungreased cookie sheet. Bake in a 350° oven about 12 minutes or till lightly browned. Remove from cookie sheet and cool on a wire rack. Makes 84 cookies.

Nutrition facts per cookie: 94 cal., 4 g total fat (1 g sat. fat), 8 mg chol., 60 mg sodium, 14 g carbo., 1 g fiber, 1 g pro.
Daily values: 1% vit. A, 1% vit. C, 1% calcium, 3% iron.

SWEDISH SHORTBREAD

Prep: 20 min. ◆ Bake: 12 min.

Choose your favorite jam to fill the centers of these tender slices.

½ cup butter
¼ cup granulated sugar
1¼ cups all-purpose flour
◆◆◆
2 Tbsp. seedless red raspberry or apricot jam
◆◆◆
½ cup sifted powdered sugar
¼ tsp. almond extract
Milk

1 In a large mixing bowl beat butter with an electric mixer on medium to high speed for 30 seconds or till softened. Beat in granulated sugar till fluffy. Beat in flour till well combined. Knead mixture with hands till smooth. Divide dough into 2 portions.

2 On an ungreased large cookie sheet pat each portion of dough into a 13×2-inch rectangle. Using your finger, make an indentation down the center of each rectangle. Carefully spoon jam into indentations. Bake cookies in a 350° oven for 12 minutes or till set and edges are lightly golden.

3 Meanwhile, for icing, stir together the powdered sugar, almond extract, and enough milk to make icing easy to drizzle (1 to 2 teaspoons). While cookies are warm, drizzle icing over jam. Cut diagonally into 1-inch slices. Cool completely on a wire rack. Makes about 20 cookies.

Nutrition facts per cookie: 91 cal., 5 g total fat (3 g sat. fat), 12 mg chol., 47 mg sodium, 12 g carbo., 0 g fiber, 1 g pro. *Daily values:* 4% vit. A, 2% iron.

RASPBERRY-ALMOND CRESCENTS

Prep: 50 min. ◆ Chill: 4 hr.
Bake: 15 min.

1 cup butter
2 cups all-purpose flour
1 egg yolk
½ cup dairy sour cream
◆◆◆
⅓ cup seedless red raspberry preserves
¼ cup ground almonds
¼ tsp. almond extract
¼ cup shredded coconut
Egg white, slightly beaten (optional)
Coarse or granulated sugar (optional)

1 Using a pastry blender, cut butter into flour till mixture resembles coarse crumbs. Beat together egg yolk and sour cream with a fork. Stir sour cream mixture into flour mixture till a ball forms. Cover; chill several hours or till easy to handle.

2 Stir together the preserves, almonds, and extract; set aside. Divide dough into fourths. On a well-floured surface roll each portion of dough into a 10-inch circle. Spread each circle with some preserve mixture and sprinkle with some coconut. Cut each circle into 12 wedges. Roll each wedge into a crescent shape, starting at the wide end. If desired, brush with egg white and sprinkle with sugar. Place, points down, 1 inch apart on a greased cookie sheet. Bake in a 350° oven for 15 minutes or till lightly browned. Cool. Makes 48.

Nutrition facts per cookie: 96 cal., 5 g total fat (3 g sat. fat), 16 mg chol., 42 mg sodium, 6 g carbo., 0 g fiber, 1 g pro.

CHOCOLATE-CHERRY OATMEAL BARS

Prep: 20 min. ◆ Bake: 30 min.

1 cup all-purpose flour
3 Tbsp. unsweetened cocoa powder
½ tsp. baking powder
½ tsp. baking soda
◆◆◆
½ cup butter or margarine, softened
¾ cup granulated sugar
½ cup packed brown sugar
2 eggs
½ tsp. vanilla
1 cup quick-cooking rolled oats
½ cup dried tart red cherries or cranberries, snipped
½ cup semisweet chocolate pieces
¼ cup chopped walnuts

1 Lightly grease an 11×7×1½-inch baking pan. In a bowl combine flour, cocoa, baking powder, and baking soda; set aside.

2 In a large mixing bowl beat together butter and sugars with an electric mixer on medium to high speed till fluffy. Add eggs and vanilla; beat till smooth. Add flour mixture; beat till combined. Using a wooden spoon, stir in oats, fruit, chocolate pieces, and nuts. Spread in prepared pan. Bake bars in a 375° oven about 30 minutes or till a wooden toothpick inserted near center comes out clean. Cool in the pan on a wire rack. Cut into bars. Makes 24.

Nutrition facts per bar: 144 cal., 6 g total fat (3 g sat. fat), 28 mg chol., 79 mg sodium, 21 g carbo., 1 g fiber, 2 g pro. *Daily values:* 5% vit. A, 2% calcium, 4% iron.

TOASTED HAZELNUT BARS

Prep: 20 min. ◆ Bake: 50 min.

This recipe earned Nancy Bruce of Florence, Oregon, $400 in the magazine's monthly contest.

2 cups all-purpose flour
2 3-oz. pkg. cream cheese, softened
½ cup butter or margarine, softened
½ cup packed brown sugar

◆◆◆

4 eggs
2 cups granulated sugar
1½ cups buttermilk
½ cup butter or margarine, melted
⅓ cup all-purpose flour
2 tsp. vanilla
¼ tsp. salt
2 cups chopped hazelnuts (filberts), toasted

◆◆◆

Sifted powdered sugar

1 In a large mixing bowl beat together the flour, cream cheese, the ½ cup softened butter or margarine, and brown sugar with an electric mixer on low to medium speed till well combined. With lightly floured hands, pat the mixture onto bottom and up sides of a 15×10×1-inch ungreased baking pan. Bake in a 350° oven for 15 minutes.

2 Meanwhile, in a large mixing bowl beat together the eggs, granulated sugar, buttermilk, the ½ cup melted butter or margarine, the ⅓ cup flour, vanilla,

and salt with an electric mixer on low speed till combined. Stir in hazelnuts. Pour mixture into pre-baked crust. Bake about 35 minutes more or till golden. Cool in pan on a wire rack.

3 To serve, cut into bars and sprinkle with powdered sugar. Cover and store in the refrigerator. Makes 48 bars.

Nutrition facts per bar: 146 cal., 9 g total fat (4 g sat. fat), 32 mg chol., 75 mg sodium, 16 g carbo., 1 g fiber, 2 g pro. *Daily values:* 5% vit. A, 2% calcium, 3% iron.

PIÑA COLADA SQUARES

Prep: 15 min. ◆ Bake: 30 min.

The secret to the simplicity of this tropical-tasting bar is the pineapple ice-cream topping used as the filling.

2 cups all-purpose flour
2 cups quick-cooking rolled oats
1⅓ cups packed brown sugar
¼ tsp. baking soda
1 cup butter or margarine

◆◆◆

1 cup pineapple ice-cream topping
1 tsp. rum extract

◆◆◆

1 cup coconut

1 In a large mixing bowl combine the flour, oats, brown sugar, and soda. Using a pastry blender, cut in butter till mixture resembles coarse crumbs. Reserve 1 cup of the crumb mixture for topping. Press the remaining mixture into the bottom of an ungreased 13×9×2-inch baking pan.

2 For filling, in a small mixing bowl combine pineapple topping

TRY A BANANA SMOOTHIE

Banana fruit smoothies are delectable, healthful, and incredibly fast to make. In a blender container combine one cup of well-chilled fruit juice with ½ cup of fresh or frozen strawberries, a cup of plain or vanilla fat-free yogurt, and one large banana. Blend till smooth, and pour into a tall chilled glass. Other fruits easily substitute for the strawberries; try seedless grapes, mango slices, papaya chunks, or any low-acid fruit.

Enjoy vitamin and mineral-packed banana smoothies as a take-along breakfast, a two-minute lunch, or mid-afternoon snack. One 12-ounce glass has less than 200 calories and only about 2 g fat.

and rum extract. Spread pineapple mixture evenly over the crust.

3 For topping, stir coconut into reserved crumb mixture. Sprinkle topping evenly over pineapple-rum filling. Bake bars in a 350° oven about 30 minutes or till golden. Cool in pan on a wire rack. To serve, cut into bars. Makes 48 bars.

Nutrition facts per bar: 108 cal., 5 g total fat (3 g sat. fat), 10 mg chol., 52 mg sodium, 16 g carbo., 1 g fiber, 1 g pro. *Daily values:* 3% vit. A, 6% vit. C, 3% iron.

OCTOBER
Autumn Warm-Up

30-minute recipes indicated in RED.
Low-fat and no-fat recipes indicated
with a ♥.
Photographs indicated in italics.

Sweaters and jackets reclaim their status on clothes hooks and closet shelves. Shorter days have a brisk freshness that invites families to rekindle their affection for the fireplace. And in kitchens, cooks seek ways to add fuel to their families' fires. Answer October's heartier appetites with meals your family can warm up to: Parsleyed New Potatoes, Cajun Beans and Burley, Sweet Potato Casserole, Shrimp Curry with Cilantro, Chicken and Sausage Gumbo, Sausage Stew Pot, Mexicali Meat Loaf, and Black Bean Chili. Just to sweeten the pot, consider Crunchy Caramel Apple Pie, Chocolate Cookie Cake, and seven kinds of coffee cake.

PARSLEYED NEW POTATOES

Prep: 10 min. ◆ Cook: 10 min.

New potatoes have a delicate taste that adds just the right touch to a meal with subtle flavors. (See the photograph on page 238.)

10 to 12 whole tiny new
   potatoes (1 lb.)
   ◆◆◆
2 Tbsp. margarine or butter,
   cut up
2 Tbsp. snipped fresh parsley
   Salt
   Pepper

1 Scrub potatoes thoroughly with a stiff brush. Cut potatoes into halves or quarters.

2 In a medium saucepan cook potatoes, covered, in a small amount of boiling, *lightly salted water* for 10 to 15 minutes or till tender; drain. Return to saucepan.

3 Add the margarine or butter and parsley to the hot potatoes, tossing gently to melt margarine and coat potatoes. Season to taste with salt and pepper. Makes 4 side-dish servings.

Nutrition facts per serving: 161 cal., 6 g total fat (1 g sat. fat), 0 mg chol., 110 mg sodium, 25 g carbo., 1 g fiber, 3 g pro. *Daily values:* 8% vit. A, 28% vit. C, 1% calcium, 13% iron.

LENTIL AND GRAINS PILAF

Prep: 15 min. ◆ Cook: 50 min.

Low on fat and long on carbos, this union of grains and legumes makes a hit with the health brigade as well as demanding diners.

3½ cups water
1 Tbsp. margarine or butter
1 tsp. instant chicken bouillon
   granules
½ cup chopped onion
⅓ cup regular brown rice
⅓ cup wheat berries
¾ tsp. dried savory, crushed
   ◆◆◆
⅓ cup dry lentils, rinsed and
   drained
2 Tbsp. snipped dried apricots
   or raisins
   Salt
   Pepper

1 In a medium saucepan combine the water, margarine or butter, and bouillon granules; heat till margarine is melted. Stir in onion, uncooked brown rice, wheat berries, and savory. Bring to boiling; reduce heat. Simmer, covered, for 20 minutes.

2 Stir the lentils into the mixture in the saucepan. Return to boiling; reduce heat. Simmer, covered, about 30 minutes more or till rice, wheat berries, and lentils are tender. Drain off excess liquid. Stir in apricots or raisins. Season to taste with salt and pepper. Makes 4 to 6 side-dish servings.

Nutrition facts per serving: 165 cal., 3 g total fat (1 g sat. fat), 0 mg chol., 262 mg sodium, 29 g carbo., 2 g fiber, 6 g pro. *Daily values:* 7% vit. A, 2% vit. C, 3% calcium, 15% iron.

CAJUN BEANS AND BARLEY

Prep: 15 min. ◆ Cook: 12 min.

Quick-cooking barley and canned pinto beans speed this zesty dish from pot to table. Chicken makes a good sidekick.

¾ cup water
½ cup quick-cooking barley
¼ cup chopped green sweet
   pepper
¼ cup chopped onion
   ◆◆◆
1 15-oz. can pinto beans,
   rinsed and drained
1 14½-oz. can stewed tomatoes
1 cup loose-pack frozen whole
   kernel corn
1 tsp. Cajun seasoning or
   ½ tsp. crushed red pepper

1 In a medium saucepan bring water to boiling. Stir in barley, sweet pepper, and onion. Return to boiling; reduce heat. Simmer, covered, 10 to 12 minutes or till barley is tender and water is absorbed.

2 Stir the beans, tomatoes, corn, and Cajun seasoning or red pepper into the mixture in the saucepan. Cook, covered, over medium heat till bubbly. Cook for 2 to 3 minutes more or till corn is tender. Makes 4 to 6 side-dish servings.

Nutrition facts per serving: 240 cal., 1 g total fat (0 g sat. fat), 0 mg chol., 810 mg sodium, 51 g carbo., 3 g fiber, 10 g pro. *Daily values:* 7% vit. A, 22% vit. C, 4% calcium, 16% iron.

Sweet Potato Casserole

Prep: 15 min. ◆ Cook: 25 min.
Bake: 25 min.

Children, grandchildren, and great-grandchildren never fail to ask for this casserole on Sunday gatherings at Odessa Sain Moore's house. To get a chunky, down-home texture, gently break up the sweet potatoes with a wooden spoon instead of mashing them.

1½ **lb. sweet potatoes**
◆◆◆
½ **cup granulated sugar**
½ **cup milk**
1 **beaten egg**
3 **Tbsp. butter, cubed**
1 **tsp. vanilla**
◆◆◆
½ **cup packed brown sugar**
⅓ **cup all-purpose flour**
2 **Tbsp. butter**
½ **cup pecan pieces**
  Pecan halves (optional)

1 Scrub and peel sweet potatoes. Cut off and discard woody portions and ends. Cut potatoes into cubes. Cook, covered, in a small amount of boiling water for 25 to 35 minutes or till potatoes are tender. Drain potatoes.

2 Combine hot sweet potatoes, granulated sugar, milk, egg, the 3 tablespoons butter, and vanilla. Using a wooden spoon, stir to break up potatoes but not completely mash them. Put mixture into a greased 2-quart square baking dish.

3 In a small mixing bowl, combine brown sugar and flour. Using a pastry blender, cut in the 2 tablespoons butter till mixture resembles coarse crumbs. Stir in pecan pieces. Sprinkle crumb mixture atop potatoes. Bake, uncovered, in a 350° oven about 25 minutes or till set. If desired, garnish with pecan halves. Makes 8 side-dish servings.

Nutrition facts per serving: 302 cal., 13 g total fat (5 g sat. fat), 47 mg chol., 98 mg sodium, 45 g carbo., 3 g fiber, 4 g pro. *Daily values:* 153% vit. A, 27% vit. C, 4% calcium, 6% iron.

Corn Pudding

Prep: 10 min. ◆ Bake: 50 min.

This flavorful side dish from Odessa Sain Moore can easily double as a dessert. It also makes a wonderful accompaniment to ham and tender dinner rolls.

1 **15¼-oz. can whole kernel corn, drained**
1 **14¾-oz. can cream-style corn**
1 **cup milk**
2 **beaten eggs**
¼ **cup margarine or butter, melted**
¼ **tsp. pepper**
½ **cup cornmeal**

1 In a large mixing bowl stir together the whole kernel corn, cream-style corn, milk, eggs, melted margarine or butter, and pepper. Add the cornmeal and stir till moistened.

2 Pour corn mixture into a 2-quart casserole. Bake casserole, uncovered, in a 350° oven for 50 to 55 minutes or till lightly browned and set in the center. Makes 8 side-dish servings.

Nutrition facts per serving: 183 cal., 8 g total fat (2 g sat. fat), 56 mg chol., 364 mg sodium, 25 g carbo., 2 g fiber, 5 g pro. *Daily values:* 12% vit. A, 9% vit. C, 4% calcium, 7% iron.

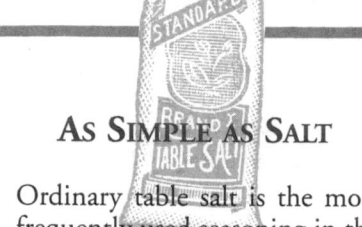

As Simple as Salt

Ordinary table salt is the most frequently used seasoning in the world. But there are several forms of salt that look different and taste different. Here are your choices:

◆ Table salt contains ingredients, such as dextrose, to keep it from clumping and maintain its pure white color. Generally, it is iodized to help provide iodine, an essential mineral in the diet. Uniodized salt also is available. All types of salt, except seasoned salts, will keep indefinitely at room temperature.

◆ Kosher salt, a coarse-ground and additive-free salt, tastes about half as salty as table salt. You've probably eaten it on pretzels or breadsticks. Kosher salt also is used by devout Jews in the preparation of meat.

◆ Pickling or canning salt is a finer grind than table salt. Free of additives, it won't cloud pickling liquids or brines.

◆ Rock salt, an inedible coarse-grain salt, often is used in freezing homemade ice cream. Because rock salt is unrefined, it retains the grayish cast of the natural mineral.

◆ Sea salt is formed by evaporating sea water. It may contain slightly more trace minerals than table salt, but has no other nutritional advantages. Many cooks prefer the taste of sea salt.

◆ Seasoned salts, such as celery, garlic, or onion salt, are blends of salt and other seasonings. Tightly capped at room temperature, these salts will remain at their best for one year.

SHRIMP CURRY WITH CILANTRO

Start to finish: 25 min.

12 oz. fresh or frozen peeled and deveined shrimp
1¼ cups orzo pasta

◆◆◆

½ cup chicken broth
⅓ cup bottled chili sauce
1 tsp. cornstarch

◆◆◆

2 Tbsp. olive oil
1 medium zucchini, quartered lengthwise and thinly sliced
1 small red sweet pepper, coarsely chopped
1 small onion, cut into thin wedges
1 clove garlic, minced
1½ to 2 tsp. curry powder

◆◆◆

¼ cup snipped fresh cilantro

1 Thaw shrimp, if frozen. Set shrimp aside. Cook the orzo according to package directions.

2 Meanwhile, for sauce stir together chicken broth, chili sauce, and cornstarch; set aside.

3 Heat *1 tablespoon* of the oil in a large skillet or wok. Add zucchini, red sweet pepper, onion, and garlic; stir-fry 2 minutes. Add curry powder; stir-fry for 1 minute more. Remove vegetables from the wok.

4 Add the remaining oil to skillet; add shrimp. Stir-fry over medium-high heat for 3 to 4 minutes or till shrimp turns opaque. Push shrimp from the center of the wok. Stir sauce; add to skillet. Cook and stir till thickened and

Menu

Ginger-Marinated Sea Bass (see below)

◆◆◆

Hot cooked rice pilaf

◆◆◆

Steamed julienned carrots, zucchini, and yellow summer squash

◆◆◆

Pumpernickel bread slices with butter

bubbly. Return vegetables to skillet; stir to coat with sauce. Cook and stir about 1 minute more or till heated through. Stir in cilantro. Drain orzo; serve shrimp mixture atop orzo. Serves 4.

Nutrition facts per serving: 375 cal., 9 g total fat (1 g sat. fat), 131 mg chol., 518 mg sodium, 50 g carbo., 1 g fiber, 23 g pro.
Daily values: 18% vit. A, 45% vit. C, 4% calcium, 31% iron.

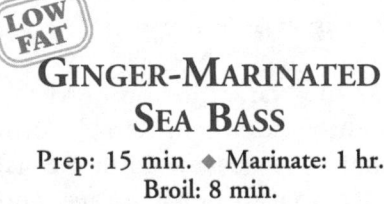

GINGER-MARINATED SEA BASS

Prep: 15 min. ◆ Marinate: 1 hr. Broil: 8 min.

4 fresh or frozen sea bass or halibut steaks, 1 inch thick (1½ to 1¾ lb. total)
¼ cup teriyaki sauce
2 Tbsp. lemon juice
1 Tbsp. grated gingerroot
2 tsp. brown sugar
2 cloves garlic, minced
⅛ tsp. ground red pepper

◆◆◆

Fresh cilantro (optional)

1 Thaw fish, if frozen. Rinse fish and pat dry with paper towels. In a shallow dish combine teriyaki sauce, lemon juice, gingerroot, brown sugar, garlic, and red pepper. Add fish; turn to coat with marinade. Cover fish and marinate in the refrigerator for 1 to 2 hours, turning the steaks occasionally.

2 Drain fish, reserving marinade. Place fish on the greased unheated rack of a broiler pan. Broil 4 inches from heat 5 minutes. Using a wide spatula, carefully turn fish over. Brush with marinade. Broil 3 to 7 minutes more or till fish flakes easily with a fork. Discard any remaining marinade. If desired, sprinkle with cilantro. Makes 4 servings.

Nutrition facts per serving: 179 cal., 3 g total fat (1 g sat. fat), 71 mg chol., 462 mg sodium, 3 g carbo., 0 g fiber, 32 g pro.
Daily values: 8% vit. A, 9% vit. C, 1% calcium, 4% iron.

POACHED SALMON STEAKS WITH CUCUMBER SALAD

Prep: 10 min. ◆ Cook: 8 min.

Barney Jacobson, known as Bestefar (Norwegian for Grandfather), honed his poaching skills during 50 years as a volunteer cook for Sons of Norway functions. These days, Bestefar Jacobson fixes his salmon specialty for smaller crowds at family gatherings in Hendersonville, North Carolina. (See the photograph on page 238.)

4 fresh or frozen salmon steaks, ¾ inch thick (about 1¼ lb. total)
2 cups water
1 Tbsp. salt

1 Tbsp. white vinegar
Freshly ground pepper
Fresh dill sprigs (optional)
Melted butter (optional)
1 recipe Cucumber Salad (see below)
1 recipe Parsleyed New Potatoes (see page 222)

1 Thaw fish, if frozen. Rinse fish and pat dry with paper towels; set aside. In a 10-inch skillet combine water, salt, and vinegar. Bring to boiling; add fish steaks. Return to boiling; reduce heat. Simmer, covered, 8 to 10 minutes or till fish flakes easily with a fork.

2 Remove fish from skillet; discard poaching liquid. Place fish on a platter; sprinkle with ground pepper. If desired, garnish with dill sprigs and serve with melted butter. Serve with Cucumber Salad and Parsleyed New Potatoes. Makes 4 servings.

Nutrition facts per serving (without salad or potatoes): 129 cal., 5 g total fat (1 g sat. fat), 25 mg chol., 351 mg sodium, 0 g carbo., 0 g fiber, 20 g pro.
Daily values: 2% vit. A, 1% calcium, 6% iron.

Cucumber Salad: In a medium bowl whisk together 1 cup *sugar*, ½ cup *vinegar*, 1 teaspoon *salt*, 1 teaspoon *celery seed*, and 1 teaspoon snipped *fresh dillweed*. Stir in 2 cups thinly sliced *cucumbers*. Toss to coat with marinade. Cover and chill 2 hours. Serve with a slotted spoon. Makes 4 side-dish servings.

Nutrition facts per serving: 105 cal., 0 g total fat, 0 mg chol., 268 mg sodium, 28 g carbo., 1 g fiber, 0 g pro.
Daily values: 1% vit. A, 4% vit. C, 1% calcium, 3% iron.

TEST KITCHEN TIP

STORING FISH

Sooner is better when it comes to cooking fish. When that's not possible, wrap fresh fish loosely in clear plastic wrap, store it in the coldest part of the refrigerator, and use it within 2 days. Cover and refrigerate any leftover cooked fish and use within 2 days.

If you purchase frozen fish, keep it in a freezer set at 0° or lower for up to 3 months. Thaw fish overnight in the refrigerator.

CHICKEN AND PASTA PRIMAVERA

Prep: 20 min. ◆ Bake: 1 hr.

Here's a homespun favorite that's a hit with Susan Manlin Katzman's whole family in St. Louis, Missouri. You can use spaghetti or any fun-shaped pasta. (See the photograph on page 238.)

2 to 2½ lb. meaty chicken pieces (breasts, thighs, and drumsticks)
♦♦♦
4 cups vegetables, peeled, trimmed, and cut into 1-inch pieces (carrots, celery, zucchini, and/or yellow summer squash)
1 medium onion, cut into wedges
2 Tbsp. Dijon-style mustard
1 Tbsp. olive oil
2 large cloves garlic, minced
1 tsp. dried oregano, crushed
½ tsp. dried thyme, crushed

½ tsp. celery salt
¼ tsp. pepper
⅛ tsp. salt
♦♦♦
6 oz. spaghetti, linguine, or farfalle (bow ties)
Freshly shredded Parmesan cheese (optional)

1 Skin chicken, if desired. Rinse chicken and pat dry with paper towels; set aside.

2 In a 13×9×2-inch baking pan combine the vegetable pieces and onion wedges. In a small bowl stir together mustard and olive oil. Drizzle about *2 tablespoons* of the mustard-oil mixture over vegetables. Sprinkle garlic, oregano, thyme, celery salt, pepper, and salt over vegetables. Toss gently to coat.

3 Arrange the chicken pieces, bone side down, on top of vegetables. Brush chicken with remaining mustard-oil mixture. Bake, uncovered, in a 350° oven about 1 hour or till chicken is tender and no longer pink. Just before removing chicken from the oven, cook pasta till just tender. Drain pasta well. Transfer the chicken pieces to a serving platter; cover and keep warm.

4 In a large serving bowl combine pasta with vegetables and juices from pan, tossing to combine. If desired, sprinkle with Parmesan cheese. Serve pasta and vegetables with chicken pieces. Makes 6 servings.

Nutrition facts per serving: 329 cal., 12 g total fat (3 g sat. fat), 69 mg chol., 410 mg sodium, 27 g carbo., 2 g fiber, 27 g pro.
Daily values: 58% vit. A, 7% vit. C, 5% calcium, 15% iron.

PRIZE TESTED RECIPE WINNER

SPICY STIR-FRIED CHICKEN WITH CASHEWS

Start to finish: 25 min.

This recipe earned Jennifer Dunklee of Oneonta, New York, $400 in the magazine's monthly contest.

- 2 Tbsp. oyster-flavored sauce
- 1 Tbsp. fish sauce or soy sauce
- 1 Tbsp. brown sugar
- 2 tsp. cornstarch
- ⅓ cup water
- 12 oz. skinless, boneless chicken breast halves

◆◆◆

- 2 Tbsp. cooking oil
- 1 medium onion, sliced
- 2 to 4 fresh red chili peppers, seeded and cut into thin strips*
- 1 clove garlic, minced
- ½ cup unsalted or lightly salted roasted cashews
- Hot cooked rice

1 For sauce, in a small bowl stir together the oyster-flavored sauce, fish sauce or soy sauce, brown sugar, and cornstarch. Stir in water; set sauce aside. Rinse chicken and pat dry. Cut into bite-size strips; set chicken aside.

2 In a large skillet or wok heat oil over medium-high heat. Add onion and stir-fry 1 minute. Add peppers and garlic and stir-fry 1 to 2 minutes more or till onion is crisp-tender. Remove with slotted spoon and set aside. Add chicken to wok. Stir-fry 3 to 4 minutes or till chicken is no longer pink. Push chicken from center of wok. Stir sauce; add to skillet. Cook and stir till thickened and bubbly. Return onion, chili peppers, and garlic to skillet. Cook and stir 1 minute more. Stir in cashews. Serve over hot cooked rice. Makes 4 servings.

*Note: Because chili peppers contain very pungent oils, be sure to protect your hands when preparing them. Put gloves or sandwich bags over your hands so your skin doesn't come in contact with the peppers. Always wash your hands and nails thoroughly in hot, soapy water after handling chili peppers.

Nutrition facts per serving: 444 cal., 18 g total fat (3 g sat. fat), 47 mg chol., 549 mg sodium, 48 g carbo., 2 g fiber, 23 g pro. *Daily values:* 1% vit. A, 21% vit. C, 22% iron.

CHICKEN AND SAUSAGE GUMBO

Prep: 15 min. ◆ Cook: 1½ hr.

Elsie Castille's secret to a great gumbo with a Cajun kick lies in the andouille, a spicy smoked sausage. If you can't find andouille, any smoked sausage will do, but you may need to spice up the gumbo with a bit more red pepper. (See the photograph on page 238.)

- 1 cup all-purpose flour
- ⅔ cup cooking oil
- ¾ cup sliced celery
- ½ cup chopped onion
- ½ cup chopped green sweet pepper
- 2 cloves garlic, minced

◆◆◆

- 2 lb. meaty chicken pieces (breasts, thighs, and drumsticks)
- 6 cups water
- 8 oz. fully cooked smoked sausage, cut into 1-inch pieces
- 8 oz. andouille sausage, cut into ½-inch pieces
- 1 tsp. salt
- 1 tsp. ground red pepper
- ¼ tsp. black pepper

◆◆◆

Hot cooked rice

1 In a large pot combine flour and oil; cook over medium-low heat about 20 minutes or till mixture is caramel-colored, stirring constantly. Add celery, onion, sweet pepper, and garlic; cook for 5 minutes, stirring occasionally.

2 Meanwhile, skin chicken, if desired. Rinse chicken; pat dry. Add the chicken, water, sausages, salt, red pepper, and black pepper to the pot. Bring to boiling; reduce heat to medium-low. Simmer, covered, about 1 hour or till chicken is tender and no longer pink. Skim off excess fat. If desired, remove chicken pieces from gumbo.

3 When chicken pieces are cool enough to handle, remove meat from bones. Discard bones. Return chicken to pot. Cook 2 to 3 minutes more or till chicken is heated through. Serve over rice. Makes 10 servings.

Nutrition facts per serving: 462 cal., 36 g total fat (9 g sat. fat), 57 mg chol., 487 mg sodium, 33 g carbo., 1 g fiber, 26 g pro. *Daily values:* 2% vit. A, 16% vit. C, 2% calcium, 16% iron.

SAUSAGE STEW POT

Prep: 20 min. ◆ **Cook:** 20 min.

This recipe earned Beverly A. Gietzen of Pismo Beach, California, $200 in the magazine's monthly contest.

1 Tbsp. cooking oil
1 lb. fully cooked Polish sausage, halved lengthwise and sliced
1 large onion, halved and sliced
1 medium yellow, red, or green sweet pepper, cut into strips
8 oz. sliced fresh mushrooms
1 clove garlic, minced
4 cups water
2 cups shredded cabbage
1 cup dry lentils, rinsed and drained
2 Tbsp. rice vinegar
1 Tbsp. brown sugar
2 tsp. instant chicken bouillon granules

1 In a large pot heat oil. Cook the sausage, onion, sweet pepper, mushrooms, and garlic in the oil about 5 minutes or till vegetables are just tender. Add the water, cabbage, lentils, vinegar, brown sugar, bouillon, and ⅛ teaspoon *freshly ground black pepper.* Bring to boiling; reduce heat. Simmer, covered, 15 to 20 minutes or till vegetables and lentils are tender. Makes 5 servings.

Nutrition facts per serving: 399 cal., 32 g total fat (9 g sat. fat), 61 mg chol., 1,281 mg sodium, 17 g carbo., 3 g fiber, 16 g pro. *Daily values:* 13% vit. A, 92% vit. C, 19% iron.

BLACK BEAN CHILI

Prep: 15 min. ◆ **Cook:** 20 min.

Top off the chili with cheese, sour cream, or extra hot sauce.

12 oz. ground beef
¾ cup sliced green onions
½ cup chopped green or red sweet pepper
⅓ cup coarsely shredded carrot
1 14½-oz. can low-sodium tomatoes, cut up
1 15-oz. can black beans, drained and rinsed
2 8-oz. cans low-sodium tomato sauce
2 fresh jalapeño or serrano peppers, seeded and chopped*
1½ to 2 tsp. chili powder
¼ tsp. ground black pepper

1 In a 3-quart saucepan cook ground beef, green onions, sweet pepper, and carrot till meat is brown. Drain fat. Stir in remaining ingredients. Bring to boiling; reduce heat. Simmer, covered, for 20 minutes. Just before serving,

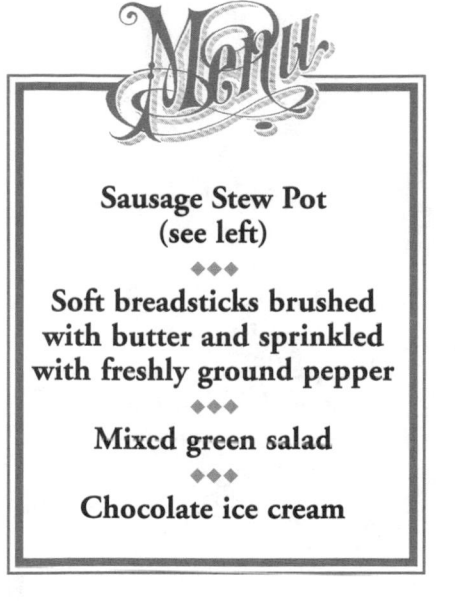

Menu

Sausage Stew Pot (see left)

◆◆◆

Soft breadsticks brushed with butter and sprinkled with freshly ground pepper

◆◆◆

Mixed green salad

◆◆◆

Chocolate ice cream

season to taste with *salt* and *pepper.* Ladle chili into bowls. Makes 4 servings.

*Note: Because chili peppers contain very pungent oils, be sure to protect your hands when preparing them. Put gloves or sandwich bags over your hands so your skin doesn't come in contact with the peppers. Always wash your hands and nails thoroughly in hot, soapy water after handling chili peppers.

Nutrition facts per serving: 311 cal., 11 g total fat (4 g sat. fat), 53 mg chol., 367 mg sodium, 31 g carbo., 8 g fiber, 26 g pro. *Daily values:* 51% vit. A, 93% vit. C, 30% iron.

Southwestern Vegetable Chili: Prepare Black Bean Chili as directed, omitting beef. Cook onion, sweet pepper, and carrot in 1 tablespoon *cooking oil.* Stir in remaining ingredients, plus one 8-ounce can *whole kernel corn,* drained. (If necessary, add *water* till chili is desired consistency.) Season to taste. If desired, top chili with *sour cream* and fresh *cilantro.* Pass *jalapeño sauce* or bottled *hot pepper sauce.*

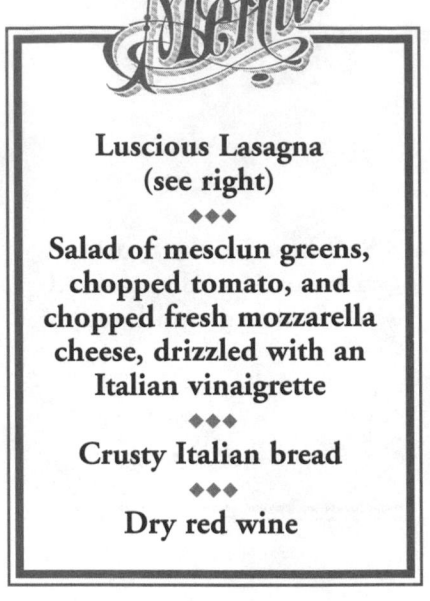

Menu

Luscious Lasagna
(see right)

♦♦♦

Salad of mesclun greens,
chopped tomato, and
chopped fresh mozzarella
cheese, drizzled with an
Italian vinaigrette

♦♦♦

Crusty Italian bread

♦♦♦

Dry red wine

CHICKEN-ASPARAGUS LASAGNA ROLLS

Prep: 40 min. ♦ Bake: 35 min.

3 sheets (10×7 inches each)
   frozen no-boil lasagna
   sheets*

♦♦♦

1 cup low-fat ricotta cheese
1 cup chopped, cooked
   chicken
1 slightly beaten egg white
¼ cup finely shredded
   Parmesan
2 Tbsp. thinly sliced green
   onion (1)
2 Tbsp. diced pimiento,
   drained
¼ tsp. salt
¼ tsp. garlic powder
½ of a 10-oz. pkg. frozen cut
   asparagus, thawed and
   drained

♦♦♦

1 8-oz. tub cream cheese with
   chives and onion
½ cup milk

1 Place frozen lasagna sheets
on a baking sheet; cover with plastic wrap and thaw for 30 minutes.
Drain and set aside.

2 In a medium mixing bowl
combine ricotta cheese, chicken,
egg white, Parmesan cheese, green
onion, pimiento, salt, and garlic
powder. Stir in asparagus.

3 Spread *one-third* of the
chicken mixture over a lasagna
sheet. Starting from the short
edge, roll up jelly-roll style. Cut
the roll crosswise into 6 pieces.
Place pasta rolls, cut side down, in
a greased 2-quart rectangular baking dish. Repeat with remaining
lasagna sheets and filling.

4 For sauce, in a small heavy
saucepan heat and stir cream
cheese over medium-low heat till
softened. Slowly add milk, stirring till smooth. Remove from
heat; cool. Pour *half* of the sauce
over rolls.

5 Bake lasagna rolls, covered,
in a 350° oven for 35 to 40 minutes or till heated through. Heat
remaining sauce over low heat,
stirring frequently. Spoon sauce
over rolls. Makes 6 servings.

*Note: Or, use 6 regular
lasagna noodles, cooked. Cut each
noodle in half crosswise. Spoon a
scant ¼ cup of chicken mixture
onto an end of the noodle. Roll
up jelly-roll style.

■ TO MAKE AHEAD ■

Prepare lasagna rolls as directed, except after assembling, cover
and chill the rolls and remaining
sauce for up to 24 hours. To serve,
bake, covered, in a 350° oven for
50 to 55 minutes or till hot. Heat
remaining sauce over low heat,
stirring frequently. Spoon sauce
over rolls.

Nutrition facts per serving: 342 cal., 18 g
total fat (7 g sat. fat), 74 mg chol., 352 mg
sodium, 23 g carbo., 2 g fiber, 21 g protein.
Daily values: 15% vit. A, 14% vit. C, 11%
calcium, 7% iron.

LUSCIOUS LASAGNA

Prep: 30 min. ♦ Bake: 30 min.

*It's traditional for Grace Charlesworth
to serve this great-tasting lasagna at
family celebrations. She still uses the
recipe from the 1953* Better Homes
and Gardens® New Cook Book.
(See the photograph on page 239.)

1 lb. bulk Italian sausage, bulk
   pork sausage, or ground
   beef
1 clove garlic, minced
1 Tbsp. snipped fresh parsley
1 Tbsp. dried basil, crushed,
   or ¼ cup snipped fresh
   basil
1 14½-oz. can tomatoes,
   undrained and cut up
1 8-oz. can tomato sauce
1 6-oz. can tomato paste

♦♦♦

10 dried lasagna noodles
2 12-oz. cartons (3 cups)
   cream-style cottage cheese
2 beaten eggs
½ cup grated Parmesan cheese
2 Tbsp. snipped fresh parsley
¼ to ½ tsp. pepper

♦♦♦

2 cups shredded mozzarella
   cheese (8 oz.)

♦♦♦

Grated Parmesan cheese
   (optional)
Fresh basil leaves (optional)

1 In a saucepan cook meat till brown; drain fat. Add garlic, the 1 tablespoon parsley, the 1 tablespoon basil, *undrained* tomatoes, tomato sauce, and tomato paste to meat. Bring just to boiling; reduce heat. Simmer, uncovered, 10 to 15 minutes or till thickened, stirring occasionally.

2 Meanwhile, cook noodles according to package directions; drain. Rinse with cold water. Drain the noodles well. In a medium mixing bowl stir together the cottage cheese, eggs, Parmesan cheese, 2 tablespoons parsley, and pepper.

3 Arrange *half* the noodles in a 3-quart rectangular baking dish. Spread with *half* the cottage cheese mixture. Sprinkle with *half* the mozzarella cheese. Spoon *half* the meat mixture over all. Repeat layers. Cover baking dish loosely with foil.

4 Bake in a 375° oven about 30 minutes or till heated through. Let stand 10 to 15 minutes before serving. If desired, sprinkle with additional Parmesan and garnish with basil leaves. Cut in squares to serve. Makes 12 servings.

TO MAKE AHEAD

Prepare lasagna as directed, except after assembling, cover and chill for up to 24 hours. To serve, bake, covered, in a 375° oven for 40 minutes. Uncover; bake about 20 minutes more or till hot. Let stand 10 minutes before serving.

Nutrition facts per serving: 343 cal., 15 g total fat (7 g sat. fat), 80 mg chol., 845 mg sodium, 26 g carbo., 1 g fiber, 24 g pro. *Daily values:* 16% vit. A, 26% vit. C, 20% calcium, 17% iron.

MEXICALI MEAT LOAF

Prep: 25 min. ◆ Bake: 1¼ hr.

Joan Gerberding of Fort Wayne, Indiana, says the grandchildren gobble up this Mexican-inspired meat loaf with gusto. They also have fun helping her mix the ingredients. (See the photograph on page 238.)

- 1 cup finely chopped celery
- 1 cup finely chopped onion and/or green onions
- ½ cup finely chopped carrot
- ½ cup finely chopped red sweet pepper
- ½ cup snipped fresh parsley
- ¼ cup finely chopped green sweet pepper
- 4 cloves garlic, minced
- 2 Tbsp. olive oil or canola oil

◆◆◆

- 2 beaten eggs
- ¾ cup fine dry bread crumbs
- ¾ cup salsa
- 1 tsp. chili powder
- 1 tsp. ground cumin
- ½ tsp. ground nutmeg
- ½ tsp. salt
- ½ tsp. black pepper
- 1 lb. lean ground beef
- 1 lb. ground raw turkey

◆◆◆

Salsa (optional)

1 In a large saucepan cook the celery, onion and/or green onions, carrot, red pepper, parsley, green pepper, and garlic in hot olive oil or canola oil till vegetables are tender but not brown. Remove from heat.

THE CLEVER COOK

MEAT LOAF WITHOUT THE MESS

Mixing together a meat loaf is a snap when you use a pastry blender to combine the ground meat with the rest of the ingredients. Your hands stay clean this way.

Barbara A. Dunbar
South Yarmouth,
Massachusetts

2 In a large mixing bowl stir together the eggs, bread crumbs, the ¾ cup salsa, chili powder, cumin, nutmeg, salt, and black pepper. Stir in the cooked vegetable mixture. Add ground beef and ground turkey. Mix well. Pat meat mixture into a 9×5×3-inch loaf pan.

3 Bake the meat loaf in a 350° oven for 1¼ to 1½ hours or till no pink remains. Remove meat loaf from the oven and let stand for 10 minutes before serving. Invert meat loaf and remove from pan. Slice to serve. If desired, top individual servings with salsa. Makes 8 servings.

Nutrition facts per serving: 295 cal., 17 g total fat (5 g sat. fat), 110 mg chol., 384 mg sodium, 13 g carbo., 1 g fiber, 22 g pro. *Daily values:* 33% vit. A, 45% vit. C, 5% calcium, 21% iron.

ORANGE AND DATE COFFEE CAKE

Prep: 20 min. ◆ Bake: 30 min.

¼ cup all-purpose flour
¼ cup packed brown sugar
2 Tbsp. butter or margarine
⅓ cup chopped walnuts

◆◆◆

1¼ cups all-purpose flour
1½ tsp. baking powder
¼ tsp. baking soda
¼ tsp. salt

◆◆◆

⅓ cup butter or margarine
½ cup granulated sugar
1 egg
1 tsp. vanilla
1 tsp. finely shredded orange
    peel
½ cup orange juice
½ cup snipped pitted dates

1 Grease and lightly flour an 8×8×2-inch baking pan. Set pan aside. For topping, in a small mixing bowl stir together the ¼ cup flour and the brown sugar. Using a pastry blender, cut in the 2 tablespoons butter or margarine till mixture resembles coarse crumbs. Stir in walnuts; set aside.

2 In another bowl stir together the 1¼ cups flour, baking powder, baking soda, and salt. Set the flour mixture aside.

3 In a medium mixing bowl beat the ⅓ cup butter or margarine with an electric mixer on medium to high speed about 30 seconds or till softened. Add granulated sugar and beat till combined. Add egg, vanilla, and orange peel; beat till well

combined (batter may appear curdled). Add flour mixture and orange juice alternately to beaten mixture, beating on low speed after each addition just till combined. Stir in dates.

4 Spread the batter into the prepared pan. Sprinkle with topping. Bake in a 350° oven about 30 minutes or till a wooden toothpick inserted near the center comes out clean. Serve warm. Makes 9 servings.

Nutrition facts per serving: 285 cal., 13 g total fat (12 g sat. fat), 43 mg chol., 263 mg sodium, 40 g carbo., 2 g fiber, and 4 g pro. *Daily values:* 10% vit. A, 12% vit. C, 6% calcium, 9% iron.

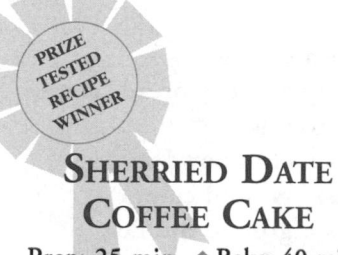

SHERRIED DATE COFFEE CAKE

Prep: 25 min. ◆ Bake: 40 min.

This recipe earned Mary A. Wirth of White Hall, Virginia, $400 in the magazine's monthly contest.
(See the photograph on page 241.)

½ cup chopped pitted whole
    dates
3 Tbsp. cream sherry
½ cup finely chopped pecans
⅓ cup packed brown sugar
¼ cup granulated sugar
1 tsp. ground cinnamon
1 Tbsp. margarine or butter,
    softened

◆◆◆

2 cups all-purpose flour
1 tsp. baking powder
1 tsp. baking soda
1 tsp. salt

1 cup granulated sugar
¼ cup margarine or butter,
    softened
1 egg
1 8-oz. carton dairy sour
    cream
1 Tbsp. cream sherry

◆◆◆

1 recipe Sherry Glaze (see
    page 231)

1 Grease an 8×8×2-inch baking pan; set aside. In a small bowl combine dates and the 3 tablespoons of sherry. Cover and let stand for 10 minutes. In another small bowl combine pecans, brown sugar, the ¼ cup granulated sugar, the cinnamon, and the 1 tablespoon margarine or butter. Stir in date mixture; set aside.

2 In a bowl stir together the flour, baking powder, baking soda, and salt. Set mixture aside.

3 In a large mixing bowl beat the 1 cup granulated sugar, the ¼ cup margarine or butter, and egg with an electric mixer till smooth. Beat in sour cream and the 1 tablespoon sherry. Add flour mixture to sour cream mixture; beat till well combined.

4 Spread *half* the batter into the prepared pan. Top with *half* the date mixture. Top with remaining batter, then date mixture. Bake in a 375° oven for 40 to 45 minutes or till a wooden toothpick inserted near center comes out clean. To prevent over-browning, cover the cake with foil for the last 15 minutes of baking. Cool slightly. Drizzle the Sherry Glaze over coffee cake. Makes 12 servings.

Sherry Glaze: In a saucepan combine 2 tablespoons *margarine or butter,* 2 tablespoons *water,* and ¼ cup *sugar.* Cook and stir till bubbly. Reduce heat; simmer for 5 minutes. Remove from heat; stir in 2 tablespoons *cream sherry.*

Nutrition facts per serving: 359 cal., 14 g total fat (4 g sat. fat), 26 mg chol., 411 mg sodium, 54 g carbo., 1 g fiber, and 4 g pro. *Daily values:* 13% vit. A, 6% calcium, 9% iron.

PRIZE TESTED RECIPE WINNER

DOUBLE-COFFEE COFFEE CAKE

Prep: 25 min. ◆ Bake: 50 min.

This recipe earned Susan Angelotti of Erie, Pennsylvania, $200 in the magazine's monthly contest. (See the photograph on page 241.)

- 4 tsp. instant coffee crystals
- 2 tsp. hot water
  ◆◆◆
- 1 cup chopped walnuts
- ¼ cup granulated sugar
- ¼ cup packed brown sugar
- 2 tsp. ground cinnamon
- 2 tsp. instant coffee crystals
  ◆◆◆
- 3 cups all-purpose flour
- 1½ tsp. baking powder
- 1½ tsp. baking soda
- ½ tsp. salt
  ◆◆◆
- ¾ cup margarine or butter
- 1¾ cups granulated sugar
- 1 8-oz. carton dairy sour cream
- 3 eggs
- ¼ cup buttermilk
- ¼ cup applesauce
- 1 tsp. vanilla

Sifted powdered sugar (optional)

1 Grease and flour a 10-inch fluted tube pan; set aside. In a small bowl dissolve the 4 teaspoons coffee crystals in hot water. Set aside.

2 In a medium bowl stir together the walnuts, the ¼ cup granulated sugar, brown sugar, cinnamon, and the 2 teaspoons coffee crystals; set aside. In another bowl stir together the flour, baking powder, baking soda, and salt; set aside.

3 In a large bowl beat margarine or butter with an electric mixer on medium speed for 30 seconds. Add the 1¾ cups granulated sugar. Beat till light and fluffy. Add sour cream, eggs, buttermilk, applesauce, vanilla, and reserved coffee-water mixture; beat well. Add flour mixture, a little at a time, beating well after each addition.

4 Pour *half* the batter into the prepared fluted tube pan. Sprinkle with *1 cup* of the nut mixture. Top with remaining batter; sprinkle with remaining nut mixture. Bake in a 350° oven about 50 minutes or till a wooden toothpick inserted near center comes out clean. Cool 10 minutes; remove from pan. If desired, sift powdered sugar on top. Serve warm. Makes 12 servings.

Nutrition facts per serving: 483 cal., 23 g total fat (6 g sat. fat), 62 mg chol., 461 mg sodium, 64 g carbo., 1 g fiber, 7 g pro. *Daily values:* 21% vit. A, 8% calcium, 14% iron.

TAKE A BREAK

Whenever you need a break, coffee cakes are a delightful choice for a tasty treat. They're an all-American concoction, closely related to biscuits, scones, muffins, quick breads, and creamed cakes, and they use many of the same simple preparation techniques.

Neither too sweet nor too rich and best served warm, coffee cake should stand for 20 to 30 minutes after you take it out of the oven before you cut it. And, as the name says, nothing goes better with it than a cup of freshly brewed coffee.

To make good coffee, start with fresh beans or ground coffee and fresh cold water. Use ¾ cup cold water and 1 to 2 tablespoons ground coffee for each 6-ounce cup.

For drip coffee, line a coffee basket with a filter, and measure the ground coffee into the lined basket. If you have an electric drip coffeemaker, pour cold water into the water compartment, place the pot on the heating element, let the water run through the basket and the coffee drip into the pot. If you have a nonelectric drip coffeemaker, pour boiling water over the ground coffee in the lined basket, and let coffee drip into the pot.

Don't let the coffee stand on the warming plate for a long time or it will develop a bitter flavor. Always wash the coffeemaker after each use.

Fresh Pear Coffee Cake

Prep: 15 min. ◆ Bake: 40 min.

⅓ cup granulated sugar
¼ cup packed brown sugar
3 Tbsp. all-purpose flour
½ tsp. ground cinnamon
2 Tbsp. butter or margarine
1¾ cups all-purpose flour
1 tsp. baking powder
½ tsp. baking soda
½ tsp. ground cinnamon
¼ tsp. salt
◆◆◆
2 eggs
¾ cup granulated sugar
¼ cup butter or margarine, softened
1 tsp. vanilla
1 8-oz. carton dairy sour cream
1½ cups peeled and chopped pears
Nonstick spray coating

1 For streusel topping, in a small mixing bowl combine the ⅓ cup granulated sugar, ¼ cup brown sugar, 3 tablespoons flour, and ½ teaspoon cinnamon. Using a pastry blender, cut in 2 tablespoons butter or margarine till crumbly; set aside. In another bowl combine 1¾ cups flour, the baking powder, baking soda, ½ teaspoon cinnamon, and salt.

2 In a large mixing bowl beat together eggs, ¾ cup granulated sugar, the softened butter or margarine, and vanilla for 2 minutes. Add the flour mixture and sour cream alternately to the beaten mixture, beating till smooth after each addition. Stir in pears.

3 Spray an 11×7×2-inch baking pan with nonstick spray coat-ing. Spread batter into pan. Sprinkle with streusel topping. Bake coffee cake in a 350° oven for 40 to 45 minutes or till a wooden toothpick inserted near center comes out clean. Serve warm. Makes 12 servings.

Nutrition facts per serving: 269 cal., 11 g total fat (6 g sat. fat), 59 mg chol., 207 mg sodium, 40 g carbo., 1 g fiber, 4 g pro. *Daily values:* 11% vit. A, 1% vit. C, 5% calcium, 8% iron.

Banana Swirl Coffee Cake

Prep: 20 min. ◆ Bake: 35 min.

1 cup finely chopped pecans
¼ cup packed brown sugar
1 tsp. ground cinnamon
2 cups all-purpose flour
1 tsp. baking powder
1 tsp. baking soda
¼ tsp. salt
◆◆◆
⅓ cup butter or margarine, softened
½ cup granulated sugar
½ cup packed brown sugar
2 eggs
◆◆◆
1 8-oz. carton dairy sour cream
1 Tbsp. brandy (optional)
¾ cup mashed bananas (2 medium)

1 Grease and lightly flour a 10-inch fluted tube pan; set aside. In a bowl stir together pecans, ¼ cup brown sugar, and cinna-mon; set aside. In another bowl stir together the flour, baking powder, baking soda, and salt.

2 In a large mixing bowl beat butter or margarine with an elec-tric mixer on medium to high speed for 30 seconds. Gradually beat in granulated sugar and ½ cup brown sugar till well com-bined. Add eggs, 1 at a time, beat-ing well after each addition.

3 Combine sour cream and, if desired, brandy. Add flour mix-ture and sour cream mixture alter-nately to sugar mixture, beating after each addition till smooth. Stir in bananas.

4 Spoon *half* the batter into prepared pan. Sprinkle with pecan mixture. Spoon remaining batter over top. Bake in a 350° oven for 35 to 40 minutes or till a wooden toothpick inserted in center comes out clean. Cool on wire rack for 10 minutes. Remove from pan. Cool at least 45 min-utes. Serve cake warm. Makes 12 to 16 servings.

Nutrition facts per serving: 319 cal., 16 g total fat (6 g sat. fat), 58 mg chol., 256 mg sodium, 41 g carbo., 1 g fiber, 5 g pro. *Daily values:* 11% vit. A, 3% vit. C, 6% calcium, 10% iron.

Praline-Apple Bread

Prep: 20 min. ◆ Bake: 55 min.

2 cups all-purpose flour
2 tsp. baking powder
½ tsp. baking soda
◆◆◆
1 cup granulated sugar
1 8-oz. carton dairy sour cream
2 eggs
2 tsp. vanilla
1¼ cups chopped, peeled tart apples
1 cup chopped pecans
◆◆◆
¼ cup butter or margarine
¼ cup packed brown sugar

1 Grease a 9×5×3-inch loaf pan; set aside. In a bowl stir together flour, baking powder, baking soda, and ½ teaspoon *salt*.

2 In a large mixing bowl beat together granulated sugar, sour cream, eggs, and vanilla with an electric mixer on low speed till combined. Beat on medium speed for 2 minutes. Add flour mixture to sour cream mixture, beating on low speed till combined. Stir in apples and *½ cup* of the pecans.

3 Spread batter into the prepared pan. Sprinkle with remaining chopped pecans; press lightly into batter. Bake in a 350° oven for 55 to 60 minutes or till a wooden toothpick inserted in center comes out clean. (If necessary, cover loosely with foil the last 10 minutes of baking to prevent overbrowning.) Cool in pan on a wire rack for 10 minutes.

4 Meanwhile, in a small saucepan combine butter or margarine and brown sugar; cook and stir till mixture begins to boil. Reduce heat and boil gently for 1 minute. Remove bread from pan. Drizzle top with brown sugar mixture; cool. Makes 1 loaf (18 servings).

Nutrition facts per serving: 203 cal., 10 g total fat (4 g sat. fat), 36 mg chol., 175 mg sodium, 27 g carbo., 1 g fiber, 3 g pro. *Daily values:* 6% vit. A, 5% calcium, 6% iron.

PUMPKIN SWIRL COFFEE CAKE

Prep: 35 min. ◆ Rise: 1¾ hr.
Bake: 25min.

2 to 2½ cups all-purpose flour
1 pkg. active dry yeast
½ cup milk
¼ cup granulated sugar
3 Tbsp. margarine or butter
1 egg

◆◆◆

1 egg yolk
¾ cup canned pumpkin
½ cup packed brown sugar
1 tsp. pumpkin pie spice
⅓ cup raisins
⅓ cup chopped walnuts

◆◆◆

½ cup sifted powdered sugar
½ tsp. vanilla
1 to 2 tsp. milk

1 In a medium mixing bowl combine *¾ cup* of the flour and the yeast; set aside. In a small saucepan heat and stir the ½ cup milk, granulated sugar, margarine, and ½ teaspoon *salt* just till warm (120° to 130°) and margarine or butter almost melts. Add milk mixture to flour-yeast mixture along with the whole egg. Beat with an electric mixer on low to medium speed for 30 seconds, scraping sides of bowl. Beat on high speed for 3 minutes. Using a wooden spoon, stir in as much of the remaining flour as you can.

2 Turn dough out onto a lightly floured surface. Knead in enough of the remaining flour to make a moderately stiff dough that is smooth and elastic (6 to 8 minutes total). Shape dough into a ball. Place in a lightly greased bowl, turning once to grease surface of dough. Cover; let rise in a warm place till double in size (1 to 1½ hours).

3 Punch dough down. Turn dough out onto a lightly floured surface. Cover; let rest 10 minutes. Grease a baking sheet; set aside. Meanwhile, in a mixing bowl combine egg yolk, pumpkin, brown sugar, pumpkin pie spice, and ⅛ teaspoon *salt*. Stir in raisins and walnuts.

4 On a lightly floured surface roll dough to a 20×10-inch rectangle. Spread pumpkin mixture to within ½ inch of edges. Roll up, jelly-roll style, beginning with a long side. Place dough, seam side down, on prepared baking sheet. Form dough into a ring; seal seam. Cover; let rise till almost double (45 to 60 minutes).

5 Bake in a 350° oven 25 to 30 minutes or till bread sounds hollow when you tap the top with your fingers. (If necessary, cover with foil the last 5 to 10 minutes of baking to prevent overbrowning.) Cool on a rack.

6 For icing, combine powdered sugar, vanilla, and enough milk to make icing easy to drizzle. Drizzle atop cooled coffee cake. Makes 1 loaf (12 servings).

Nutrition facts per serving: 213 cal., 6 g total fat (1 g sat. fat), 36 mg chol., 160 mg sodium, 36 g carbo., 2 g fiber, 4 g pro. *Daily values:* 41% vit. A, 1% vit. C, 3% calcium, 11% iron.

APPLE-DATE COFFEE CAKE

Prep: 25 min. ◆ Rise: 30 min.
Bake: 30 min.

Betty Hessler of Belding, Michigan, makes use of the fall apple harvest to create this fruit-filled coffee cake. It's bound to become a special addition to your weekend or holiday brunch menu. (See the photograph on page 240.)

2 cups chopped, peeled apples
    (2 medium)
1 cup chopped pitted dates
½ cup granulated sugar
¼ cup water

◆◆◆

½ recipe Grandma's Yeast
    Dough (see page 235)
1 Tbsp. butter, softened

◆◆◆

1 recipe Powdered Sugar Icing
    (see right)
    Maraschino cherry pieces
    (optional)
    Sliced almonds (optional)

1 In a medium saucepan combine apples, dates, granulated sugar, and water. Cook and stir the mixture over medium heat for 5 to 7 minutes or till apples are tender and liquid is absorbed. Set apple-date mixture aside to cool.

2 Grease a baking sheet; set aside. On a lightly floured surface roll the prepared dough to a 15×10-inch rectangle. Spread softened butter over dough. Spread cooled apple-date mixture evenly over dough. Roll up, jelly-roll style, starting from a long side; seal seam.

3 Place roll on the prepared baking sheet. Shape dough into a ring; seal seam. Using sharp

kitchen shears, cut slits about ½ inch deep and 1 inch apart atop loaf (see below). Cover the loaf and let rise in a warm place till nearly double in size (30 to 40 minutes).

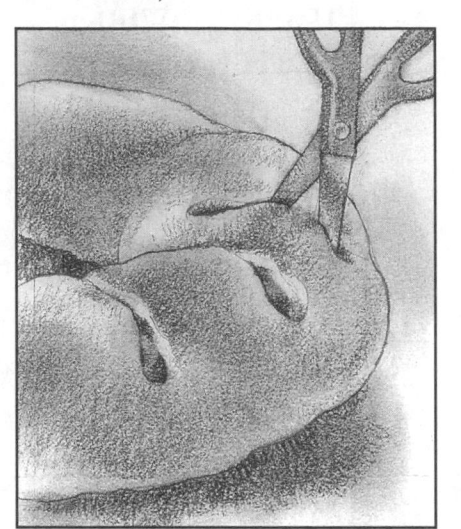

4 Bake in a 375° oven about 30 minutes or till bread sounds hollow when you tap the top with your fingers. (If necessary, cover coffee cake loosely with foil the last 10 minutes of baking to prevent overbrowning.) Immediately remove coffee cake from baking sheet. Cool on a wire rack.

5 Drizzle with the Powdered Sugar Icing. If desired, garnish with cherry pieces and sliced almonds. Makes 1 loaf (12 to 16 servings).

Powdered Sugar Icing: In a small mixing bowl combine 1 cup *sifted powdered sugar* and ½ teaspoon *vanilla*. Stir in enough *milk* (1 to 2 tablespoons) to make icing easy to drizzle.

Nutrition facts per serving: 323 cal., 6 g total fat (3 g sat. fat), 32 mg chol., 241 mg sodium, 63 g carbo., 3 g fiber, 5 g pro. *Daily values:* 6% vit. A, 1% vit. C, 3% calcium, 13% iron.

APRICOT-GINGER LADDER LOAF

Prep: 25 min. ◆ Rise: 45 min.
Bake: 25 min.

1 16-oz. loaf frozen sweet roll
    or white bread dough,
    thawed
2 Tbsp. butter or margarine,
    softened

◆◆◆

3 Tbsp. granulated sugar
2 Tbsp. all-purpose flour
2 Tbsp. finely chopped
    crystallized ginger
2 cups thinly sliced apricots,
    nectarines, or peeled
    peaches

◆◆◆

½ cup sifted powdered sugar
2 to 3 tsp. milk

1 Line a baking sheet with foil; grease foil. On a lightly floured surface roll dough to a 12×9-inch rectangle. Transfer dough to prepared baking sheet. Spread with the softened butter or margarine.

2 For filling, in a medium mixing bowl stir together granulated sugar, flour, and ginger. Add fruit, tossing to coat. Spread filling in a 3-inch-wide strip down the center of the dough to within 1 inch of the ends.

3 On long sides, make 3-inch cuts from the edges toward the center at 1-inch intervals. Starting at an end, alternately fold opposite strips of dough, at an angle, across the filling. Slightly press ends together in center to seal. Cover dough and let rise in a warm place till nearly double (45 to 60 minutes).

4 Bake in a 350° oven about 25 minutes or till golden. Carefully remove loaf from baking sheet and cool on a wire rack about 30 minutes.

5 For icing, combine powdered sugar and enough milk to make icing easy to drizzle. Drizzle icing atop loaf. Serve warm. Makes 1 loaf (10 servings).

Nutrition facts per serving: 196 cal., 5 g total fat (3 g sat. fat), 29 mg chol., 97 mg sodium, 35 g carbo., 1 g fiber, 4 g pro. *Daily values:* 12% vit. A, 6% vit. C, 2% calcium, 12% iron.

GRANDMA'S YEAST DOUGH
Prep: 20 min. ◆ Rise: 1½ hr.

Follow Betty Hessler's example and divide this dough in half. Use one portion of the dough to create Golden Dinner Rolls (see right), and use the other portion to make Apple-Date Coffee Cake (see page 234).

   2 pkg. active dry yeast
   ½ cup warm water (105° to 115°)

◆◆◆

 1½ cups milk
   ½ cup butter or margarine
   ½ cup sugar
   2 tsp. salt

◆◆◆

   2 slightly beaten eggs
 7½ to 8 cups all-purpose flour

1 In a small bowl dissolve the yeast in the warm water; set aside.

2 Meanwhile, in a medium saucepan combine milk, butter or margarine, sugar, and salt. Heat and stir just till warm (120° to 130°) and butter almost melts.

3 In a large bowl combine yeast mixture, warmed milk mixture, and eggs. Using a wooden spoon, stir in as much of the flour as you can.

4 Turn the dough out onto a lightly floured surface. Knead in enough of the remaining flour to make a moderately soft dough that is smooth and elastic (3 to 5 minutes total). Shape dough into a ball. Place in a lightly greased bowl, turning once to grease surface of the dough. Cover; let rise in a warm place till double in size (about 1½ hours).

5 Punch dough down. Turn dough out onto a lightly floured surface. Divide dough in half. Cover; let rest 10 minutes. Use one portion of the dough to prepare Golden Dinner Rolls, and use the remaining portion to make Apple-Date Coffee Cake.

LOW FAT

GOLDEN DINNER ROLLS
Prep: 15 min. ◆ Rise: 30 min.
Bake: 15 min.

When the aroma of Betty Hessler's fresh-from-the-oven rolls wafts through your house, your family will immediately follow their noses to the dinner table.
(See the photograph on page 240.)

 ½ recipe Grandma's Yeast Dough (see left)

1 Grease a 13×9×2-inch baking pan; set aside. Divide the prepared dough into 18 pieces. To shape, gently pull each dough piece into a ball, tucking edges underneath. Place the shaped rolls into the prepared pan. Cover and let rise in a warm place till nearly double in size (30 to 40 minutes).

2 Bake in a 400° oven about 15 minutes or till golden brown. Remove rolls from pan. Cool on wire racks. Makes 18 rolls.

Nutrition facts per roll: 131 cal., 3 g total fat (2 g sat. fat), 19 mg chol., 153 mg sodium, 22 g carbo., 1 g fiber, 3 g pro. *Daily values:* 3% vit. A, 1% calcium, 8% iron.

THE CLEVER COOK

A CRUMBLY SOLUTION
Put your leftover rolls and bread crusts to good use by turning them into soft crumbs in your food processor. Store the crumbs in a freezer container and keep them in the freezer. Use the crumbs plain in recipes or make seasoned bread crumbs. Just combine 2 cups of bread crumbs with ¼ cup grated Parmesan cheese, 2 tablespoons dried parsley flakes, and ½ teaspoon garlic powder. The seasoned crumbs are great when mixed with a little melted butter and sprinkled over a green bean casserole.

Angela Thomas
Indian Springs, Ohio

SWEDISH RYE BREAD

Prep: 25 min. ◆ Rise: 2 hr.
Bake: 35 min.

Violet Nelson's Scandinavian heritage was the inspiration for these wonderful loaves.
(See the photograph on page 237.)

1 pkg. active dry yeast
¼ cup warm water (105° to 115°)
½ cup margarine or butter, cut up
⅓ cup sugar
¼ cup light-flavored molasses
2 tsp. salt
2 cups boiling water
2 cups rye flour
4¾ to 5½ cups all-purpose flour

◆◆◆

Margarine or butter, softened

1 In a small bowl dissolve yeast in the warm water; set aside.

2 In a large mixing bowl place the ½ cup margarine or butter, sugar, molasses, and salt. Add the boiling water; stir till margarine is melted. Add rye flour. Beat with an electric mixer on low speed till combined. Beat on medium speed 3 minutes. Gradually beat in yeast mixture till combined. Using a wooden spoon, stir in as much of the all-purpose flour as you can.

3 Turn dough out onto a lightly floured surface. Knead in enough of the remaining all-purpose flour to make a moderately stiff dough that is smooth and elastic (6 to 8 minutes total). Shape dough into a ball. Place in a greased bowl; turn once. Cover; let rise in a warm place till double in size (1¼ to 1½ hours).

4 Punch dough down. Turn dough out onto a lightly floured surface. Divide dough in half. Cover; let rest 10 minutes. Grease two 8×4×2-inch or 9×5×3-inch loaf pans. Shape each half into a loaf and place in prepared pans. Cover; let rise in a warm place till nearly double (40 to 50 minutes).

5 Bake in a 350° oven 35 to 45 minutes or till done. Remove from pans. Brush tops of warm loaves with a little softened margarine. Cool on wire rack. Makes 2 loaves (24 servings).

Nutrition facts per serving: 171 cal., 5 g total fat (1 g sat. fat), 0 mg chol., 230 mg sodium, 29 g carbo., 2 g fiber, 3 g pro. *Daily values:* 5% vit. A, 1% calcium, 9% iron.

DILL BREAD

Prep: 25 min. ◆ Rise: 1½ hr.
Bake: 40 min.
See the photograph on page 237.

1 pkg. active dry yeast
¼ cup warm water (105° to 115°)
1 Tbsp. sugar

◆◆◆

1 cup cream-style cottage cheese
1 Tbsp. sugar
1 Tbsp. minced dried onion
1 Tbsp. butter or margarine
2½ tsp. dillseed
¼ tsp. baking soda

◆◆◆

1 slightly beaten egg
2¼ to 2½ cups bread flour or all-purpose flour

1 In a small bowl combine the yeast, warm water, and the 1 tablespoon sugar. Set aside to dissolve yeast.

2 Meanwhile, in a medium saucepan combine cottage cheese, the 1 tablespoon sugar, onion, the 1 tablespoon butter, *2 teaspoons* of the dillseed, the baking soda, and 1 teaspoon *salt.* Heat and stir just till mixture is warm (120° to 130°) and butter almost melts.

3 Combine dissolved yeast mixture, cottage cheese mixture, and egg. Stir in as much of the flour as you can. Turn dough out onto a floured surface. Knead in enough remaining flour to make a moderately soft dough that is smooth and elastic (3 to 5 minutes total). Shape dough into a ball; place in a greased bowl, turning once. Cover; let rise in a warm place till double (about 1 hour).

4 Grease a 1½-quart casserole. Punch dough down. Turn dough out onto a lightly floured surface. Shape dough into a 7-inch round. Place dough into the prepared casserole. Cover and let dough rise in a warm place till nearly double in size (30 to 40 minutes).

5 Brush dough with 1 teaspoon *melted butter or margarine.* Sprinkle surface with the remaining dillseed. Bake in a 350° oven 40 to 45 minutes or till golden brown and bread sounds hollow when tapped. (If necessary, cover the bread loosely with foil the last 15 minutes of baking to prevent overbrowning.) Immediately remove bread from casserole. Cool on wire rack. Makes 1 large loaf (16 servings).

Nutrition facts per serving: 108 cal., 2 g total fat (1 g sat. fat), 18 mg chol., 223 mg sodium, 17 g carbo., 1 g fiber, 5 g pro. *Daily values:* 2% vit. A, 1% calcium, 6% iron.

Above: *Dill Bread (page 236)*
Right: *Swedish Rye Bread (page 236)*

Top: *Poached Salmon Steaks with Cucumber Salad*
(page 224) and *Parsleyed New Potatoes (page 222)*
Above: *Chicken and Sausage Gumbo (page 226)*

Top: *Chicken and Pasta Primavera (page 225)*
Above: *Mexicali Meat Loaf (page 229)*
Page 239: *Luscious Lasagna (page 228)*

Top: *Sherried Date Coffee Cake (page 230)*
Above: *Paul's Pumpkin Bars (page 247)*
Page 240: *Apple-Date Coffee Cake (page 234)* and *Golden Dinner Rolls (page 235)*

Top: *Double-Coffee Coffee Cake (page 231)*
Above: *Gâteau de Sirop (Syrup Cake) (page 247)*

Left: *Swedish Rice Pudding (page 245)*
Below: *Chocolate Cookie Cake (page 246)*
Page 243: *Bestefar's Favorite Cookies* and *Hjortetakk Bakkels (Reindeer Antler Cookies) (page 248)*

Crunchy Caramel Apple Pie (page 245)

CRUNCHY CARAMEL APPLE PIE

Prep: 35 min. ◆ Bake: 50 min.

Betty Hessler likes to use moderately tart apples, such as Idareds, Jonathans, or Northern Spys, for her pie. With or without a scoop of vanilla ice cream, a piece of this pie is a memorable indulgence.
(See the photograph on page 244.)

1 recipe Pastry for Single-
  Crust Pie (see right)

◆◆◆

½ cup sugar
3 Tbsp. all-purpose flour
1 tsp. ground cinnamon
⅛ tsp. salt
6 cups thinly sliced, peeled
  cooking apples
1 recipe Crumb Topping
  (see right)

◆◆◆

½ cup chopped pecans
¼ cup caramel ice-cream
  topping

1 Prepare Pastry for Single-Crust Pie. On a lightly floured surface, roll dough into a 12-inch circle. Transfer pastry to a 9-inch pie plate. Ease pastry into pie plate, being careful not to stretch pastry. Trim and crimp edge.

2 In a large mixing bowl stir together sugar, flour, cinnamon, and salt. Add apple slices and gently toss till coated. Transfer apple mixture to the pastry-lined pie plate. Sprinkle Crumb Topping over apple mixture.

3 To prevent overbrowning, cover edge of pie with foil. Bake in a 375° oven for 25 minutes. Remove foil. Bake pie for 25 to 30 minutes more or till top is golden. Remove from oven; sprin-kle pie with pecans and drizzle with caramel topping. Cool on a wire rack. Makes 8 servings.

Pastry for Single-Crust Pie: In a bowl stir together 1¼ cups *all-purpose flour* and ¼ teaspoon *salt*. Using a pastry blender, cut in ⅓ cup *shortening* till pieces are pea-size. Using 4 to 5 tablespoons *cold water* total, sprinkle 1 tablespoon of water at a time over the flour mixture, tossing with a fork till all of the dough is moistened. Form dough into a ball.

Crumb Topping: Stir together 1 cup *packed brown sugar*, ½ cup *all-purpose flour*, and ½ cup *quick-cooking rolled oats*. Using a pastry blender, cut in ½ cup *butter or margarine* till the topping mixture resembles coarse crumbs.

Nutrition facts per serving: 554 cal., 25 g total fat (10 g sat. fat), 31 mg chol., 260 mg sodium, 81 g carbo., 3 g fiber, 5 g pro. *Daily values:* 11% vit. A, 6% vit. C, 3% calcium, 15% iron.

SWEDISH RICE PUDDING

Prep: 35 min. ◆ Bake: 15 min.

Violet Nelson of Humboldt, Iowa, stirs a whole, unblanched almond into her rice pudding mixture before baking to follow an old Swedish custom. Tradition has it that whoever gets the almond will marry within a year.
(See the photograph on page 242.)

4 cups milk
½ cup long-grain rice
½ tsp. salt

◆◆◆

4 egg yolks
½ cup sugar
2 Tbsp. butter, softened
1 tsp. vanilla

4 egg whites
3 Tbsp. sugar

1 Grease a 2-quart casserole; set aside. In a large heavy saucepan bring milk just to boiling (watch carefully to prevent milk from foaming); stir in rice and salt. Reduce heat to medium-low. Cook rice, uncovered, about 18 minutes or till tender, stirring frequently.

2 In a medium mixing bowl combine egg yolks, the ½ cup sugar, butter, and vanilla. Beat till well combined but not foamy. Stir *1 cup* of hot rice mixture into egg mixture. While stirring, pour all of the egg mixture into rice mixture in saucepan. Bring mixture to boiling, stirring constantly. Cook and stir 1 minute more or till thickened. Pour rice mixture into the prepared casserole.

3 Meanwhile, in a large bowl beat the 4 egg whites with an electric mixer on medium speed about 1 minute or till soft peaks form (tips curl). Gradually add the 3 tablespoons sugar, 1 tablespoon at a time, beating on high speed about 4 minutes more or till mixture forms stiff, glossy peaks (tips stand straight) and sugar dissolves.

4 Immediately spread the meringue over rice pudding mixture, carefully sealing to the edge. Bake in a 350° oven 15 minutes. Serve warm or cold. To store, cover and chill. Serves 8.

Nutrition facts per serving: 234 cal., 8 g total fat (4 g sat. fat), 123 mg chol., 255 mg sodium, 33 g carbo., 0 g fiber, 8 g pro. *Daily values:* 26% vit. A, 1% vit. C, 13% calcium, 5% iron.

CHOCOLATE COOKIE CAKE

Prep: 50 min.
Bake: 20 min. per batch

This decadent sensation is "the ultimate granny treat," says Susan Manlin Katzman of St. Louis, Missouri, whose family clamors for the cake whenever it's time to celebrate a birthday. (See the photograph on page 242.)

2⅔ cups all-purpose flour
2¼ cups granulated sugar
1¼ tsp. baking soda
¾ tsp. salt
½ tsp. baking powder
1⅓ cups milk
1 8-oz. carton dairy sour cream
5 oz. unsweetened chocolate, melted and cooled
⅓ cup butter, softened
3 eggs
2 tsp. vanilla

1 recipe Chocolate Sandwich Cookie Filling (see below right)

◆◆◆

1 recipe Chocolate Frosting (see below right)

◆◆◆

4 chocolate sandwich cookies, crushed

1 Grease and lightly flour two 8- or 9×1½-inch round cake pans. Set pans aside.

2 In an extra-large mixing bowl combine flour, sugar, baking soda, salt, and baking powder. Add milk, sour cream, melted chocolate, butter, eggs, and vanilla. Beat with an electric mixer on low speed about 1 minute or till mixture is well combined. Beat on high speed 3 minutes, scraping sides of bowl occasionally.

3 Place *half* of the batter in a medium bowl; cover and chill. Divide remaining half of batter evenly between the prepared pans. Bake in a 350° oven for 20 to 25 minutes for 9-inch layers and 25 to 30 minutes for 8-inch layers or till a wooden toothpick inserted in centers comes out clean. Cool cakes in pans on wire racks for 10 minutes. Remove cakes from pans and let layers cool completely on wire racks.

4 Wash the 2 cake pans. Grease and lightly flour pans. Divide reserved, chilled batter evenly between pans. Bake and cool as directed above.

5 Prepare Chocolate Sandwich Cookie Filling; reserve ¾ cup of the filling for the cake garnish.

6 To assemble the cake, put a cake layer on a serving plate and top with *one-third* of the remaining cookie filling, spreading filling evenly over layer. Add a second layer of cake and spread with another one-third portion of the cookie filling. Add another cake layer and spread with remaining cookie filling. Top with the final cake layer.

7 Prepare the Chocolate Frosting. Spread top and sides of cake with frosting. Stir reserved cookie filling and enough milk (about 2 to 3 teaspoons) to make it a drizzling consistency. Spoon onto the center top of cake. Carefully spread filling to force some down sides of cake. Garnish top of cake with the crushed chocolate sandwich cookies. Makes 16 servings.

Chocolate Sandwich Cookie Filling: In a large mixing bowl combine 4 cups *sifted powdered sugar;* ⅓ cup *butter, softened;* 2 tablespoons *milk;* and 1 teaspoon *vanilla.* Beat with electric mixer on low speed till mixture is combined. Beat on medium speed till very smooth. Beat in 1 to 2 tablespoons more *milk* till frosting is easy to spread.

Put ¾ cup of the mixture in a small bowl and reserve for top of cake. Crush 10 *chocolate sandwich cookies* (1 cup crushed) and stir into remaining filling. Use filling as directed above. Makes about 1½ cups filling plus ¾ cup reserved filling.

Chocolate Frosting: In a small saucepan melt ⅓ cup *butter* and 3 ounces *unsweetened chocolate* over low heat.

In a large mixing bowl combine 3 cups *sifted powdered sugar,* ⅔ cup *dairy sour cream,* and 1½ teaspoons *vanilla.* Add melted chocolate mixture and beat with an electric mixer on low speed till combined. Beat on high speed about 1 minute or till mixture is smooth and creamy. Cool for 3 to 5 minutes or till thick enough to spread. Makes about 2½ cups.

Nutrition facts per serving: 629 cal., 27 g total fat (14 g sat. fat), 83 mg chol., 402 mg sodium, 98 g carbo., 2 g fiber, 7 g pro. *Daily values:* 19% vit. A, 7% calcium, 15% iron.

GÂTEAU DE SIROP (SYRUP CAKE)

Prep: 20 min. ◆ Bake: 45 min.

Although cane syrup (made from sugar cane) is what makes this an authentic Southern sweet, you can substitute a mix of dark corn syrup and molasses. Elsie Castille of Breux Bridge, Louisiana, likes to serve this spice cake with fresh fruit or sweetened cream. (See the photograph on page 241.)

2½ **cups all-purpose flour**
2 **tsp. baking powder**
2 **tsp. ground allspice**
½ **tsp. baking soda**
   Dash salt
1 **cup sugar**
¾ **cup cane syrup or ½ cup dark-colored corn syrup plus ¼ cup molasses**
¾ **cup cooking oil**
2 **eggs**
¾ **cup water**
   ◆◆◆
1 **recipe Sweetened Whipped Cream (see above right) (optional)**
   Ground nutmeg (optional)

1 Grease a 13×9×2-inch baking pan; set aside. In a medium mixing bowl combine flour, baking powder, allspice, baking soda, and salt; set aside. In a large bowl beat sugar, cane syrup or corn syrup plus molasses, oil, and eggs with an electric mixer on low speed till combined. Add flour mixture and water alternately to syrup mixture, beating till combined after each addition. Pour mixture batter into prepared pan.

2 Bake in a 350° oven about 45 minutes or till a wooden toothpick inserted near center comes out clean. (Cake may dip slightly in center.) Cool slightly in pan on a wire rack. Serve warm with Sweetened Whipped Cream and sprinkle with nutmeg, if desired. Makes 16 servings.

Sweetened Whipped Cream: In a large mixing bowl beat 1 cup *whipping cream* with 2 tablespoons *cane syrup or sugar* till stiff peaks form.

Nutrition facts per serving: 259 cal., 11 g total fat (2 g sat. fat), 27 mg chol., 113 mg sodium, 38 g carbo., 0 g fiber, 3 g pro. *Daily values:* 1% vit. A, 4% calcium, 10% iron.

PAUL'S PUMPKIN BARS

Prep: 15 min. ◆ Bake: 25 min.

How do we love these bars? Let Glenna Smith, an Indian Springs, Ohio, reader, count the ways: "They're easy to make, taste great, are very moist, feed a lot of people, and everyone loves the cream cheese frosting." (See the photograph on page 241.)

2 **cups all-purpose flour**
2 **tsp. baking powder**
2 **tsp. ground cinnamon**
1 **tsp. baking soda**
¼ **tsp. salt**
   ◆◆◆
4 **eggs**
1 **15-oz. can pumpkin**
1⅔ **cups granulated sugar**
1 **cup cooking oil**
¾ **cup chopped pecans (optional)**
1 **recipe Cream Cheese Frosting (see below)**
   Pecan halves (optional)

1 In a bowl stir together flour, baking powder, cinnamon, baking soda, and salt; set aside.

2 In a large mixing bowl beat together eggs, pumpkin, sugar, and oil with an electric mixer on medium speed. Add the flour mixture; beat till well combined. If desired, stir in chopped pecans.

3 Spread batter into an ungreased 15×10×1-inch baking pan. Bake in a 350° oven for 25 to 30 minutes or till a wooden toothpick inserted in the center comes out clean. Cool on a wire rack. Frost with Cream Cheese Frosting. If desired, top with additional pecan halves. Cut into squares. Store in the refrigerator. Makes 24 bars.

Cream Cheese Frosting: In a medium bowl beat together one 3-ounce package *cream cheese, softened;* ¼ cup *butter or margarine, softened;* and 1 teaspoon *vanilla* till fluffy. Gradually add 2 cups *sifted powdered sugar,* beating till smooth.

Nutrition facts per bar: 250 cal., 13 g total fat (4 g sat. fat), 45 mg chol., 147 mg sodium, 31 g carbo., 1 g fiber, 3 g pro. *Daily values:* 19% vit. A, 1% vit. C, 3% calcium, 6% iron.

BESTEFAR'S FAVORITE COOKIES

Prep: 20 min.
Bake: 8 min. per batch

We've added an orange-flavored icing to update Barney Jacobson's family recipe that dates back at least 50 years. (See the photograph on page 243.)

2¾ cups all-purpose flour
2 tsp. ground cinnamon
1 tsp. baking soda
¼ tsp. salt
1½ cups raisins or chopped pitted dates
1 cup coarsely chopped pecans or walnuts

❖❖❖

1 cup butter, softened
1½ cups packed brown sugar
3 eggs
1 Tbsp. finely shredded orange peel
2 Tbsp. fresh orange juice

❖❖❖

1 recipe Orange Icing (see above right)

1 In a medium bowl stir together flour, cinnamon, baking soda, and salt. Stir in raisins or pitted dates and pecans or walnuts; set aside.

2 In a large mixing bowl beat butter and brown sugar with an electric mixer on medium to high speed till well combined. Add eggs, 1 at a time, beating well after each. Beat in the orange peel and about half of the flour mixture. Add orange juice and remaining flour mixture, beating till mixture is combined.

3 Drop by rounded teaspoons 2 inches apart on a greased or parchment-lined cookie sheet.

Bake in a 375° oven for 8 to 10 minutes or till edges are golden. Cool on wire rack. Frost with Orange Icing. Makes about 60.

Orange Icing: In a mixing bowl combine 2 cups *sifted powdered sugar,* ½ teaspoon *finely shredded orange peel,* and 1 to 2 tablespoons *orange juice* to make icing easy to spread.

Nutrition facts per cookie: 103 cal., 5 g total fat (2 g sat. fat), 19 mg chol., 66 mg sodium, 15 g carbo., 0 g fiber, 1 g pro.
Daily values: 3% vit. A, 3% iron.

HJORTETAKK BAKKELS (REINDEER ANTLER COOKIES)

Prep: 30 min. ◆ Chill: Overnight
Fry: 30 sec. per cookie

With a little imagination you can see the head of a reindeer, complete with antlers, in the finished cookie. Gather the family, as Barney Jacobson does, to create an assembly line for shaping these Norwegian treats. (See the photograph on page 243.)

1½ tsp. dairy sour cream
½ tsp. baker's dry ammonia* or baking powder
2 eggs
½ cup granulated sugar
¼ cup butter, melted
1 Tbsp. rum or brandy
1½ tsp. ground cardamom
½ tsp. lemon extract
2 cups sifted cake flour

❖❖❖

Cooking oil for deep-fat frying
Sifted powdered sugar (optional)

1 If using dry ammonia, place sour cream in a small bowl. Stir in dry ammonia; set aside. In a large bowl combine eggs, sugar, melted butter, rum or brandy, cardamom, lemon extract, and the dry ammonia mixture or the baking powder and the 1½ teaspoons sour cream. Beat with an electric mixer on medium speed just till combined. Stir in cake flour. Chill overnight.

2 On a lightly floured surface, roll about *2 tablespoons* of dough at a time into a 15-inch-long rope. Cut into three 5-inch-long ropes. Using 1 rope per cookie, cross 1 end of rope over the other about 1 inch from each end to form a circle with "antlers." Press dough firmly together where ends meet. Keep dough chilled and work with only a few pieces of dough at a time to prevent it from becoming sticky.

3 In a heavy, deep, 3-quart saucepan or deep-fat fryer, heat oil to 375°. Using a spoon, carefully add 4 or 5 cookies at a time to hot oil. Fry for 30 seconds on each side or till golden, turning once with a slotted spoon. Carefully remove cookies from hot oil with slotted spoon. Drain cookies on paper towels. If desired, dust with sifted powdered sugar. Repeat with remaining cookies. Makes about 60 cookies.

***Note:** Baking ammonia was the typical leavening agent for baking in Norway in the early part of the century. It's available today in most pharmacies.

Nutrition facts per cookie: 46 cal., 3 g total fat (1 g sat. fat), 9 mg chol., 13 mg sodium, 5 g carbo., 0 g fiber, and 1 g pro.
Daily values: 1% vit. A, 1% iron.

NOVEMBER
Winter's First Bite

> 30-minute recipes indicated in RED.
> Low-fat and no-fat recipes indicated with a ♥.
> Photographs indicated in italics.

The brilliance of early fall fades in November. Meals can be the bright spots in overcast days, an opportunity to add warmth, color, and zest to your outlook. Mosaic Potatoes or colorful Glazed Chicken Rolls dress up an evening table. For November nights, consider one of several kinds of chili. And you can delight your family this Thanksgiving with Smoked Trout Appetizers, our tips for better turkeys, Glazed Roasted Vegetables, and an All-Ages Glacier Punch. We also offer hints for roasting chestnuts and, for a more daring holiday finale, Raspberry-Chocolate Cake. All in all, it's cause for thanksgiving.

GLACIER PUNCH

Prep: 15 min. ◆ Freeze: 3 hr.

To ensure that the punch retains its sparkle, mix the ingredients just before guests arrive. For a version without alcohol, see the recipe below right. (See the photograph on page 279.)

2 cups raspberry-, cherry-, or citrus-flavored vodka, chilled
⅔ cup orange liqueur
2 Tbsp. kirsch
4 cups ice cubes
1 750-ml bottle sparkling wine or champagne, chilled
2 cups sparkling water, chilled
Sugar (optional)
1 recipe Raspberry Brittle (see below)

1 In a medium punch bowl combine vodka, orange liqueur, kirsch, and ice cubes. To preserve carbonation, carefully pour sparkling wine or champagne and sparkling water down side of bowl. If desired, sweeten to taste with a little sugar. Top with some chunks of Raspberry Brittle. Serve each glass of punch with a piece of the Raspberry Brittle. Makes about 20 (4-oz.) servings.

Raspberry Brittle: Pour 1 cup *water* into bottom of 15×10×1-inch baking pan with sides (or use a 13×9×2-inch baking pan). Sprinkle surface of water evenly with about ½ cup *edible flowers* (such as marigolds, calendula, violets, pansies, or dianthus). Sprinkle surface of water evenly with 1 cup *fresh raspberries or other fresh fruit*. Freeze 3 hours or overnight. To unmold, allow to

stand at room temperature 5 to 10 minutes or till ice can be removed. Remove from pan and break into large chunks. Place in punch just before serving.

Nutrition facts per serving: 108 cal., 0 g total fat, 0 mg chol., 5 mg sodium, 5 g carbo., 1 g fiber, 0 g pro.
Daily values: 5% vit. C.

ALL-AGES GLACIER PUNCH

Prep: 15 min. ◆ Freeze: 3 hr.

When the occasion calls for drinks without alcohol, try this sparkling, fruity punch.

1 23-oz. bottle raspberry- or blackberry-flavored sparkling water, chilled
1 750-ml bottle sparkling white grape juice or sparkling apple cider, chilled
1 10-oz. bottle citrus- or tropical-flavored sparkling water, chilled
1 recipe Raspberry Brittle (see left)

1 In a medium punch bowl, combine raspberry- or blackberry-flavored sparkling water, sparkling grape juice or cider, and citrus- or tropical-flavored sparkling water. Top with some chunks of Raspberry Brittle. Serve each glass of punch with a piece of the Raspberry Brittle. Makes about 14 (4-oz.) servings.

Nutrition facts per serving: 40 cal., 0 g total fat, 0 mg chol., 17 mg sodium, 10 g carbo., 1 g fiber, 0 g pro.
Daily values: 28% vit. C.

THE CLEVER COOK

INSTANT RECIPE CARDS

If you enjoy clipping recipes from magazines, preserve them for years to come by "laminating" them with clear contact paper. The coating will keep the clippings from being torn and make them easier to slide in and out of your recipe box. What's more, you can wipe off any cooking spills.

Lori Lange
Overland Park, Kansas

CURRY CHICKEN POT STICKERS

Prep: 45 min. ◆ Cook: 15 min.

Pot stickers are proof that the best things come in small packages. A top pick for dim sum, the appetizer course served in Asian restaurants, pot stickers encase a flavorful filling inside a paper-thin dough.

2 Tbsp. soy sauce
1 Tbsp. cornstarch
1 to 1½ tsp. curry powder
1 tsp. toasted sesame oil (optional)
½ tsp. sugar
1 cup packaged shredded broccoli (broccoli slaw mix) or cabbage with carrot (coleslaw mix)
8 oz. ground raw chicken

1 Tbsp. finely chopped onion
30 pot sticker or wonton
   wrappers
   ◆◆◆
   Cooking oil
⅔ cup water

1 For filling, in a medium mixing bowl combine soy sauce, cornstarch, curry powder, toasted sesame oil (if desired), and sugar. Finely chop the shredded slaw mix. Add slaw mix, chicken, and onion to the soy sauce mixture; mix well. Cover and chill up to 24 hours.

2 Spoon 2 teaspoons filling onto each wrapper. Moisten edges with water. Fold wrappers in half over filling. (For wonton wrappers, fold one corner over filling to opposite corner.) Fold pleats along edges; press to seal.

3 Arrange pot stickers, pleated edges up, on a lightly floured baking sheet, pressing gently to flatten the bottoms. Cover till ready to cook.

4 In a 12-inch skillet heat *2 tablespoons* oil. Arrange half of the pot stickers, pleated edges up, in skillet. Cook, uncovered, over medium heat for 1 to 2 minutes or till bottoms are light brown. Reduce heat to low.

5 Remove from heat; carefully add the water all at once near edge (oil may splatter). Return to heat. Cook, covered, 10 minutes more. Increase heat to medium-high. Uncover; cook 3 to 5 minutes or till filling is no longer pink and water is evaporated.

6 Add *2 teaspoons* oil. Lift and tilt skillet to coat pot-sticker bottoms. Cook, uncovered, 1 minute more. Gently remove pot stickers from skillet. Drain on paper towels. Keep warm in a 300° oven. Makes 30 pot stickers.

TO MAKE AHEAD

Assemble pot stickers as directed. Place the uncooked pot stickers in a single layer in a covered freezer container; freeze for up to 2 months. To serve, thaw at room temperature for 30 minutes before cooking. Cook as directed.

Nutrition facts per pot sticker: 45 cal., 2 g total fat (0 g sat. fat), 5 mg chol., 119 mg sodium, 5 g carbo., 0 g fiber, 2 g pro. *Daily values:* 4% vit. C, 2% iron.

SMOKED TROUT APPETIZERS

Prep: 35 min. ◆ Bake: 12 min.

The smoked trout also can be served on plain crackers or small rounds of party pumpernickel or rye bread. (See the photograph on page 282.)

½ of a 17¼-oz. pkg. frozen
   puff pastry (1 sheet)
1 egg yolk
1 Tbsp. water
   ◆◆◆
8 oz. cooked smoked trout,
   skinned and flaked
½ cup dairy sour cream
1 Tbsp. lemon juice
1 Tbsp. grated fresh
   horseradish
½ tsp. honey mustard
   Fresh dill sprigs (optional)
2 oz. fresh red and/or gold
   caviar or one 2-oz. jar red
   or gold caviar*

1 Thaw puff pastry according to package directions. On a lightly floured surface, roll puff pastry sheet to a 14-inch square. Cut puff pastry into 2-inch squares. Line cups of 1¾-inch muffin pans with pastry squares, allowing corners to extend above cups. In a cup or small bowl beat together egg yolk and water. Brush pastry cups with egg yolk mixture.

2 Bake pastry in a 375° oven for 12 to 15 minutes or till golden brown. (Pastry will puff, leaving small indentations.) Remove pastry cups from pans and cool on a wire rack.

3 Meanwhile, in a medium mixing bowl or food processor bowl, combine smoked trout, sour cream, lemon juice, horseradish, and honey mustard. Beat with an electric mixer or cover and process till almost smooth. Fit a pastry bag with a large star tip and fill with smoked trout mixture. (Or, fill a self-sealing plastic bag with mixture and snip ¼ inch off one corner.) Pipe filling on top of each pastry. If desired, top each appetizer with a sprig of dill. Spoon ⅛ *teaspoon* caviar onto each. Cover and chill till serving time. Makes about 4 dozen.

*Note: When using caviar from a jar, place in a tea strainer and rinse gently to remove excess salt and dye before using.

Nutrition facts per appetizer: 39 cal., 3 g total fat (0 g sat. fat), 16 mg chol., 40 mg sodium, 2 g carbo., 0 g fiber, 2 g pro. *Daily values:* 1% vit. A, 0% vit. C, 0% calcium, 1% iron.

SALMON MOUSSE

Prep: 25 min. ◆ Chill: 5 hr.

A luscious flash from the past, this make-ahead spread has been a reader favorite for more than 15 years. Serve it with assorted crackers and cucumber slices.

1   15½-oz. can salmon
    ◆◆◆
2   envelopes unflavored gelatin
2   cups mayonnaise or salad
      dressing
½   cup chili sauce
2   Tbsp. lemon juice
1   Tbsp. Worcestershire sauce
½   tsp. dried dillweed
¼   tsp. pepper
1   6½-oz. can tuna, drained
      and finely flaked
4   hard-cooked eggs, chopped
½   cup pimiento-stuffed olives,
      finely chopped
¼   cup finely chopped onion
    ◆◆◆
    Pimiento-stuffed olives,
      sliced (optional)

1 Lightly oil a 6-cup mold; set aside. Drain salmon, reserving liquid; add *water,* if needed, to equal ½ cup total. Remove and discard skin and bones. Finely flake salmon; set aside.

2 In a small saucepan combine reserved salmon liquid and gelatin. Let stand 5 minutes. Cook and stir over medium heat till gelatin is dissolved; transfer to a bowl. Gradually stir in mayonnaise or salad dressing. Stir in the chili sauce, lemon juice, Worcestershire sauce, dillweed, and pepper. Fold in salmon, tuna, eggs, olives, and onion.

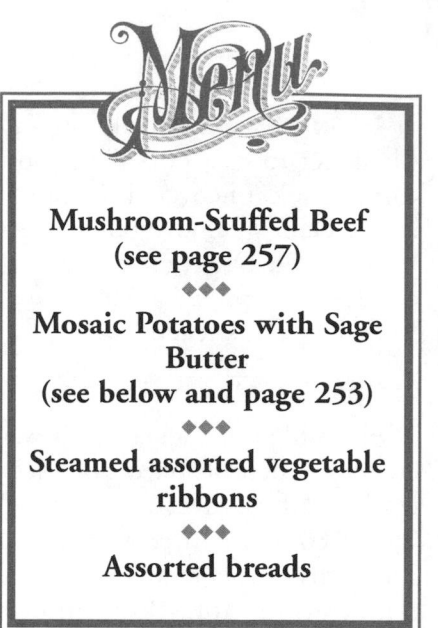

Menu

**Mushroom-Stuffed Beef
(see page 257)**

◆◆◆

**Mosaic Potatoes with Sage
Butter
(see below and page 253)**

◆◆◆

**Steamed assorted vegetable
ribbons**

◆◆◆

Assorted breads

3 Turn mousse mixture into prepared mold. Cover surface with plastic wrap. Chill for 5 hours or till firm. Unmold. If desired, garnish with sliced olives. Makes 6 cups spread.

Nutrition facts per tablespoon: 48 cal., 4 g total fat (1 g sat. fat), 15 mg chol., 92 mg sodium, 1 g carbo., 0 g fiber, 2 g pro. *Daily values:* 1% vit. A, 1% vit. C, 1% calcium, 5% iron.

EASY OVEN RISOTTO

Prep: 10 min. ◆ Bake: 55 min.

Frozen green beans substitute well for snow pea pods. Just stir in the beans during the last 15 minutes of baking.

3¼   cups water
1   10¾-oz. can condensed
       cream of chicken with
       herbs soup or condensed
       cream of chicken soup
1¼   cups Arborio or medium-
       grain white rice
⅓   cup shredded carrot
½   cup frozen snow pea pods,
       bias-cut in half
     ◆◆◆
½   cup grated Parmesan cheese

1 In a 2-quart casserole stir together water, soup, uncooked rice, and shredded carrot. Bake, covered, in a 375° oven 55 to 60 minutes or till rice is tender, stirring twice during baking. Stir in peas the last 5 minutes of baking.

2 Remove casserole from oven; gently stir in the Parmesan cheese. Let the risotto stand for 10 minutes before serving. If desired, garnish with *rosemary sprigs.* Makes 6 side-dish servings.

Nutrition facts per serving: 233 cal., 6 g total fat (3 g sat. fat), 11 mg chol., 563 mg sodium, 36 g carbo., 1 g fiber, 8 g pro. *Daily values:* 21% vit. A, 4% vit. C, 12% calcium, 14% iron.

LOW FAT
MOSAIC POTATOES

Prep: 30 min. ◆ Bake: 35 min.

When baked, the cut surface of the potato becomes transparent and the herb leaf shows through. (See the photograph on page 282.)

     Olive oil
24   1¼- to 1½-inch white or
       yellow whole tiny new
       potatoes, scrubbed (about
       1½ lb.)
1   bunch fresh Italian parsley*
       or 48 small fresh sage
       leaves (one ½- to ¾-oz.
       pkg.)
     ◆◆◆
1   recipe Sage Butter (optional)
       (see page 253)

1 Place a sheet of parchment paper or brown paper on a baking sheet. Brush paper with olive oil; set aside. Scrub potatoes; cut each in half crosswise. Using a sharp vegetable peeler, knife, or slicer, cut a paper-thin slice off the cut side of each potato half. Place a leaf of Italian parsley or sage on each potato half; replace the thin potato slice over each half, covering herb leaf.

2 Place potato halves, cut sides down, on prepared baking sheet. Brush potatoes with more olive oil. Bake, uncovered, in a 375° oven 35 minutes or till tender. If desired, serve with Sage Butter. Season to taste with *salt* and *pepper*. Makes 8 servings.

*Note: If small leaves are not available, cut larger leaves in half.

Nutrition facts per serving: 103 cal., 2 g total fat (0 g sat. fat), 0 mg chol., 7 mg sodium, 20 g carbo., 0 g fiber, 2 g pro. *Daily values:* 21% vit. C, 6% iron.

SAGE BUTTER

Prep: 10 min. ◆ Chill: 2 hr.

Besides being a delightful addition to Mosaic Potatoes, this savory spread adds a fantastic herb flavor to other vegetables, such as green beans, brussels sprouts, peas, or zucchini.

1 **cup butter, softened**
1 **Tbsp. finely snipped fresh sage or 1 tsp. dried sage**

1 In a small bowl combine butter and sage. Shape into individual serving-size portions with a butter mold. Chill at least 2 hours or overnight. (Or, place butter onto a sheet of plastic wrap; shape into a log. Chill and cut into serving-size pats.) If desired, garnish serving plate with *fresh herb sprigs.*

Nutrition facts per tablespoon: 100 cal., 11 g total fat (7 g sat. fat), 31 mg chol., 116 mg sodium, 0 g carbo., 0 g fiber, 0 g pro. *Daily values:* 10% vit. A.

SMASH POTATOES

Smile, spud lovers. The potato bin in the supermarket is brighter than ever. Besides the white and red potato varieties, purple and yellow spuds are now available in some parts of the country. You can substitute these pretty veggies in any recipe that calls for red or white potatoes, but expect to pay a little more per pound. For a special occasion meal, prepare them simply so their color really stands out.

◆ **Yukon Gold:** When it's cooked, you'll understand why this buttery-looking potato is called Yukon Gold. Actually, these spuds taste like a baking potato but have a smoother, creamier texture. Try them baked, boiled, or mashed. During frying, the potato turns slightly orange. Yukon Gold potatoes are available year-round.

◆ **Peruvian Blue or Peruvian Purple:** This Peru native is named for its subdued purple-tinged skin and deep violet interior. The shape and size is similar to a medium russet potato (an oblong white baking potato). During cooking, the potato skin darkens and the inside color intensifies. When fried, watch out: The purple color appears almost fluorescent. The cooked potato has a moist, smooth texture and rich potato flavor. Available September through March.

◆ **Yellow Finnish:** These round little potatoes have a smooth texture and turn light yellow when cooked. The buttery taste is a bonus because these potatoes have the same number of calories as other varieties. With a dry, mealy texture, they're ideal baked or oiled and diced for salads. Look for pretty Yellow Finnish potatoes from October through April.

---

30 MIN. LOW FAT

STIR-FRIED RABE WITH SESAME AND GINGER

Start to finish: 25 min.

1 **lb. broccoli rabe**
2 **tsp. cooking oil**
1 **tsp. toasted sesame oil**
1 **Tbsp. grated gingerroot**
¼ **tsp. crushed red pepper**
2 **Tbsp. soy sauce**
2 **Tbsp. sesame seed, toasted**

1 Rinse rabe; cut off and discard any thick woody stems. Slice remaining stems into 1-inch pieces; set aside. Coarsely chop leaves and flowerets; set aside. In a wok or 12-inch skillet heat oils over medium-high heat. (Add more cooking oil if necessary during cooking.) Stir-fry rabe stems in hot oil for 3 to 4 minutes or till crisp-tender; remove from wok. Add rabe leaves and flowerets, gingerroot, and red pepper; stir-fry 1 to 2 minutes or till crisp-tender. Stir in rabe stems and soy sauce; heat through. Sprinkle with sesame seed. Makes 6 servings.

Nutrition facts per serving: 63 cal., 4 g total fat (1 g sat. fat), 0 mg chol., 364 mg sodium, 5 g carbo., 3 g fiber, 3 g pro. *Daily values:* 33% vit. A, 72% vit. C, 4% calcium, 6% iron.

HERBED MAYONNAISE

Prep: 10 min. ◆ Chill: 1 hr.

This velvety, dill-flavored mayonnaise makes a superb sandwich spread as well as an accompaniment to Carrot-Spinach Terrine (see below).

½ cup mayonnaise or salad
   dressing
½ cup dairy sour cream
3 Tbsp. snipped fresh dillweed
   or 1 Tbsp. dried dillweed
2 Tbsp. snipped fresh parsley
1 clove garlic, minced

1 In a blender container or food processor bowl, combine mayonnaise or salad dressing, sour cream, dillweed, parsley, and garlic. Cover and blend or process till almost smooth. Pour into a storage container. Cover and chill at least 1 hour. Serve with the terrine. Makes 1¼ cups.

Nutrition facts per tablespoon: 65 cal., 7 g total fat (2 g sat. fat), 7 mg chol., 43 mg sodium, 1 g carbo., 0 g fiber, 0 g pro. *Daily values:* 2% vit. A, 1% vit. C.

CARROT-SPINACH TERRINE

Prep: 45 min. ◆ Bake: 1½ hr.
Chill: 4 hr.

Before baking, tap the filled pan firmly on the countertop to eliminate air bubbles that might spoil the appearance of the loaf.
(See the photograph on page 282.)

1½ lb. carrots, halved crosswise,
   then cut in half lengthwise
   ◆◆◆
1 12-oz. pkg. goat cheese
3 eggs
⅛ tsp. ground nutmeg
⅛ tsp. ground red pepper

⅛ tsp. salt
⅛ tsp. black pepper
   ◆◆◆
1 10-oz. pkg. frozen chopped
   spinach, thawed and well
   drained
2 cloves garlic, minced
⅛ tsp. salt
⅛ tsp. black pepper
   ◆◆◆
1 recipe Herbed Mayonnaise
   (optional) (see left)
   Fresh chives (optional)

1 Line an 8×4×2-inch loaf pan with foil; grease well and set aside. Cook carrots, covered, in a small amount of *boiling salted water* for 10 to 12 minutes or till carrots are very tender. Drain and cool slightly. Arrange about *one-fourth* of the cooked carrots, diagonally, in the bottom of the pan, trimming to fit as necessary.

2 Place remaining carrots in a blender container or food processor bowl with *one-third* of the goat cheese (about ½ cup), *2* of the eggs, the nutmeg, ground red pepper, ⅛ teaspoon salt, and ⅛ teaspoon black pepper. Cover and blend or process till smooth. Spoon *half* of the carrot puree atop carrots in loaf pan, shaking slightly to ensure puree coats all the carrots.

3 Rinse blender or food processor. Place spinach in blender container or food processor bowl with remaining goat cheese, remaining egg, garlic, ⅛ teaspoon salt, and ⅛ teaspoon black pepper. Cover and blend till smooth. Spoon over top of carrot puree. Spoon remaining carrot puree over spinach layer.

4 Cover loaf pan with foil. Place the loaf pan in a roasting pan half filled with *boiling water*. Bake in a 325° oven for 1½ hours or till set and a knife inserted in center comes out clean.

5 Allow terrine to cool at room temperature. Cover and chill thoroughly. Turn the terrine out onto a plate; slice to serve. If desired, serve with Herbed Mayonnaise and garnish with snipped chives. Makes 6 servings.

Nutrition facts per serving: 281 cal., 19 g total fat (9 g sat. fat), 157 mg chol., 546 mg sodium, 13 g carbo., 4 g fiber, 16 g pro. *Daily values:* 292% vit. A, 11% vit. C, 12% calcium, 2% iron.

LOW FAT
GLAZED ROASTED VEGETABLES

Prep: 30 min. ◆ Bake: 65 min.

The cooking time of this dish has been adjusted to make it dovetail with the timing of the Nut-Crusted Turkey. See tip on page 260 for preparation hints.
(See the photograph on page 280.)

8 medium carrots, bias-sliced
   1 inch thick (4 cups)
4 medium parsnips, bias-sliced
   1 inch thick (4 cups)
   ◆◆◆
12 baby beets, peeled and
   halved, or 3 small whole
   beets, quartered
   (about 12 oz.)
2 Tbsp. snipped fresh parsley
2 tsp. snipped fresh marjoram,
   thyme, or rosemary, or
   ½ tsp. dried marjoram,
   thyme, or rosemary
¼ tsp. salt
3 Tbsp. olive oil or cooking oil

4 cups peeled, seeded winter
  squash cut into 1½-inch
  pieces (about 2 lb. before
  trimming)
¼ cup packed brown sugar

1 In a large saucepan cook carrots and parsnips, covered, in a small amount of *boiling water* for 3 minutes. Drain.

2 In a 13×9×2-inch baking pan combine the partially cooked carrots and parsnips and the beets. Sprinkle with parsley; marjoram, thyme, or rosemary; and salt. Drizzle with olive oil. Toss gently to coat.

3 Cover pan with foil. Bake in a 375° oven for 30 minutes, stirring once. Stir in squash; cover and bake about 20 minutes more or just till barely done. Remove from oven. Increase oven temperature to 450°. Stir brown sugar into vegetables. Return to oven and bake vegetables, uncovered, 15 to 20 minutes more or till vegetables are tender and glazed. Makes 8 to 10 side-dish servings.

Nutrition facts per serving: 155 cal., 4 g total fat (1 g sat. fat), 0 mg chol., 112 mg sodium, 29 g carbo., 7 g fiber, 2 g pro. *Daily values:* 170% vit. A, 31% vit. C, 5% calcium, 8% iron.

WILD RICE-STUFFED SQUASH

Prep: 45 min. ◆ Bake: 1 hr.

If your market doesn't carry the kind of squash specified, substitute any hard-skinned winter variety.
(See the photograph on page 280.)

1 14½-oz. can reduced-sodium
  chicken broth

½ tsp. dried thyme, crushed
⅓ cup wild rice, rinsed
½ cup chopped leeks
⅓ cup long-grain rice

◆◆◆

6 small winter squash (such as
  acorn, Sweet Dumpling, or
  Golden Nugget), each
  about 3½ to 4 inches in
  diameter

◆◆◆

¼ cup dried cranberries or
  dried currants
¼ cup snipped dried apricots
3 Tbsp. margarine or butter,
  melted
⅛ tsp. salt
⅛ tsp. pepper

◆◆◆

Six 6- to 8-inch twig wreaths
  (optional)
Pansies or other edible
  flowers (optional)
Fresh sage leaves (optional)

1 In a heavy medium saucepan bring the chicken broth and thyme to a boil. Add the uncooked wild rice; reduce heat. Simmer, covered, for 30 minutes. Add the leeks and uncooked long-grain rice. Cover and simmer mixture for 15 minutes more or till rice is tender. Let stand, covered, 5 minutes. Drain excess liquid, if necessary.

2 Meanwhile, wash squash and cut off the top third including the stem end. With a teaspoon, remove seeds. Place squash, cut sides down, in a shallow baking pan. Bake squash in a 350° oven for 30 minutes. Turn cut sides up. Cover pan with foil and bake about 20 minutes more or till tender. Remove from oven and set aside.

3 In a large bowl combine the rice mixture, dried cranberries or currants, and dried apricots. Stir in melted margarine or butter, salt, and pepper.

4 Mound stuffing into the squash. Place in a shallow baking pan. Bake in a 425° oven about 10 minutes or till heated through. If desired, serve atop twig wreaths and garnish plate with pansies or other edible flowers and sage leaves. Makes 6 side-dish servings.

Nutrition facts per serving: 262 cal., 7 g total fat (1 g sat. fat), 0 mg chol., 320 mg sodium, 50 g carbo., 7 g fiber, 5 g pro. *Daily values:* 177% vit. A, 63% vit. C, 10% calcium, 19% iron.

THE CLEVER COOK

COLORFUL BOWLS

Make your holiday buffet or appetizer table look more festive by using red, green, yellow, or orange bell peppers as containers for serving. Remove the tops of the peppers and scoop out the seeds. Rinse the peppers with water and fill them with savory dips, sauces, or relishes.

Kristin Couch
Tampa, Florida

TRUFFLE OIL SALAD

Prep: 20 min.

There are three options for serving cheese with this salad. Pick the one that fits best with your available time and family tastes.
(See the photograph on page 279.)

- ¼ cup rice vinegar
- 2 Tbsp. lemon juice
- 2 Tbsp. salad oil
- 2 Tbsp. truffle oil*, sesame oil, or walnut oil
- 2 tsp. sugar
- ¼ to ½ tsp. salt
- ¼ to ½ tsp. pepper

◆◆◆

- 6 cups torn mixed salad greens
- 2 medium unpeeled tart red apples, such as Braeburn or Jonathan, cut into thin wedges or strips
- 1 turnip, peeled and cut into thin strips
- 2 Tbsp. chopped walnuts
- 1 recipe Cheese Croutons (see right), 1 recipe Cheese Cups (see right), and/or 1 recipe Goat Cheese Slices (see page 257) (optional)

1 In a screw-top jar combine rice vinegar, lemon juice, salad oil, truffle oil, sugar, salt, and pepper. Cover; shake to mix thoroughly.

2 Divide salad greens among 6 plates. Arrange apples and turnip over greens. Sprinkle walnuts atop. Shake dressing and drizzle each serving with about 1 tablespoon dressing. Refrigerate remaining dressing for another use. If desired, arrange Cheese Croutons, Cheese Cups, and/or Goat Cheese Slices on plate with salad. Makes 6 side-dish servings.

*Note: Truffle oil is available at food specialty stores and from food mail-order companies.

Nutrition facts per serving without cheese garnish: 74 cal., 5 g total fat (0 g sat. fat), 0 mg chol., 76 mg sodium, 7 g carbo., 2 g fiber, 2 g pro.
Daily values: 18% vit. A, 26% vit. C, 3% calcium, 6% iron.

CHEESE CROUTONS

Prep: 20 min. ◆ Chill: 2 hr.

These crumb-coated cheese patties turn ordinary salad into an extraordinary dining experience.

- 4 oz. reduced-fat cream cheese (Neufchâtel), softened
- ½ cup shredded Havarti cheese, such as dill or other herb flavor, or smoked cheddar cheese
- 1 beaten egg
- 1 Tbsp. water
- 2 Tbsp. cornmeal
- 1 Tbsp. fine dry bread crumbs
- 1 Tbsp. sesame seed, toasted
- 2 tsp. grated Parmesan cheese

◆◆◆

- 2 Tbsp. cooking oil
- 1 Tbsp. margarine or butter

1 In a medium mixing bowl beat cream cheese and Havarti cheese together using an electric mixer till combined. Cover and chill cheese mixture for 1 hour. Meanwhile, combine egg and water in a small bowl. In a shallow dish combine cornmeal, bread crumbs, sesame seed, and Parmesan cheese. Shape chilled cheese mixture into twelve 1-inch balls; flatten to form patties. Dip into egg mixture and coat with the cornmeal mixture. Cover and chill for 1 hour till firm.

2 In a large skillet heat cooking oil and margarine or butter. Add cheese patties; cook on medium-high heat for 1 to 2 minutes or till light golden, turning once. Drain on paper towels. Serve warm. Makes 12 croutons.

■ **TO MAKE AHEAD** ■

After cooking let cool. Cover and chill till serving time. Place chilled croutons on a baking sheet. Bake in a 400° oven about 3 minutes or till warm (do not overbake or they will melt).

Nutrition facts per crouton: 89 cal., 8 g total fat (3 g sat. fat), 30 mg chol., 75 mg sodium, 2 g carbo., 0 g fiber, 3 g pro.
Daily values: 6% vit. A, 5% calcium, 1% iron.

CHEESE CUPS

Prep: 15 min. ◆ Bake: 5 min.

Looking for an elegant, but easy, appetizer? Try these impressive mini cheese tarts.

- 2 oz. reduced-fat cream cheese (Neufchâtel), softened
- ¼ cup shredded Havarti cheese, such as dill or other herb flavor, or smoked cheddar cheese (1 oz.)
- 12 1- to 2-inch prebaked pastry cups

1 In a medium mixing bowl beat cream cheese and Havarti cheese together using an electric mixer till combined. Fill each pastry cup with about 1 teaspoon of cheese filling. Place filled cups on an ungreased baking sheet. Bake in a 350° oven for 5 to 7 minutes or till hot and cheese has softened. Serve warm. Makes 12 cups.

After filling cups with cheese, cover and chill till serving time. Bake in a 400° oven about 5 to 7 minutes or till hot and cheese has softened.

Nutrition facts per cheese cup: 65 cal., 5 g total fat (2 g sat. fat), 10 mg chol., 60 mg sodium, 3 g carbo., 0 g fiber, 3 g pro. *Daily values:* 4% vit. A, 4% calcium, 1% iron.

GOAT CHEESE SLICES

Start to finish: 10 min.

Another time, serve this herb-accented cheese with slices of French bread as a first course.

4 oz. semisoft goat cheese
2 Tbsp. snipped fresh tarragon or dillweed or 2 tsp. dried tarragon or dillweed, crushed

1 Cut the goat cheese into 6 slices. Coat the cheese slices with the herbs. Makes 6 slices.

Nutrition facts per cheese slice: 62 cal., 5 g total fat (3 g sat. fat), 17 mg chol., 110 mg sodium, 0 g carbo., 0 g fiber, 3 g pro. *Daily values:* 2% vit. A, 1% calcium.

MUSHROOM-STUFFED BEEF

Prep: 40 min. ◆ Roast: 50 min.

Roll the beef as tightly as possible and tie with kitchen string to ensure it will keep its shape when cut. (See the photograph on page 278.)

· 1 lb. fresh mushrooms, such as button, porcini, shiitake, and/or morel
½ cup shredded carrot

3 Tbsp. finely chopped onion
1 Tbsp. butter or olive oil
2 Tbsp. white wine vinegar or water
2 Tbsp. dry white wine, vermouth, or water
1 Tbsp. snipped fresh tarragon or ½ tsp. dried tarragon, crushed
¾ cup soft bread crumbs
½ cup shredded fresh Parmesan or Monterey Jack cheese

◆◆◆

1 2- to 2½-lb. beef tenderloin

◆◆◆

3 Tbsp. all-purpose flour
¼ cup dry white wine or beef broth
¼ cup beef broth
½ cup whipping cream
2 to 3 tsp. Dijon-style mustard
1 Tbsp. snipped fresh tarragon or ½ tsp. dried tarragon, crushed

1 For stuffing, place mushrooms, one-fourth at a time, in a food processor bowl or blender container; process or blend till mushrooms are finely chopped. In a large skillet cook mushrooms, carrot, and onion in hot butter or olive oil over low heat till mushrooms are tender. Continue cooking till liquid evaporates. Add the vinegar or water; the 2 tablespoons wine, vermouth, or water; and 1 tablespoon fresh tarragon. Continue cooking till only about 1 tablespoon of liquid remains. Remove from heat. Stir in bread crumbs and cheese; set aside.

2 To butterfly the tenderloin, make a lengthwise slit down the center to within ½ inch of bottom. On each side of the V formed by the first cut, make another lengthwise slit. Open flat

and pound with a meat mallet to about ½-inch thickness. Sprinkle lightly with *salt* and *pepper.*

3 Spread the stuffing mixture on the tenderloin. Roll up from the long side, tucking in ends; secure with kitchen string tied tightly at 2-inch intervals. Place on rack in shallow roasting pan. Insert a meat thermometer into the center of the roll.

4 Roast meat, uncovered, in a 325° oven till meat thermometer registers 140° for medium-rare (about 50 minutes) or 155° for medium (about 65 minutes). Remove from oven. Cover with foil. Let stand 15 minutes (the temperature of the meat will rise 5 degrees during standing).

5 While meat is standing, prepare gravy. Pour off pan drippings, reserving 2 tablespoons fat. Return the 2 tablespoons fat to the roasting pan. Using a wire whisk, stir in flour. Add the ¼ cup wine and broth to flour mixture; scrape up brown bits that have stuck to pan. Cook and stir for 1 minute. Add whipping cream, Dijon-style mustard, and 1 tablespoon fresh tarragon. Cook and stir over medium heat till thickened and bubbly. Cook and stir for 1 minute more. Season to taste with *salt* and *pepper.* Slice meat and serve with gravy. Makes 8 to 10 servings.

Nutrition facts per serving: 298 cal., 16 g total fat (7 g sat. fat), 93 mg chol., 250 mg sodium, 9 g carbo., 1 g fiber, 27 g pro. *Daily values:* 28% vit. A, 4% vit. C, 7% calcium, 27% iron.

CROWN ROAST

Prep: 40 min. ◆ Roast: 2¾ hr.

Check with your butcher a few weeks early to be sure you can get a crown roast. Handle the meat carefully so that it will keep its shape. (See the photograph on page 283.)

- 1 12-rib pork rib crown roast (about 5½ lb.)

◆◆◆

- 2 medium fennel bulbs, chopped (about 2 cups)
- ⅓ cup chopped onion
- ¼ cup margarine or butter
- 4 cups dry sourdough bread cubes (6 to 7 slices)*
- 2 tart apples, cored and chopped (2 cups)
- 2 Tbsp. snipped fresh thyme or 1 tsp. dried thyme, crushed
- 1 Tbsp. snipped fresh parsley
- 2 beaten eggs
- ½ to ¾ cup apple juice
- 2 Tbsp. apple brandy (optional)

◆◆◆

- ¼ cup apple jelly
- 2 tsp. snipped fresh thyme or ½ tsp. dried thyme, crushed

◆◆◆

  Rosemary sprigs (optional)
  Sage flowers or other edible flowers (optional)

1 Trim fat from meat. Sprinkle meat lightly with *salt* and *pepper*. Place roast, bone tips up, on rack in shallow roasting pan. Make a ball of foil and press it into cavity to hold open. Wrap the bone tips with foil. Roast in a 325° oven for 1¼ hours.

2 Meanwhile, in a medium skillet cook fennel and onion in hot margarine or butter till tender. In a very large mixing bowl, toss together the bread cubes, apples, the 2 tablespoons fresh thyme, parsley, and onion-fennel mixture. Combine eggs, ½ cup of the apple juice, and, if desired, apple brandy. Gradually add to bread mixture, tossing to moisten. If desired, add remaining ¼ cup apple juice for a moister stuffing.

3 Remove roast from oven. Lift foil from roast cavity. Loosely pack stuffing into the center of the roast. Cover stuffing loosely with foil. Insert meat thermometer through foil into center of the stuffing. Place any remaining stuffing in a lightly greased casserole; cover with foil or casserole lid. Roast stuffed meat for 1½ hours more or till thermometer in stuffing reaches 160° and temperature of meat reaches 155°, adding the casserole to the oven the last 1 hour of baking.

4 In a small saucepan heat apple jelly and the 2 teaspoons fresh thyme just till jelly is melted. Brush over meat during the last 20 minutes of roasting.

5 Remove roast from oven. Cover with additional foil; let stand 15 minutes before carving. (The temperature will rise 5° during standing.) Remove foil from roast, top of stuffing, and ends of ribs. If desired, tuck rosemary sprigs and edible flowers into string around roast. Serve additional stuffing in casserole along with roast. To serve, slice roast between ribs. Makes 12 servings.

*Note: To dry fresh bread cubes, bake them in a shallow baking pan in a 300° oven for 10 to 15 minutes or till dry, stirring once or twice.

Nutrition facts per serving with stuffing: 300 cal., 15 g total fat (4 g sat. fat), 103 mg chol., 203 mg sodium, 17 g carbo., 4 g fiber, 24 g pro.
Daily values: 6% vit. A, 6% vit. C, 2% calcium, 10% iron.

LOW FAT

CHOPS AND CABBAGE WITH CIDER GRAVY

Start to finish: 35 min.

- 4 pork chops, cut ½ inch thick (1¼ lb. total)
  Nonstick spray coating
- 3 cups packaged coleslaw mix
- 1 medium onion, cut into wedges
- 1¼ cups apple cider or juice
- 1 Tbsp. cider vinegar
- 2 to 3 tsp. prepared horseradish
- 1 medium red or green apple, cored and sliced

◆◆◆

- 1 Tbsp. cornstarch
- 1 tsp. instant beef bouillon granules

1 Trim fat from meat. Spray a cold, large skillet with nonstick coating. In the skillet brown chops over medium heat 4 minutes on each side. Add coleslaw mix, onion, *1 cup* of the apple cider, vinegar, and horseradish. Bring to boiling; reduce heat. Simmer, covered, 7 to 8 minutes or till pork is done and cabbage is crisp-tender. Add apple; cook 2 to 3 minutes more. Transfer chops and mixture to a platter, reserving liquid in skillet; keep warm.

2 For gravy, stir together the remaining ¼ cup apple cider, cornstarch, bouillon granules, and ¼ teaspoon *pepper*. Stir into liquid in skillet. Cook and stir till thickened and bubbly. Cook and stir for 2 minutes more. Serve with pork chops and apple-vegetable mixture. Makes 4 servings.

Nutrition facts per serving: 227 cal., 6 g total fat (3 g sat. fat), 58 mg chol., 308 mg sodium, 21 g carbo., 3 g fiber, 24 g pro. *Daily values:* 50% vit. A, 50% vit. C, 6% calcium, 8% iron.

Nuevo Pork 'n' Beans

Prep: 20 min. ◆ Broil: 1 min.

Add a Mexican accent to a knife-and-fork sandwich by corralling a can of refried beans, chorizo sausage, and cheese.

- **6 oz. spicy chorizo or bulk Italian sausage, casing removed**
- **1 16-oz. can fat-free refried beans**
- **1 4½-oz. can diced green chili peppers, drained**
- **3 8-inch pieces baguette-style French bread, split lengthwise and toasted**
- **½ medium red sweet pepper, cut into thin strips**
- **½ medium green sweet pepper, cut into thin strips**
- **½ cup shredded reduced-fat Monterey Jack cheese**

1 In a skillet crumble sausage; cook over medium heat till brown. Drain in colander; wipe skillet with paper towels. Return sausage to skillet. Stir in refried beans and chili peppers; heat through. Spread sausage-bean mixture on bottom halves of bread; arrange bread on unheated rack of a broiler pan. Top with sweet pepper strips; sprinkle with cheese. Broil 4 inches from heat for 1 to 2 minutes or till cheese melts. Place toasted bread tops over filling; cut each portion in half crosswise. Makes 6 servings.

Nutrition facts per serving: 311 cal., 15 g total fat (6 g sat. fat), 7 mg chol., 865 mg sodium, 53 g carbo., 4 g fiber, 20 g pro. *Daily values:* 9% vit. A, 48% vit. C, 14% calcium, 20% iron.

Glazed Chicken Rolls

Start to finish: 30 min.

- **2 medium carrots**
- **1 medium yellow, red, or green sweet pepper, cut into strips**
  ◆◆◆
- **4 medium skinless, boneless chicken breast halves**
  ◆◆◆
- **2 tsp. margarine or butter**
- **¼ tsp. curry powder**
  ◆◆◆
- **¼ cup orange marmalade**

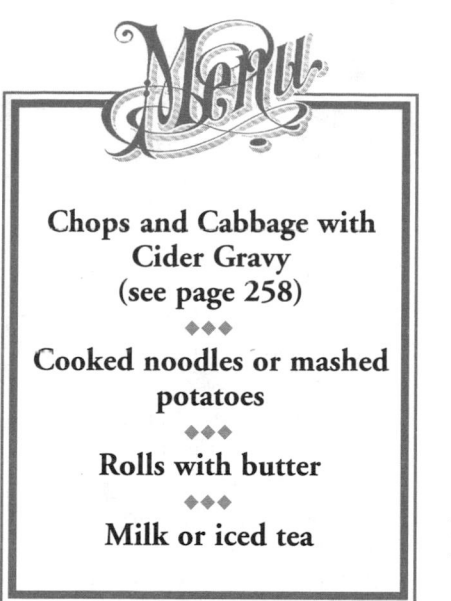

Menu

Chops and Cabbage with Cider Gravy (see page 258)

◆◆◆

Cooked noodles or mashed potatoes

◆◆◆

Rolls with butter

◆◆◆

Milk or iced tea

1 Halve carrots crosswise; cut lengthwise into 8 sticks total. In a 1-quart microwave-safe casserole microwave carrots in ¼ cup *water*, covered, on 100% power (high) 2 minutes or till crisp-tender. Stir in peppers; cook, covered, on high 1 minute more. Drain; set aside.

2 Rinse chicken; pat dry. Place, boned side up, between 2 pieces of plastic wrap. Pound lightly with a meat mallet to ¼-inch thickness.

3 In a custard cup combine margarine or butter and curry powder. Microwave, uncovered, on high for 30 to 40 seconds or till melted; brush one side of chicken. Place carrots and peppers crosswise on short ends of chicken pieces; roll up. Secure the rolls with wooden toothpicks.

4 Arrange rolls, seam side down, in a 2-quart square microwave-safe baking dish. Cover with microwave-safe plastic wrap, leaving a corner vented to allow steam to escape. Microwave on high for 5 to 7 minutes or till chicken is no longer pink, rearranging pieces of chicken after 3 minutes.

5 For glaze, in a custard cup microwave marmalade, uncovered, on high for 30 to 45 seconds or till marmalade is melted. Spoon marmalade over chicken. Makes 4 servings.

Nutrition facts per serving: 192 cal., 4 g total fat (1 g sat. fat), 45 mg chol., 99 mg sodium, 21 g carbo., 0 g fiber, 17 g pro. *Daily values:* 164% vit. A, 60% vit. C, 4% calcium, 7% iron.

TUNA MUFFIN MELT

Prep: 15 min. ◆ Broil: 4 min.

Chances are, the ingredients for the filling are ready and waiting on your pantry shelf. Accompany the sandwich with pickles.

1 **5-oz. jar cream cheese spread with olives or pimiento or American cheese spread**
1 **6½-oz. can tuna, drained and broken into chunks**
3 **English muffins, split and toasted**

◆◆◆

6 **slices tomato, halved**
  Pimiento-stuffed olives, quartered or sliced (optional)
  Pickle spears (optional)

1 In a mixing bowl combine *⅓ cup* of the cheese spread and the tuna. Spread tuna mixture onto muffin halves. Place halves on the unheated rack of a broiler pan. Broil 4 inches from the heat about 3 minutes or till sandwiches are heated through.

2 Top each tuna-topped muffin half with 2 tomato-slice halves and a spoonful of the remaining cheese spread. Broil about 1 minute more or till heated through. If desired, top each sandwich with olives and serve with pickle spears. Makes 3 main-dish servings.

Nutrition facts per serving: 367 cal., 12 g total fat (7 g sat. fat), 61 mg chol., 1,235 mg sodium, 33 g carbo., 2 g fiber, 32 g pro. *Daily values:* 18% vit. A, 14% vit. C, 46% calcium, 16% iron.

TO COOK TURKEY AND GLAZED ROASTED VEGETABLES TOGETHER

If you want to roast the Nut-Crusted Turkey (see right) and the Glazed Roasted Vegetables (see page 254) in the same oven, you may find that the oven is not wide enough for both large pans side by side. Here are some hints on how to cook them together:

Arrange oven racks to accommodate both pans. Place the roasting pan with the turkey breast on the lower rack at beginning of roasting time. The covered 13×9×2-inch pan of vegetables can go on the upper rack.

After turkey and vegetables have baked 30 minutes, remove both pans. Add marmalade and nuts to turkey; stir squash into vegetables. Cover vegetables again. Place vegetables on lower rack now, and the turkey breast on the upper rack. (This will allow nuts to brown more easily. If nuts begin to overbrown but the turkey is not yet done, cover the turkey breast loosely with foil.)

If vegetables get done before the turkey, remove the pan of vegetables from oven and let stand, covered, while turkey finishes. Then, after removing turkey, increase oven temperature to 450° and bake the vegetables, uncovered, during the 15 minute standing time for the turkey.

NUT-CRUSTED TURKEY

Prep: 15 min. ◆ Roast: 1 hr.

When a whole bird won't fit into your holiday dinner plans, try this version that's less fuss but is still a striking presence (and makes fine sandwiches the next day as well). For guidance on cooking a whole turkey, see our Turkey Roasting Guide on page 261. (See the photograph on page 280.)

1 **3- to 3½-lb. boneless whole turkey breast**
1 **Tbsp. olive oil or cooking oil**
1 **clove garlic, minced**
¼ **tsp. salt**

◆◆◆

⅓ **cup slivered almonds**
⅓ **cup pine nuts or slivered almonds**
1 **tsp. ground coriander**
¼ **tsp. ground cinnamon**
¼ **tsp. coarsely ground pepper**

◆◆◆

¼ **cup orange marmalade**

◆◆◆

  Fresh thyme sprigs (optional)
1 **recipe Glazed Roasted Vegetables (see page 254) (optional)**

1 Remove skin from turkey breast. Rinse turkey breast and pat dry with paper towels. Place turkey breast on a lightly greased rack in a shallow roasting pan. In a small bowl stir together the olive oil or cooking oil, garlic, and salt. Brush mixture over turkey breast. Insert a meat thermometer into the thickest part of the breast.

2 Roast turkey, uncovered, in a 375° oven for 30 minutes. Meanwhile, in a blender container or food processor bowl, combine the almonds and pine nuts. Cover and blend or process till nuts are just finely chopped. Place the chopped nuts in a small mixing bowl. Stir in the coriander, cinnamon, and pepper; set aside.

3 Remove turkey breast from oven. Brush surface with marmalade; sprinkle nut mixture over, pressing gently so nuts adhere. Continue roasting, uncovered, for 30 to 45 minutes longer or till meat thermometer registers 170°. Remove from oven. Let stand about 15 minutes before slicing.

4 To serve, slice turkey.* If desired, garnish with fresh thyme sprigs and serve turkey with Glazed Roasted Vegetables. Makes 8 to 10 servings.

*Note: To carve a turkey breast, start at the outside of the breast and slice downward, keeping slices thin. Continue slicing, moving slightly higher up on the breast with each slice.

Nutrition facts per serving without vegetables: 218 cal., 9 g total fat (2 g sat. fat), 59 mg chol., 109 mg sodium, 7 g carbo., 1 g fiber, 28 g pro.
Daily values: 1% vit. C, 3% calcium, 13% iron.

TURKEY: SMART WAYS TO STUFF IT

Play-It-Safe Stuffing
Good stuffing begins with prudent preparation—mix the stuffing just before you stuff and roast. Pack it loosely into neck and body cavities.

To roast, place the stuffed bird in an oven that's preheated to at least 325°. When juices run clear, check temperature in center of stuffing and innermost part of thigh. The stuffing must reach a temperature of 165°, and the meat must be 180° for safe eating.

Thawing Fast and Safe
Be sure your bird is completely thawed before stuffing or roasting. (If the center is still frozen, it may not cook evenly.) To thaw a whole frozen turkey, place the wrapped bird on a tray in the refrigerator for 1 to 5 days. Allow 24 hours for every 5 pounds. Or, place it in a sink of cold water. Change the water every 30 minutes. Allow 30 minutes per pound. Do not thaw at room temperature or in warm water. Remove the giblets and neck. Rinse bird and pat dry with paper towels. Do not stuff the bird until you're ready to roast it.

Preparing the Bird
To stuff, spoon some stuffing loosely into neck cavity. (Allow no more than ¾ cup stuffing per pound of turkey.) Pull the neck skin over stuffing; fasten to back with a short skewer. Loosely spoon stuffing into the body cavity; do not pack. Spoon any remaining stuffing into a casserole; cover and chill till ready to roast. If you prefer not to stuff your turkey, place quartered onions and celery in the body cavity to add flavor. Pull the neck skin to the back; fasten with a short skewer. Tuck the drumsticks under the band of skin that crosses the tail. If there isn't a band, tie the drumsticks to the tail. Twist the wing tips under the back.

Turkey Roasting Guide

Type of turkey	Ready-to-cook weight	Oven temperature	Roasting time
Stuffed whole turkey (open roasting)	8 to 12 lb.	325°	3 to 3½ hours
	12 to 14 lb.	325°	3½ to 4 hours
	14 to 18 lb.	325°	4 to 4¼ hours
	18 to 20 lb.	325°	4¼ to 4¾ hours
	20 to 24 lb.	325°	4¾ to 5¼ hours
Stuffed whole turkey (in oven cooking bag)	12 to 16 lb.	350°	2½ to 3 hours
	16 to 20 lb.	350°	3 to 3½ hours
	20 to 24 lb.	350°	3½ to 4 hours

For unstuffed turkeys of the same weight, reduce the total cooking time by 15 to 30 minutes.

ROASTING CHESTNUTS

To shell chestnuts, use the tip of a sturdy paring knife to carefully cut an "X" on the flat side of each chestnut. Place in a shallow baking pan and roast in a 400° oven about 15 minutes or till corners of Xs curl up. Peel while warm; remove papery skin by rolling peeled chestnuts in a towel. Four cups unshelled chestnuts will yield about 2½ cups shelled.

Whole, fresh chestnuts are available from November to January. They will keep for up to two weeks in the refrigerator, or several months in the freezer, in an airtight container. You also can find them canned or dried in many supermarkets.

CHESTNUT AND PARSNIP SOUP

Prep: 30 min. ◆ Cook: 40 min.

The sweet, nutty flavor of parsnips is a natural with chestnuts in this rich and velvety soup.

1 Tbsp. walnut oil or cooking oil
1 lb. parsnips, peeled and chopped (about 3½ cups)
2½ cups roasted chestnuts (see method, above) or one 15-oz. can whole chestnuts, drained
½ cup chopped onion
2 cloves garlic

⅛ tsp. ground white pepper
3 14½-oz. cans reduced-sodium chicken broth
2 sprigs fresh marjoram

◆◆◆

1 cup half-and-half or light cream
Fresh chives or edible flowers (optional)

1 In a large saucepan heat oil. Add parsnips, chestnuts, onion, garlic, and white pepper. Cook, covered, about 10 minutes or till parsnips are tender, stirring often. Carefully add broth. Bring mixture to boiling; reduce heat. Simmer, uncovered, for 20 minutes. Add marjoram; cook for 10 minutes more. Remove marjoram and discard. Cool soup.

2 Place *one-third* of mixture in a blender container. Cover; blend till smooth.* Return mixture to new saucepan. Repeat with remaining soup. Stir in *½ cup* of the half-and-half or light cream; heat through. Ladle soup into bowls. Swirl 1 tablespoon or remaining half-and-half or light cream into each serving. Makes 8 side-dish servings.

***Note:** When blending heated mixtures, fill blender container only one-third full. Cover tightly, leaving center slightly open to vent hot air; cover blender with a clean towel while operating.

Nutrition facts per serving: 227 cal., 7 g total fat (2 g sat. fat), 11 mg chol., 454 mg sodium, 38 g carbo., 6 g fiber, 5 g pro. *Daily values:* 3% vit. A, 42% vit. C, 5% calcium, 7% iron.

VEGETABLE CHILI WITH CHEESE TOPPING

Prep: 20 min. ◆ Cook: 45 min.

This recipe earned Jan Curry of Raleigh, North Carolina, $400 in the magazine's monthly contest.

Nonstick spray coating
1¼ cups finely chopped zucchini
¾ cup finely chopped carrot
2 Tbsp. chopped green onion (1)
2 cloves garlic, minced
2 15-oz. cans hot-style chili beans in chili sauce, undrained
2 14½-oz. cans diced tomatoes, undrained
¼ cup catsup
1 Tbsp. unsweetened cocoa powder
1 tsp. chili powder
1 tsp. ground cumin
1 tsp. bottled hot pepper sauce
¼ tsp. dried oregano, crushed

◆◆◆

½ of an 8-oz. tub cream cheese with chives and onion
2 Tbsp. milk
½ cup shredded cheddar cheese (2 oz.)
Green onion strips (optional)

1 Spray a large saucepan with nonstick coating. Cook zucchini, carrot, green onion, and garlic in saucepan over medium heat for 2 minutes. Add undrained chili beans, undrained tomatoes, catsup, cocoa powder, chili powder, cumin, hot sauce, and oregano. Heat to boiling; reduce heat. Simmer, uncovered, for 45 minutes or till desired consistency, stirring occasionally. Season to taste with *salt* and *pepper*.

2 Meanwhile, in a small bowl stir together cream cheese and milk till smooth. Stir in cheddar cheese. To serve, ladle chili into bowls. Spoon cream cheese mixture onto each serving. If desired, garnish with green onion strips. Makes 6 main-dish servings.

Nutrition facts per serving: 281 cal., 13 g total fat (5 g sat. fat), 30 mg chol., 1,183 mg sodium, 39 g carbo., 5 g fiber, 13 g pro. *Daily values:* 69% vit. A, 48% vit. C, 17% calcium, 26% iron.

PRIZE TESTED RECIPE WINNER

INDO-TEXAN CURRY CHILI

Prep: 20 min. ◆ Cook: 1½ hr.

This recipe earned Loanne Chiu of Fort Worth, Texas, $200 in the magazine's monthly contest.

2 **lb. coarsely ground beef**
4 **cloves garlic, minced**
1 **Tbsp. hot Madras curry powder, salt-free curry seasoning blend, or curry powder**
2 **tsp. ground coriander**
1 **tsp. ground cumin**
1 **tsp. finely shredded lemon peel**
2 **cups chopped red sweet pepper**
1 **15-oz. can tomato puree**
2 **10-oz. cans diced tomatoes and chilies, undrained**
1 **10½-oz. can condensed beef broth**
1 **cup canned unsweetened coconut milk**
¼ **cup catsup**

Hot cooked rice
Snipped fresh basil (optional)
Chopped peanuts, raisins, and/or chutney (optional)

1 In a 4-quart pot cook ground beef and garlic till meat is brown. Drain fat. Stir in curry powder, coriander, cumin, and lemon peel. Stir in sweet pepper, tomato puree, undrained tomatoes, broth, coconut milk, and catsup. Bring to boiling; reduce heat. Simmer chili, uncovered, 1½ hours or till desired consistency.

2 To serve, ladle chili into bowls over hot cooked rice. If desired, garnish with snipped basil. If desired, serve with peanuts, raisins, and/or chutney. Makes 6 main-dish servings.

Nutrition facts per serving: 511 cal., 23 g total fat (12 g sat. fat), 95 mg chol., 923 mg sodium, 42 g carbo., 3 g fiber, 34 g pro. *Daily values:* 42% vit. A, 140% vit. C, 6% calcium, 46% iron.

30 MIN.

CHICKEN CHILI WITH RICE

Start to finish: 30 min.

If you're searching for ways to use up leftover turkey, substitute it for the chicken in this stewlike version of "white chili."

3 **cloves garlic, minced**
1 **fresh jalapeño pepper, seeded and finely chopped***
1 **Tbsp. cooking oil**
2 **cups frozen whole small onions**
1 **cup reduced-sodium chicken broth or regular chicken broth**

2 to 3 **tsp. green chili powder or chili powder**
1 **tsp. white wine Worcestershire sauce**
½ **tsp. ground cumin**
⅛ **tsp. ground white pepper**
1 **19-oz. can white kidney beans (cannellini beans), rinsed and drained**
1 **cup chopped cooked chicken**

◆◆◆

2 **cups hot cooked rice or couscous**
Dairy sour cream or plain yogurt
Snipped fresh chives

1 In a large saucepan cook the garlic and jalapeño in hot oil for 30 seconds. Carefully stir in onions, chicken broth, chili powder, Worcestershire sauce, cumin, white pepper, and ¼ teaspoon *salt*. Bring to boiling; reduce heat. Simmer, covered, for 20 minutes. Add beans and chicken; cook and stir till heated through.

2 To serve, ladle chili into bowls over rice or couscous. Top each serving with sour cream or yogurt and chives. Makes 4 main-dish servings.

***Note:** Because chili peppers contain very pungent oils, be sure to protect your hands when preparing them. Put gloves or sandwich bags over your hands so your skin doesn't come in contact with the peppers. Always wash your hands and nails thoroughly in hot, soapy water after handling chili peppers.

Nutrition facts per serving: 397 cal., 12 g total fat (4 g sat. fat), 35 mg chol., 655 mg sodium, 56 g carbo., 9 g fiber, 25 g pro. *Daily values:* 10% vit. A, 16% vit. C, 8% calcium, 29% iron.

TRIPLE-BEAN CHILI

Prep: 15 min. ◆ Cook: 20 min.

1½ cups sliced fresh mushrooms
1 cup chopped green sweet
    pepper
1 cup chopped onion
1 clove garlic, minced
1 Tbsp. olive oil
1 28-oz. can tomatoes,
    undrained and cut up
1½ cups water
3 Tbsp. bottled barbecue sauce
1 Tbsp. chili powder
1 tsp. dried oregano, crushed
½ tsp. ground cumin
1 16-oz. can vegetarian baked
    beans, undrained
1 15½-oz. can Mexican-style
    chili beans, undrained
1 15-oz. can red kidney beans,
    rinsed and drained
¼ cup snipped fresh cilantro

◆◆◆

Dairy sour cream (optional)
Chopped fresh tomatoes
(optional)

1 In a 4-quart pot cook mushrooms, sweet pepper, onion, and garlic in hot oil till tender. Stir in undrained tomatoes, water, barbecue sauce, chili powder, oregano, and cumin. Bring to boiling; reduce heat. Simmer, covered, 20 minutes. Stir in un-drained baked and chili beans, drained kidney beans, and cilantro. Heat through.

2 To serve, ladle chili into bowls. If desired, top each serving with sour cream and fresh tomatoes. Makes 6 main-dish servings.

Nutrition facts per serving: 271 cal., 4 g total fat (0 g sat. fat), 0 mg chol., 1,303 mg sodium, 49 g carbo., 10 g fiber, 14 g pro. *Daily values:* 34% vit. A, 59% vit. C, 9% calcium, 27% iron.

POTATO, BLACK BEAN, AND SAUSAGE CHILI

Prep: 15 min. ◆ Cook: 30 min.

Choose low-sodium tomato sauce and beans to help lower the tally of sodium in this hearty bowl of red.

1 lb. ground turkey sausage
1 clove garlic, minced
1½ cups water
1½ cups cubed potatoes
1 14½-oz. can diced tomatoes,
    undrained
½ cup tomato sauce
1 Tbsp. brown sugar
2 to 3 tsp. chili powder
¼ tsp. pepper
¼ tsp. dried oregano or basil,
    crushed
1 15-oz. can black beans or
    red kidney beans, rinsed
    and drained

◆◆◆

Shredded Monterey Jack or
cheddar cheese (optional)

1 In a large saucepan cook sausage and garlic till meat is no longer pink. Drain, if necessary. Stir in water, potatoes, undrained tomatoes, tomato sauce, brown sugar, chili powder, pepper, and oregano or basil. Bring to boiling; reduce heat. Simmer, covered, for 30 minutes or till potatoes are tender. Stir in black beans or kidney beans. Heat through.

2 To serve, ladle chili into bowls. If desired, sprinkle each serving with Monterey Jack or cheddar cheese. Makes 4 main-dish servings.

Nutrition facts per serving: 346 cal., 13 g total fat (4 g sat. fat), 82 mg chol., 1,344 mg sodium, 38 g carbo., 7 g fiber, 28 g pro. *Daily values:* 13% vit. A, 47% vit. C, 11% calcium, 30% iron.

MOLE-STYLE PORK AND SQUASH CHILI

Prep: 15 min. ◆ Cook: 30 min.

A miniscule amount of chocolate puts the "mole" on a humble bowl of chili. Mole is a classic Mexican red pepper sauce that's gently spiked with chocolate.

12 oz. boneless pork sirloin
    chops or pork shoulder
    steaks, cut ½ inch thick
½ cup chopped onion
2 cloves garlic, minced
2 Tbsp. olive oil or cooking oil
2 14½-oz. cans stewed
    tomatoes, undrained
8 oz. butternut squash, peeled
    and cut into ½-inch cubes
    (about 1½ cups)
1 16-oz. can red kidney beans,
    rinsed and drained
1 15-oz. can black beans,
    rinsed drained
1 cup frozen loose-pack whole
    kernel corn
1 cup water
1 Tbsp. chili powder
½ tsp. ground cumin
¼ tsp. ground cinnamon
¼ tsp. dried oregano, crushed
1 Tbsp. grated unsweetened
    chocolate

◆◆◆

Tortilla Crisps (optional)

1 Cut pork into ½-inch cubes. In a large pot cook pork, onion, and garlic in hot oil till meat is browned. Stir in undrained tomatoes, squash, kidney beans, black beans, corn, water, chili powder, cumin, cinnamon, oregano, and chocolate. Bring to boiling; reduce heat. Simmer, covered, for 30 minutes or till squash and pork are tender, stirring occasionally.

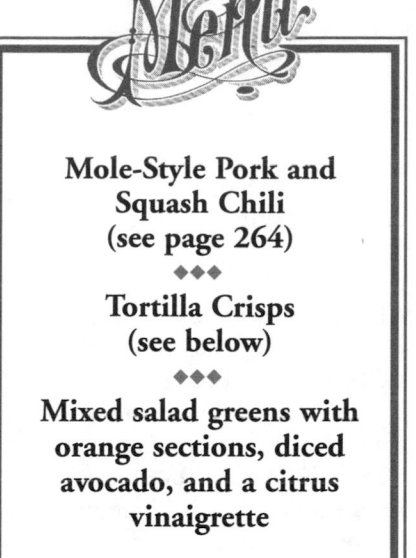

Mole-Style Pork and Squash Chili
(see page 264)

◆◆◆

Tortilla Crisps
(see below)

◆◆◆

Mixed salad greens with orange sections, diced avocado, and a citrus vinaigrette

---

2 To serve, ladle chili into bowls. If desired, serve chili with Tortilla Crisps. Makes 6 main-dish servings.

Tortilla Crisps: Cut three 7- or 8-inch *flour tortillas* into 8 wedges each. Spread the wedges in a 15×10×1-inch baking pan. Bake in a 350° oven for 5 to 10 minutes or till dry and crisp; cool. Store in an airtight container at room temperature up to 4 days. Makes 24 crisps.

Nutrition facts per serving: 289 cal., 9 g total fat (2 g sat. fat), 23 mg chol., 678 mg sodium, 41 g carbo., 11 g fiber, 20 g pro. *Daily values:* 41% vit. A, 58% vit. C, 10% calcium, 24% iron.

Mole-Style Beef and Squash Chili: Prepare the chili as directed on page 264, except substitute *beef stew meat,* cut into ½-inch pieces, for the pork. Brown the beef in the hot oil along with the onion and garlic. Add the undrained tomatoes, water, and seasonings. Cook, covered, for

---

30 minutes. Add the squash, kidney beans, black beans, corn, and chocolate. Simmer chili, covered, for 30 minutes more. Serve as directed.

SIMPLY SPICED CHILI

Prep: 15 min. ◆ Cook: 20 min.

Sweet and spicy flavor hints from the French or Catalina salad dressing make for a mellow background flavor to what would be a basic chili.

8 oz. ground beef
½ cup chopped onion
2 15- to 16-oz. cans navy, pinto, great northern, and/or red kidney beans, rinsed and drained
1 cup water
1 8-oz. can tomato sauce
⅓ cup French or Catalina salad dressing
⅓ cup picante sauce or salsa
1 to 2 Tbsp. chili powder
½ tsp. ground cumin

◆◆◆

Finely shredded cheddar cheese (optional)
Tortilla chips (optional)

1 In a large saucepan cook ground beef and onion till meat is browned and onion is tender. Drain off fat. Stir in the beans, water, tomato sauce, French or Catalina salad dressing, picante sauce or salsa, chili powder, and cumin. Bring to boiling; reduce heat. Simmer, covered, for 20 minutes.

---

2 To serve, ladle chili into bowls. If desired, top each serving with finely shredded cheddar cheese and tortilla chips. Makes 4 main-dish servings.

Nutrition facts per serving: 443 cal., 9 g total fat (3 g sat. fat), 36 mg chol., 1668 mg sodium, 63 g carbo., 2 g fiber, 30 g pro. *Daily values:* 14% vit. A, 32% vit. C, 11% calcium, 44% iron.

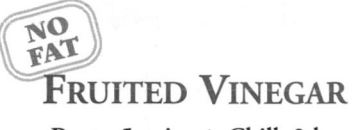

FRUITED VINEGAR

Prep: 5 min. ◆ Chill: 2 hr.

The perfect holiday food gift—a flavored vinegar that's easy to make and welcomed when received. Pour the vinegar into clean, decorative bottles, then tie on ribbons and a note card including ideas for use.

1 cup rice vinegar or white vinegar
1 bag raspberry-, orange-, blackberry-, or cranberry-flavored tea

1 In a glass measure combine the vinegar and tea bag. Cover and chill for 2 hours. Remove tea bag. Pour into a clean glass bottle with a lid. Use vinegar in salad dressings and in meat marinades that call for a fruit-flavored vinegar. Makes 1 cup.

Gingered Orange Vinegar: Add ½ teaspoon grated *gingerroot* with the orange tea bag and the 1 cup vinegar. Strain vinegar before pouring into the clean bottle.

Nutrition facts per tablespoon: no measurable values.

THINK ZINC

Zinc is a common metal with an uncommonly powerful nutritional impact. The same metal that's used for durability in house siding and for energy in batteries also is essential for hundreds of functions in the human body—from sense of taste to development of healthy babies. Adults need 12 to 15 mg of zinc per day—about as much as the amount in a large steak or a bowl of fortified oatmeal. But according to the American Dietetic Association, the majority of us are getting only about two-thirds of the required amounts. "Zinc is essential for the immune system, wound healing, taste, and protein production," says Dr. Arthur Grider, nutrition researcher at the University of Georgia. "Hundreds of different enzymes (protein compounds that trigger or assist in chemical processes) rely on zinc to help them do their work. For example, zinc is needed for maintaining insulin, yet it also helps red blood cells dispose of carbon dioxide. Zinc even serves as an integral part of an important antioxidant system in our body's cells."

WHAT HAPPENS WITHOUT ZINC

With so many functions depending on the metal, zinc deficiency leads to a rather long list of complications, ranging from skin rashes, hair loss, and decreased senses of taste and smell to delayed fetal development, nerve damage, and birth defects. Some research even suggests zinc deficiency may significantly increase the risk of cancer of the esophagus.

Low zinc intake for even a relatively short period of time during adolescence retards bone growth, posing greater risk for the bone disease osteoporosis in later life. Most of these afflictions are reversible, but only if the sufferer gets enough zinc before the maladies become permanent.

Agreeing with the assessment that Americans aren't getting enough zinc, Dr. Harold Sandstead of the University of Texas Medical School's Department of Preventive Medicine says, "This is likely due to a diet pattern that includes a decrease in red meat consumption. Red meat is the best practical food source of available zinc."

Why all this hasn't raised a red flag is largely because pertinent studies have not been conducted. Sandstead says, "In this country, the problem is one of mild moderate zinc deficiency. America doesn't have a large population with a severe deficiency, so the possible effects widespread marginal zinc intake may have on our population haven't been looked at closely."

In a study in China of moderately zinc-deficient children with learning difficulties, zinc supplementation led to improved mental ability. One problem in determining whether nominal zinc deficiencies lead to similar afflictions is that the threshold at which general health begins to suffer is unknown. Sandstead says, "There may be ongoing health issues in our total population (caused by low dietary zinc intake) that we are not addressing."

The implication is that many widely experienced symptoms, which sufferers might dismiss when considered individually (for example, skin rashes, certain types of hair loss, and slow wound healing), could be because of an overall marginal intake of dietary zinc.

GETTING ENOUGH ZINC

The body more efficiently absorbs zinc from animal sources than from plant sources—up to several times as much, in fact. This is because plants contain phytates, compounds that are unabsorbable yet bind to minerals. The richest common source of dietary zinc is red meat—beef, lamb, and game. Other excellent sources are eggs, poultry, and seafood, especially oysters, which have more natural zinc than any other single food.

Fortified cereals are high in zinc, with about 15 mg of the mineral per ounce. Peas, beans, nuts, nut butters, whole grains, and whole-grain breads are good plant sources of zinc, but also are high in phytates, so the zinc is less available to be absorbed. It will take about four times as much plant-sourced zinc to meet your zinc needs.

ZINC SUPPLEMENTS

If you're a healthy adult eating a wide variety of foods on a nonrestrictive diet, you probably don't need additional zinc. Seniors, growing children, pregnant or lactating women, and vegetarians who don't eat sufficient legumes, nuts, or fortified grains may benefit from 10 to 15 mg extra zinc per day.

Like many minerals, zinc can be toxic in high amounts—more than 50 mg zinc per day over time. Also, different minerals compete with each other for absorption in the body. Low levels of some, such as iron and copper, lead to anemia, increased cholesterol, bone abnormalities, and other problems. If possible, take zinc and iron supplements at opposite times of the day. On the other hand, excess calcium inhibits zinc absorption. Taking different mineral supplements several hours apart helps.

Acute zinc toxicity symptoms include a metallic taste and nausea or vomiting accompanied by cramps, dizziness, and chills. Use supplements only when recommended by your health professional, and take only the recommended dosage.

WHERE TO GET YOUR ZINC

Food Item	Approx. Zinc Content (mg/oz.)
• cereals, fortified	15.00
• oysters, steamed	9.00
• beef, cooked	2.00
• pork, cooked	0.90
• nuts, peanut butter*	0.90
• oatmeal, nonfortified, cooked*	0.90
• chicken (dark meat), cooked	0.75
• chicken (light meat), cooked	0.35
• soybean products, cooked*	0.35
• bread, multigrain*	0.30
• fish, cooked	0.25
• eggs, boiled	0.25
• milk	0.25
• potatoes, cooked	0.15

less efficiently absorbed

PRIZE TESTED RECIPE WINNER

ASIAN PICKLED CARROTS

Prep: 30 min. plus chilling

This recipe earned Janice Elder of Charlotte, North Carolina, $200 in the magazine's monthly contest.

1　16-oz. bag peeled baby carrots
1　tsp. salt
¼　cup gingerroot, peeled and cut into thin strips
3　whole allspice

◆◆◆

¾　cup water
¾　cup rice vinegar
⅓　cup packed brown sugar
4　whole cloves
4　whole black peppercorns

1 Cook carrots and salt, covered, in a small amount of *boiling water* about 3 minutes or till crisp-tender. Drain and place in 3 hot clean half-pint jars. Place some of the gingerroot and one whole allspice in each jar.

2 In a medium saucepan combine the ¾ cup water, rice vinegar, brown sugar, cloves, and peppercorns. Bring mixture to boiling; reduce heat. Simmer, uncovered, for 5 minutes. Pour over carrots. Seal jars and refrigerate for up to 3 months. Makes 3 half-pints (about 6 appetizer servings per half-pint).

Nutrition facts per serving: 18 cal., 0 g total fat, 0 mg chol., 135 mg sodium, 5 g carbo., 1 g fiber, 0 g pro.
Daily values: 56% vit. A, 1% iron.

NO FAT

PICKLED CARAMBOLA

Prep: 30 min. plus standing and chilling

Choose fruit that is shiny and firm; allow it to ripen at room temperature until yellow-orange in color. In some regions, carambola is sold under the name star fruit.

3　cups water
3　Tbsp. salt
4　medium carambola (star fruit) (10 oz. total or 2½ cups), sliced ⅜ inch thick

◆◆◆

1　cup sugar
½　cup white vinegar
½　cup water
4　inches stick cinnamon
½　tsp. whole cloves

◆◆◆

1　Tbsp. finely shredded orange peel

1 In a large glass or ceramic bowl combine 3 cups water and salt. Stir in carambola. Allow to stand at room temperature for 4 hours or overnight. Drain in colander and rinse under cold running water for 3 minutes. Drain well. Return to bowl.

2 For syrup, in a medium saucepan combine sugar, vinegar, ½ cup water, the cinnamon, and cloves. Bring to boiling, stirring to dissolve sugar; reduce heat. Simmer sugar mixture, uncovered, for 7 minutes.

3 Using a slotted spoon, remove the spices from syrup; discard. Add the orange peel to syrup in saucepan. Pour syrup over carambola in bowl. Cool to room temperature.

4 Ladle into hot clean screw-top jars or a storage container. Cover and refrigerate for at least 4 hours (or up to 2 weeks) before using. Makes about 2 cups (12 servings).

Nutrition facts per serving: 14 cal., 0 g total fat, 0 mg chol., 91 mg sodium, 3 g carbo., 0 g fiber, 0 g pro.
Daily values: 1% vit. A, 11% vit. C.

NO FAT

MARINATED ZUCCHINI

Prep: 25 min. plus chilling

2　medium zucchini (about 8 oz. total), sliced thinly lengthwise*
1　small onion, cut into wedges
1　clove garlic, minced
1　Tbsp. pickling salt
　　Cracked ice or cold water

◆◆◆

¾　cup cider vinegar